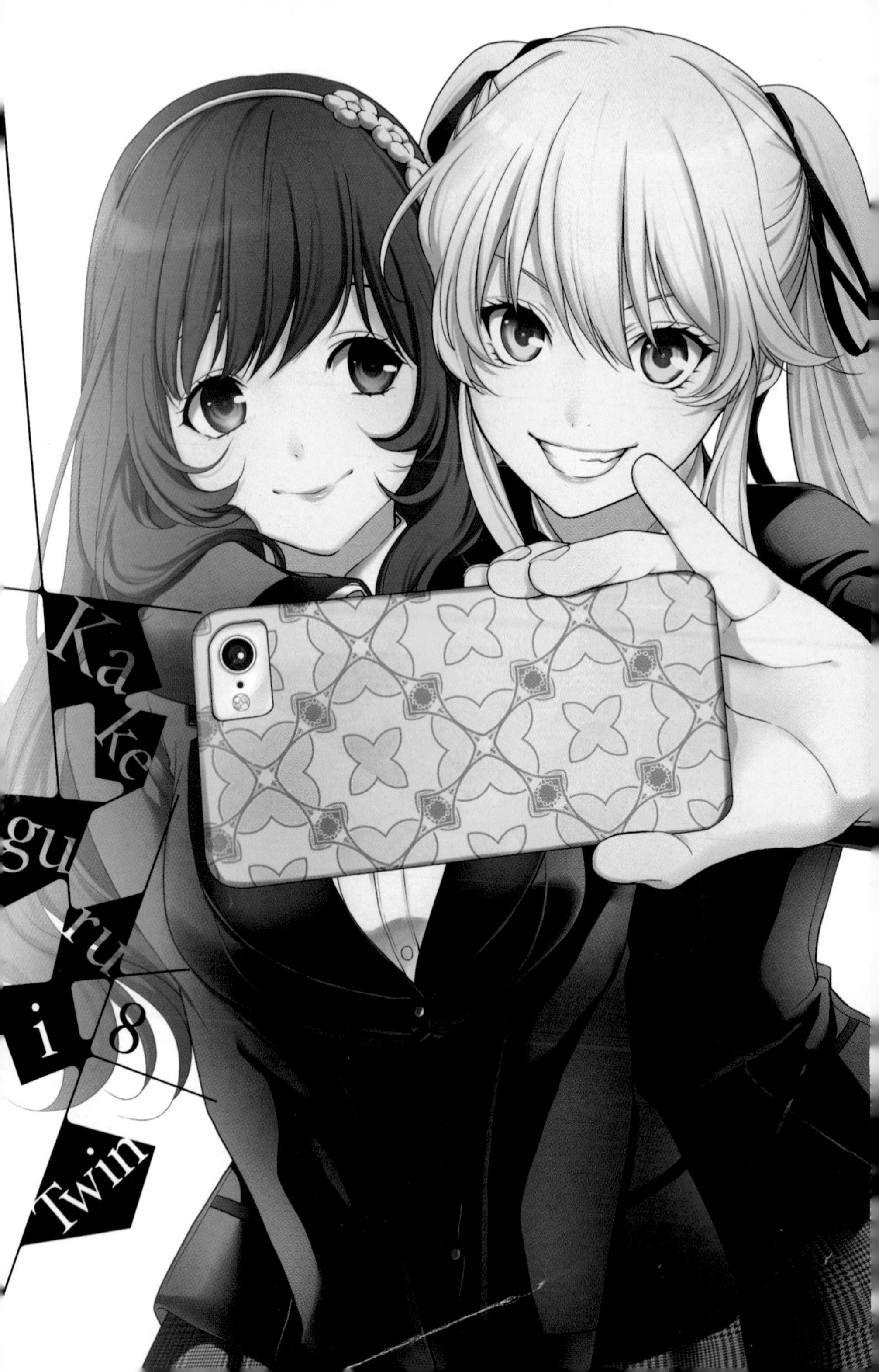
Kakegurui
8
Twin

⑧

# KAKEGURUI TWIN

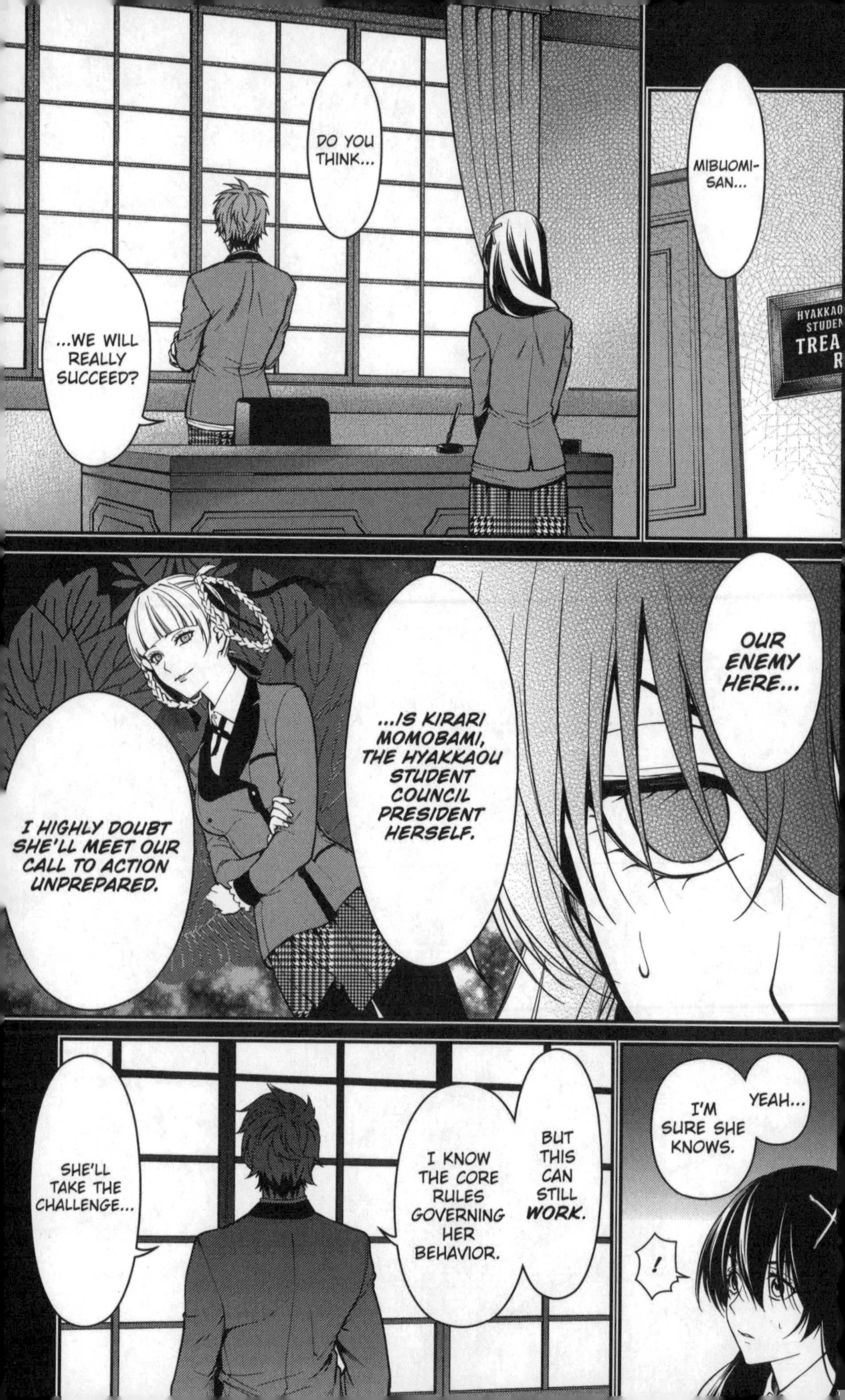
MIBUOMI-SAN...
HYAKKAO
STUDEN
TREA
R
DO YOU THINK...
...WE WILL REALLY SUCCEED?
OUR ENEMY HERE...
...IS KIRARI MOMOBAMI, THE HYAKKAOU STUDENT COUNCIL PRESIDENT HERSELF.
I HIGHLY DOUBT SHE'LL MEET OUR CALL TO ACTION UNPREPARED.
YEAH...
I'M SURE SHE KNOWS.
!
BUT THIS CAN STILL WORK.
I KNOW THE CORE RULES GOVERNING HER BEHAVIOR.
SHE'LL TAKE THE CHALLENGE...

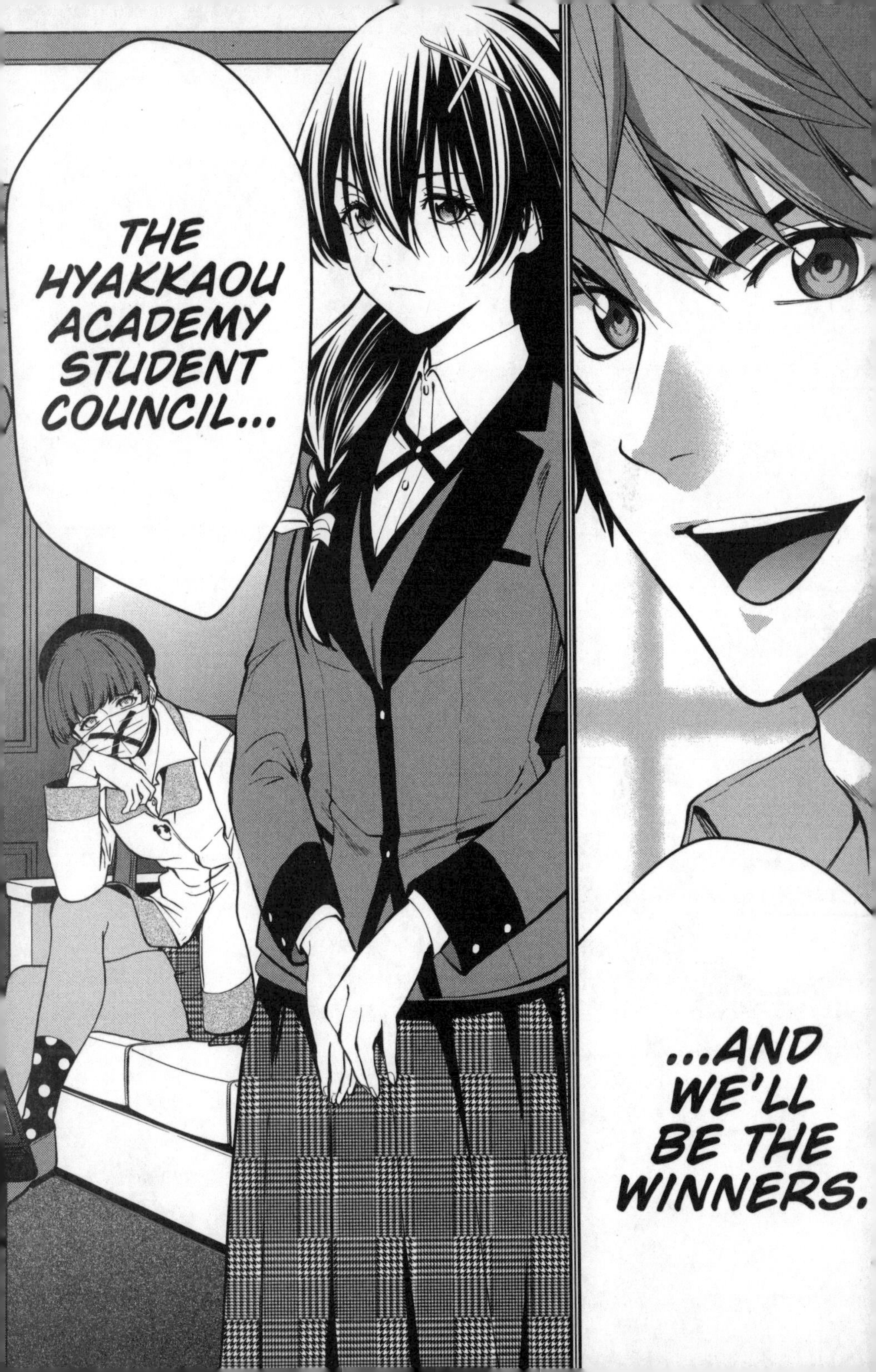
THE HYAKKAOU ACADEMY STUDENT COUNCIL...
...AND WE'LL BE THE WINNERS.

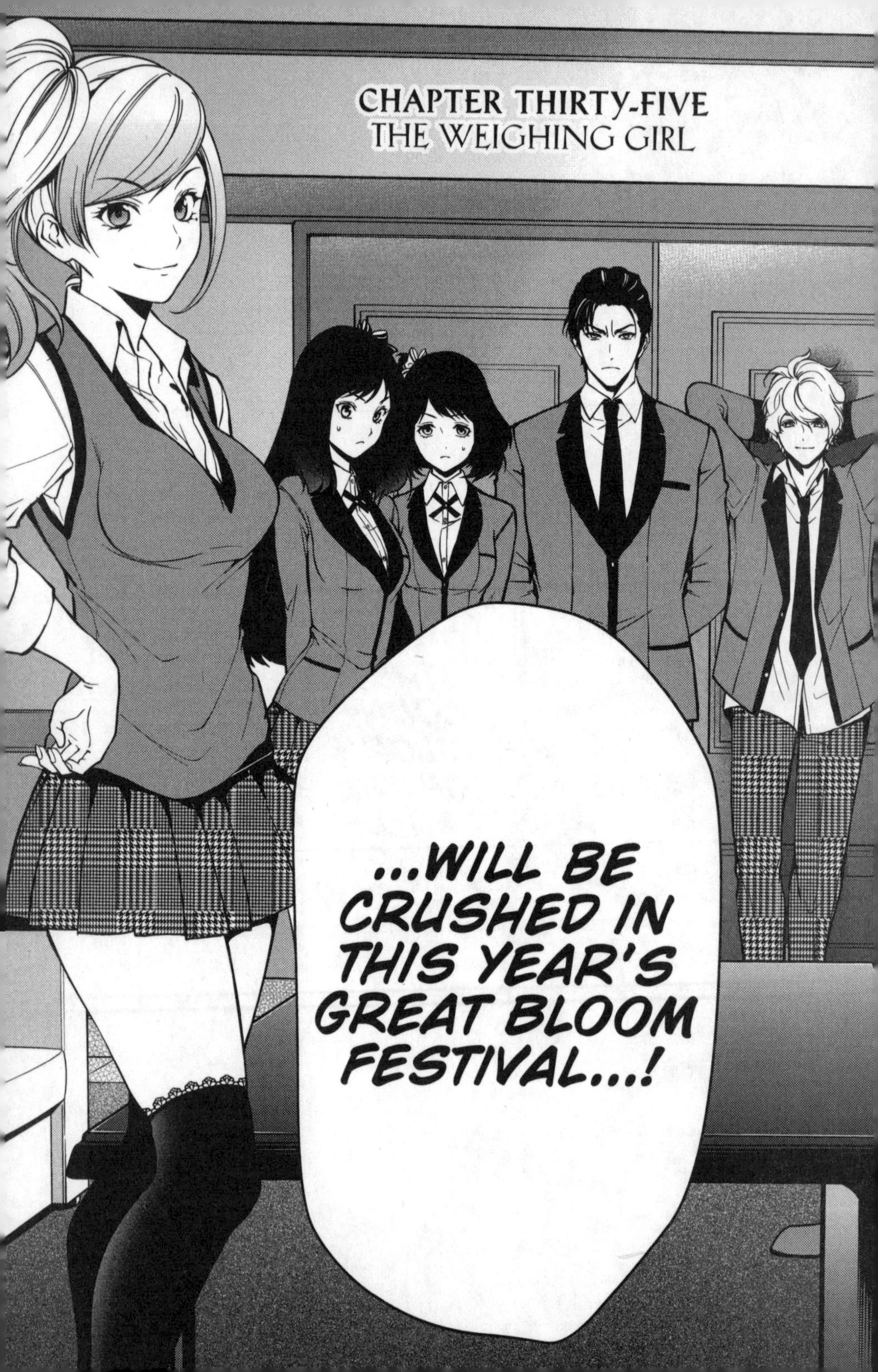
CHAPTER THIRTY-FIVE
THE WEIGHING GIRL
...WILL BE CRUSHED IN THIS YEAR'S GREAT BLOOM FESTIVAL...!

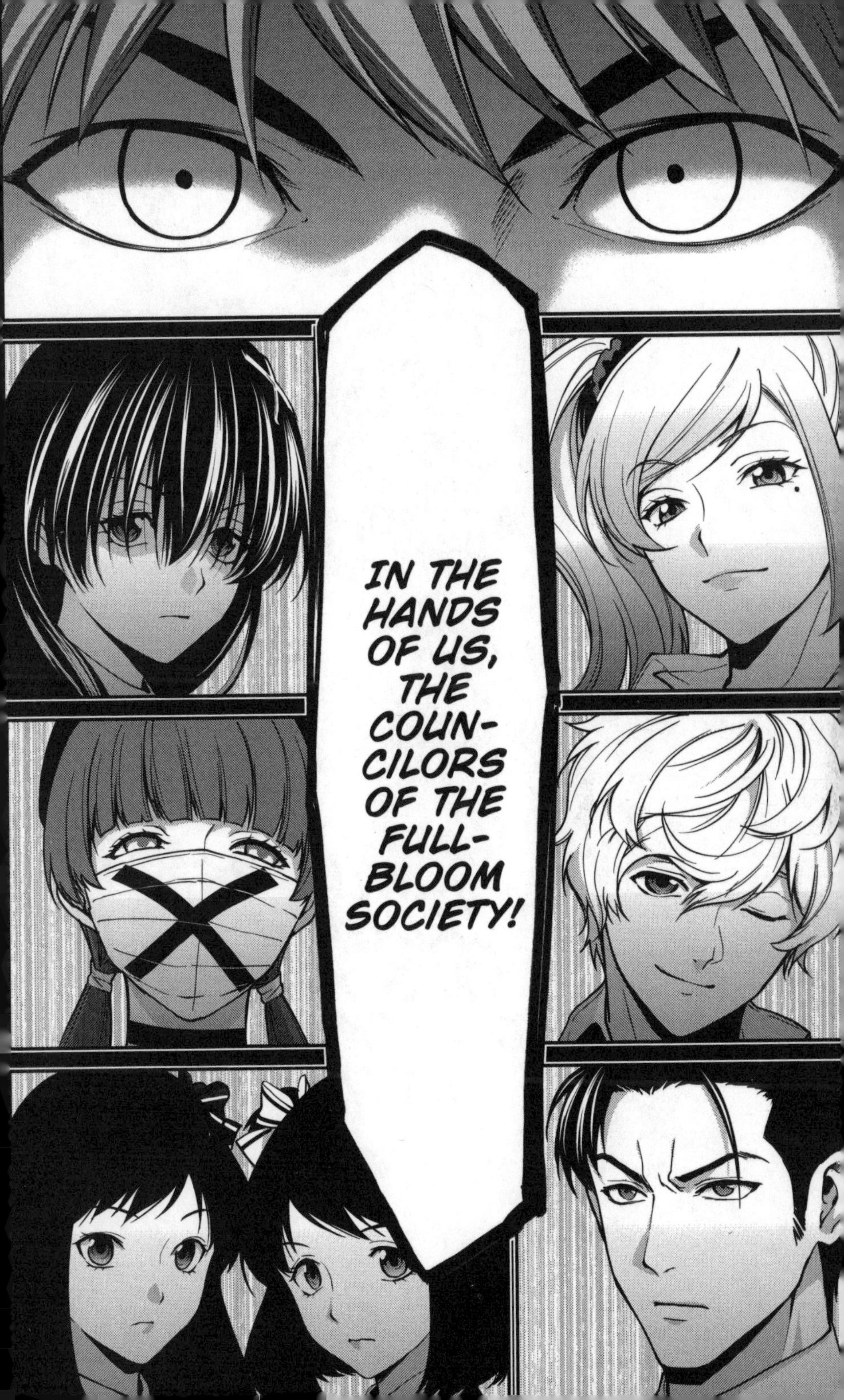
IN THE HANDS OF US, THE COUN-CILORS OF THE FULL-BLOOM SOCIETY!

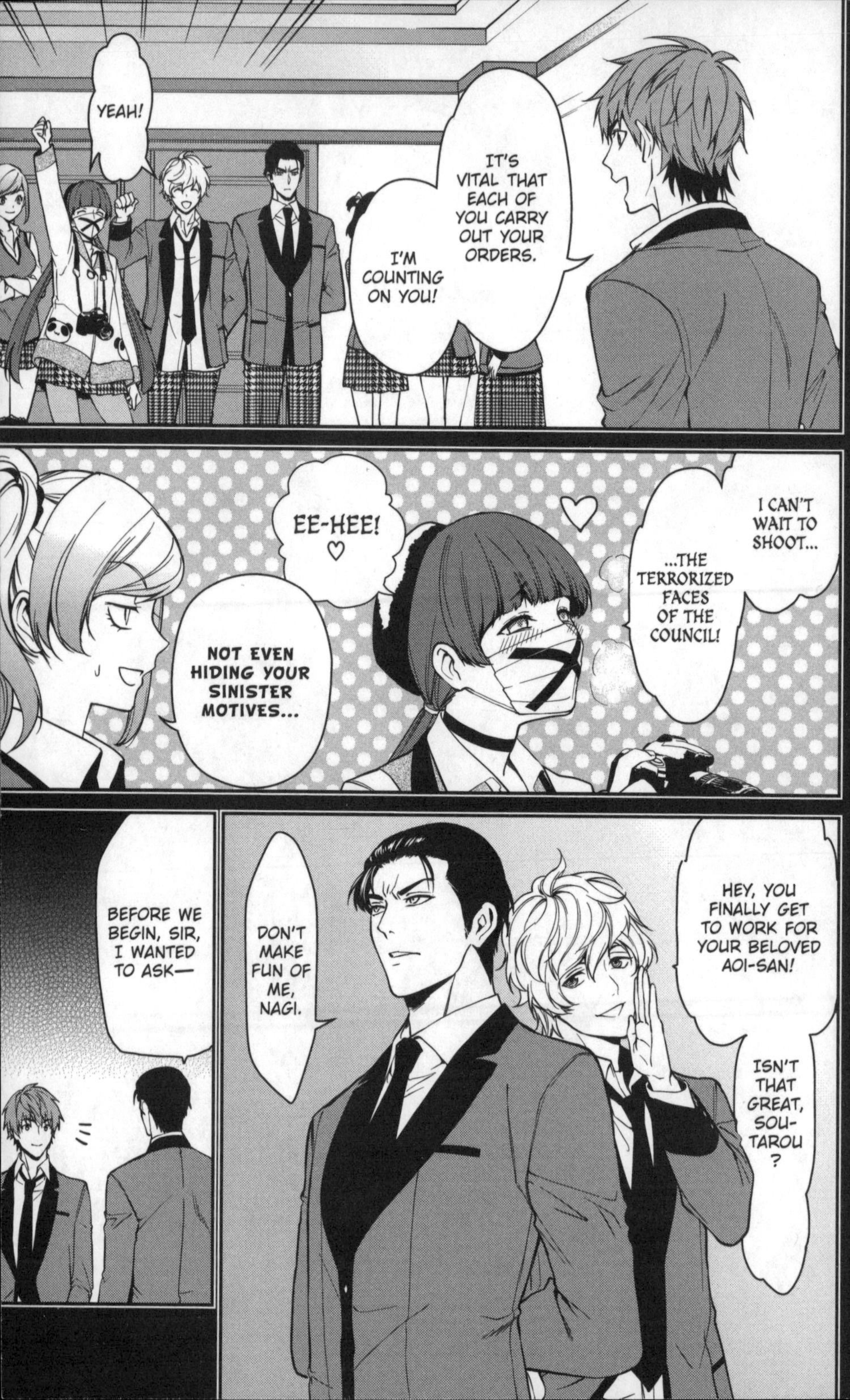
IT'S VITAL THAT EACH OF YOU CARRY OUT YOUR ORDERS.
I'M COUNTING ON YOU!
YEAH!
I CAN'T WAIT TO SHOOT...
...THE TERRORIZED FACES OF THE COUNCIL!
EE-HEE! ♡
NOT EVEN HIDING YOUR SINISTER MOTIVES...
HEY, YOU FINALLY GET TO WORK FOR YOUR BELOVED AOI-SAN!
ISN'T THAT GREAT, SOU-TAROU?
DON'T MAKE FUN OF ME, NAGI.
BEFORE WE BEGIN, SIR, I WANTED TO ASK—

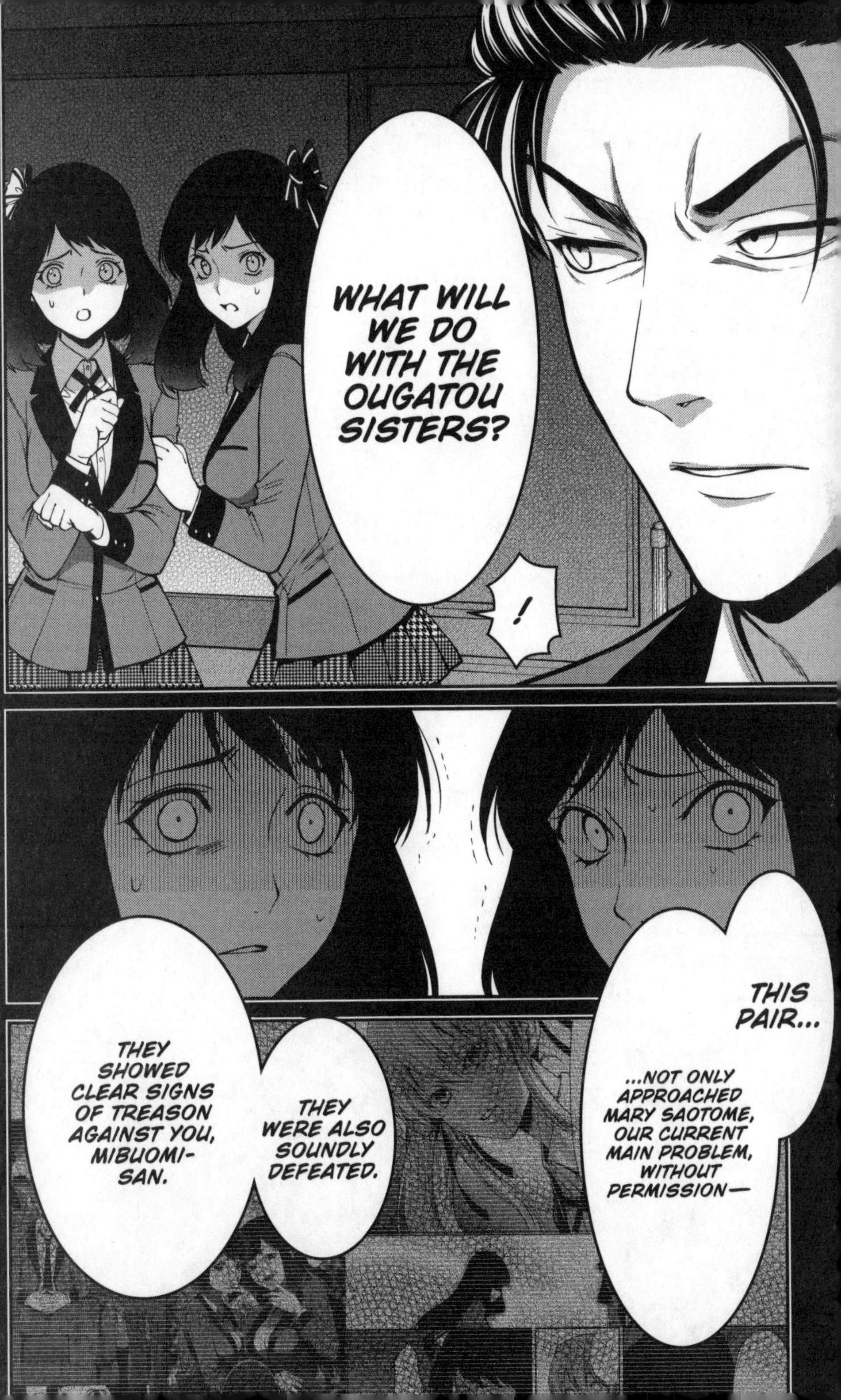
WHAT WILL WE DO WITH THE OUGATOU SISTERS?
!
THIS PAIR...
...NOT ONLY APPROACHED MARY SAOTOME, OUR CURRENT MAIN PROBLEM, WITHOUT PERMISSION—
THEY WERE ALSO SOUNDLY DEFEATED.
THEY SHOWED CLEAR SIGNS OF TREASON AGAINST YOU, MIBUOMI-SAN.

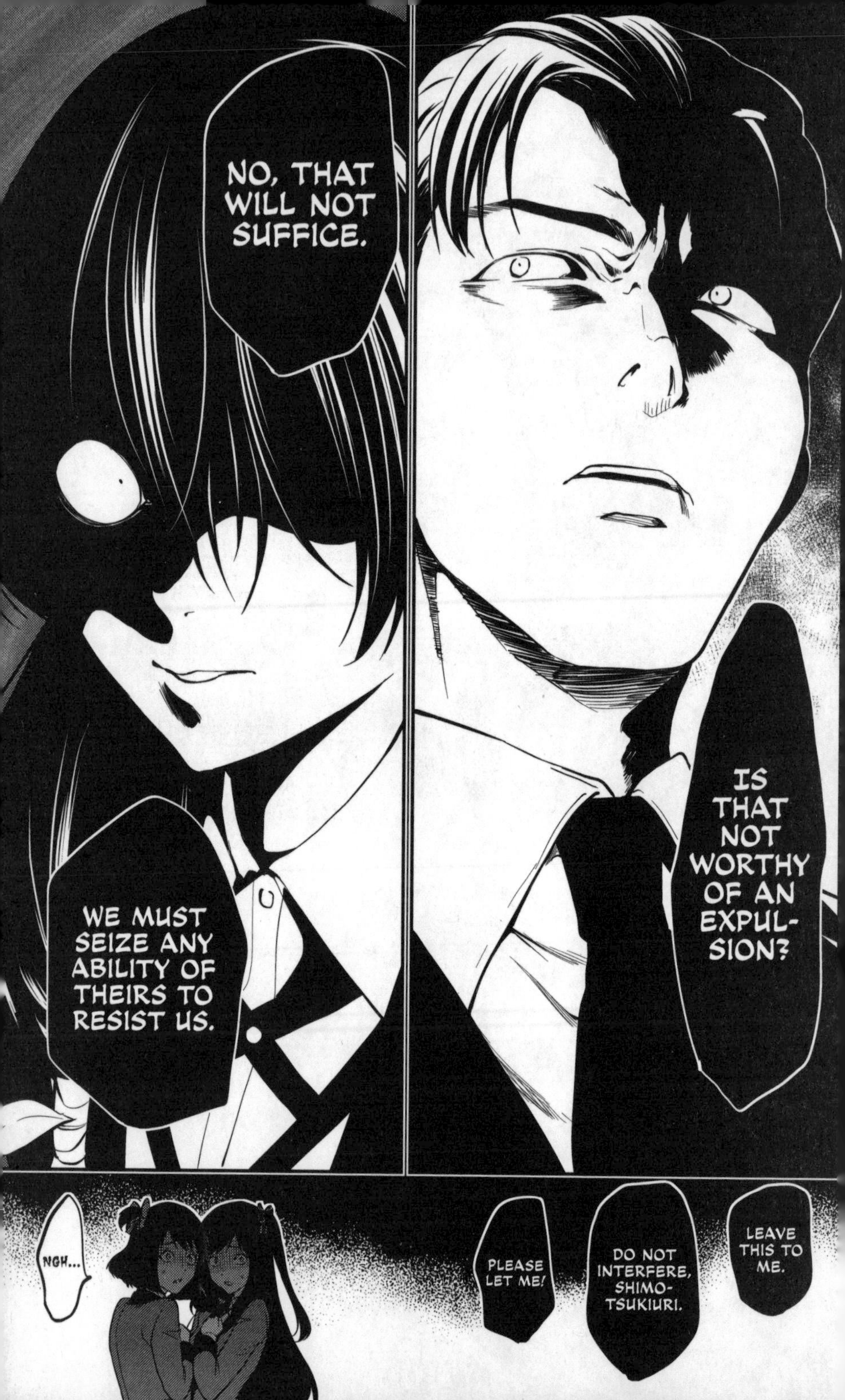
IS THAT NOT WORTHY OF AN EXPUL-SION?
NO, THAT WILL NOT SUFFICE.
WE MUST SEIZE ANY ABILITY OF THEIRS TO RESIST US.
LEAVE THIS TO ME.
DO NOT INTERFERE, SHIMO-TSUKIURI.
PLEASE LET ME!
NGH...

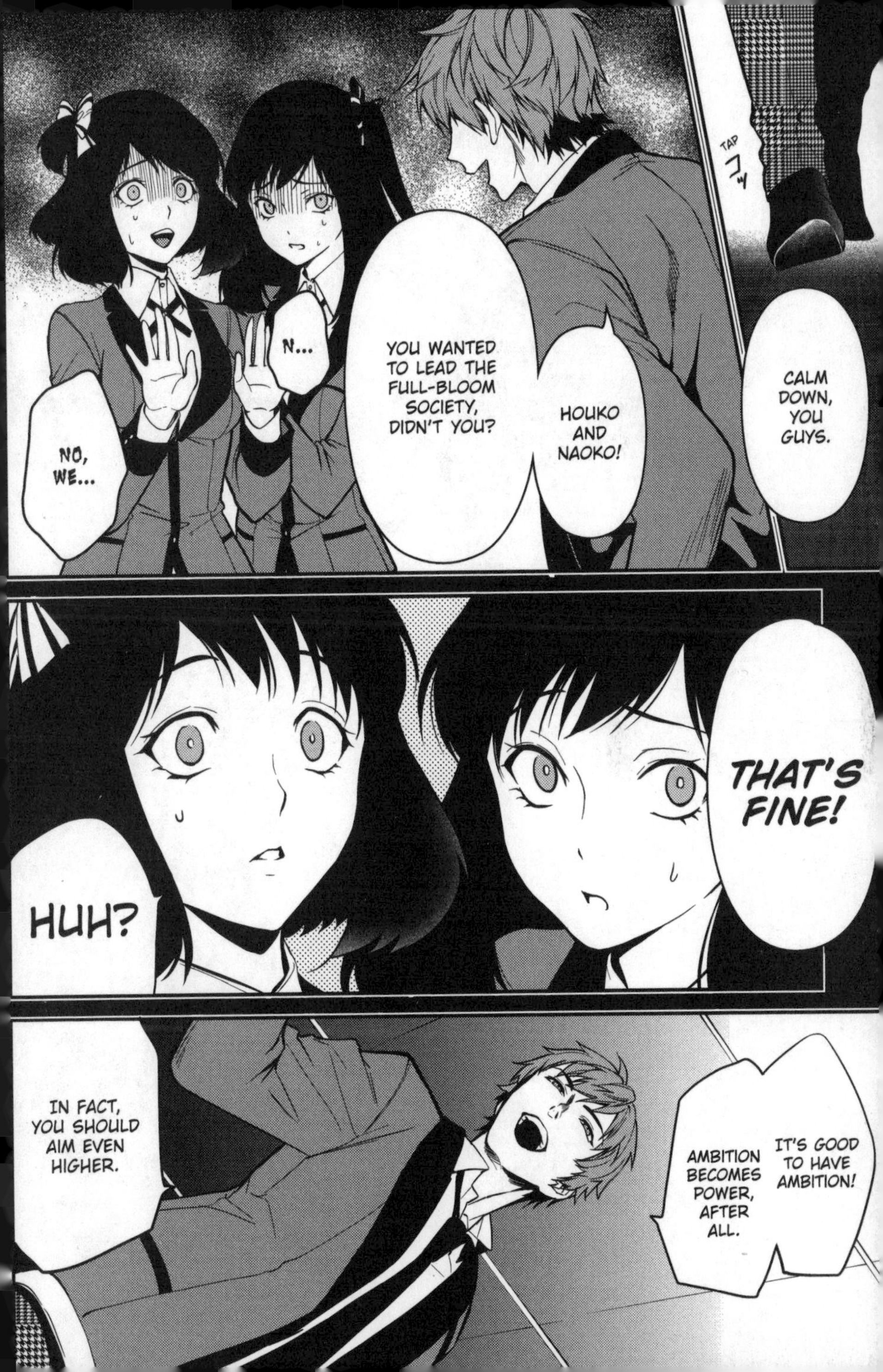
TAP
コッ
CALM DOWN, YOU GUYS.
HOUKO AND NAOKO!
YOU WANTED TO LEAD THE FULL-BLOOM SOCIETY, DIDN'T YOU?
N...
NO, WE...
THAT'S FINE!
HUH?
IT'S GOOD TO HAVE AMBITION!
AMBITION BECOMES POWER, AFTER ALL.
IN FACT, YOU SHOULD AIM EVEN HIGHER.

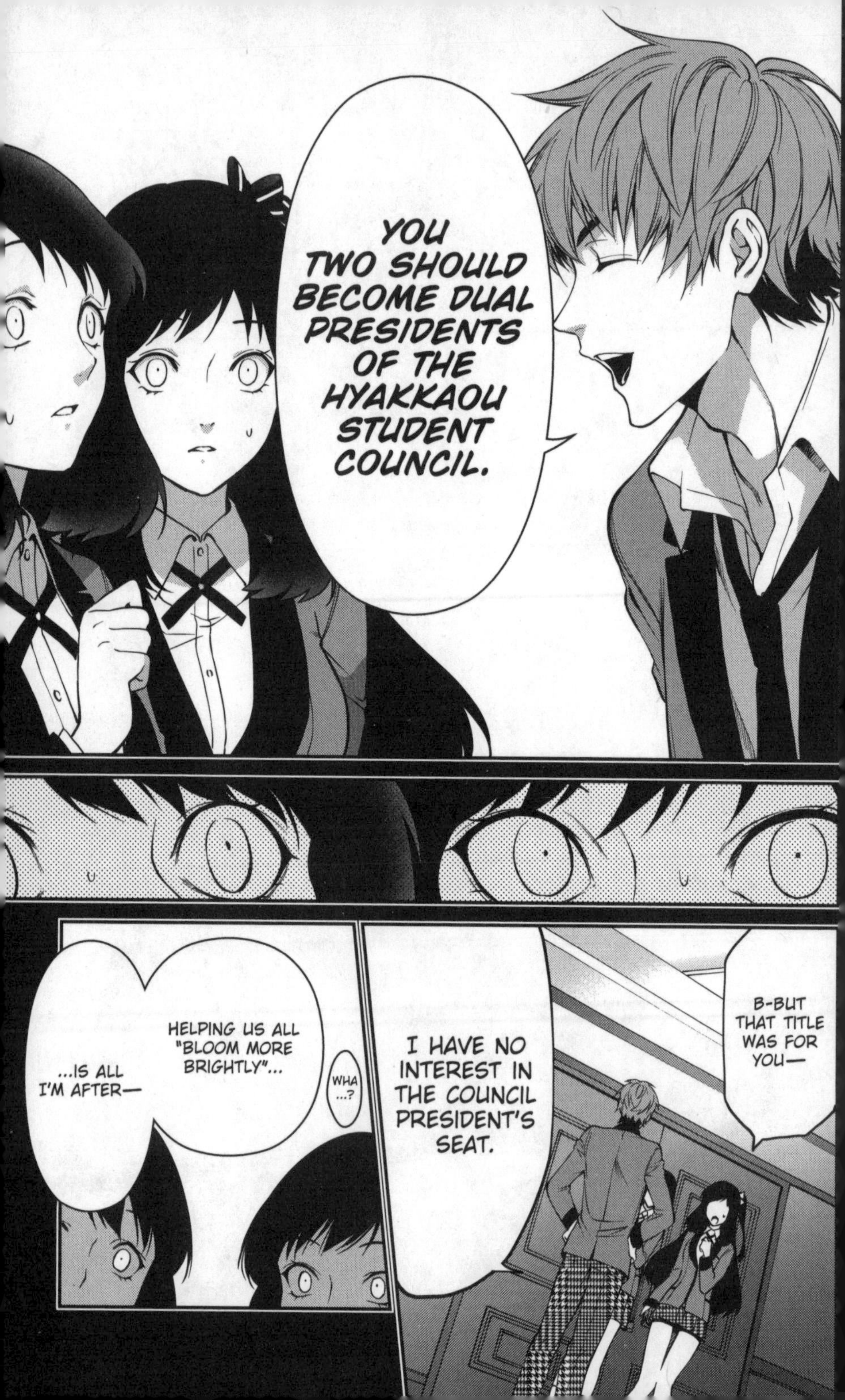
YOU TWO SHOULD BECOME DUAL PRESIDENTS OF THE HYAKKAOU STUDENT COUNCIL.
B-BUT THAT TITLE WAS FOR YOU—
I HAVE NO INTEREST IN THE COUNCIL PRESIDENT'S SEAT.
WHA ...?
HELPING US ALL "BLOOM MORE BRIGHTLY"...
...IS ALL I'M AFTER—

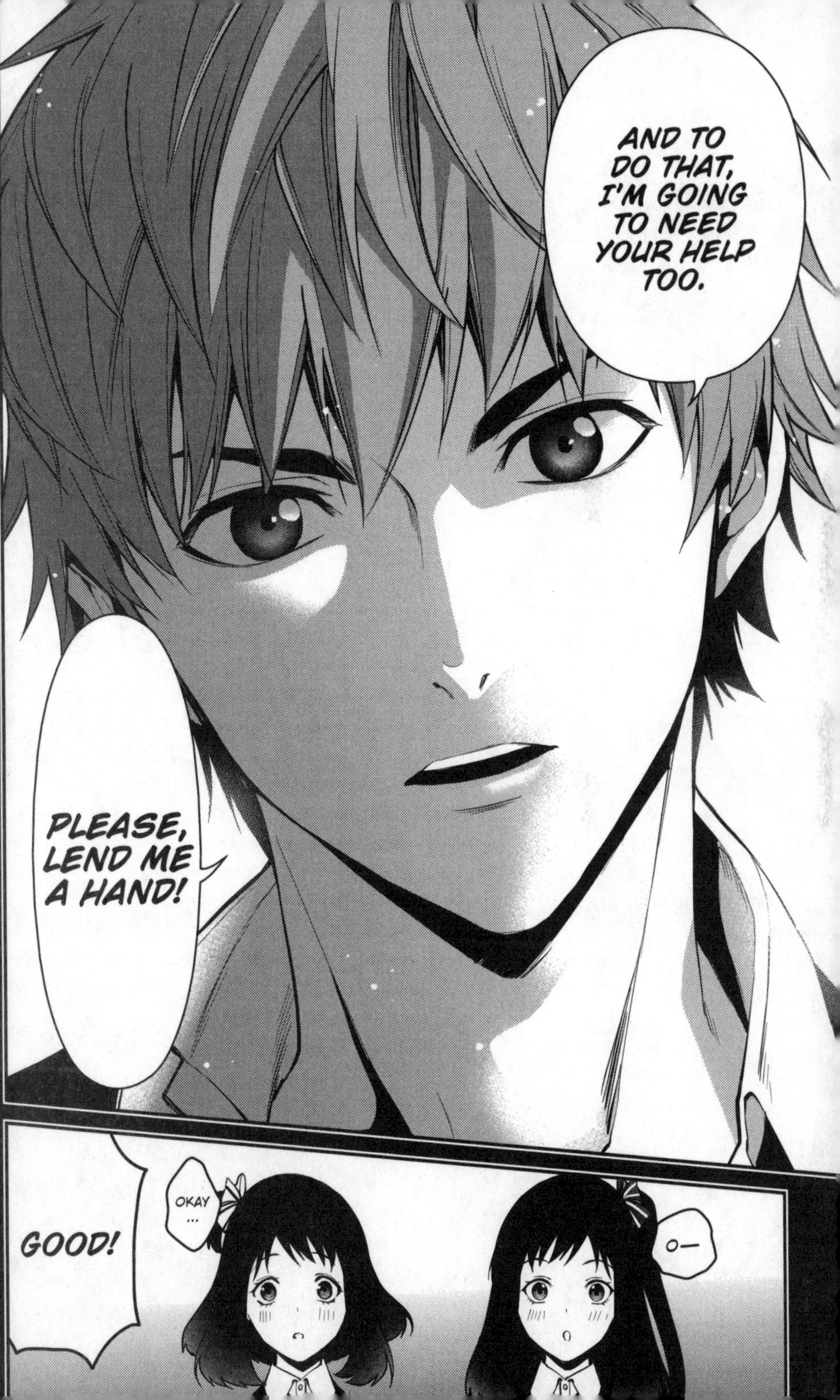
AND TO DO THAT, I'M GOING TO NEED YOUR HELP TOO.
PLEASE, LEND ME A HAND!
O—
OKAY ...
GOOD!

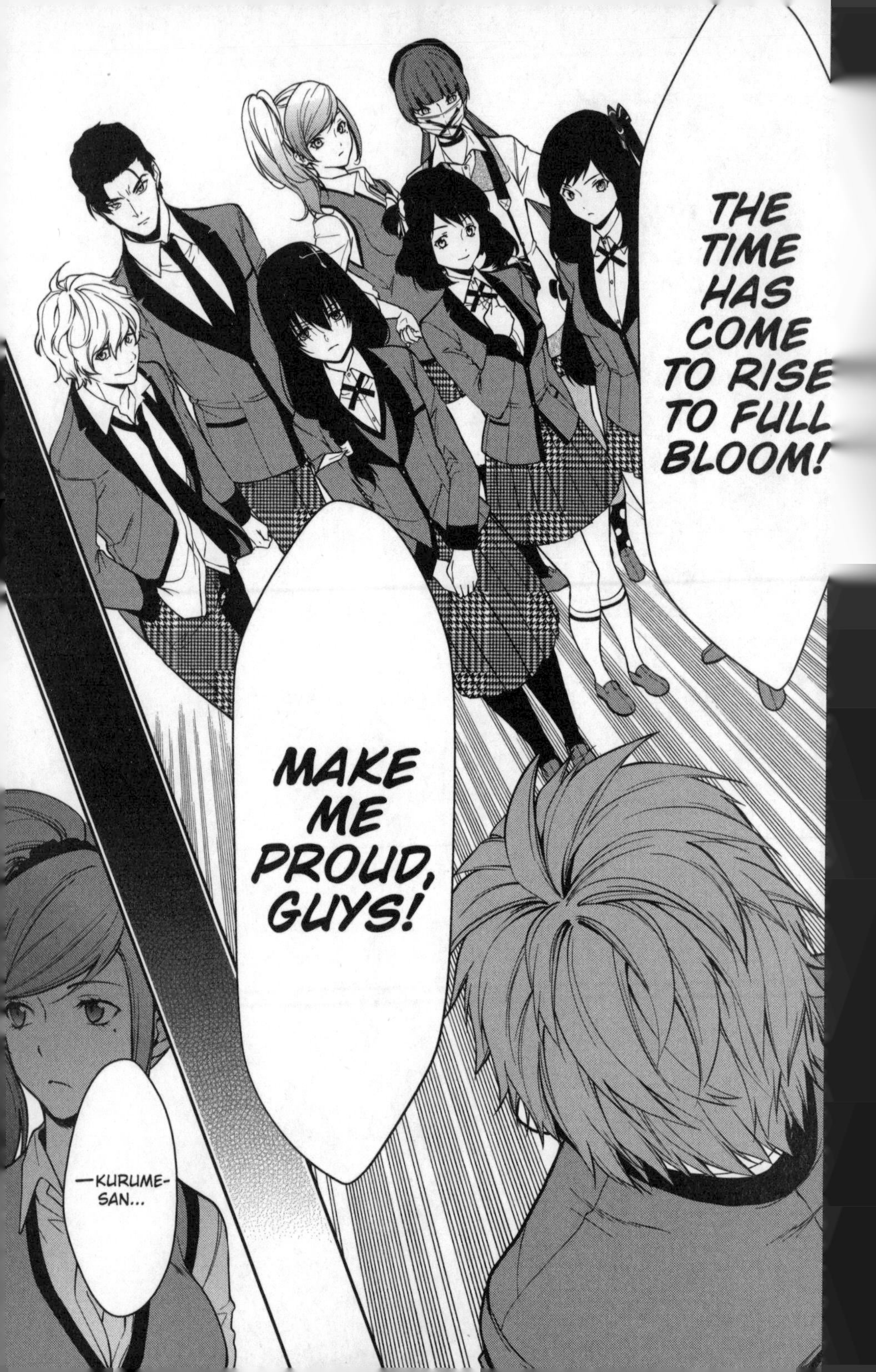
THE TIME HAS COME TO RISE TO FULL BLOOM!
MAKE ME PROUD, GUYS!
—KURUME-SAN...

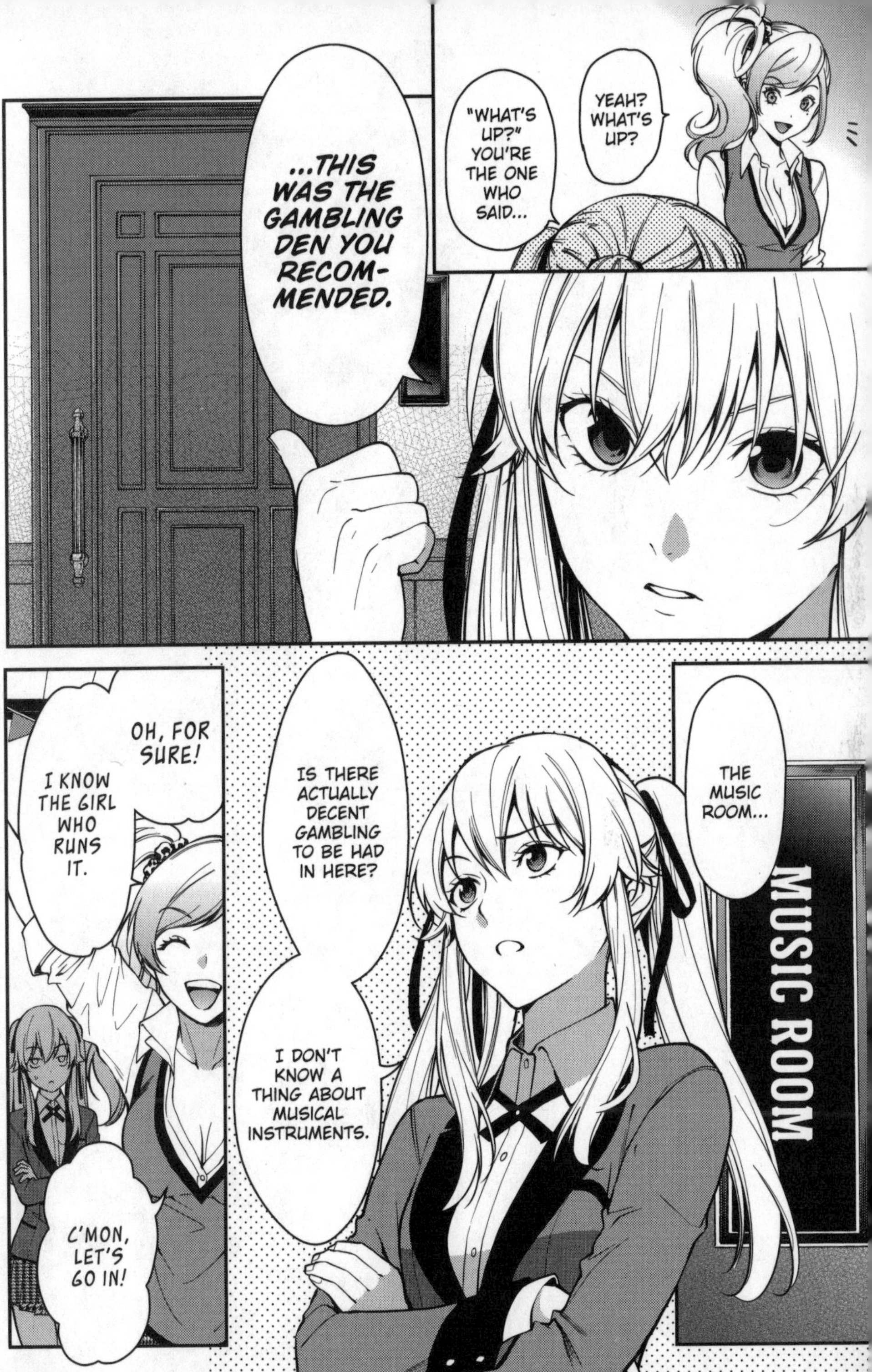
YEAH? WHAT'S UP?
"WHAT'S UP?" YOU'RE THE ONE WHO SAID...
...THIS WAS THE GAMBLING DEN YOU RECOMMENDED.
THE MUSIC ROOM...
MUSIC ROOM
IS THERE ACTUALLY DECENT GAMBLING TO BE HAD IN HERE?
I DON'T KNOW A THING ABOUT MUSICAL INSTRUMENTS.
OH, FOR SURE!
I KNOW THE GIRL WHO RUNS IT.
C'MON, LET'S GO IN!

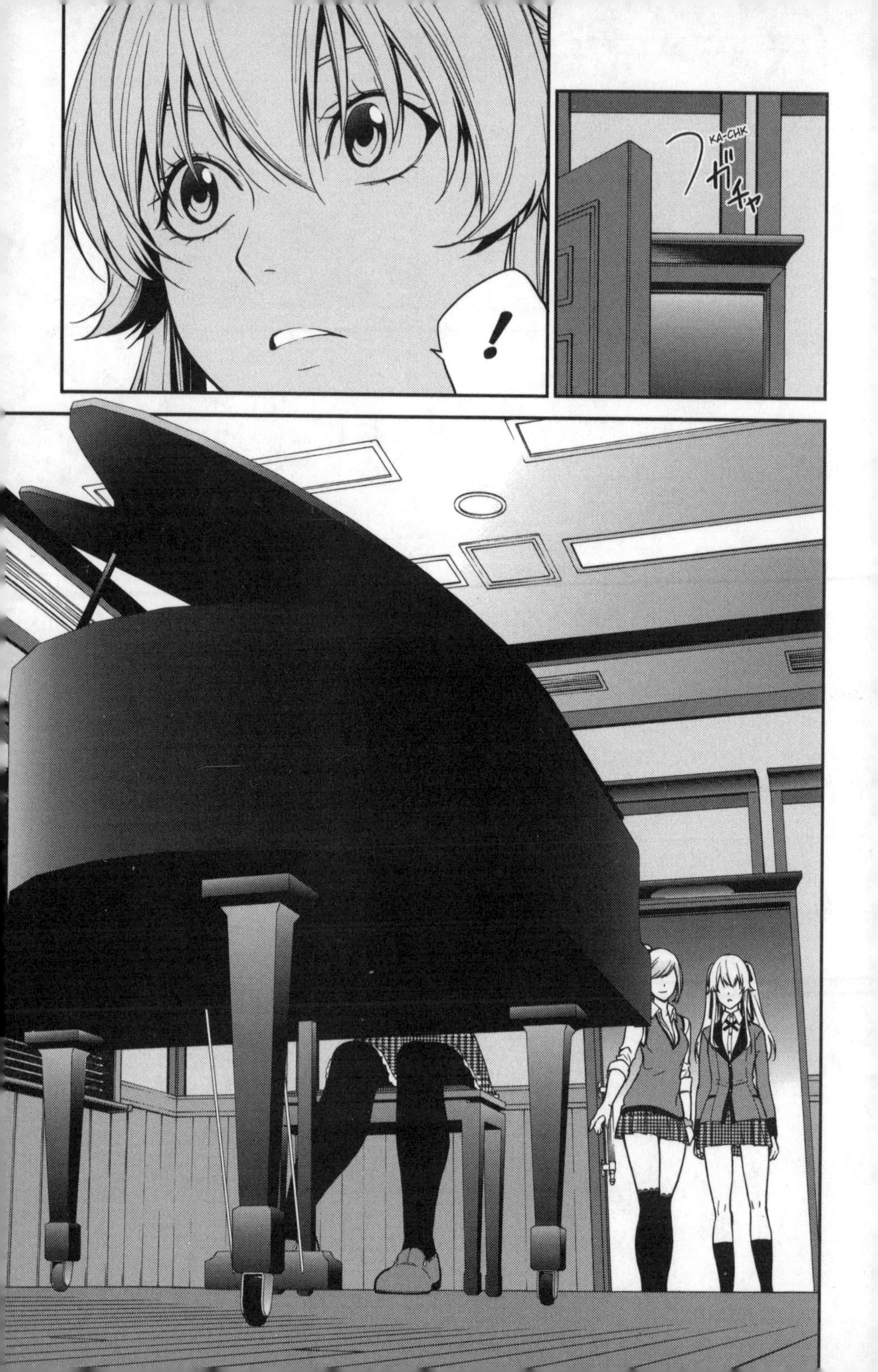
KA-CHK
ガチャ
!

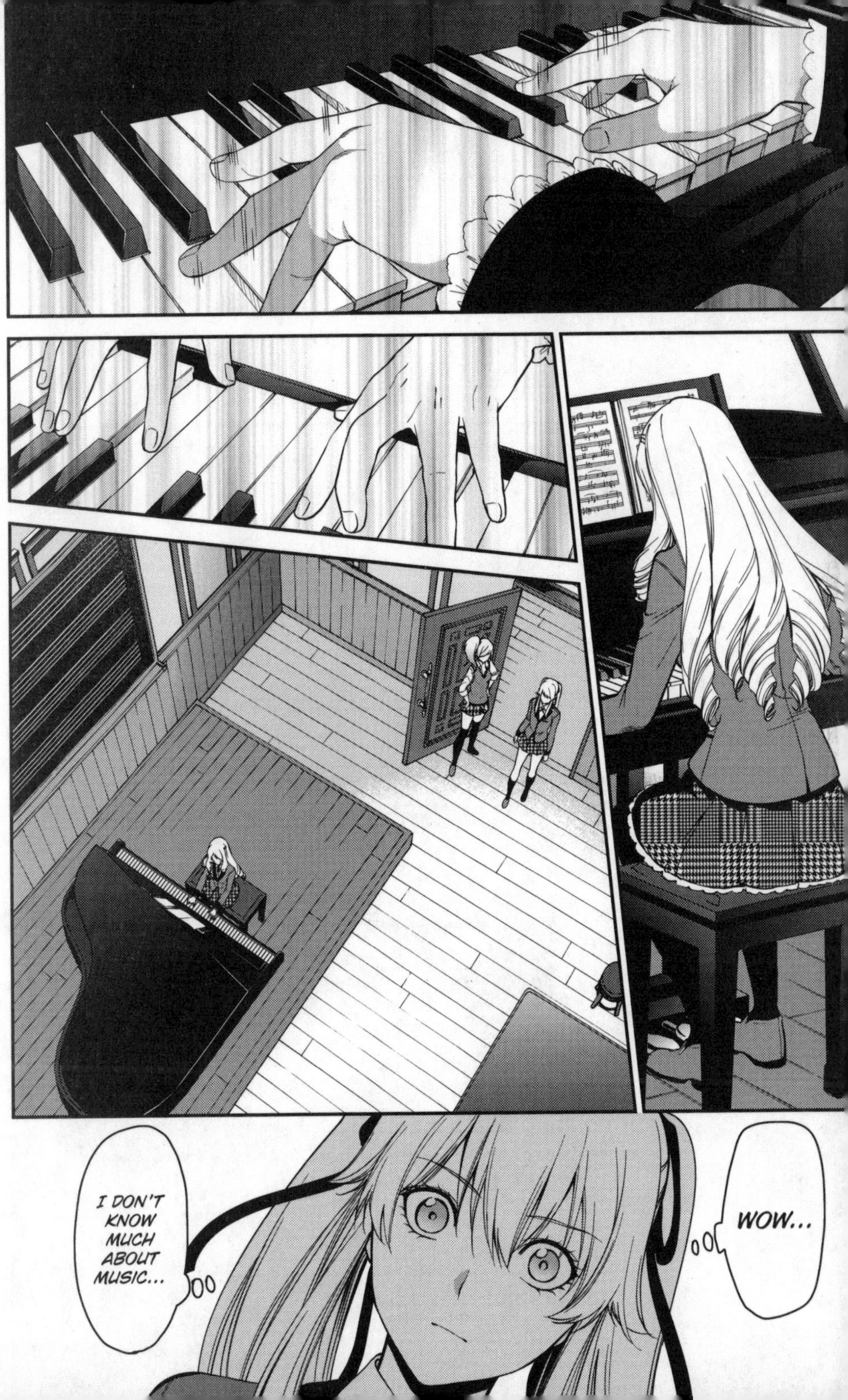
WOW...
I DON'T KNOW MUCH ABOUT MUSIC...

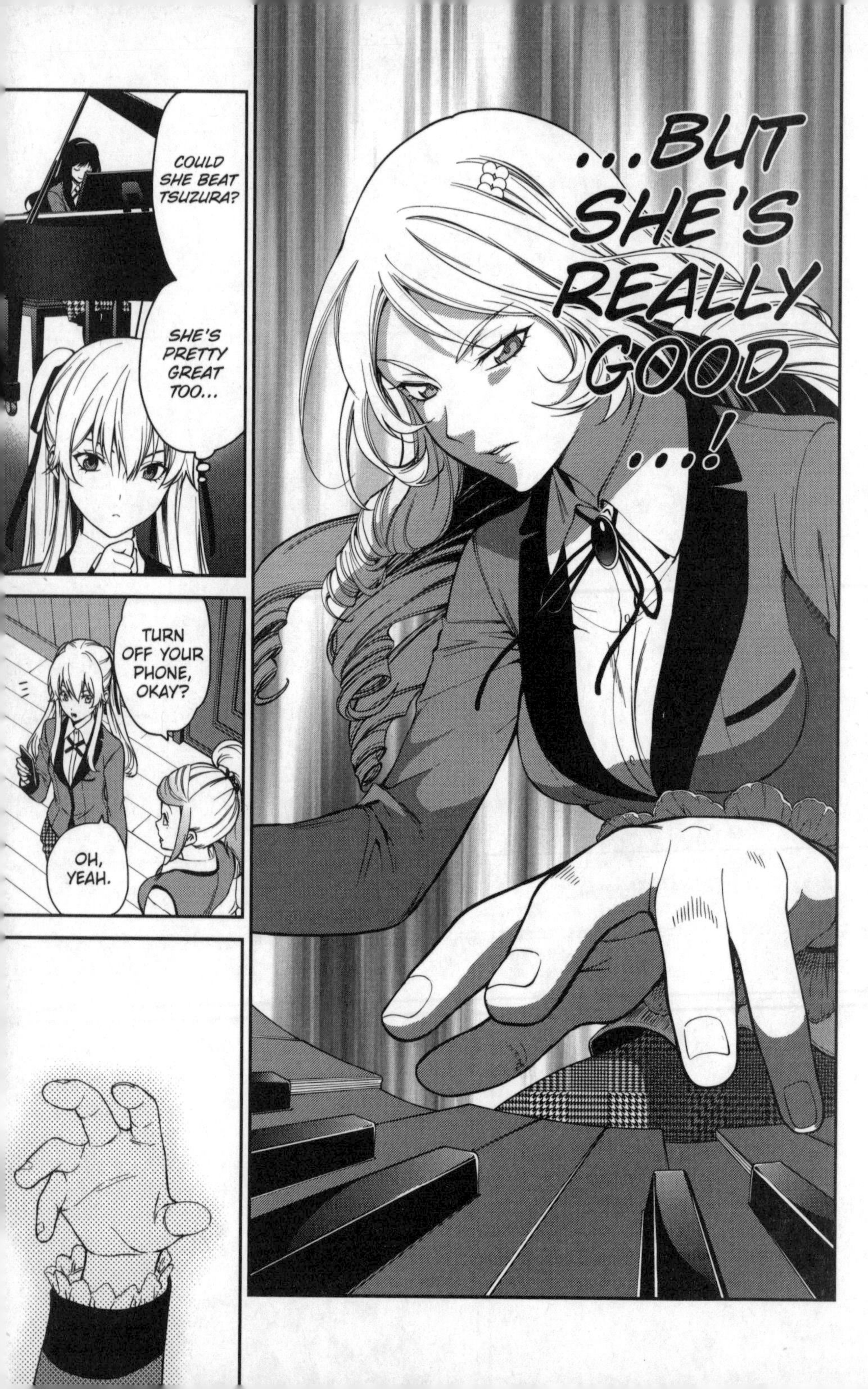
...BUT SHE'S REALLY GOOD ....!
COULD SHE BEAT TSUZURA?
SHE'S PRETTY GREAT TOO...
TURN OFF YOUR PHONE, OKAY?
OH, YEAH.

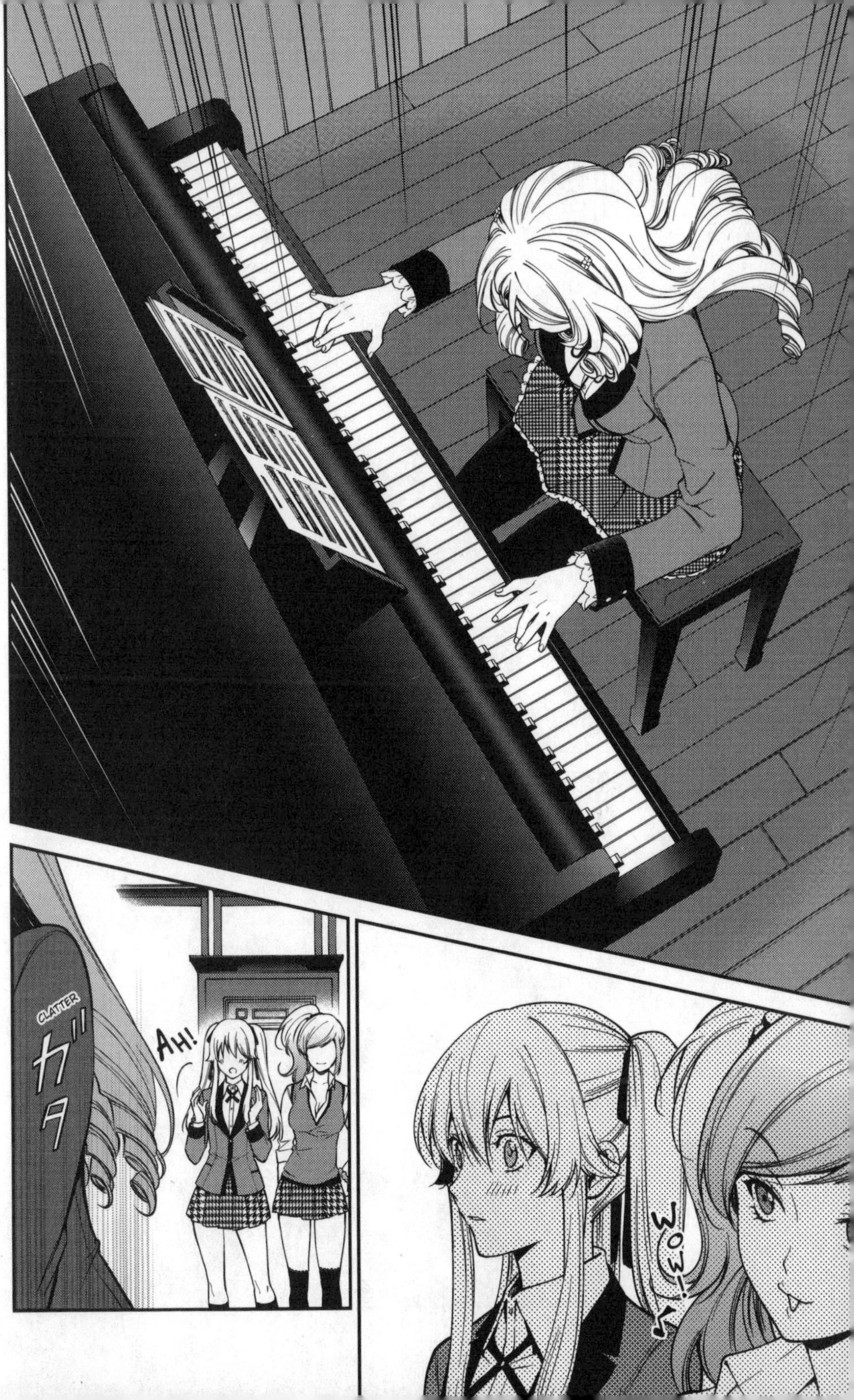
WOW!
AH!
CLATTER
ガタ

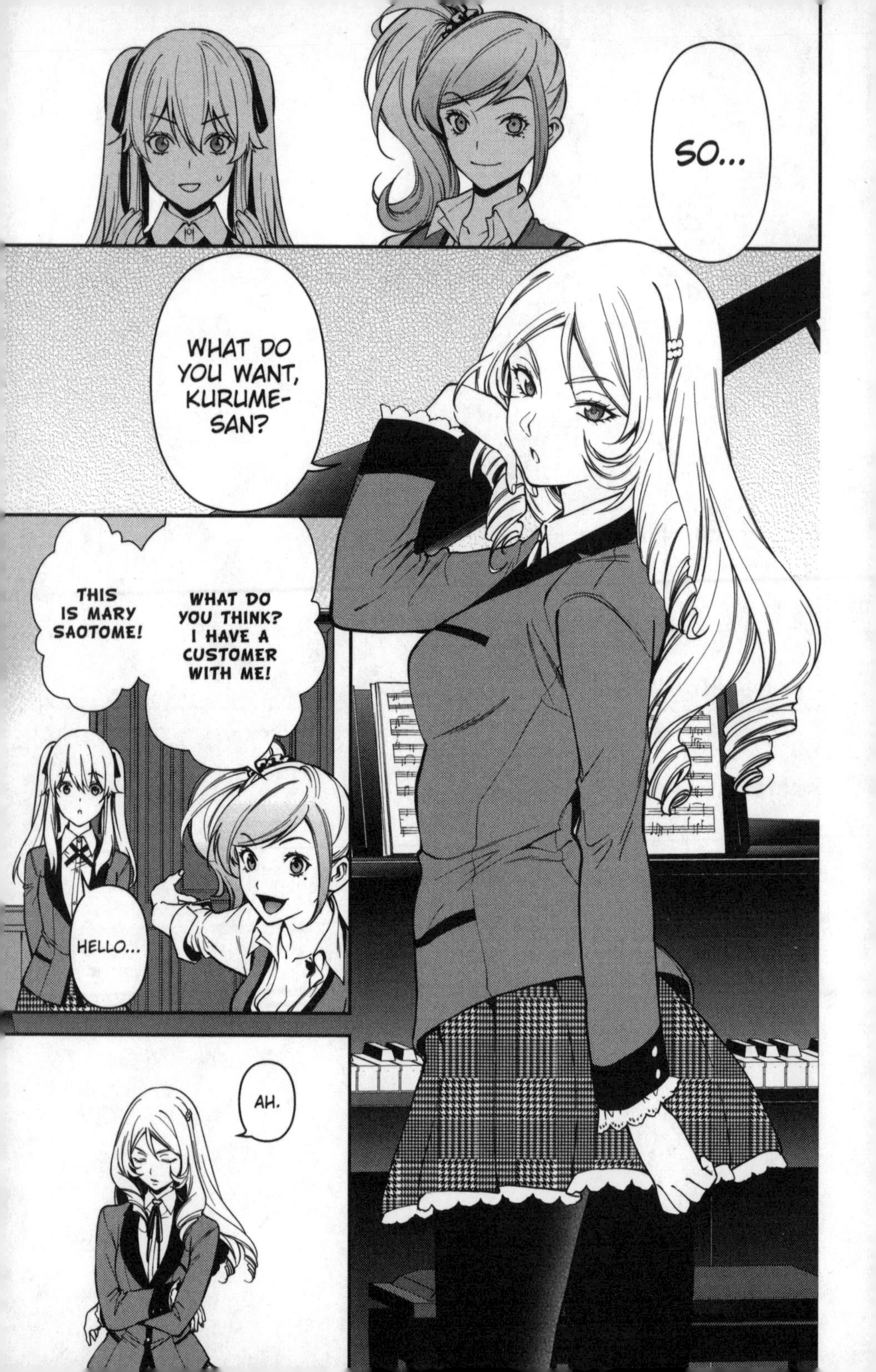
SO...
WHAT DO YOU WANT, KURUME-SAN?
WHAT DO YOU THINK? I HAVE A CUSTOMER WITH ME!
THIS IS MARY SAOTOME!
HELLO...
AH.

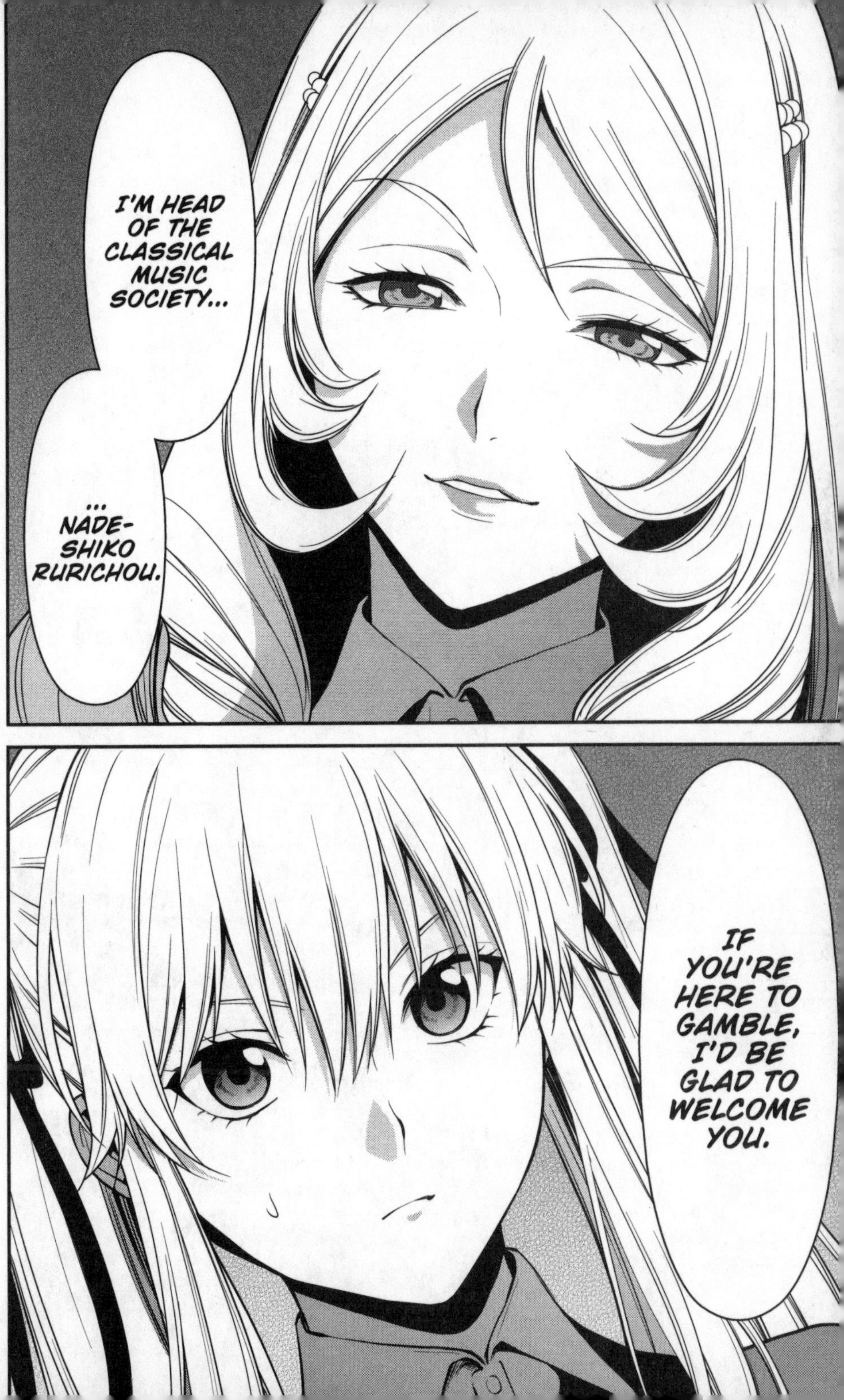
I'M HEAD OF THE CLASSICAL MUSIC SOCIETY...
...NADE-SHIKO RURICHOU.
IF YOU'RE HERE TO GAMBLE, I'D BE GLAD TO WELCOME YOU.

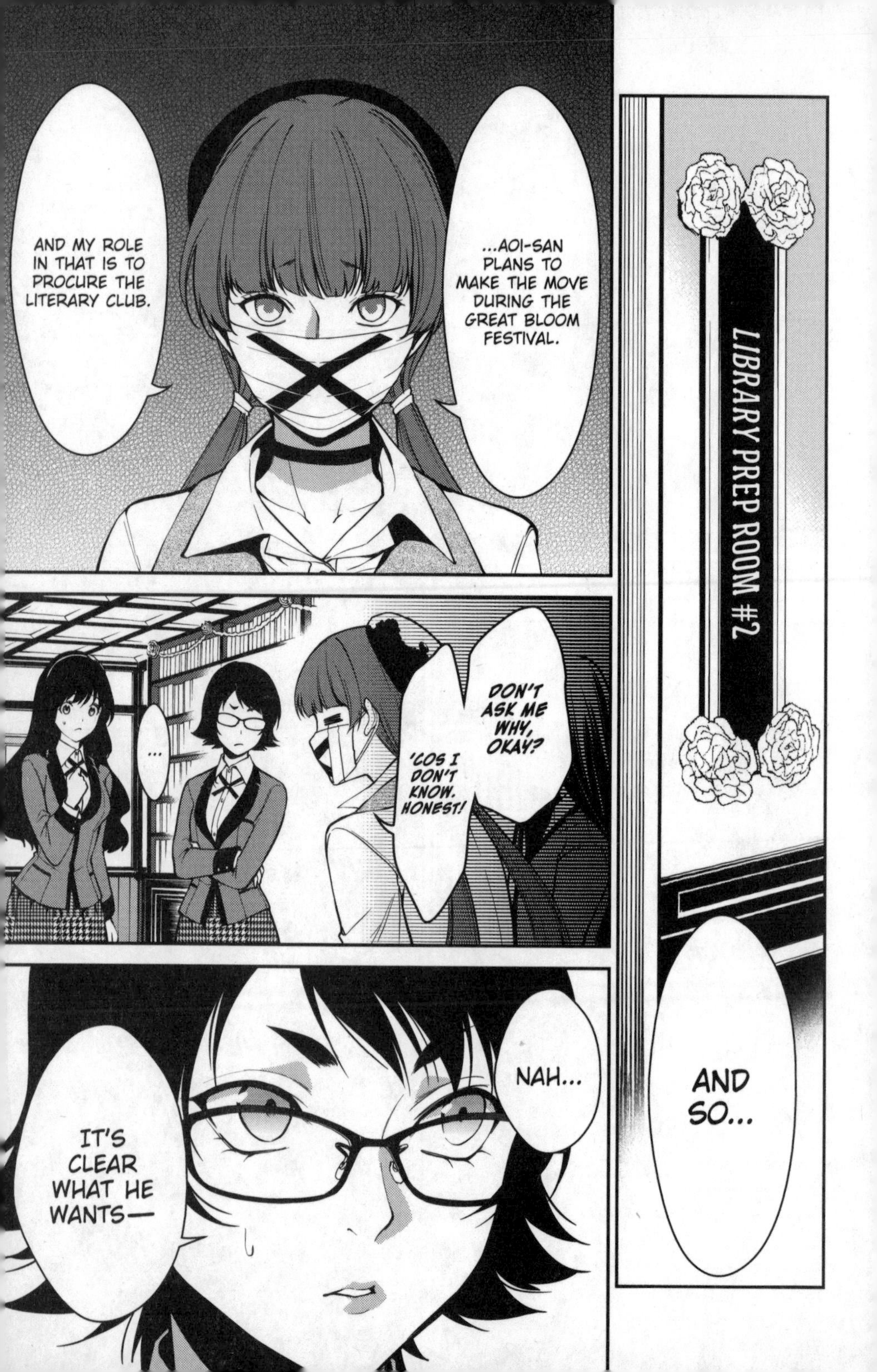
LIBRARY PREP ROOM #2
AND SO...
...AOI-SAN PLANS TO MAKE THE MOVE DURING THE GREAT BLOOM FESTIVAL.
AND MY ROLE IN THAT IS TO PROCURE THE LITERARY CLUB.
DON'T ASK ME WHY, OKAY?
'COS I DON'T KNOW. HONEST!
...
NAH...
IT'S CLEAR WHAT HE WANTS—

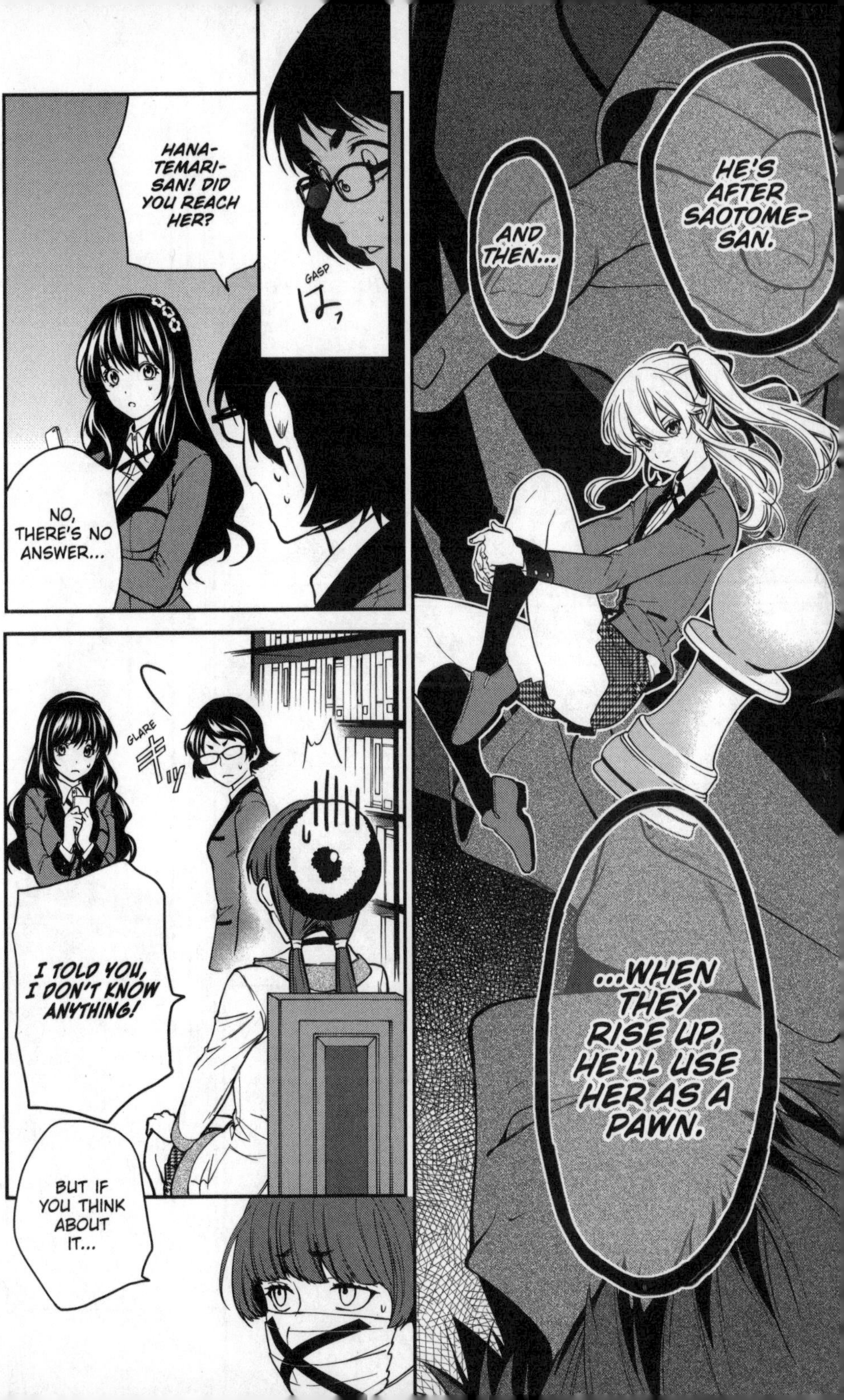
HE'S AFTER SAOTOME-SAN.
AND THEN...
...WHEN THEY RISE UP, HE'LL USE HER AS A PAWN.
GASP
は，
HANA-TEMARI-SAN! DID YOU REACH HER?
NO, THERE'S NO ANSWER...
GLARE
キッ
I TOLD YOU, I DON'T KNOW ANYTHING!
BUT IF YOU THINK ABOUT IT...

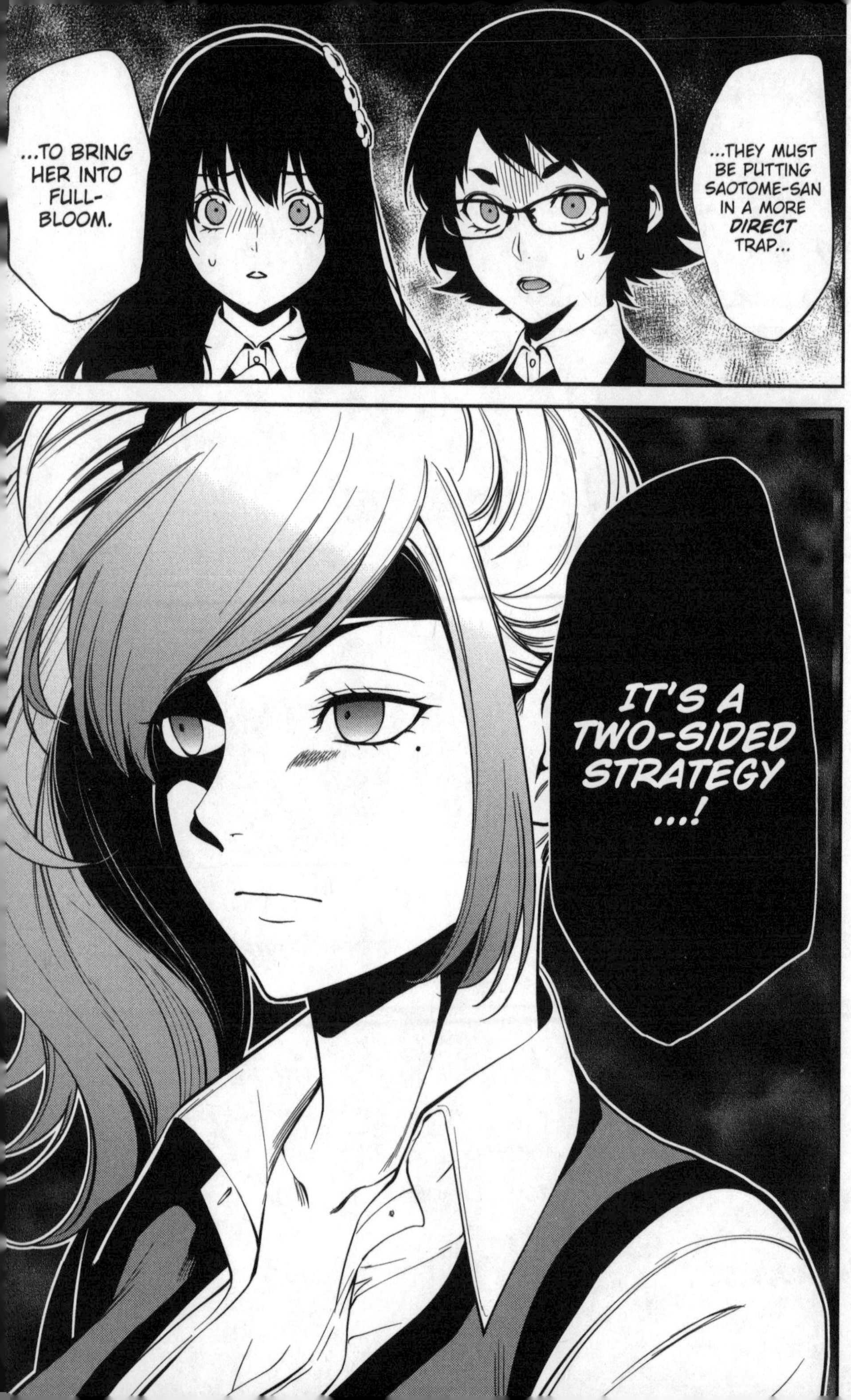
...THEY MUST BE PUTTING SAOTOME-SAN IN A MORE DIRECT TRAP...
...TO BRING HER INTO FULL-BLOOM.
IT'S A TWO-SIDED STRATEGY ...!

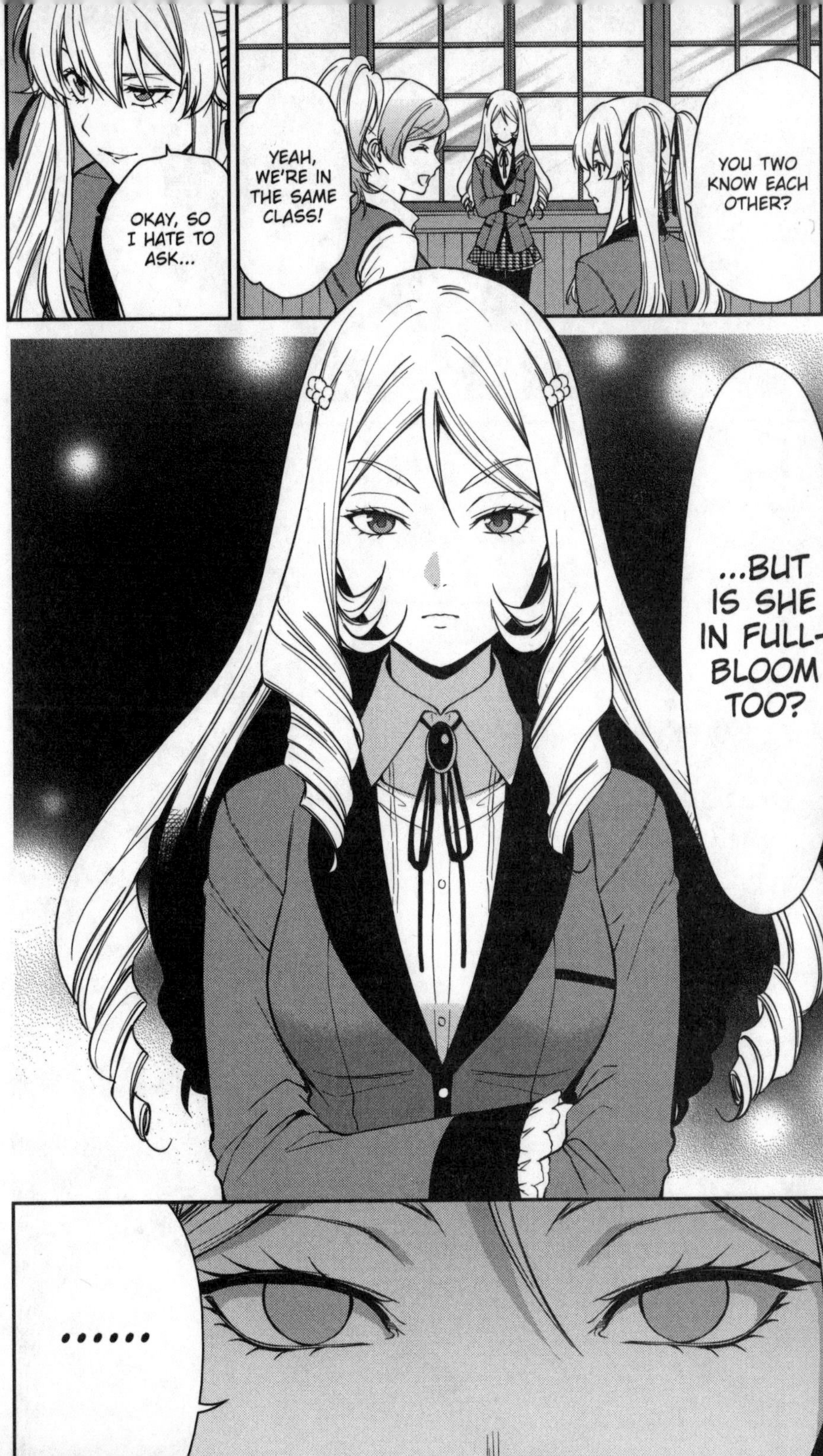
YOU TWO KNOW EACH OTHER?
YEAH, WE'RE IN THE SAME CLASS!
OKAY, SO I HATE TO ASK...
...BUT IS SHE IN FULL-BLOOM TOO?
......

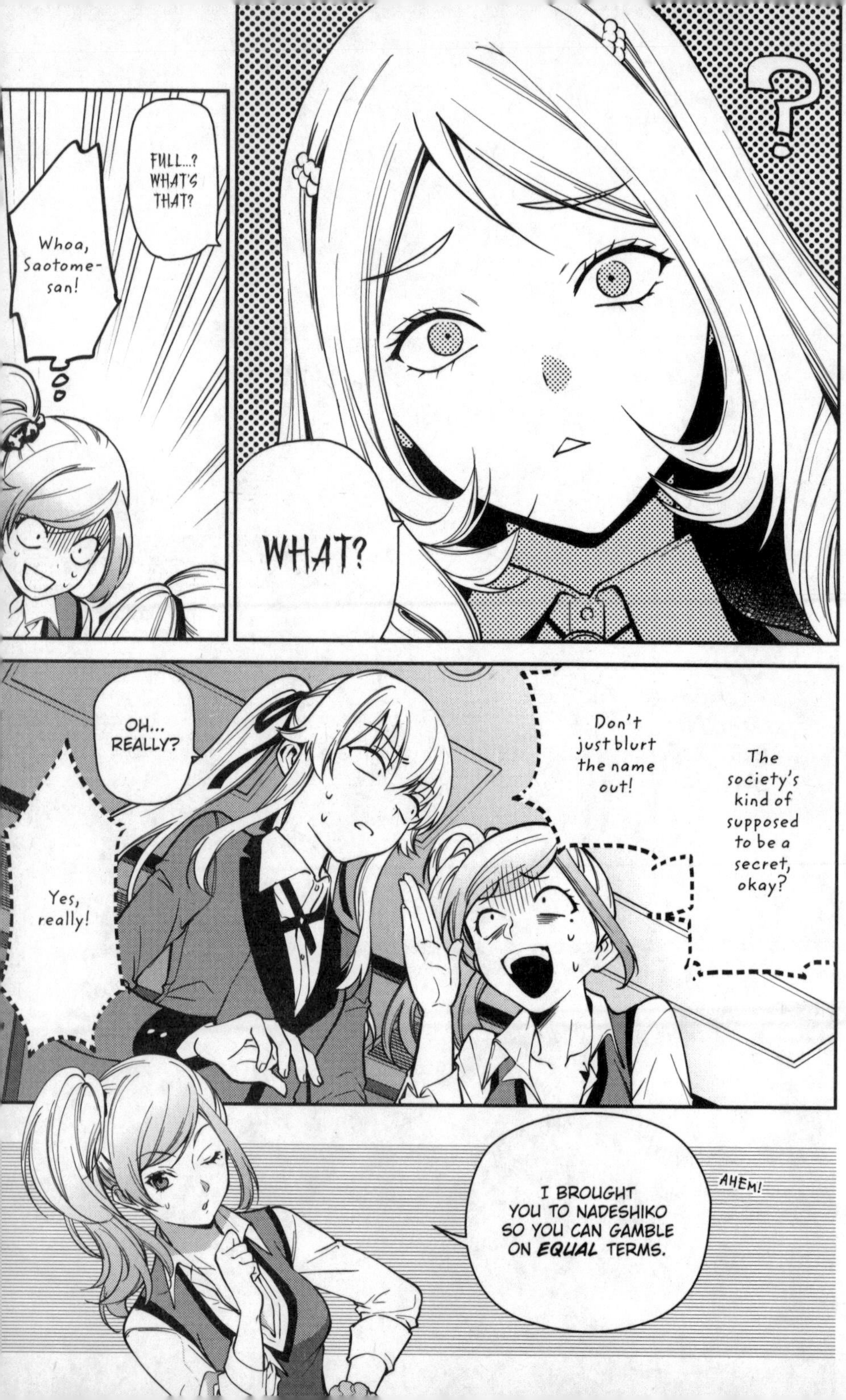
?
WHAT?
FULL...? WHAT'S THAT?
Whoa, Saotome-san!
Don't just blurt the name out! The society's kind of supposed to be a secret, okay?
OH... REALLY?
Yes, really!
AHEM!
I BROUGHT YOU TO NADESHIKO SO YOU CAN GAMBLE ON *EQUAL* TERMS.

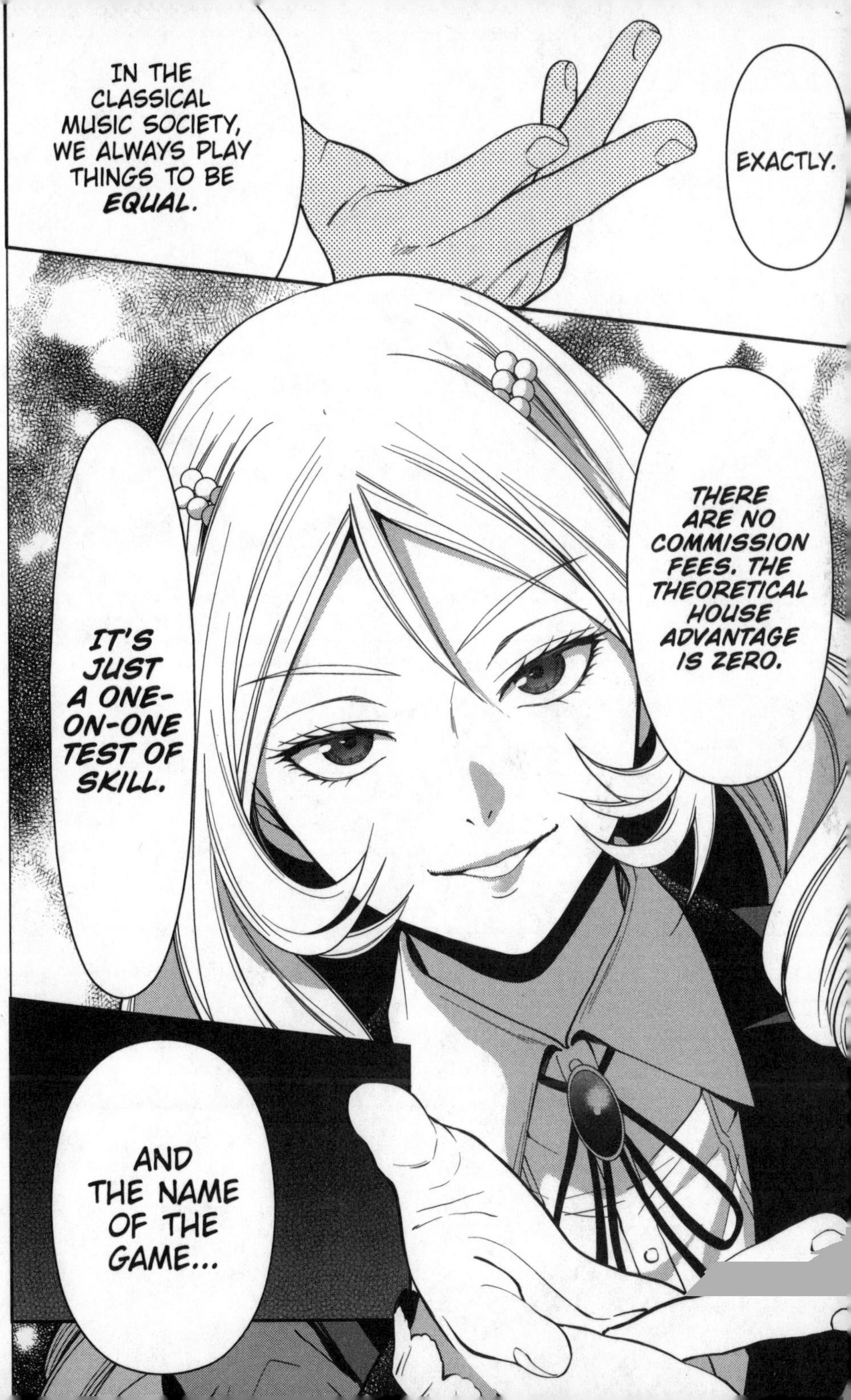
EXACTLY.
IN THE CLASSICAL MUSIC SOCIETY, WE ALWAYS PLAY THINGS TO BE *EQUAL*.
THERE ARE NO COMMISSION FEES. THE THEORETICAL HOUSE ADVANTAGE IS ZERO.
*IT'S JUST A ONE-ON-ONE TEST OF SKILL.*
AND THE NAME OF THE GAME...

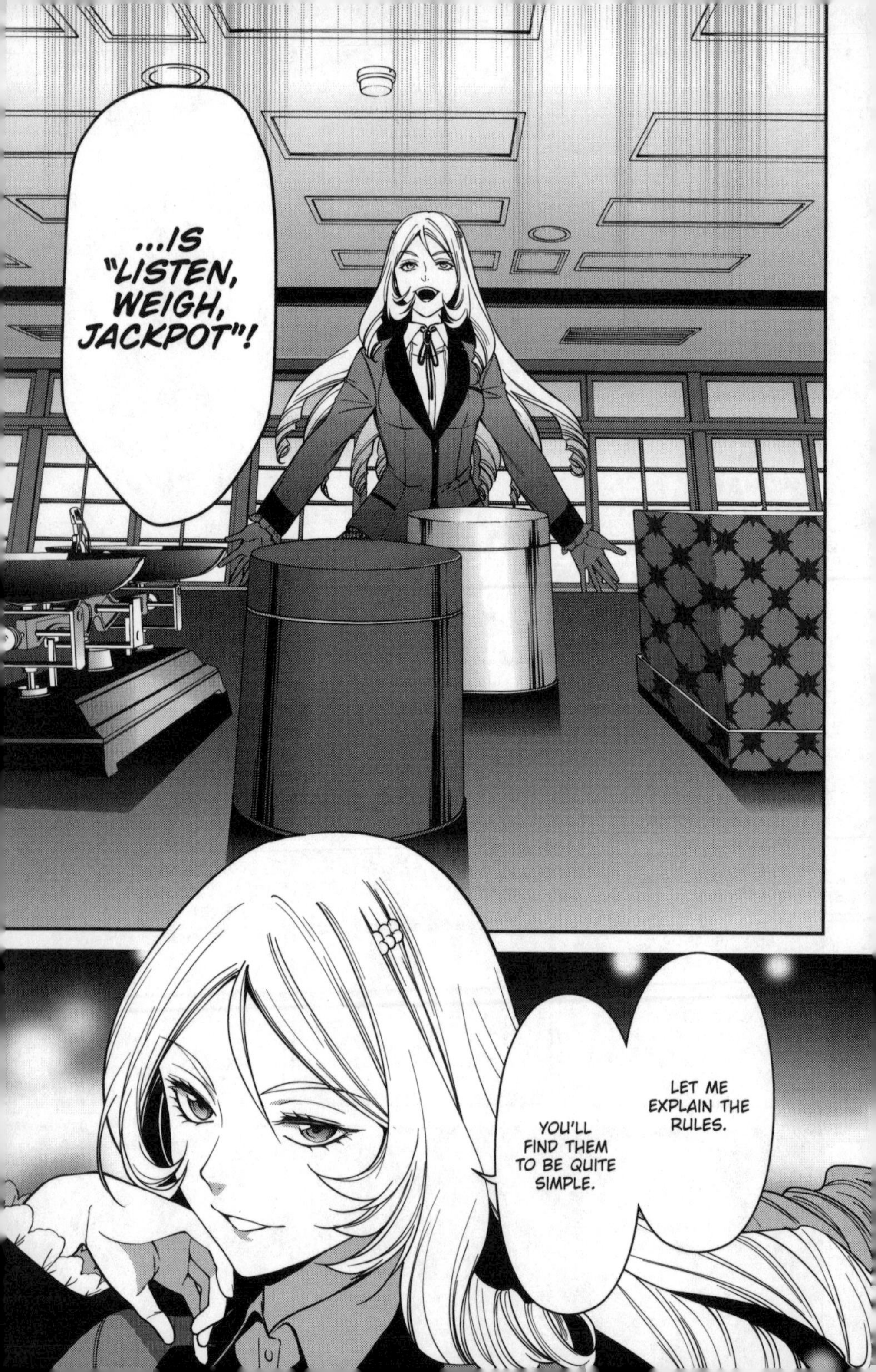
...IS "LISTEN, WEIGH, JACKPOT"!
LET ME EXPLAIN THE RULES.
YOU'LL FIND THEM TO BE QUITE SIMPLE.

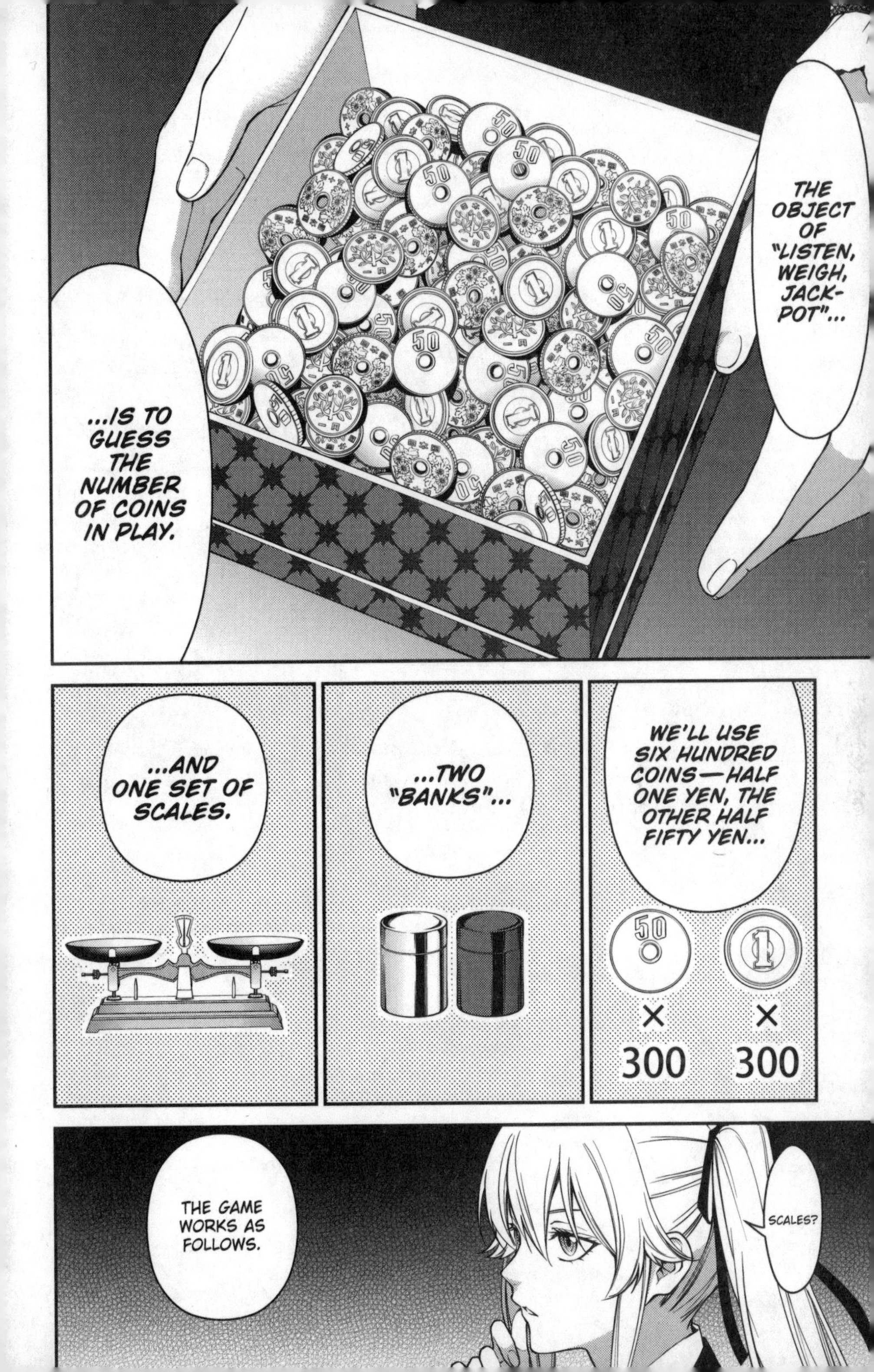
THE OBJECT OF "LISTEN, WEIGH, JACKPOT"...
...IS TO GUESS THE NUMBER OF COINS IN PLAY.
WE'LL USE SIX HUNDRED COINS—HALF ONE YEN, THE OTHER HALF FIFTY YEN...
50
×
300
1
×
300
...TWO "BANKS"...
...AND ONE SET OF SCALES.
SCALES?
THE GAME WORKS AS FOLLOWS.

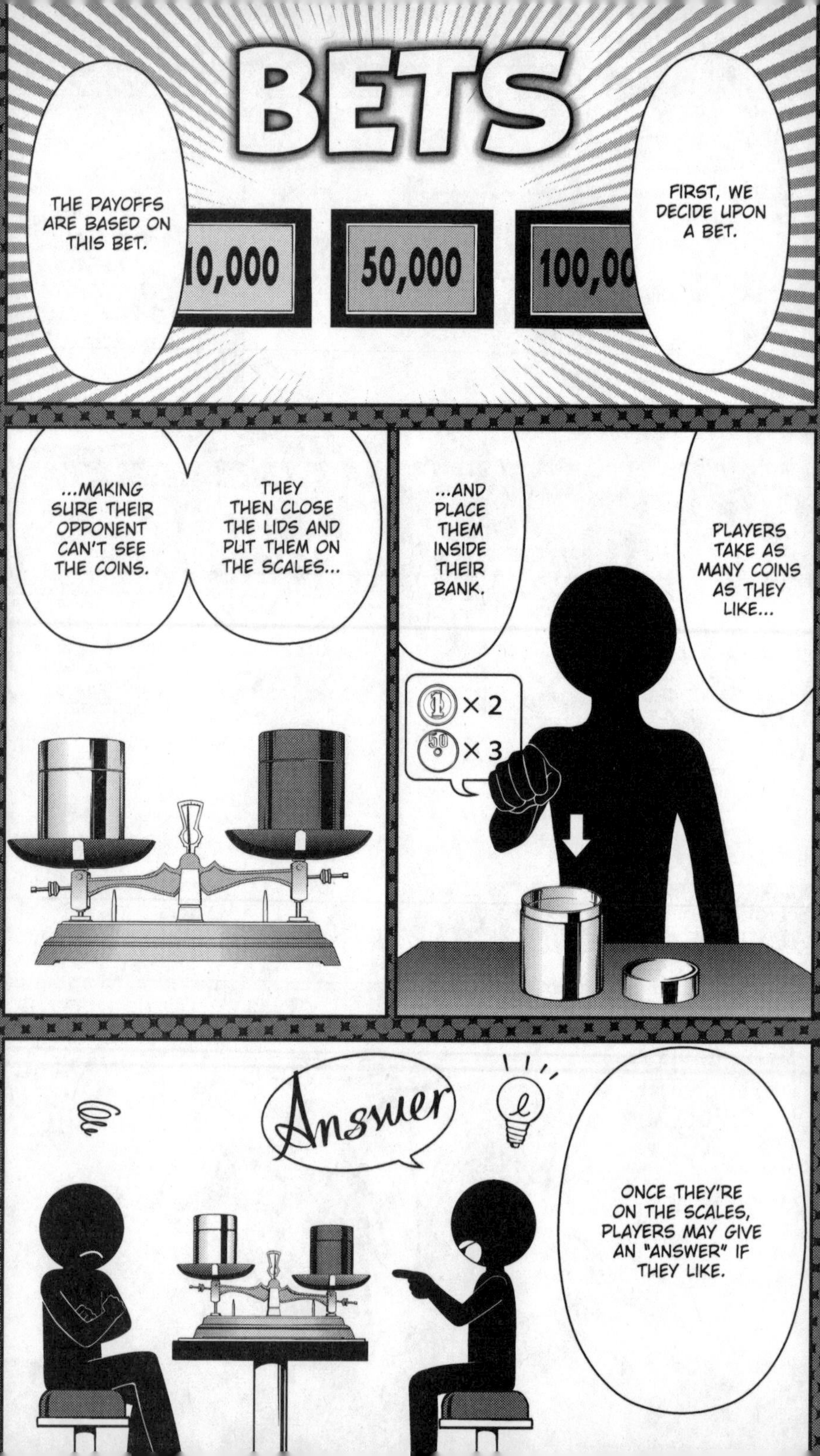
BETS
FIRST, WE DECIDE UPON A BET.
100,00
50,000
10,000
THE PAYOFFS ARE BASED ON THIS BET.
PLAYERS TAKE AS MANY COINS AS THEY LIKE...
...AND PLACE THEM INSIDE THEIR BANK.
1 × 2
50 × 3
THEY THEN CLOSE THE LIDS AND PUT THEM ON THE SCALES...
...MAKING SURE THEIR OPPONENT CAN'T SEE THE COINS.
ONCE THEY'RE ON THE SCALES, PLAYERS MAY GIVE AN "ANSWER" IF THEY LIKE.
Answer

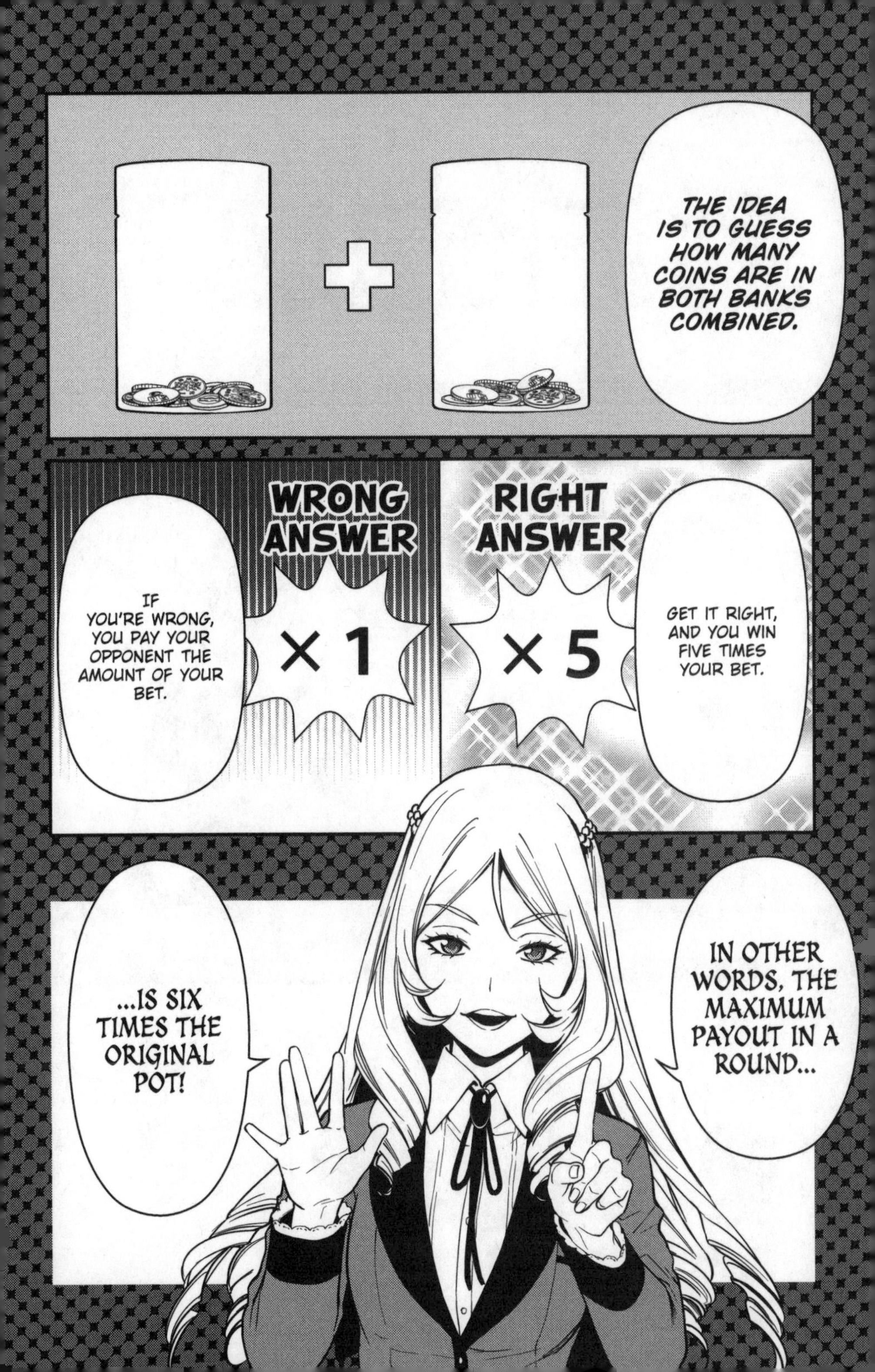
THE IDEA IS TO GUESS HOW MANY COINS ARE IN BOTH BANKS COMBINED.
RIGHT ANSWER
×5
GET IT RIGHT, AND YOU WIN FIVE TIMES YOUR BET.
WRONG ANSWER
×1
IF YOU'RE WRONG, YOU PAY YOUR OPPONENT THE AMOUNT OF YOUR BET.
IN OTHER WORDS, THE MAXIMUM PAYOUT IN A ROUND...
...IS SIX TIMES THE ORIGINAL POT!

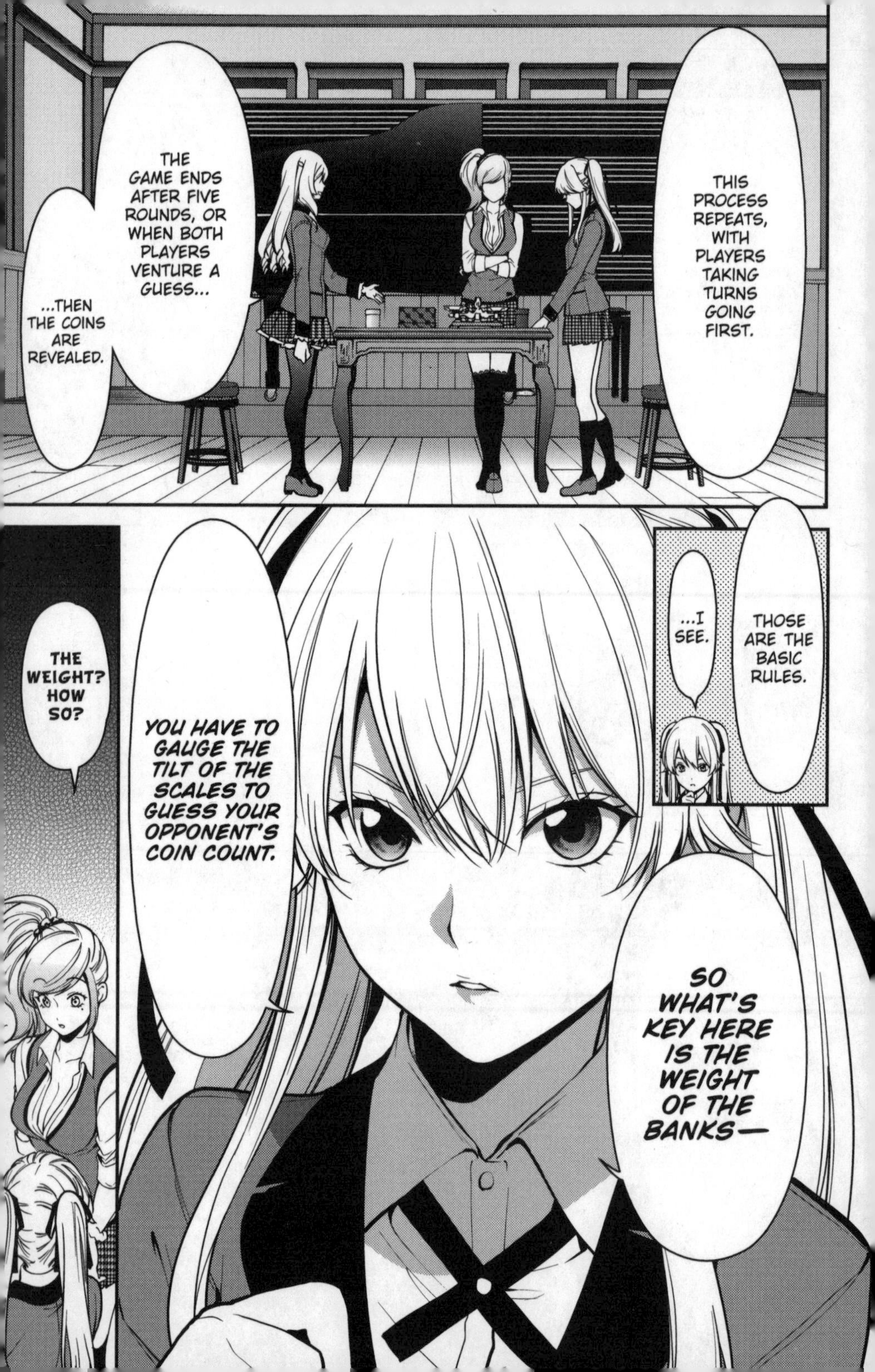
THIS PROCESS REPEATS, WITH PLAYERS TAKING TURNS GOING FIRST.
THE GAME ENDS AFTER FIVE ROUNDS, OR WHEN BOTH PLAYERS VENTURE A GUESS...
...THEN THE COINS ARE REVEALED.
THOSE ARE THE BASIC RULES.
...I SEE.
SO WHAT'S KEY HERE IS THE WEIGHT OF THE BANKS—
THE WEIGHT? HOW SO?
YOU HAVE TO GAUGE THE TILT OF THE SCALES TO GUESS YOUR OPPONENT'S COIN COUNT.

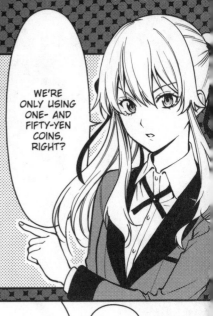

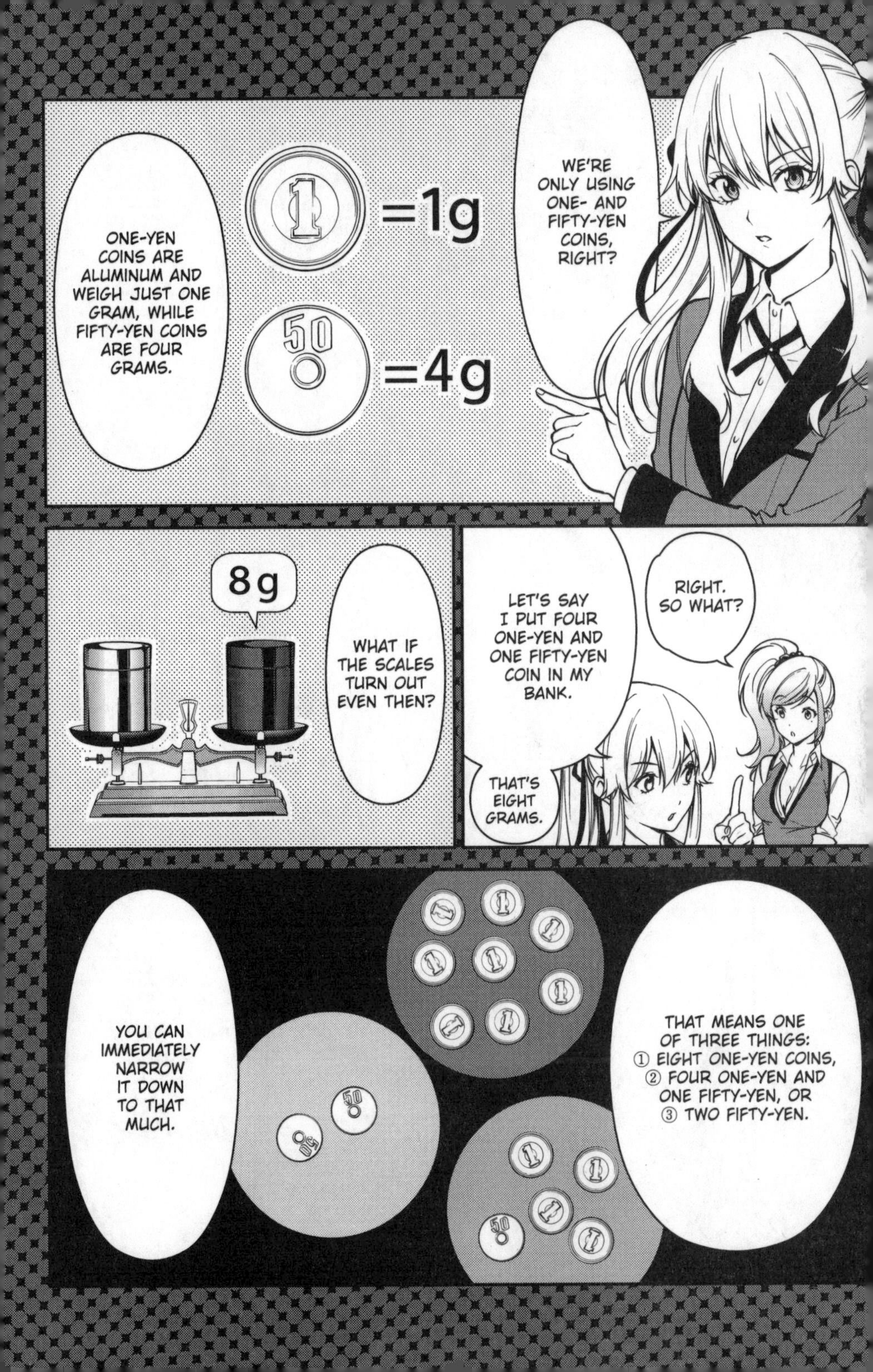

WE'RE ONLY USING ONE- AND FIFTY-YEN COINS, RIGHT?
ONE-YEN COINS ARE ALUMINUM AND WEIGH JUST ONE GRAM, WHILE FIFTY-YEN COINS ARE FOUR GRAMS.
=1g
50
=4g
RIGHT. SO WHAT?
LET'S SAY I PUT FOUR ONE-YEN AND ONE FIFTY-YEN COIN IN MY BANK.
THAT'S EIGHT GRAMS.
8g
WHAT IF THE SCALES TURN OUT EVEN THEN?
THAT MEANS ONE OF THREE THINGS: ① EIGHT ONE-YEN COINS, ② FOUR ONE-YEN AND ONE FIFTY-YEN, OR ③ TWO FIFTY-YEN.
YOU CAN IMMEDIATELY NARROW IT DOWN TO THAT MUCH.

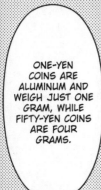

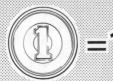

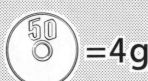

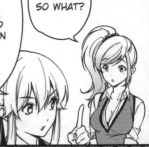

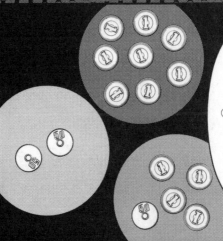

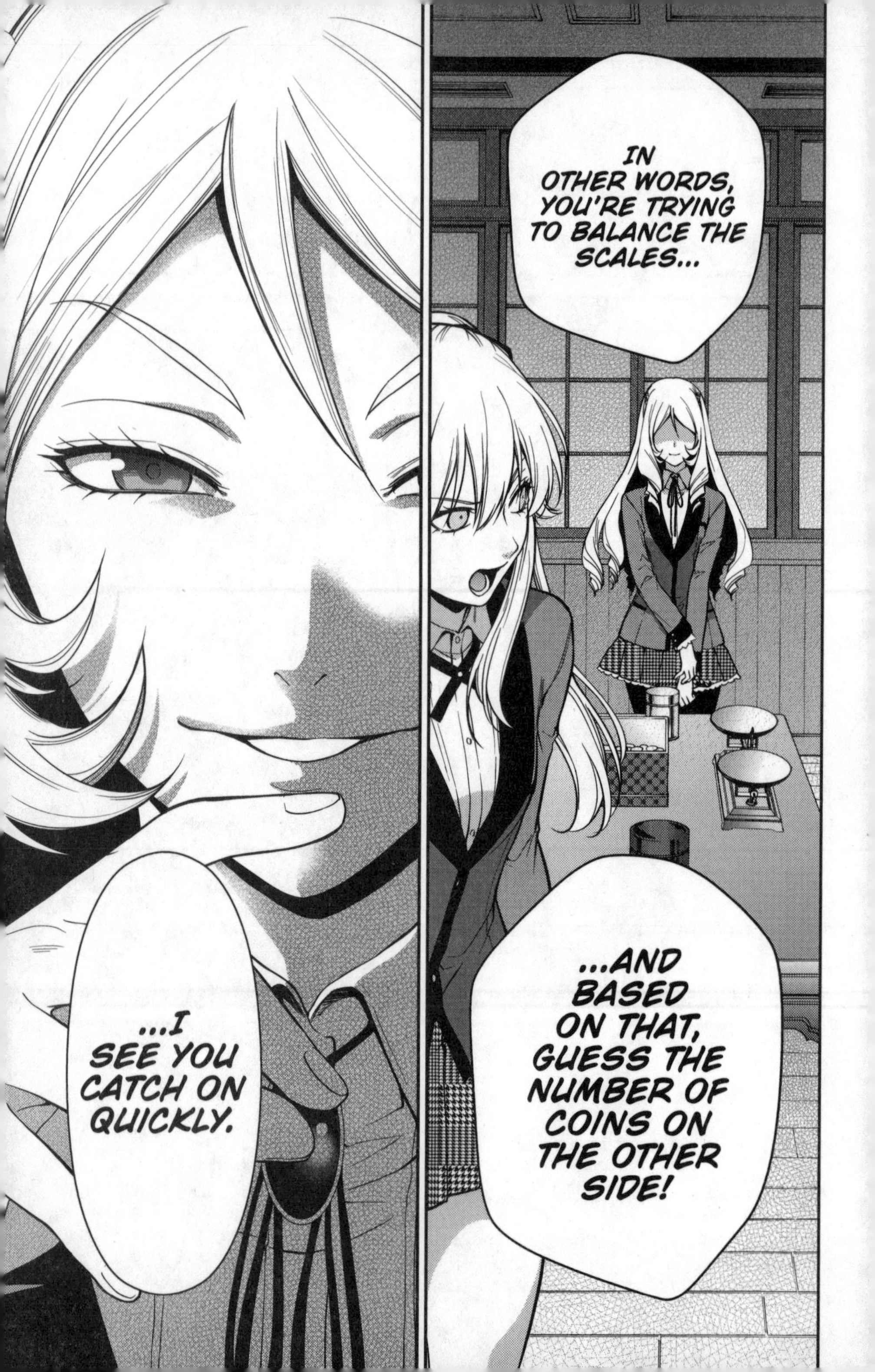
IN OTHER WORDS, YOU'RE TRYING TO BALANCE THE SCALES...
...AND BASED ON THAT, GUESS THE NUMBER OF COINS ON THE OTHER SIDE!
...I SEE YOU CATCH ON QUICKLY.

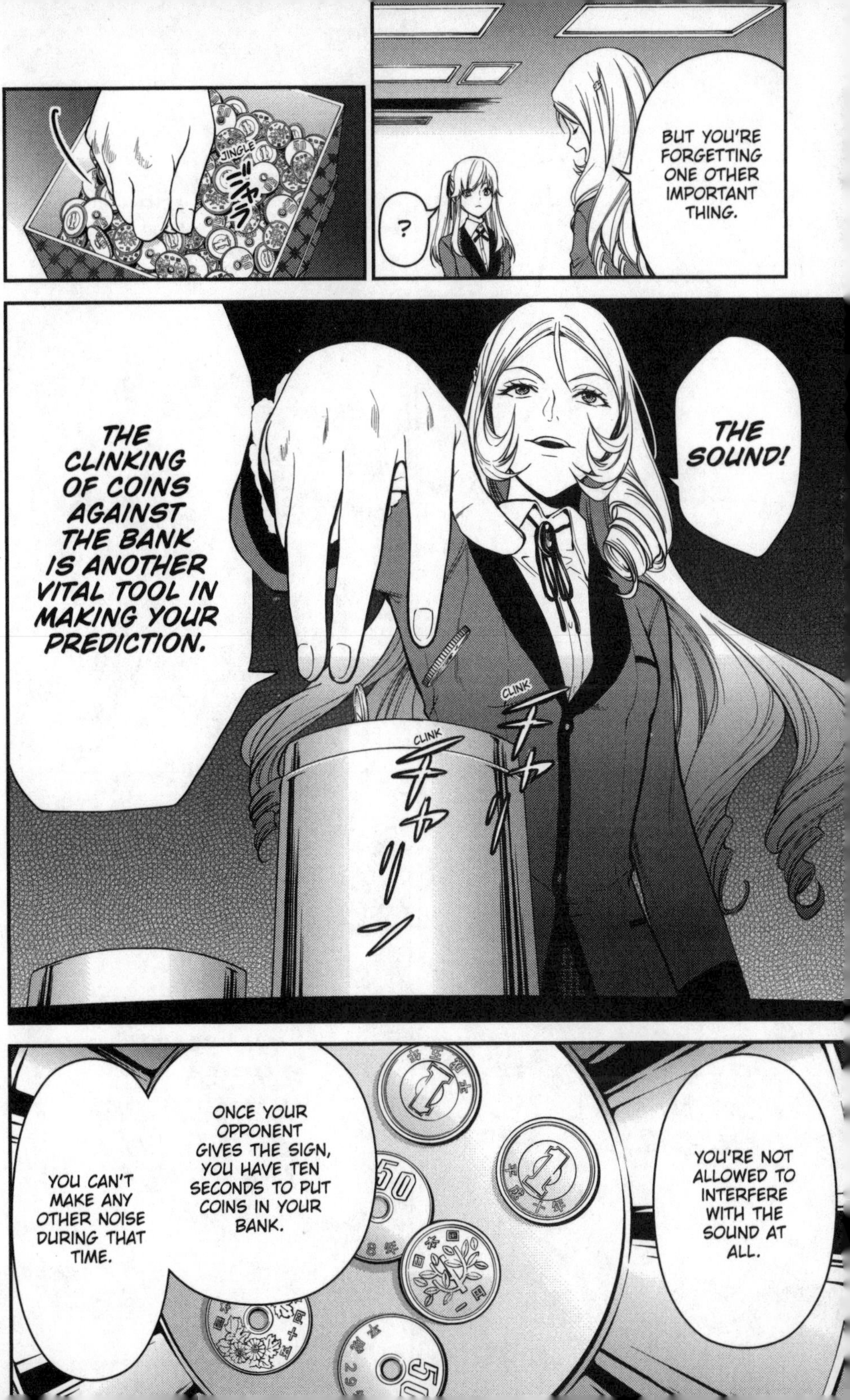
BUT YOU'RE FORGETTING ONE OTHER IMPORTANT THING.
?
JINGLE
ジャラ
THE SOUND!
THE CLINKING OF COINS AGAINST THE BANK IS ANOTHER VITAL TOOL IN MAKING YOUR PREDICTION.
CLINK
CLINK
YOU'RE NOT ALLOWED TO INTERFERE WITH THE SOUND AT ALL.
ONCE YOUR OPPONENT GIVES THE SIGN, YOU HAVE TEN SECONDS TO PUT COINS IN YOUR BANK.
YOU CAN'T MAKE ANY OTHER NOISE DURING THAT TIME.

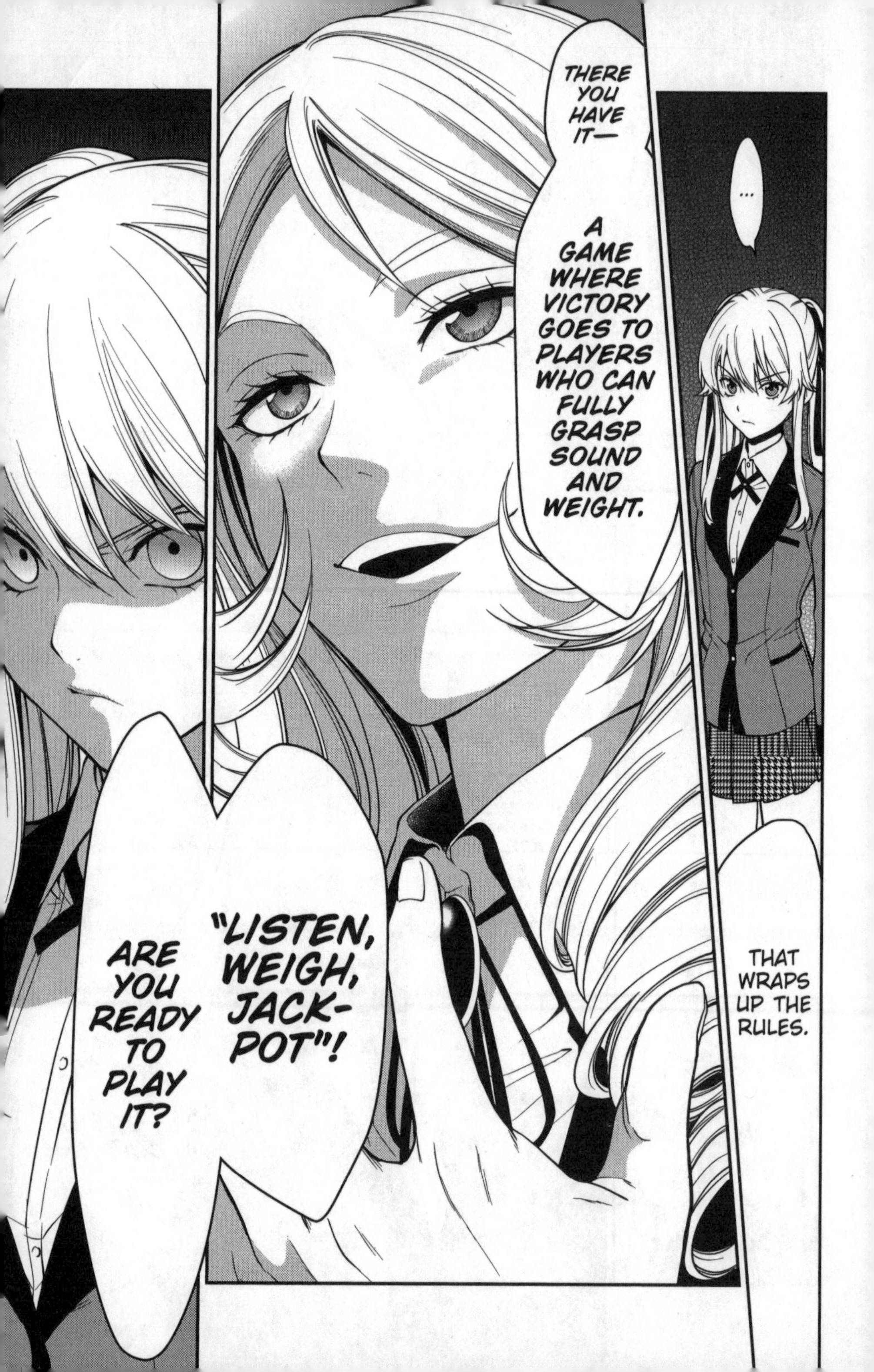
...
THAT WRAPS UP THE RULES.
THERE YOU HAVE IT—
A GAME WHERE VICTORY GOES TO PLAYERS WHO CAN FULLY GRASP SOUND AND WEIGHT.
"LISTEN, WEIGH, JACK-POT"!
ARE YOU READY TO PLAY IT?

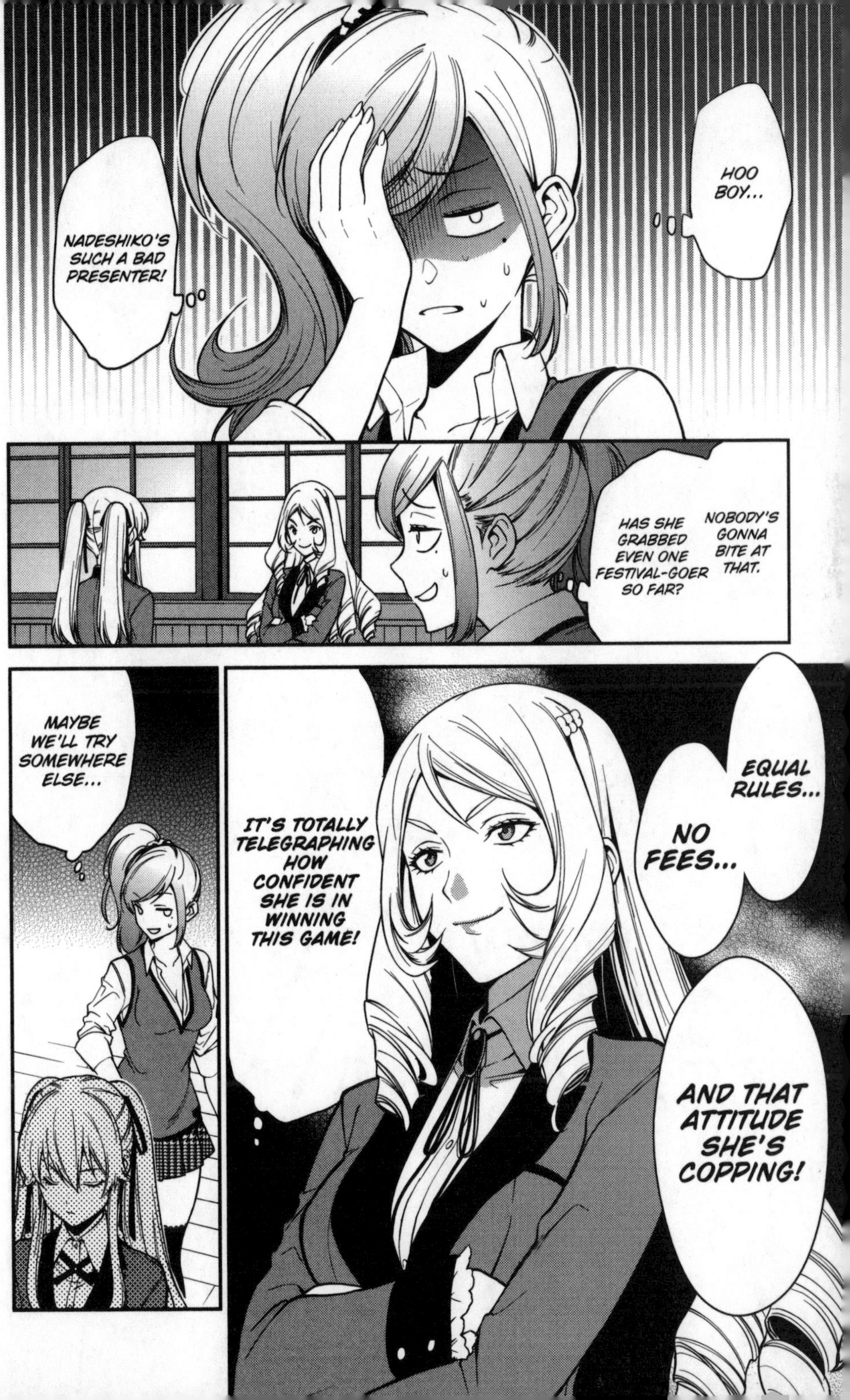
HOO BOY...
NADESHIKO'S SUCH A BAD PRESENTER!
NOBODY'S GONNA BITE AT THAT.
HAS SHE GRABBED EVEN ONE FESTIVAL-GOER SO FAR?
EQUAL RULES...
NO FEES...
AND THAT ATTITUDE SHE'S COPPING!
IT'S TOTALLY TELEGRAPHING HOW CONFIDENT SHE IS IN WINNING THIS GAME!
MAYBE WE'LL TRY SOMEWHERE ELSE...

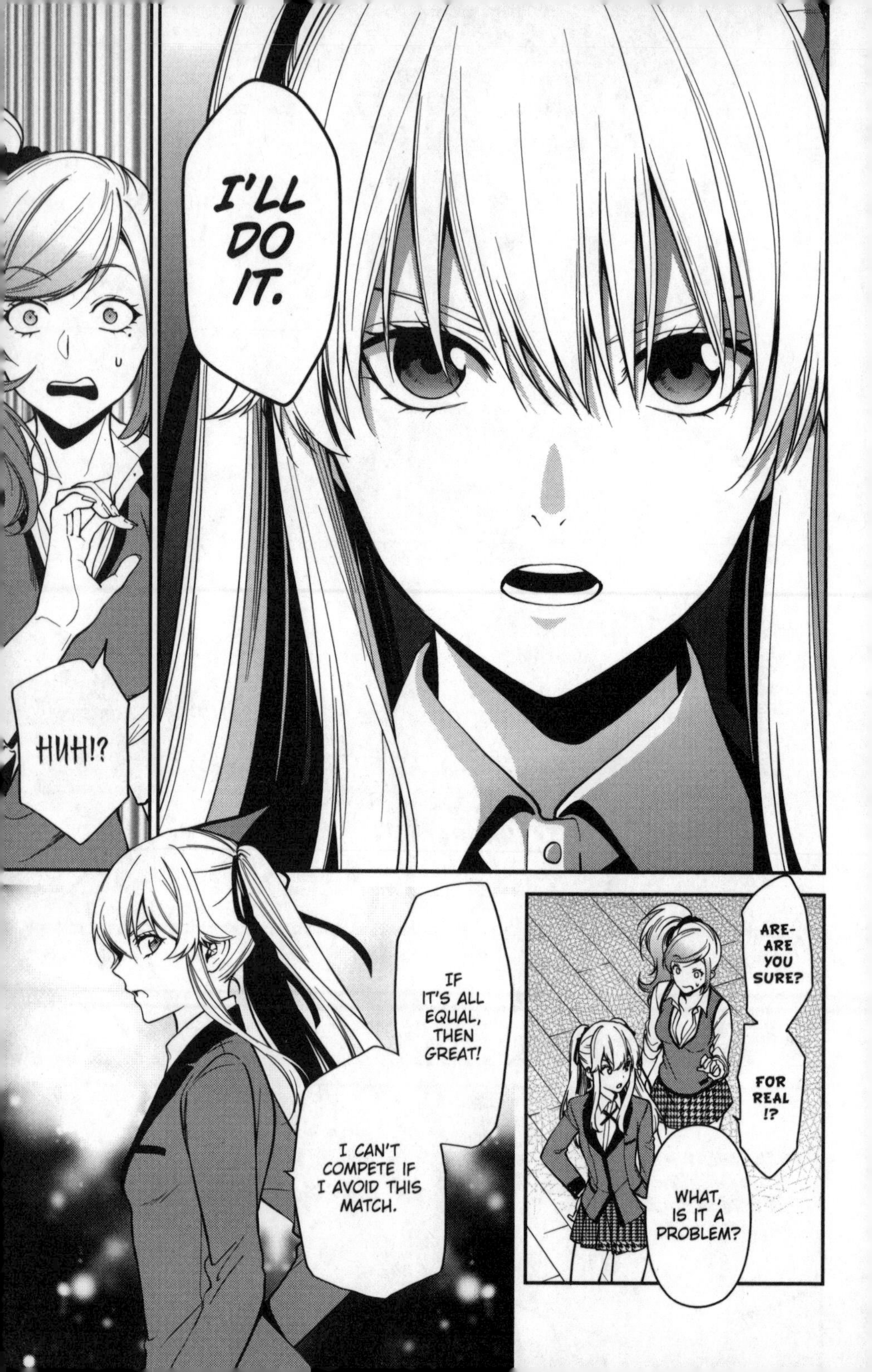
I'LL DO IT.
HUH!?
ARE-ARE YOU SURE?
FOR REAL!?
WHAT, IS IT A PROBLEM?
IF IT'S ALL EQUAL, THEN GREAT!
I CAN'T COMPETE IF I AVOID THIS MATCH.

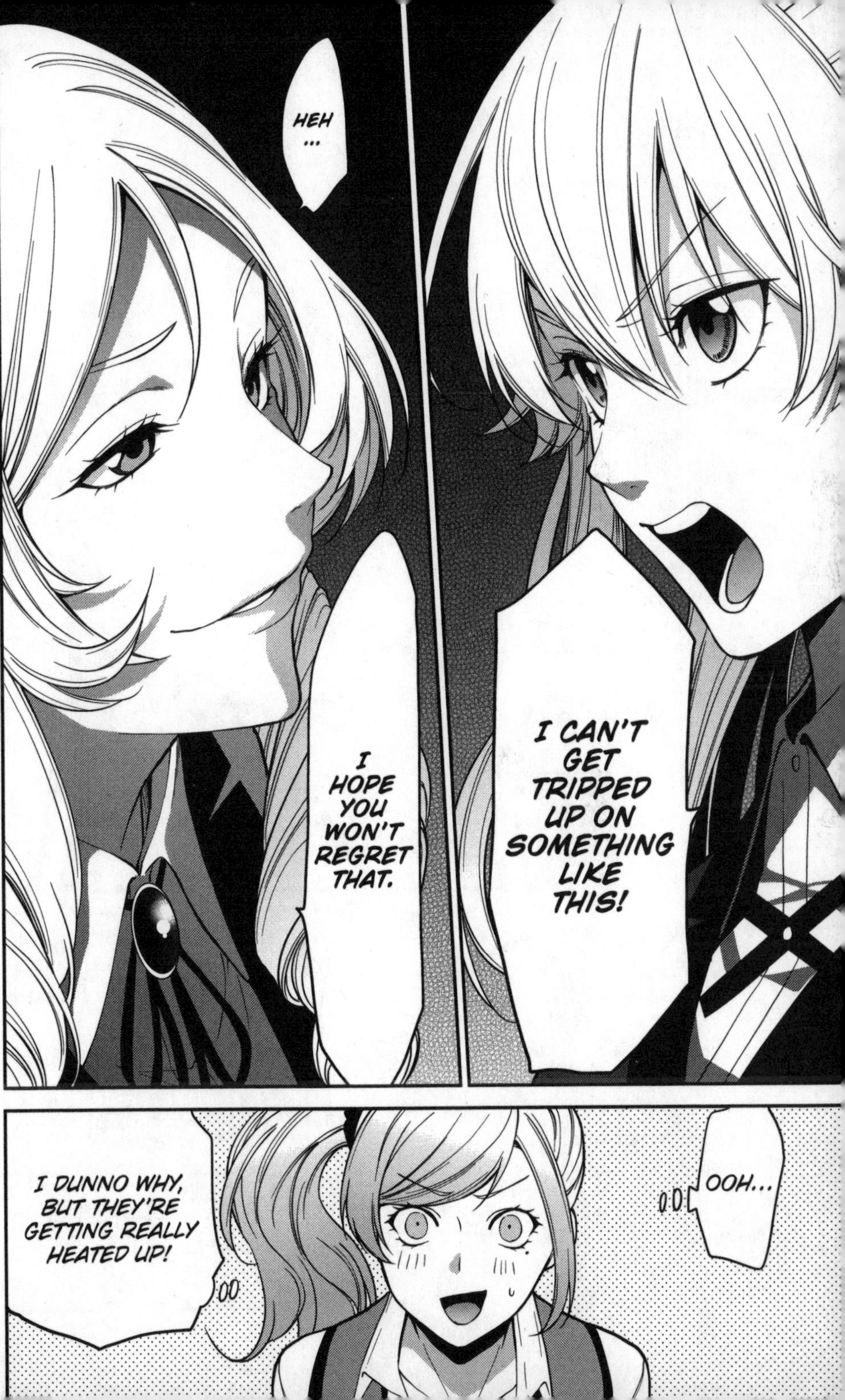
I CAN'T GET TRIPPED UP ON SOMETHING LIKE THIS!
HEH...
I HOPE YOU WON'T REGRET THAT.
OOH...
I DUNNO WHY, BUT THEY'RE GETTING REALLY HEATED UP!

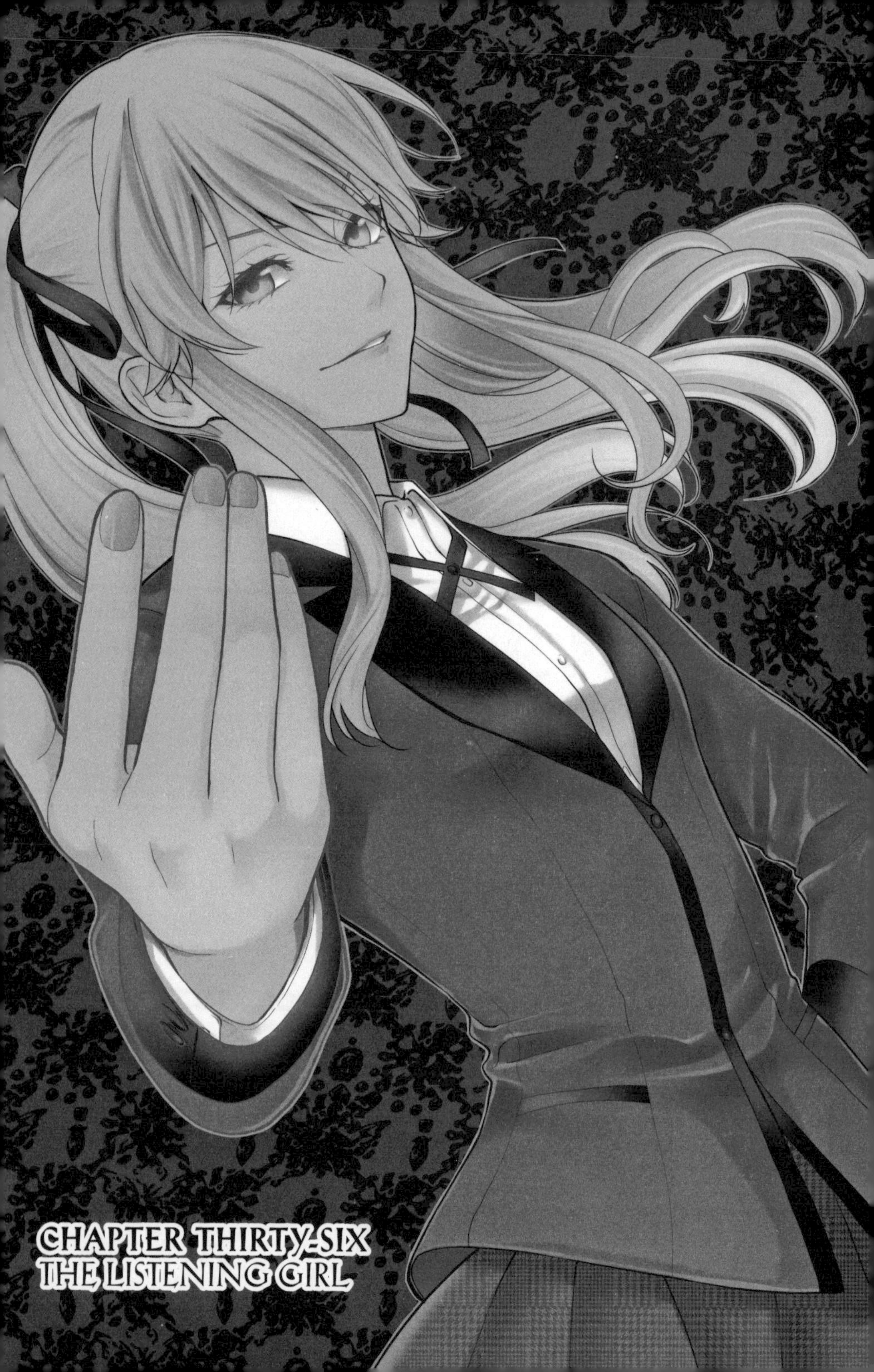
CHAPTER THIRTY-SIX
THE LISTENING GIRL

Kakegurui Twin

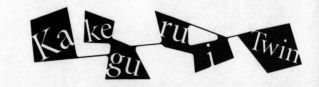

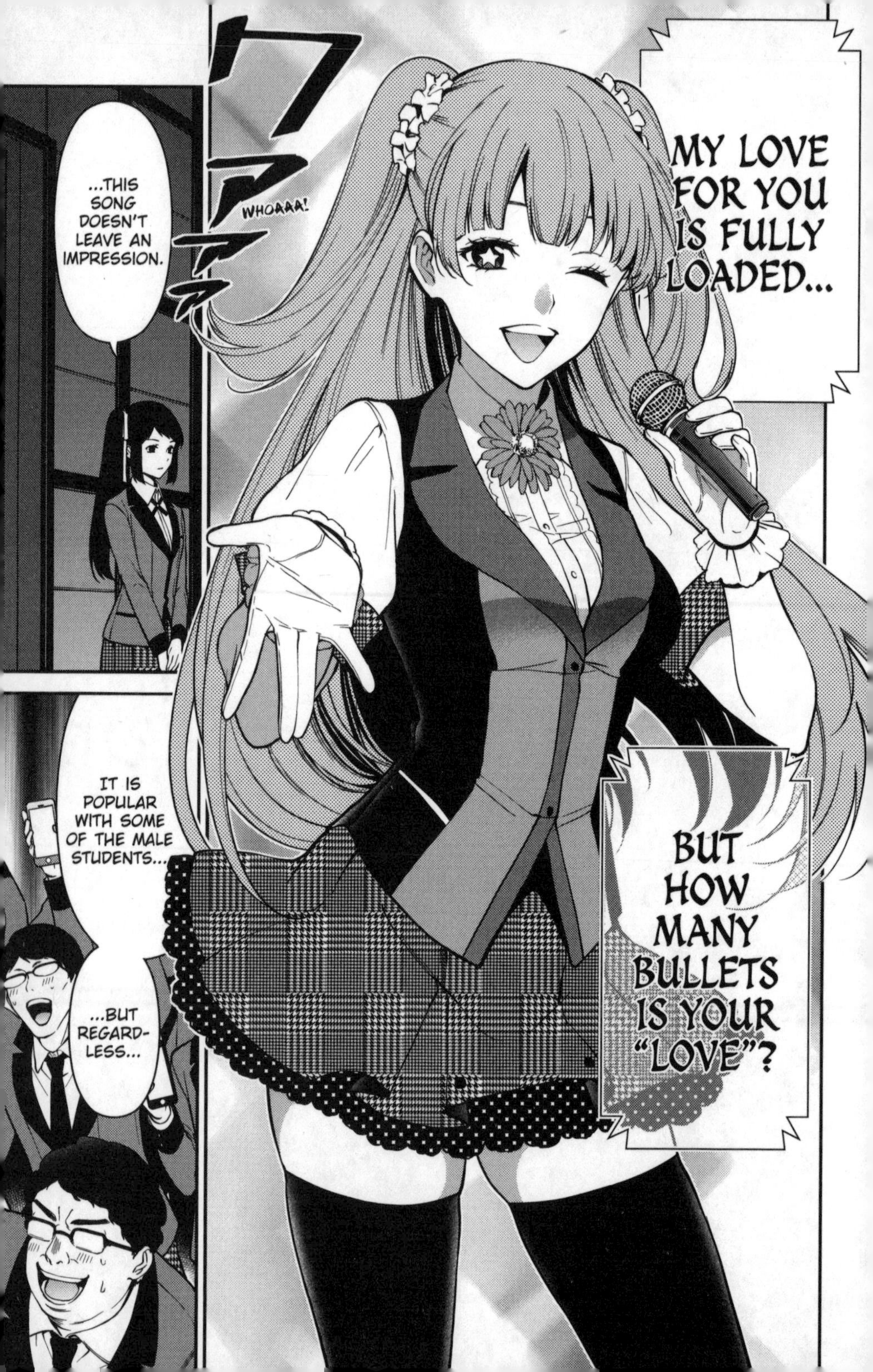
MY LOVE FOR YOU IS FULLY LOADED...
WHOAAA!
BUT HOW MANY BULLETS IS YOUR "LOVE"?
...THIS SONG DOESN'T LEAVE AN IMPRESSION.
IT IS POPULAR WITH SOME OF THE MALE STUDENTS...
...BUT REGARDLESS...

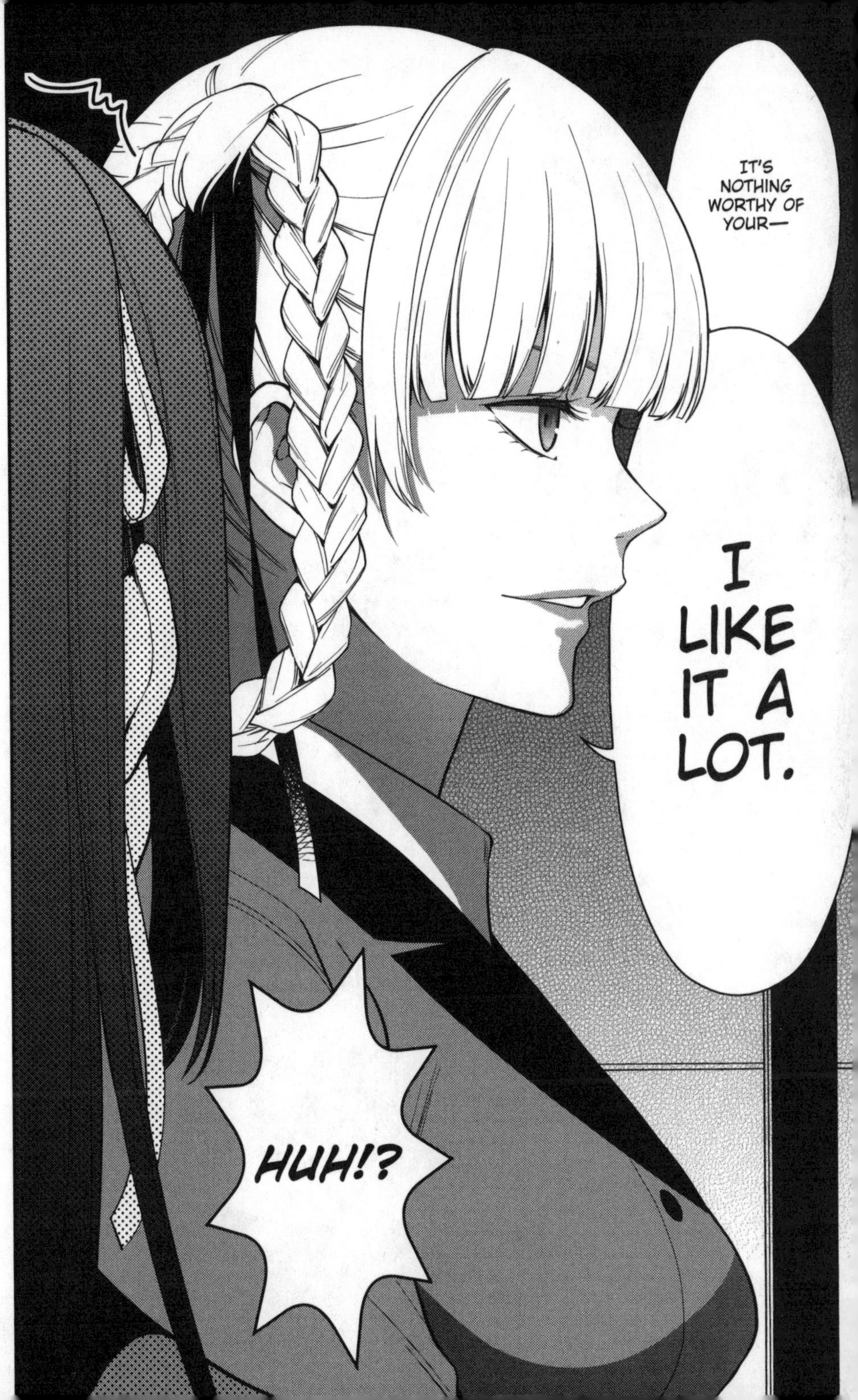
IT'S NOTHING WORTHY OF YOUR—
I LIKE IT A LOT.
HUH!?

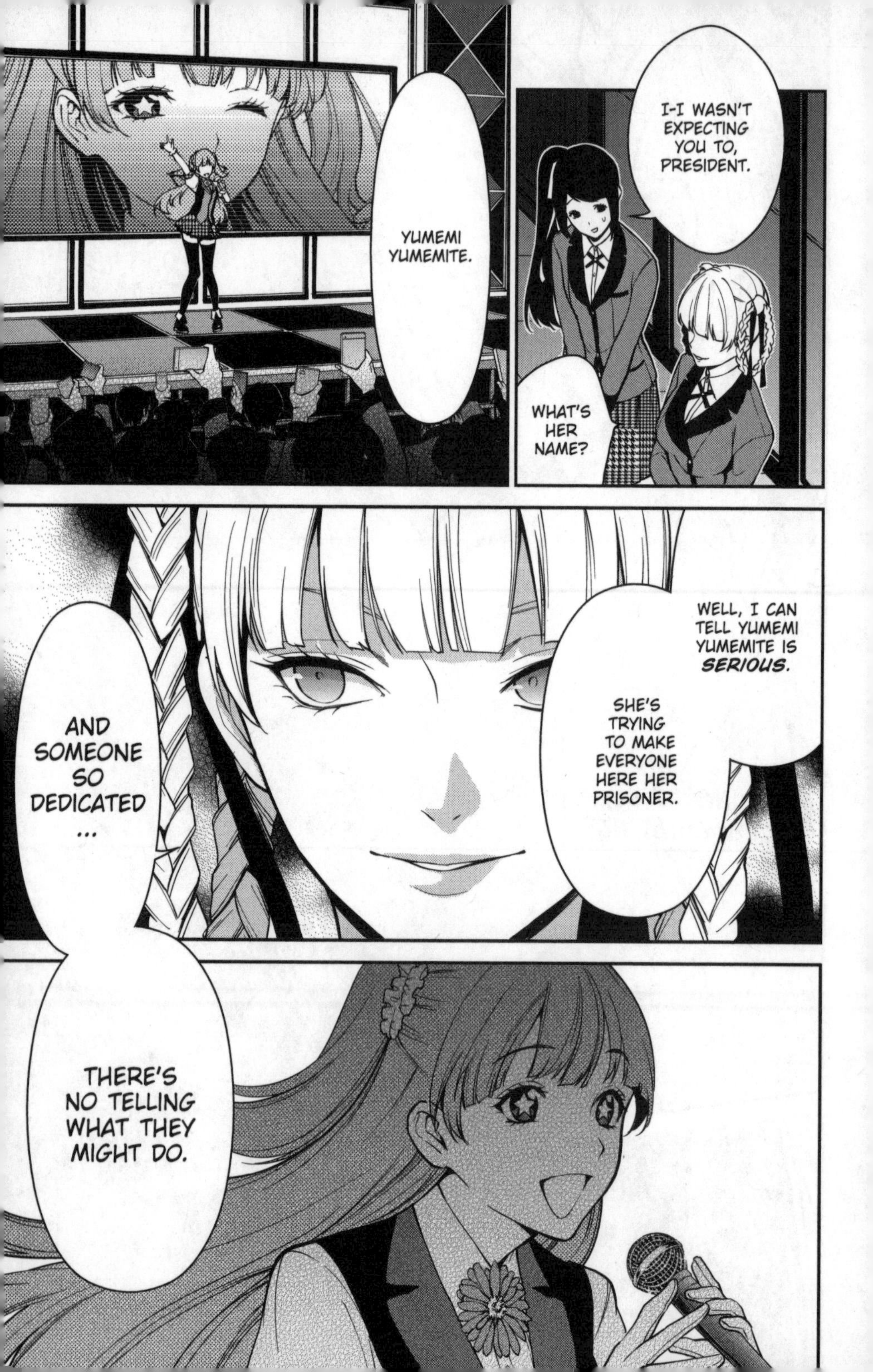
I-I WASN'T EXPECTING YOU TO, PRESIDENT.
WHAT'S HER NAME?
YUMEMI YUMEMITE.
WELL, I CAN TELL YUMEMI YUMEMITE IS ***SERIOUS***.
SHE'S TRYING TO MAKE EVERYONE HERE HER PRISONER.
AND SOMEONE SO DEDICATED ...
THERE'S NO TELLING WHAT THEY MIGHT DO.

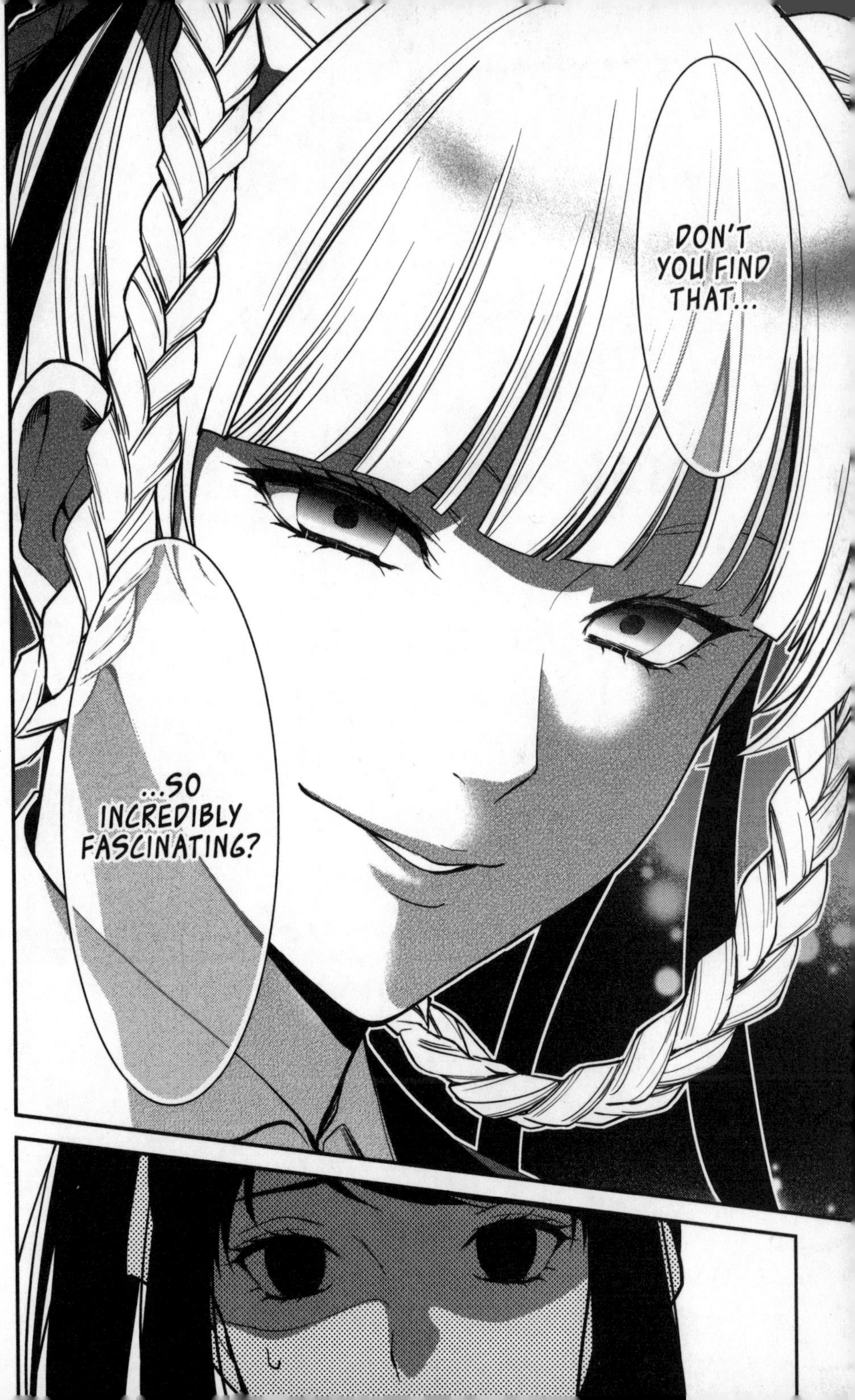
DON'T YOU FIND THAT...
...SO INCREDIBLY FASCINATING?

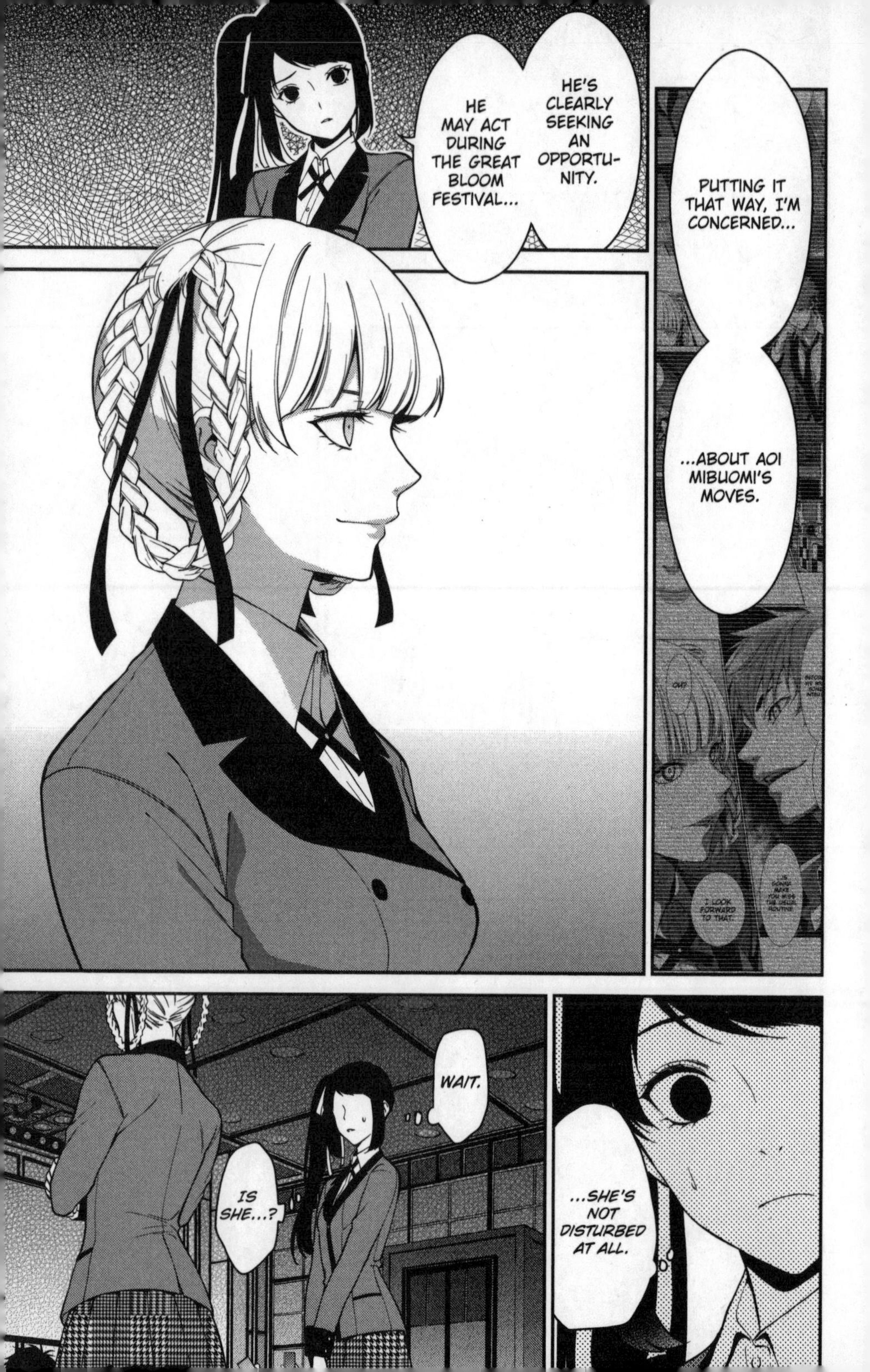
HE'S CLEARLY SEEKING AN OPPORTUNITY.
HE MAY ACT DURING THE GREAT BLOOM FESTIVAL...
PUTTING IT THAT WAY, I'M CONCERNED...
...ABOUT AOI MIBUOMI'S MOVES.
I LOOK FORWARD TO THAT.
WAIT.
IS SHE...?
...SHE'S NOT DISTURBED AT ALL.

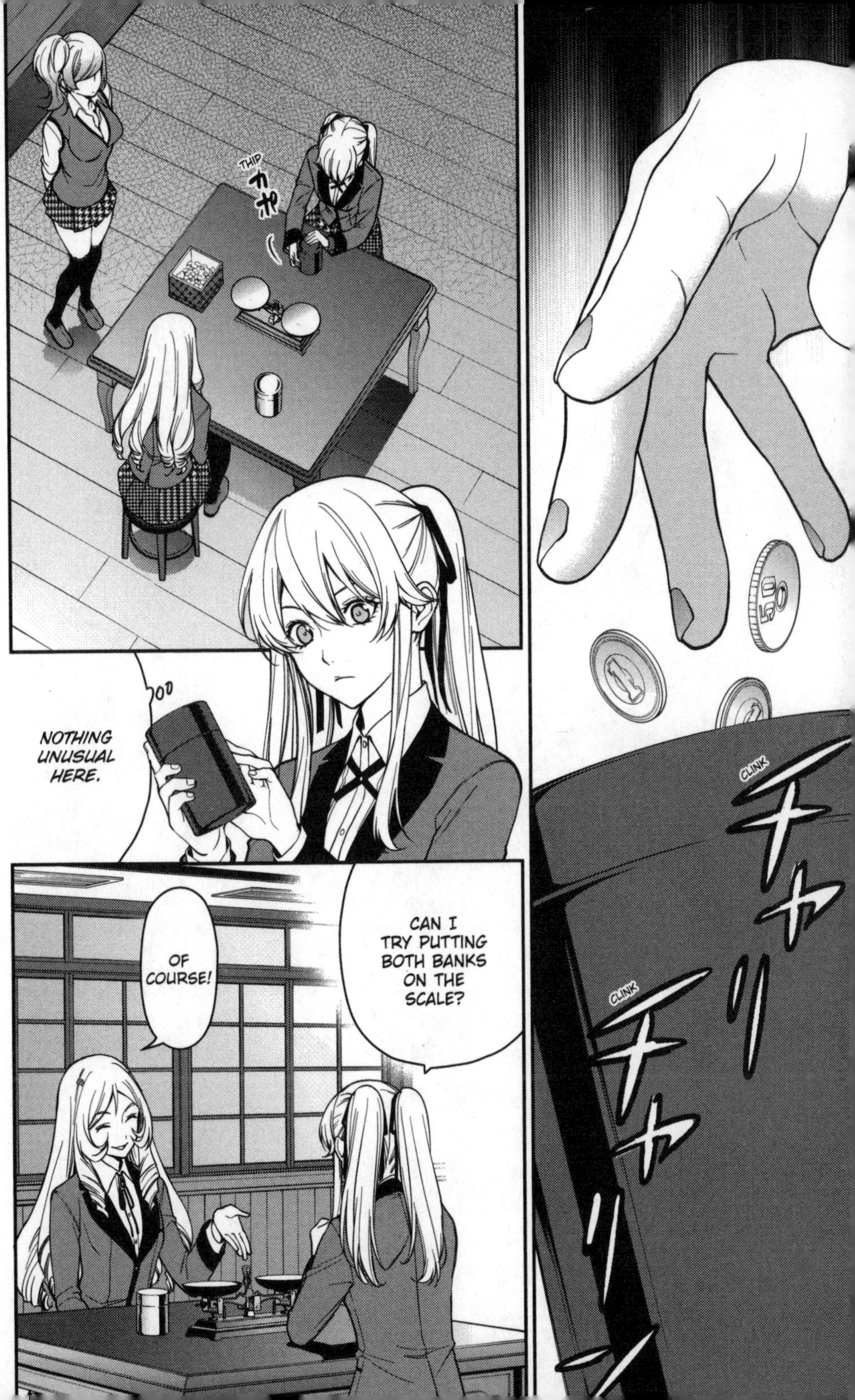
CLINK
チャリ
CLINK
チャリ
THIP
カパ
NOTHING UNUSUAL HERE.
CAN I TRY PUTTING BOTH BANKS ON THE SCALE?
OF COURSE!

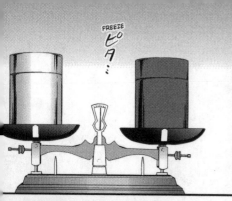
FREEZE

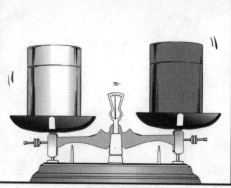

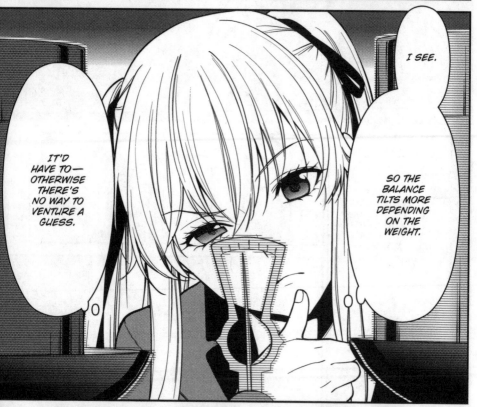

I SEE.

SO THE BALANCE TILTS MORE DEPENDING ON THE WEIGHT.

IT'D HAVE TO— OTHERWISE THERE'S NO WAY TO VENTURE A GUESS.

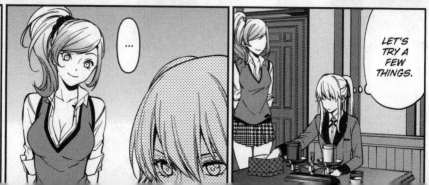

...

LET'S TRY A FEW THINGS.

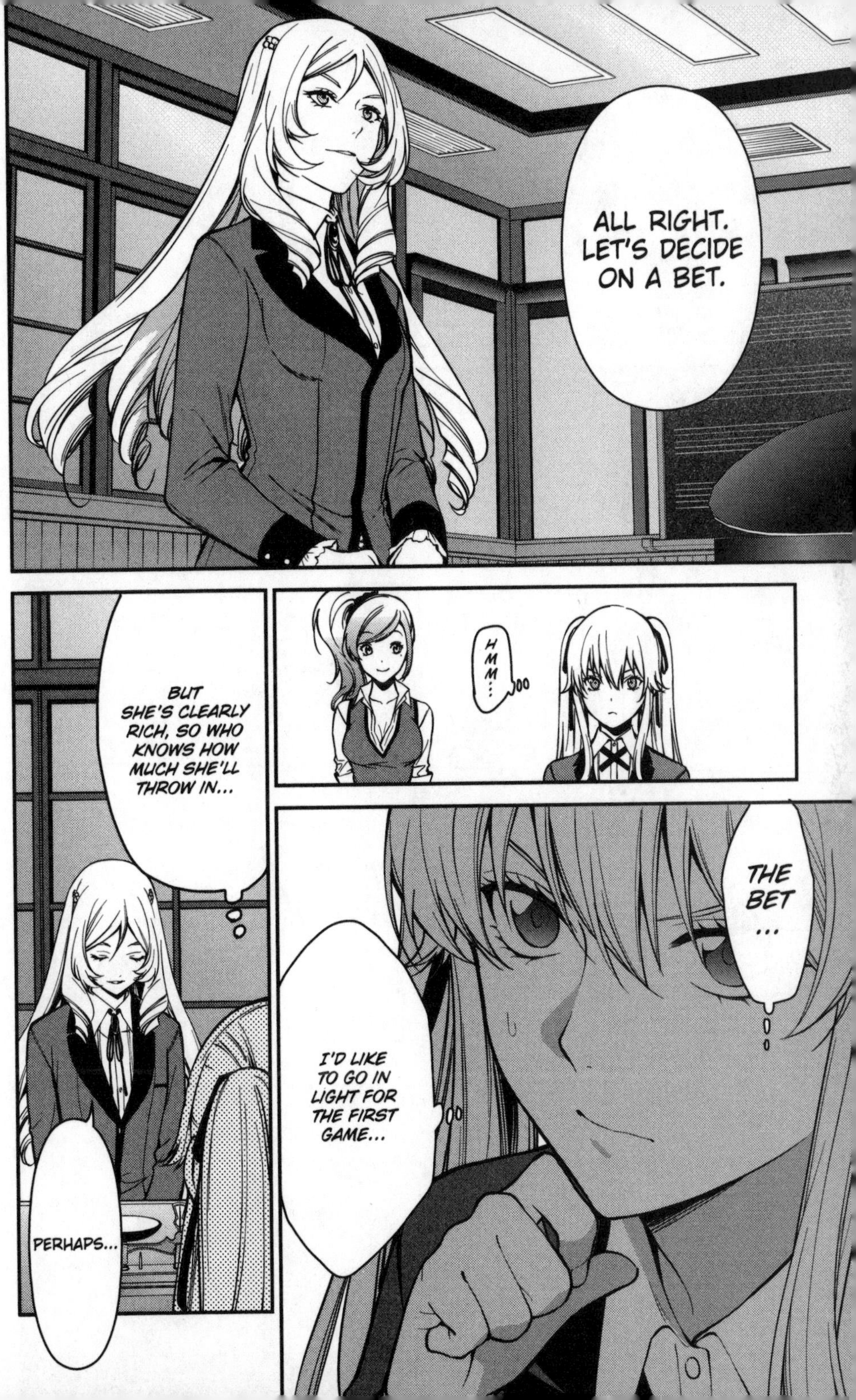
ALL RIGHT. LET'S DECIDE ON A BET.
HMM...
THE BET...
I'D LIKE TO GO IN LIGHT FOR THE FIRST GAME...
BUT SHE'S CLEARLY RICH, SO WHO KNOWS HOW MUCH SHE'LL THROW IN...
PERHAPS...

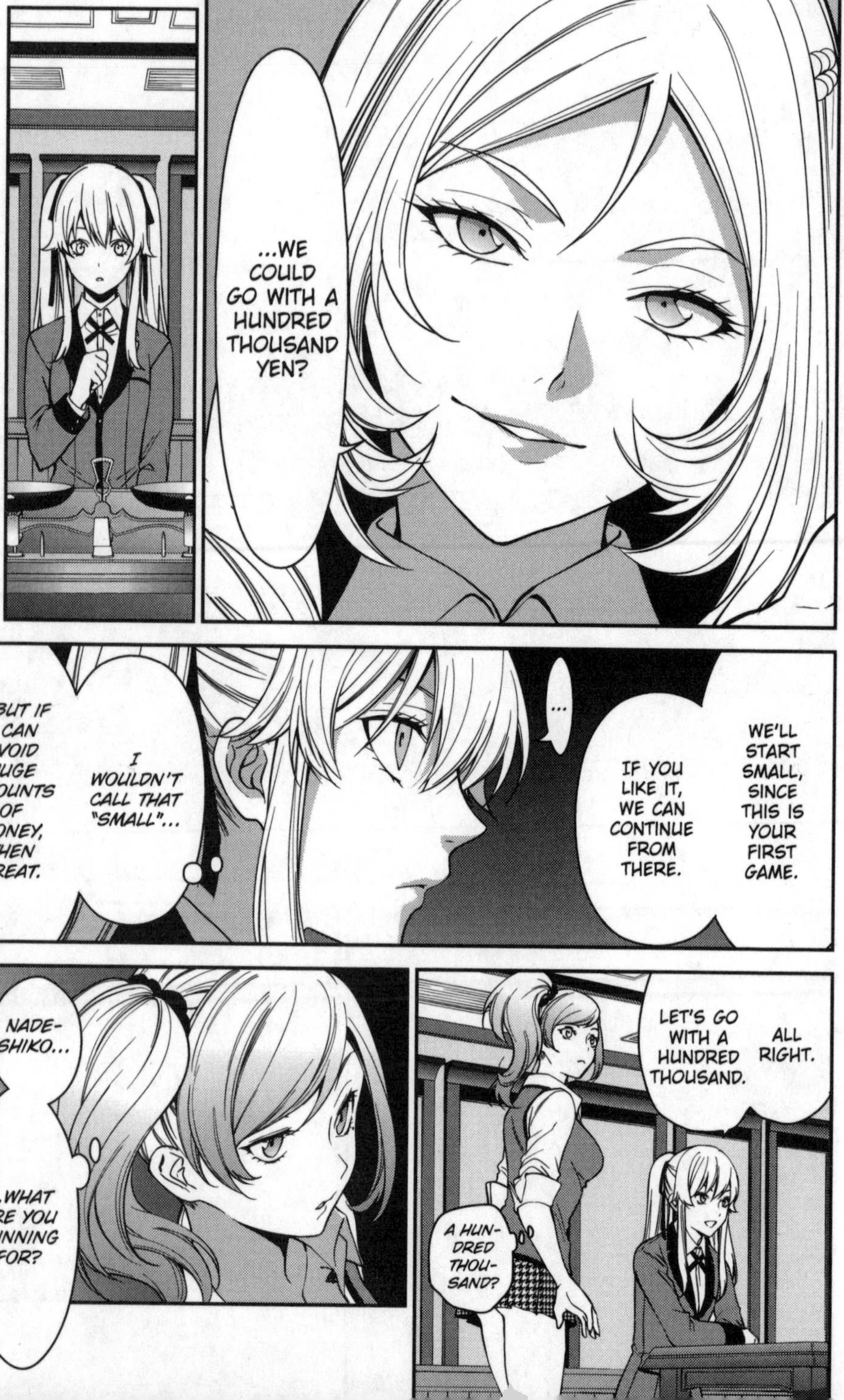
...WE COULD GO WITH A HUNDRED THOUSAND YEN?
WE'LL START SMALL, SINCE THIS IS YOUR FIRST GAME.
IF YOU LIKE IT, WE CAN CONTINUE FROM THERE.
...
I WOULDN'T CALL THAT "SMALL"...
...BUT IF I CAN AVOID HUGE AMOUNTS OF MONEY, THEN GREAT.
ALL RIGHT.
LET'S GO WITH A HUNDRED THOUSAND.
A HUN-DRED THOU-SAND?
NADE-SHIKO...
...WHAT ARE YOU GUNNING FOR?

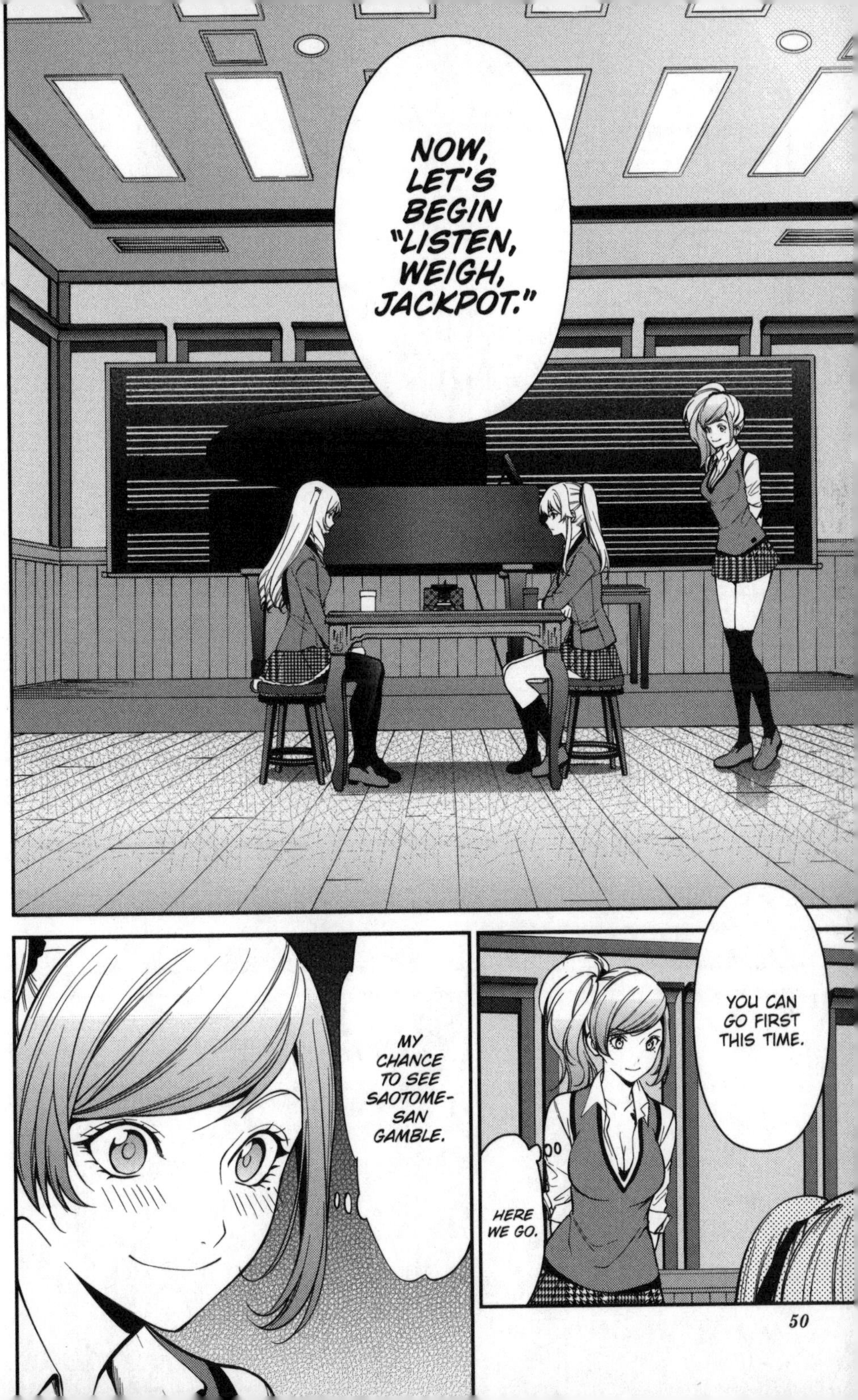
NOW, LET'S BEGIN "LISTEN, WEIGH, JACKPOT."
YOU CAN GO FIRST THIS TIME.
HERE WE GO.
MY CHANCE TO SEE SAOTOME-SAN GAMBLE.

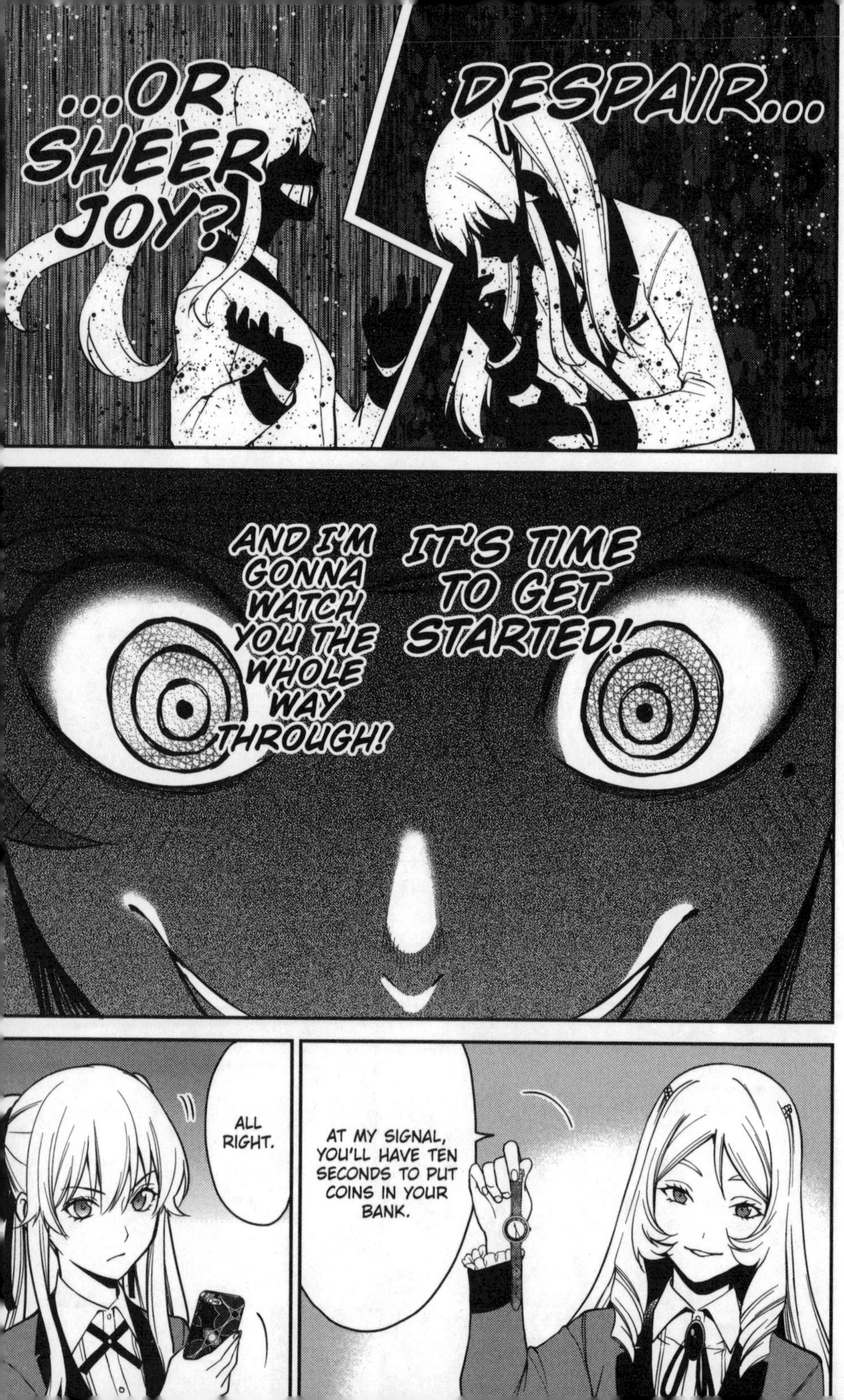
DESPAIR...
...OR SHEER JOY?
IT'S TIME TO GET STARTED!
AND I'M GONNA WATCH YOU THE WHOLE WAY THROUGH!
AT MY SIGNAL, YOU'LL HAVE TEN SECONDS TO PUT COINS IN YOUR BANK.
ALL RIGHT.

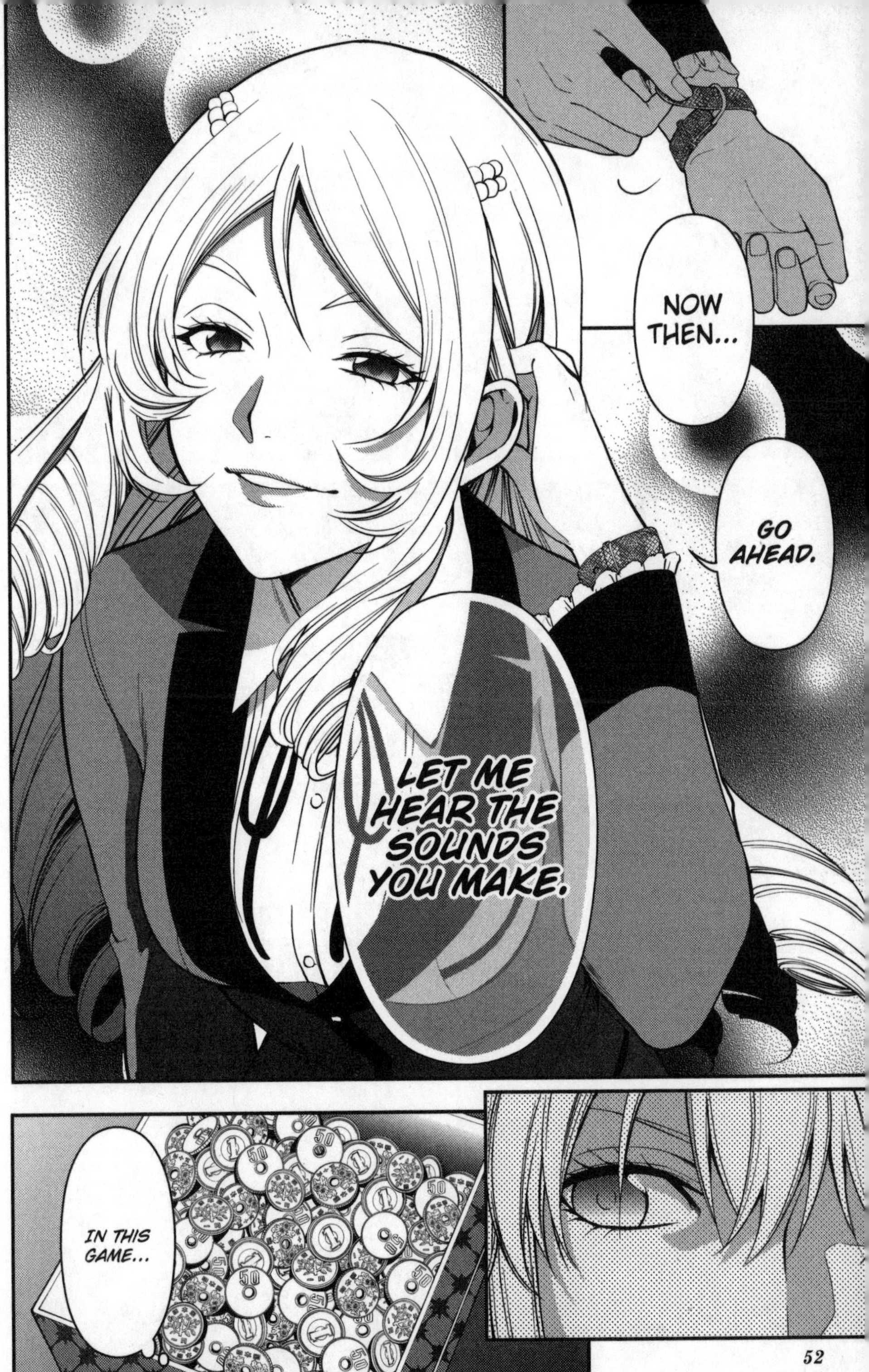
NOW THEN...
GO AHEAD.
LET ME HEAR THE SOUNDS YOU MAKE.
IN THIS GAME...

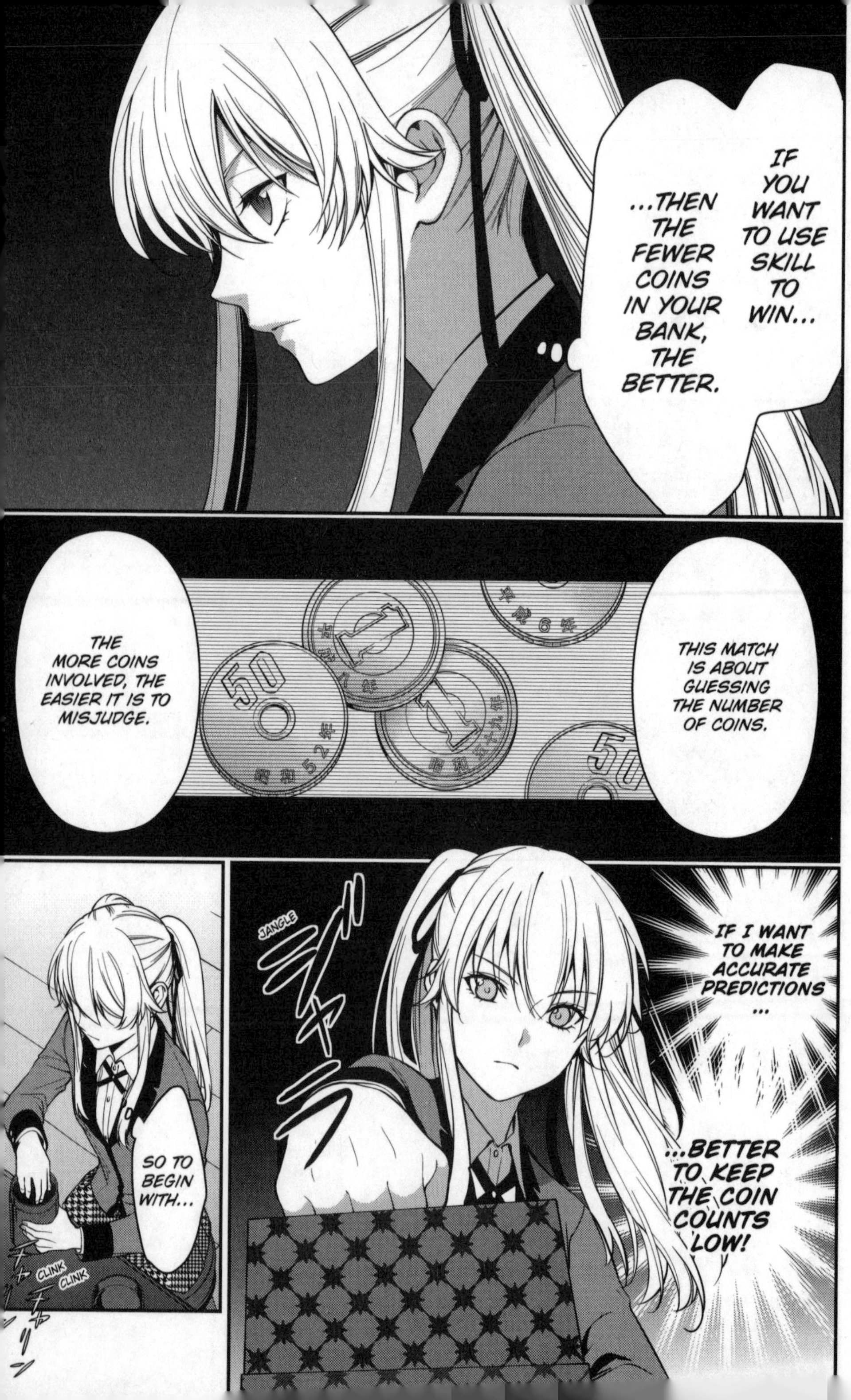
IF YOU WANT TO USE SKILL TO WIN...
...THEN THE FEWER COINS IN YOUR BANK, THE BETTER.
THIS MATCH IS ABOUT GUESSING THE NUMBER OF COINS.
THE MORE COINS INVOLVED, THE EASIER IT IS TO MISJUDGE.
IF I WANT TO MAKE ACCURATE PREDICTIONS ...
...BETTER TO KEEP THE COIN COUNTS LOW!
JANGLE
SO TO BEGIN WITH...
CLINK CLINK

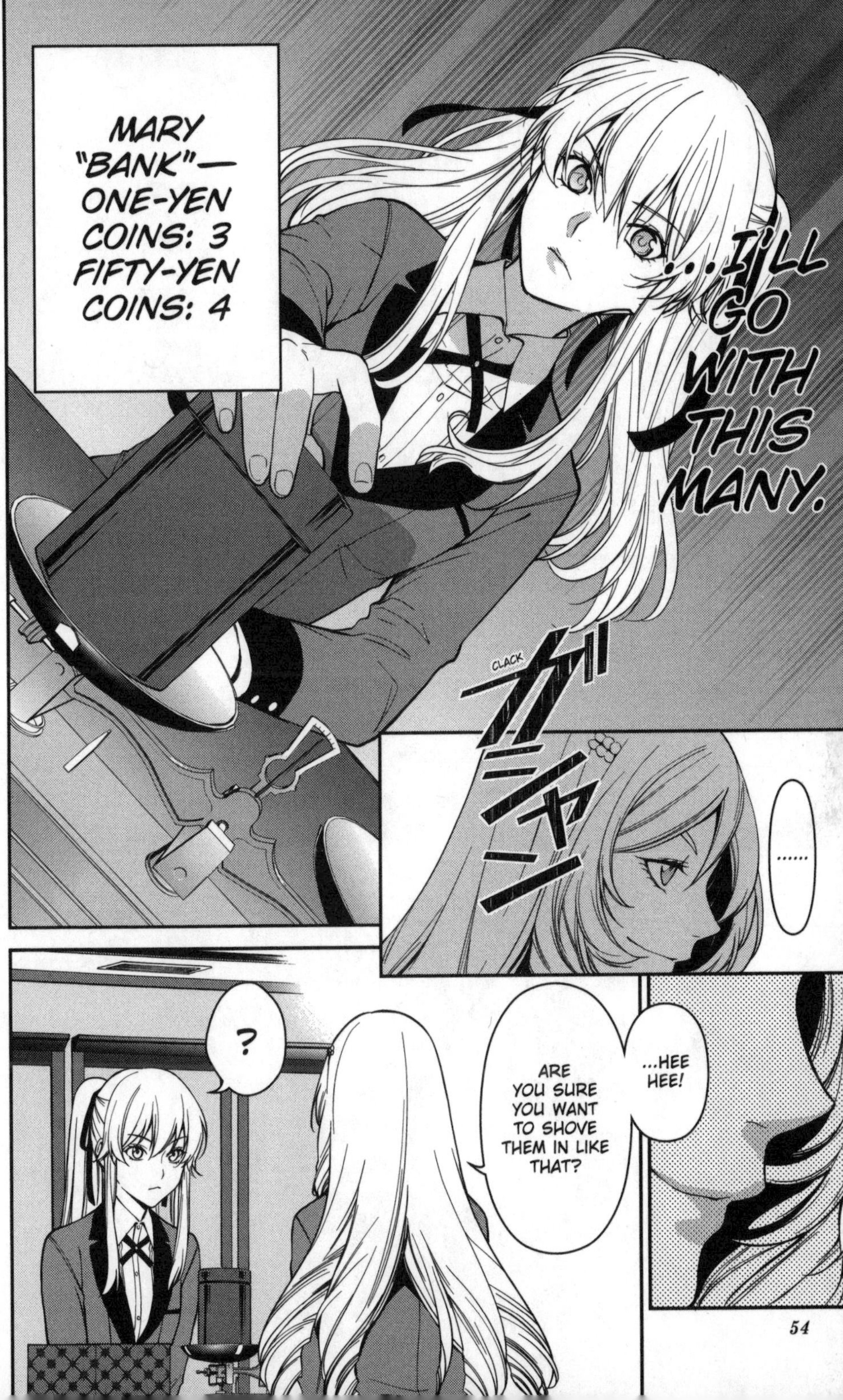
MARY "BANK"— ONE-YEN COINS: 3 FIFTY-YEN COINS: 4
...I'LL GO WITH THIS MANY.
CLACK
......
...HEE HEE!
ARE YOU SURE YOU WANT TO SHOVE THEM IN LIKE THAT?
?

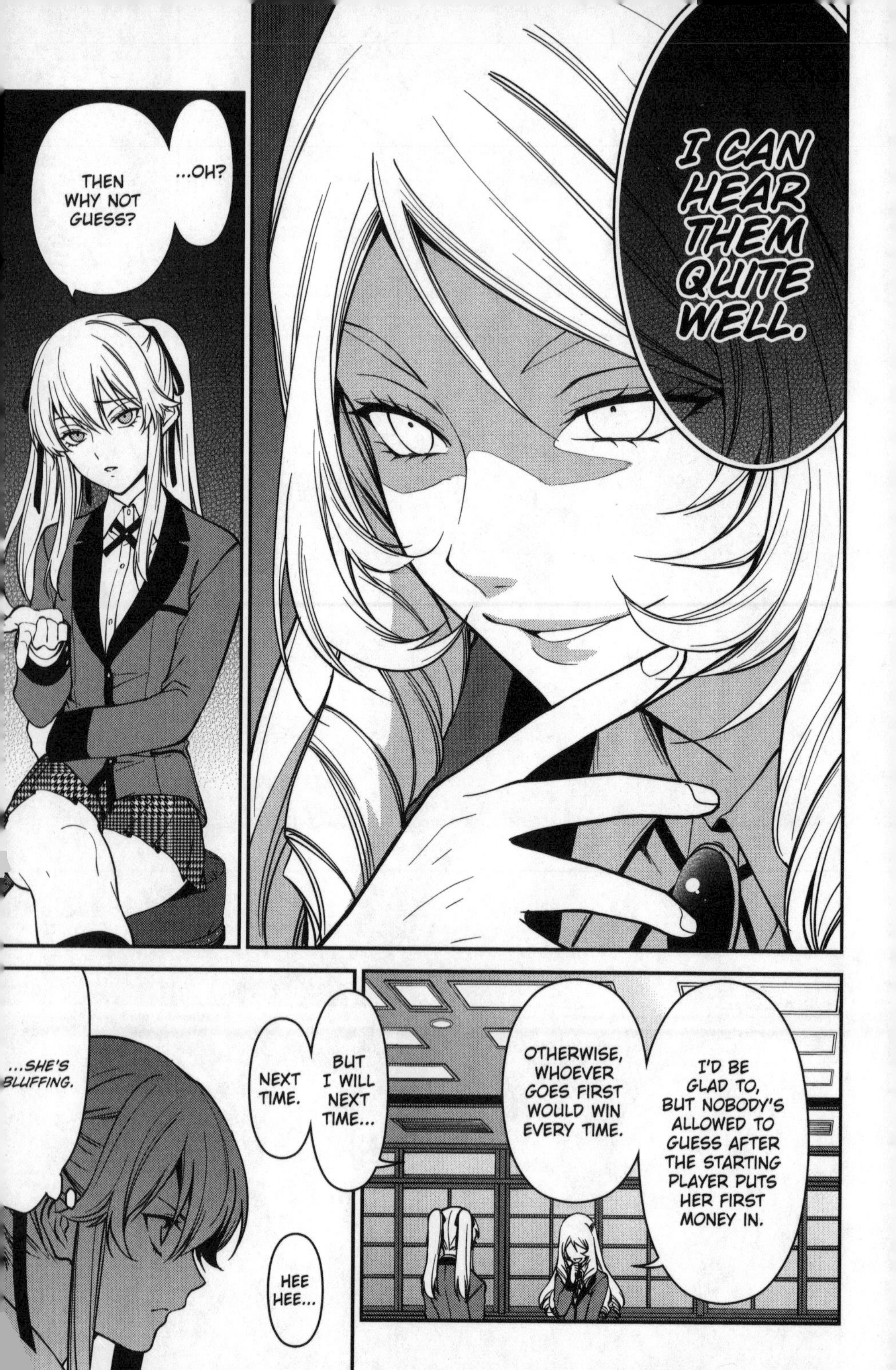
I CAN HEAR THEM QUITE WELL.
...OH?
THEN WHY NOT GUESS?
I'D BE GLAD TO, BUT NOBODY'S ALLOWED TO GUESS AFTER THE STARTING PLAYER PUTS HER FIRST MONEY IN.
OTHERWISE, WHOEVER GOES FIRST WOULD WIN EVERY TIME.
BUT I WILL NEXT TIME...
NEXT TIME.
...SHE'S BLUFFING.
HEE HEE...

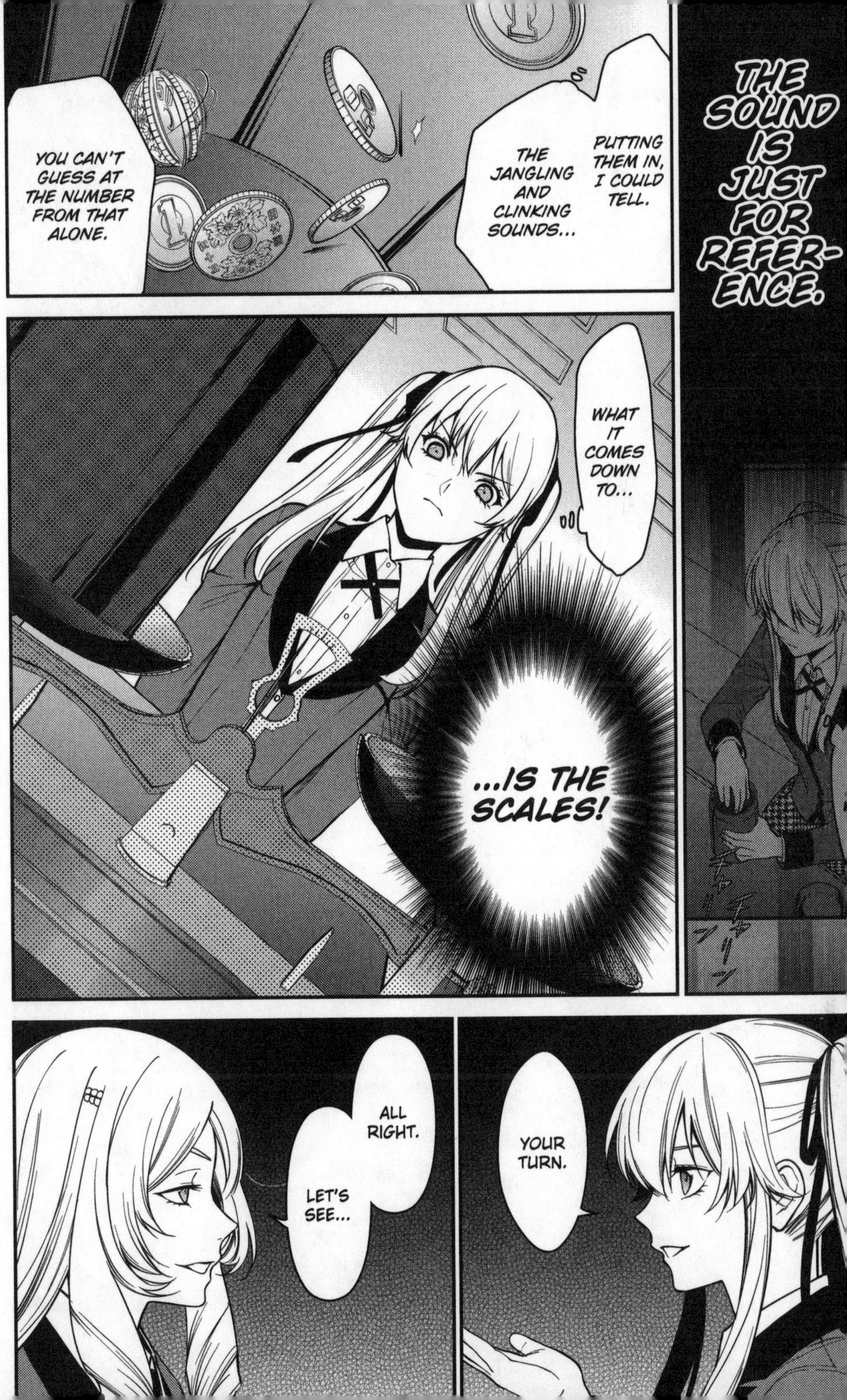
THE SOUND IS JUST FOR REFERENCE.
PUTTING THEM IN, I COULD TELL.
THE JANGLING AND CLINKING SOUNDS...
YOU CAN'T GUESS AT THE NUMBER FROM THAT ALONE.
WHAT IT COMES DOWN TO...
...IS THE SCALES!
YOUR TURN.
ALL RIGHT.
LET'S SEE...

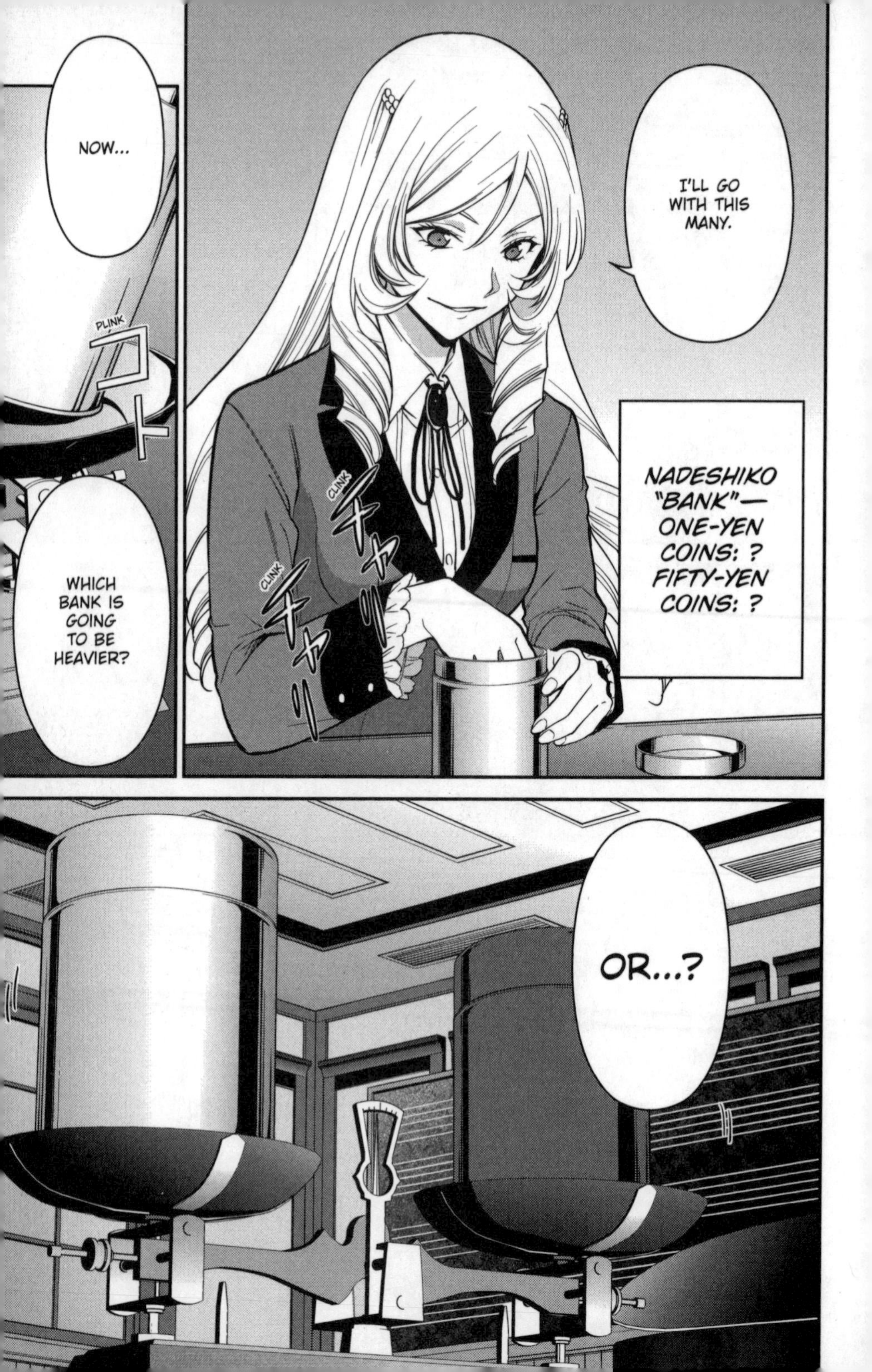
I'LL GO WITH THIS MANY.
NADESHIKO "BANK"— ONE-YEN COINS: ? FIFTY-YEN COINS: ?
CLINK
CLINK
NOW...
PLINK
WHICH BANK IS GOING TO BE HEAVIER?
OR...?

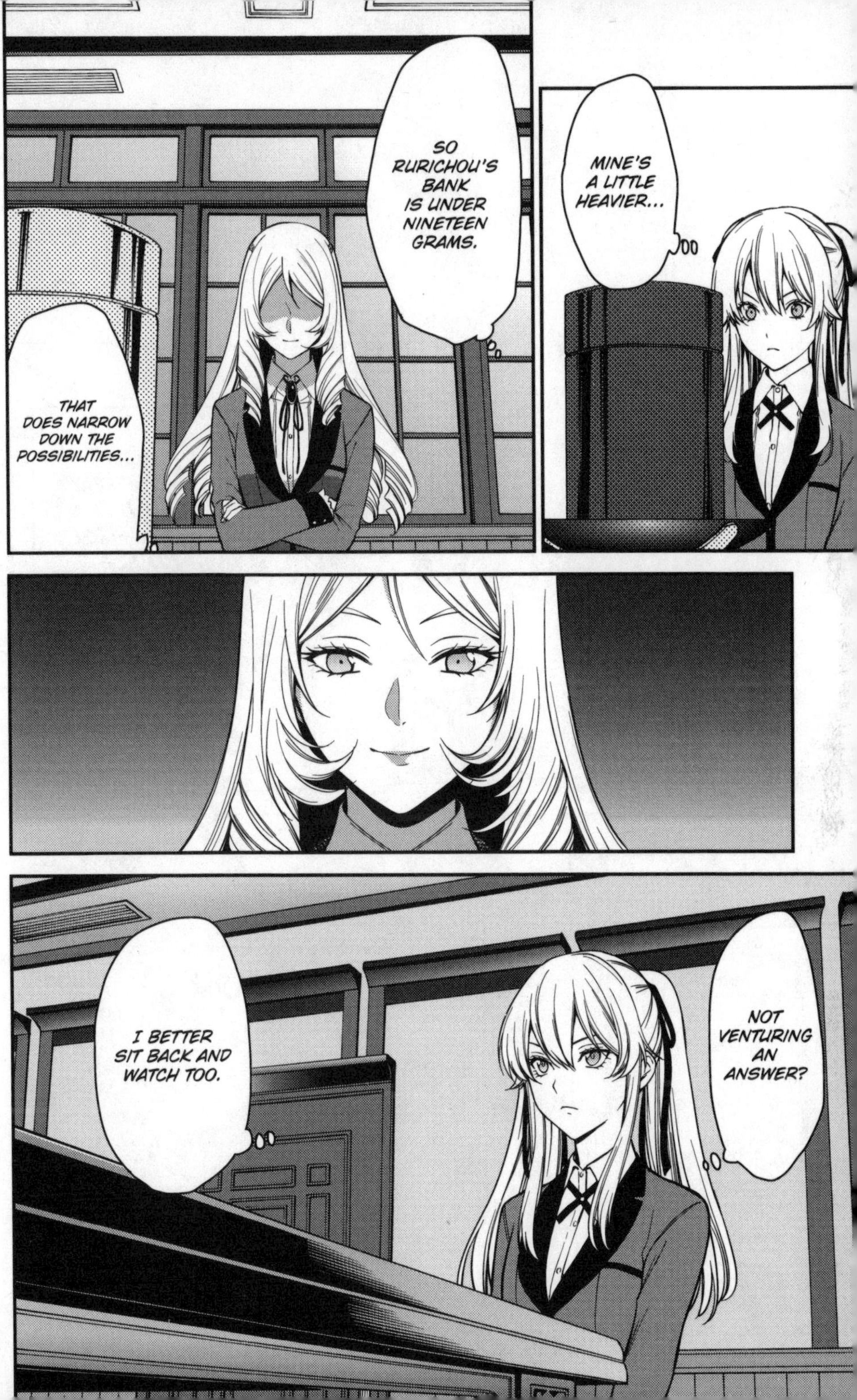
MINE'S A LITTLE HEAVIER...
SO RURICHOU'S BANK IS UNDER NINETEEN GRAMS.
THAT DOES NARROW DOWN THE POSSIBILITIES...
NOT VENTURING AN ANSWER?
I BETTER SIT BACK AND WATCH TOO.

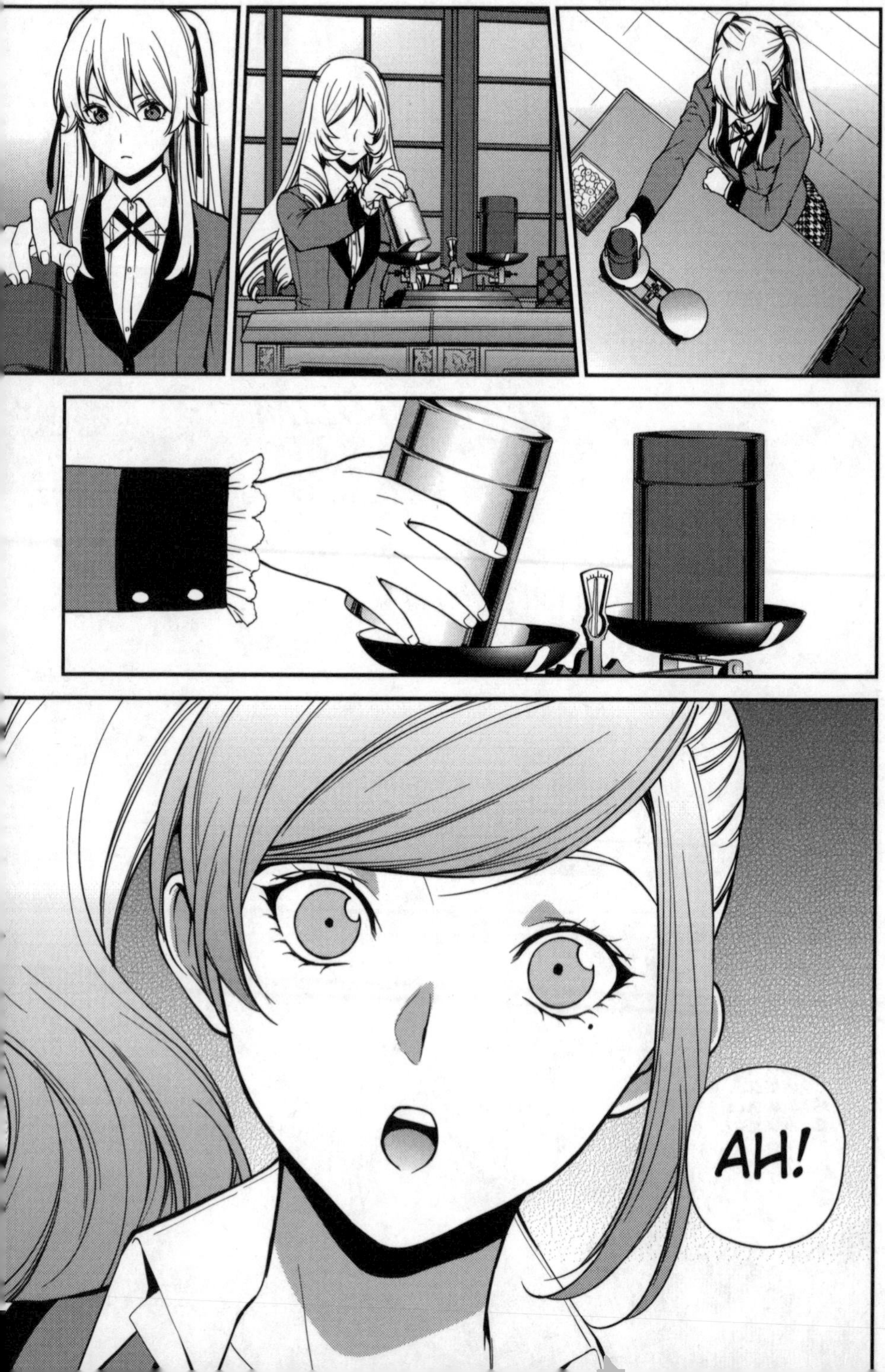
AH!

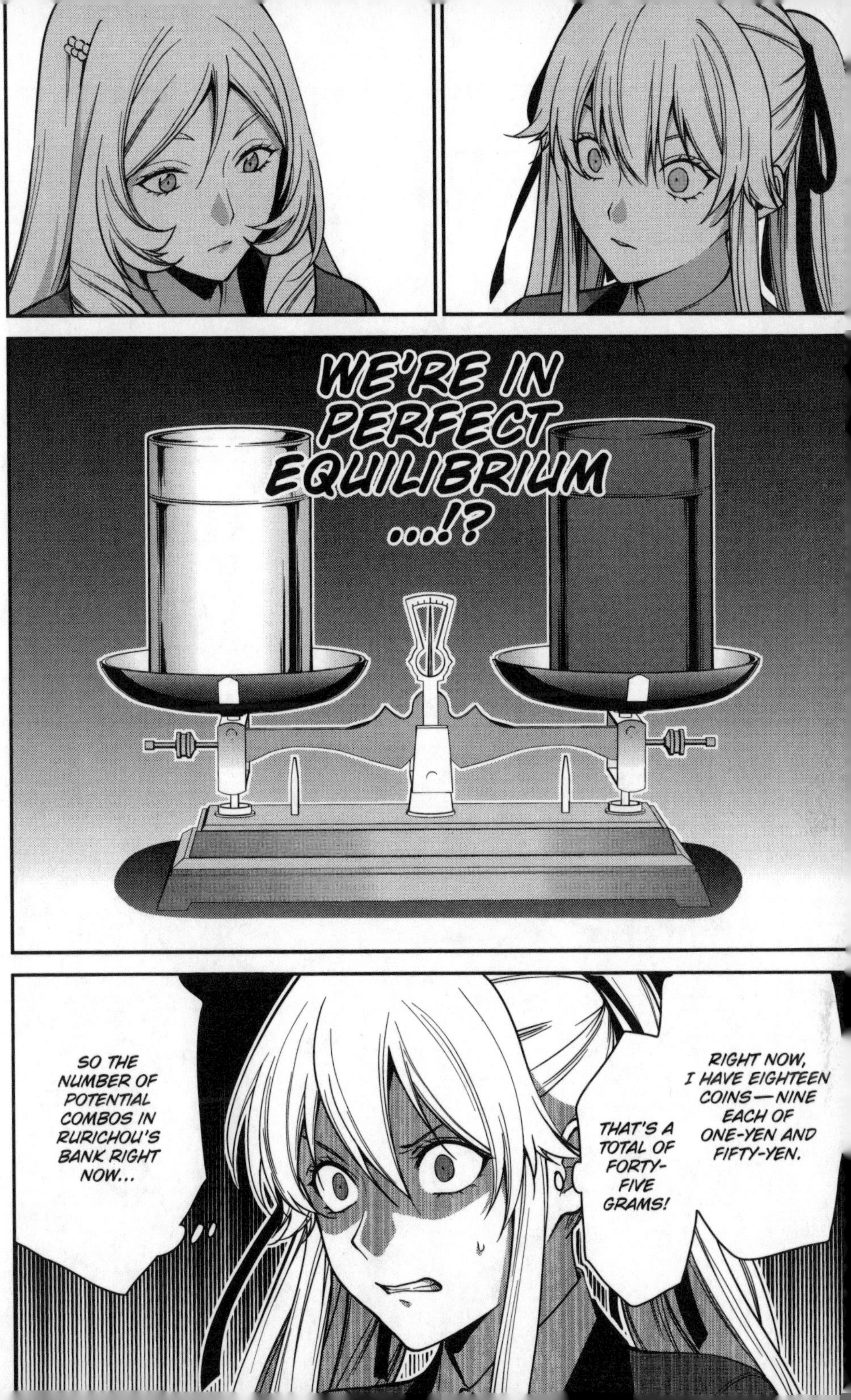
WE'RE IN PERFECT EQUILIBRIUM ...!?
RIGHT NOW, I HAVE EIGHTEEN COINS—NINE EACH OF ONE-YEN AND FIFTY-YEN.
THAT'S A TOTAL OF FORTY-FIVE GRAMS!
SO THE NUMBER OF POTENTIAL COMBOS IN RURICHOU'S BANK RIGHT NOW...
...

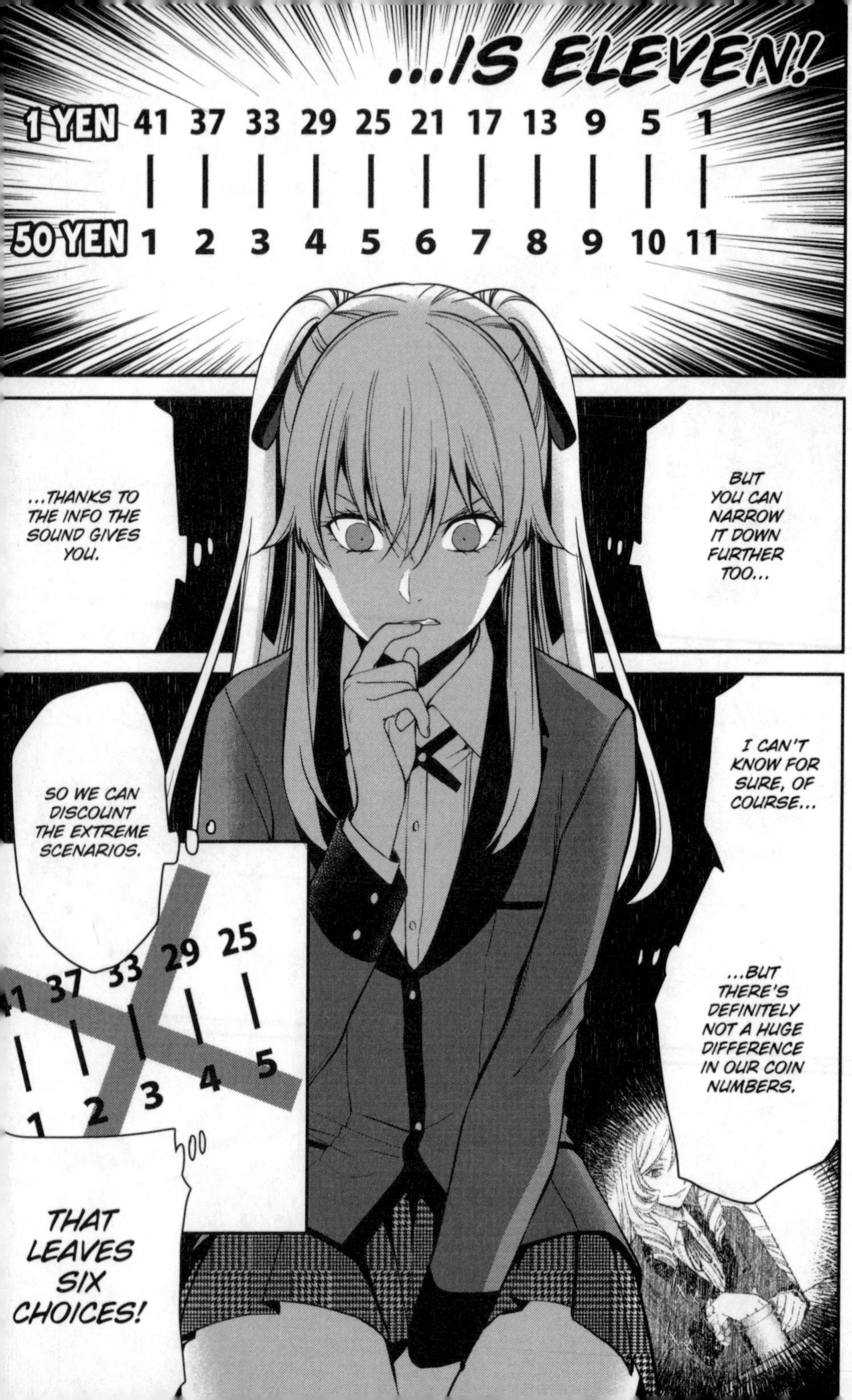
...IS ELEVEN!
1 YEN 41 37 33 29 25 21 17 13 9 5 1
50 YEN 1 2 3 4 5 6 7 8 9 10 11
BUT YOU CAN NARROW IT DOWN FURTHER TOO...
...THANKS TO THE INFO THE SOUND GIVES YOU.
I CAN'T KNOW FOR SURE, OF COURSE...
...BUT THERE'S DEFINITELY NOT A HUGE DIFFERENCE IN OUR COIN NUMBERS.
SO WE CAN DISCOUNT THE EXTREME SCENARIOS.
37 33 29 25
1 2 3 4 5
THAT LEAVES SIX CHOICES!

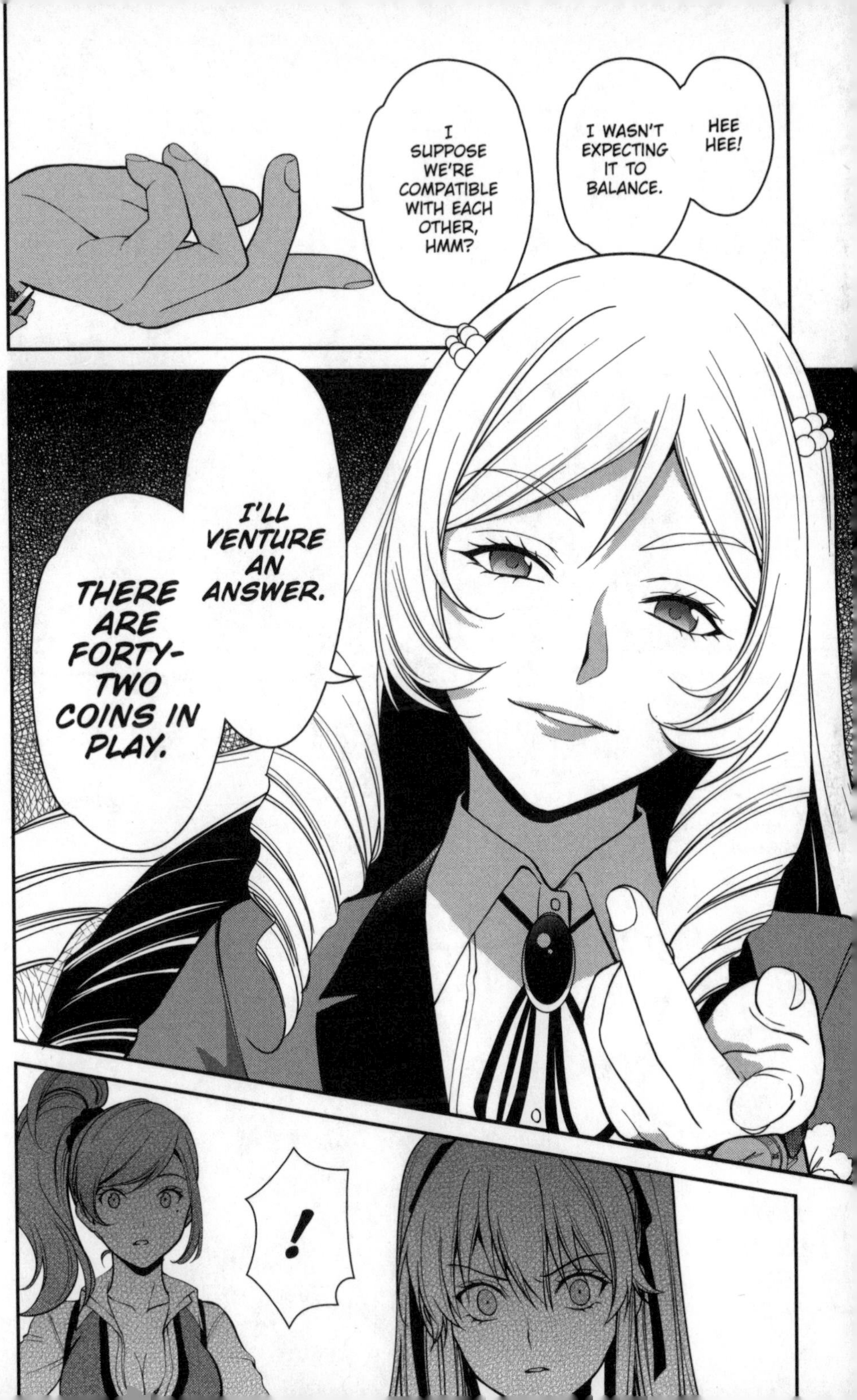
HEE HEE!
I WASN'T EXPECTING IT TO BALANCE.
I SUPPOSE WE'RE COMPATIBLE WITH EACH OTHER, HMM?
I'LL VENTURE AN ANSWER.
THERE ARE FORTY-TWO COINS IN PLAY.
!

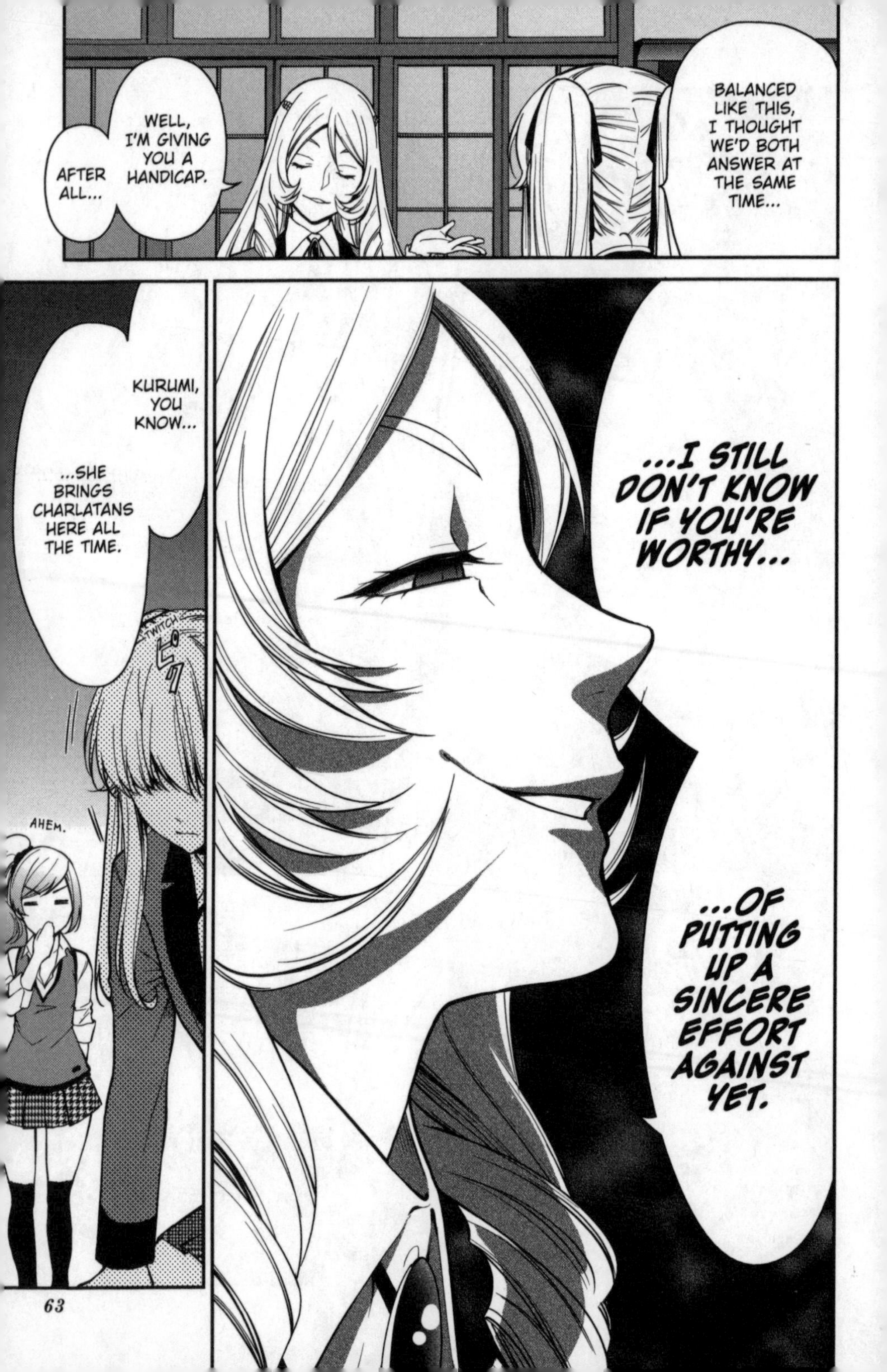
BALANCED LIKE THIS, I THOUGHT WE'D BOTH ANSWER AT THE SAME TIME...
WELL, I'M GIVING YOU A HANDICAP.
AFTER ALL...
...I STILL DON'T KNOW IF YOU'RE WORTHY...
...OF PUTTING UP A SINCERE EFFORT AGAINST YET.
KURUMI, YOU KNOW...
...SHE BRINGS CHARLATANS HERE ALL THE TIME.
TWITCH
AHEM.

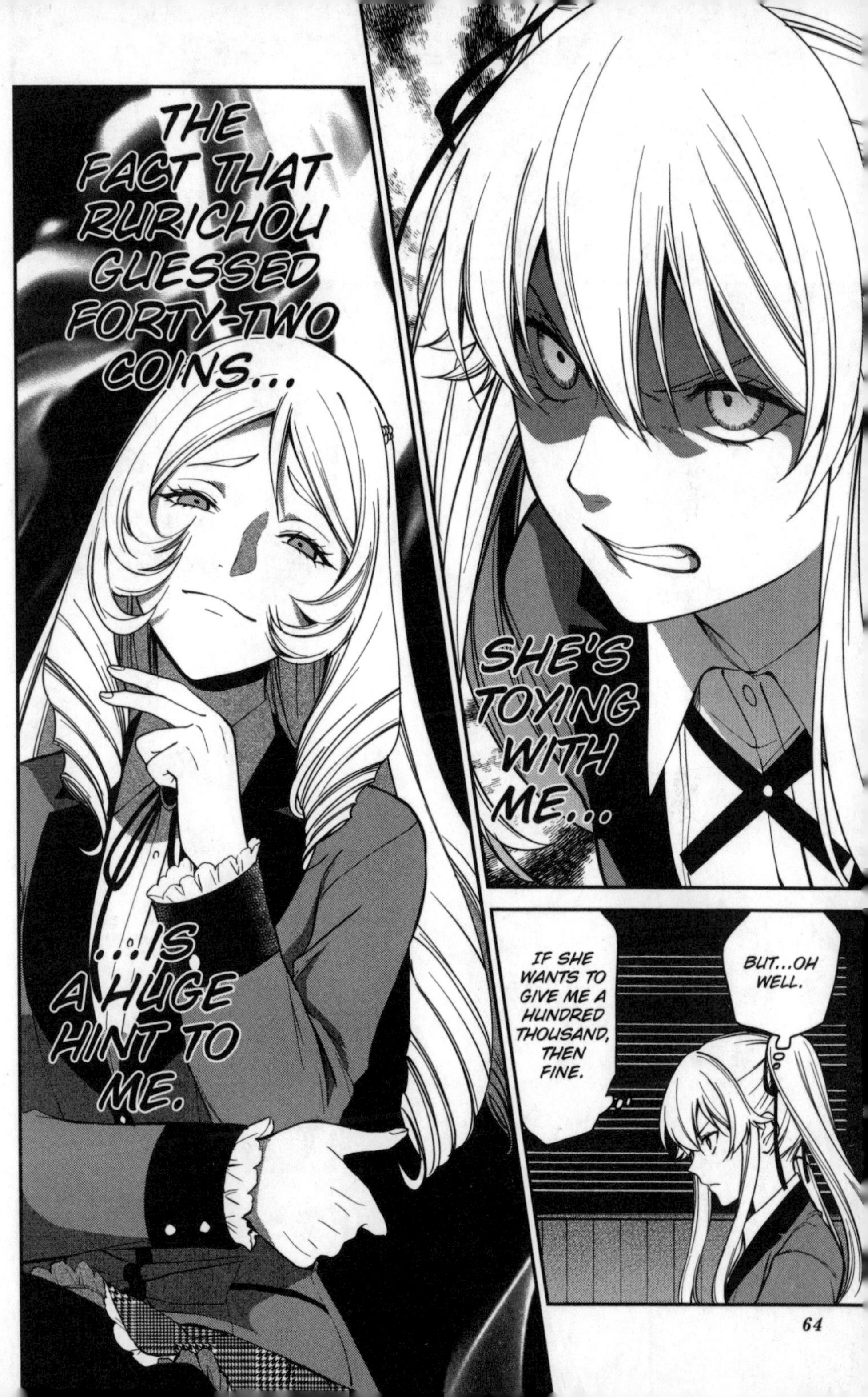
SHE'S TOYING WITH ME...
BUT...OH WELL.
IF SHE WANTS TO GIVE ME A HUNDRED THOUSAND, THEN FINE.
THE FACT THAT RURICHOU GUESSED FORTY-TWO COINS...
...IS A HUGE HINT TO ME.

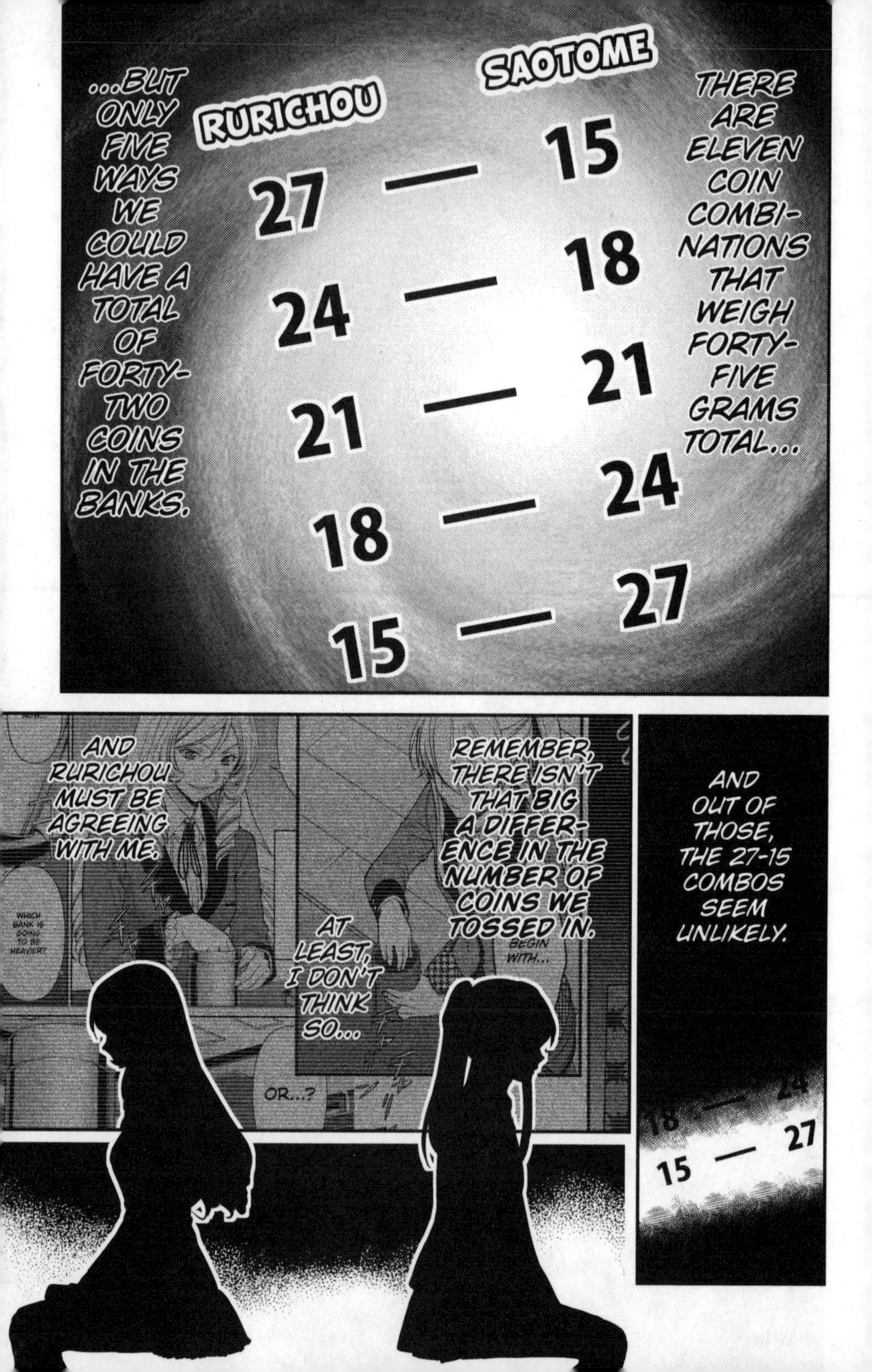
THERE ARE ELEVEN COIN COMBINATIONS THAT WEIGH FORTY-FIVE GRAMS TOTAL...
SAOTOME
RURICHOU
27 — 15
24 — 18
21 — 21
18 — 24
15 — 27
...BUT ONLY FIVE WAYS WE COULD HAVE A TOTAL OF FORTY-TWO COINS IN THE BANKS.
AND OUT OF THOSE, THE 27-15 COMBOS SEEM UNLIKELY.
18 — 24
15 — 27
REMEMBER, THERE ISN'T THAT BIG A DIFFERENCE IN THE NUMBER OF COINS WE TOSSED IN.
BEGIN WITH...
AT LEAST, I DON'T THINK SO...
AND RURICHOU MUST BE AGREEING WITH ME.
WHICH BANK IS GOING TO BE HEAVIER?
OR...?

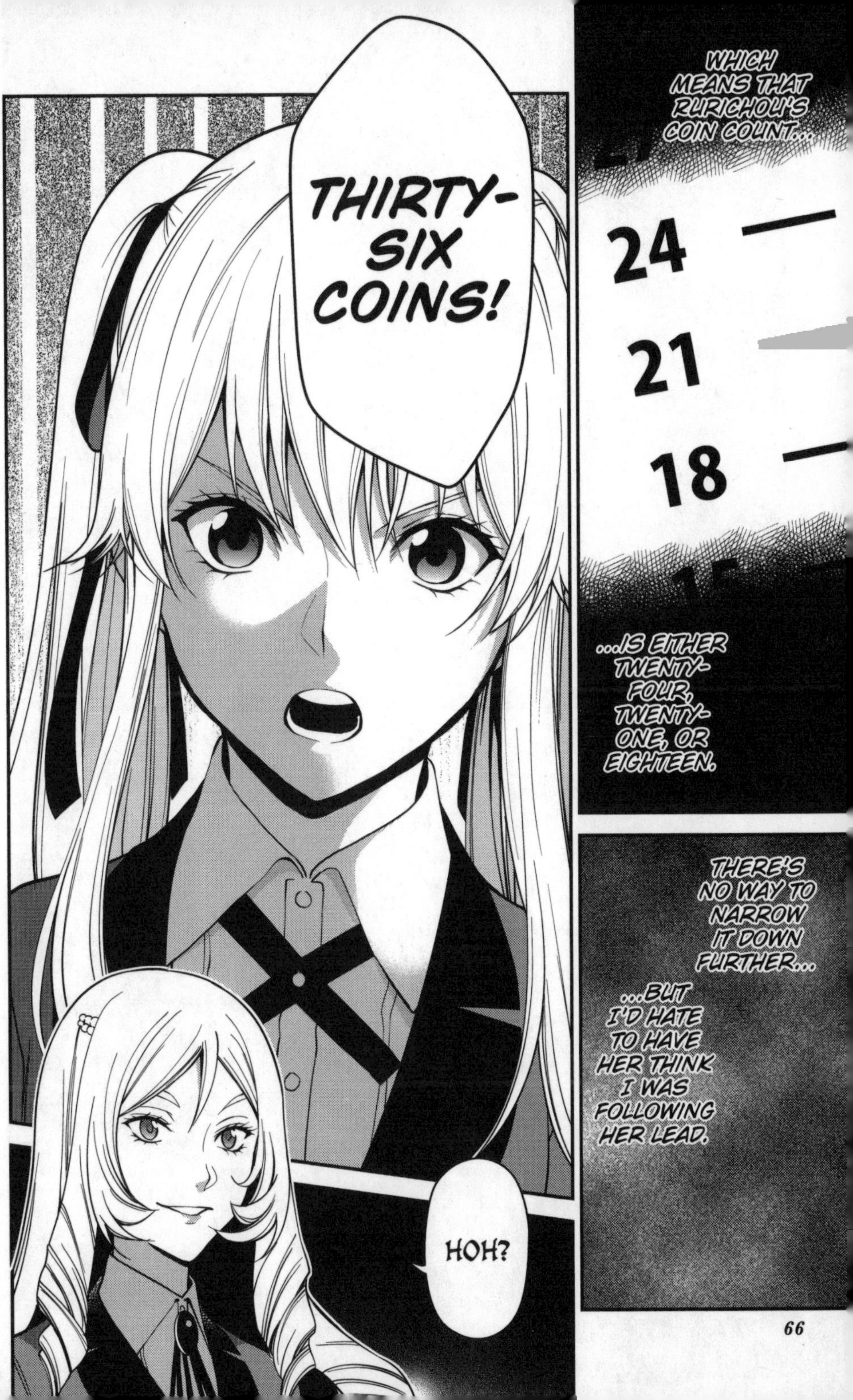
WHICH MEANS THAT RURICHOU'S COIN COUNT...
24
21
18
...IS EITHER TWENTY-FOUR, TWENTY-ONE, OR EIGHTEEN.
THERE'S NO WAY TO NARROW IT DOWN FURTHER...
...BUT I'D HATE TO HAVE HER THINK I WAS FOLLOWING HER LEAD.
THIRTY-SIX COINS!
HOH?

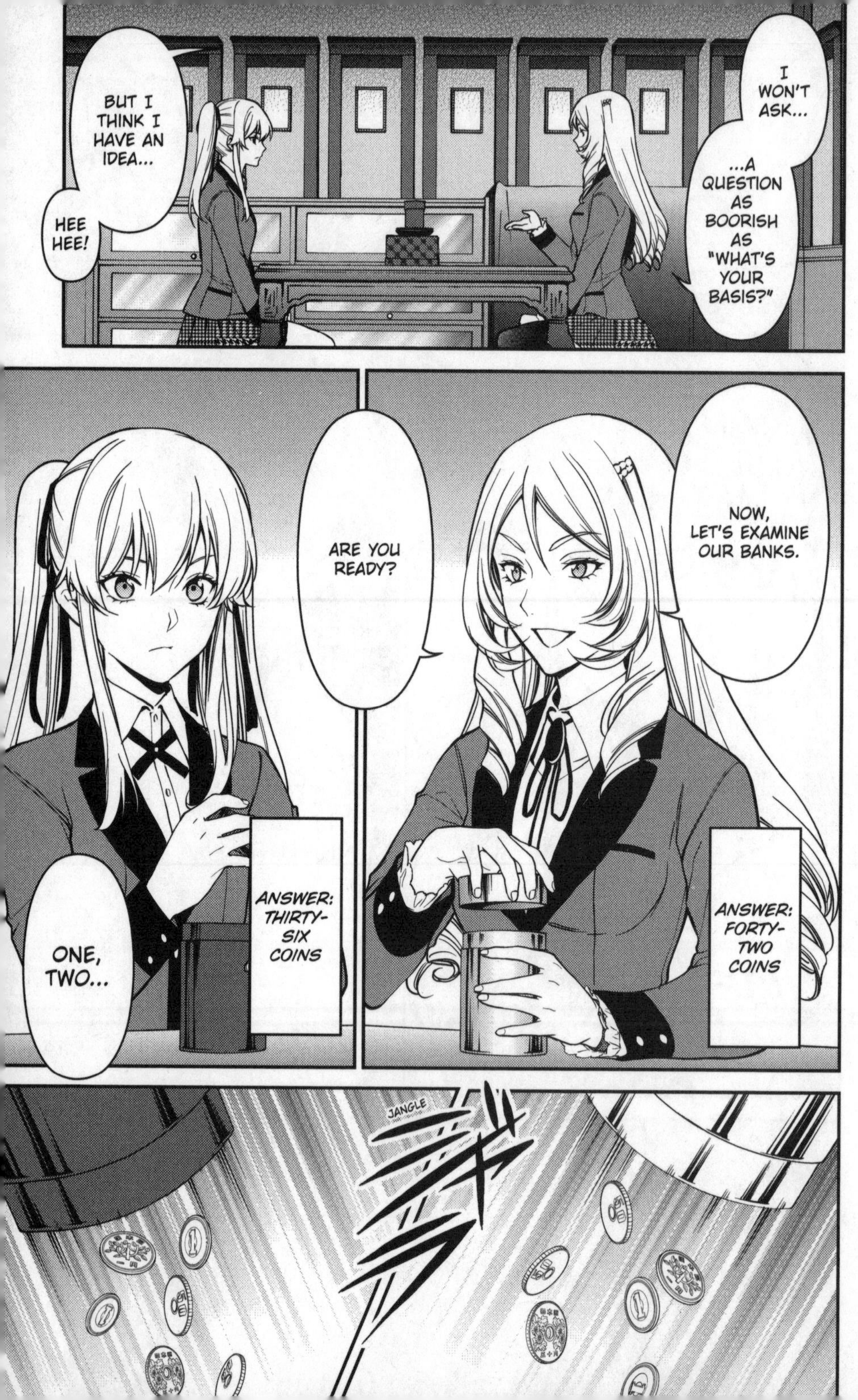
I WON'T ASK...
...A QUESTION AS BOORISH AS "WHAT'S YOUR BASIS?"
BUT I THINK I HAVE AN IDEA...
HEE HEE!
NOW, LET'S EXAMINE OUR BANKS.
ANSWER: FORTY-TWO COINS
ARE YOU READY?
ANSWER: THIRTY-SIX COINS
ONE, TWO...
JANGLE

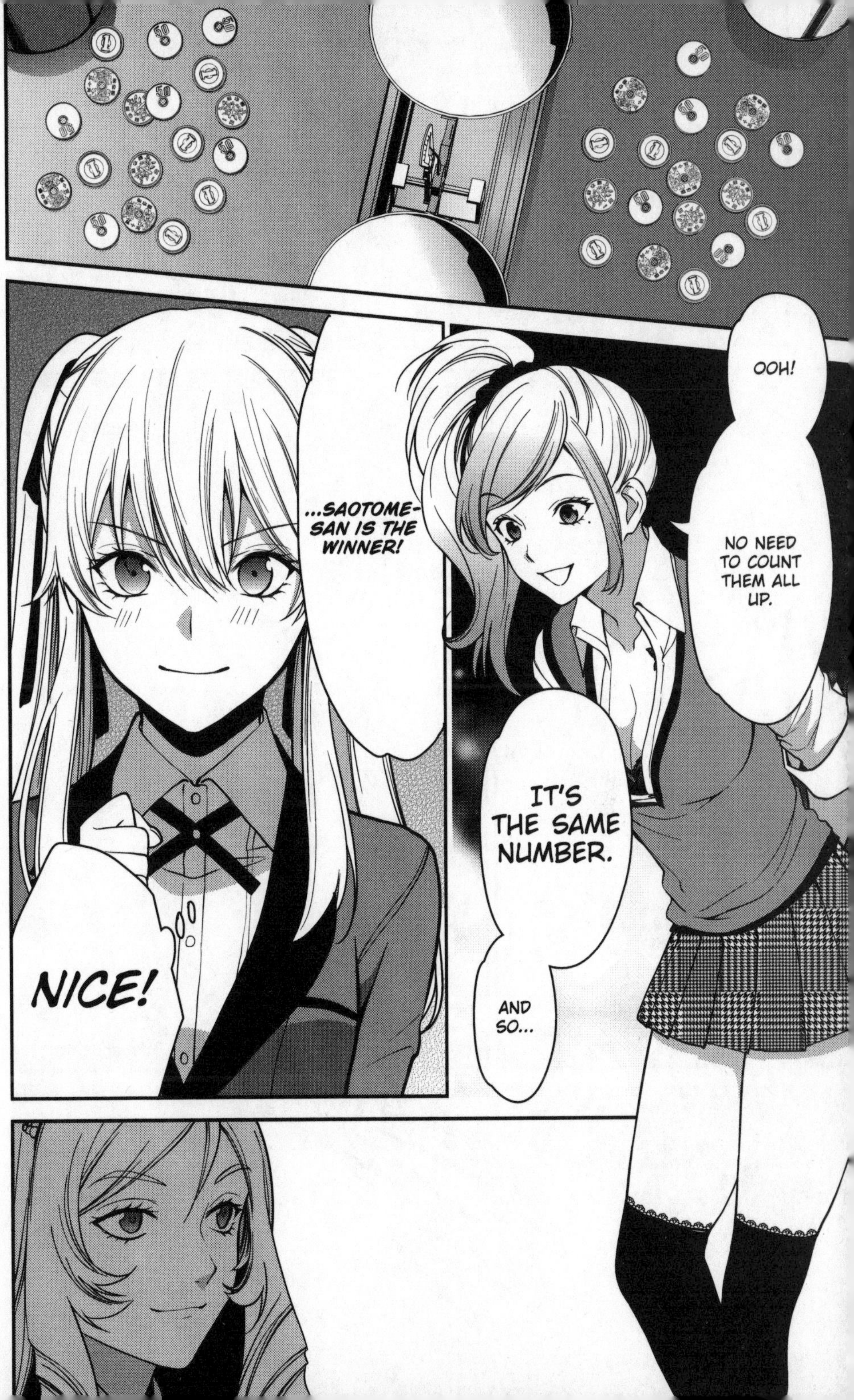
OOH!
NO NEED TO COUNT THEM ALL UP.
IT'S THE SAME NUMBER.
AND SO...
...SAOTOME-SAN IS THE WINNER!
NICE!

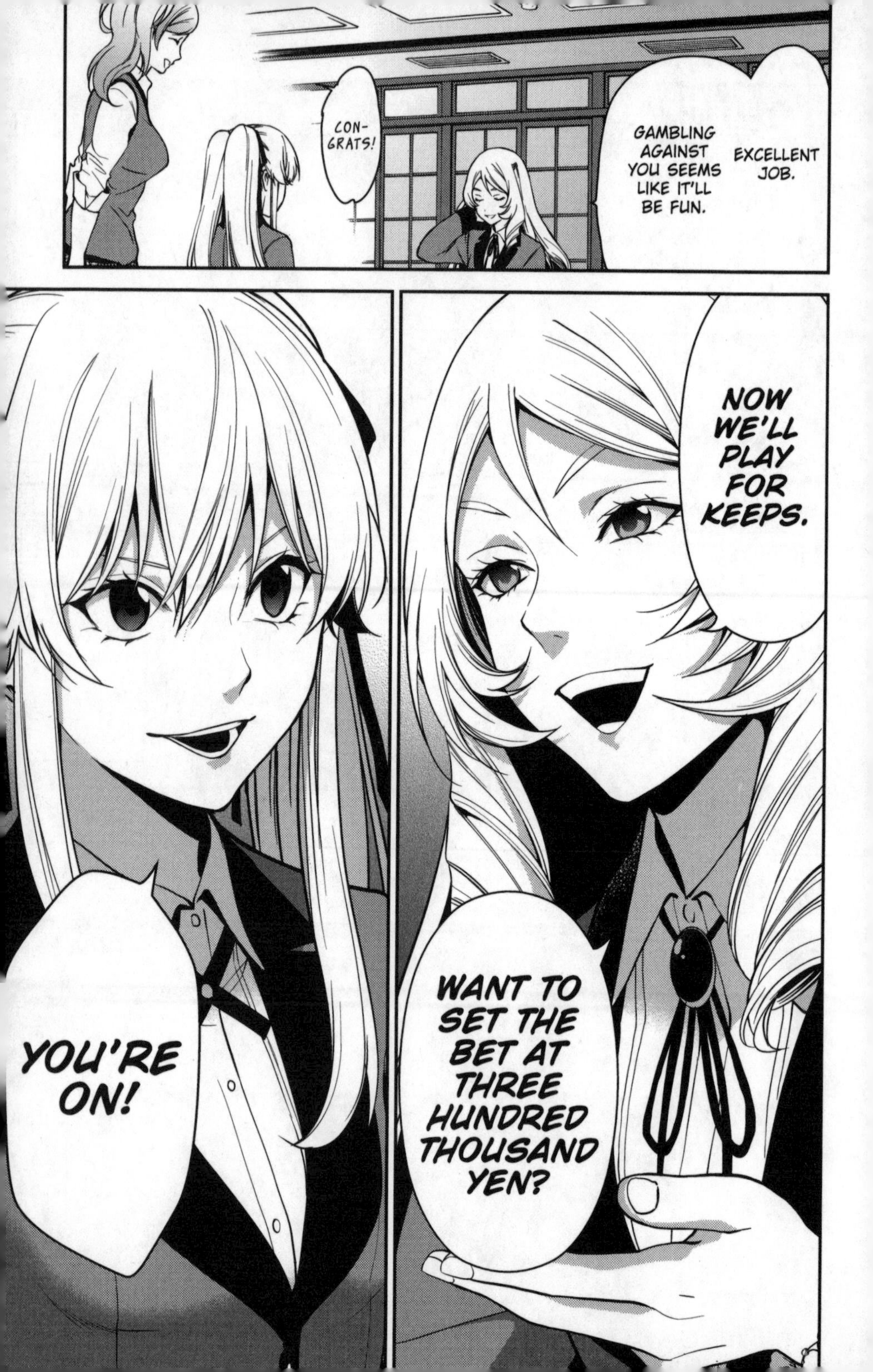
EXCELLENT JOB.
GAMBLING AGAINST YOU SEEMS LIKE IT'LL BE FUN.
CON-GRATS!
NOW WE'LL PLAY FOR KEEPS.
WANT TO SET THE BET AT THREE HUNDRED THOUSAND YEN?
YOU'RE ON!

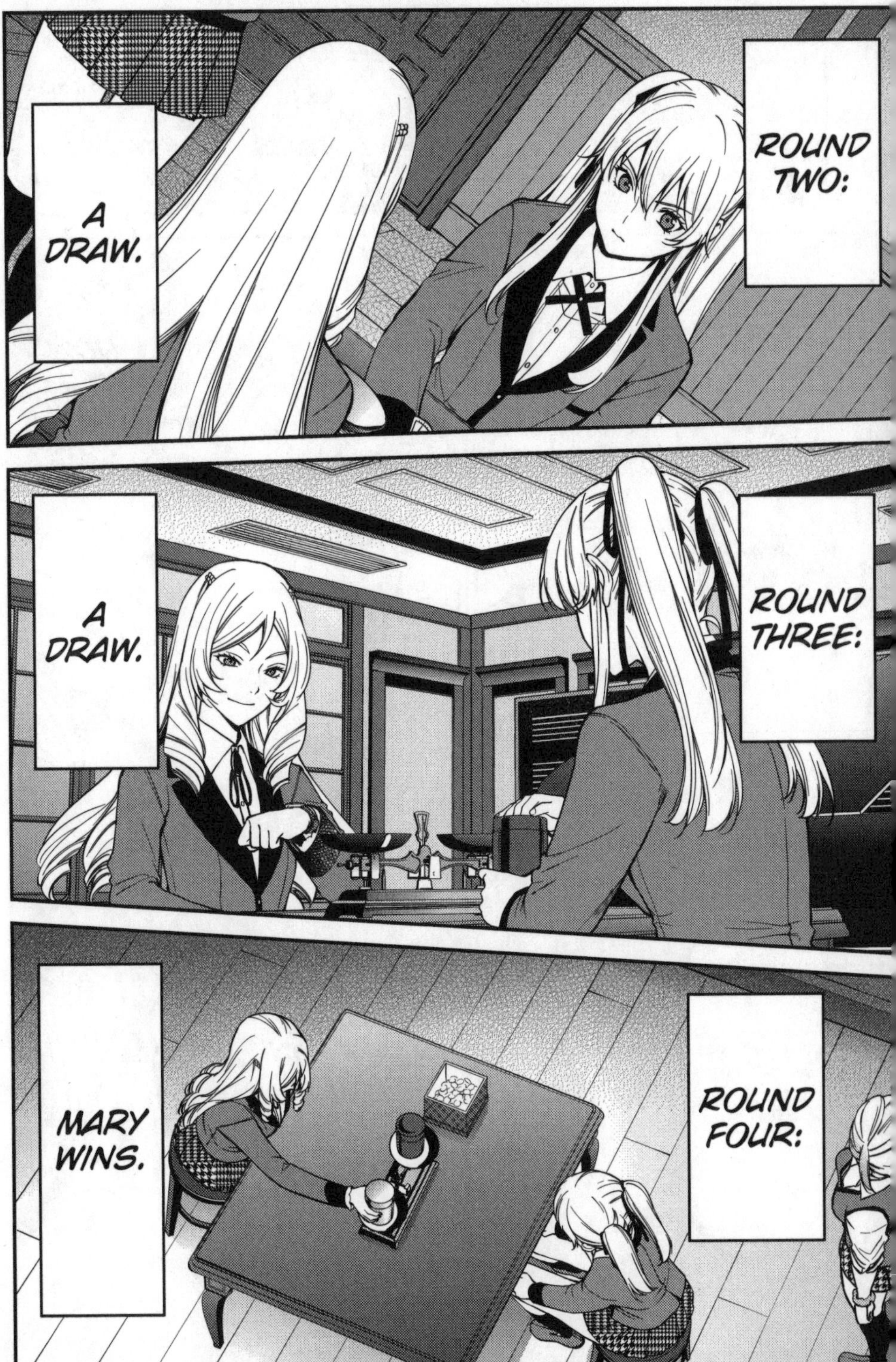
ROUND TWO:
A DRAW.
ROUND THREE:
A DRAW.
ROUND FOUR:
MARY WINS.

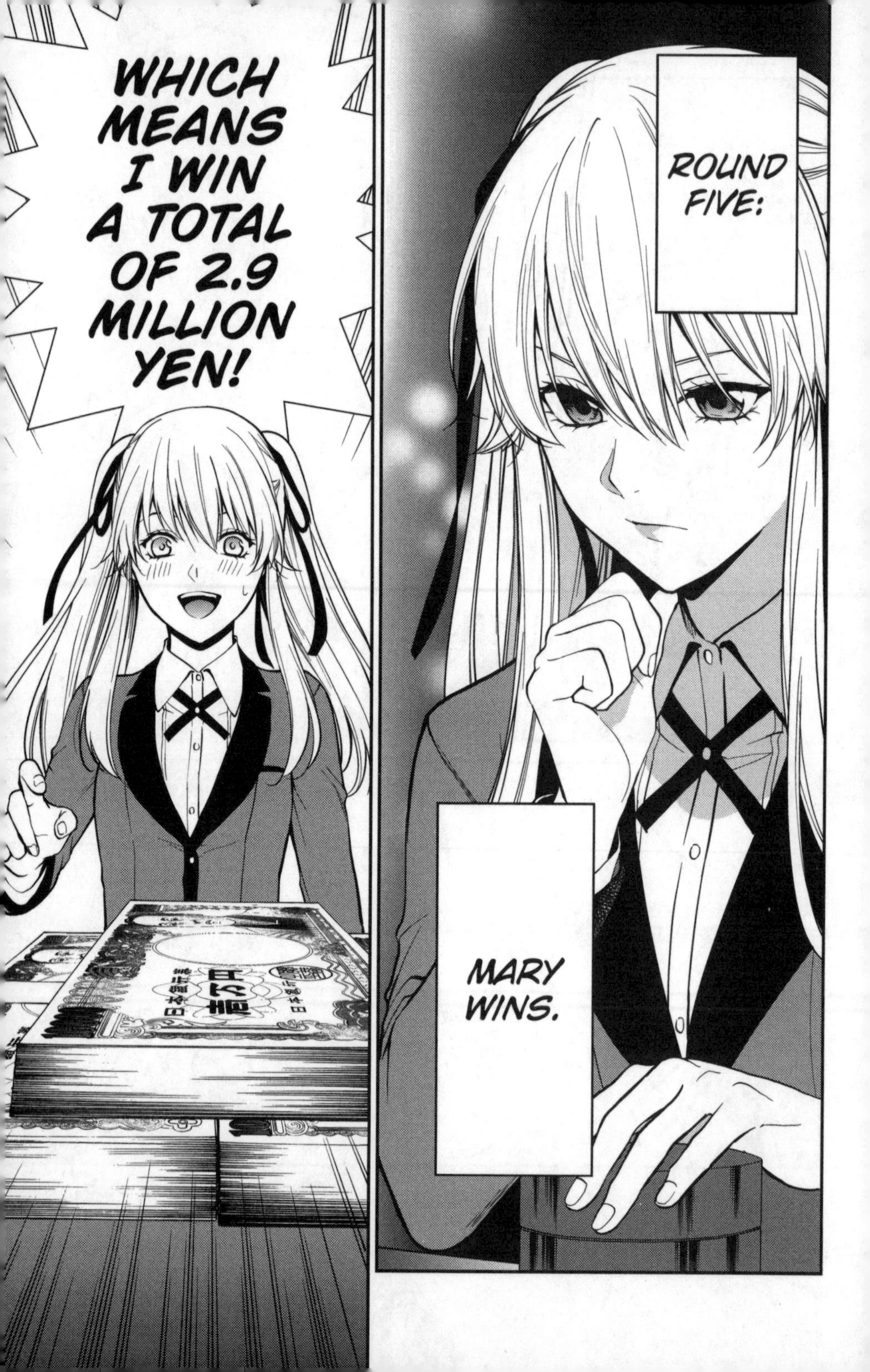
ROUND FIVE:
MARY WINS.
WHICH MEANS I WIN A TOTAL OF 2.9 MILLION YEN!

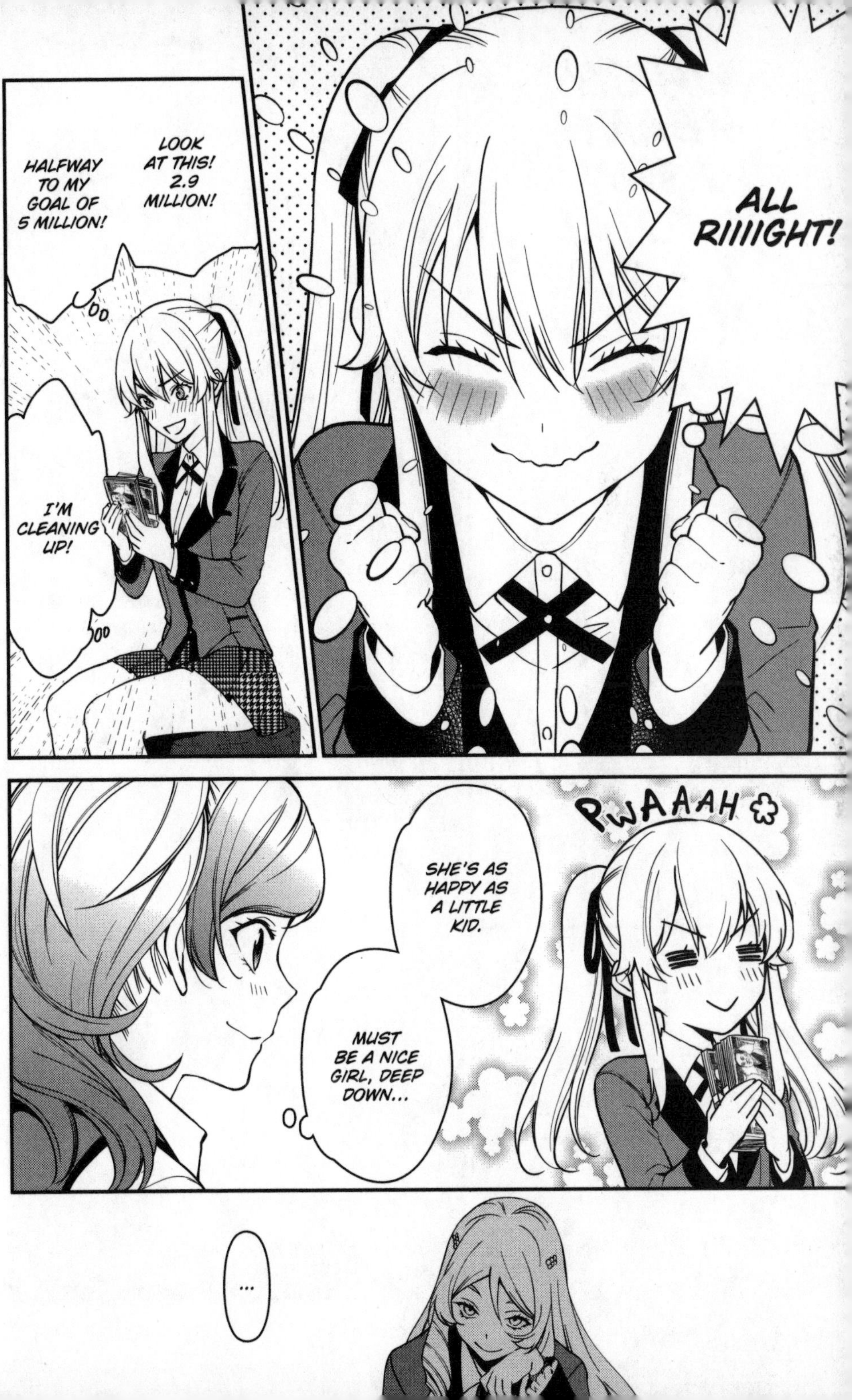
ALL RIIIIGHT!
LOOK AT THIS! 2.9 MILLION!
HALFWAY TO MY GOAL OF 5 MILLION!
I'M CLEANING UP!
PWAAAH
SHE'S AS HAPPY AS A LITTLE KID.
MUST BE A NICE GIRL, DEEP DOWN...
...

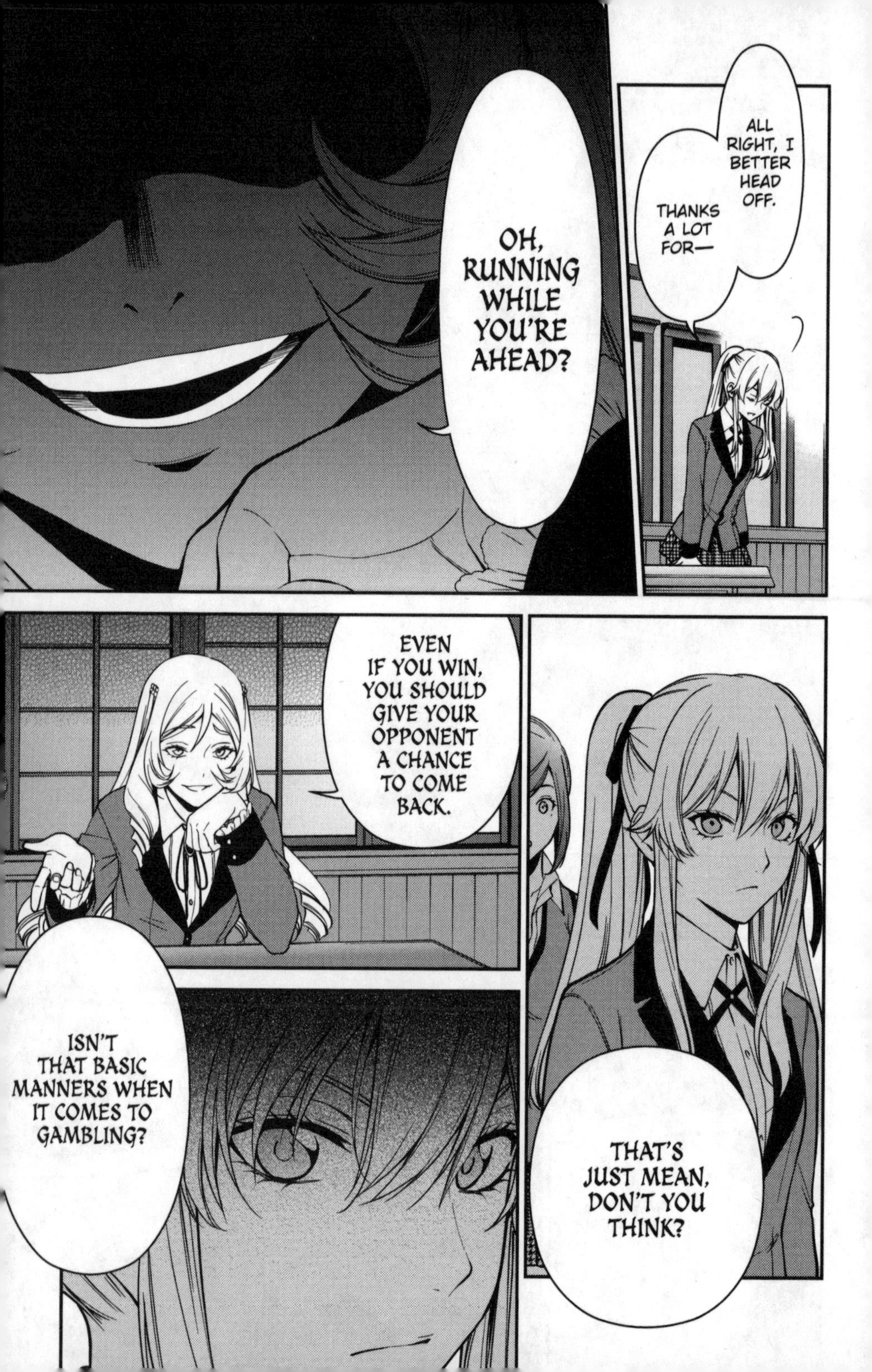
ALL RIGHT, I BETTER HEAD OFF.
THANKS A LOT FOR—
OH, RUNNING WHILE YOU'RE AHEAD?
THAT'S JUST MEAN, DON'T YOU THINK?
EVEN IF YOU WIN, YOU SHOULD GIVE YOUR OPPONENT A CHANCE TO COME BACK.
ISN'T THAT BASIC MANNERS WHEN IT COMES TO GAMBLING?

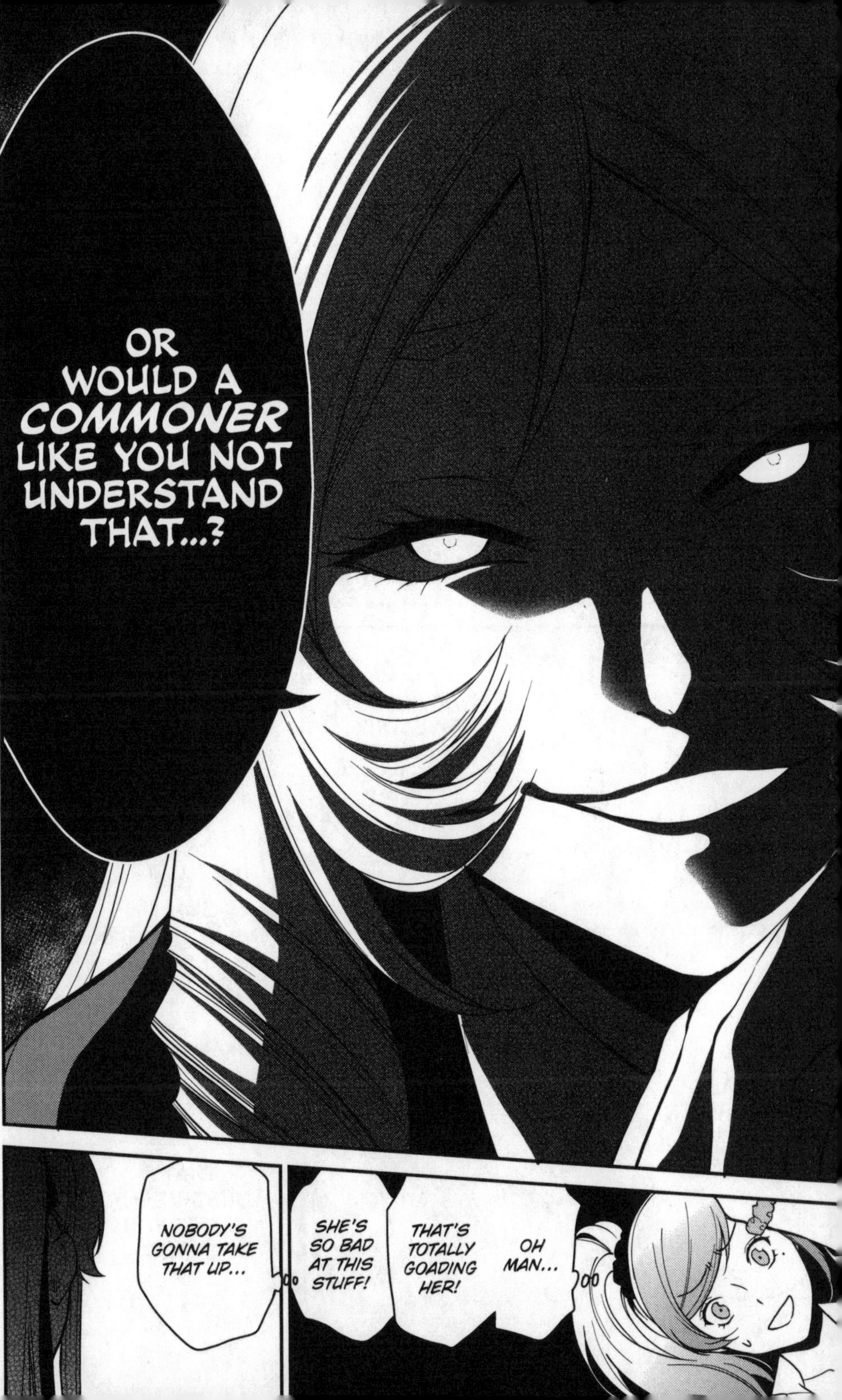
OR WOULD A COMMONER LIKE YOU NOT UNDERSTAND THAT...?
OH MAN...
THAT'S TOTALLY GOADING HER!
SHE'S SO BAD AT THIS STUFF!
NOBODY'S GONNA TAKE THAT UP...

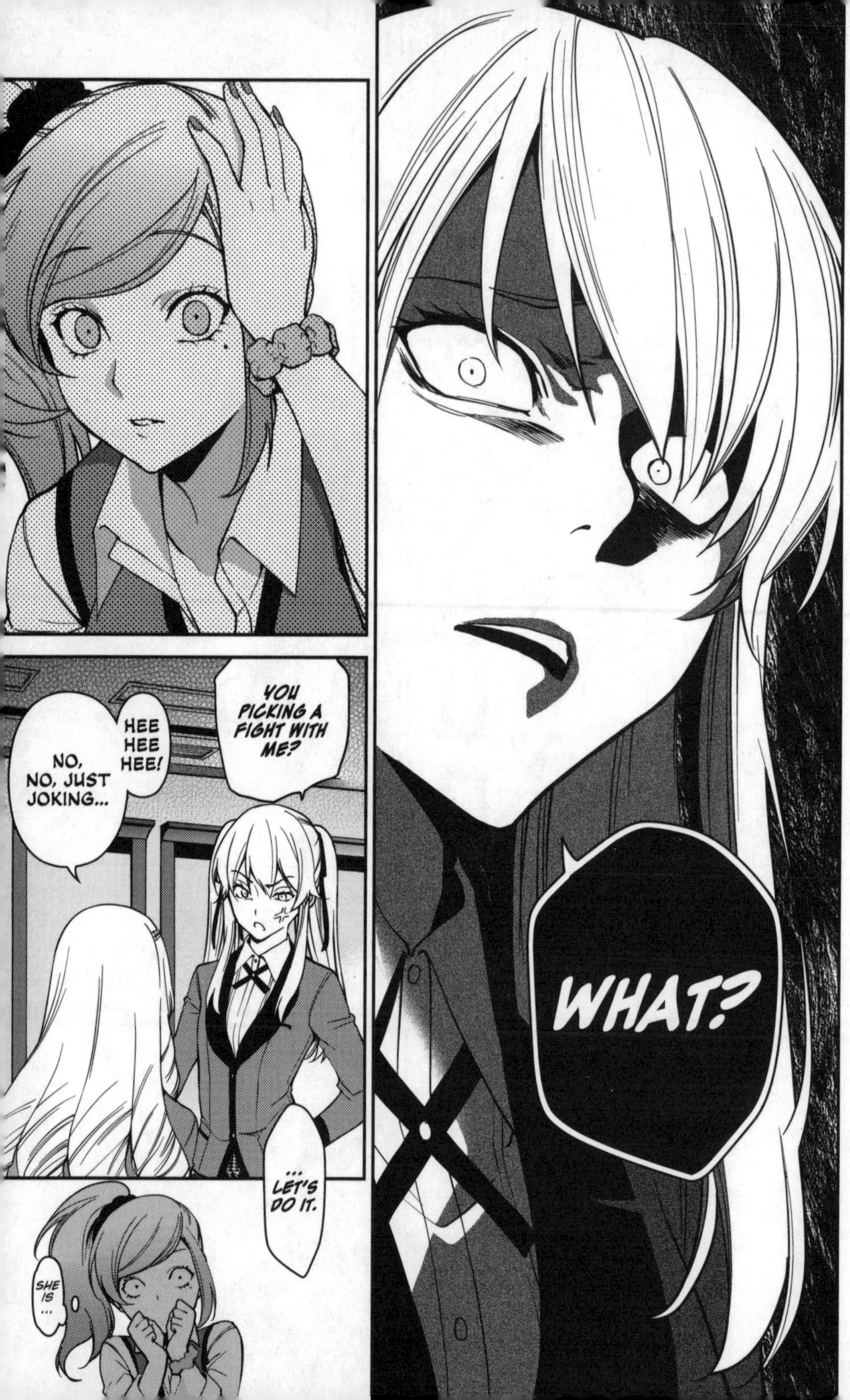
WHAT?
YOU PICKING A FIGHT WITH ME?
HEE HEE HEE!
NO, NO, JUST JOKING...
... LET'S DO IT.
SHE IS ...

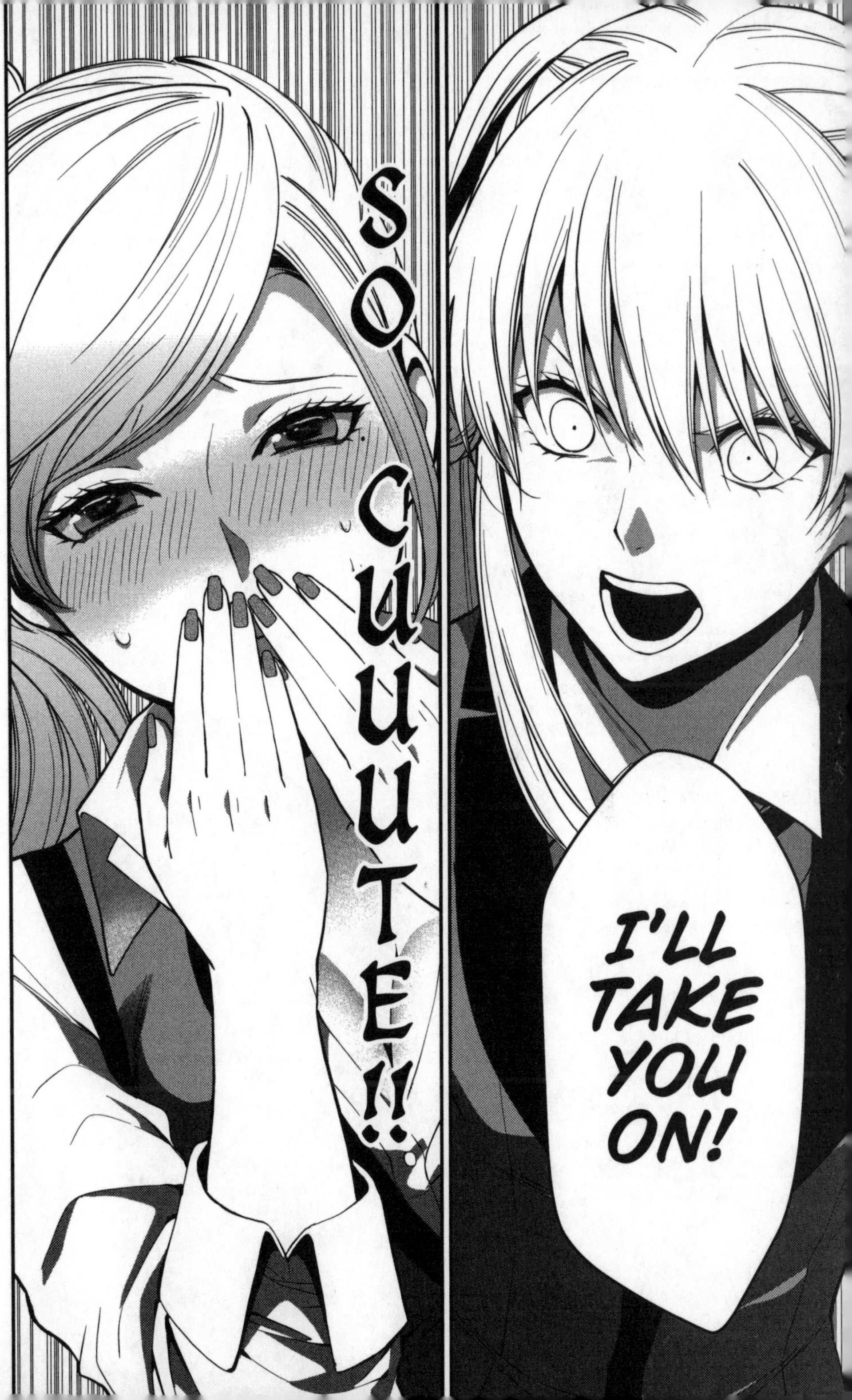
I'LL TAKE YOU ON!
SO CUUUTE!!

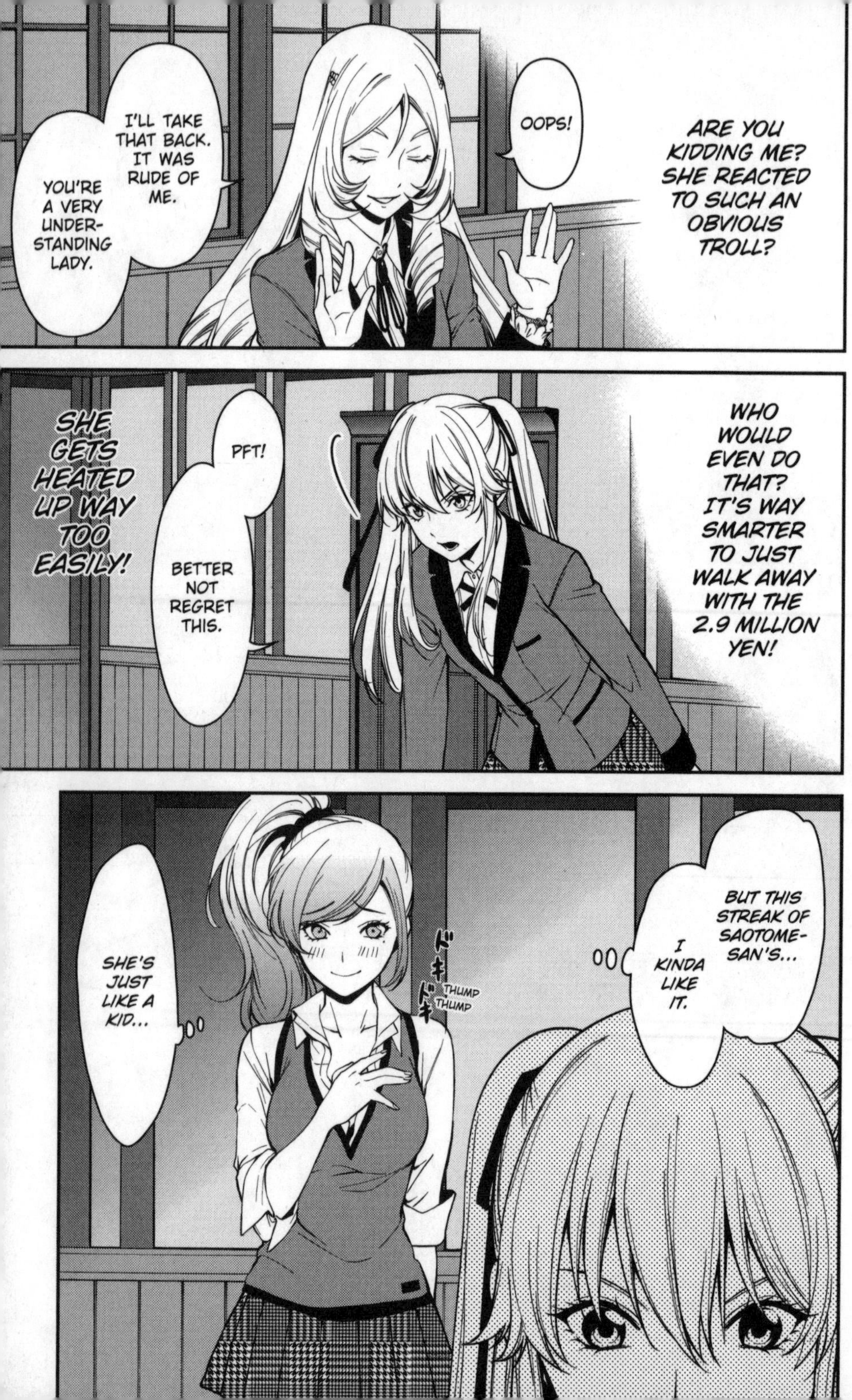
ARE YOU KIDDING ME? SHE REACTED TO SUCH AN OBVIOUS TROLL?
OOPS!
I'LL TAKE THAT BACK. IT WAS RUDE OF ME.
YOU'RE A VERY UNDER-STANDING LADY.
WHO WOULD EVEN DO THAT? IT'S WAY SMARTER TO JUST WALK AWAY WITH THE 2.9 MILLION YEN!
PFT!
BETTER NOT REGRET THIS.
SHE GETS HEATED UP WAY TOO EASILY!
BUT THIS STREAK OF SAOTOME-SAN'S...
I KINDA LIKE IT.
ドキドキ THUMP THUMP
SHE'S JUST LIKE A KID...

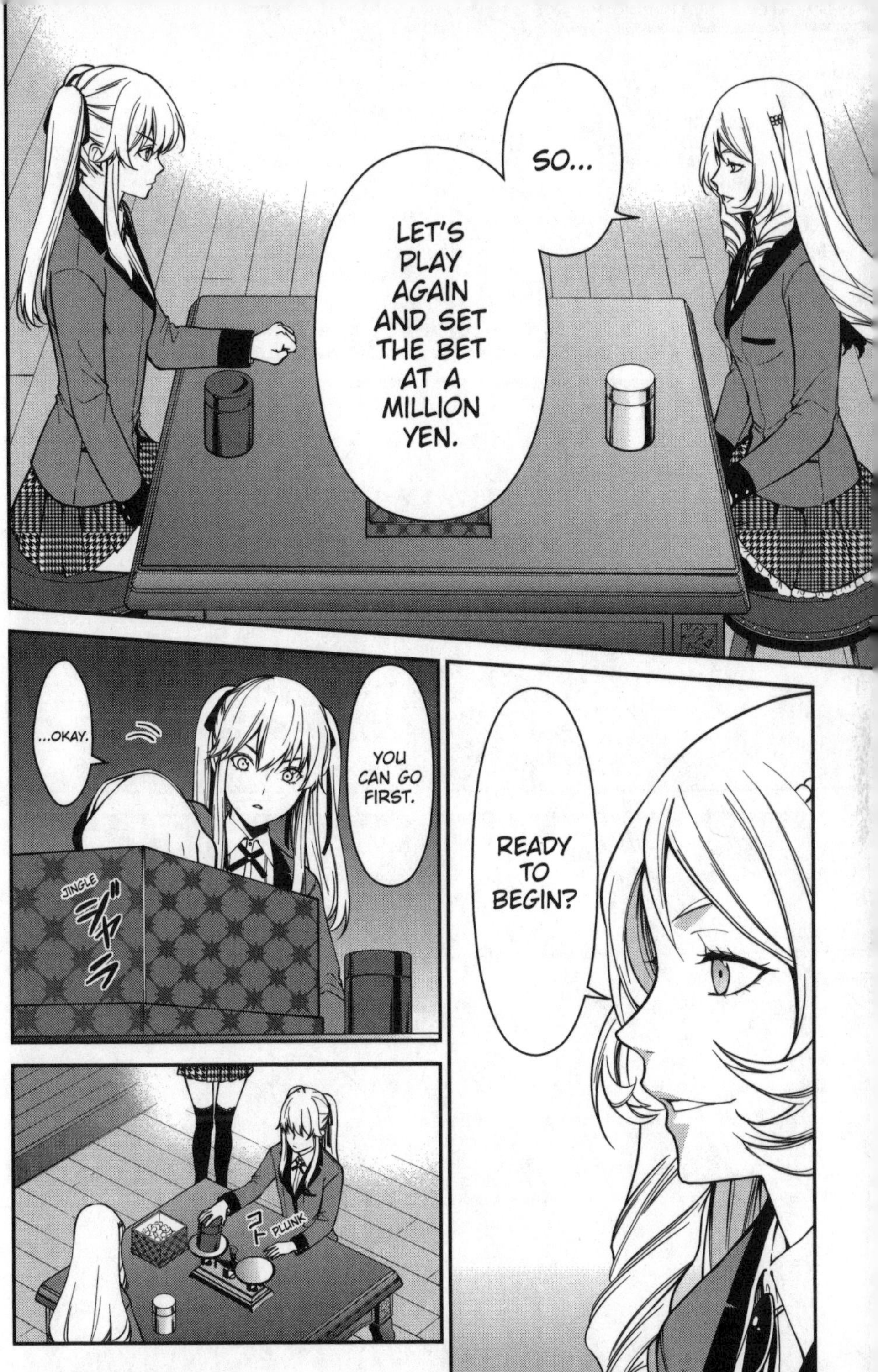
SO...
LET'S PLAY AGAIN AND SET THE BET AT A MILLION YEN.
READY TO BEGIN?
YOU CAN GO FIRST.
...OKAY.
JINGLE
PLUNK

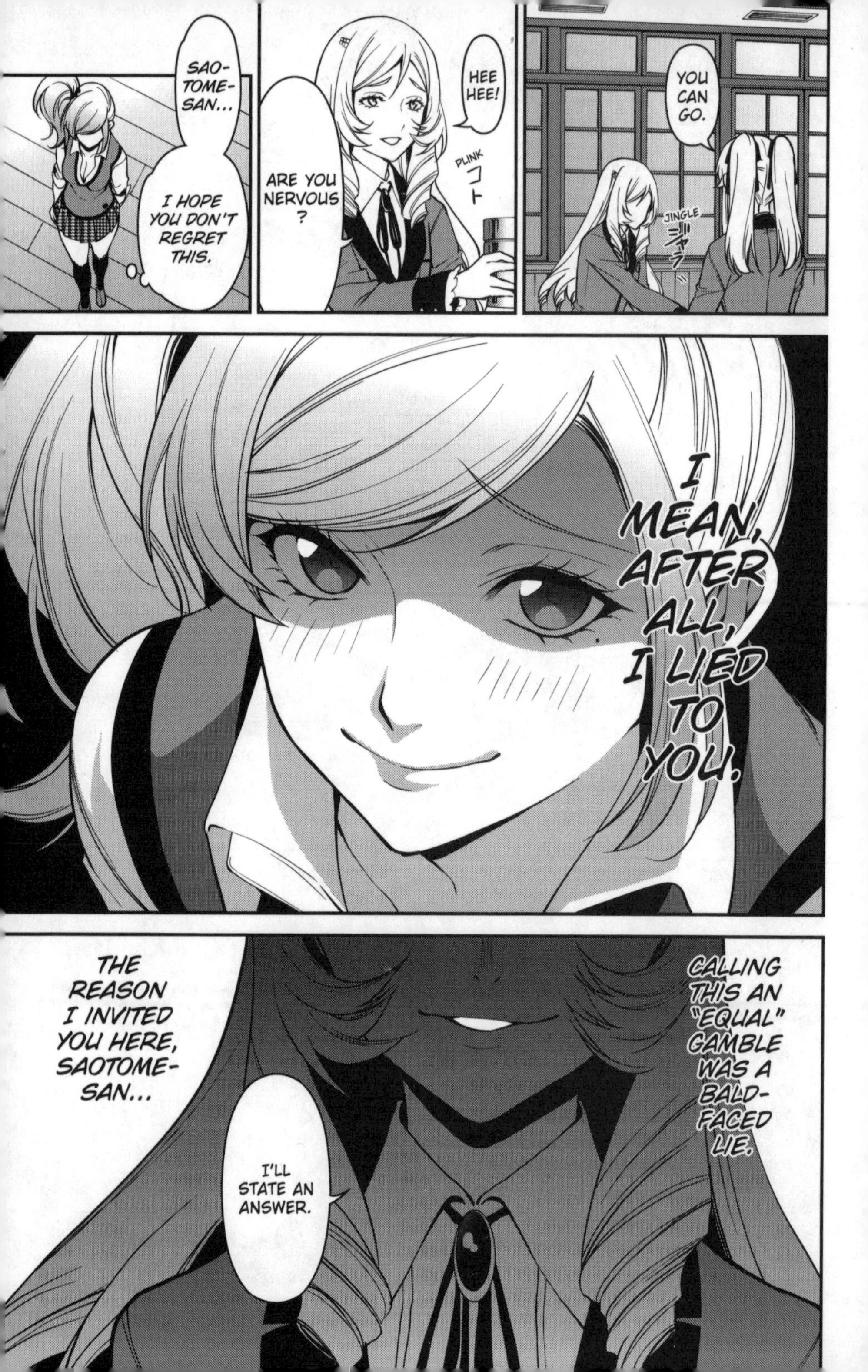
YOU CAN GO.
JINGLE
HEE HEE!
PLINK
コト
ARE YOU NERVOUS?
SAO-TOME-SAN...
I HOPE YOU DON'T REGRET THIS.
I MEAN, AFTER ALL, I LIED TO YOU.
CALLING THIS AN "EQUAL" GAMBLE WAS A BALD-FACED LIE.
THE REASON I INVITED YOU HERE, SAOTOME-SAN...
I'LL STATE AN ANSWER.

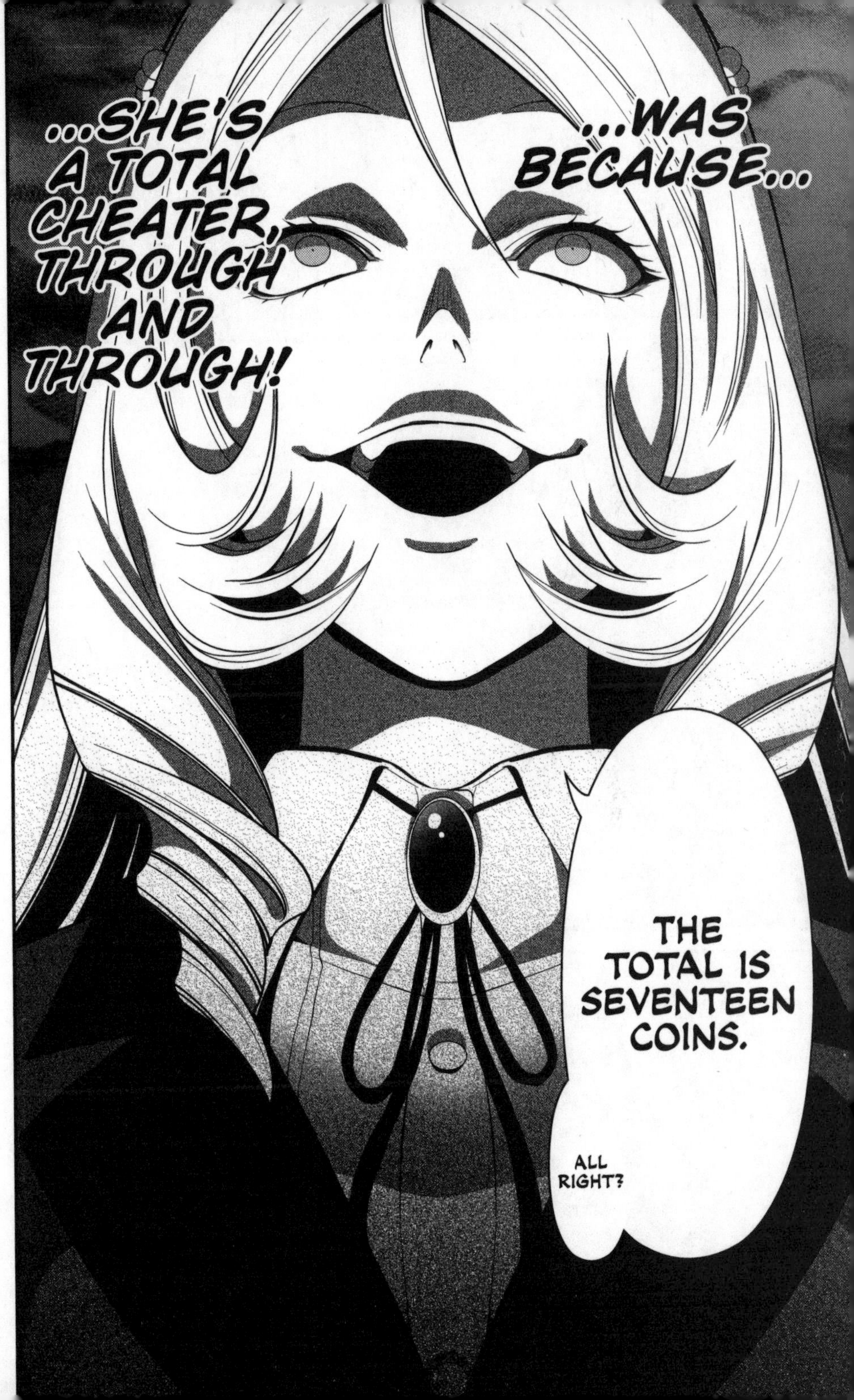
...WAS BECAUSE...
...SHE'S A TOTAL CHEATER, THROUGH AND THROUGH!
THE TOTAL IS SEVENTEEN COINS.
ALL RIGHT?

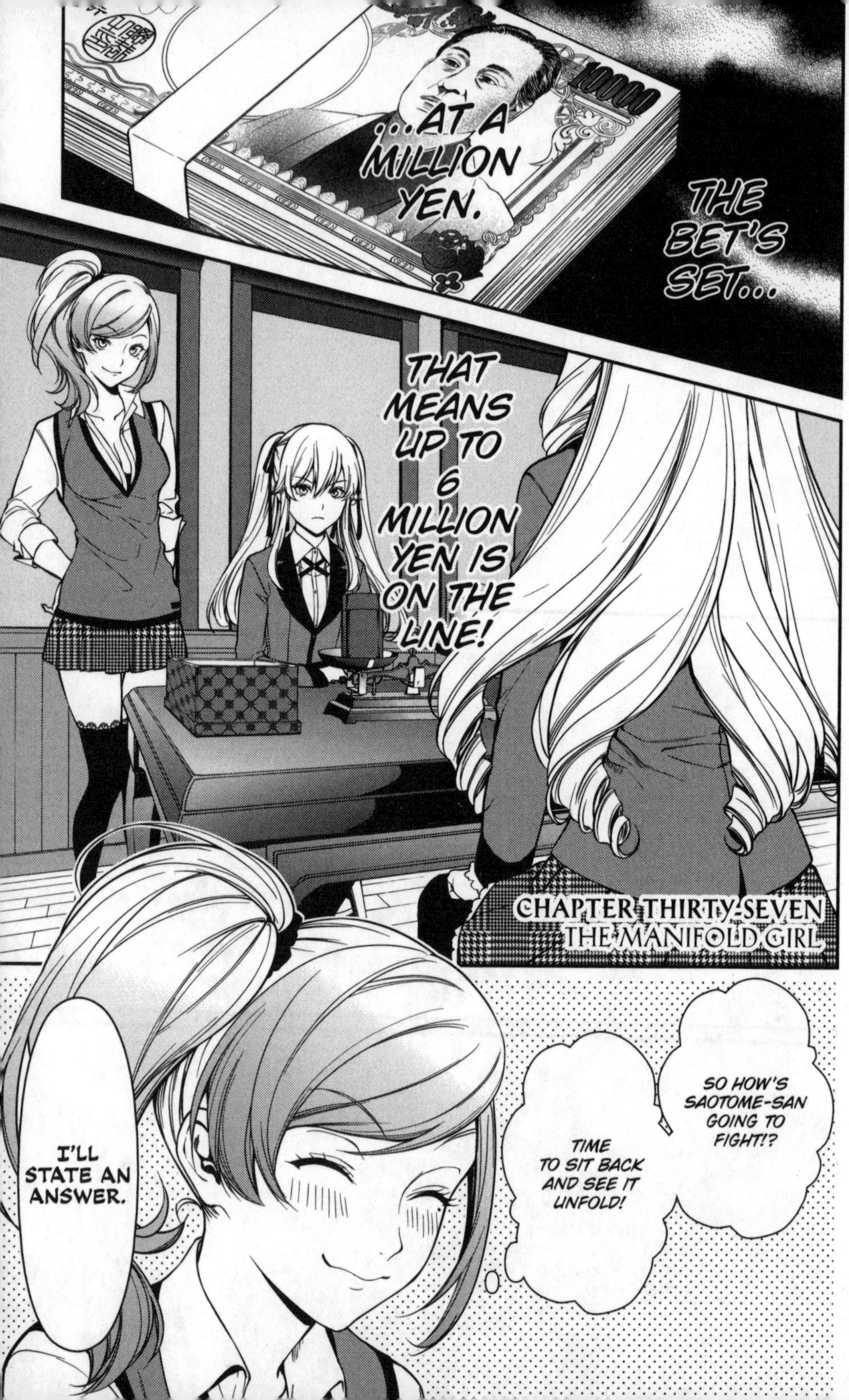
THE BET'S SET...
...AT A MILLION YEN.
THAT MEANS UP TO 6 MILLION YEN IS ON THE LINE!
CHAPTER THIRTY-SEVEN
THE MANIFOLD GIRL
SO HOW'S SAOTOME-SAN GOING TO FIGHT!?
TIME TO SIT BACK AND SEE IT UNFOLD!
I'LL STATE AN ANSWER.

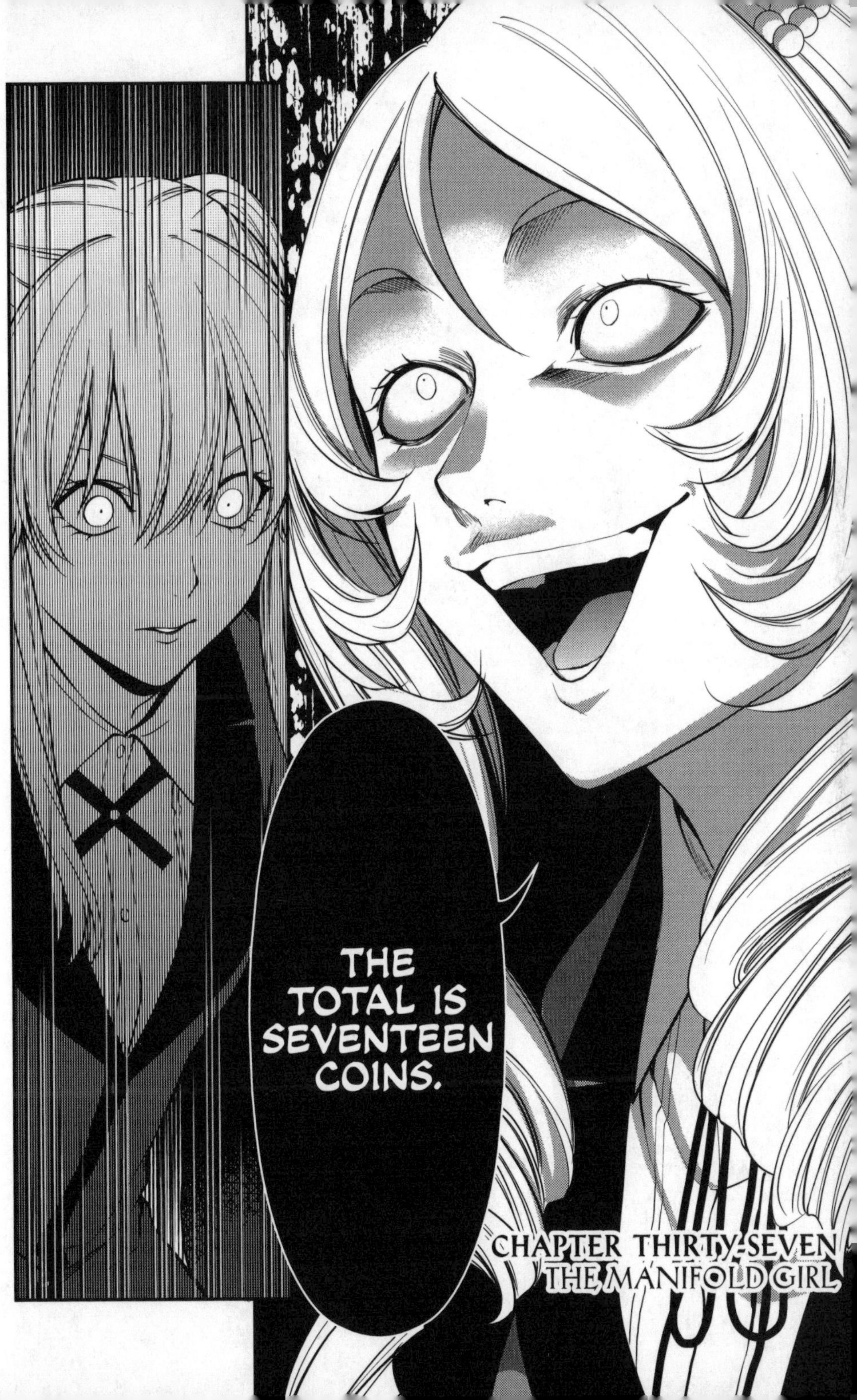
THE TOTAL IS SEVENTEEN COINS.
CHAPTER THIRTY-SEVEN
THE MANIFOLD GIRL

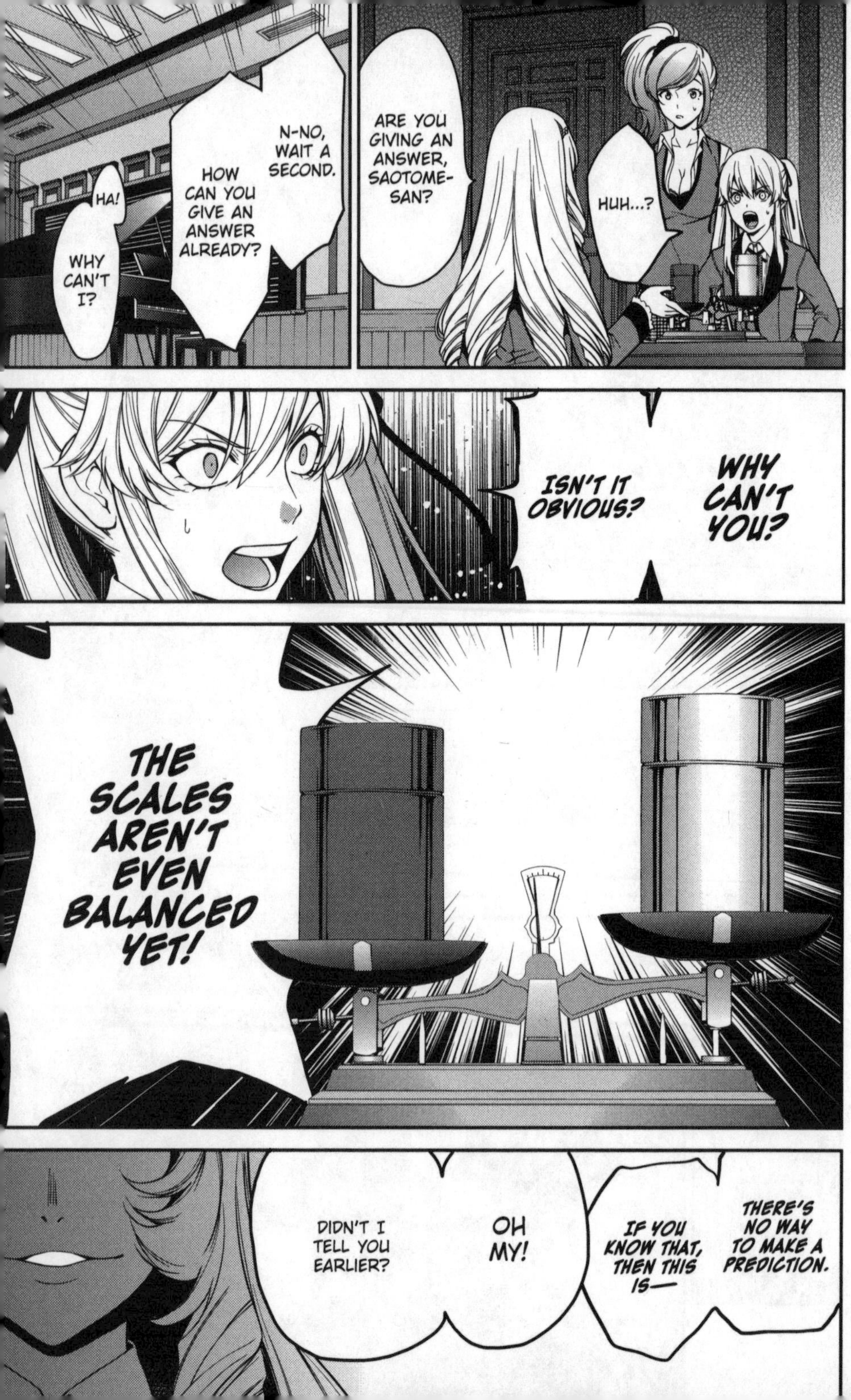
ARE YOU GIVING AN ANSWER, SAOTOME-SAN?
HUH...?
N-NO, WAIT A SECOND.
HOW CAN YOU GIVE AN ANSWER ALREADY?
HA!
WHY CAN'T I?
WHY CAN'T YOU?
ISN'T IT OBVIOUS?
THE SCALES AREN'T EVEN BALANCED YET!
THERE'S NO WAY TO MAKE A PREDICTION.
IF YOU KNOW THAT, THEN THIS IS—
OH MY!
DIDN'T I TELL YOU EARLIER?

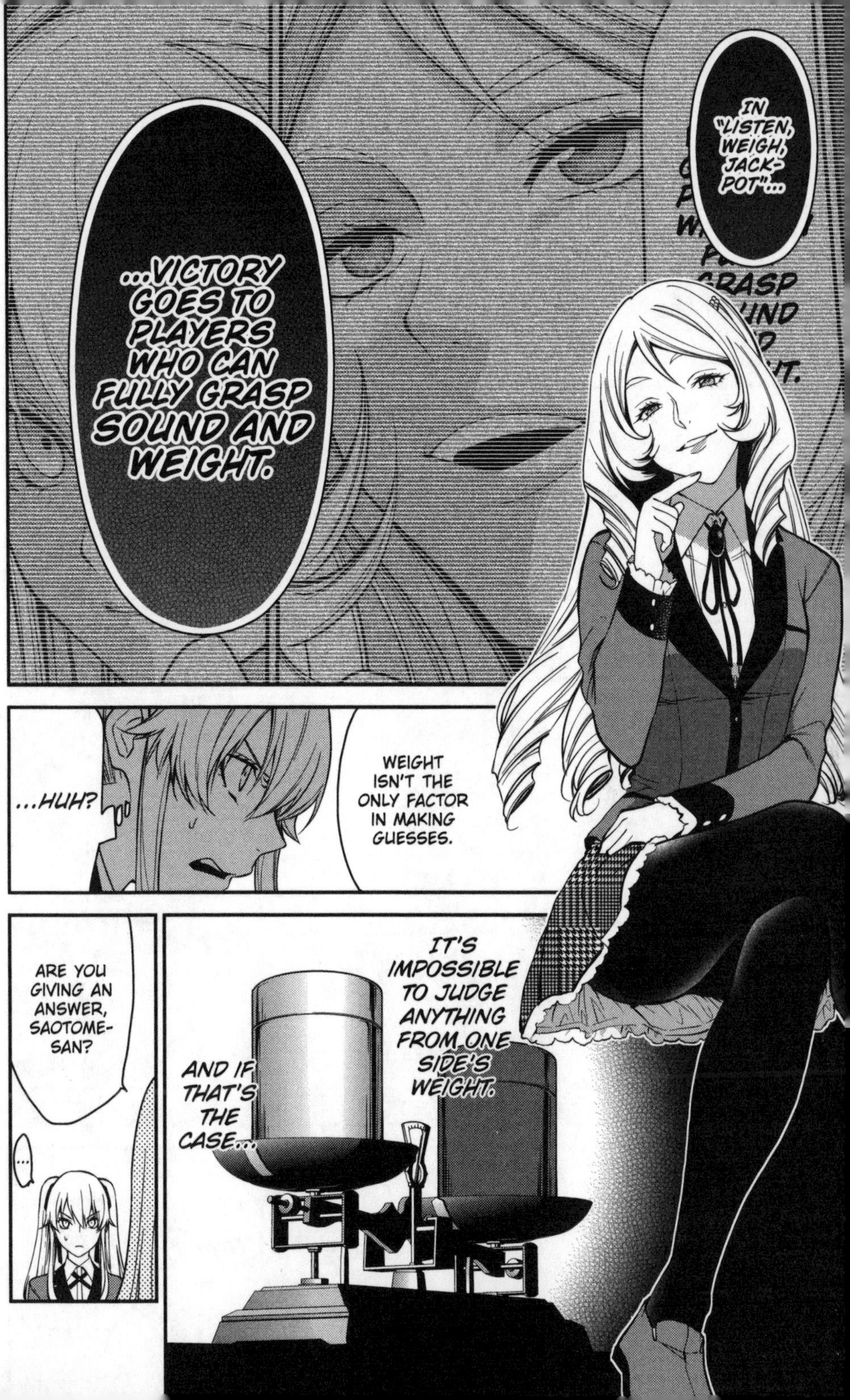
IN "LISTEN, WEIGH, JACK-POT"...
...VICTORY GOES TO PLAYERS WHO CAN FULLY GRASP SOUND AND WEIGHT.
WEIGHT ISN'T THE ONLY FACTOR IN MAKING GUESSES.
...HUH?
IT'S IMPOSSIBLE TO JUDGE ANYTHING FROM ONE SIDE'S WEIGHT.
AND IF THAT'S THE CASE...
ARE YOU GIVING AN ANSWER, SAOTOME-SAN?
...

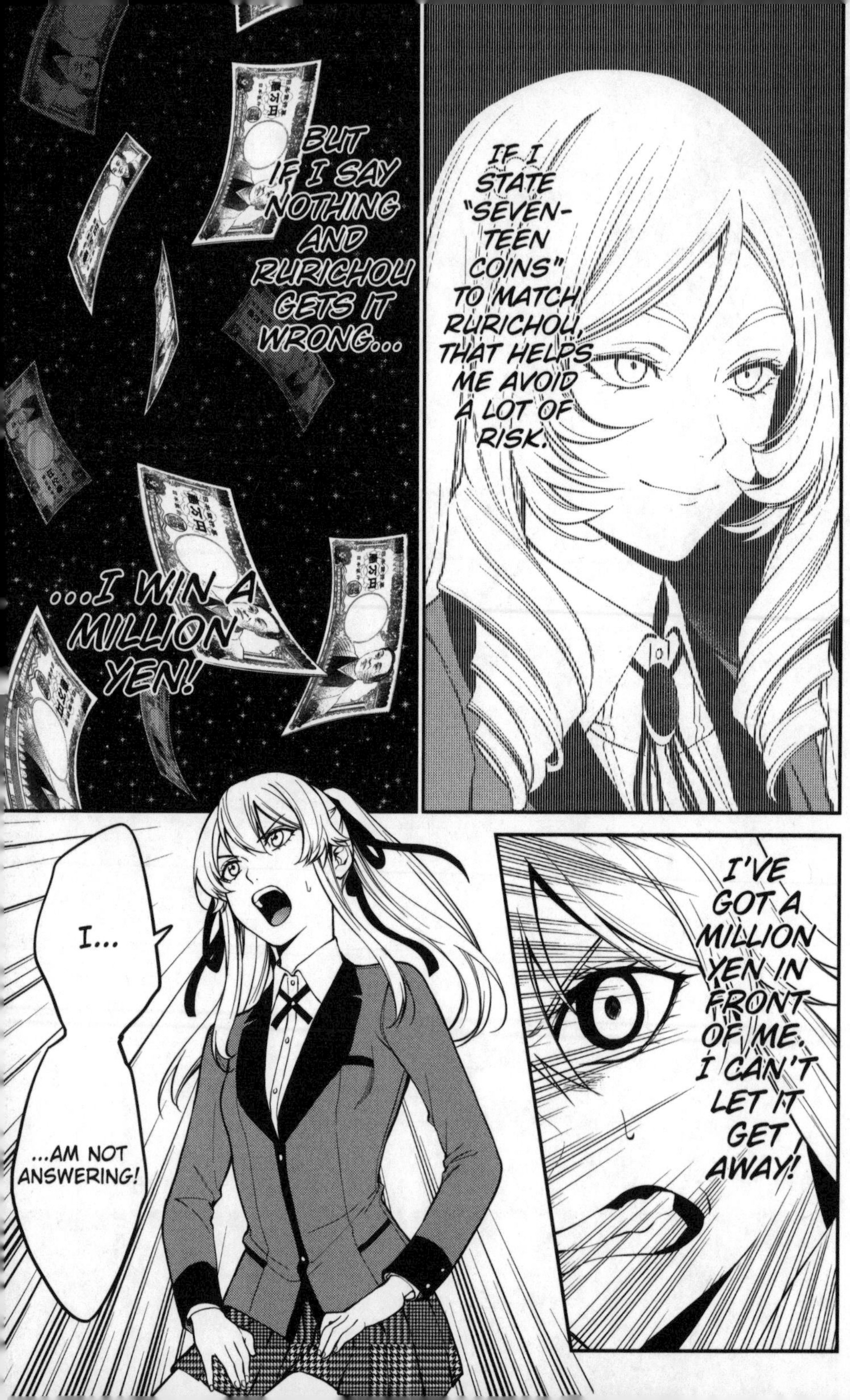
IF I STATE "SEVENTEEN COINS" TO MATCH RURICHOU, THAT HELPS ME AVOID A LOT OF RISK.
BUT IF I SAY NOTHING AND RURICHOU GETS IT WRONG...
...I WIN A MILLION YEN!
I'VE GOT A MILLION YEN IN FRONT OF ME. I CAN'T LET IT GET AWAY!
I...
...AM NOT ANSWERING!

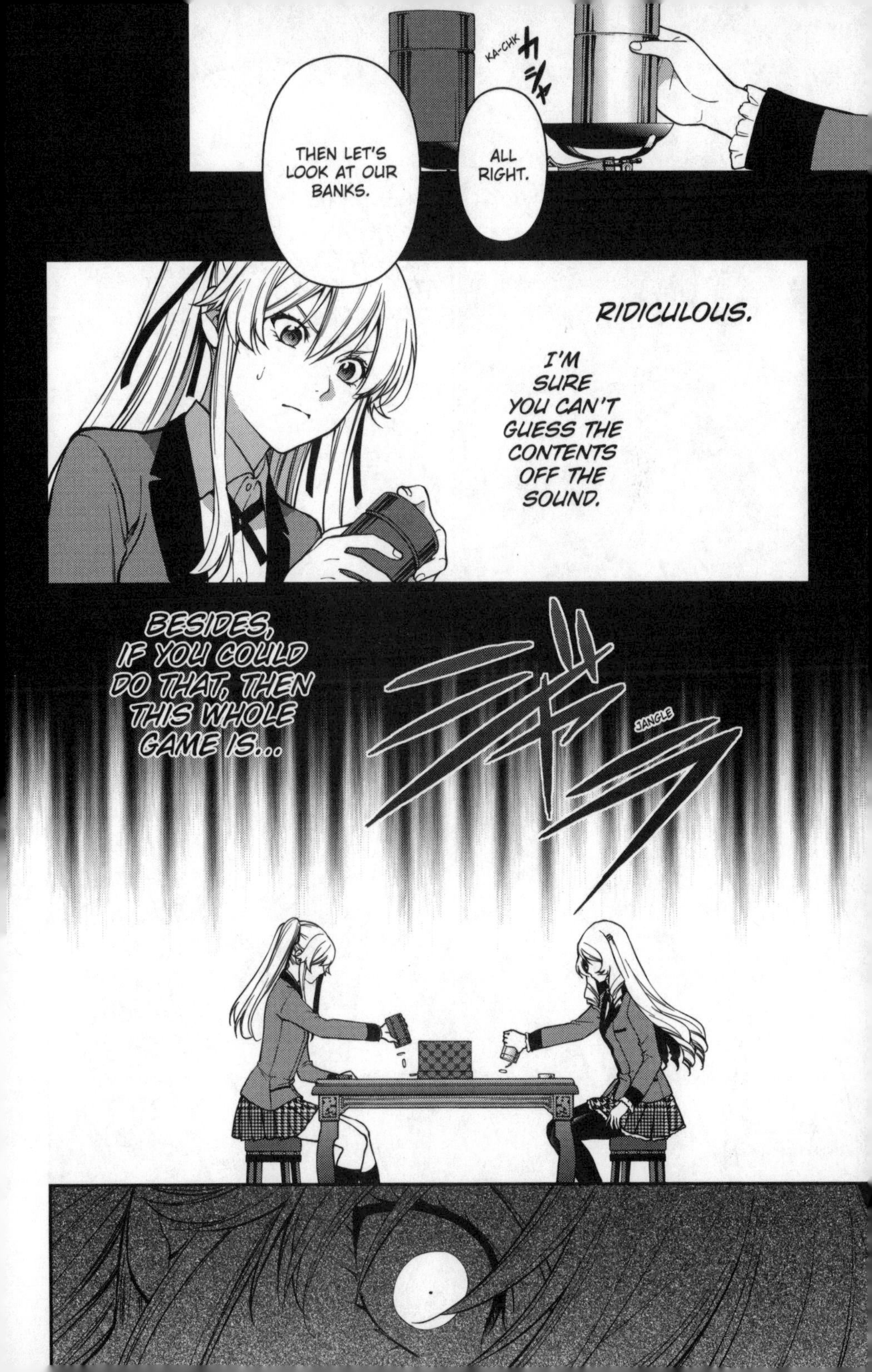
KA-CHK
ALL RIGHT.
THEN LET'S LOOK AT OUR BANKS.
RIDICULOUS.
I'M SURE YOU CAN'T GUESS THE CONTENTS OFF THE SOUND.
BESIDES, IF YOU COULD DO THAT, THEN THIS WHOLE GAME IS...
JANGLE

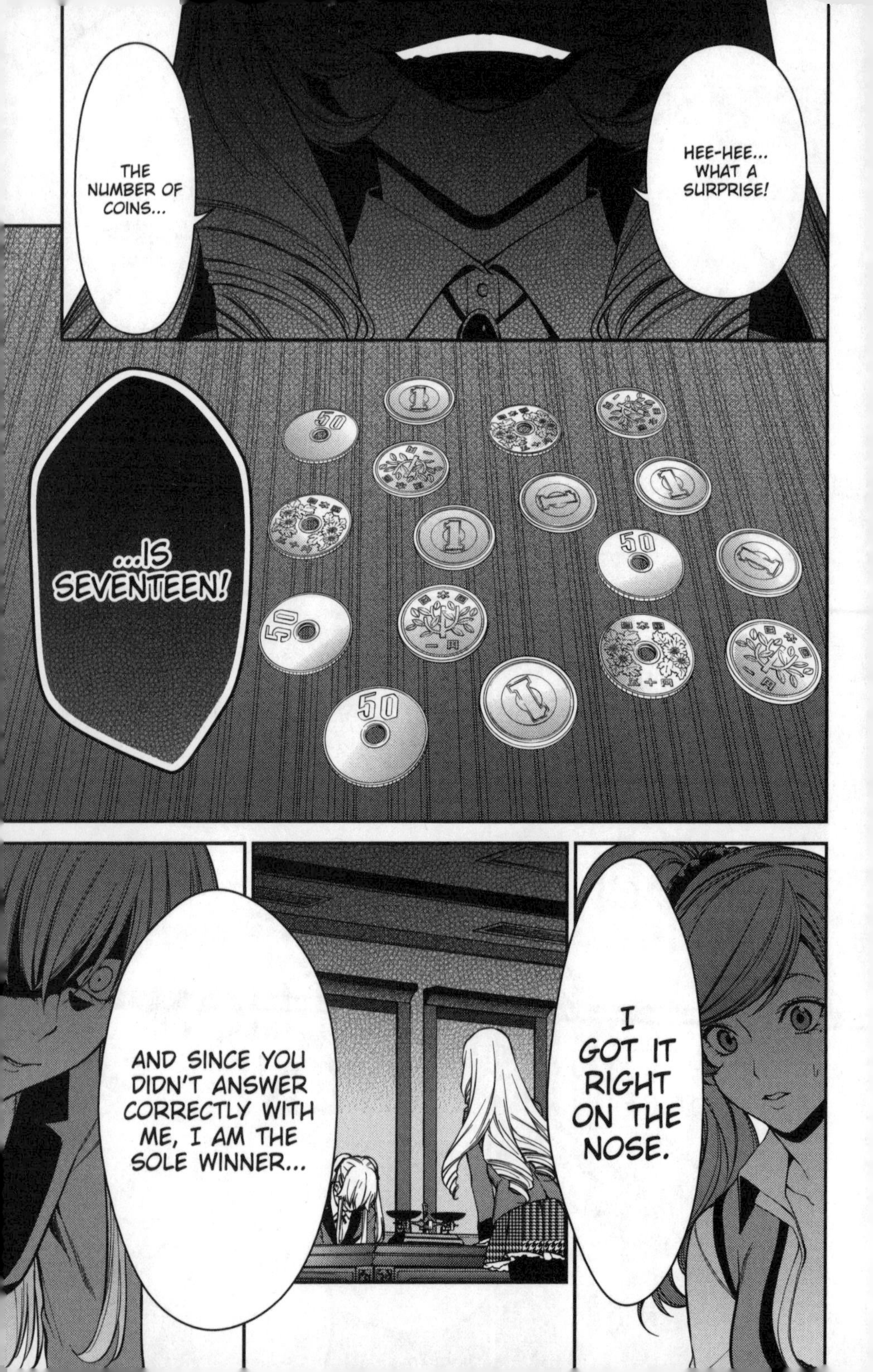
HEE-HEE... WHAT A SURPRISE!
THE NUMBER OF COINS...
...IS SEVENTEEN!
I GOT IT RIGHT ON THE NOSE.
AND SINCE YOU DIDN'T ANSWER CORRECTLY WITH ME, I AM THE SOLE WINNER...

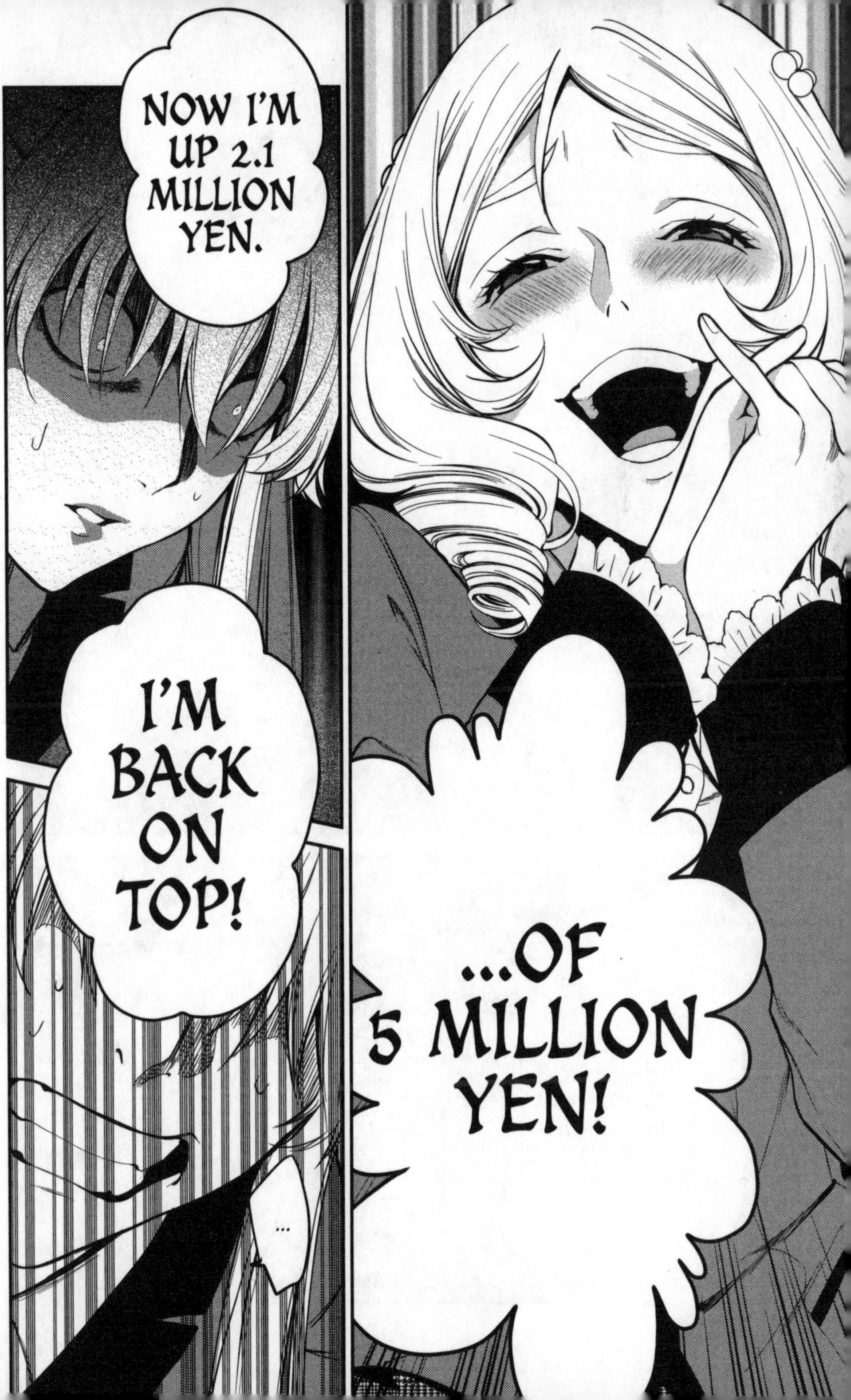
NOW I'M UP 2.1 MILLION YEN.
I'M BACK ON TOP!
...
...OF 5 MILLION YEN!

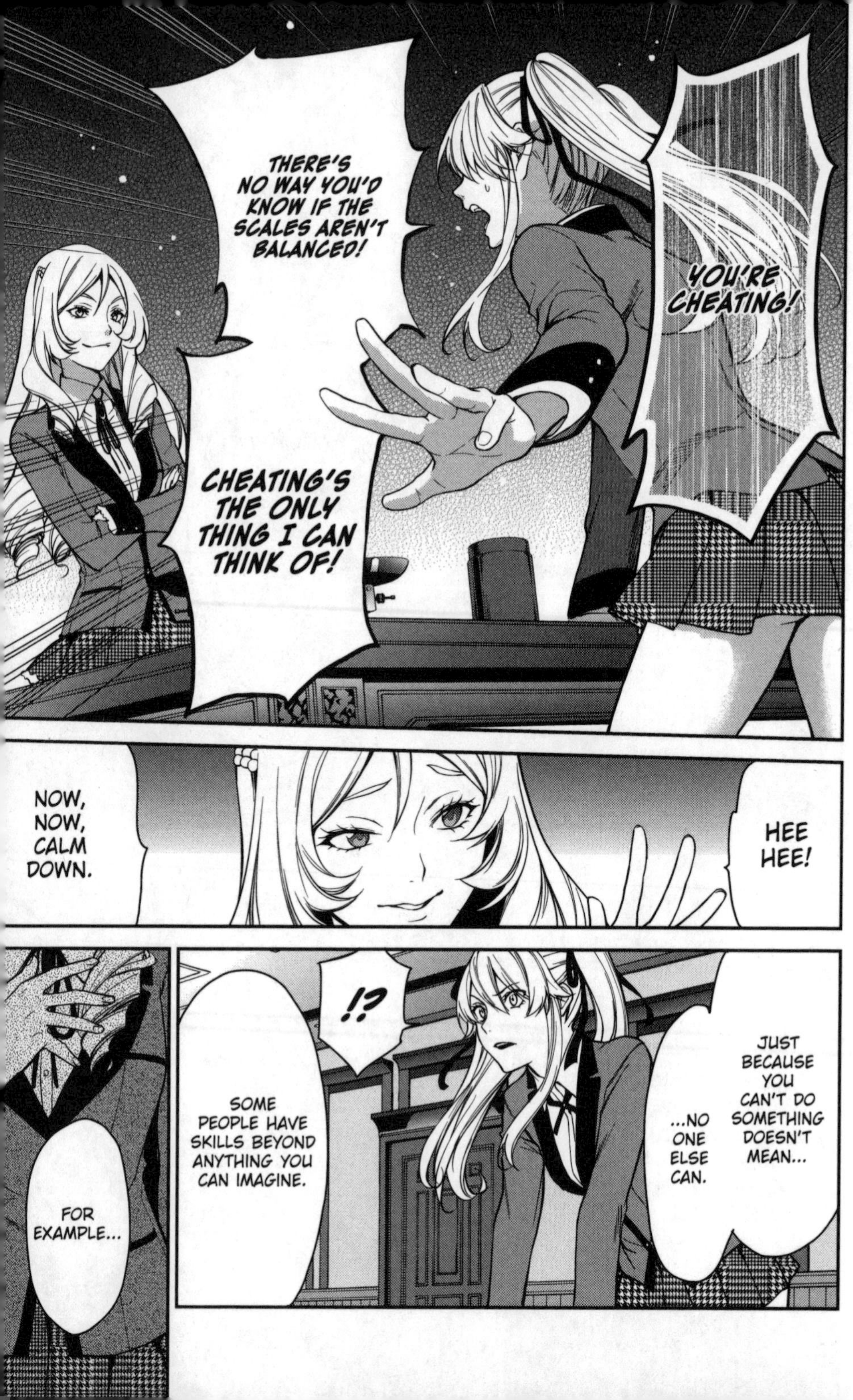
YOU'RE CHEATING!
THERE'S NO WAY YOU'D KNOW IF THE SCALES AREN'T BALANCED!
CHEATING'S THE ONLY THING I CAN THINK OF!
HEE HEE!
NOW, NOW, CALM DOWN.
JUST BECAUSE YOU CAN'T DO SOMETHING DOESN'T MEAN...
...NO ONE ELSE CAN.
!?
SOME PEOPLE HAVE SKILLS BEYOND ANYTHING YOU CAN IMAGINE.
FOR EXAMPLE...

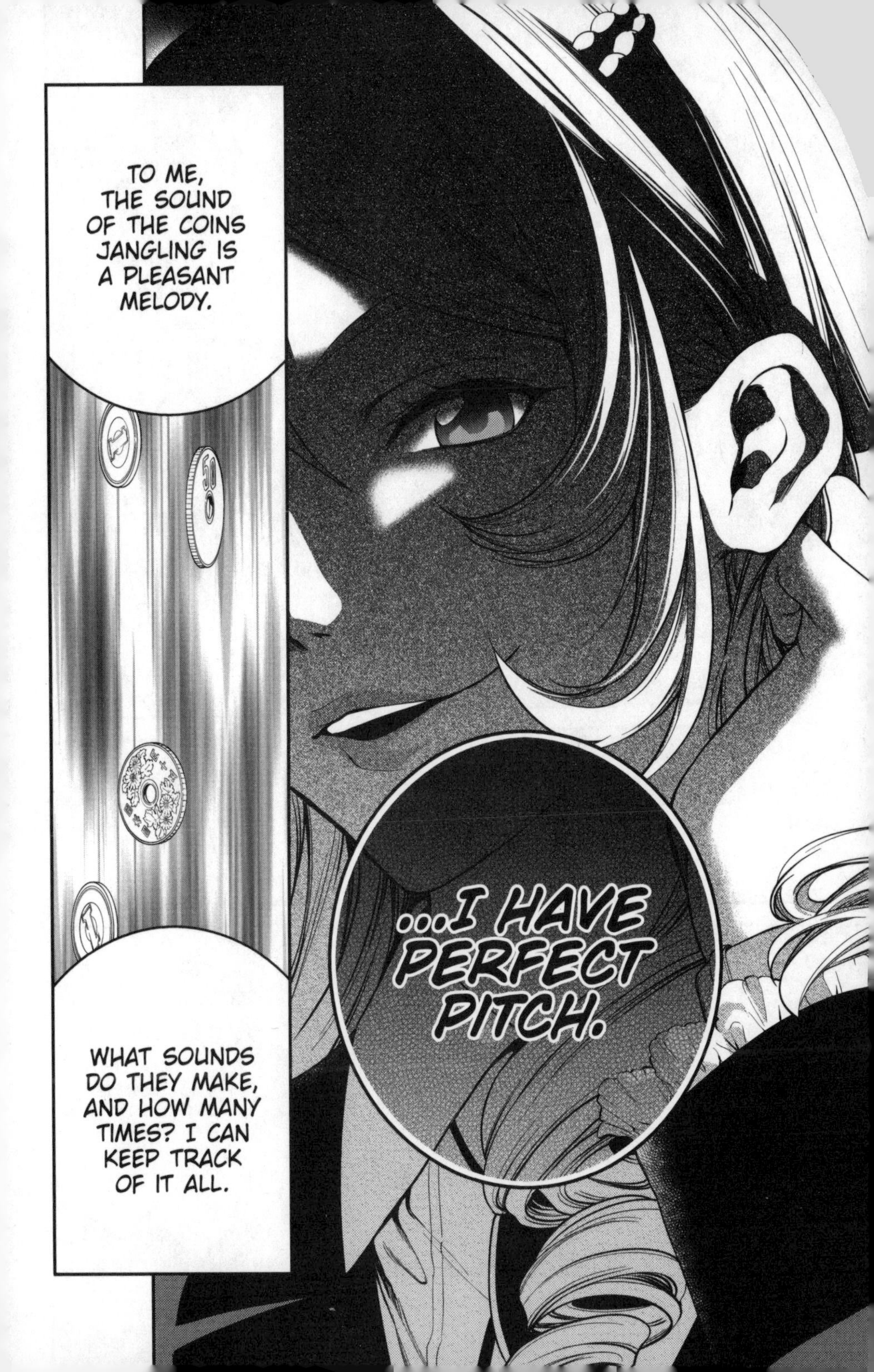
TO ME, THE SOUND OF THE COINS JANGLING IS A PLEASANT MELODY.
...I HAVE PERFECT PITCH.
WHAT SOUNDS DO THEY MAKE, AND HOW MANY TIMES? I CAN KEEP TRACK OF IT ALL.

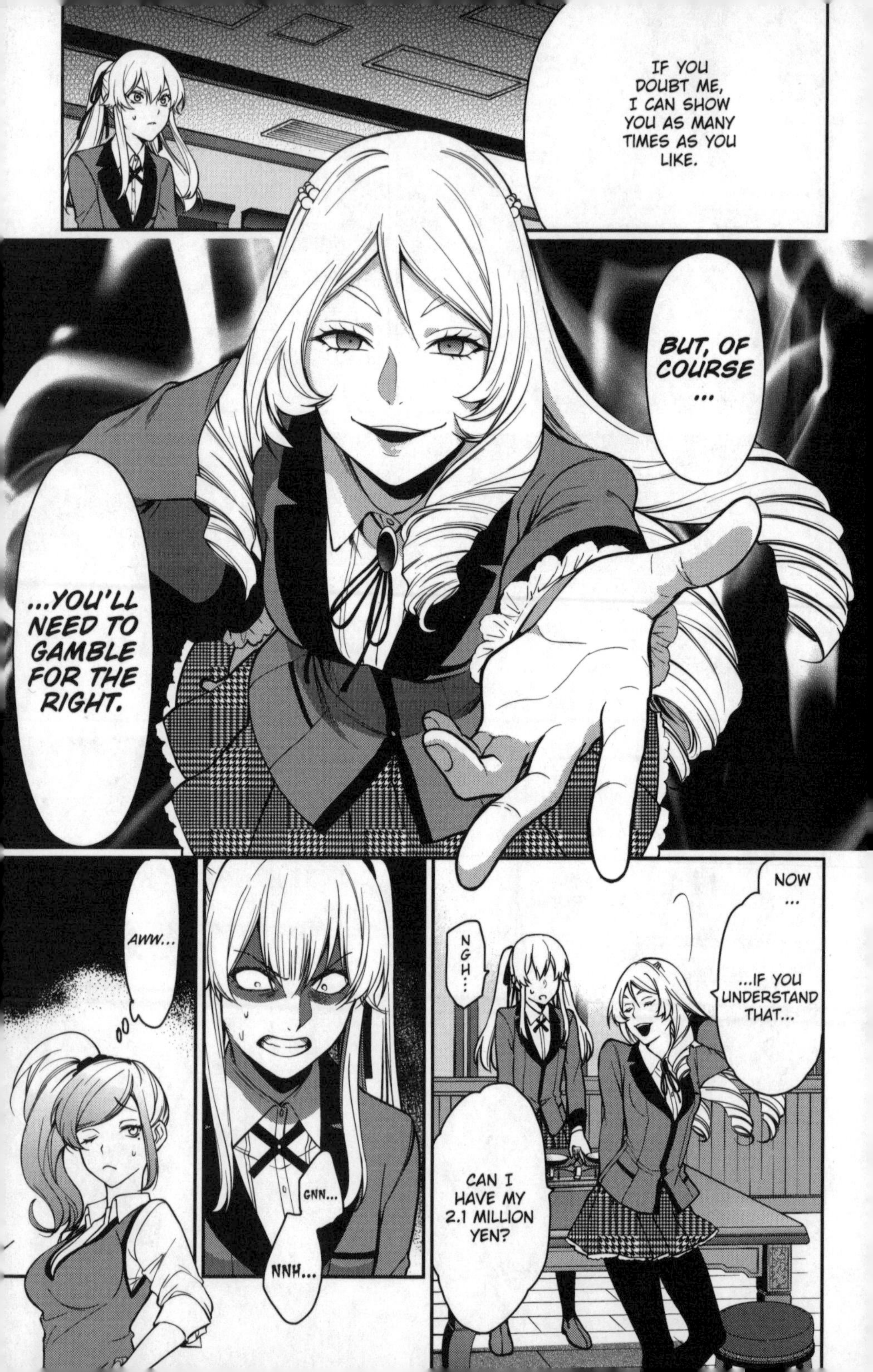
IF YOU DOUBT ME, I CAN SHOW YOU AS MANY TIMES AS YOU LIKE.
BUT, OF COURSE...
...YOU'LL NEED TO GAMBLE FOR THE RIGHT.
NOW...
...IF YOU UNDERSTAND THAT...
NGH...
CAN I HAVE MY 2.1 MILLION YEN?
GNN...
NNH...
AWW...

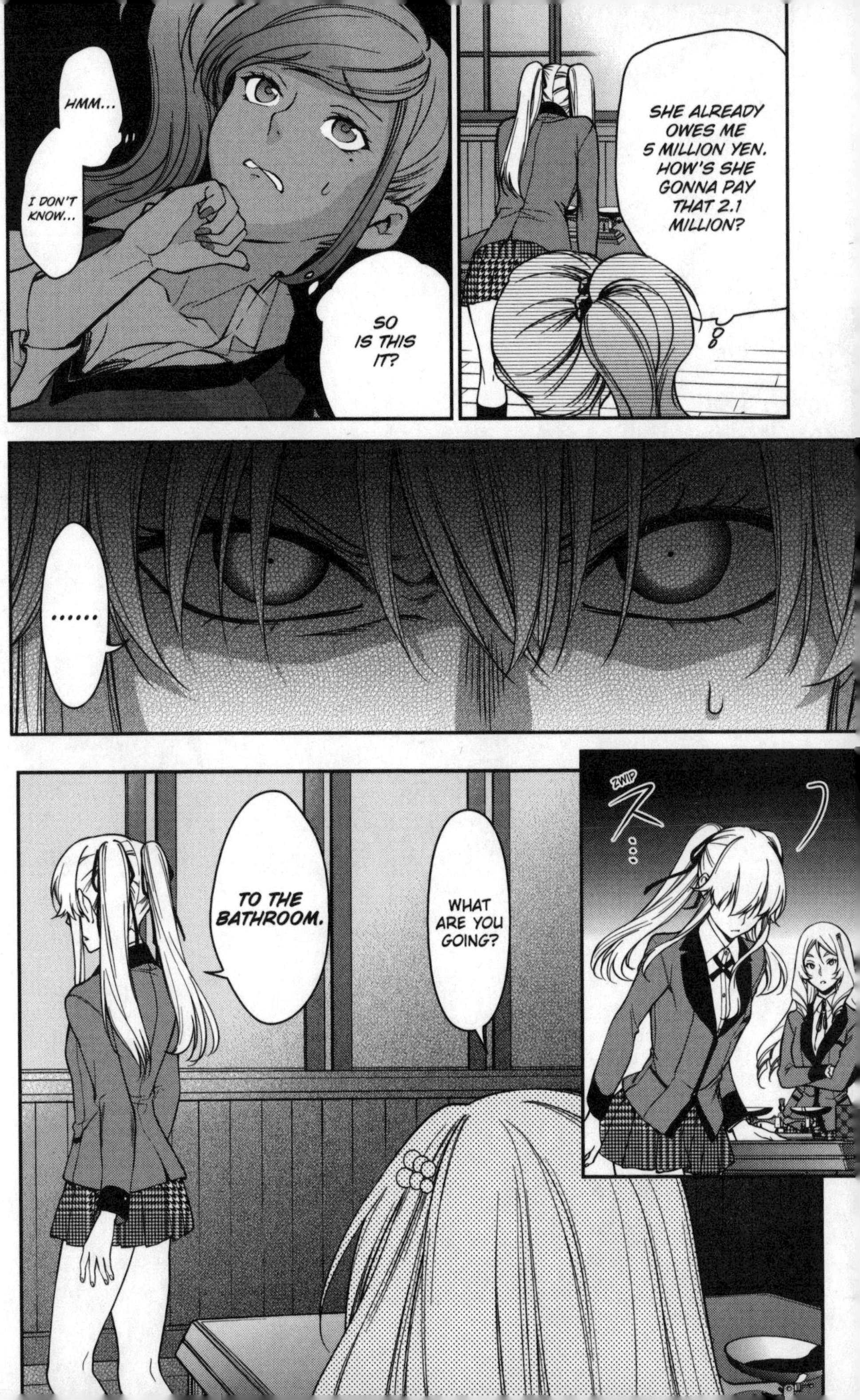
SHE ALREADY OWES ME 5 MILLION YEN. HOW'S SHE GONNA PAY THAT 2.1 MILLION?
HMM...
I DON'T KNOW...
SO IS THIS IT?
......
ZWIP
WHAT ARE YOU GOING?
TO THE BATHROOM.

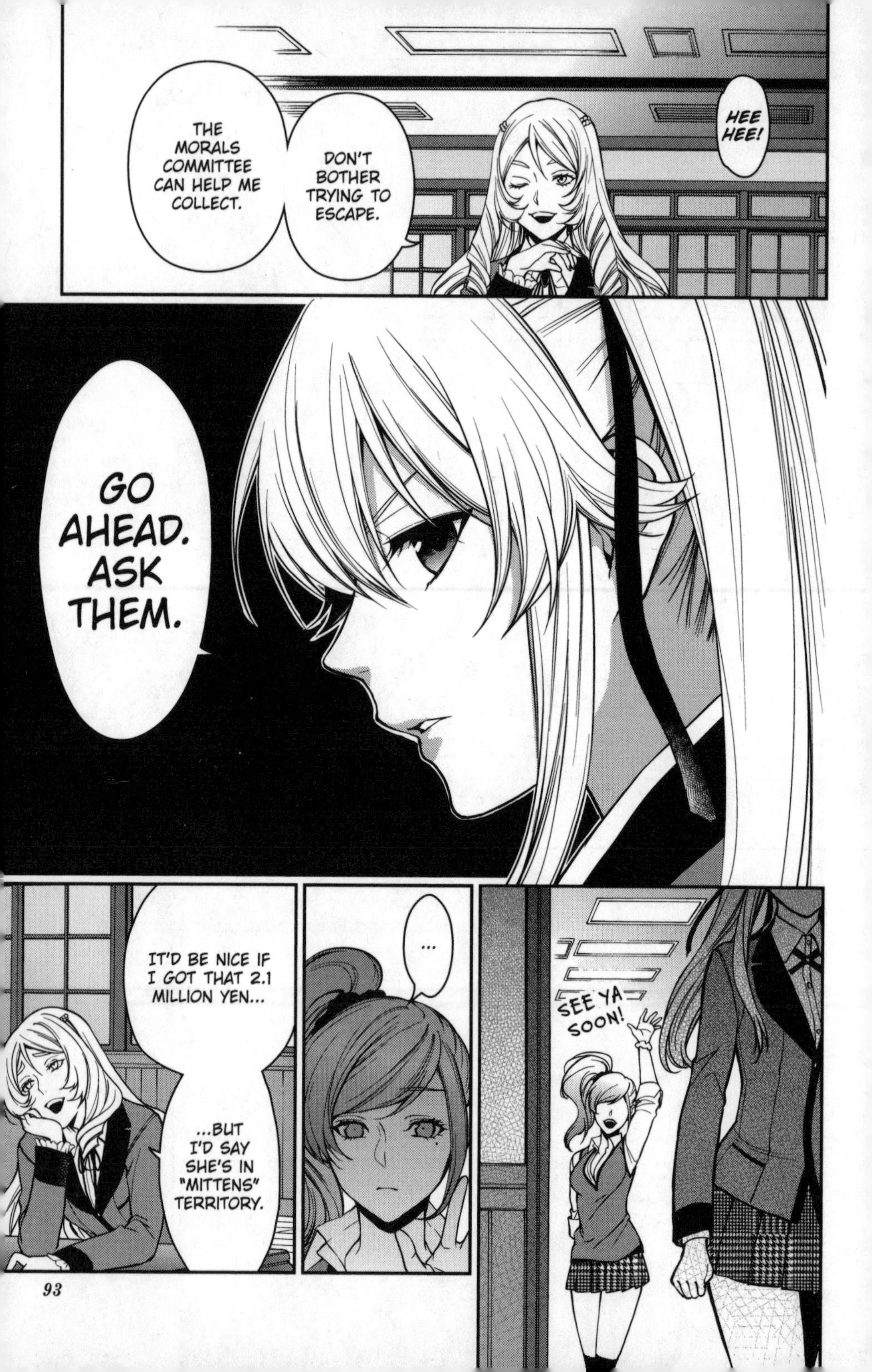
HEE HEE!
DON'T BOTHER TRYING TO ESCAPE.
THE MORALS COMMITTEE CAN HELP ME COLLECT.
GO AHEAD. ASK THEM.
SEE YA SOON!
...
IT'D BE NICE IF I GOT THAT 2.1 MILLION YEN...
...BUT I'D SAY SHE'S IN "MITTENS" TERRITORY.

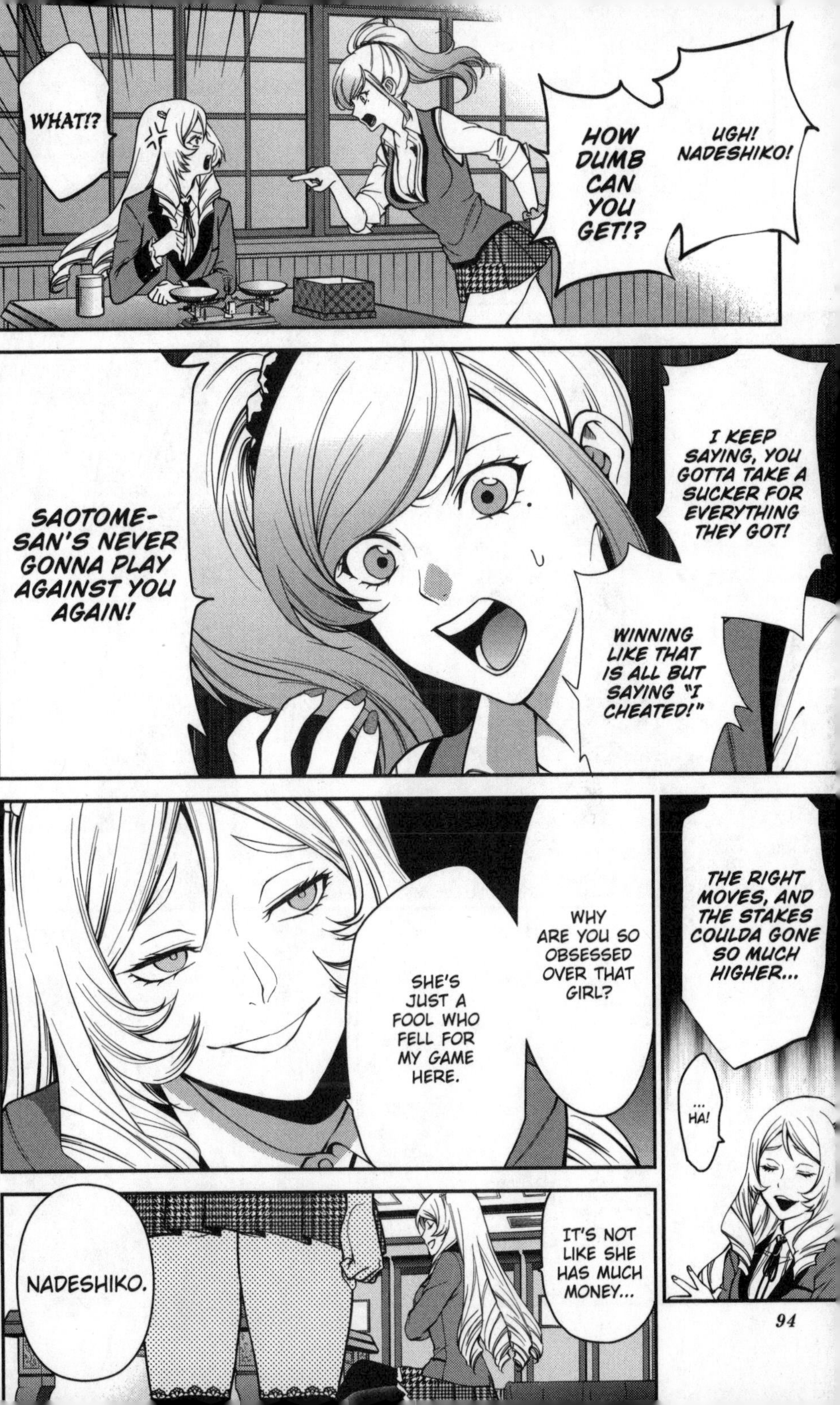
UGH! NADESHIKO!
HOW DUMB CAN YOU GET!?
WHAT!?
I KEEP SAYING, YOU GOTTA TAKE A SUCKER FOR EVERYTHING THEY GOT!
WINNING LIKE THAT IS ALL BUT SAYING "I CHEATED!"
SAOTOME-SAN'S NEVER GONNA PLAY AGAINST YOU AGAIN!
THE RIGHT MOVES, AND THE STAKES COULDA GONE SO MUCH HIGHER...
... HA!
WHY ARE YOU SO OBSESSED OVER THAT GIRL?
SHE'S JUST A FOOL WHO FELL FOR MY GAME HERE.
IT'S NOT LIKE SHE HAS MUCH MONEY...
NADESHIKO.

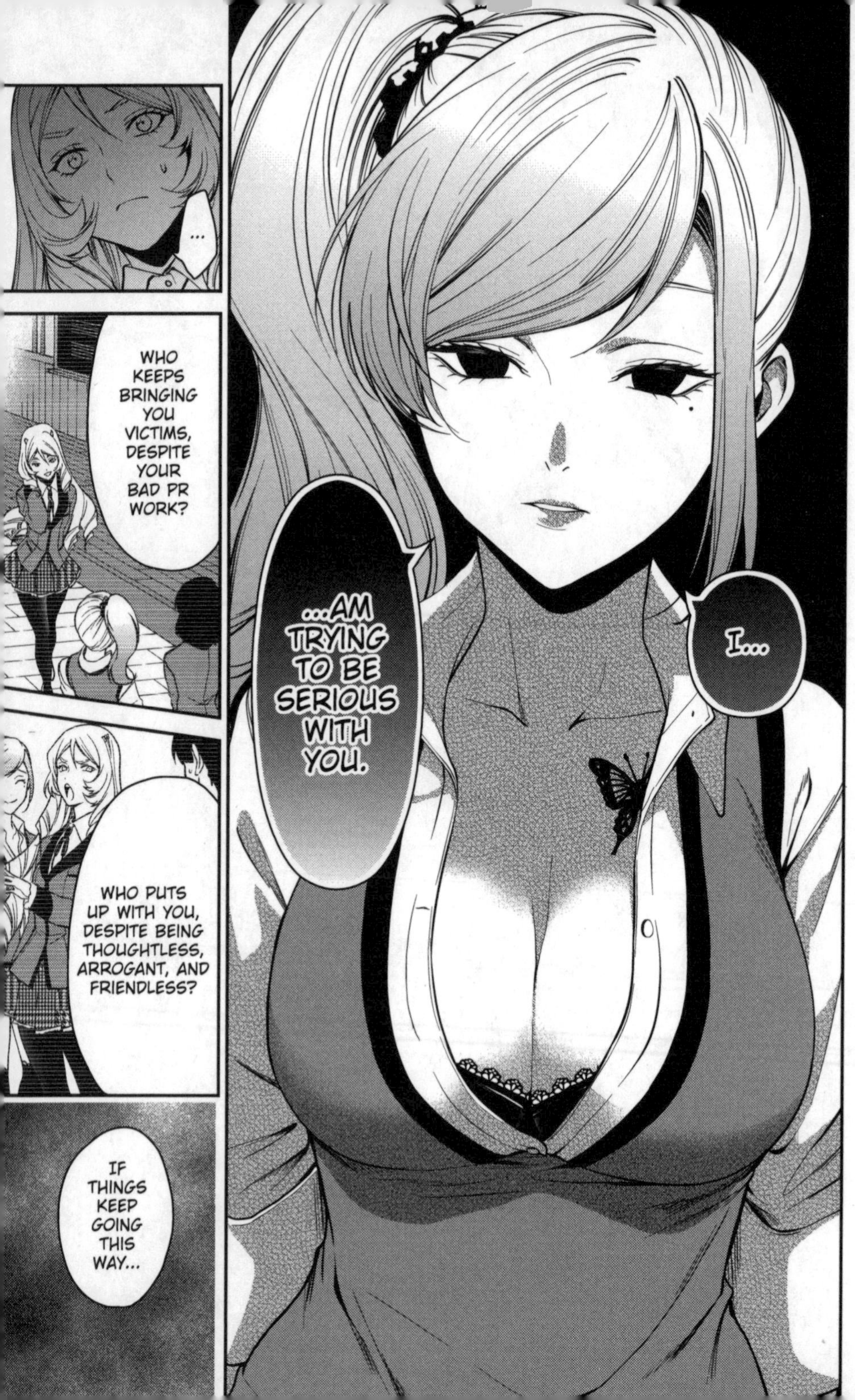
I...
...AM TRYING TO BE SERIOUS WITH YOU.
...
WHO KEEPS BRINGING YOU VICTIMS, DESPITE YOUR BAD PR WORK?
WHO PUTS UP WITH YOU, DESPITE BEING THOUGHTLESS, ARROGANT, AND FRIENDLESS?
IF THINGS KEEP GOING THIS WAY...

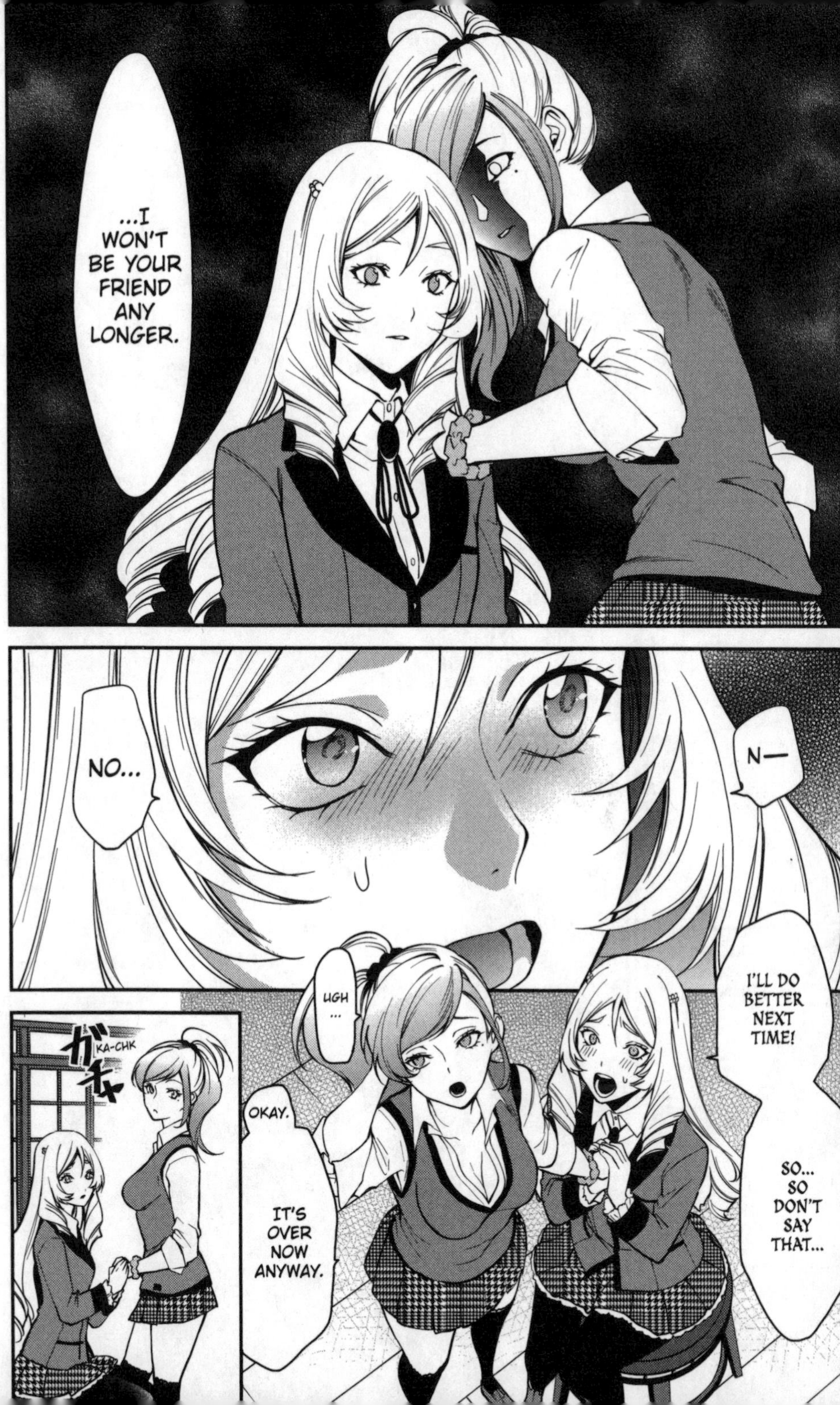
...I WON'T BE YOUR FRIEND ANY LONGER.
N—
NO...
I'LL DO BETTER NEXT TIME!
SO... SO DON'T SAY THAT...
UGH ...
OKAY.
IT'S OVER NOW ANYWAY.
ガチャ
KA-CHK

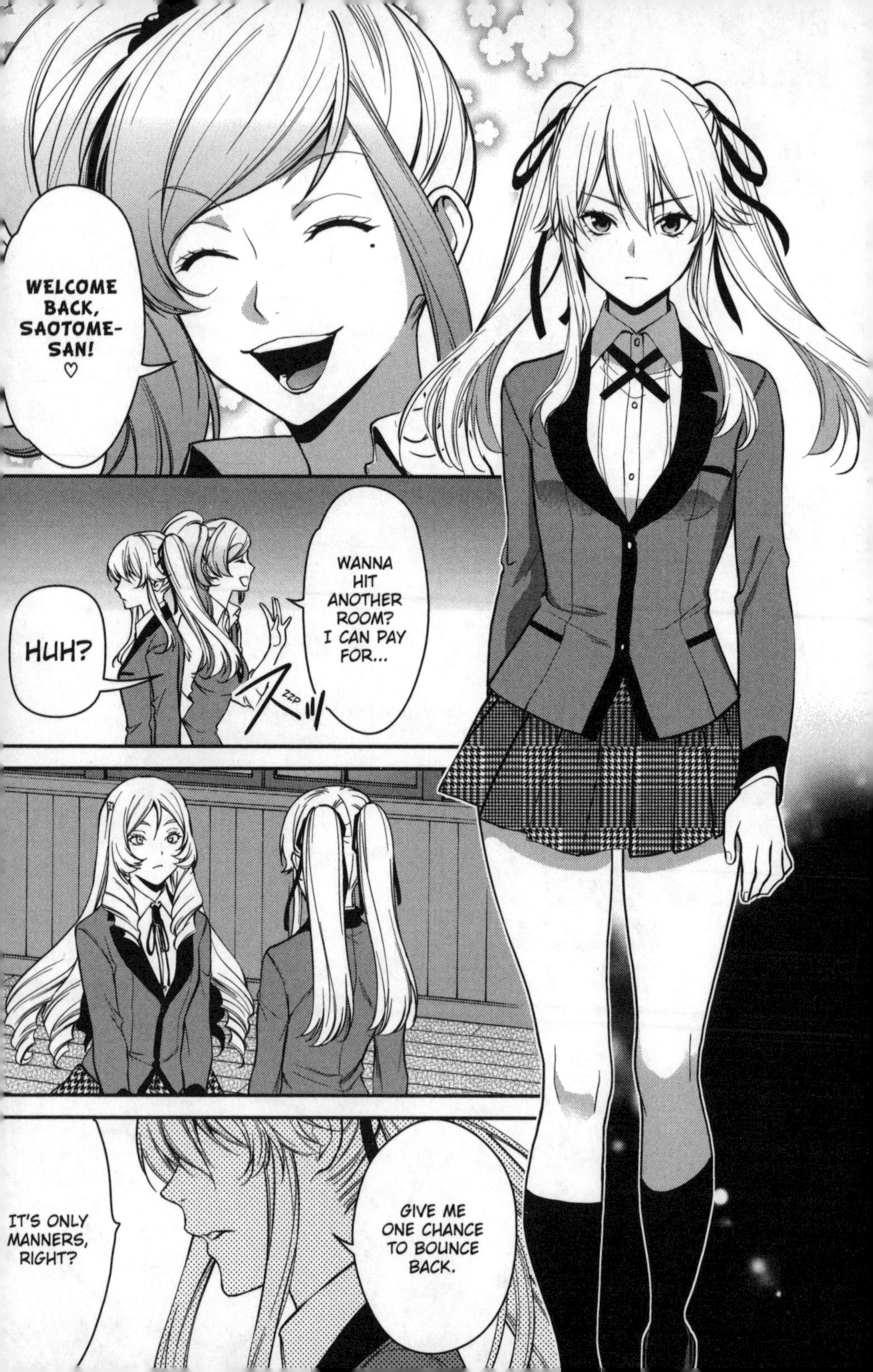
WELCOME BACK, SAOTOME-SAN! ♡
WANNA HIT ANOTHER ROOM? I CAN PAY FOR...
HUH?
ZZP
GIVE ME ONE CHANCE TO BOUNCE BACK.
IT'S ONLY MANNERS, RIGHT?

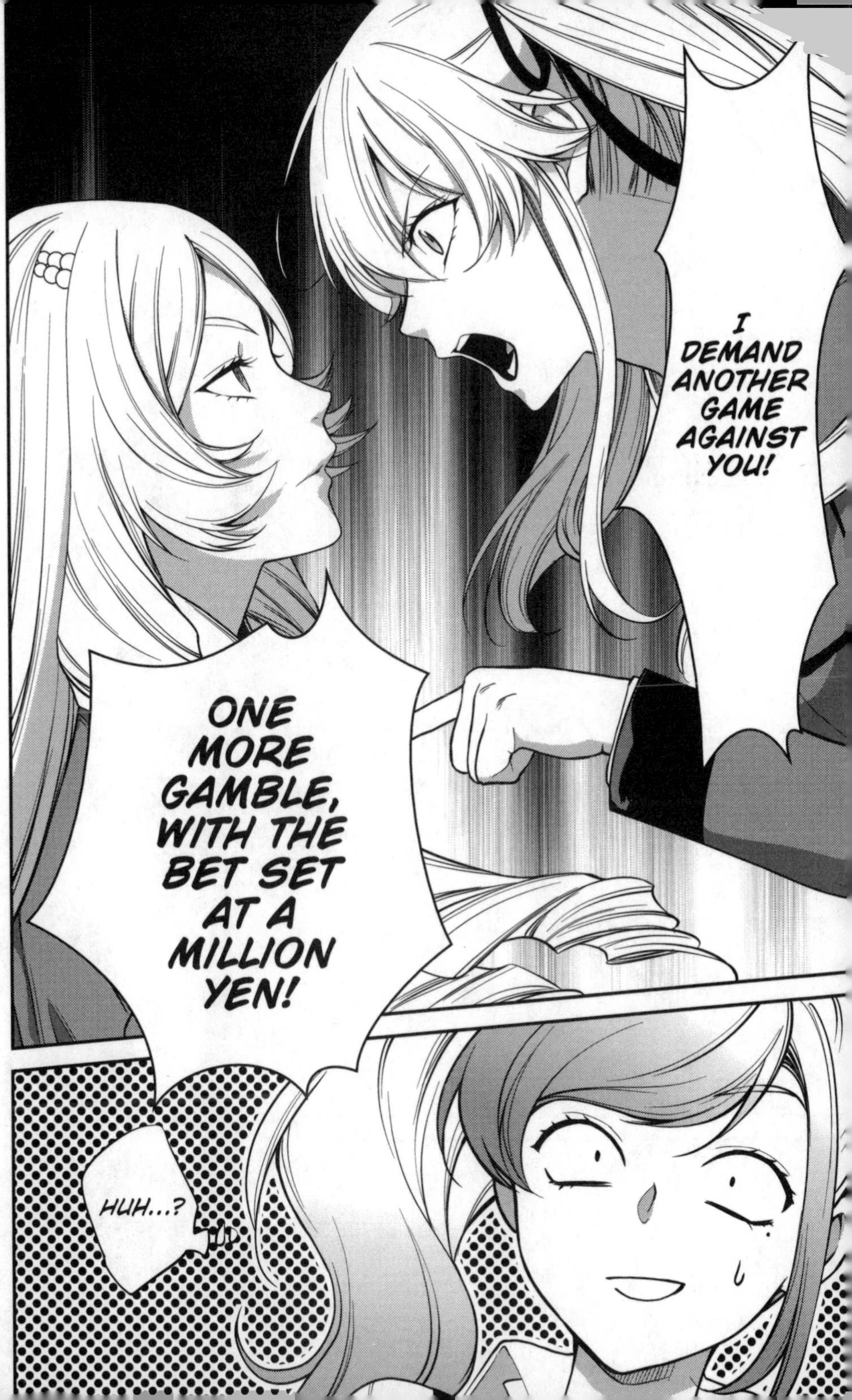
I DEMAND ANOTHER GAME AGAINST YOU!
ONE MORE GAMBLE, WITH THE BET SET AT A MILLION YEN!
HUH...?

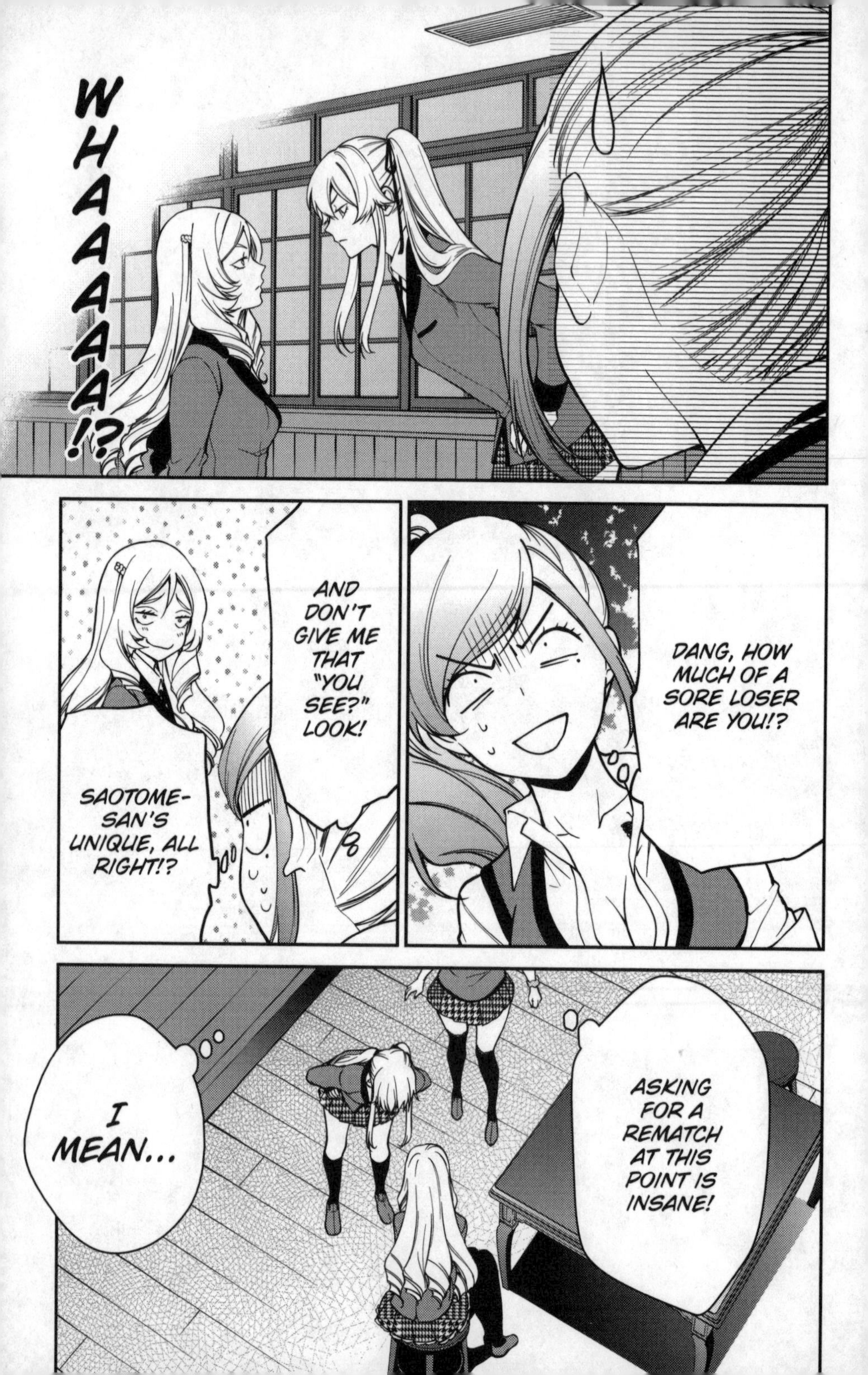
WHAAAAAA!?
DANG, HOW MUCH OF A SORE LOSER ARE YOU!?
AND DON'T GIVE ME THAT "YOU SEE?" LOOK!
SAOTOME-SAN'S UNIQUE, ALL RIGHT!?
ASKING FOR A REMATCH AT THIS POINT IS INSANE!
I MEAN...

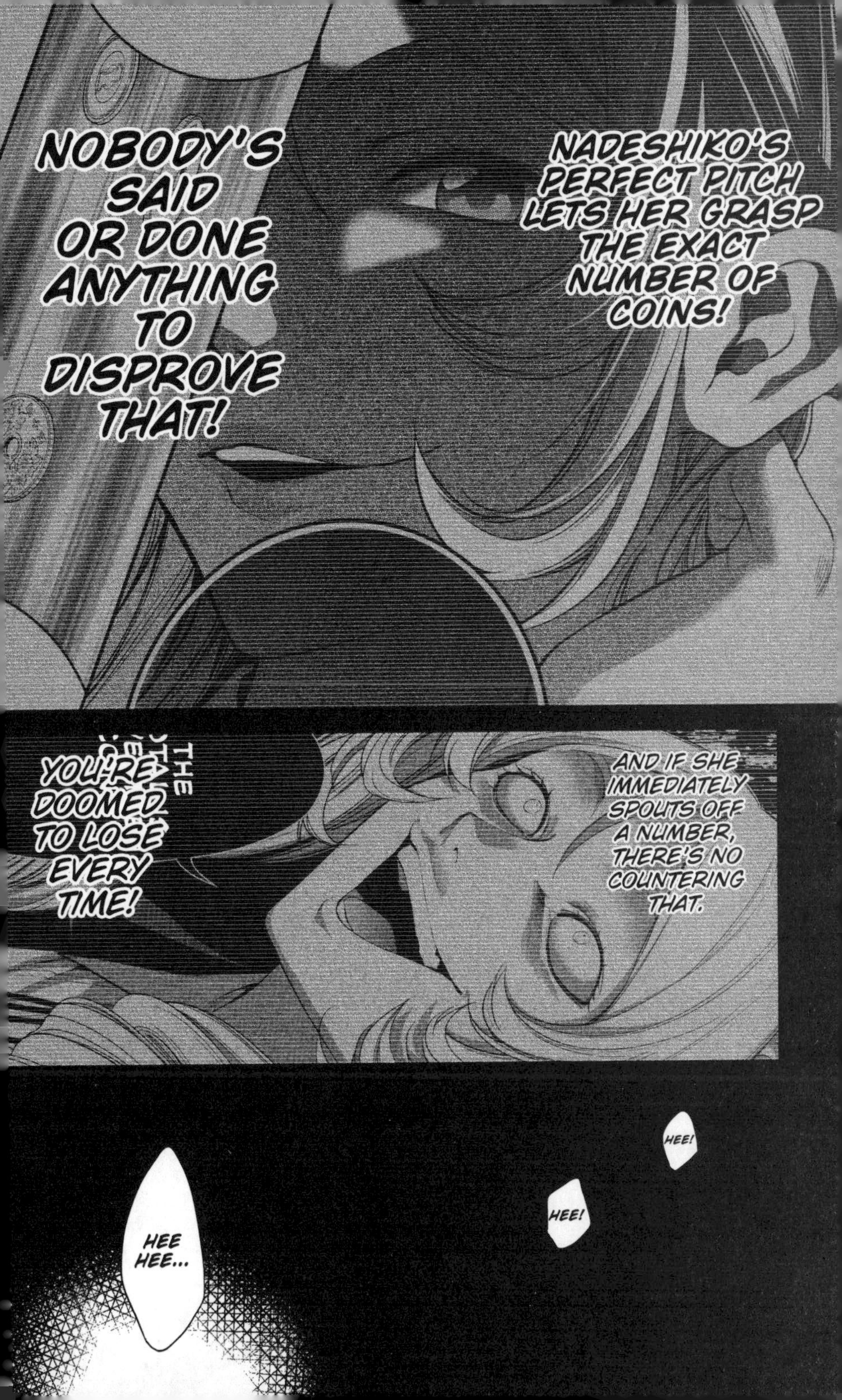
NADESHIKO'S PERFECT PITCH LETS HER GRASP THE EXACT NUMBER OF COINS!
NOBODY'S SAID OR DONE ANYTHING TO DISPROVE THAT!
AND IF SHE IMMEDIATELY SPOUTS OFF A NUMBER, THERE'S NO COUNTERING THAT.
YOU'RE DOOMED TO LOSE EVERY TIME!
HEE!
HEE!
HEE HEE...

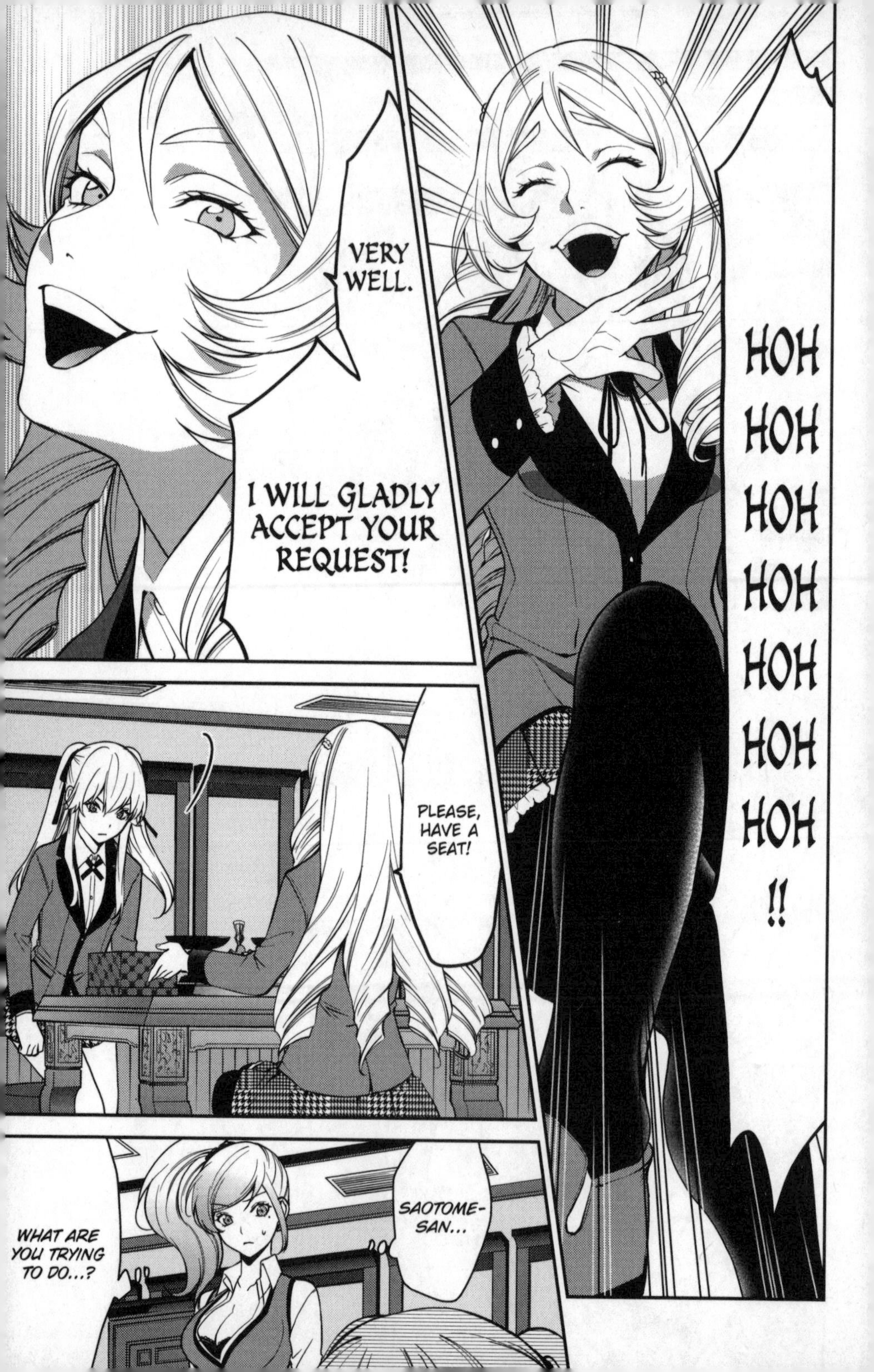
HOH HOH HOH HOH HOH HOH HOH !!
VERY WELL.
I WILL GLADLY ACCEPT YOUR REQUEST!
PLEASE, HAVE A SEAT!
SAOTOME-SAN...
WHAT ARE YOU TRYING TO DO...?

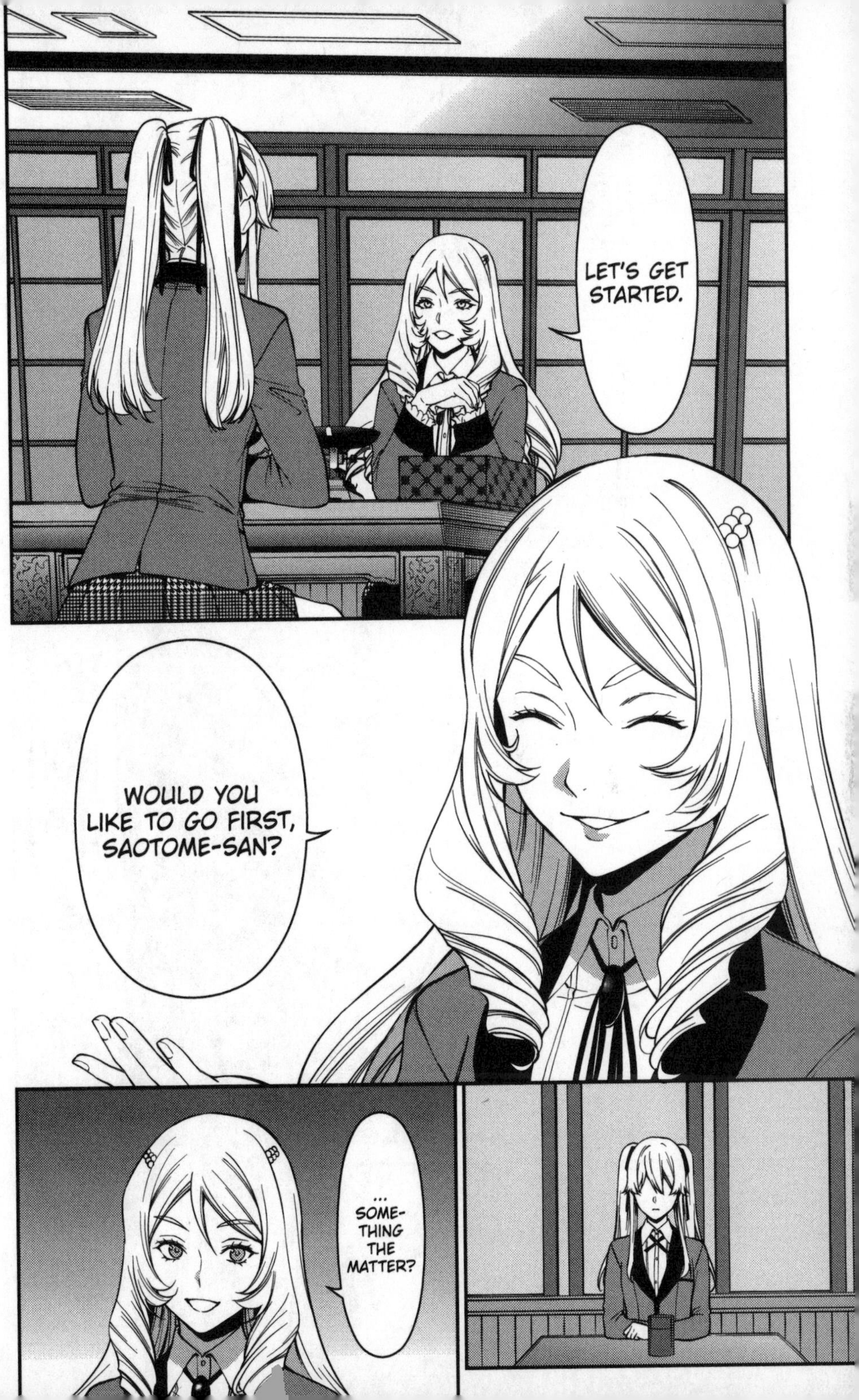
LET'S GET STARTED.
WOULD YOU LIKE TO GO FIRST, SAOTOME-SAN?
...SOME-THING THE MATTER?

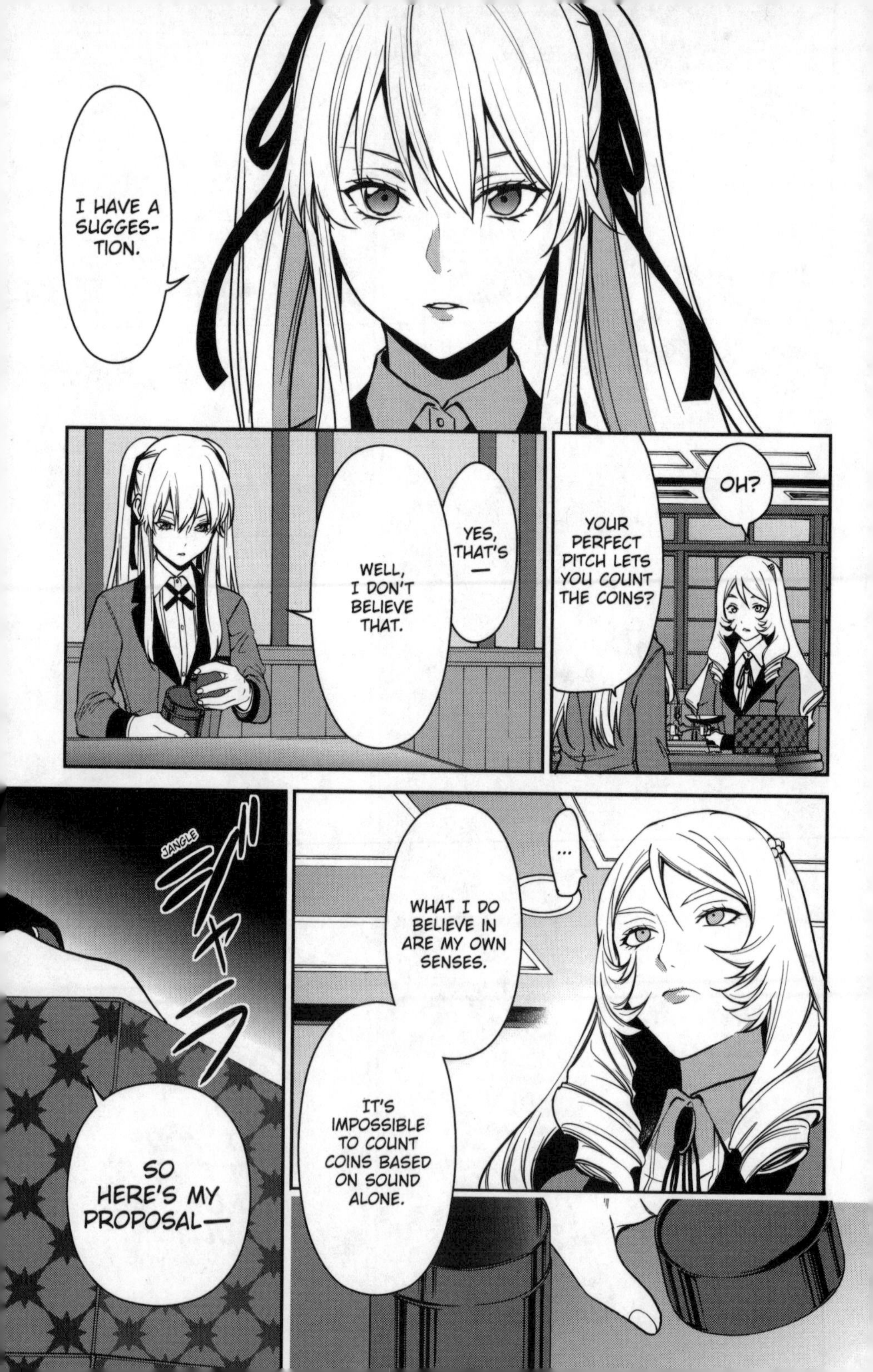
I HAVE A SUGGES-TION.
OH?
YOUR PERFECT PITCH LETS YOU COUNT THE COINS?
YES, THAT'S—
WELL, I DON'T BELIEVE THAT.
...
WHAT I DO BELIEVE IN ARE MY OWN SENSES.
IT'S IMPOSSIBLE TO COUNT COINS BASED ON SOUND ALONE.
JANGLE
SO HERE'S MY PROPOSAL—

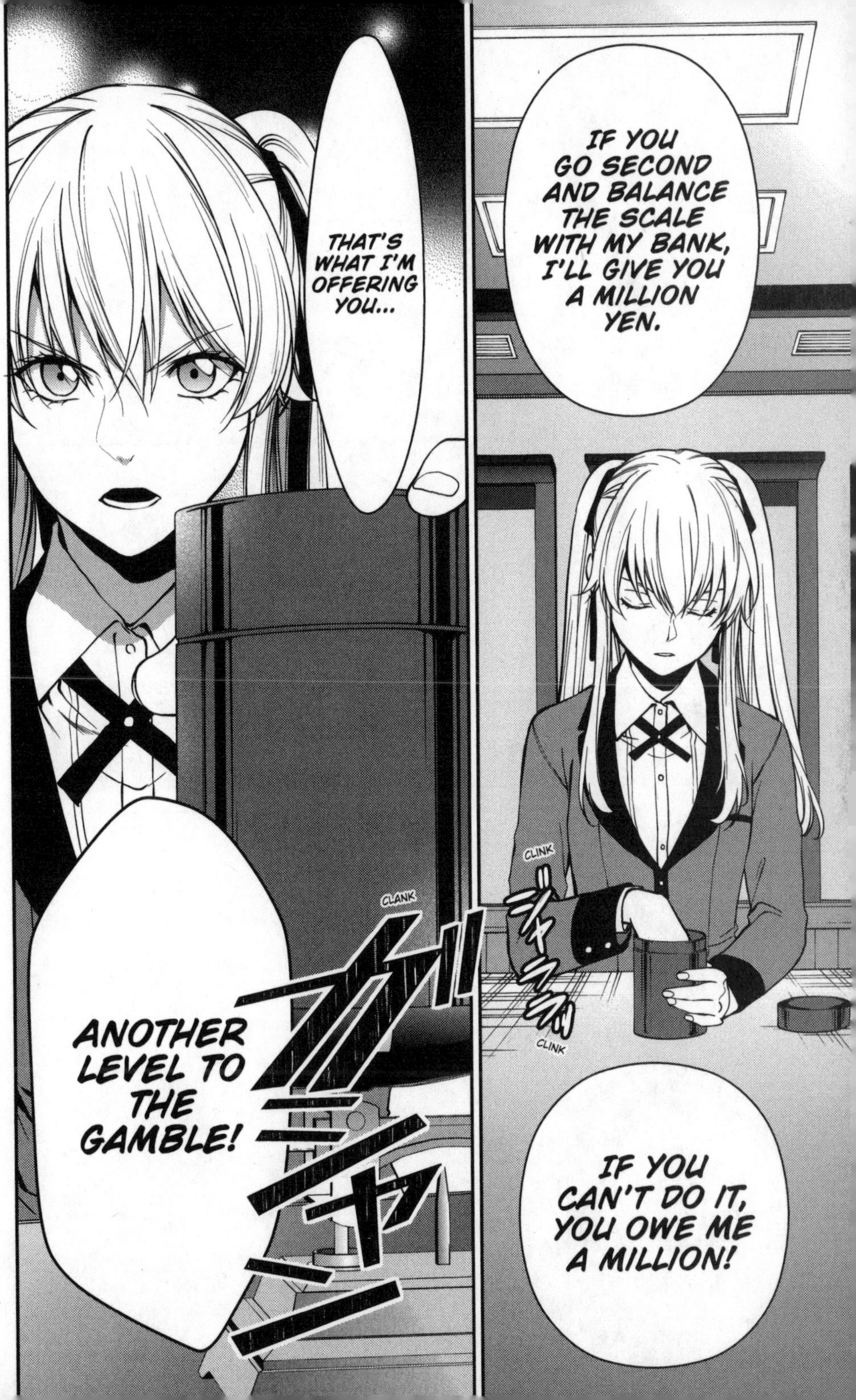
IF YOU GO SECOND AND BALANCE THE SCALE WITH MY BANK, I'LL GIVE YOU A MILLION YEN.
CLINK
CLINK
IF YOU CAN'T DO IT, YOU OWE ME A MILLION!
THAT'S WHAT I'M OFFERING YOU...
CLANK
ANOTHER LEVEL TO THE GAMBLE!

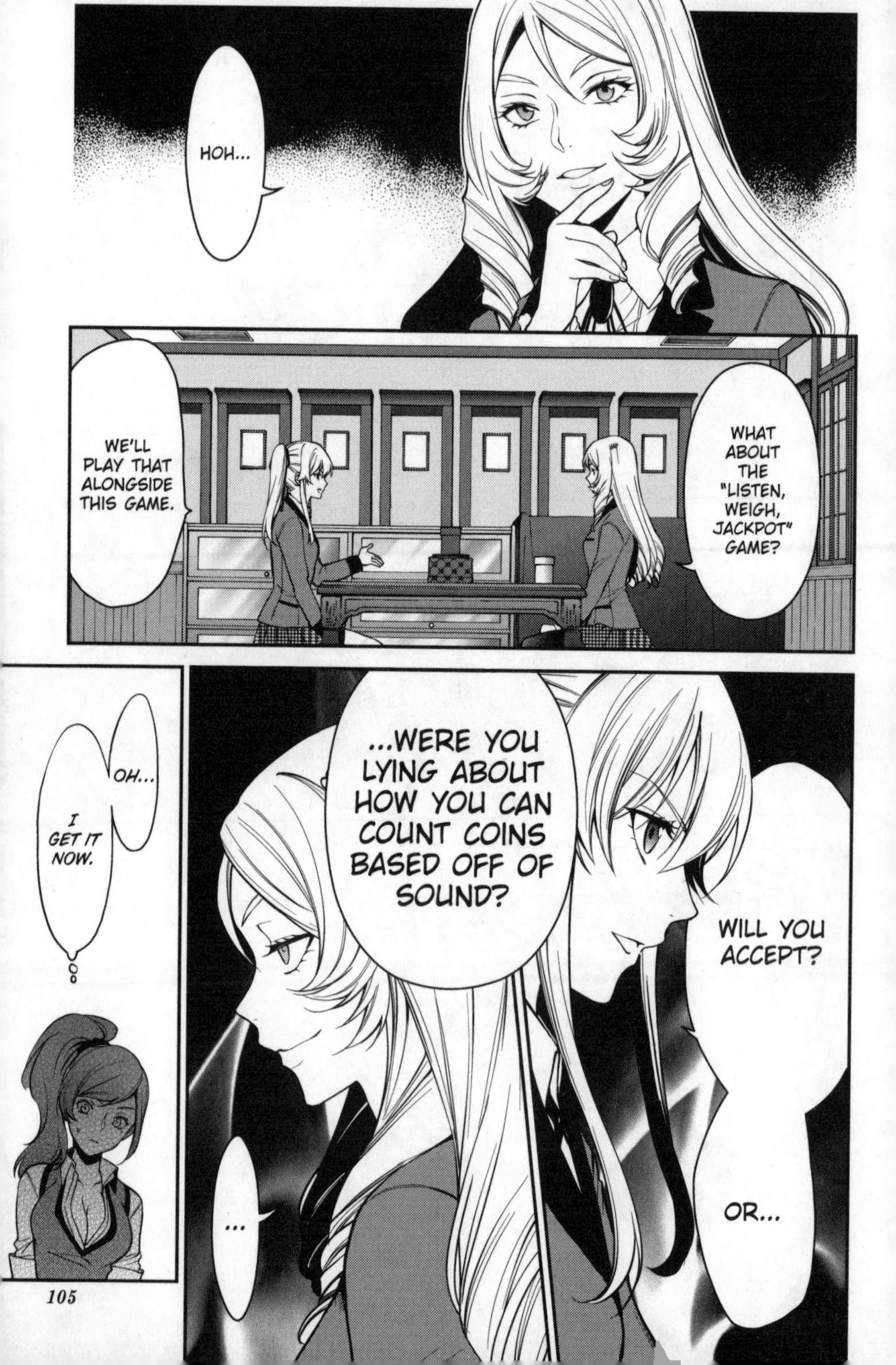
HOH...
WHAT ABOUT THE "LISTEN, WEIGH, JACKPOT" GAME?
WE'LL PLAY THAT ALONGSIDE THIS GAME.
WILL YOU ACCEPT?
OR...
...WERE YOU LYING ABOUT HOW YOU CAN COUNT COINS BASED OFF OF SOUND?
...
OH...
I GET IT NOW.

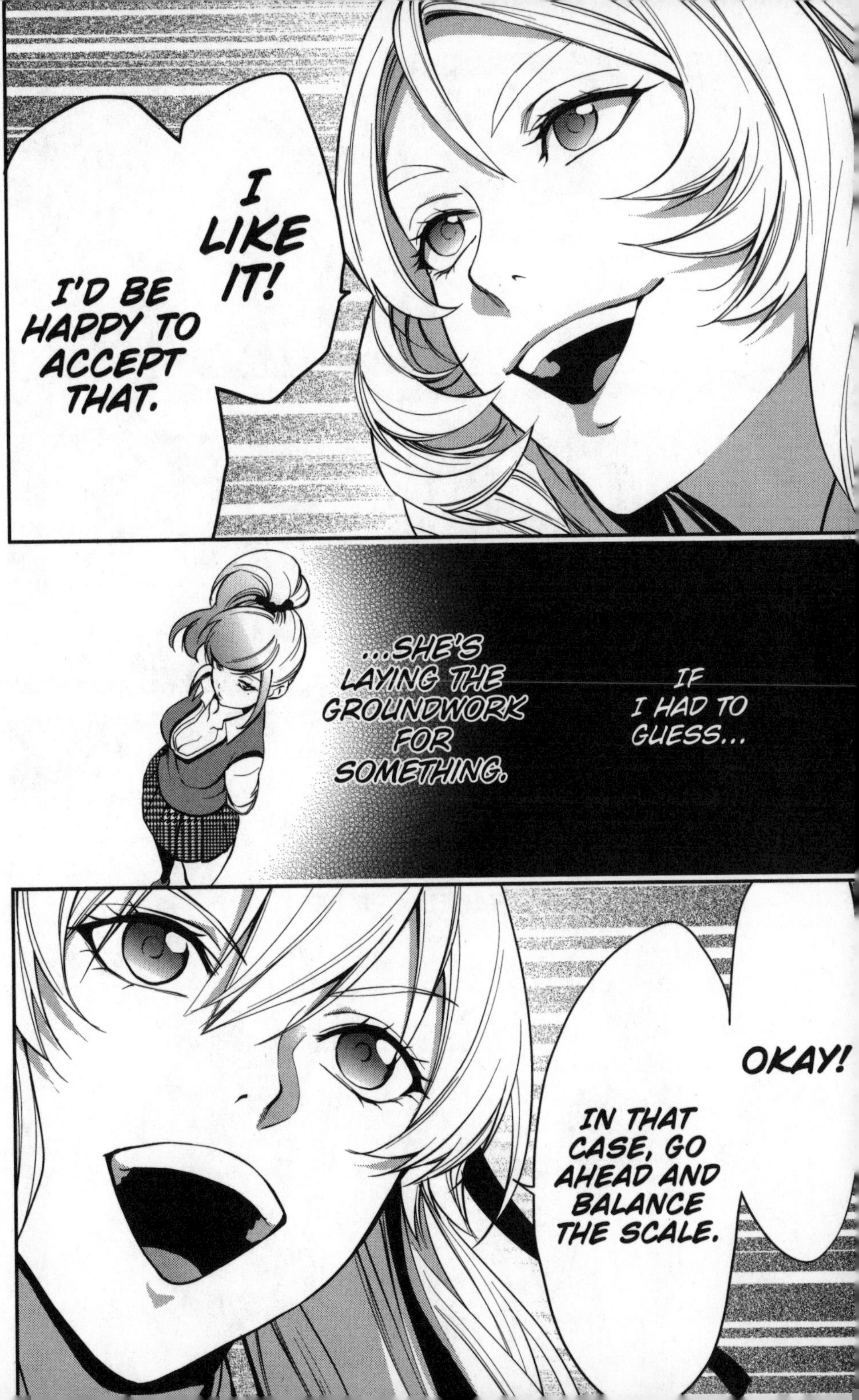
I LIKE IT!
I'D BE HAPPY TO ACCEPT THAT.
IF I HAD TO GUESS...
...SHE'S LAYING THE GROUNDWORK FOR SOMETHING.
OKAY!
IN THAT CASE, GO AHEAD AND BALANCE THE SCALE.

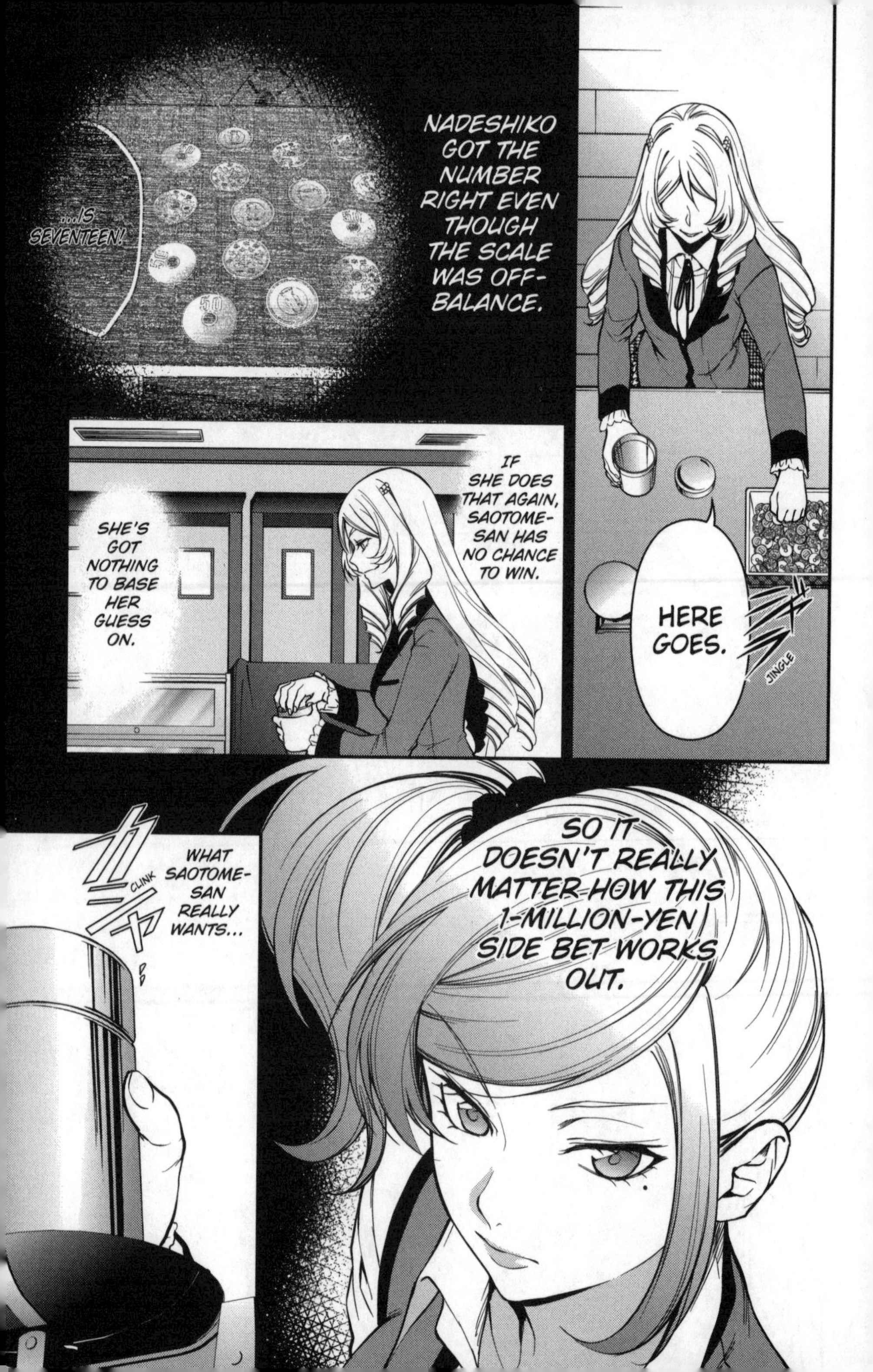
HERE GOES.
JINGLE
NADESHIKO GOT THE NUMBER RIGHT EVEN THOUGH THE SCALE WAS OFF-BALANCE.
...IS SEVENTEEN!
IF SHE DOES THAT AGAIN, SAOTOME-SAN HAS NO CHANCE TO WIN.
SHE'S GOT NOTHING TO BASE HER GUESS ON.
SO IT DOESN'T REALLY MATTER HOW THIS 1-MILLION-YEN SIDE BET WORKS OUT.
WHAT SAOTOME-SAN REALLY WANTS...
CLINK

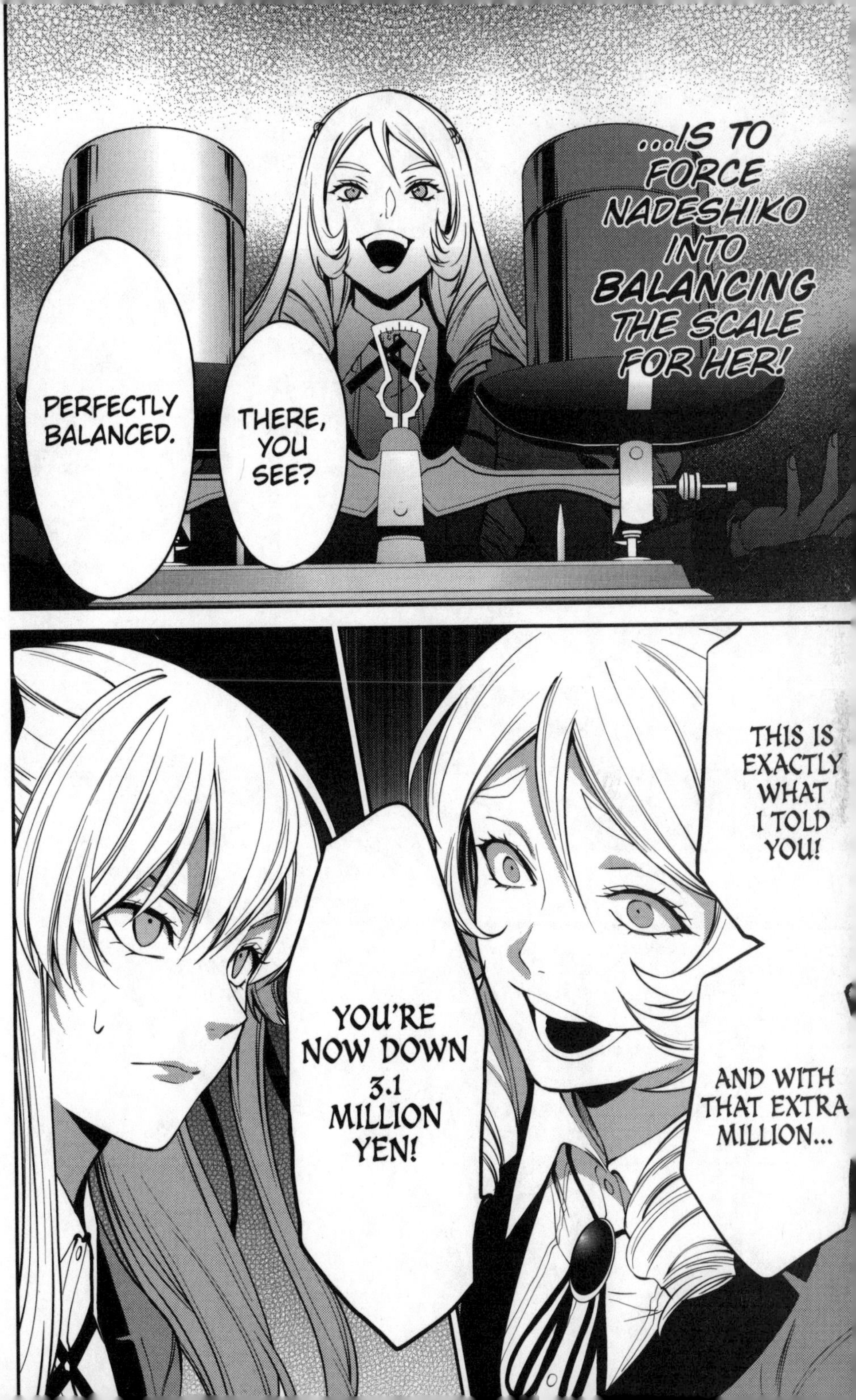
...IS TO FORCE NADESHIKO INTO BALANCING THE SCALE FOR HER!
THERE, YOU SEE?
PERFECTLY BALANCED.
THIS IS EXACTLY WHAT I TOLD YOU!
AND WITH THAT EXTRA MILLION...
YOU'RE NOW DOWN 3.1 MILLION YEN!

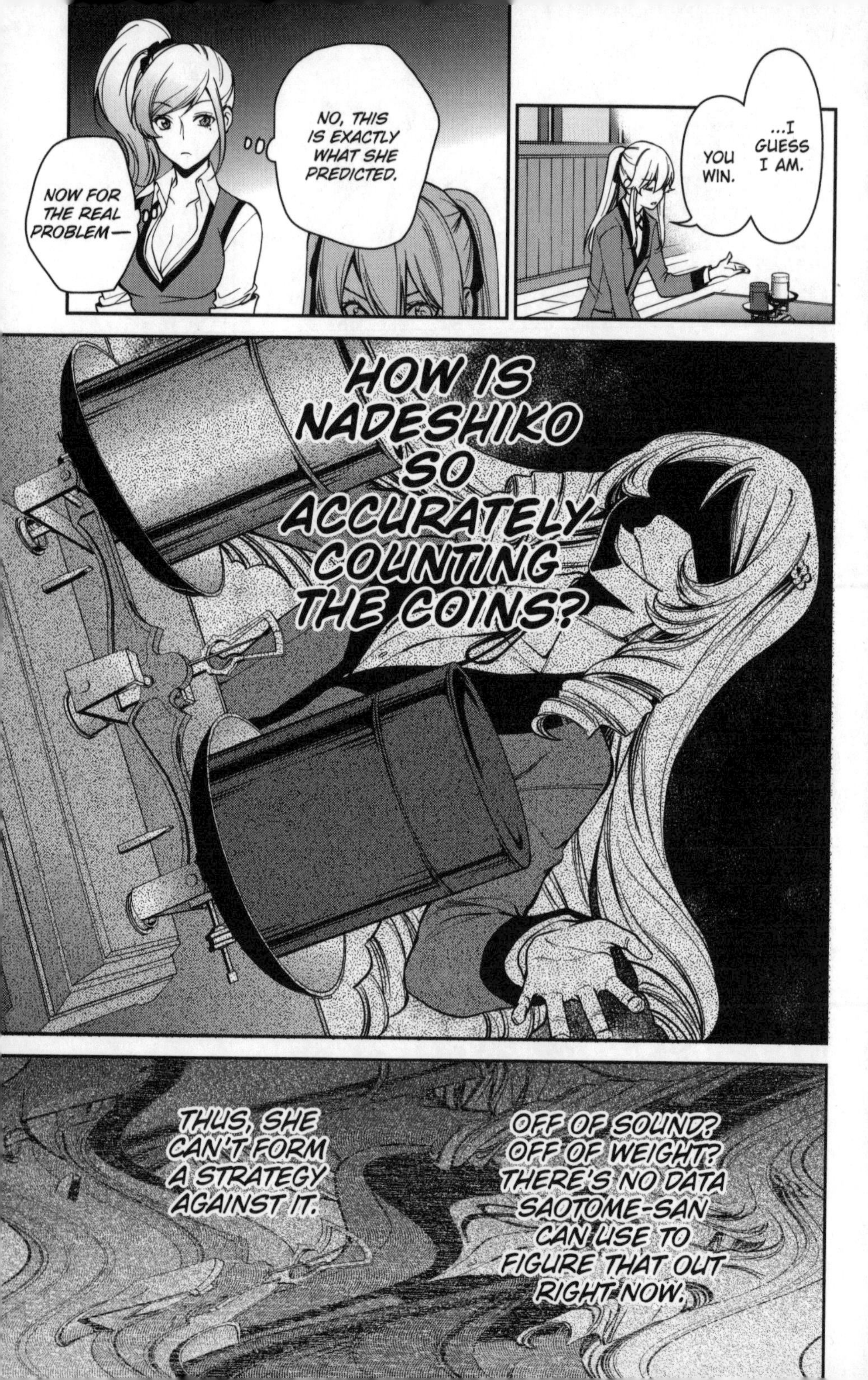
...I GUESS I AM.
YOU WIN.
NO, THIS IS EXACTLY WHAT SHE PREDICTED.
NOW FOR THE REAL PROBLEM—
HOW IS NADESHIKO SO ACCURATELY COUNTING THE COINS?
OFF OF SOUND? OFF OF WEIGHT? THERE'S NO DATA SAOTOME-SAN CAN USE TO FIGURE THAT OUT RIGHT NOW.
THUS, SHE CAN'T FORM A STRATEGY AGAINST IT.

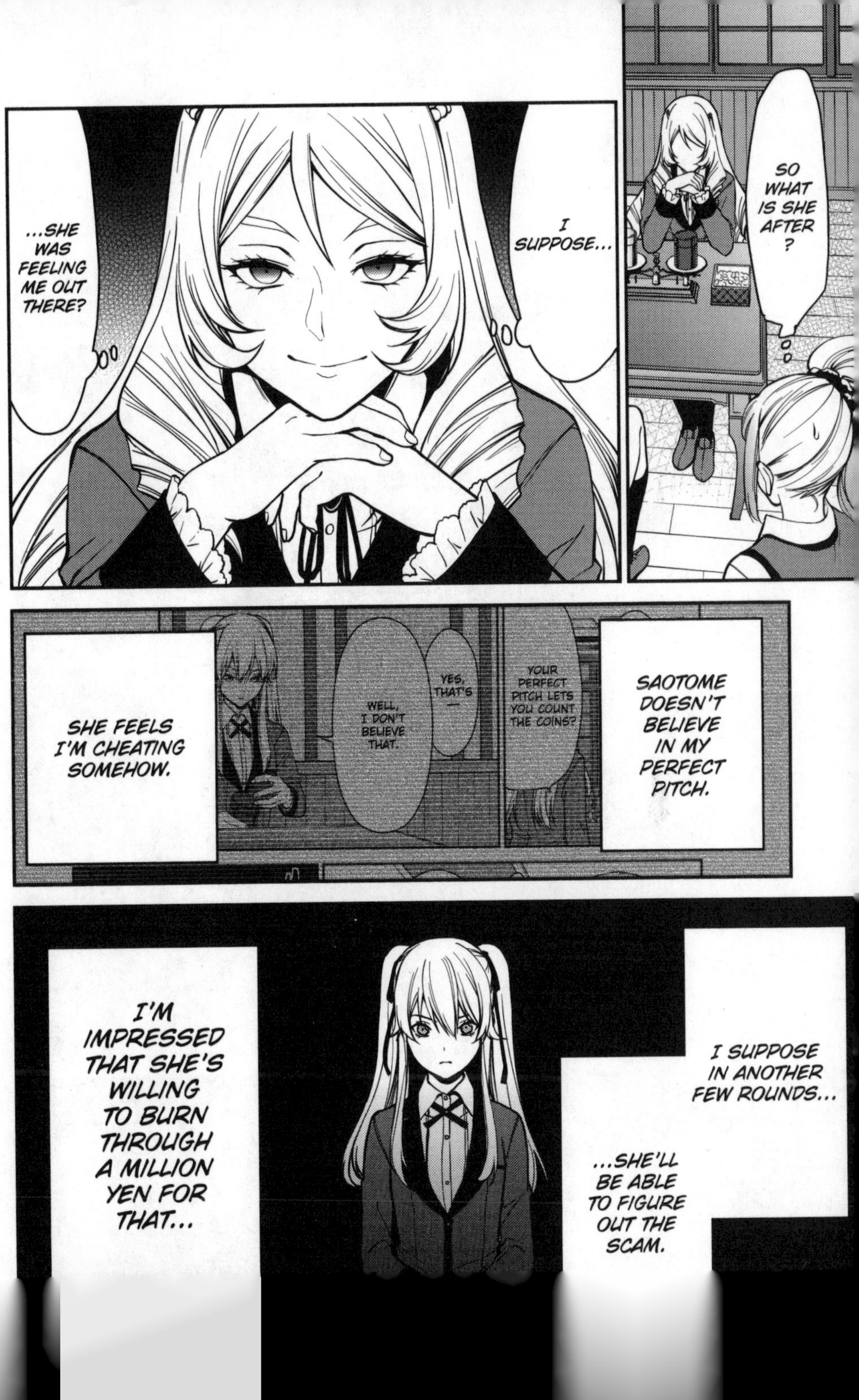
SO WHAT IS SHE AFTER?
I SUPPOSE...
...SHE WAS FEELING ME OUT THERE?
SAOTOME DOESN'T BELIEVE IN MY PERFECT PITCH.
YOUR PERFECT PITCH LETS YOU COUNT THE COINS?
YES, THAT'S —
WELL, I DON'T BELIEVE THAT.
SHE FEELS I'M CHEATING SOMEHOW.
I SUPPOSE IN ANOTHER FEW ROUNDS...
...SHE'LL BE ABLE TO FIGURE OUT THE SCAM.
I'M IMPRESSED THAT SHE'S WILLING TO BURN THROUGH A MILLION YEN FOR THAT...

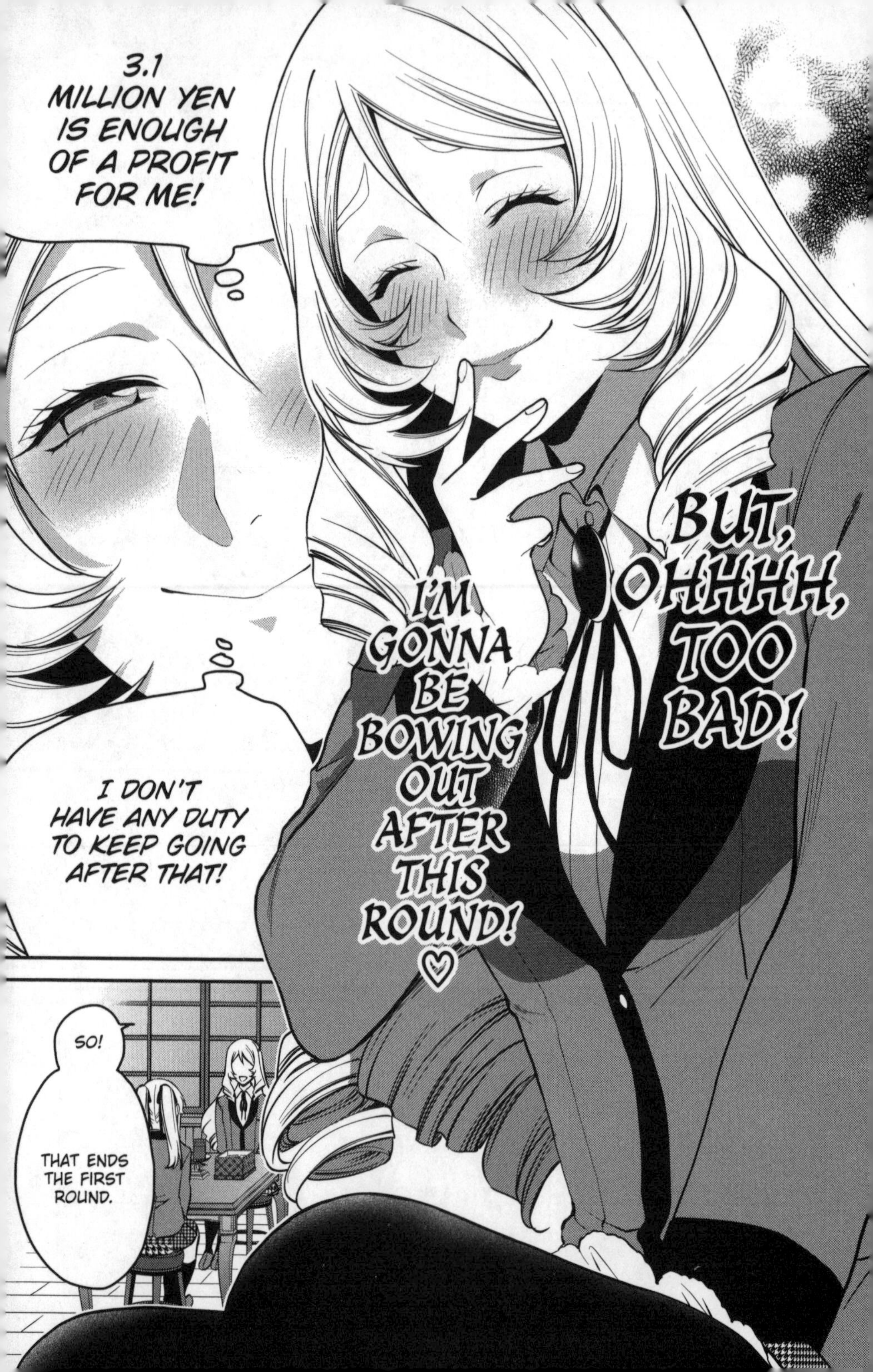

3.1 MILLION YEN IS ENOUGH OF A PROFIT FOR ME!
I DON'T HAVE ANY DUTY TO KEEP GOING AFTER THAT!
BUT, OHHHH, TOO BAD!
I'M GONNA BE BOWING OUT AFTER THIS ROUND! ♡
SO!
THAT ENDS THE FIRST ROUND.

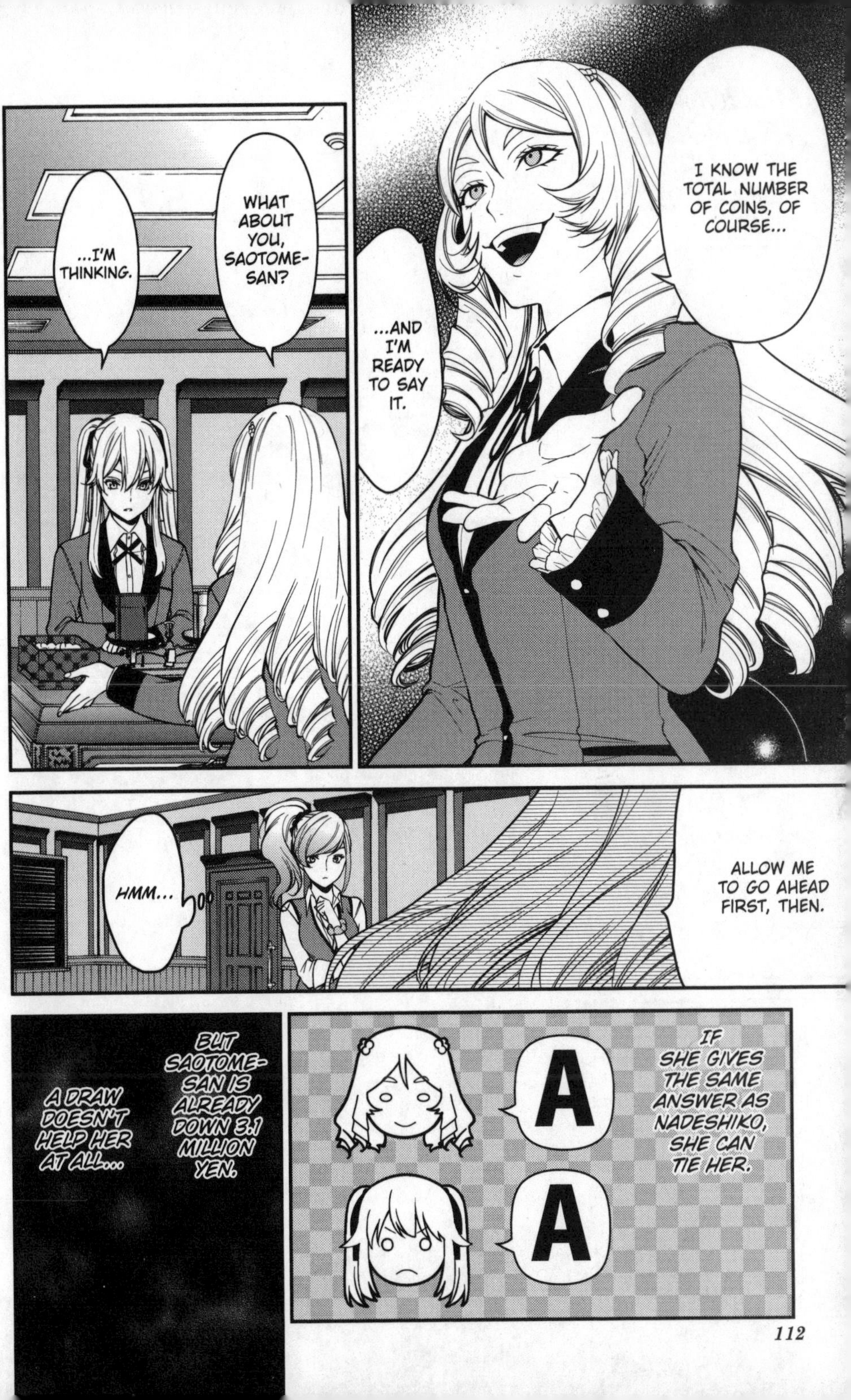
I KNOW THE TOTAL NUMBER OF COINS, OF COURSE...
...AND I'M READY TO SAY IT.
WHAT ABOUT YOU, SAOTOME-SAN?
...I'M THINKING.
ALLOW ME TO GO AHEAD FIRST, THEN.
HMM...
IF SHE GIVES THE SAME ANSWER AS NADESHIKO, SHE CAN TIE HER.
A
A
BUT SAOTOME-SAN IS ALREADY DOWN 3.1 MILLION YEN.
A DRAW DOESN'T HELP HER AT ALL...

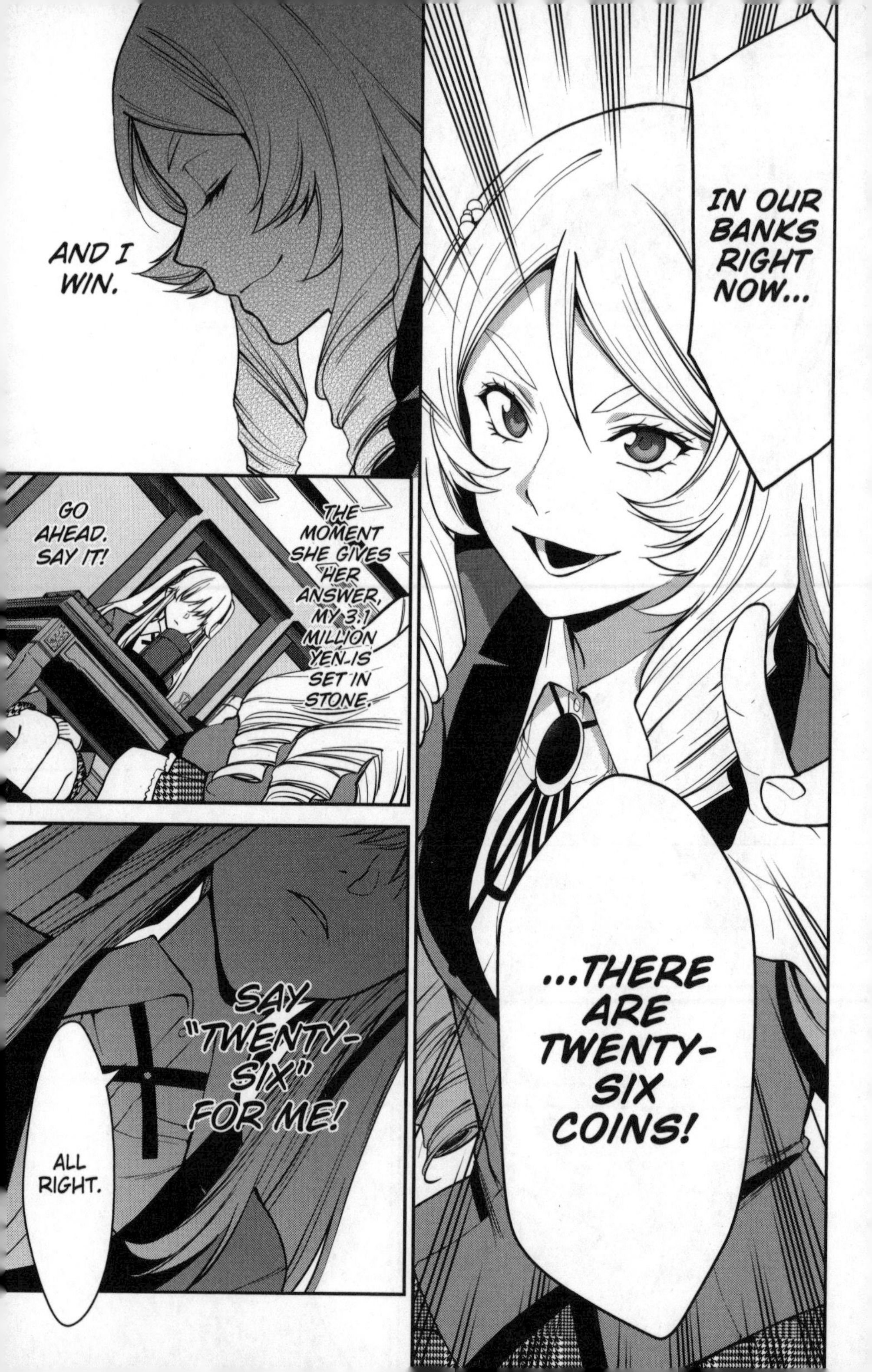
IN OUR BANKS RIGHT NOW...
...THERE ARE TWENTY-SIX COINS!
AND I WIN.
THE MOMENT SHE GIVES HER ANSWER, MY 3.1 MILLION YEN IS SET IN STONE.
GO AHEAD. SAY IT!
SAY "TWENTY-SIX" FOR ME!
ALL RIGHT.

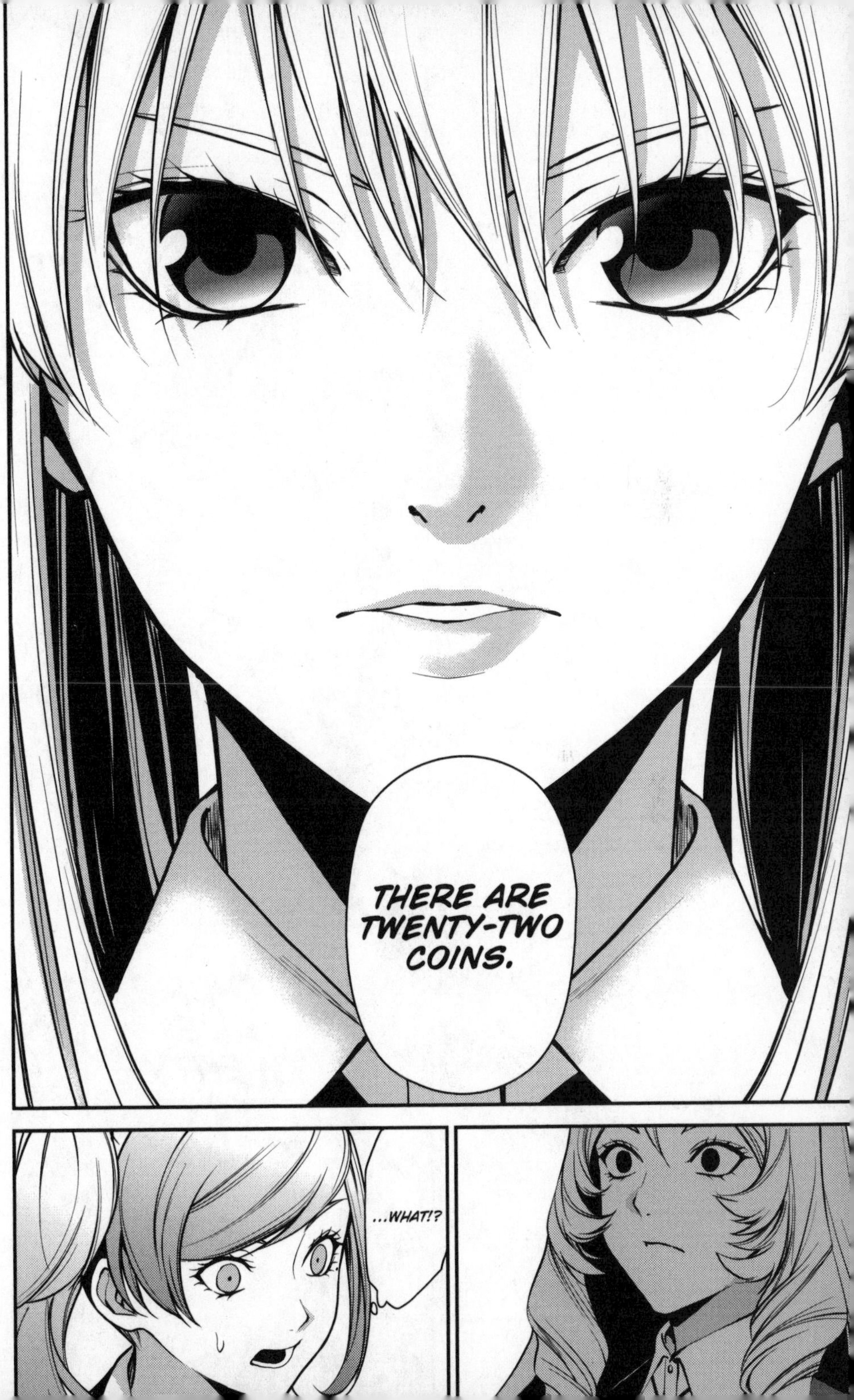
THERE ARE TWENTY-TWO COINS.
...WHAT!?

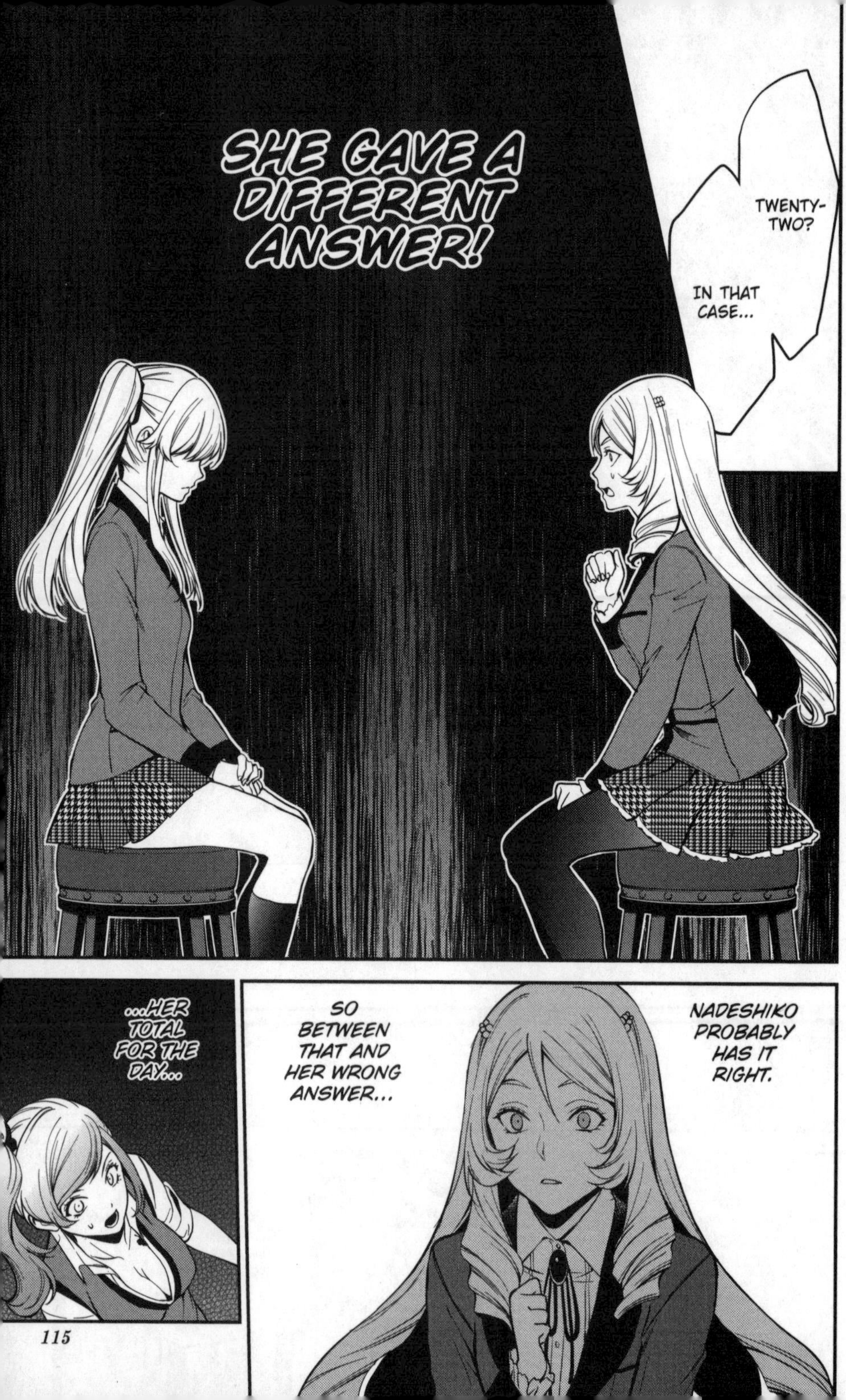
TWENTY-TWO?
IN THAT CASE...
SHE GAVE A DIFFERENT ANSWER!
NADESHIKO PROBABLY HAS IT RIGHT.
SO BETWEEN THAT AND HER WRONG ANSWER...
...HER TOTAL FOR THE DAY...

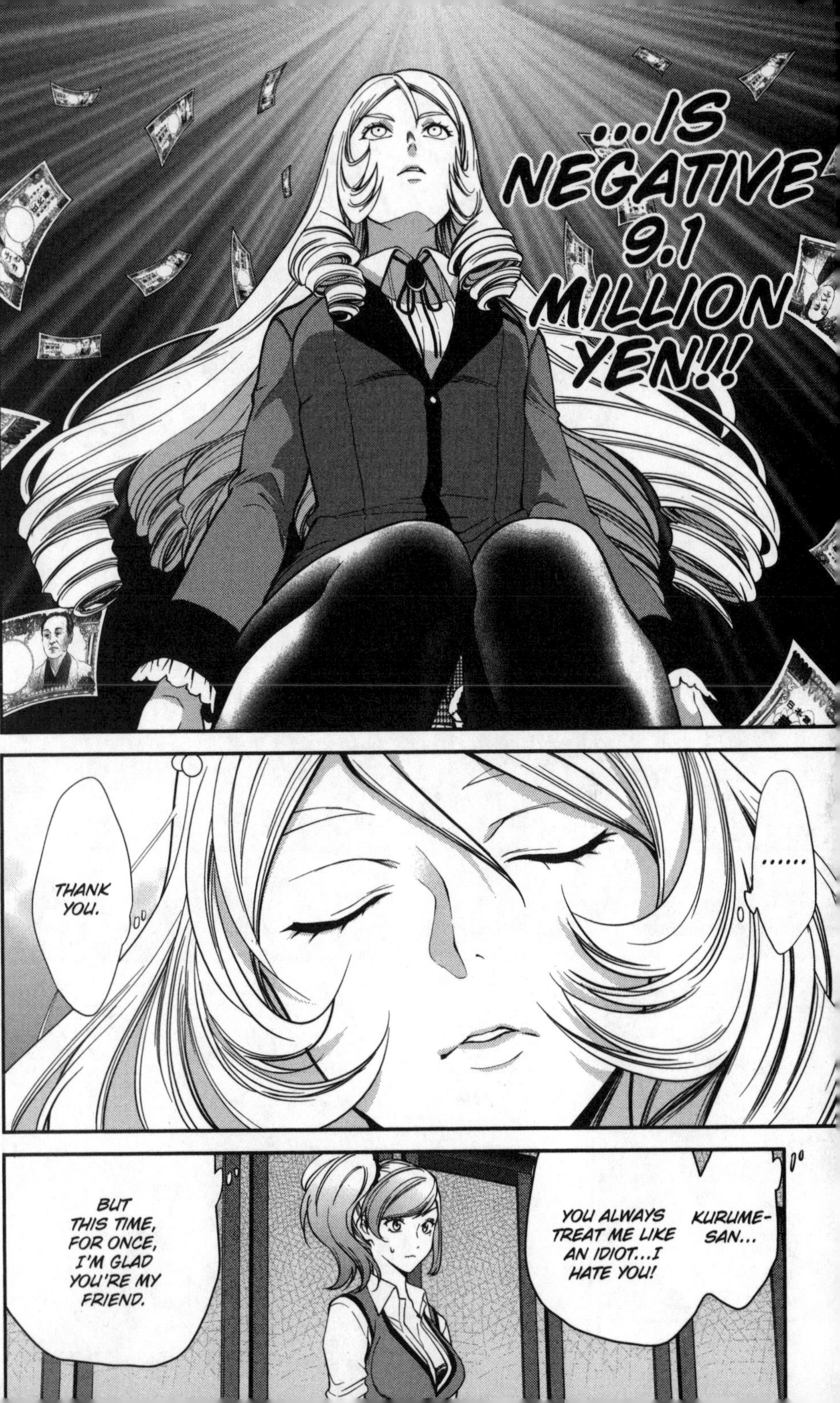
...IS NEGATIVE 9.1 MILLION YEN!!
......
THANK YOU.
KURUME-SAN...
YOU ALWAYS TREAT ME LIKE AN IDIOT...I HATE YOU!
BUT THIS TIME, FOR ONCE, I'M GLAD YOU'RE MY FRIEND.

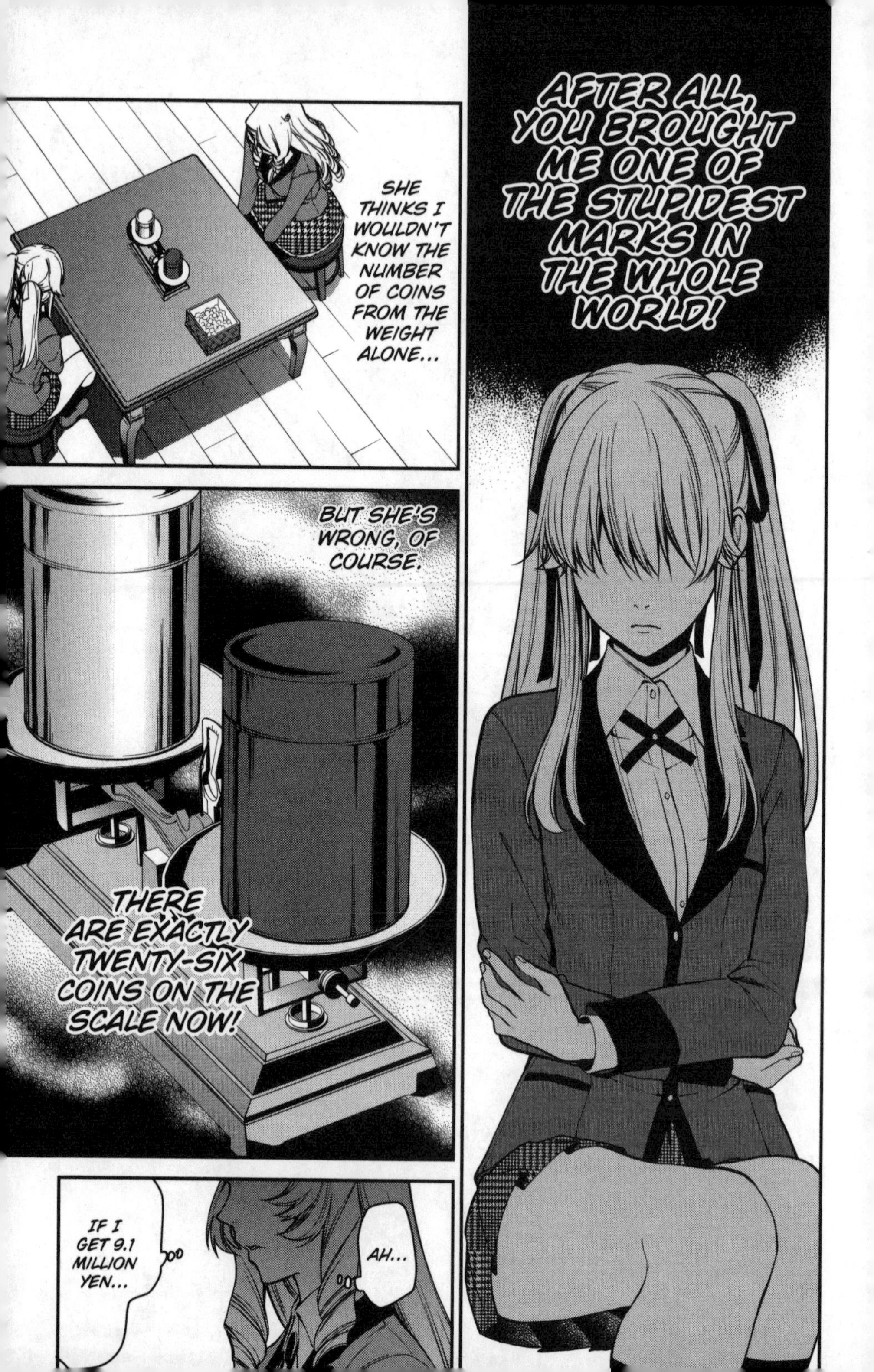
AFTER ALL, YOU BROUGHT ME ONE OF THE STUPIDEST MARKS IN THE WHOLE WORLD!
SHE THINKS I WOULDN'T KNOW THE NUMBER OF COINS FROM THE WEIGHT ALONE...
BUT SHE'S WRONG, OF COURSE.
THERE ARE EXACTLY TWENTY-SIX COINS ON THE SCALE NOW!
AH...
IF I GET 9.1 MILLION YEN...

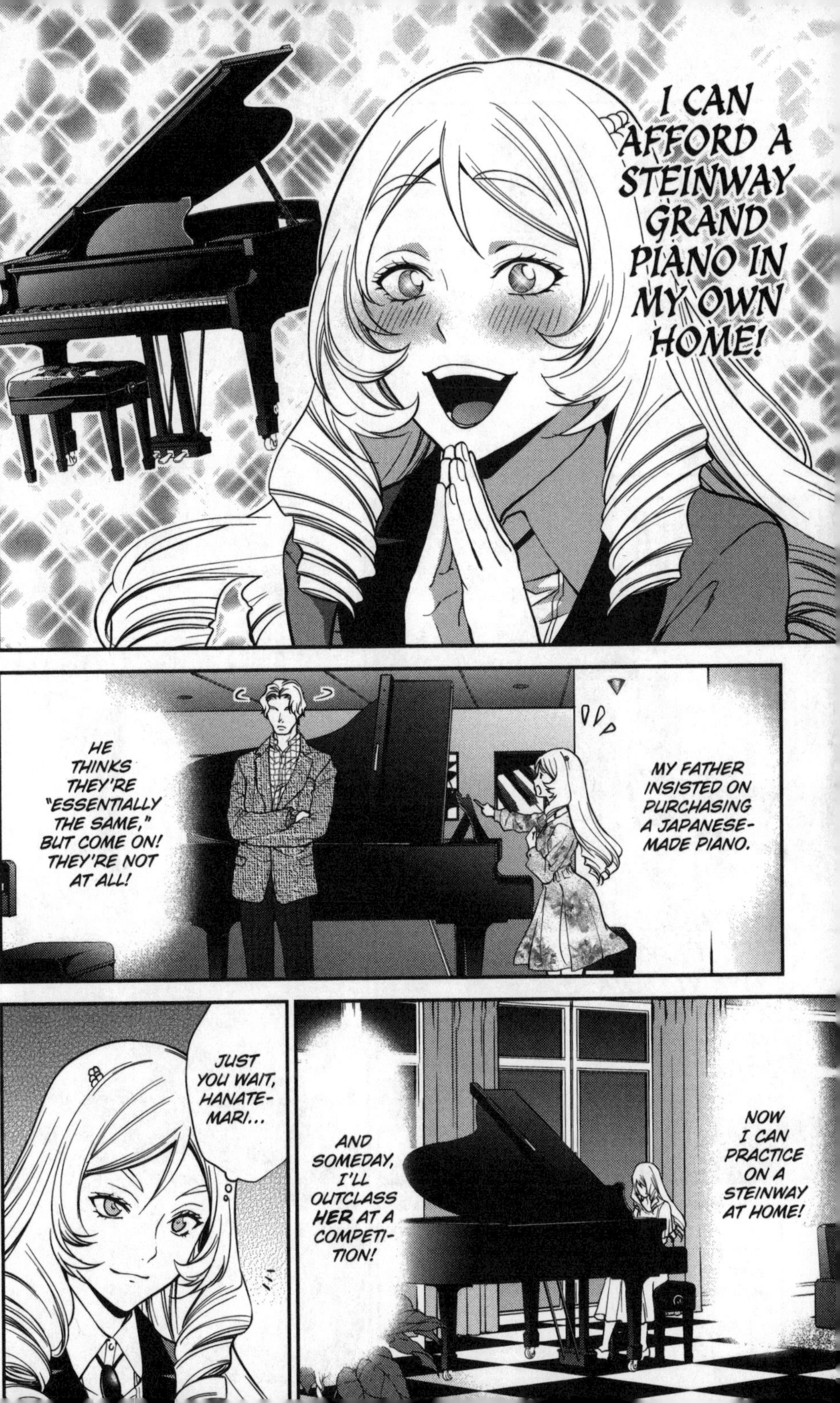
I CAN AFFORD A STEINWAY GRAND PIANO IN MY OWN HOME!
MY FATHER INSISTED ON PURCHASING A JAPANESE-MADE PIANO.
HE THINKS THEY'RE "ESSENTIALLY THE SAME," BUT COME ON! THEY'RE NOT AT ALL!
NOW I CAN PRACTICE ON A STEINWAY AT HOME!
AND SOMEDAY, I'LL OUTCLASS HER AT A COMPETITION!
JUST YOU WAIT, HANATEMARI...

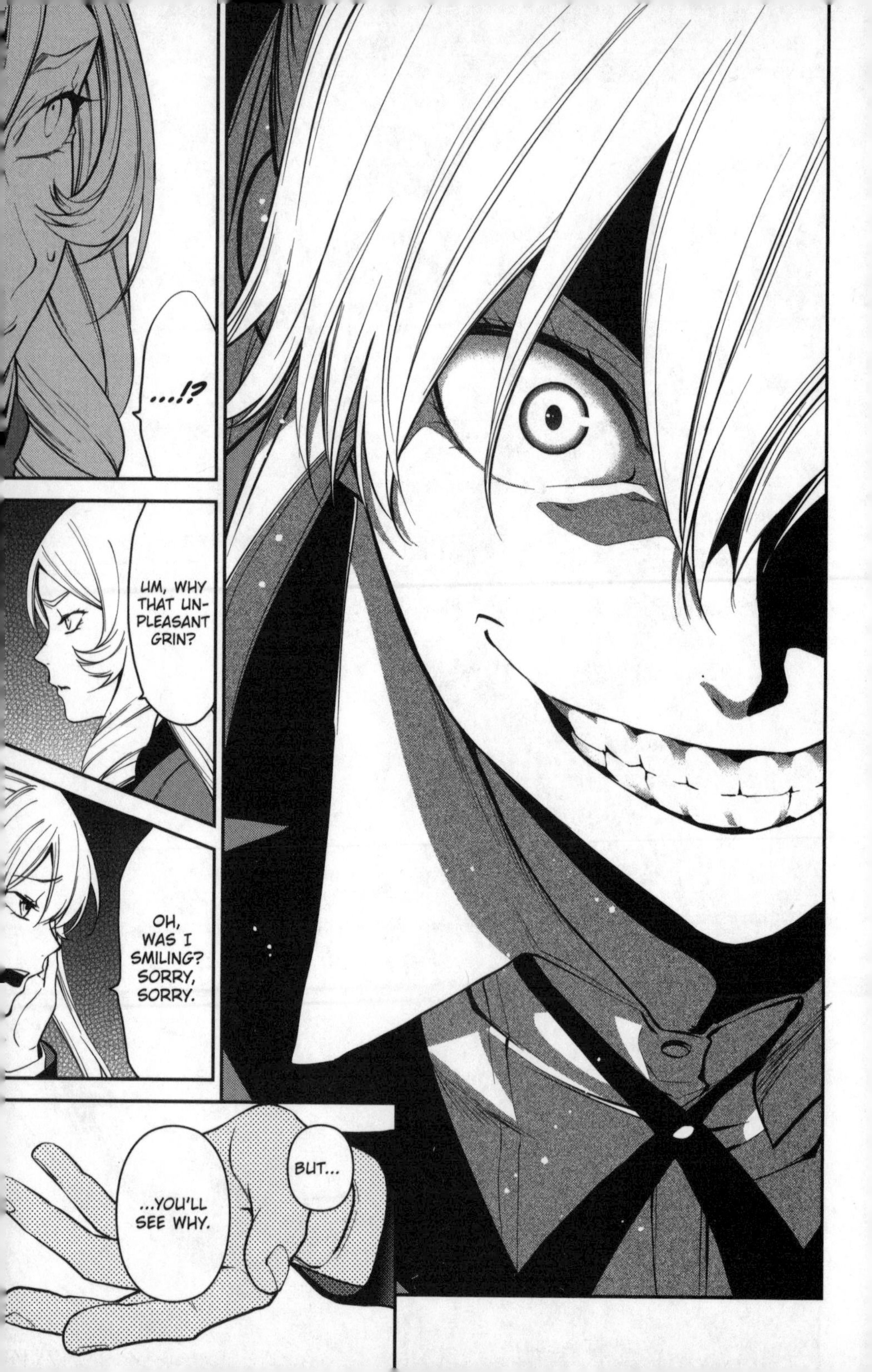
...!?
UM, WHY THAT UN-PLEASANT GRIN?
OH, WAS I SMILING? SORRY, SORRY.
BUT...
...YOU'LL SEE WHY.

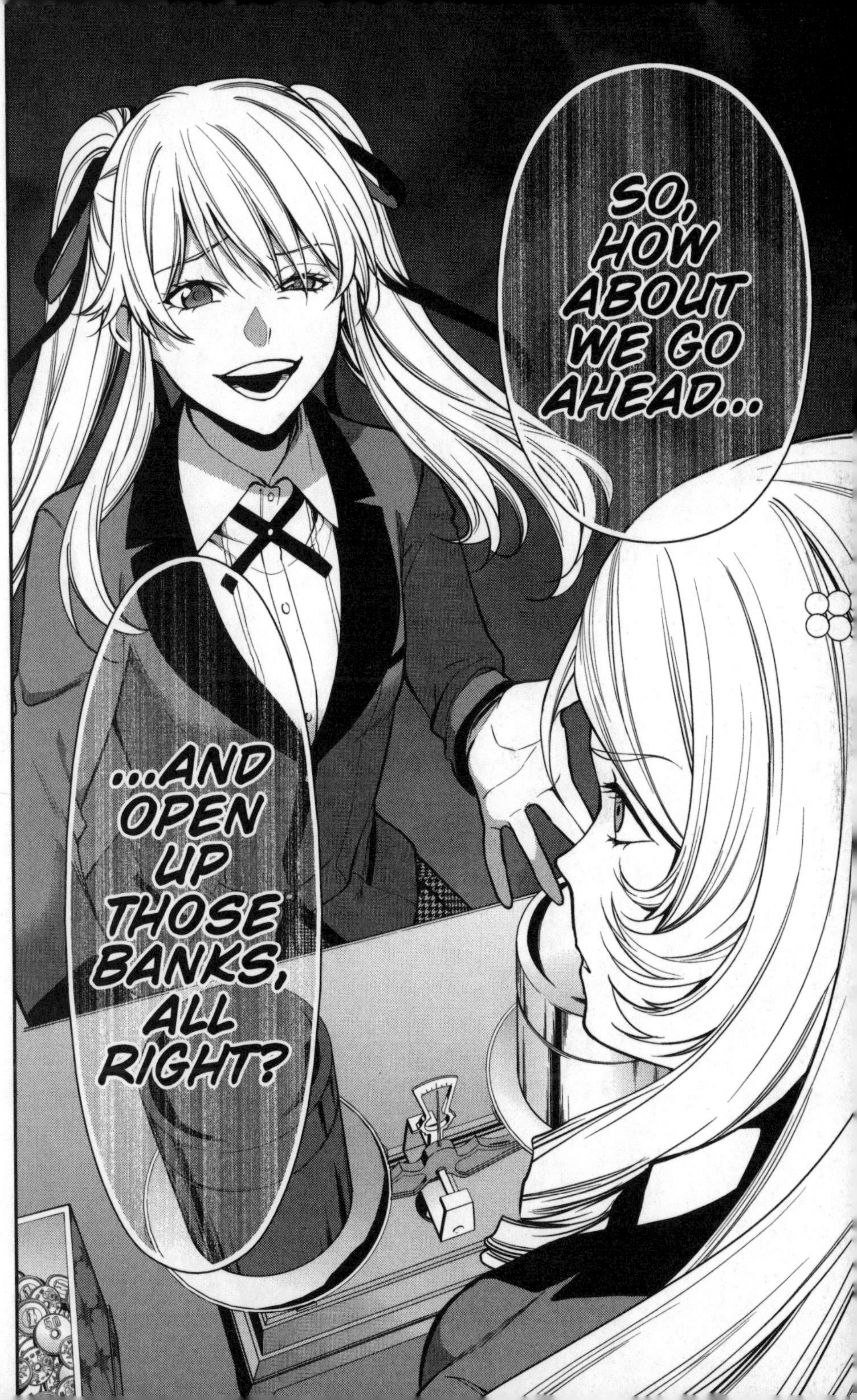
SO, HOW ABOUT WE GO AHEAD...
...AND OPEN UP THOSE BANKS, ALL RIGHT?

Kakegurui Twin

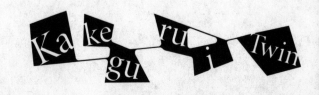

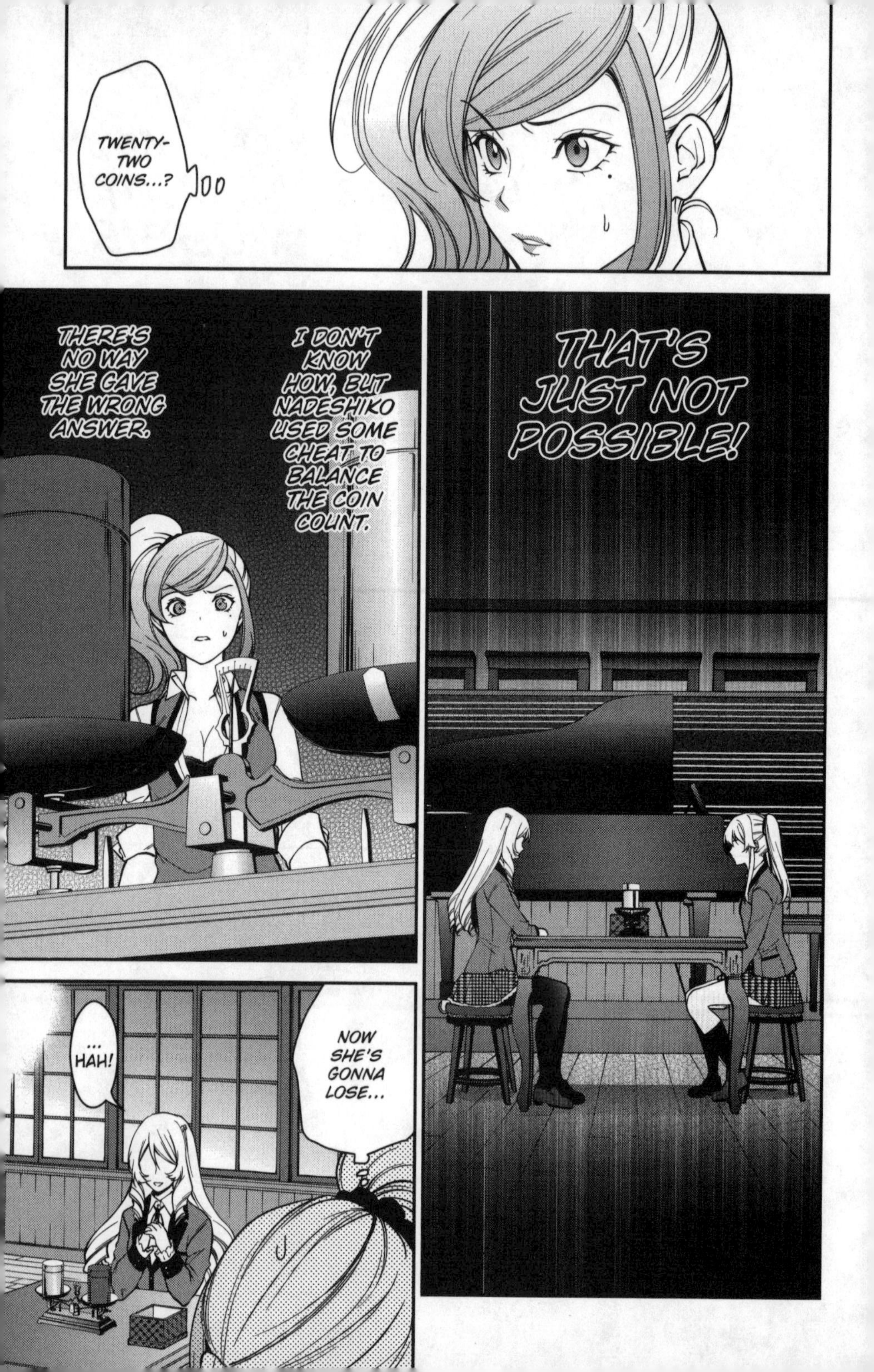
TWENTY-TWO COINS...?
THAT'S JUST NOT POSSIBLE!
I DON'T KNOW HOW, BUT NADESHIKO USED SOME CHEAT TO BALANCE THE COIN COUNT.
THERE'S NO WAY SHE GAVE THE WRONG ANSWER.
NOW SHE'S GONNA LOSE...
...HAH!

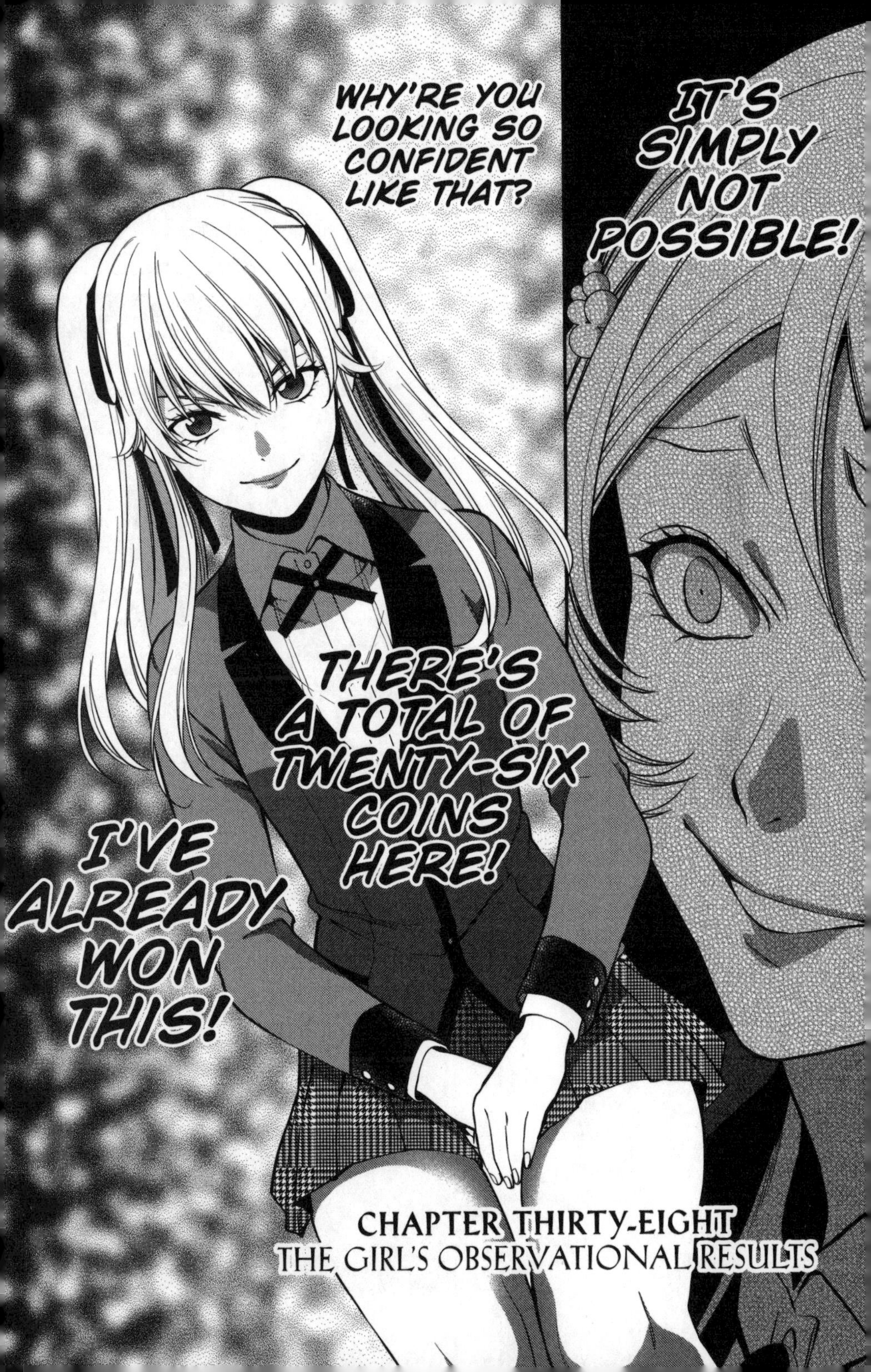
IT'S SIMPLY NOT POSSIBLE!
WHY'RE YOU LOOKING SO CONFIDENT LIKE THAT?
THERE'S A TOTAL OF TWENTY-SIX COINS HERE!
I'VE ALREADY WON THIS!

# CHAPTER THIRTY-EIGHT
## THE GIRL'S OBSERVATIONAL RESULTS

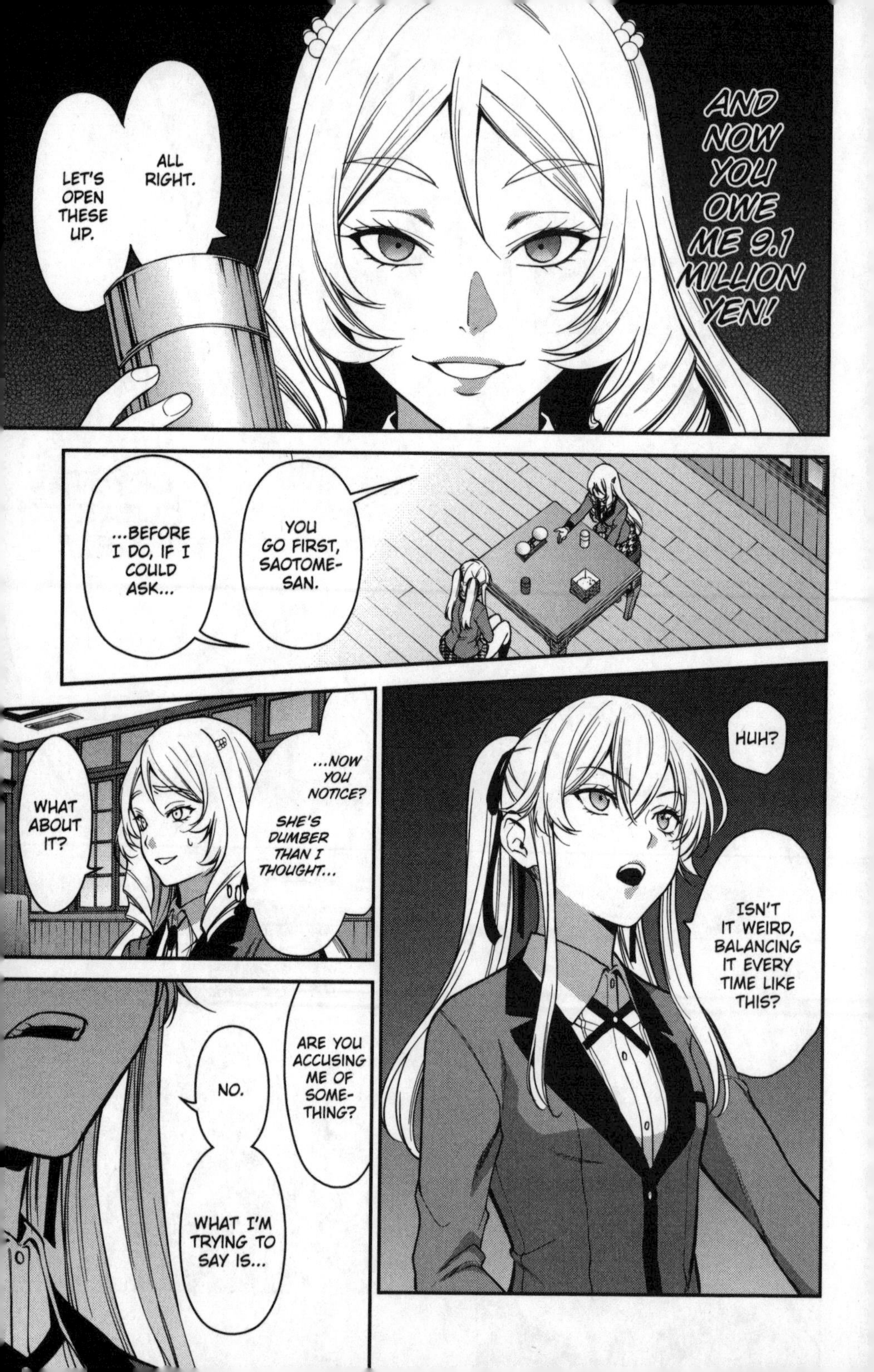
AND NOW YOU OWE ME 9.1 MILLION YEN!
ALL RIGHT.
LET'S OPEN THESE UP.
YOU GO FIRST, SAOTOME-SAN.
...BEFORE I DO, IF I COULD ASK...
HUH?
ISN'T IT WEIRD, BALANCING IT EVERY TIME LIKE THIS?
...NOW YOU NOTICE? SHE'S DUMBER THAN I THOUGHT...
WHAT ABOUT IT?
ARE YOU ACCUSING ME OF SOMETHING?
NO.
WHAT I'M TRYING TO SAY IS...

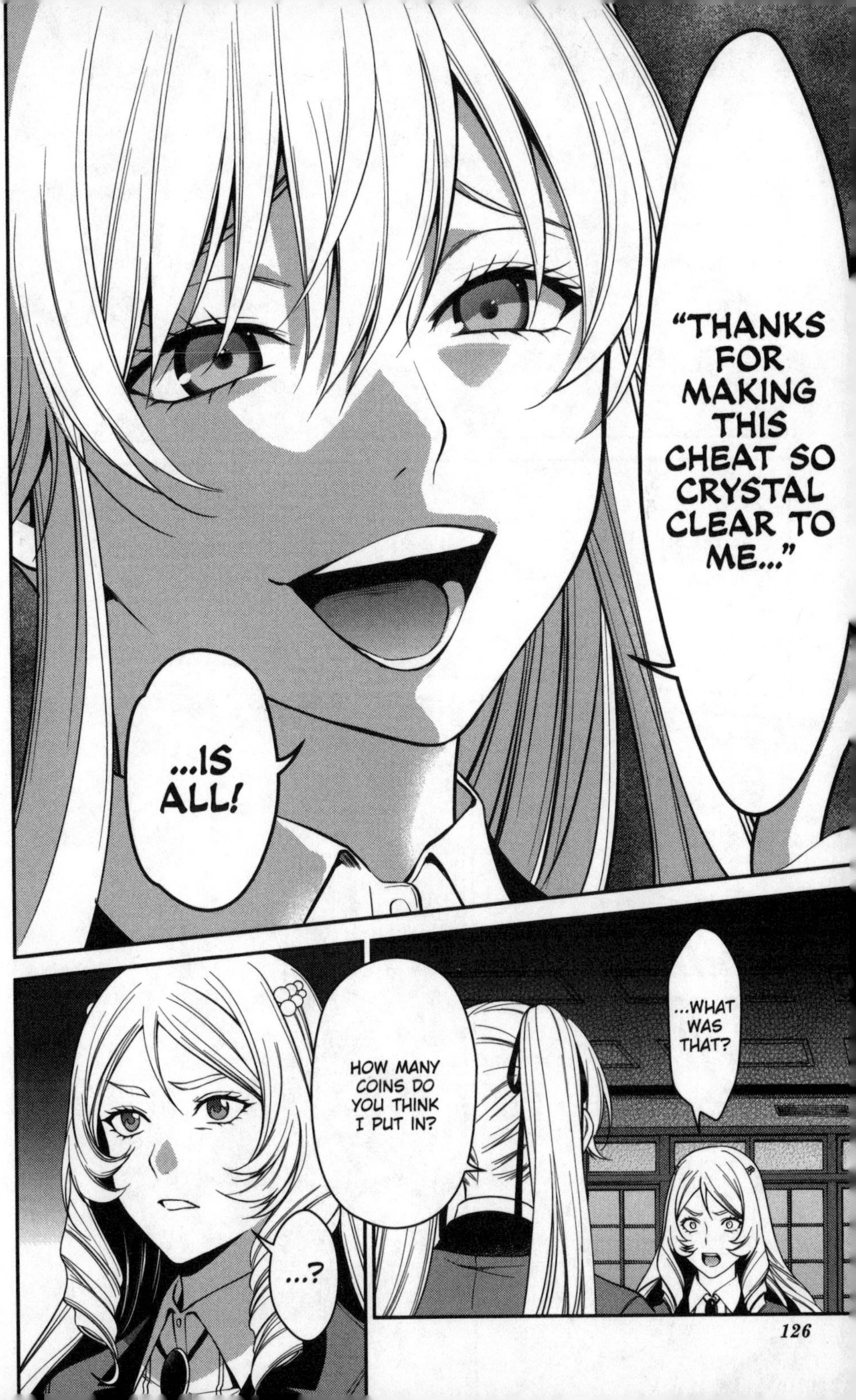

"THANKS FOR MAKING THIS CHEAT SO CRYSTAL CLEAR TO ME..."
...IS ALL!
...WHAT WAS THAT?
HOW MANY COINS DO YOU THINK I PUT IN?
...?

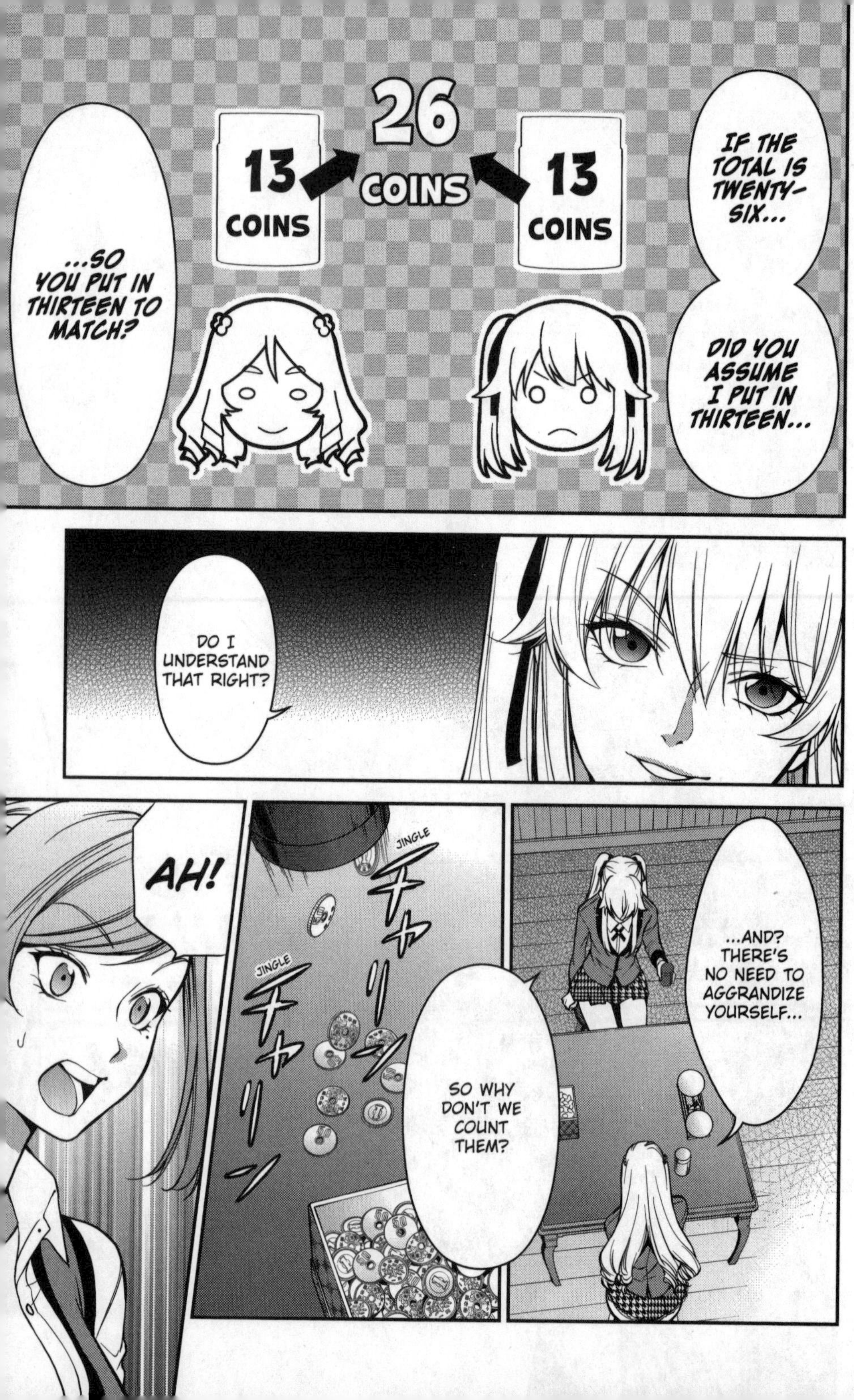
IF THE TOTAL IS TWENTY-SIX...
DID YOU ASSUME I PUT IN THIRTEEN...
13 COINS
26 COINS
13 COINS
...SO YOU PUT IN THIRTEEN TO MATCH?
DO I UNDERSTAND THAT RIGHT?
...AND? THERE'S NO NEED TO AGGRANDIZE YOURSELF...
SO WHY DON'T WE COUNT THEM?
JINGLE
JINGLE
AH!

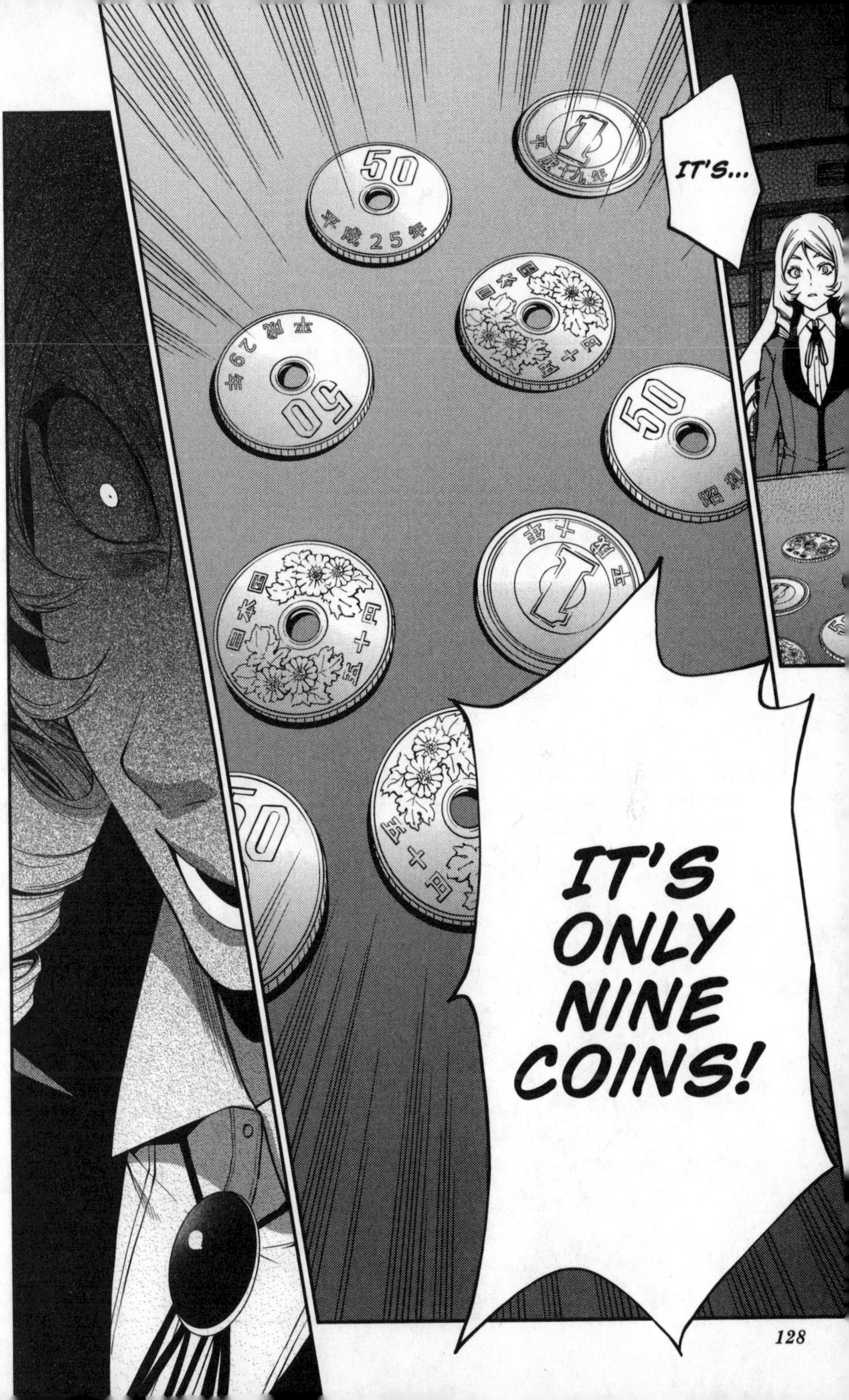
IT'S...
IT'S ONLY NINE COINS!

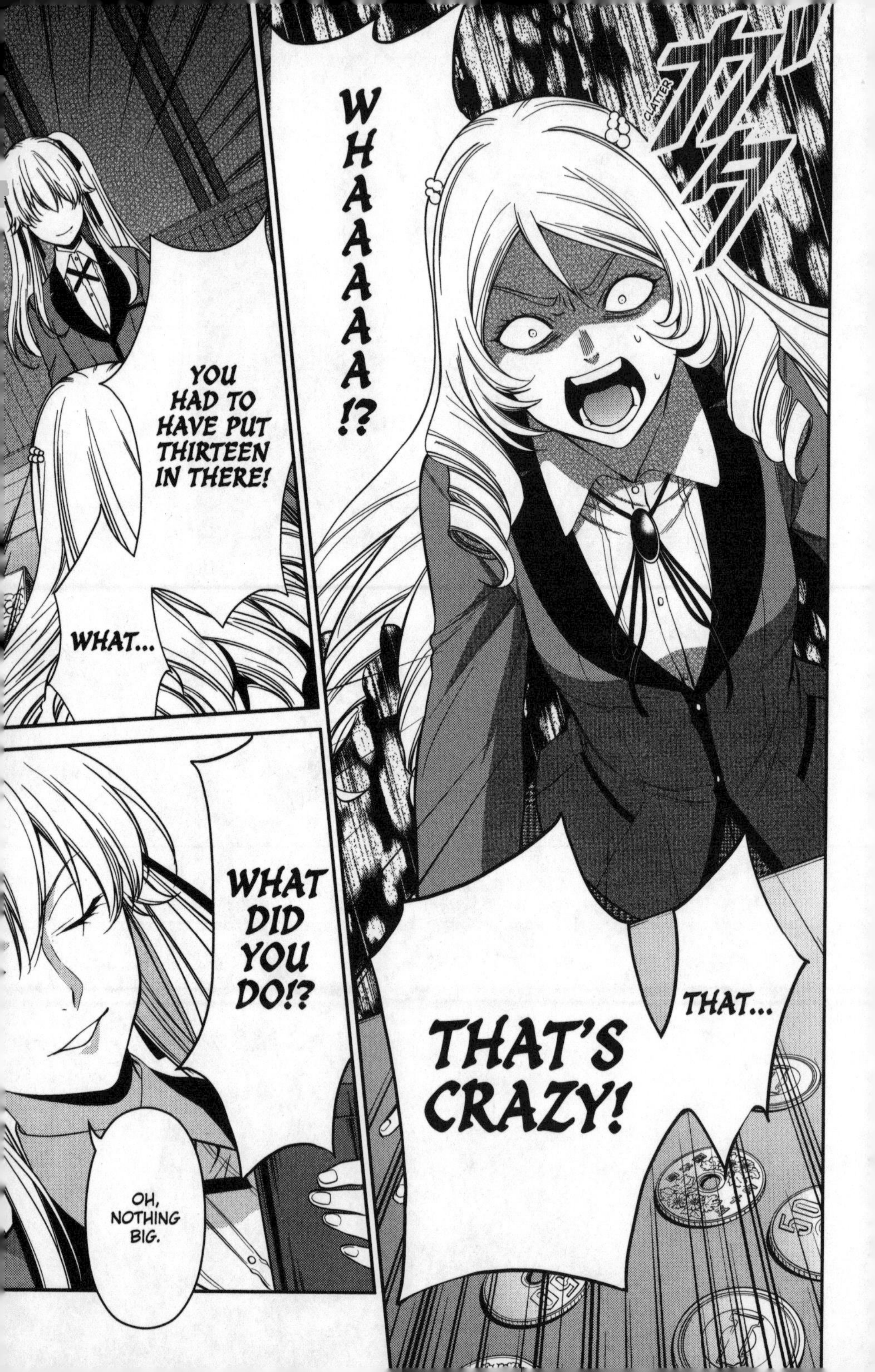

CLATTER
WHAAAAAA!?
THAT...
THAT'S CRAZY!
YOU HAD TO HAVE PUT THIRTEEN IN THERE!
WHAT...
WHAT DID YOU DO!?
OH, NOTHING BIG.

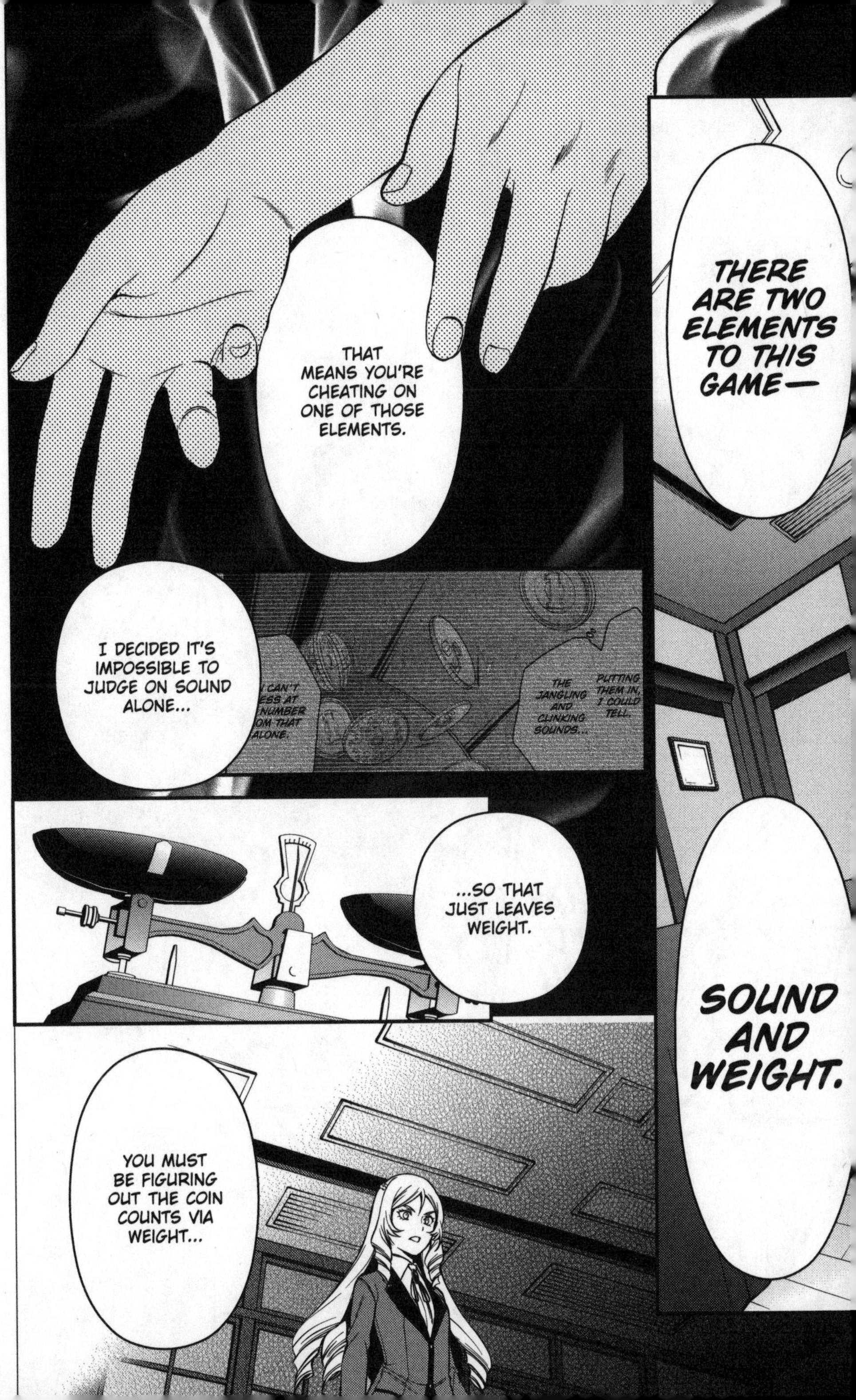
THERE ARE TWO ELEMENTS TO THIS GAME—
SOUND AND WEIGHT.
THAT MEANS YOU'RE CHEATING ON ONE OF THOSE ELEMENTS.
PUTTING THEM IN, I COULD TELL.
THE JANGLING AND CLINKING SOUNDS...
I DECIDED IT'S IMPOSSIBLE TO JUDGE ON SOUND ALONE...
...SO THAT JUST LEAVES WEIGHT.
YOU MUST BE FIGURING OUT THE COIN COUNTS VIA WEIGHT...

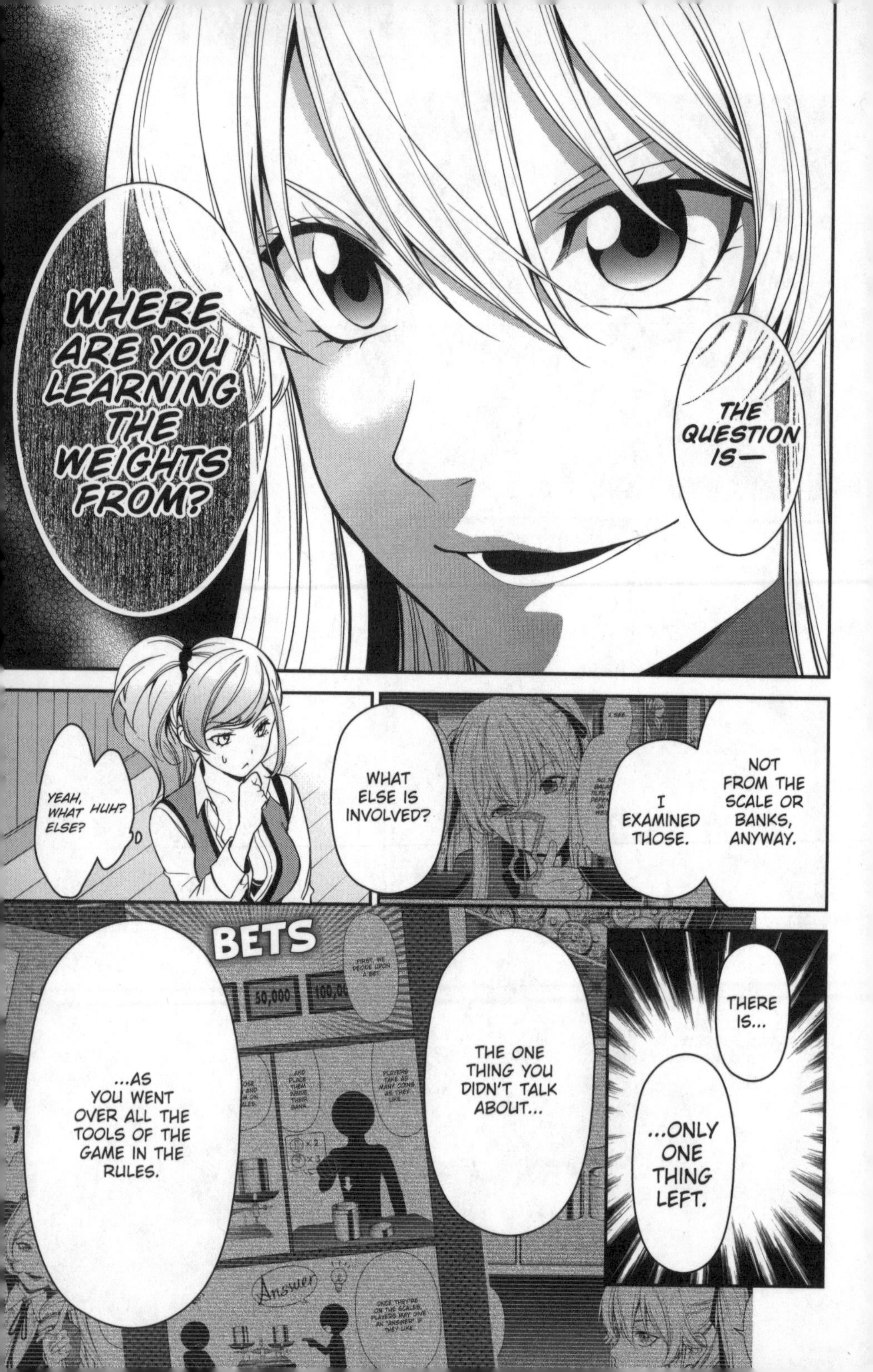
THE QUESTION IS—
WHERE ARE YOU LEARNING THE WEIGHTS FROM?
NOT FROM THE SCALE OR BANKS, ANYWAY.
I EXAMINED THOSE.
WHAT ELSE IS INVOLVED?
HUH?
YEAH, WHAT ELSE?
THERE IS...
...ONLY ONE THING LEFT.
THE ONE THING YOU DIDN'T TALK ABOUT...
BETS
FIRST, WE DECIDE UPON A BET.
50,000
Answer
...AS YOU WENT OVER ALL THE TOOLS OF THE GAME IN THE RULES.

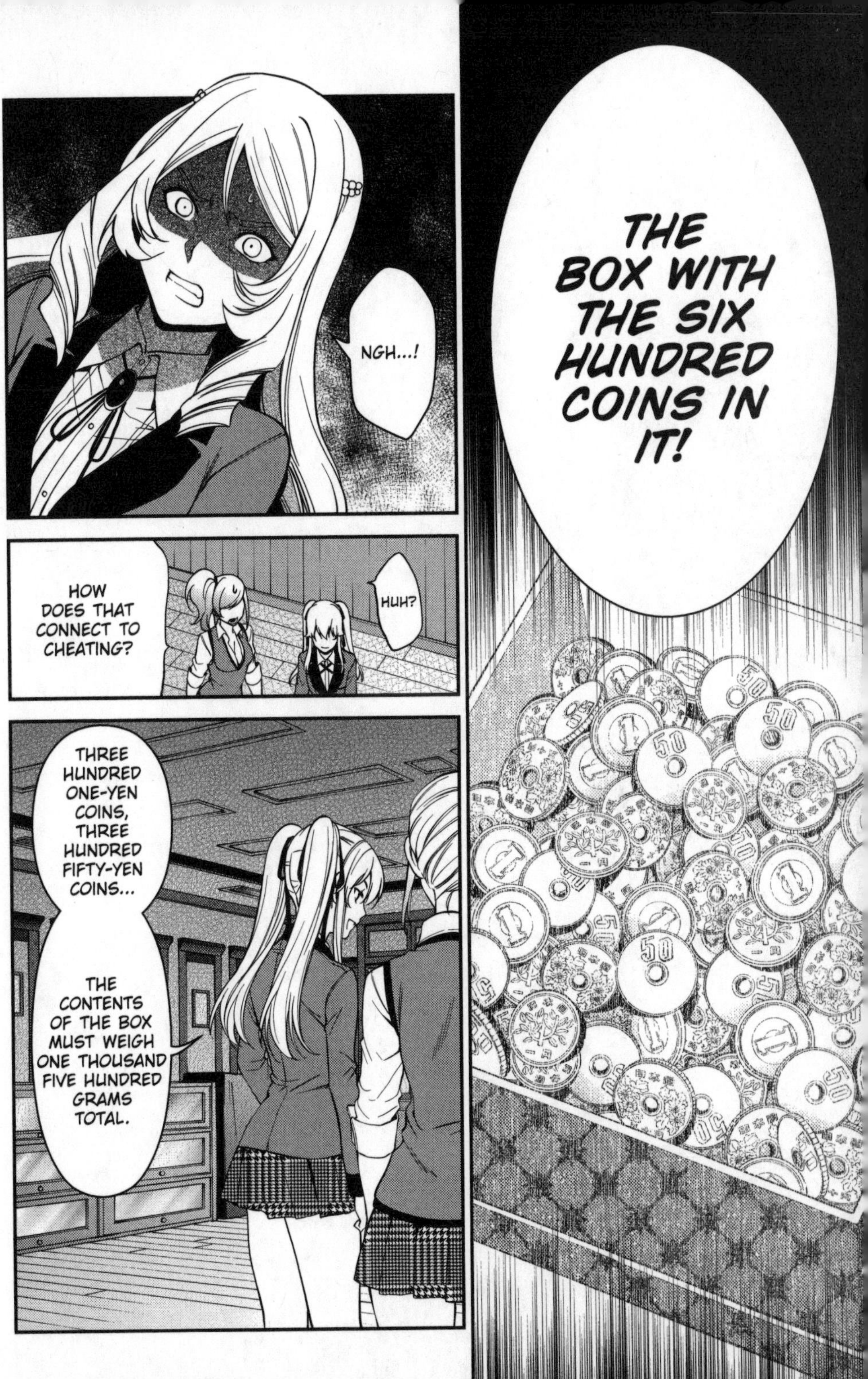
THE BOX WITH THE SIX HUNDRED COINS IN IT!
NGH...!
HUH?
HOW DOES THAT CONNECT TO CHEATING?
THREE HUNDRED ONE-YEN COINS, THREE HUNDRED FIFTY-YEN COINS...
THE CONTENTS OF THE BOX MUST WEIGH ONE THOUSAND FIVE HUNDRED GRAMS TOTAL.

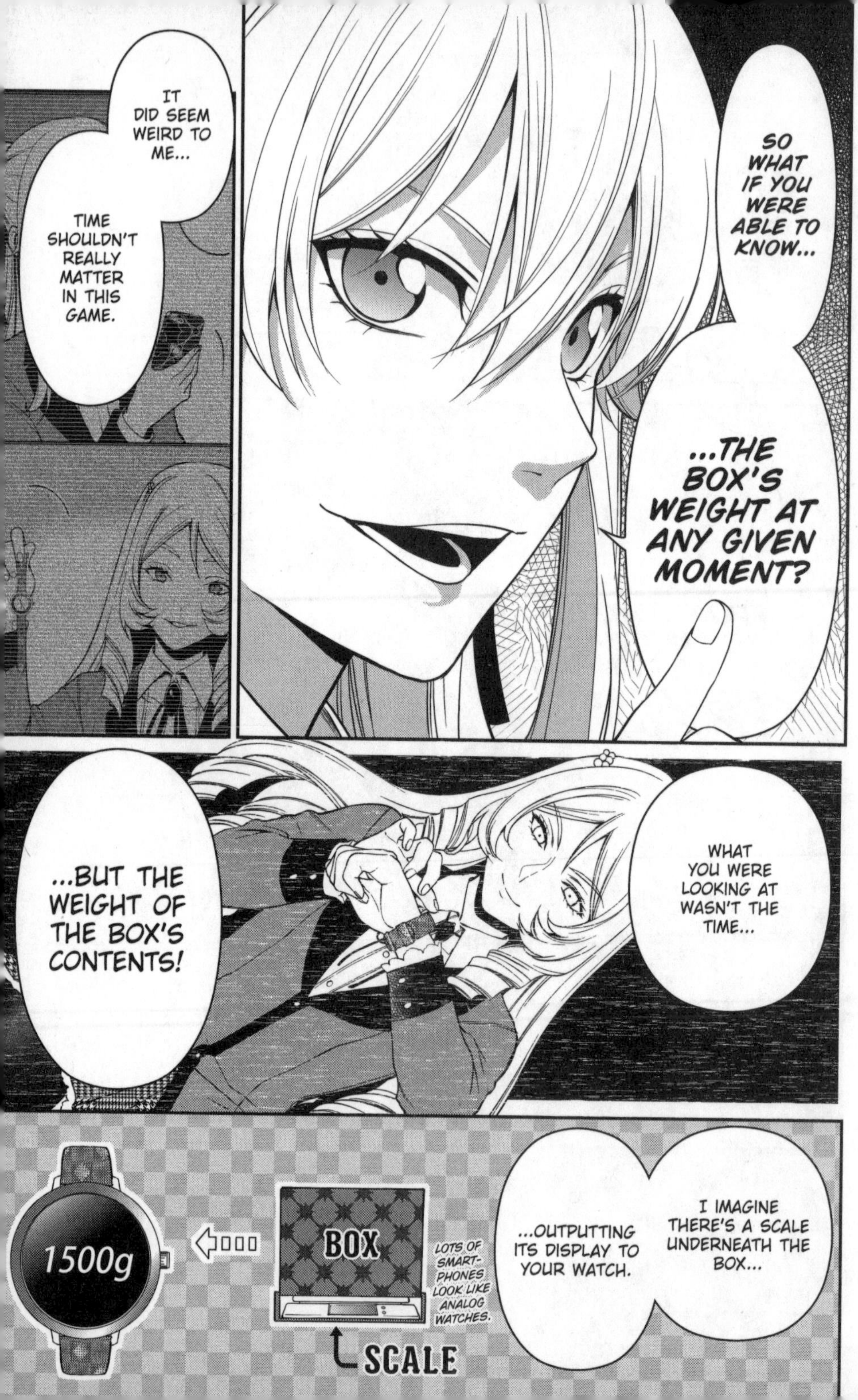
SO WHAT IF YOU WERE ABLE TO KNOW...
...THE BOX'S WEIGHT AT ANY GIVEN MOMENT?
IT DID SEEM WEIRD TO ME...
TIME SHOULDN'T REALLY MATTER IN THIS GAME.
WHAT YOU WERE LOOKING AT WASN'T THE TIME...
...BUT THE WEIGHT OF THE BOX'S CONTENTS!
I IMAGINE THERE'S A SCALE UNDERNEATH THE BOX...
...OUTPUTTING ITS DISPLAY TO YOUR WATCH.
LOTS OF SMART-PHONES LOOK LIKE ANALOG WATCHES.
BOX
SCALE
1500g

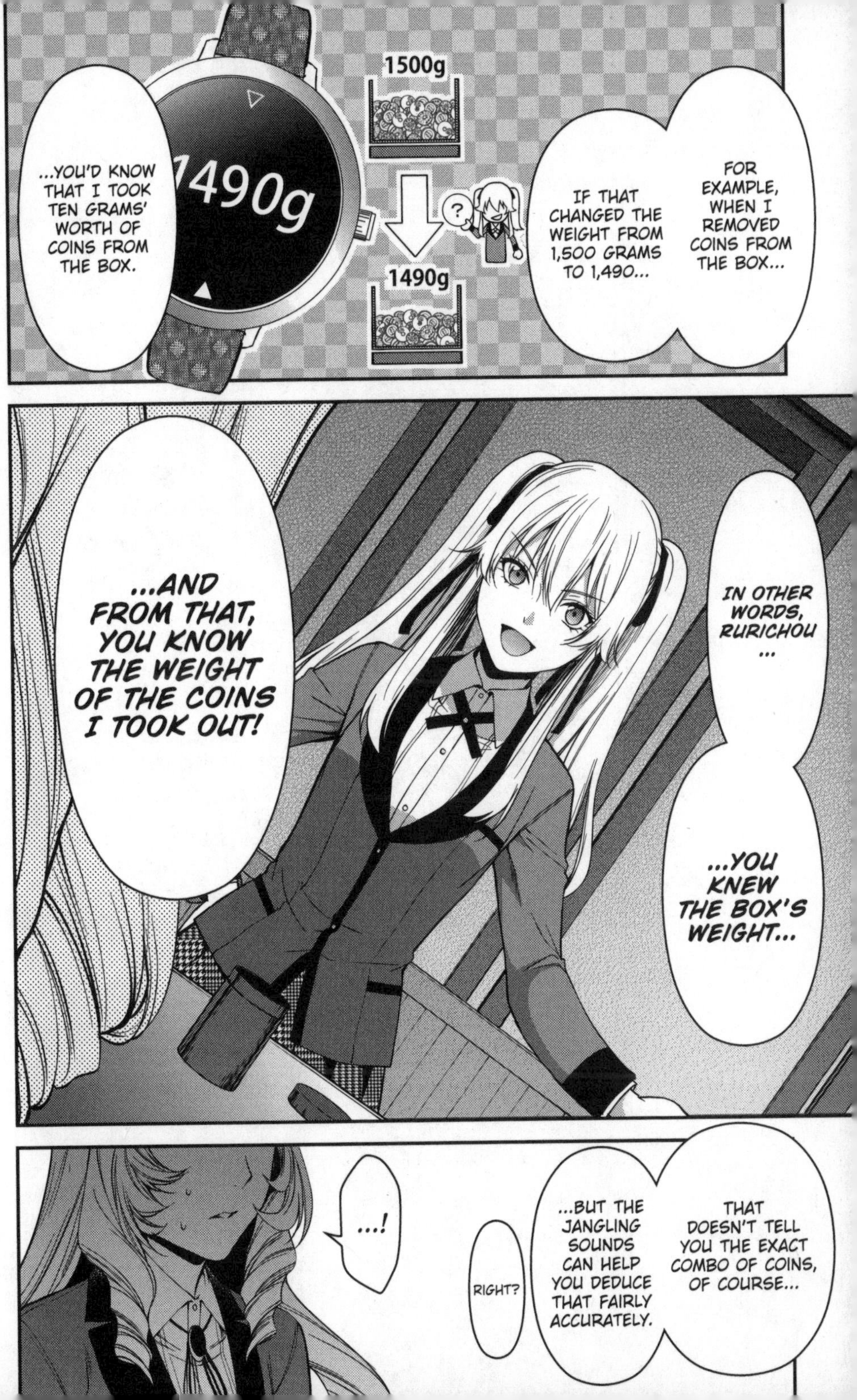
FOR EXAMPLE, WHEN I REMOVED COINS FROM THE BOX...
IF THAT CHANGED THE WEIGHT FROM 1,500 GRAMS TO 1,490...
1500g
?
1490g
1490g
...YOU'D KNOW THAT I TOOK TEN GRAMS' WORTH OF COINS FROM THE BOX.
IN OTHER WORDS, RURICHOU ...
...YOU KNEW THE BOX'S WEIGHT...
...AND FROM THAT, YOU KNOW THE WEIGHT OF THE COINS I TOOK OUT!
THAT DOESN'T TELL YOU THE EXACT COMBO OF COINS, OF COURSE...
...BUT THE JANGLING SOUNDS CAN HELP YOU DEDUCE THAT FAIRLY ACCURATELY.
RIGHT?
...!

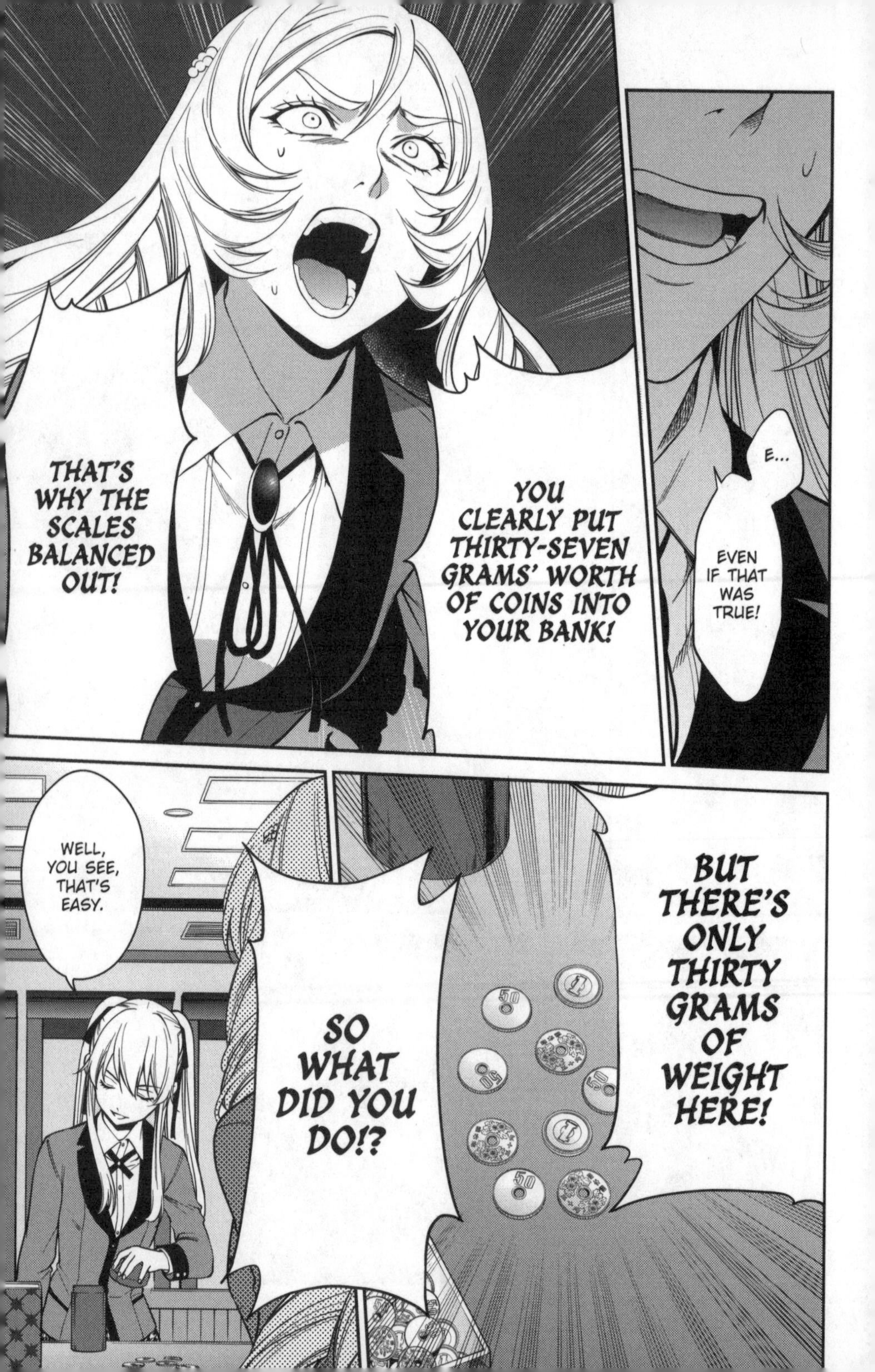
E...
EVEN IF THAT WAS TRUE!
YOU CLEARLY PUT THIRTY-SEVEN GRAMS' WORTH OF COINS INTO YOUR BANK!
THAT'S WHY THE SCALES BALANCED OUT!
BUT THERE'S ONLY THIRTY GRAMS OF WEIGHT HERE!
SO WHAT DID YOU DO!?
WELL, YOU SEE, THAT'S EASY.

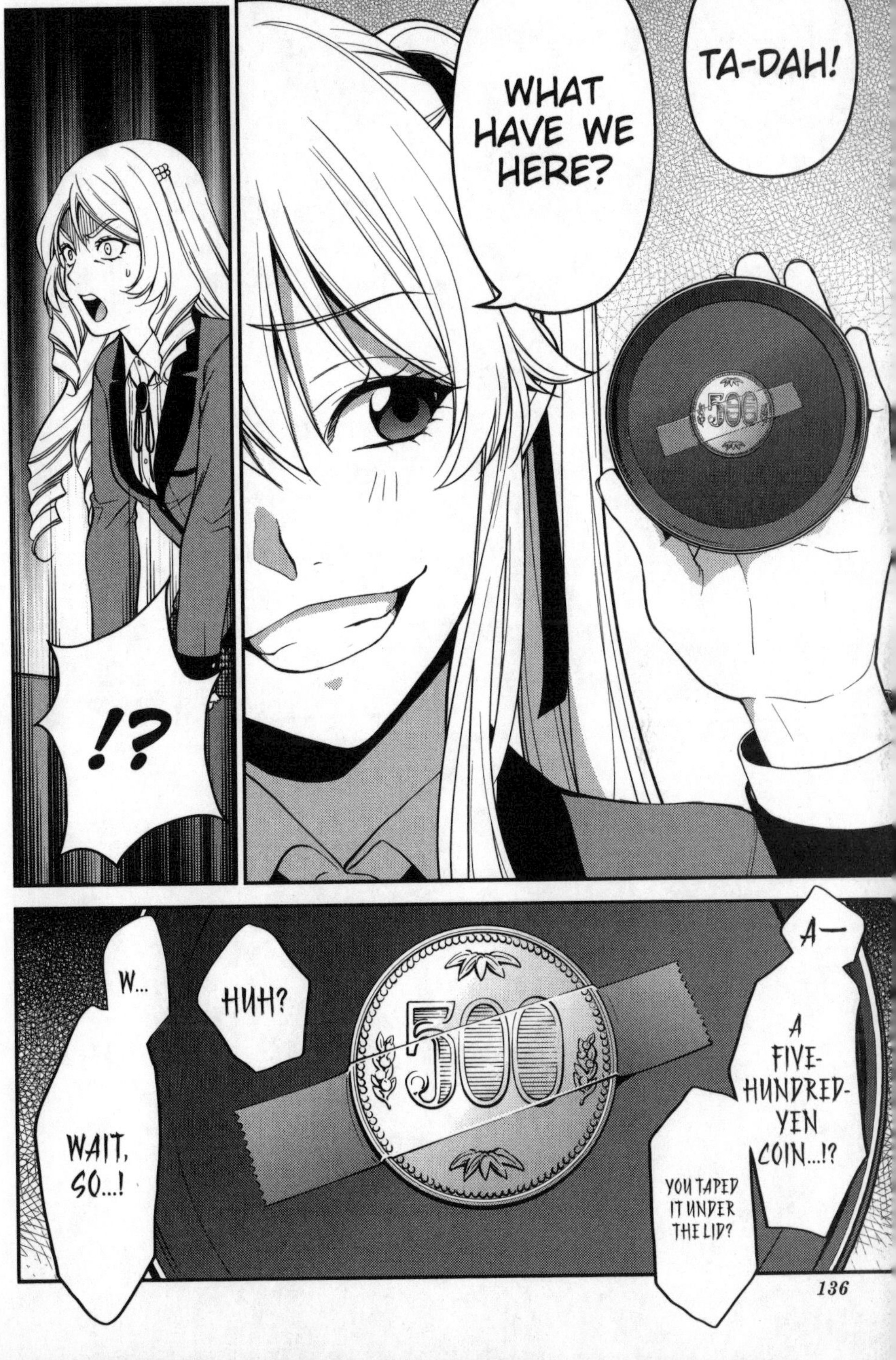

TA-DAH!
WHAT HAVE WE HERE?
!?
A—
A FIVE-HUNDRED-YEN COIN...!?
YOU TAPED IT UNDER THE LID?
HUH?
W...
WAIT, SO...!

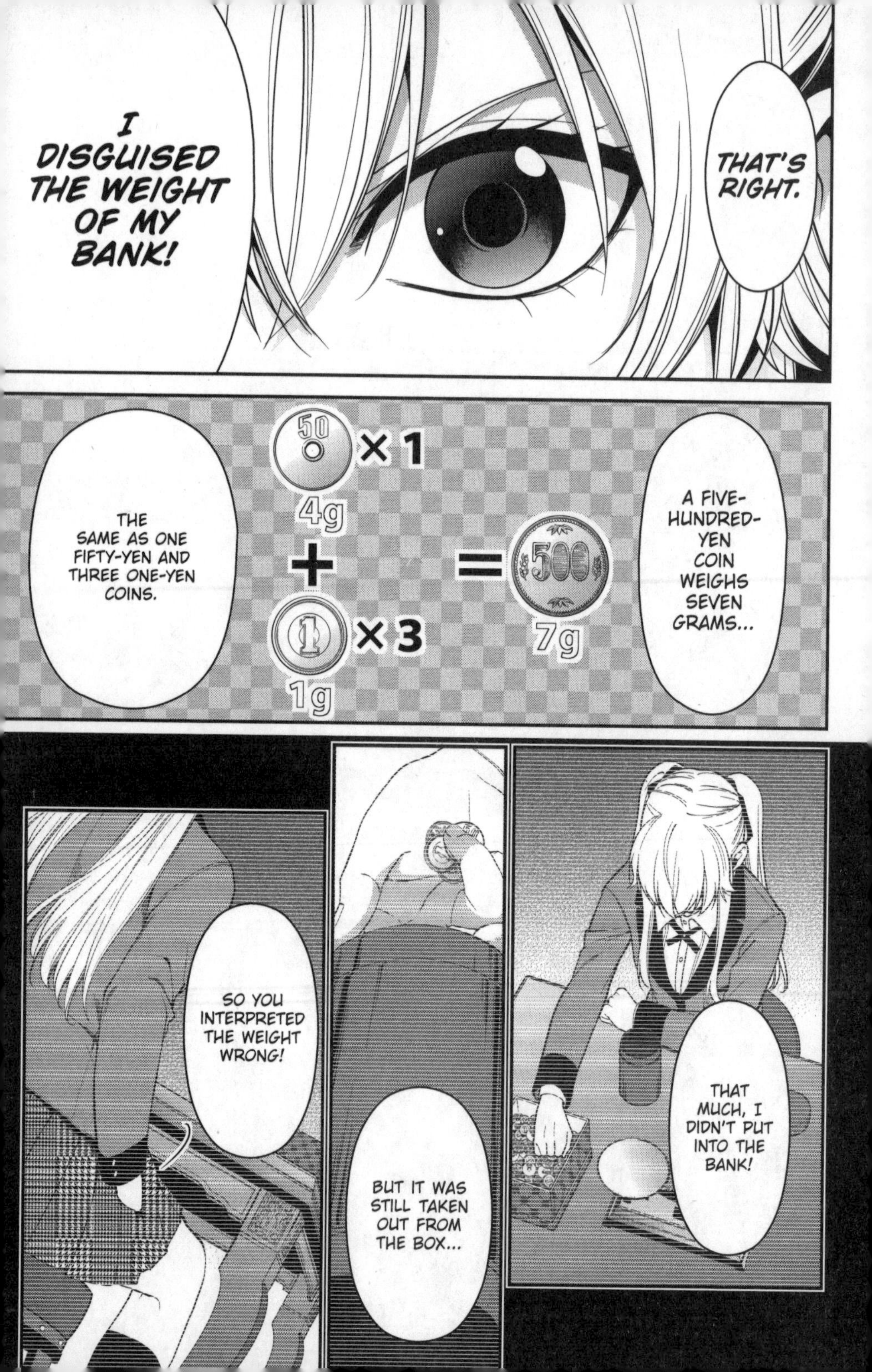
THAT'S RIGHT.
I DISGUISED THE WEIGHT OF MY BANK!
A FIVE-HUNDRED-YEN COIN WEIGHS SEVEN GRAMS...
× 1
4g
+
× 3
1g
=
7g
THE SAME AS ONE FIFTY-YEN AND THREE ONE-YEN COINS.
THAT MUCH, I DIDN'T PUT INTO THE BANK!
BUT IT WAS STILL TAKEN OUT FROM THE BOX...
SO YOU INTERPRETED THE WEIGHT WRONG!

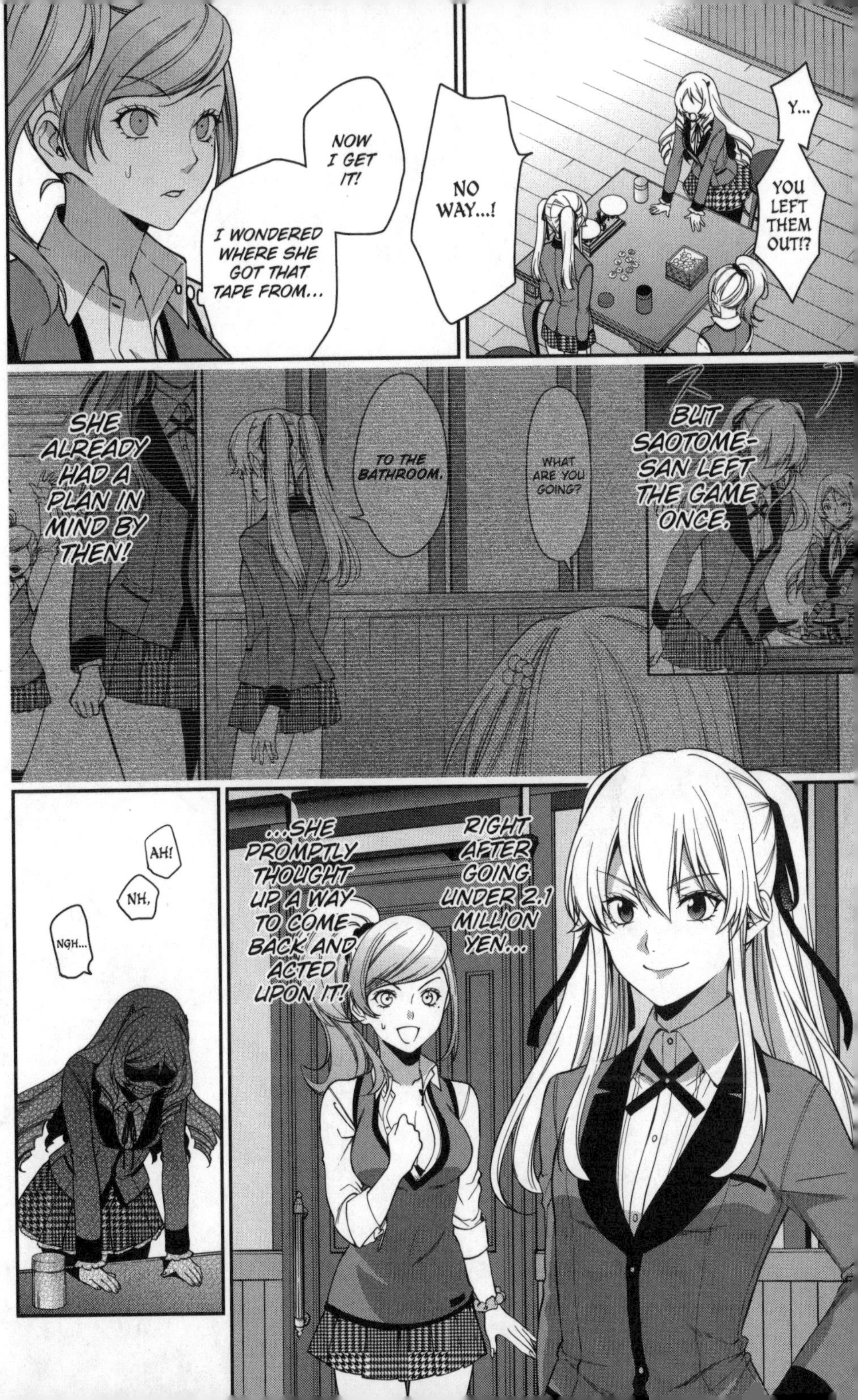
Y...
YOU LEFT THEM OUT!?
NO WAY...!
NOW I GET IT!
I WONDERED WHERE SHE GOT THAT TAPE FROM...
BUT SAOTOME-SAN LEFT THE GAME ONCE.
WHAT ARE YOU GOING?
TO THE BATHROOM.
SHE ALREADY HAD A PLAN IN MIND BY THEN!
RIGHT AFTER GOING UNDER 2.1 MILLION YEN...
...SHE PROMPTLY THOUGHT UP A WAY TO COME BACK AND ACTED UPON IT!
AH!
NH,
NGH...

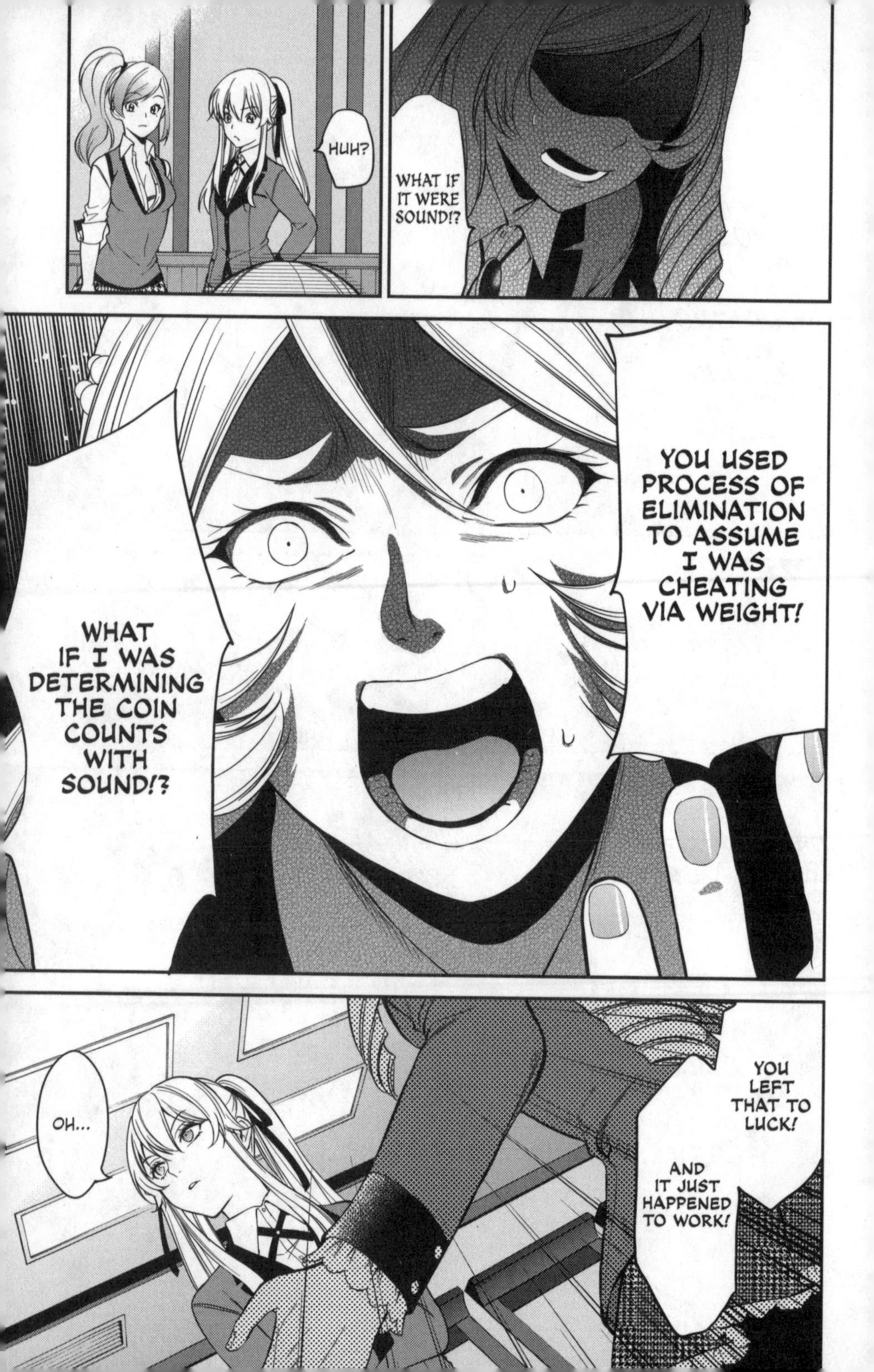
WHAT IF IT WERE SOUND!?
HUH?
YOU USED PROCESS OF ELIMINATION TO ASSUME I WAS CHEATING VIA WEIGHT!
WHAT IF I WAS DETERMINING THE COIN COUNTS WITH SOUND!?
YOU LEFT THAT TO LUCK!
AND IT JUST HAPPENED TO WORK!
OH...

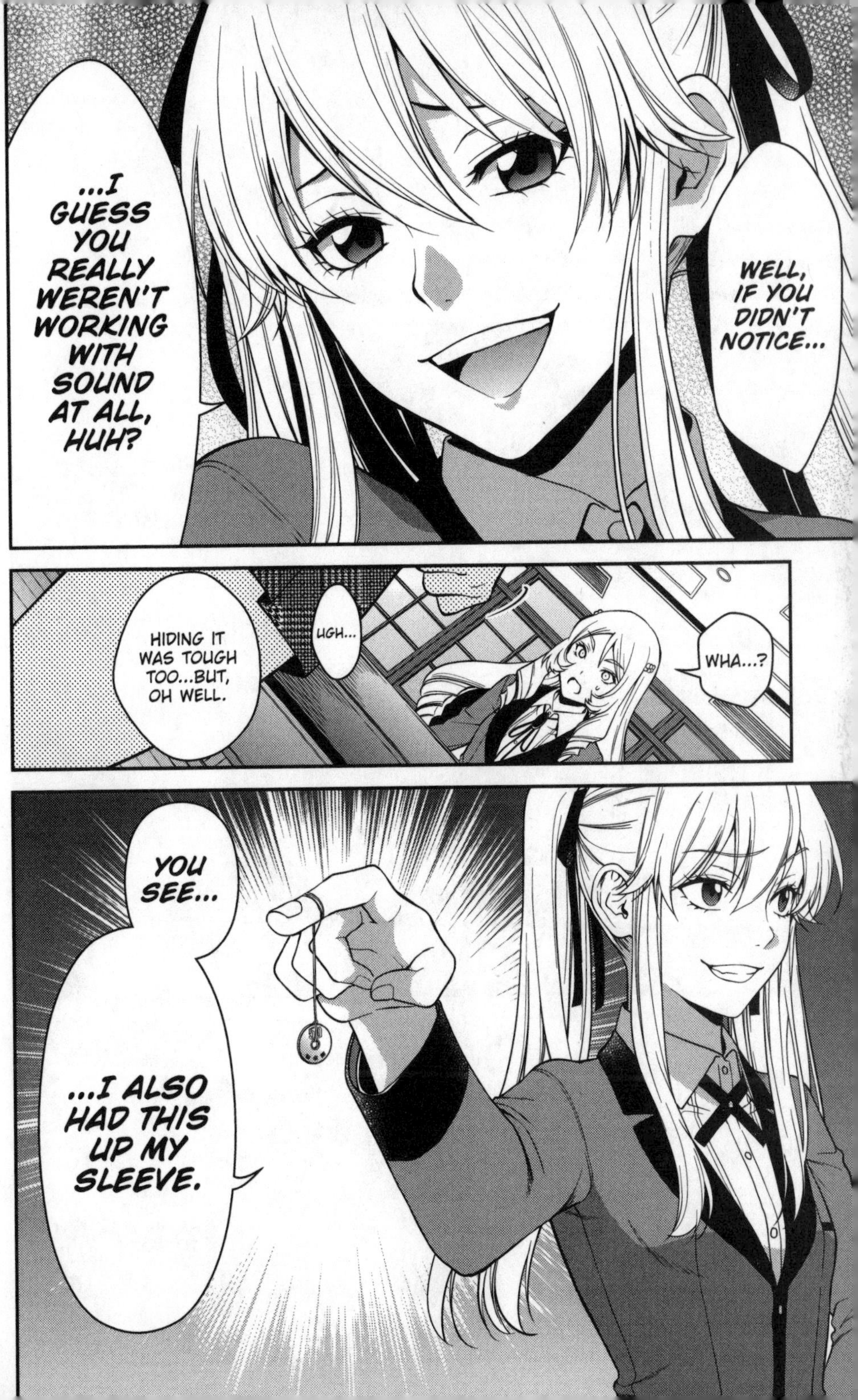
WELL, IF YOU DIDN'T NOTICE...
...I GUESS YOU REALLY WEREN'T WORKING WITH SOUND AT ALL, HUH?
WHA...?
UGH...
HIDING IT WAS TOUGH TOO...BUT, OH WELL.
YOU SEE...
...I ALSO HAD THIS UP MY SLEEVE.

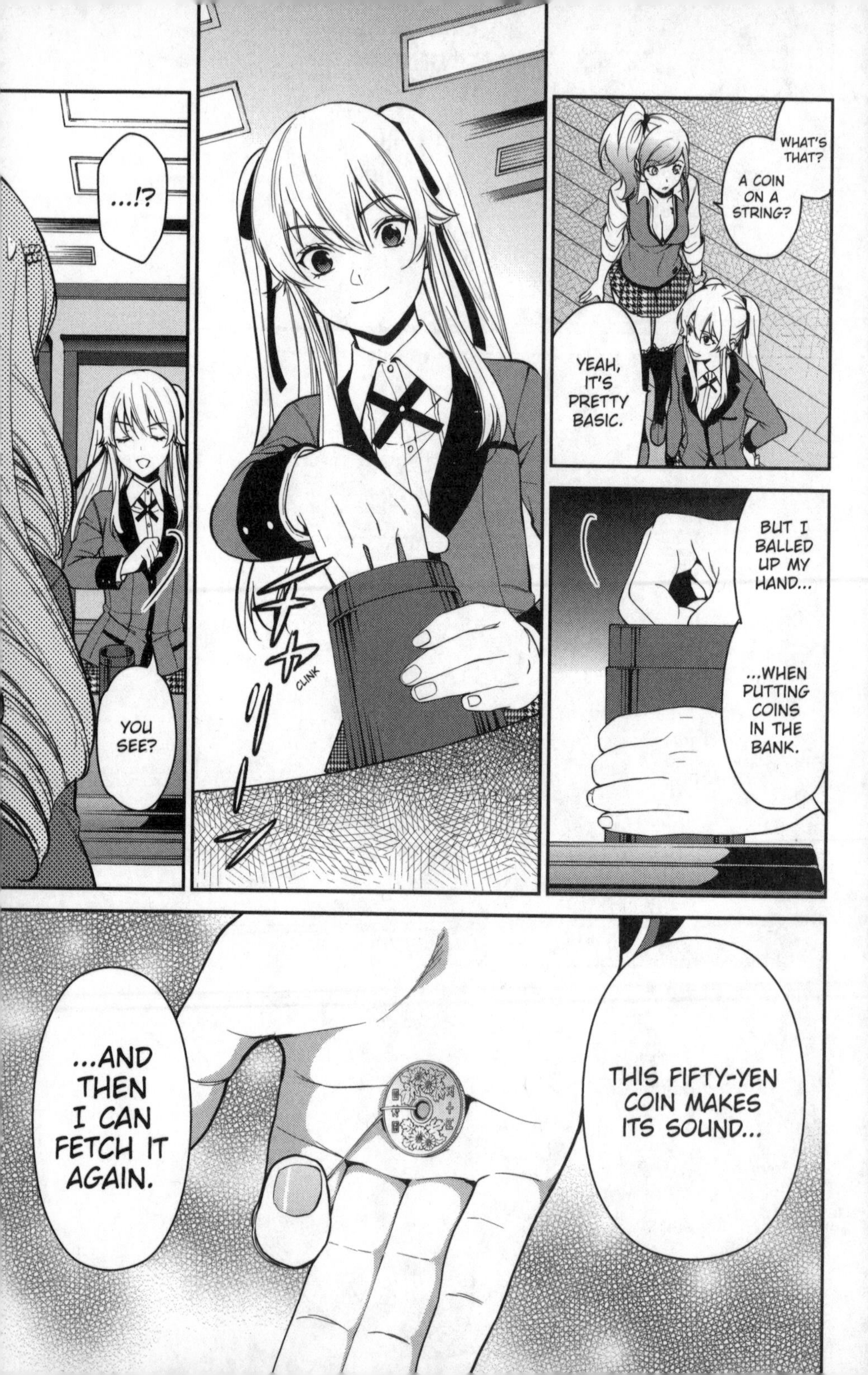
WHAT'S THAT? A COIN ON A STRING?
YEAH, IT'S PRETTY BASIC.
BUT I BALLED UP MY HAND...
...WHEN PUTTING COINS IN THE BANK.
CLINK
...!?
YOU SEE?
THIS FIFTY-YEN COIN MAKES ITS SOUND...
...AND THEN I CAN FETCH IT AGAIN.

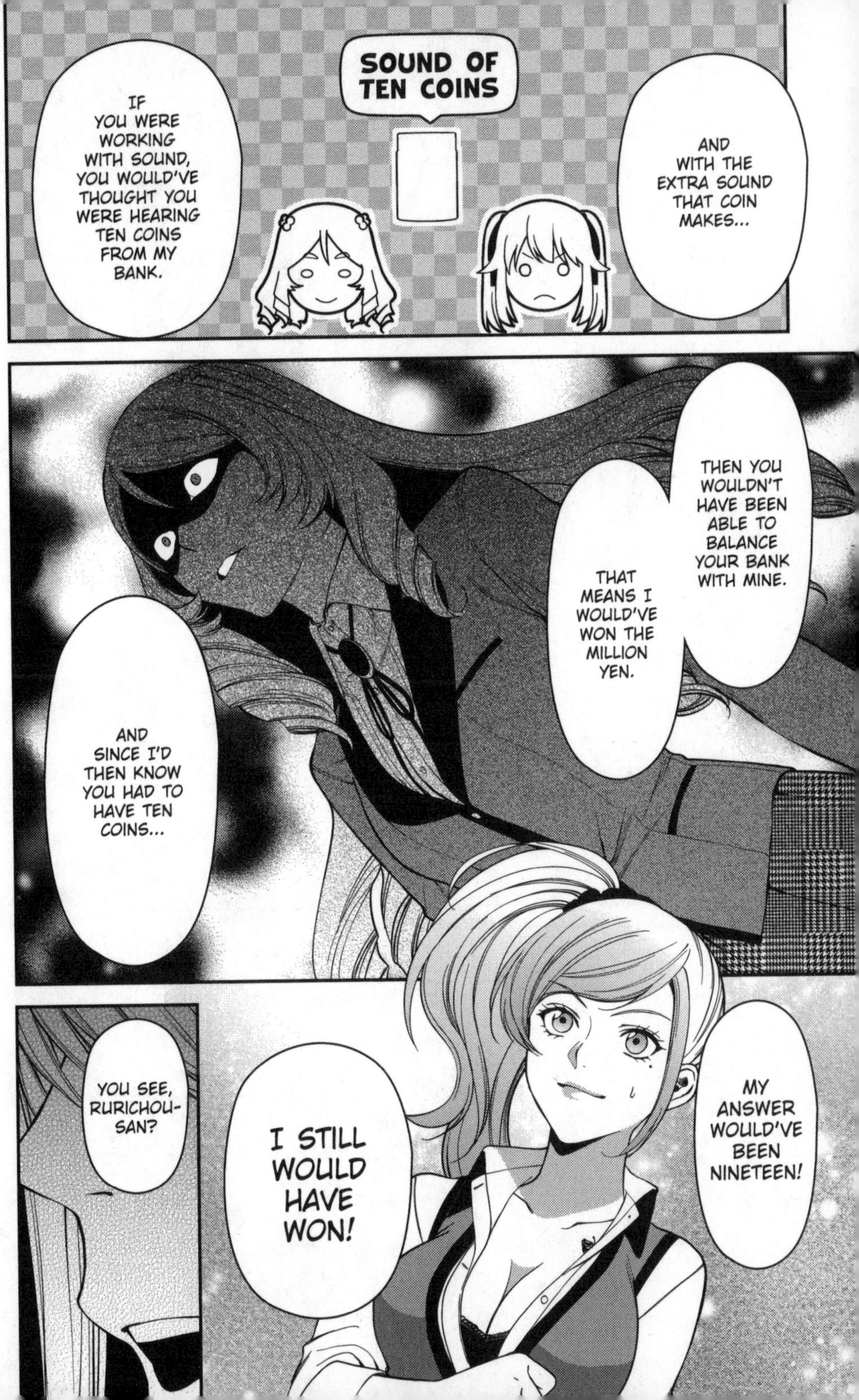
AND WITH THE EXTRA SOUND THAT COIN MAKES...
SOUND OF TEN COINS
IF YOU WERE WORKING WITH SOUND, YOU WOULD'VE THOUGHT YOU WERE HEARING TEN COINS FROM MY BANK.
THEN YOU WOULDN'T HAVE BEEN ABLE TO BALANCE YOUR BANK WITH MINE.
THAT MEANS I WOULD'VE WON THE MILLION YEN.
AND SINCE I'D THEN KNOW YOU HAD TO HAVE TEN COINS...
MY ANSWER WOULD'VE BEEN NINETEEN!
I STILL WOULD HAVE WON!
YOU SEE, RURICHOU-SAN?

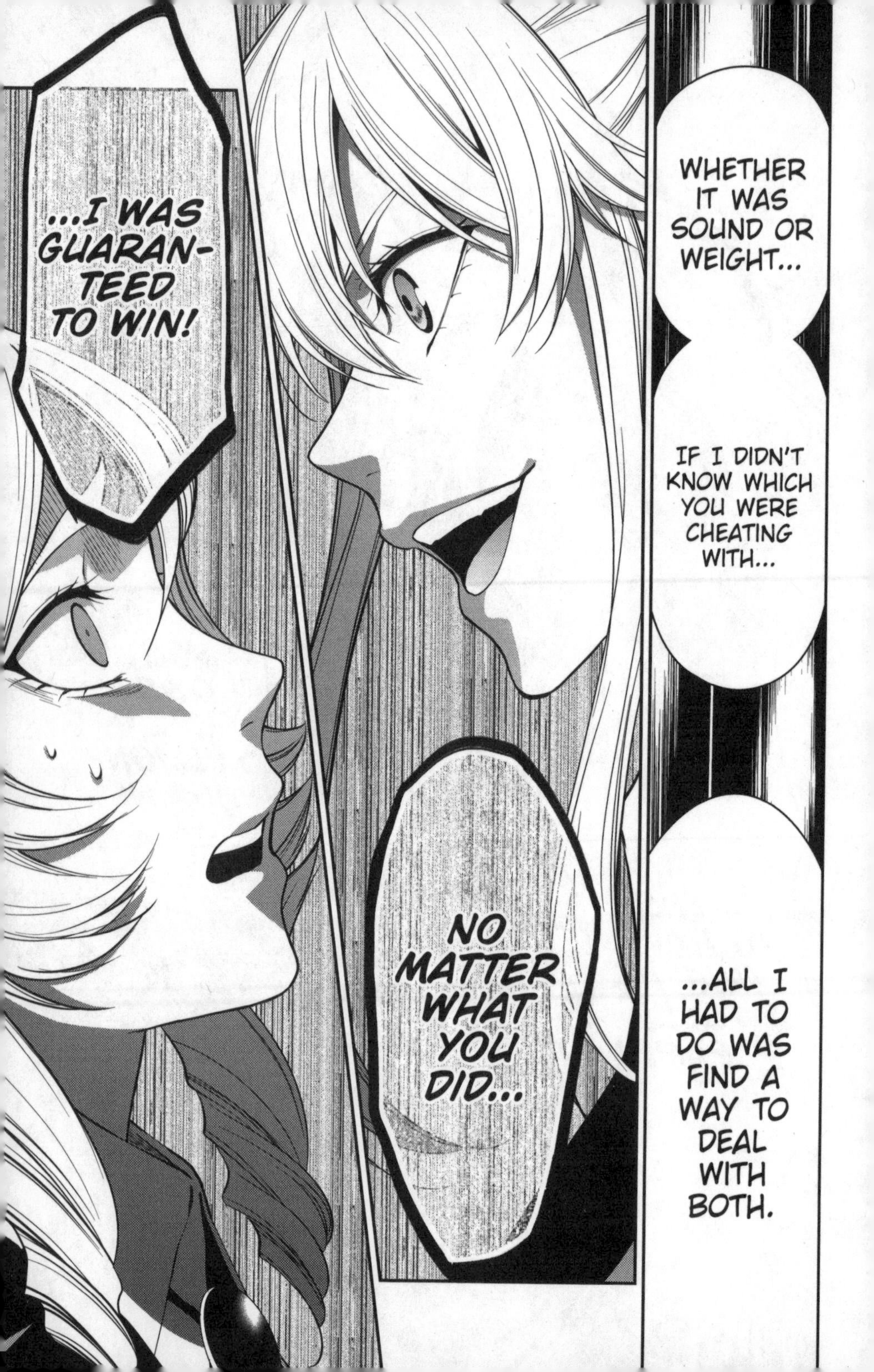
WHETHER IT WAS SOUND OR WEIGHT...
IF I DIDN'T KNOW WHICH YOU WERE CHEATING WITH...
...ALL I HAD TO DO WAS FIND A WAY TO DEAL WITH BOTH.
NO MATTER WHAT YOU DID...
...I WAS GUARAN-TEED TO WIN!

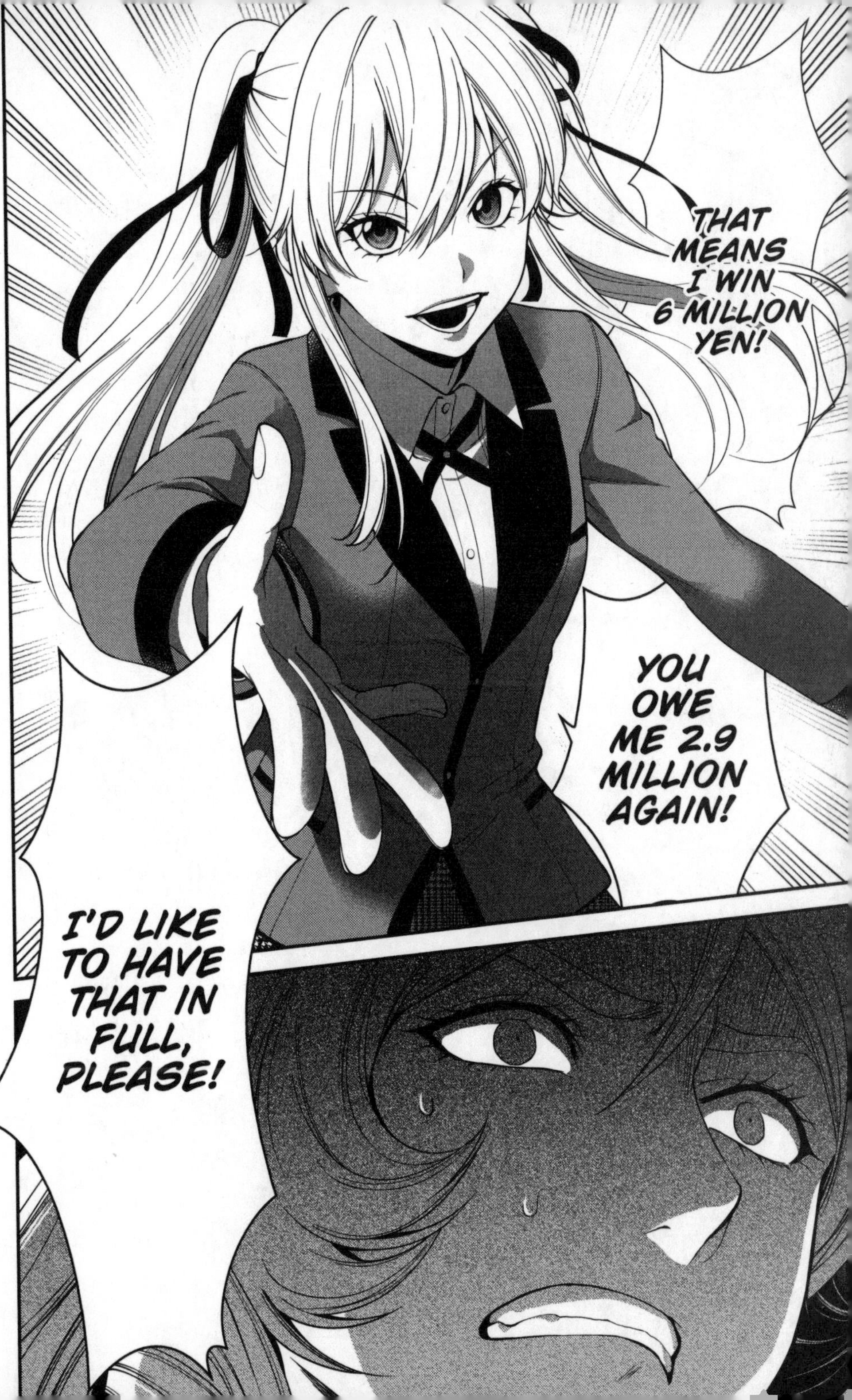
THAT MEANS I WIN 6 MILLION YEN!
YOU OWE ME 2.9 MILLION AGAIN!
I'D LIKE TO HAVE THAT IN FULL, PLEASE!

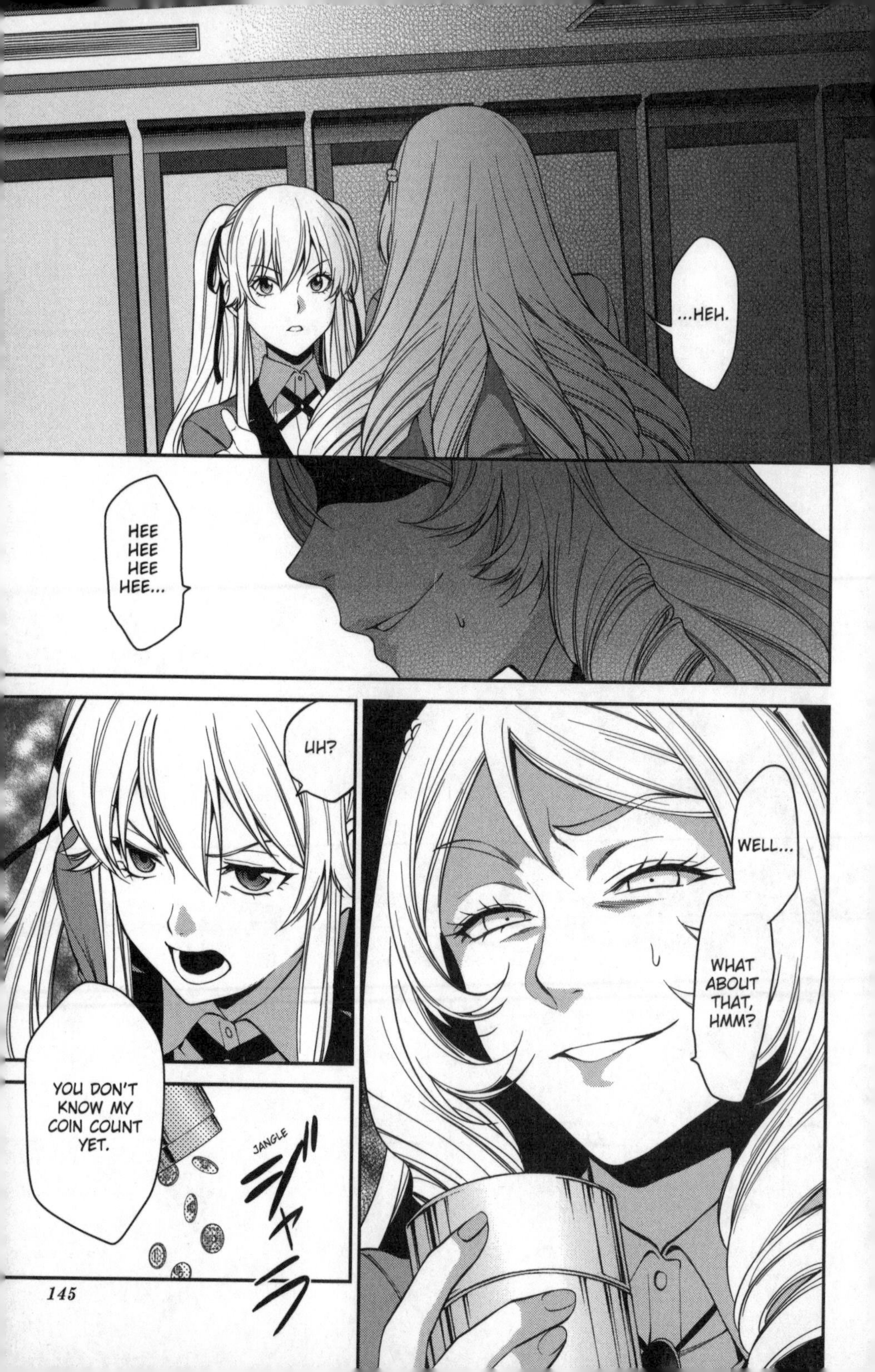
...HEH.
HEE HEE HEE HEE...
WELL...
WHAT ABOUT THAT, HMM?
UH?
YOU DON'T KNOW MY COIN COUNT YET.
JANGLE

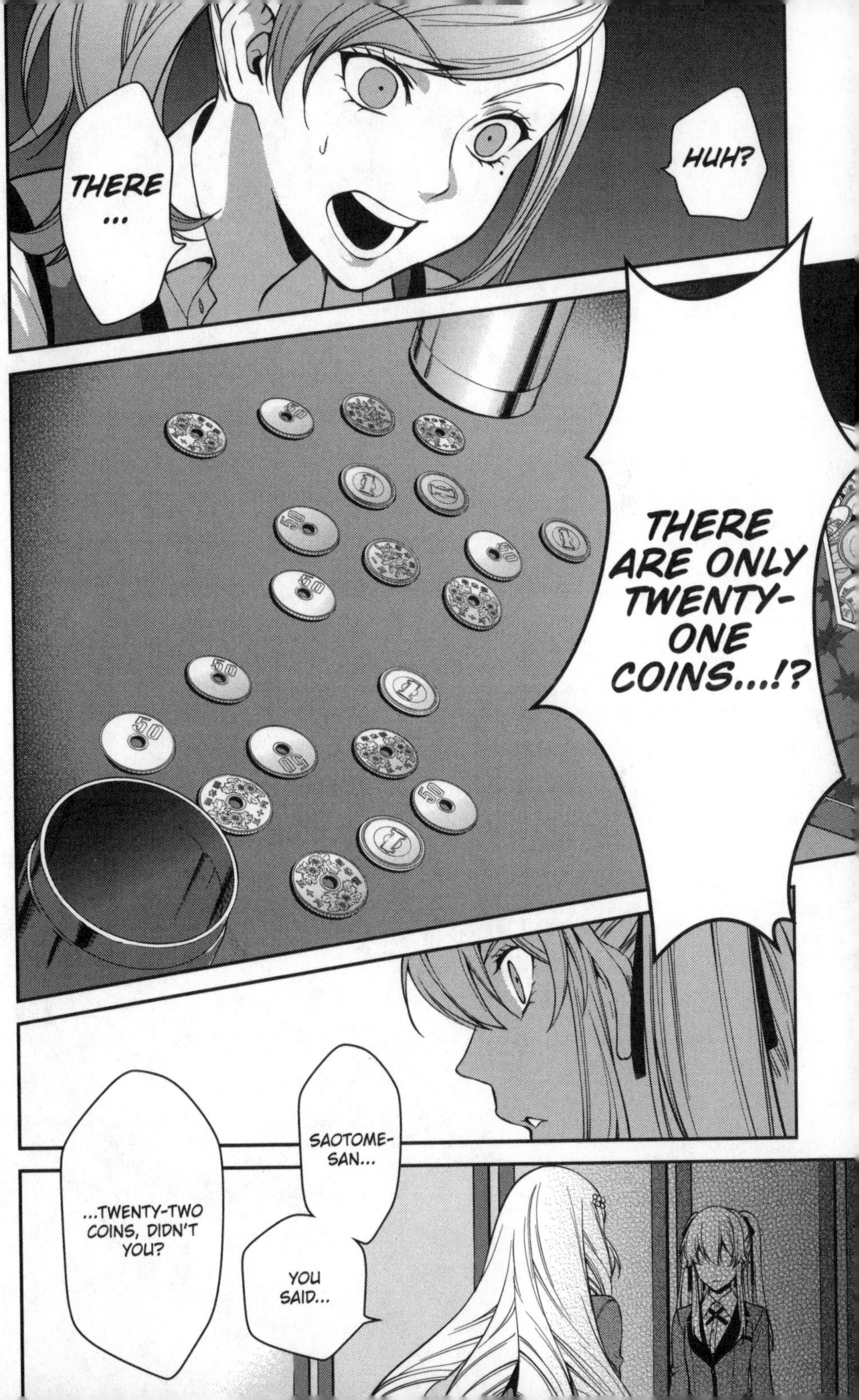
HUH?
THERE ...
THERE ARE ONLY TWENTY-ONE COINS...!?
SAOTOME-SAN...
YOU SAID...
...TWENTY-TWO COINS, DIDN'T YOU?

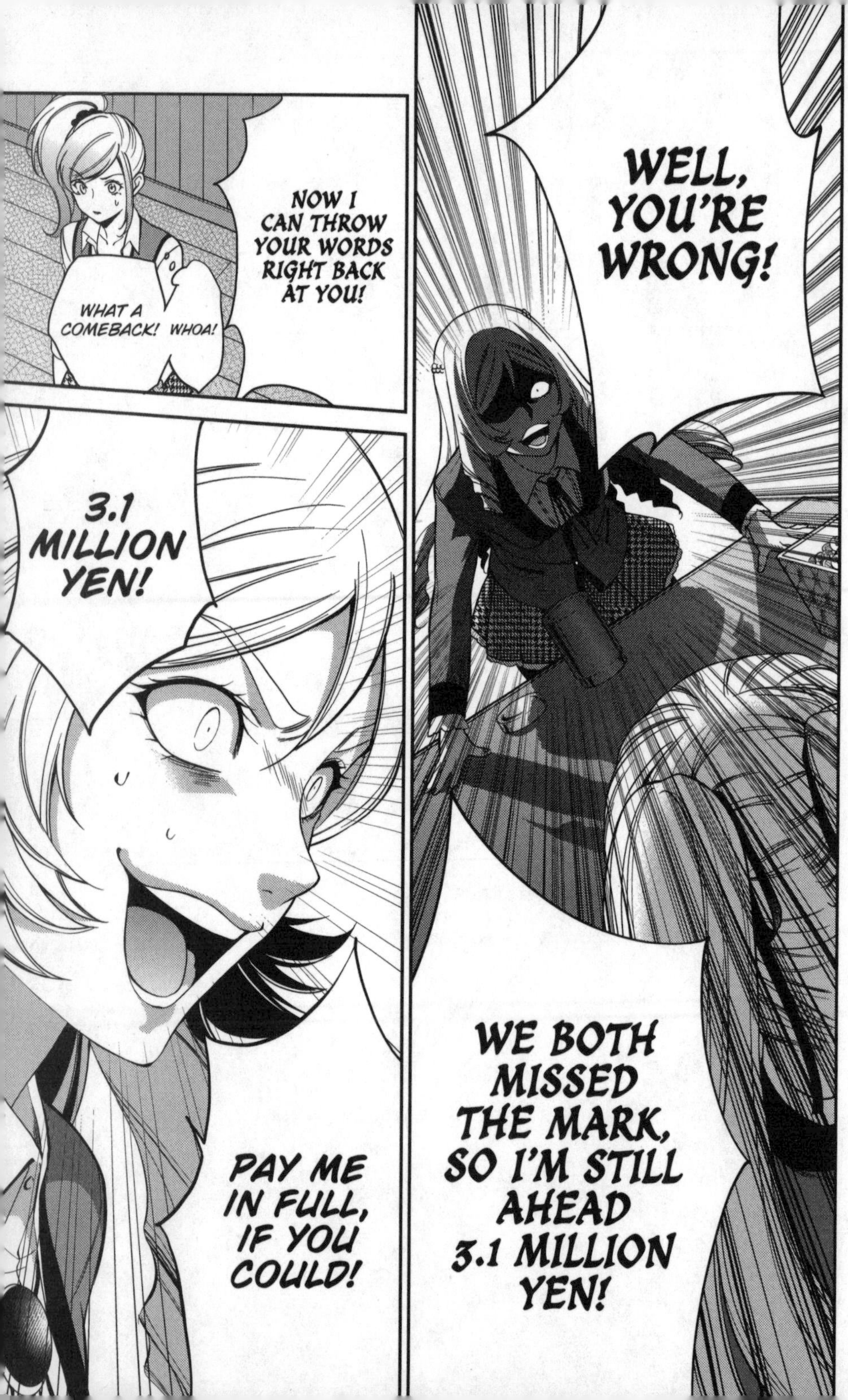
WELL, YOU'RE WRONG!
WE BOTH MISSED THE MARK, SO I'M STILL AHEAD 3.1 MILLION YEN!
NOW I CAN THROW YOUR WORDS RIGHT BACK AT YOU!
WHOA!
WHAT A COMEBACK!
3.1 MILLION YEN!
PAY ME IN FULL, IF YOU COULD!

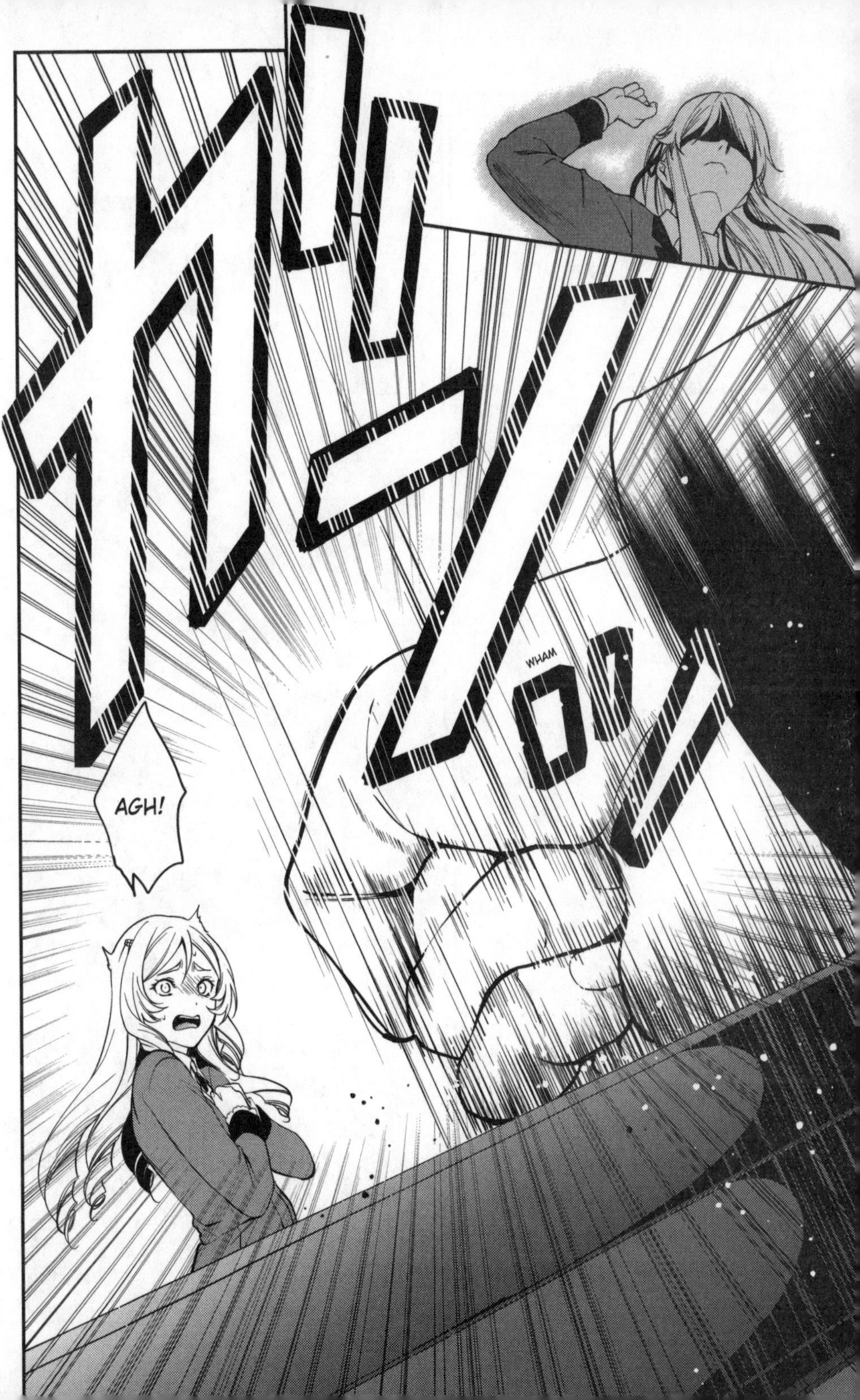
WHAM
AGH!

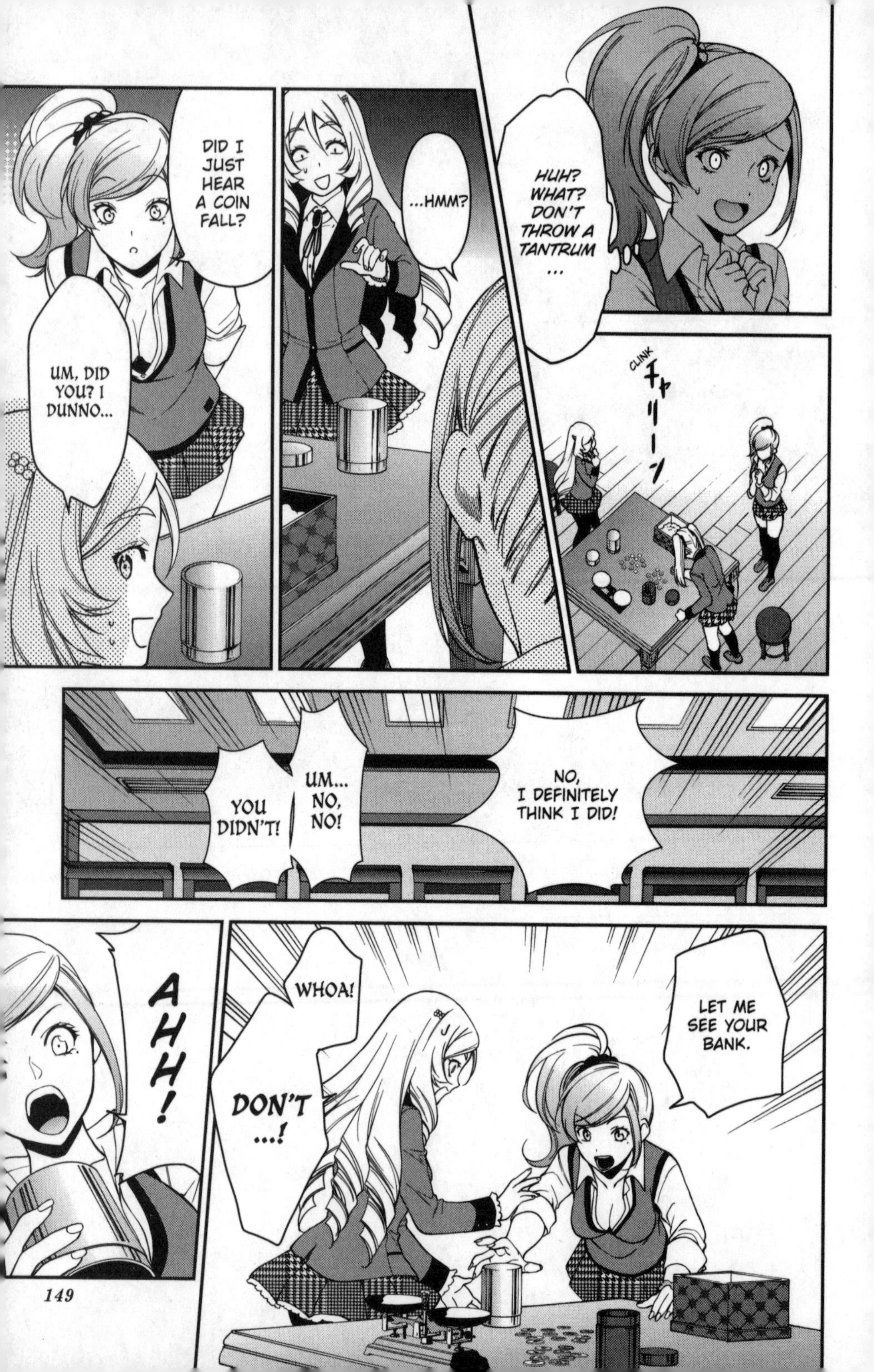
HUH? WHAT? DON'T THROW A TANTRUM ...
CLINK
チャリーン
...HMM?
DID I JUST HEAR A COIN FALL?
UM, DID YOU? I DUNNO...
NO, I DEFINITELY THINK I DID!
UM... NO, NO!
YOU DIDN'T!
LET ME SEE YOUR BANK.
WHOA!
DON'T ...!
AHH!

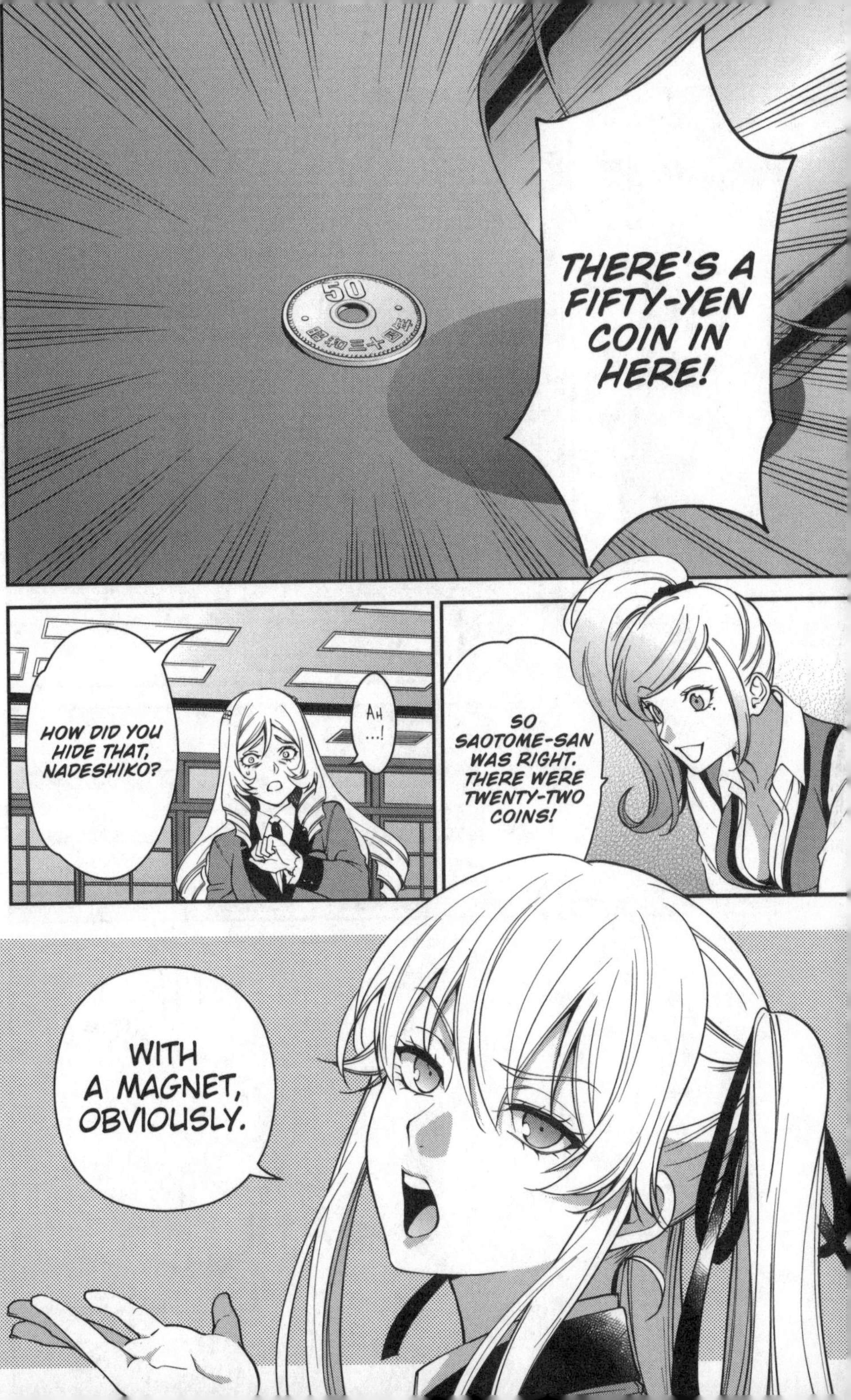
THERE'S A FIFTY-YEN COIN IN HERE!
50
SO SAOTOME-SAN WAS RIGHT. THERE WERE TWENTY-TWO COINS!
AH ...!
HOW DID YOU HIDE THAT, NADESHIKO?
WITH A MAGNET, OBVIOUSLY.

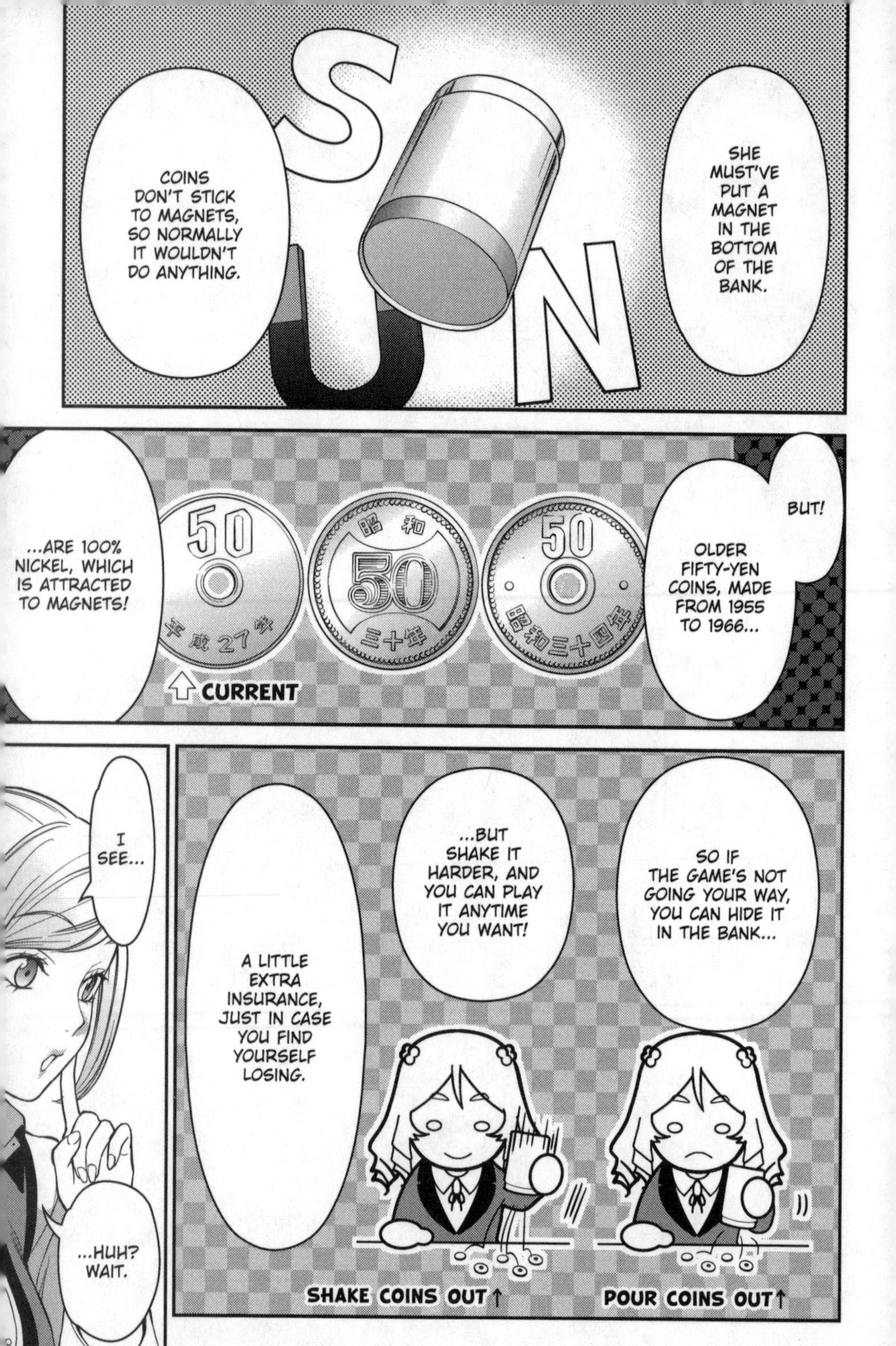
SHE MUST'VE PUT A MAGNET IN THE BOTTOM OF THE BANK.
SUN
COINS DON'T STICK TO MAGNETS, SO NORMALLY IT WOULDN'T DO ANYTHING.
BUT!
OLDER FIFTY-YEN COINS, MADE FROM 1955 TO 1966...
50
昭和三十四年
昭和
50
三十年
50
平成27年
↑ CURRENT
...ARE 100% NICKEL, WHICH IS ATTRACTED TO MAGNETS!
SO IF THE GAME'S NOT GOING YOUR WAY, YOU CAN HIDE IT IN THE BANK...
...BUT SHAKE IT HARDER, AND YOU CAN PLAY IT ANYTIME YOU WANT!
A LITTLE EXTRA INSURANCE, JUST IN CASE YOU FIND YOURSELF LOSING.
POUR COINS OUT↑
SHAKE COINS OUT↑
I SEE...
...HUH? WAIT.

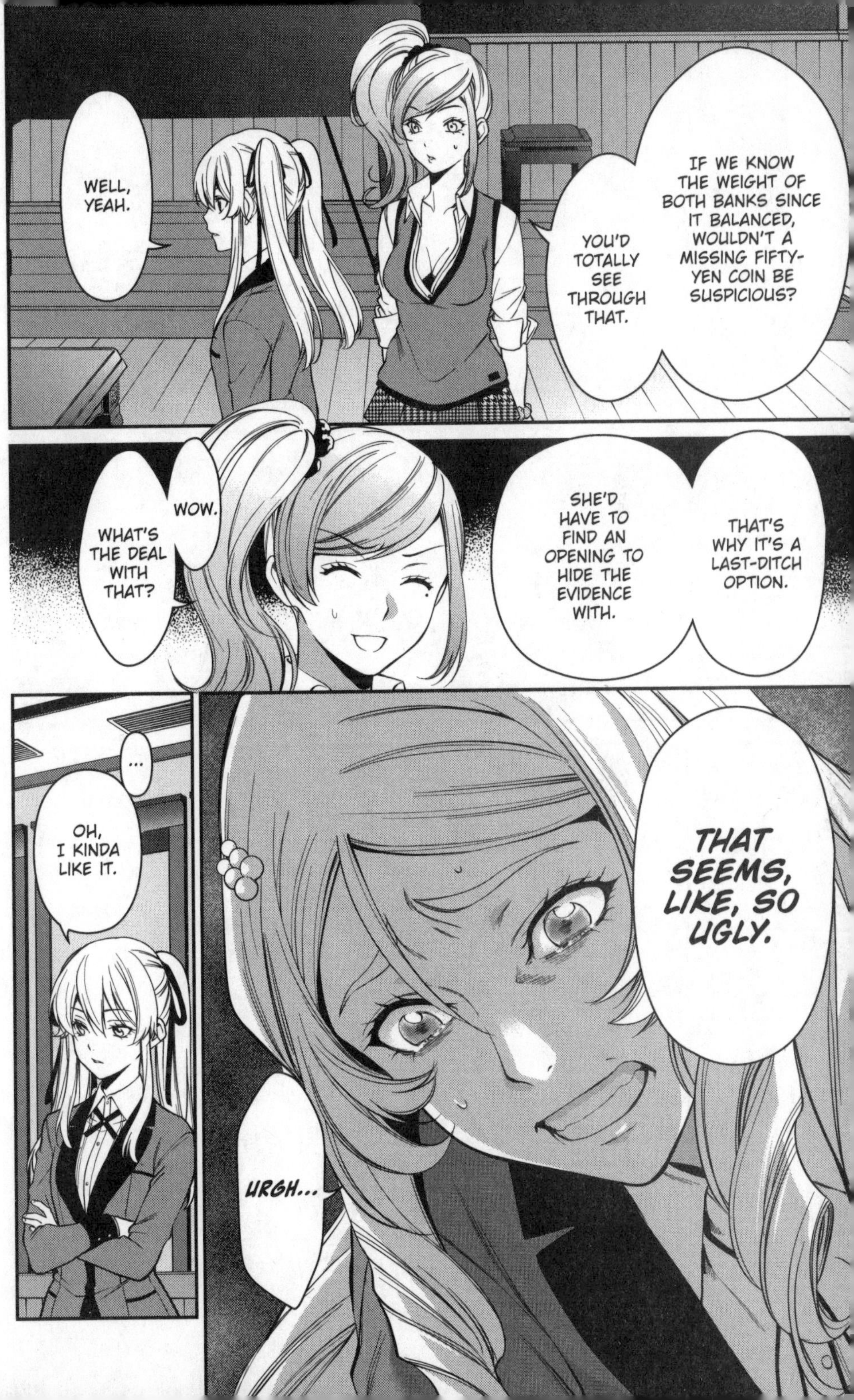
IF WE KNOW THE WEIGHT OF BOTH BANKS SINCE IT BALANCED, WOULDN'T A MISSING FIFTY-YEN COIN BE SUSPICIOUS?
YOU'D TOTALLY SEE THROUGH THAT.
WELL, YEAH.
THAT'S WHY IT'S A LAST-DITCH OPTION.
SHE'D HAVE TO FIND AN OPENING TO HIDE THE EVIDENCE WITH.
WOW.
WHAT'S THE DEAL WITH THAT?
THAT SEEMS, LIKE, SO UGLY.
URGH...
...
OH, I KINDA LIKE IT.

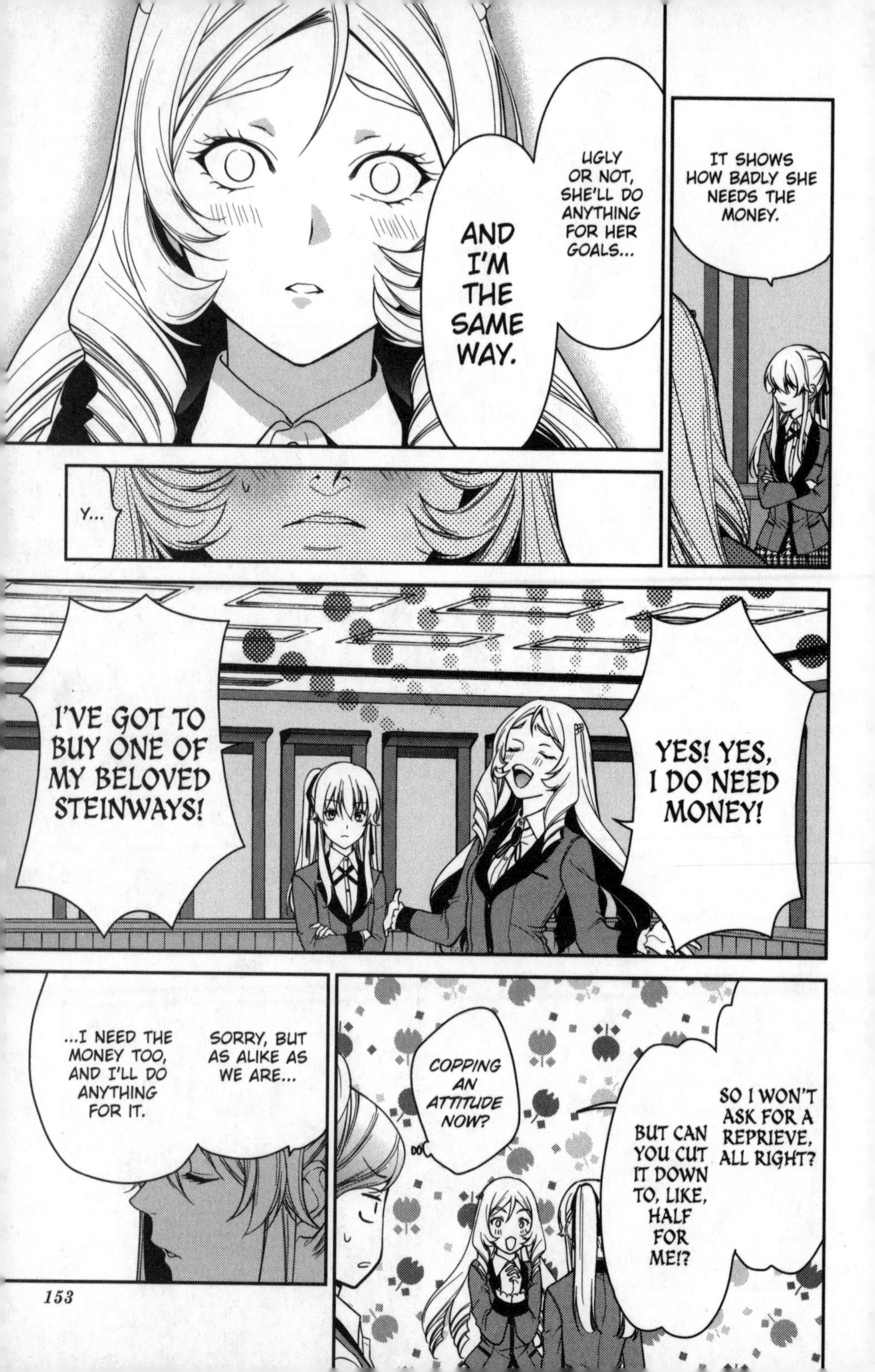
IT SHOWS HOW BADLY SHE NEEDS THE MONEY.
UGLY OR NOT, SHE'LL DO ANYTHING FOR HER GOALS...
AND I'M THE SAME WAY.
Y...
YES! YES, I DO NEED MONEY!
I'VE GOT TO BUY ONE OF MY BELOVED STEINWAYS!
SO I WON'T ASK FOR A REPRIEVE, ALL RIGHT?
BUT CAN YOU CUT IT DOWN TO, LIKE, HALF FOR ME!?
COPPING AN ATTITUDE NOW?
SORRY, BUT AS ALIKE AS WE ARE...
...I NEED THE MONEY TOO, AND I'LL DO ANYTHING FOR IT.

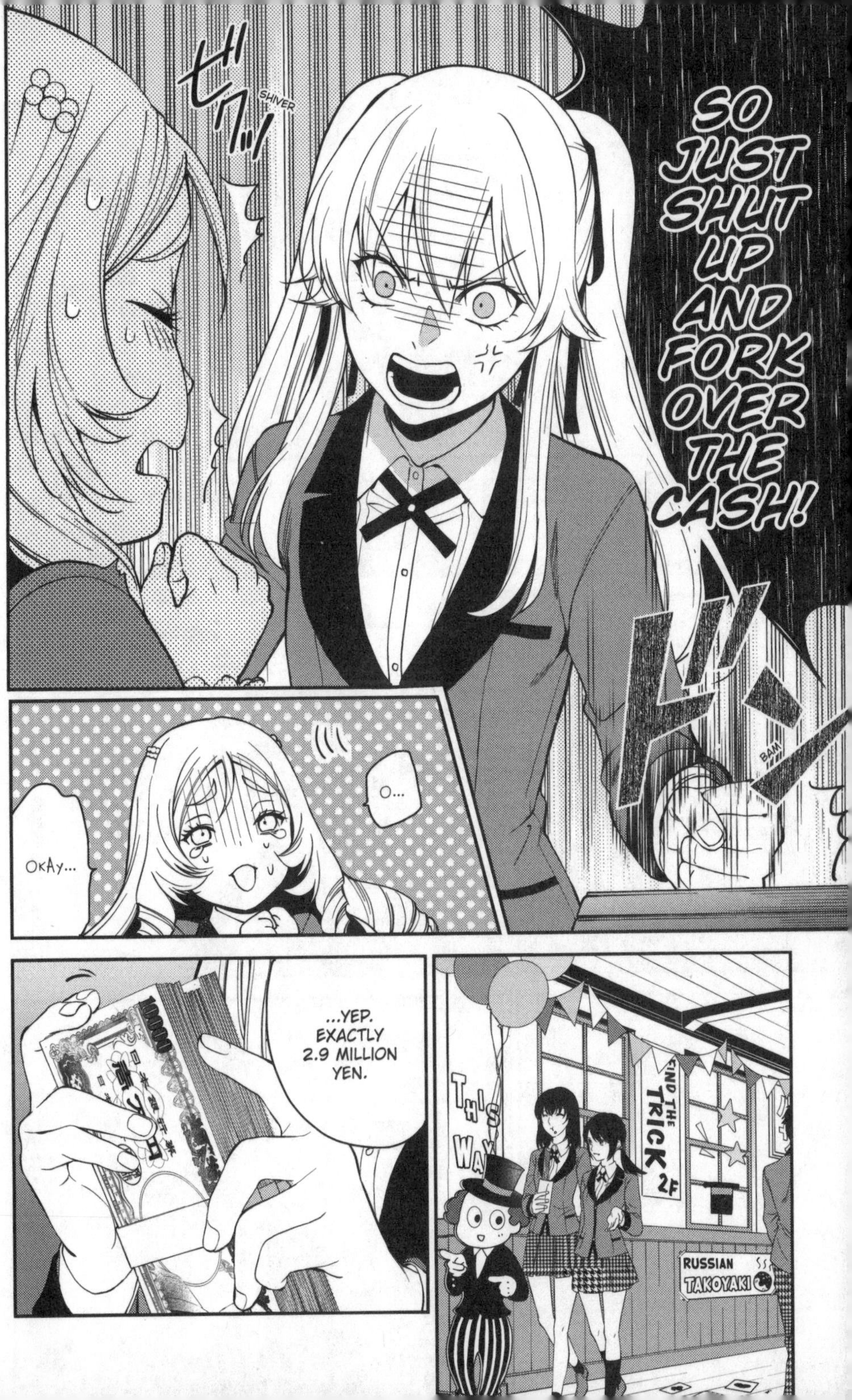
SO JUST SHUT UP AND FORK OVER THE CASH!
ゾクッ
SHIVER
BAM
O...
OKAY...
THIS WAY
FIND THE TRICK 2F
RUSSIAN TAKOYAKI
...YEP. EXACTLY 2.9 MILLION YEN.

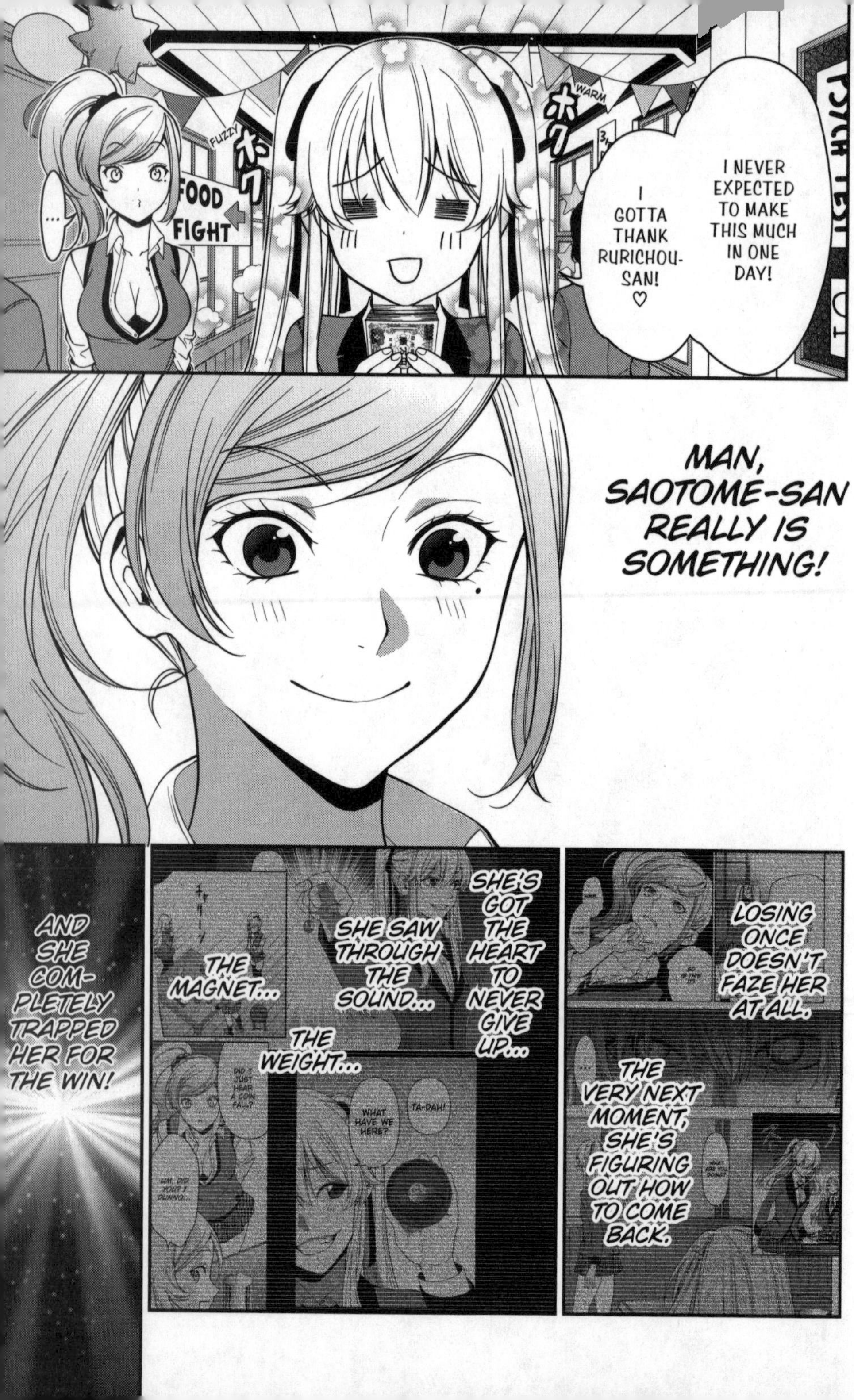
I NEVER EXPECTED TO MAKE THIS MUCH IN ONE DAY!
I GOTTA THANK RURICHOU-SAN! ♡
WARM
FUZZY
FOOD FIGHT
...
MAN, SAOTOME-SAN REALLY IS SOMETHING!
LOSING ONCE DOESN'T FAZE HER AT ALL.
THE VERY NEXT MOMENT, SHE'S FIGURING OUT HOW TO COME BACK.
SHE'S GOT THE HEART TO NEVER GIVE UP...
SHE SAW THROUGH THE SOUND...
THE MAGNET...
THE WEIGHT...
TA-DAH!
WHAT HAVE WE HERE?
DID I JUST HEAR A COIN FALL?
AND SHE COMPLETELY TRAPPED HER FOR THE WIN!

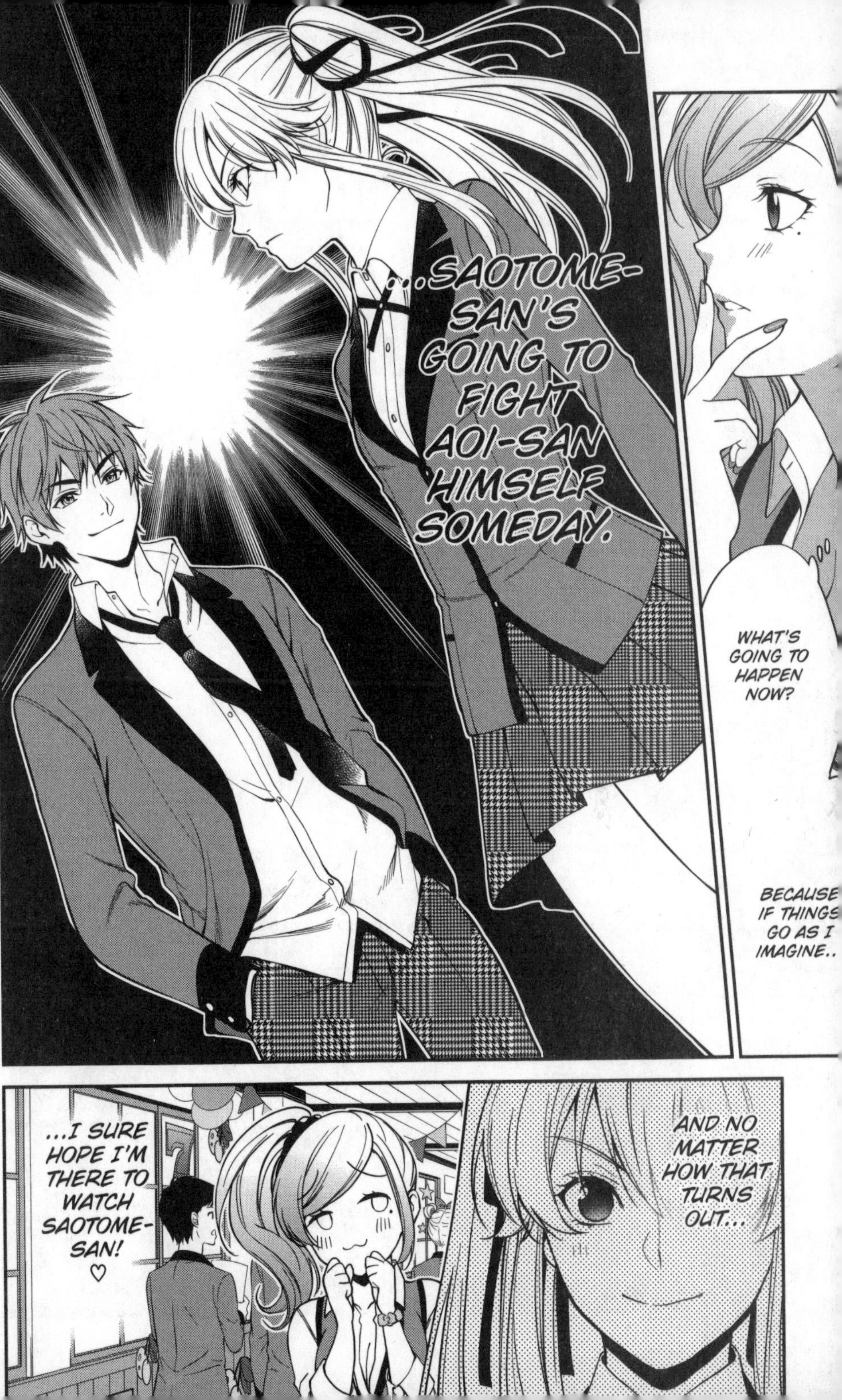
WHAT'S GOING TO HAPPEN NOW?
BECAUSE IF THINGS GO AS I IMAGINE...
...SAOTOME-SAN'S GOING TO FIGHT AOI-SAN HIMSELF SOMEDAY.
AND NO MATTER HOW THAT TURNS OUT...
...I SURE HOPE I'M THERE TO WATCH SAOTOME-SAN! ♡

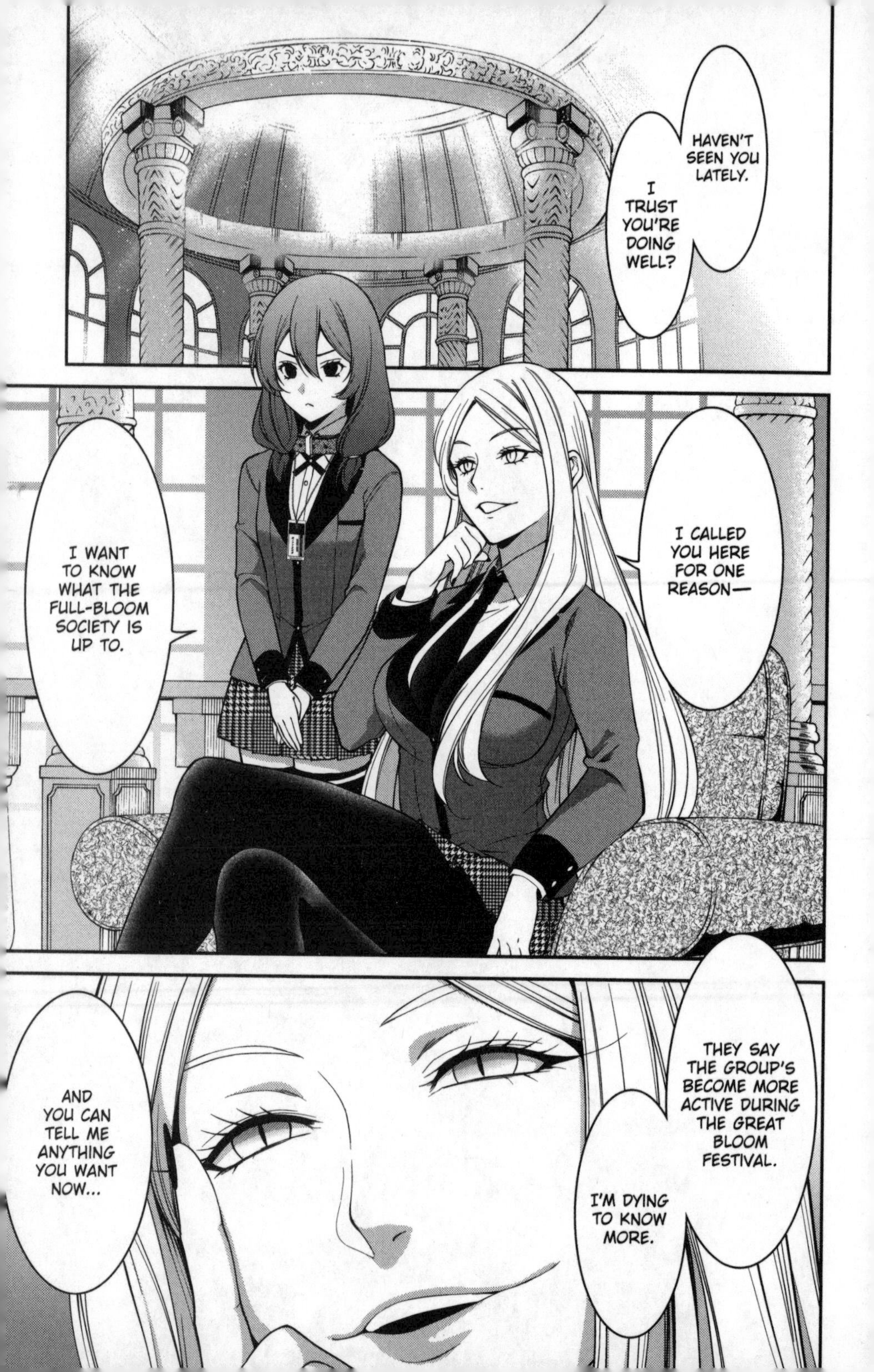
HAVEN'T SEEN YOU LATELY.
I TRUST YOU'RE DOING WELL?
I CALLED YOU HERE FOR ONE REASON—
I WANT TO KNOW WHAT THE FULL-BLOOM SOCIETY IS UP TO.
THEY SAY THE GROUP'S BECOME MORE ACTIVE DURING THE GREAT BLOOM FESTIVAL.
I'M DYING TO KNOW MORE.
AND YOU CAN TELL ME ANYTHING YOU WANT NOW...

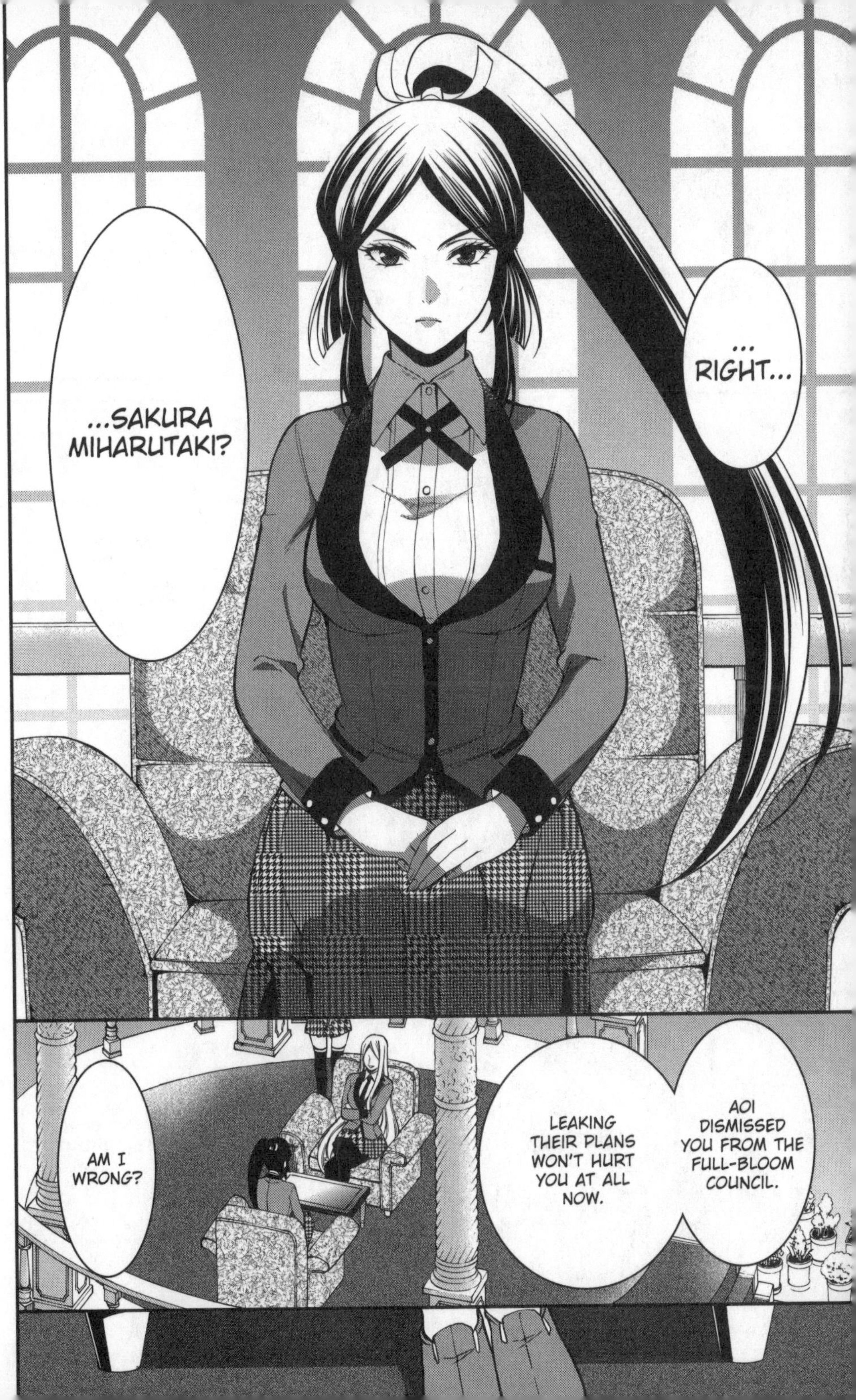
... RIGHT...
...SAKURA MIHARUTAKI?
AOI DISMISSED YOU FROM THE FULL-BLOOM COUNCIL.
LEAKING THEIR PLANS WON'T HURT YOU AT ALL NOW.
AM I WRONG?

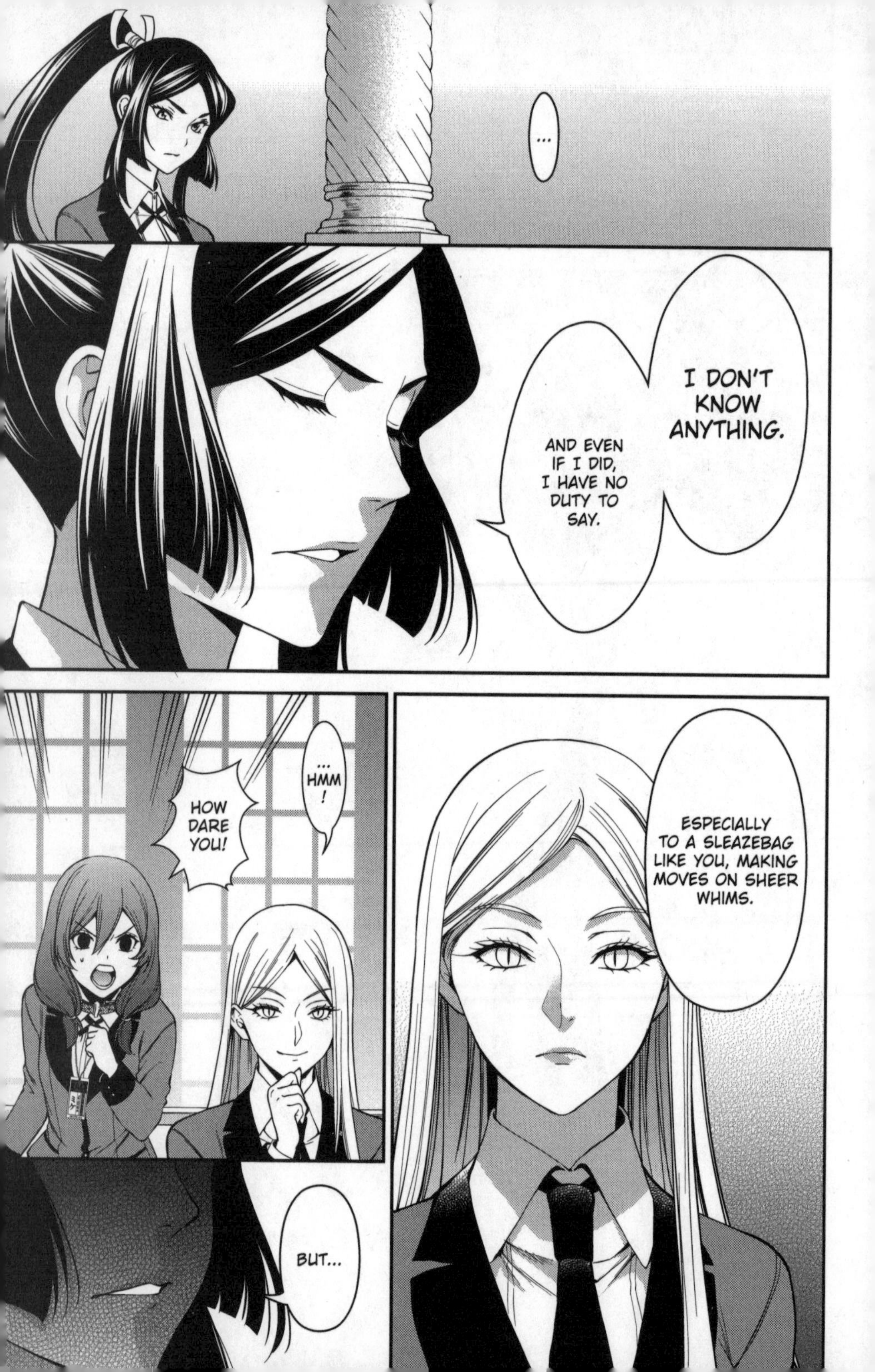
...
I DON'T KNOW ANYTHING.
AND EVEN IF I DID, I HAVE NO DUTY TO SAY.
ESPECIALLY TO A SLEAZEBAG LIKE YOU, MAKING MOVES ON SHEER WHIMS.
...HMM!
HOW DARE YOU!
BUT...

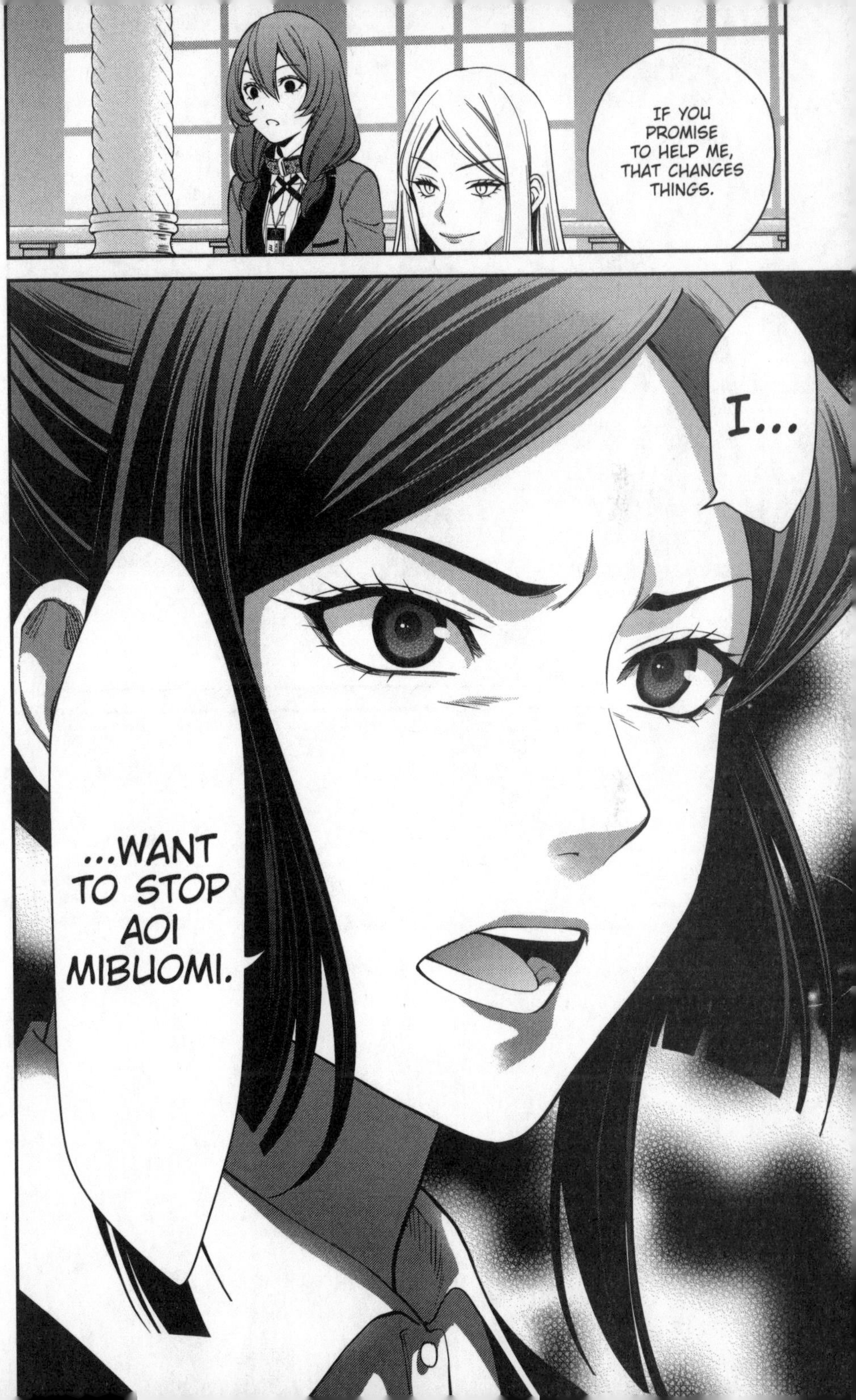
IF YOU PROMISE TO HELP ME, THAT CHANGES THINGS.
I...
...WANT TO STOP AOI MIBUOMI.

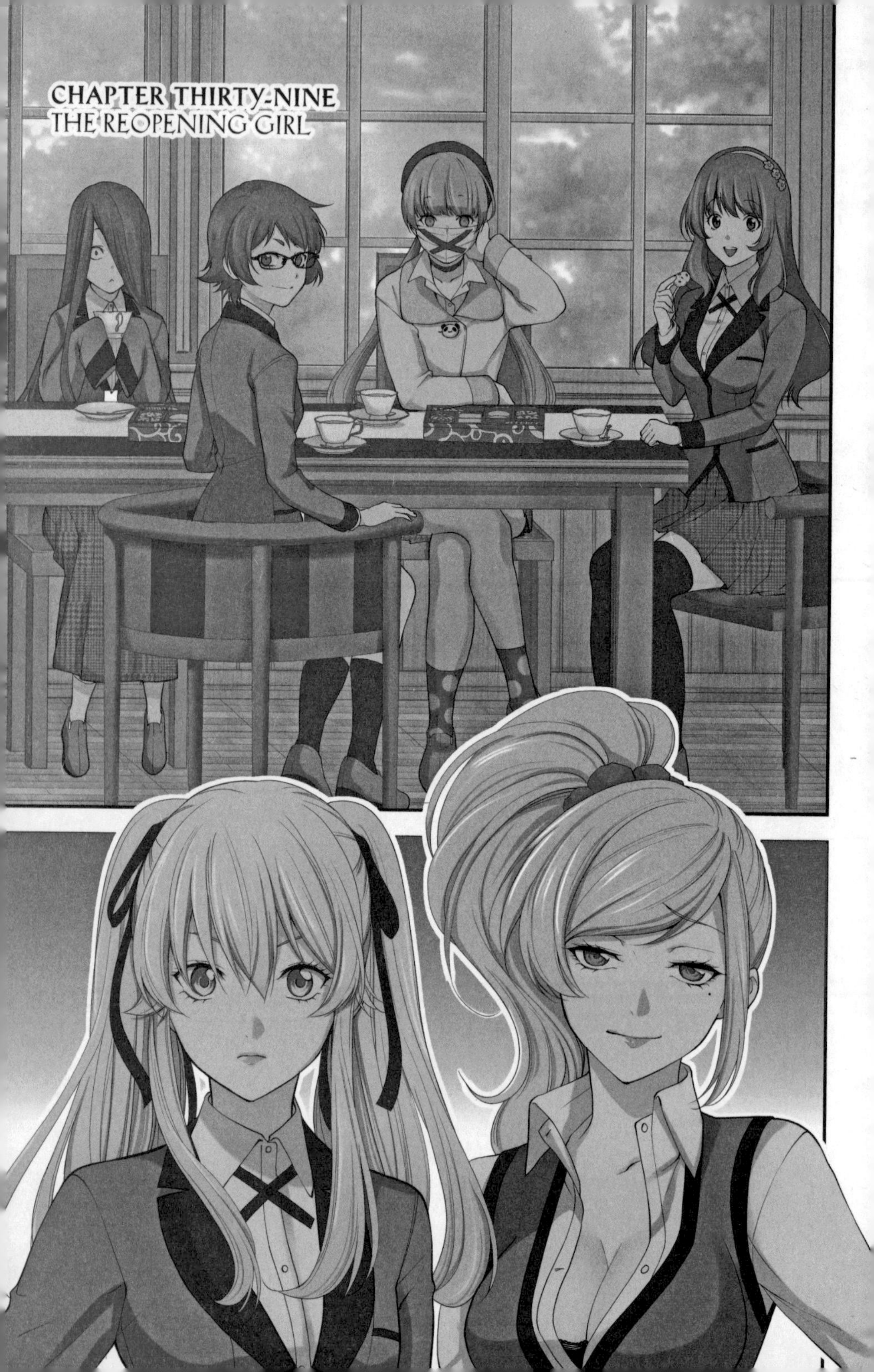
CHAPTER THIRTY-NINE
THE REOPENING GIRL

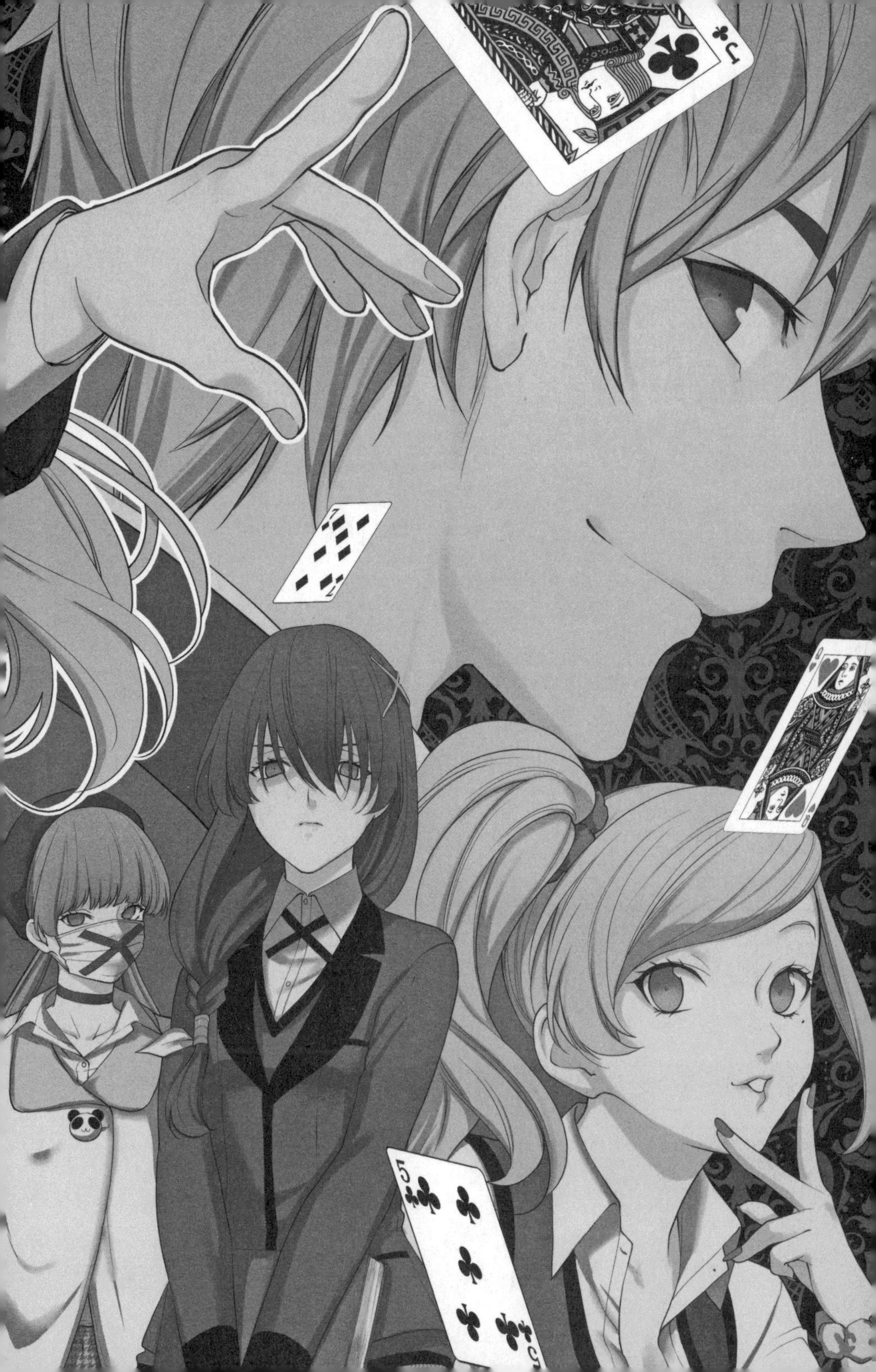

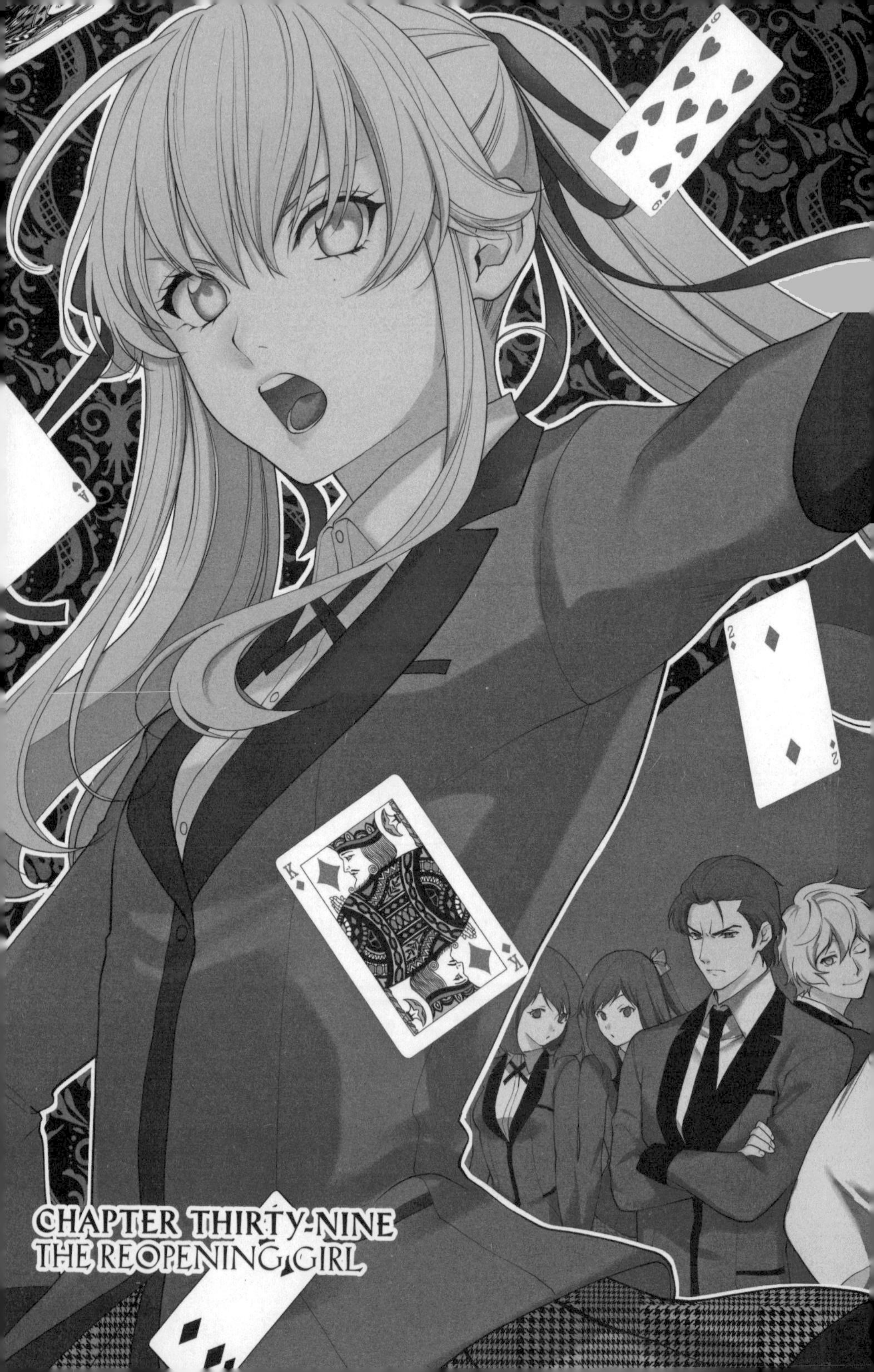
CHAPTER THIRTY-NINE
THE REOPENING GIRL

Kakegurui Twin

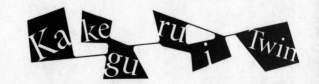

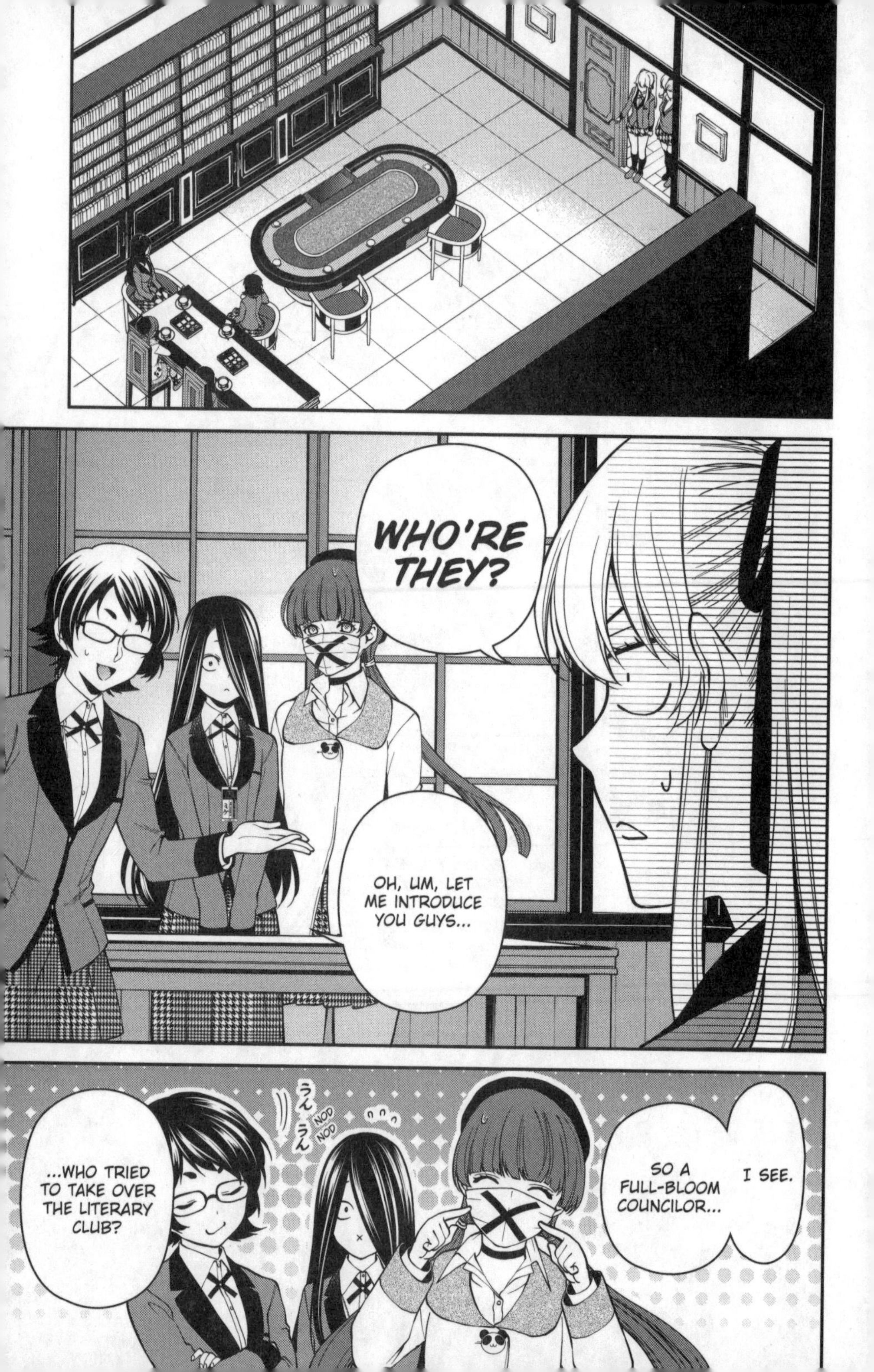
WHO'RE THEY?
OH, UM, LET ME INTRODUCE YOU GUYS...
I SEE.
SO A FULL-BLOOM COUNCILOR...
うん うん
NOD NOD
...WHO TRIED TO TAKE OVER THE LITERARY CLUB?

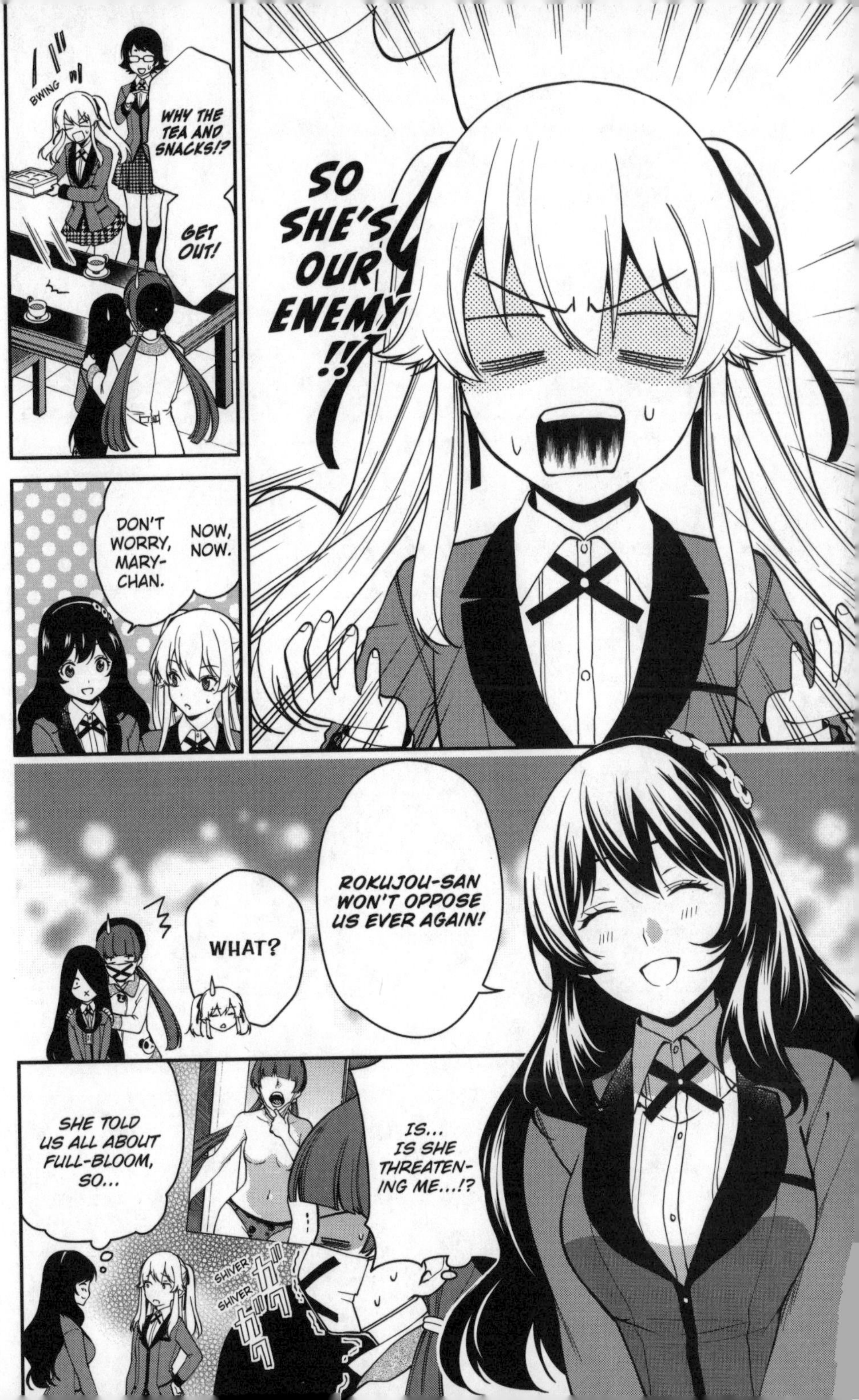
SO SHE'S OUR ENEMY!!
WHY THE TEA AND SNACKS!?
GET OUT!
BWING
NOW, NOW.
DON'T WORRY, MARY-CHAN.
ROKUJOU-SAN WON'T OPPOSE US EVER AGAIN!
WHAT?
IS... IS SHE THREATENING ME...!?
SHIVER SHIVER
SHE TOLD US ALL ABOUT FULL-BLOOM, SO...

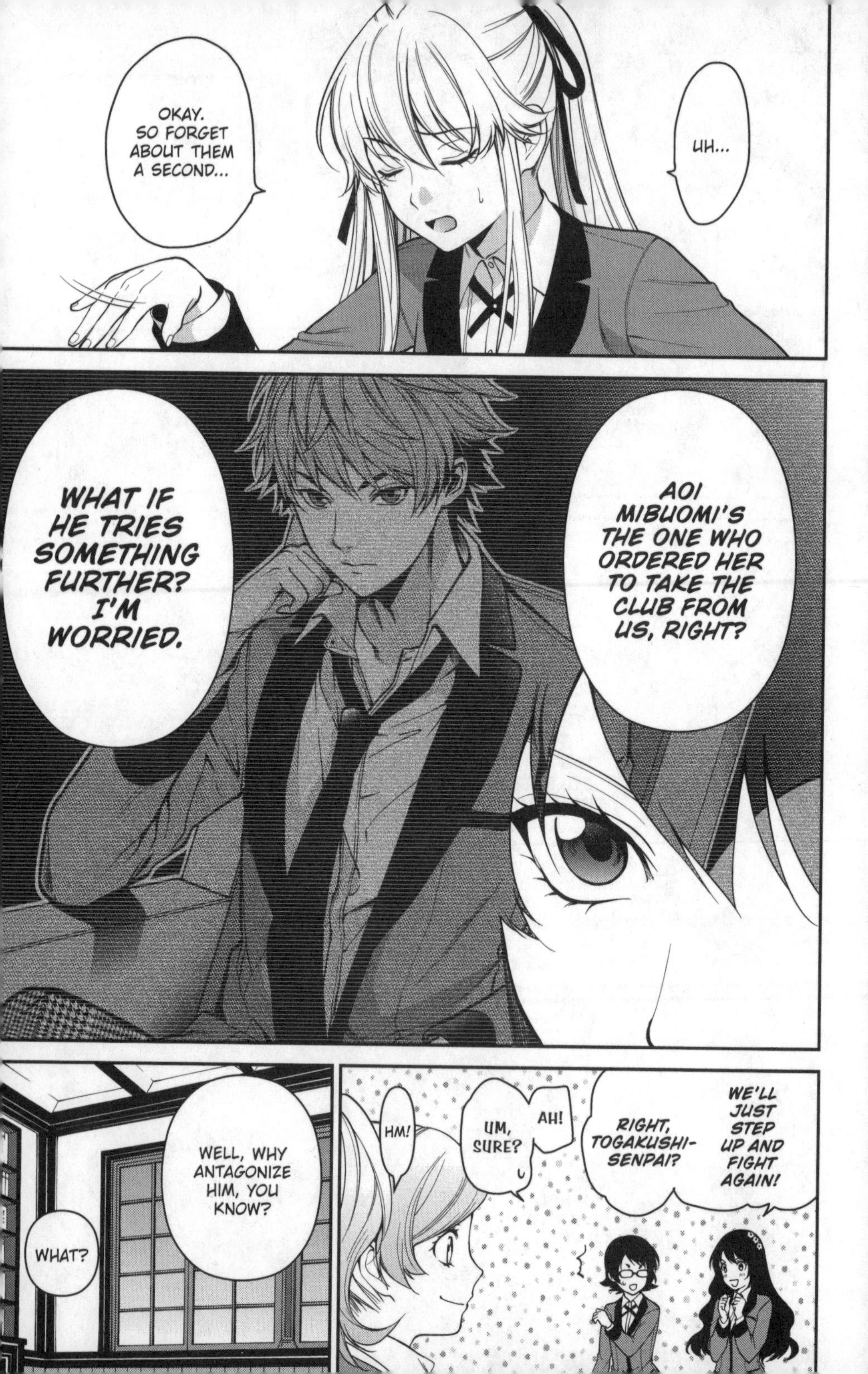
UH...
OKAY. SO FORGET ABOUT THEM A SECOND...
AOI MIBUOMI'S THE ONE WHO ORDERED HER TO TAKE THE CLUB FROM US, RIGHT?
WHAT IF HE TRIES SOMETHING FURTHER? I'M WORRIED.
WE'LL JUST STEP UP AND FIGHT AGAIN!
RIGHT, TOGAKUSHI-SENPAI?
AH!
UM, SURE?
HM!
WELL, WHY ANTAGONIZE HIM, YOU KNOW?
WHAT?

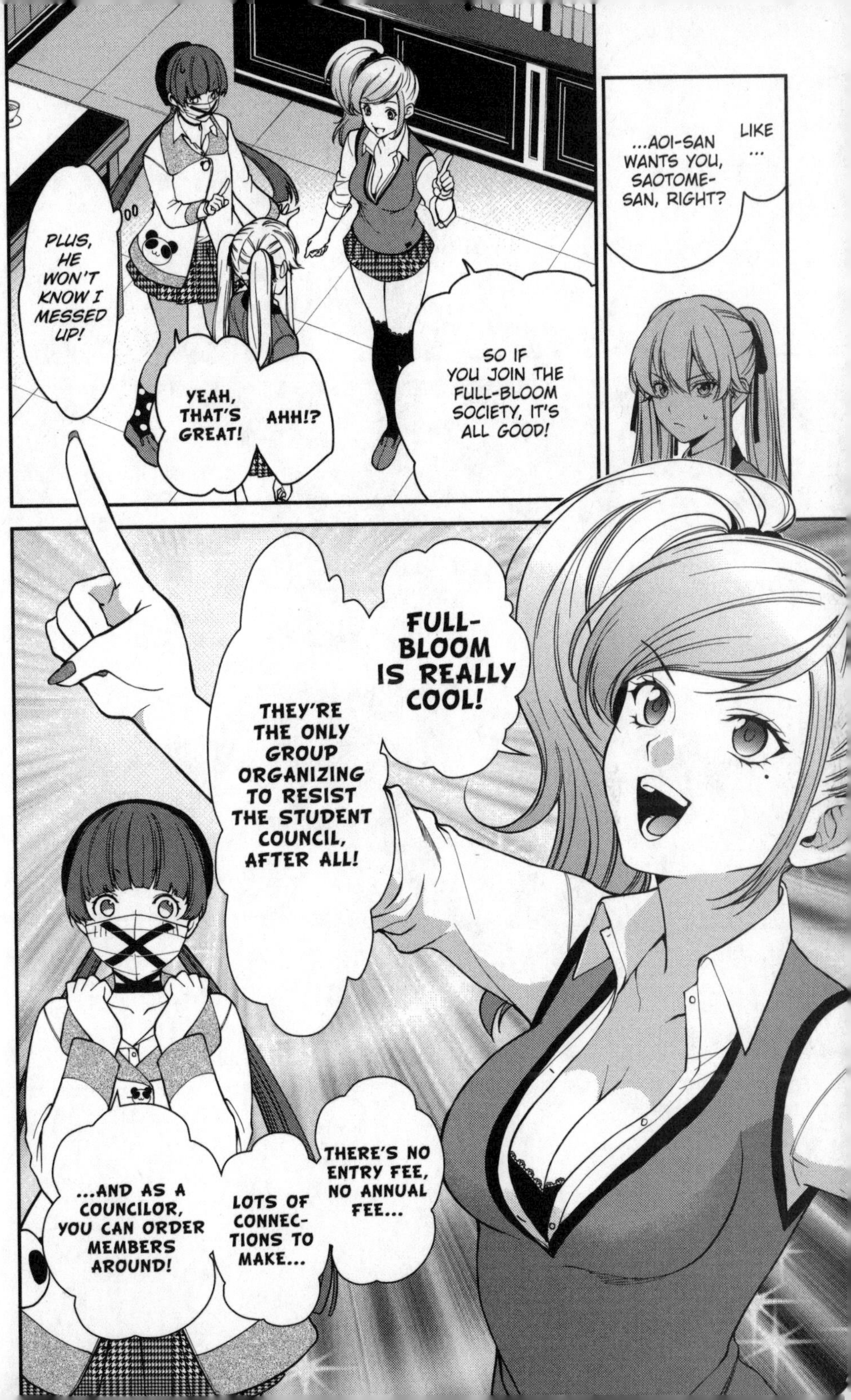
LIKE ...
...AOI-SAN WANTS YOU, SAOTOME-SAN, RIGHT?
SO IF YOU JOIN THE FULL-BLOOM SOCIETY, IT'S ALL GOOD!
AHH!?
YEAH, THAT'S GREAT!
PLUS, HE WON'T KNOW I MESSED UP!
FULL-BLOOM IS REALLY COOL!
THEY'RE THE ONLY GROUP ORGANIZING TO RESIST THE STUDENT COUNCIL, AFTER ALL!
THERE'S NO ENTRY FEE, NO ANNUAL FEE...
LOTS OF CONNECTIONS TO MAKE...
...AND AS A COUNCILOR, YOU CAN ORDER MEMBERS AROUND!

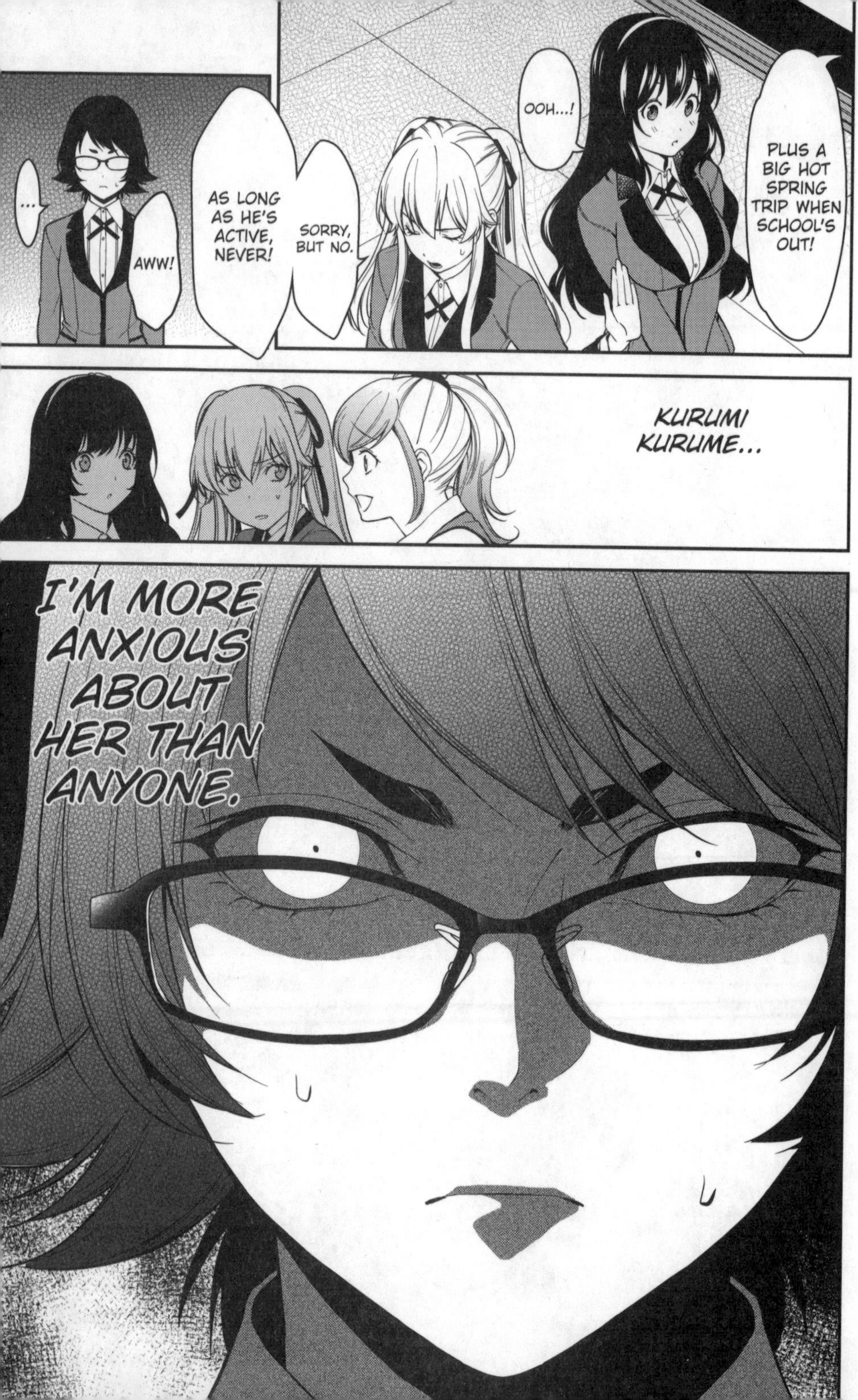
PLUS A BIG HOT SPRING TRIP WHEN SCHOOL'S OUT!
OOH...!
SORRY, BUT NO.
AS LONG AS HE'S ACTIVE, NEVER!
AWW!
...
KURUMI KURUME...
I'M MORE ANXIOUS ABOUT HER THAN ANYONE.

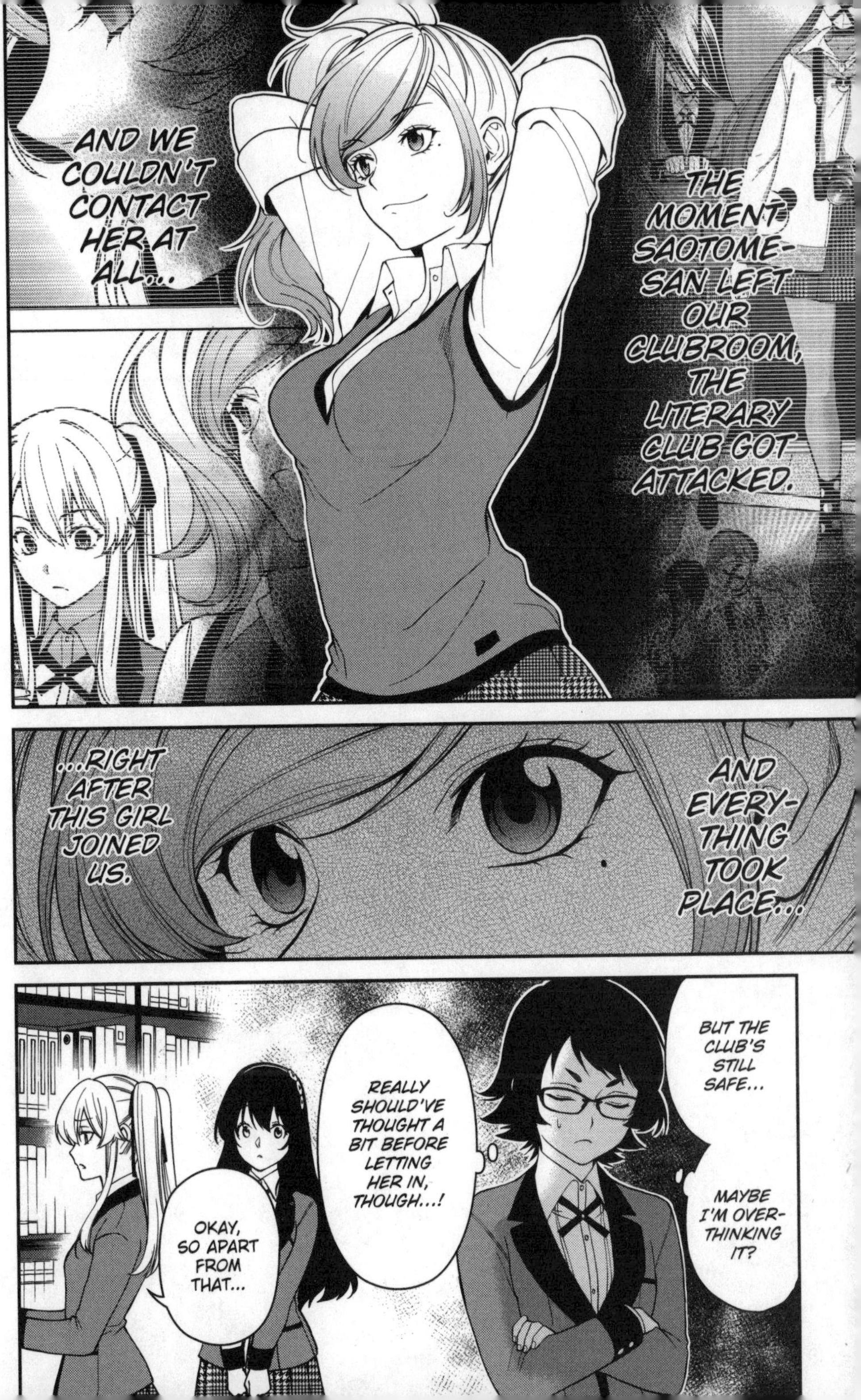
THE MOMENT SAOTOME-SAN LEFT OUR CLUBROOM, THE LITERARY CLUB GOT ATTACKED.
AND WE COULDN'T CONTACT HER AT ALL...
AND EVERY-THING TOOK PLACE...
...RIGHT AFTER THIS GIRL JOINED US.
BUT THE CLUB'S STILL SAFE...
MAYBE I'M OVER-THINKING IT?
REALLY SHOULD'VE THOUGHT A BIT BEFORE LETTING HER IN, THOUGH...!
OKAY, SO APART FROM THAT...

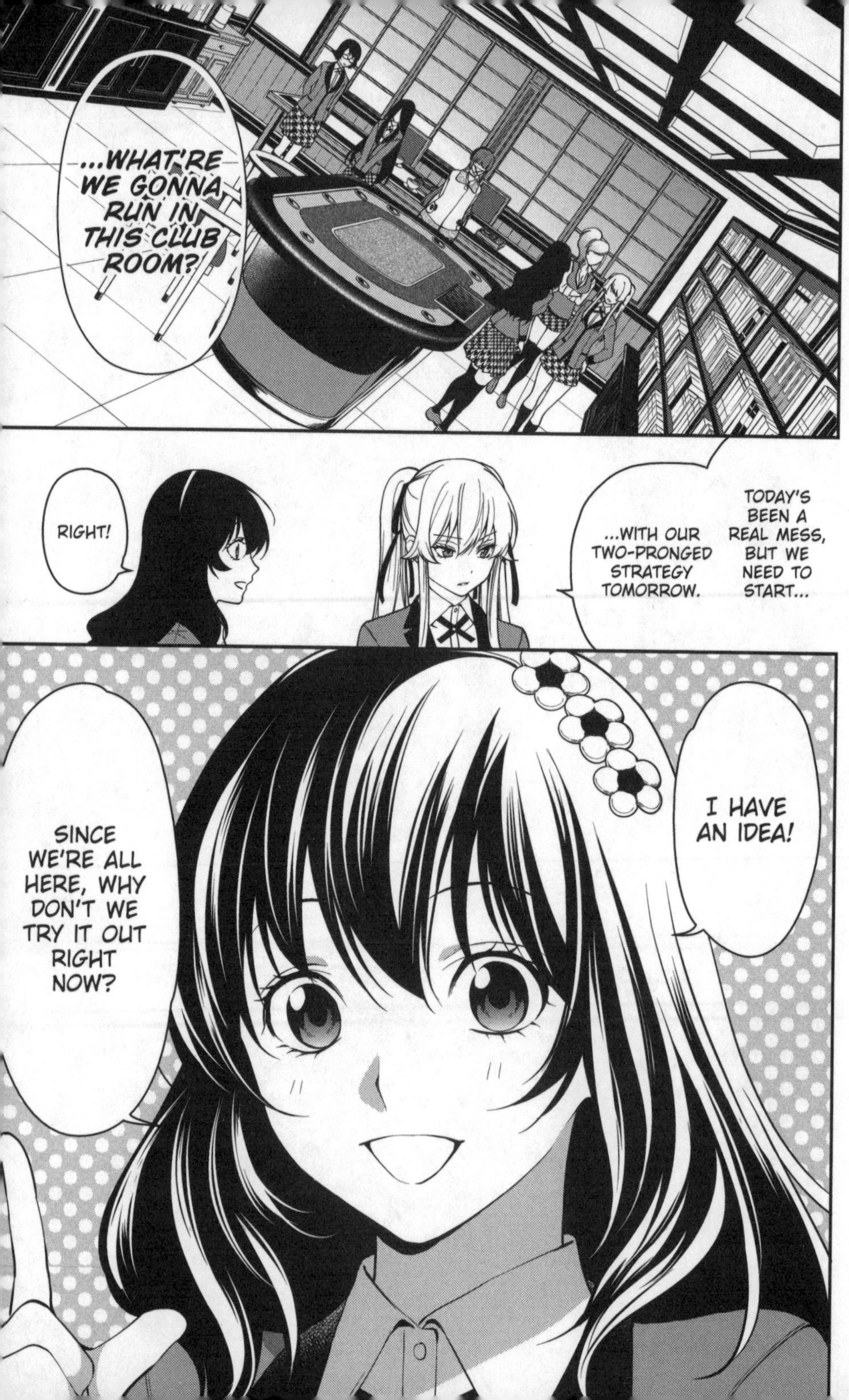
...WHAT'RE WE GONNA RUN IN THIS CLUB ROOM?
TODAY'S BEEN A REAL MESS, BUT WE NEED TO START...
...WITH OUR TWO-PRONGED STRATEGY TOMORROW.
RIGHT!
I HAVE AN IDEA!
SINCE WE'RE ALL HERE, WHY DON'T WE TRY IT OUT RIGHT NOW?

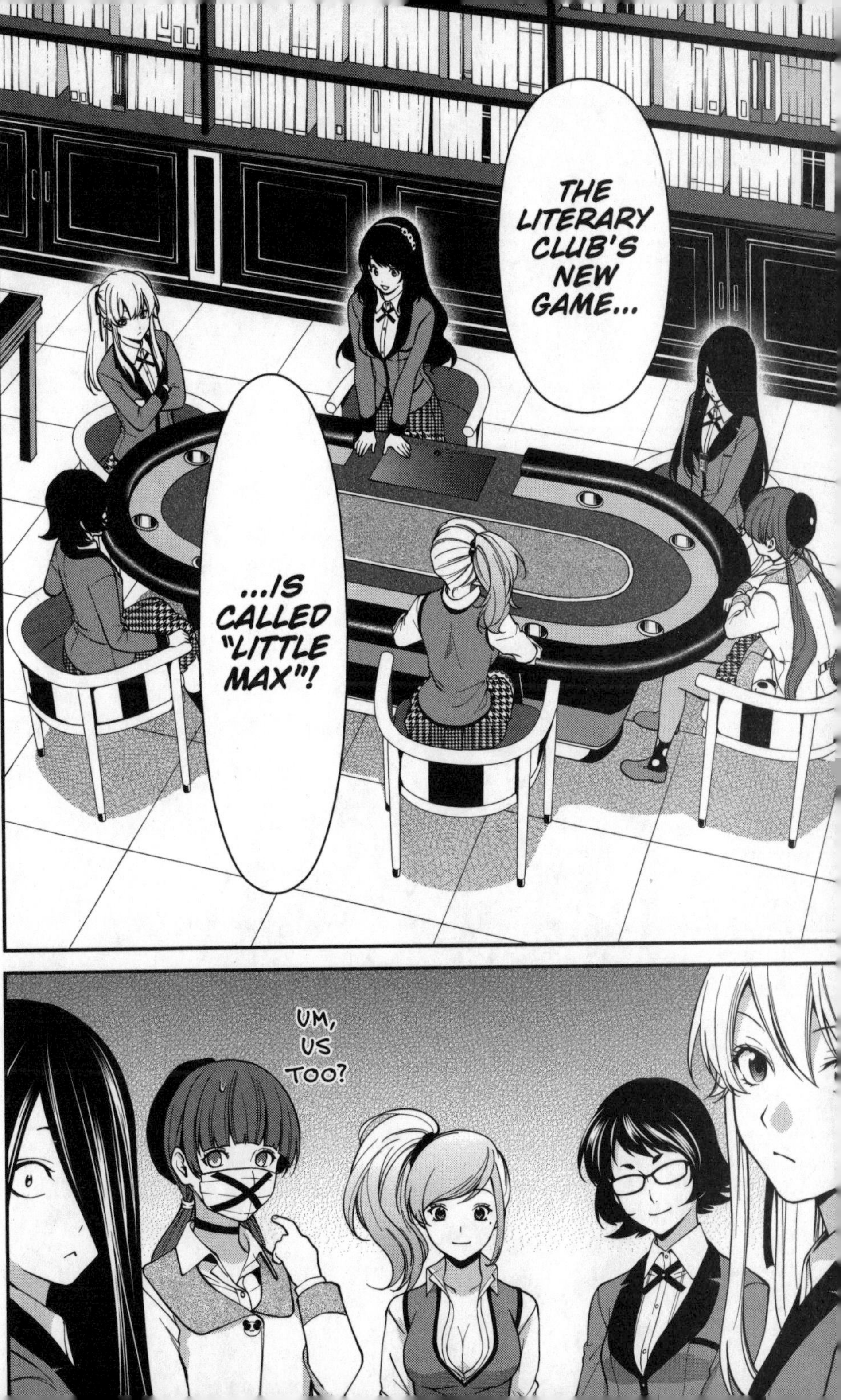
THE LITERARY CLUB'S NEW GAME...
...IS CALLED "LITTLE MAX"!
UM, US TOO?

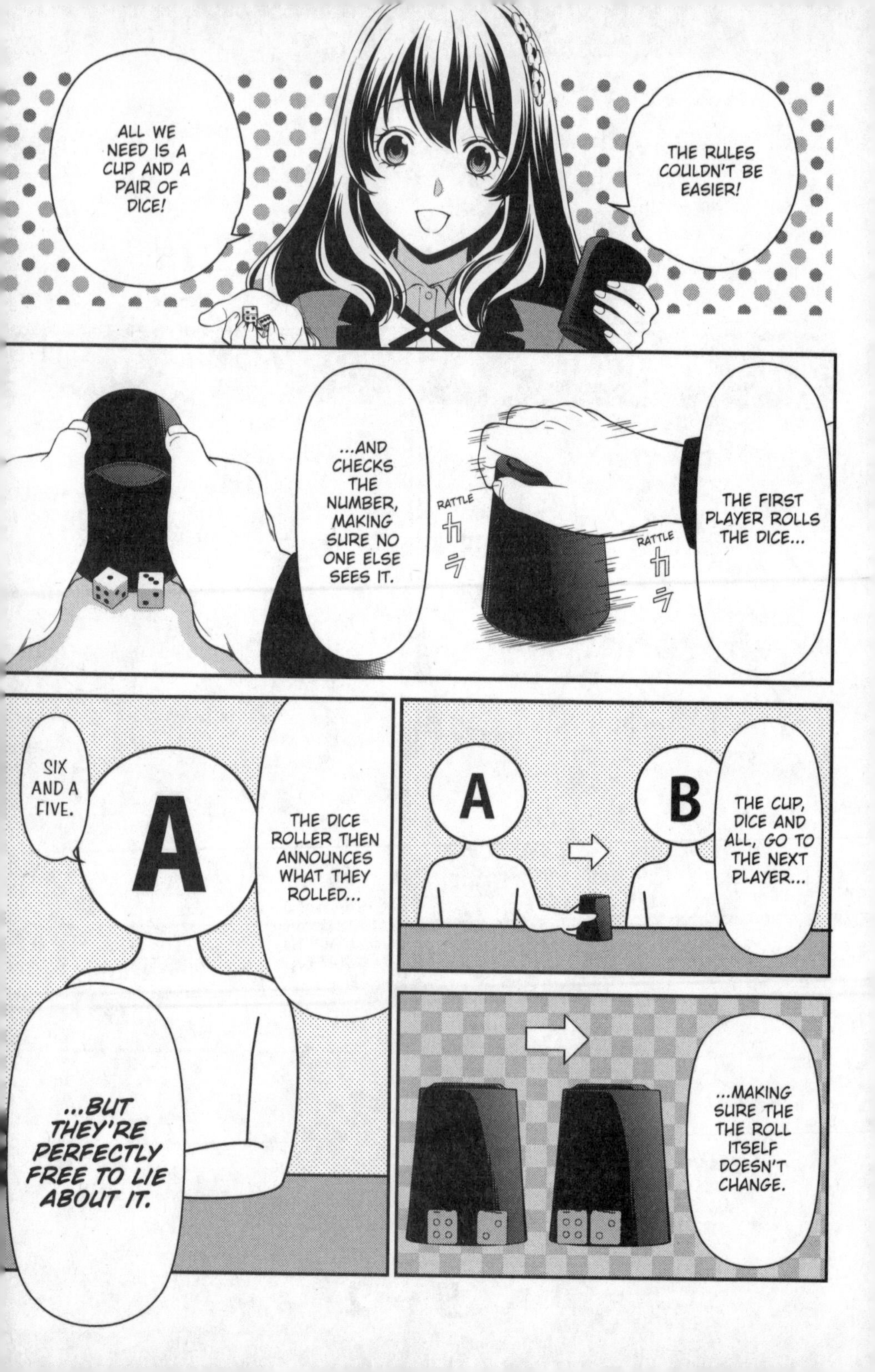
THE RULES COULDN'T BE EASIER!
ALL WE NEED IS A CUP AND A PAIR OF DICE!
THE FIRST PLAYER ROLLS THE DICE...
RATTLE
カラ
RATTLE
カラ
...AND CHECKS THE NUMBER, MAKING SURE NO ONE ELSE SEES IT.
A
B
THE CUP, DICE AND ALL, GO TO THE NEXT PLAYER...
...MAKING SURE THE THE ROLL ITSELF DOESN'T CHANGE.
A
THE DICE ROLLER THEN ANNOUNCES WHAT THEY ROLLED...
SIX AND A FIVE.
...BUT THEY'RE PERFECTLY FREE TO LIE ABOUT IT.

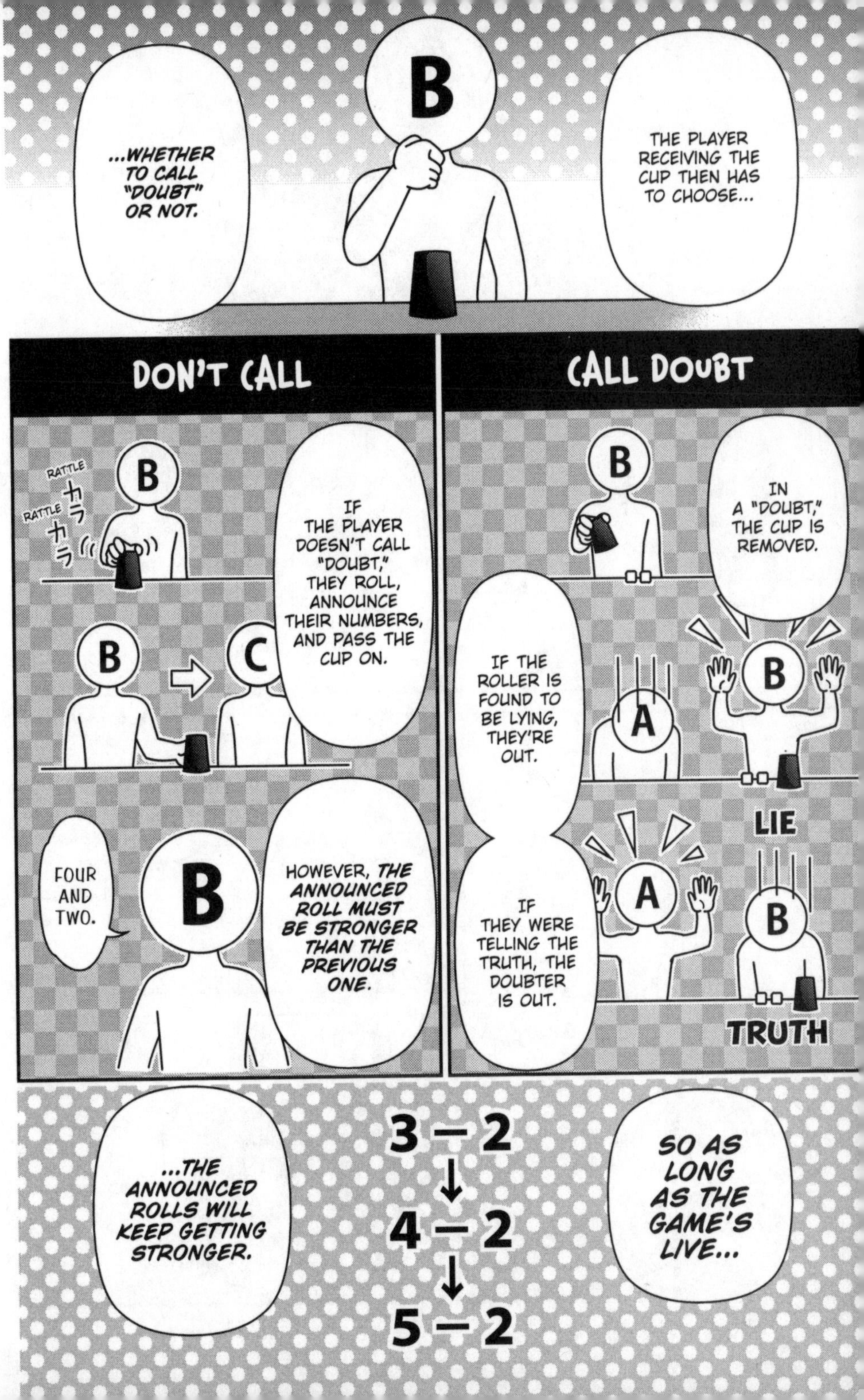
THE PLAYER RECEIVING THE CUP THEN HAS TO CHOOSE...
...WHETHER TO CALL "DOUBT" OR NOT.
CALL DOUBT
IN A "DOUBT," THE CUP IS REMOVED.
IF THE ROLLER IS FOUND TO BE LYING, THEY'RE OUT.
LIE
IF THEY WERE TELLING THE TRUTH, THE DOUBTER IS OUT.
TRUTH
DON'T CALL
RATTLE カラ
RATTLE カラ
IF THE PLAYER DOESN'T CALL "DOUBT," THEY ROLL, ANNOUNCE THEIR NUMBERS, AND PASS THE CUP ON.
HOWEVER, THE ANNOUNCED ROLL MUST BE STRONGER THAN THE PREVIOUS ONE.
FOUR AND TWO.
SO AS LONG AS THE GAME'S LIVE...
3 – 2 ↓ 4 – 2 ↓ 5 – 2
...THE ANNOUNCED ROLLS WILL KEEP GETTING STRONGER.

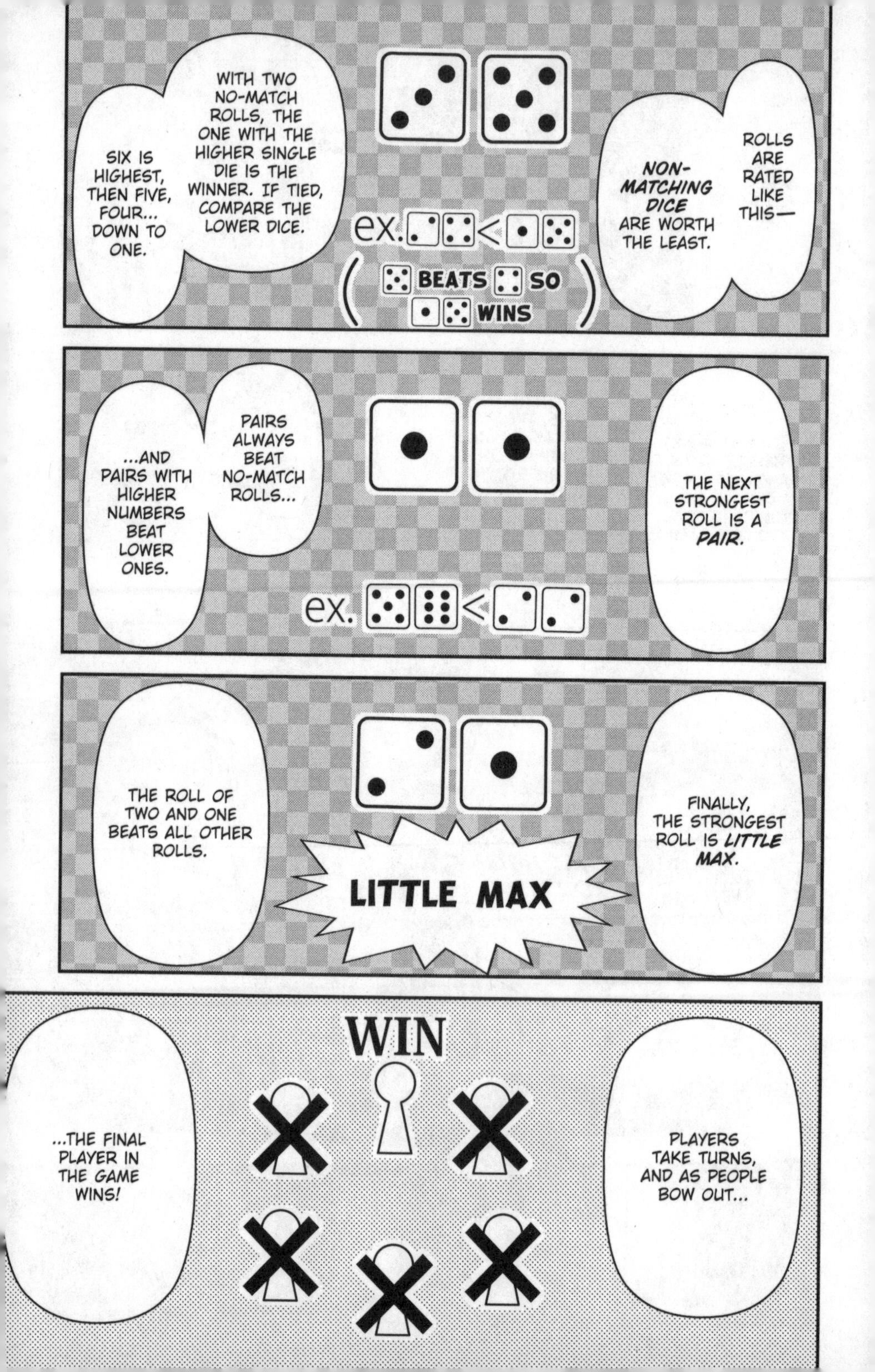
ROLLS ARE RATED LIKE THIS—
NON-MATCHING DICE ARE WORTH THE LEAST.
ex. <
BEATS SO WINS
WITH TWO NO-MATCH ROLLS, THE ONE WITH THE HIGHER SINGLE DIE IS THE WINNER. IF TIED, COMPARE THE LOWER DICE.
SIX IS HIGHEST, THEN FIVE, FOUR... DOWN TO ONE.
THE NEXT STRONGEST ROLL IS A PAIR.
ex. <
PAIRS ALWAYS BEAT NO-MATCH ROLLS...
...AND PAIRS WITH HIGHER NUMBERS BEAT LOWER ONES.
FINALLY, THE STRONGEST ROLL IS LITTLE MAX.
LITTLE MAX
THE ROLL OF TWO AND ONE BEATS ALL OTHER ROLLS.
PLAYERS TAKE TURNS, AND AS PEOPLE BOW OUT...
WIN
...THE FINAL PLAYER IN THE GAME WINS!

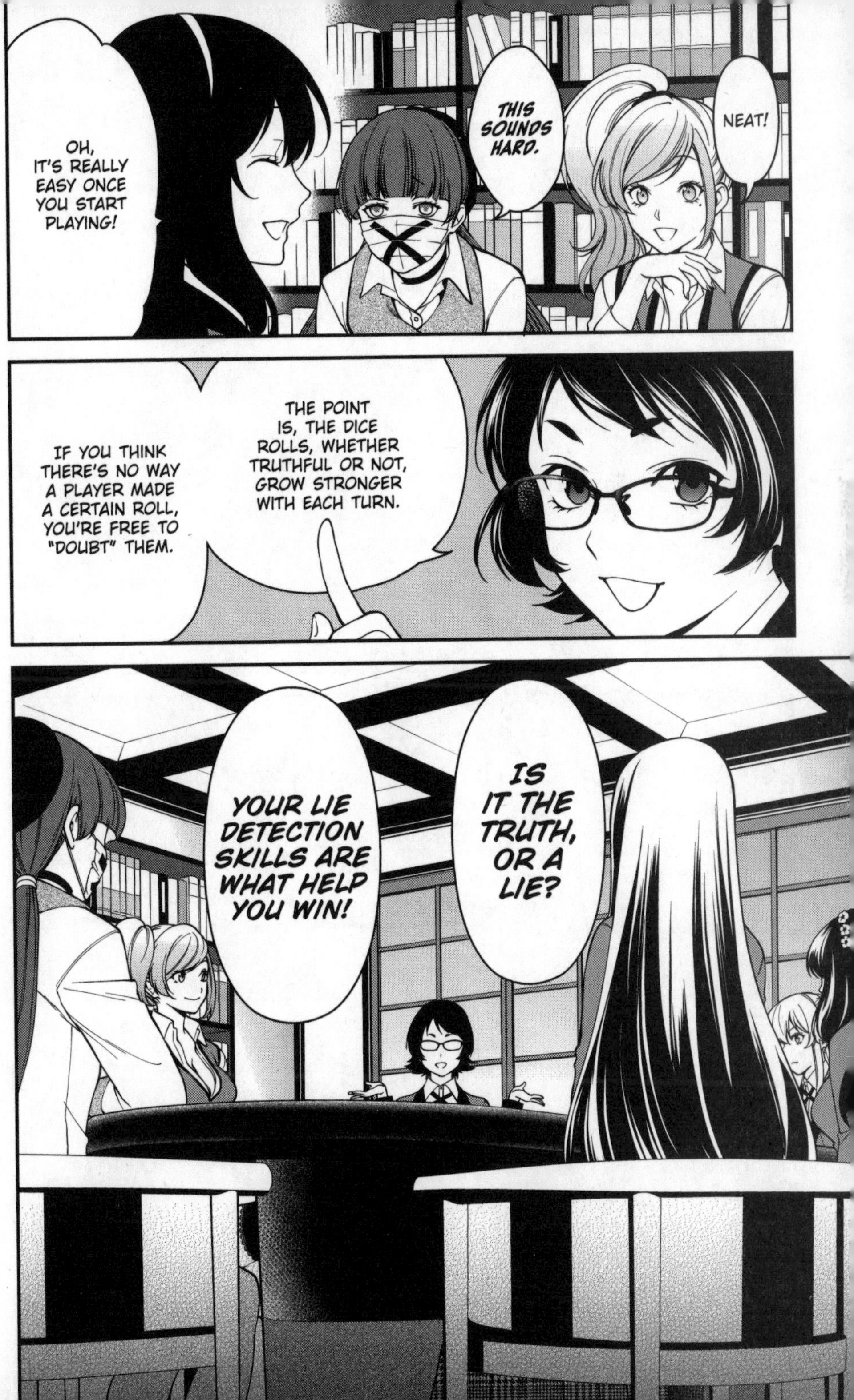
NEAT!
THIS SOUNDS HARD.
OH, IT'S REALLY EASY ONCE YOU START PLAYING!
THE POINT IS, THE DICE ROLLS, WHETHER TRUTHFUL OR NOT, GROW STRONGER WITH EACH TURN.
IF YOU THINK THERE'S NO WAY A PLAYER MADE A CERTAIN ROLL, YOU'RE FREE TO "DOUBT" THEM.
IS IT THE TRUTH, OR A LIE?
YOUR LIE DETECTION SKILLS ARE WHAT HELP YOU WIN!

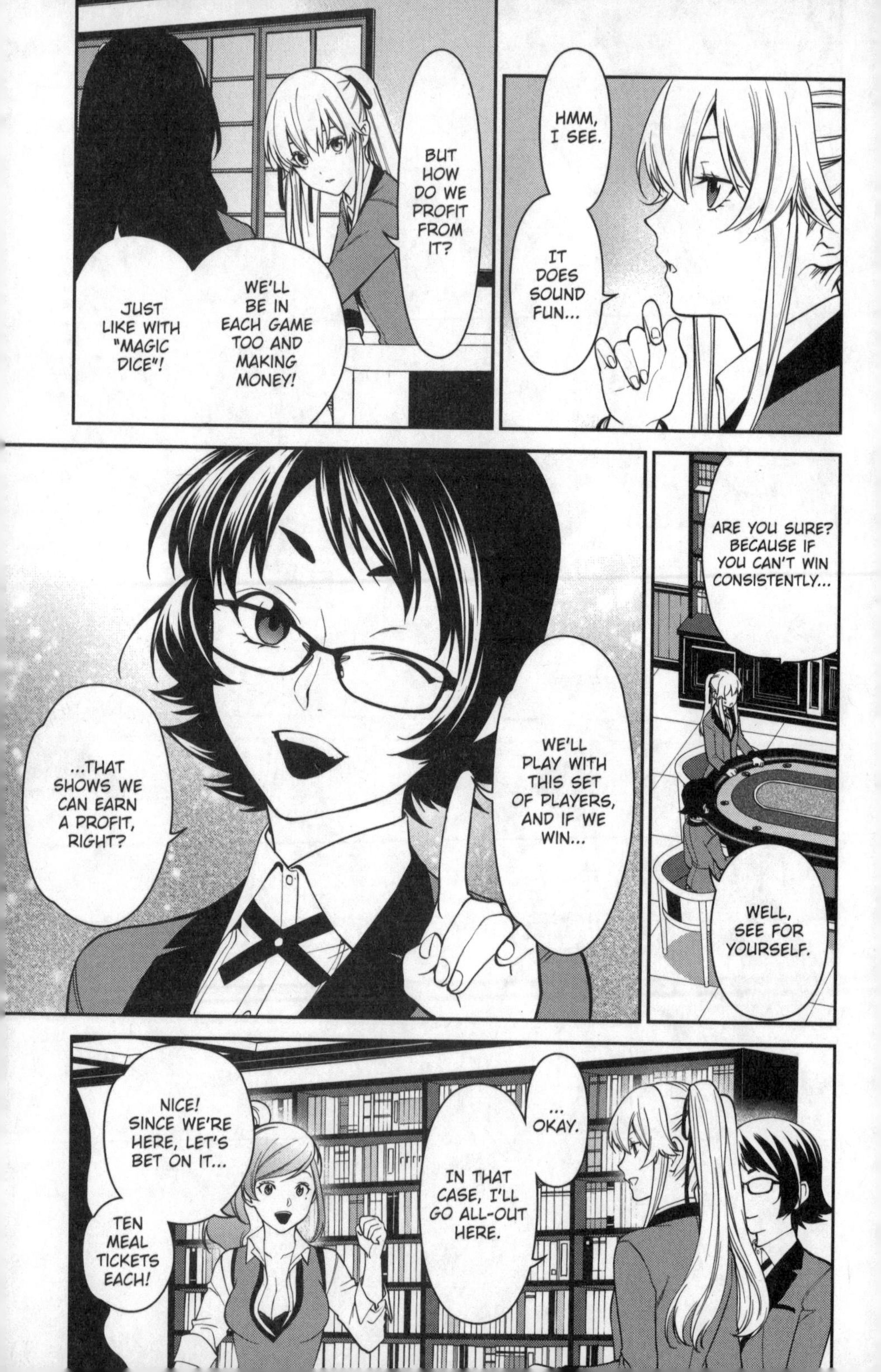
HMM, I SEE.
IT DOES SOUND FUN...
BUT HOW DO WE PROFIT FROM IT?
WE'LL BE IN EACH GAME TOO AND MAKING MONEY!
JUST LIKE WITH "MAGIC DICE"!
ARE YOU SURE? BECAUSE IF YOU CAN'T WIN CONSISTENTLY...
WELL, SEE FOR YOURSELF.
WE'LL PLAY WITH THIS SET OF PLAYERS, AND IF WE WIN...
...THAT SHOWS WE CAN EARN A PROFIT, RIGHT?
... OKAY.
IN THAT CASE, I'LL GO ALL-OUT HERE.
NICE! SINCE WE'RE HERE, LET'S BET ON IT...
TEN MEAL TICKETS EACH!

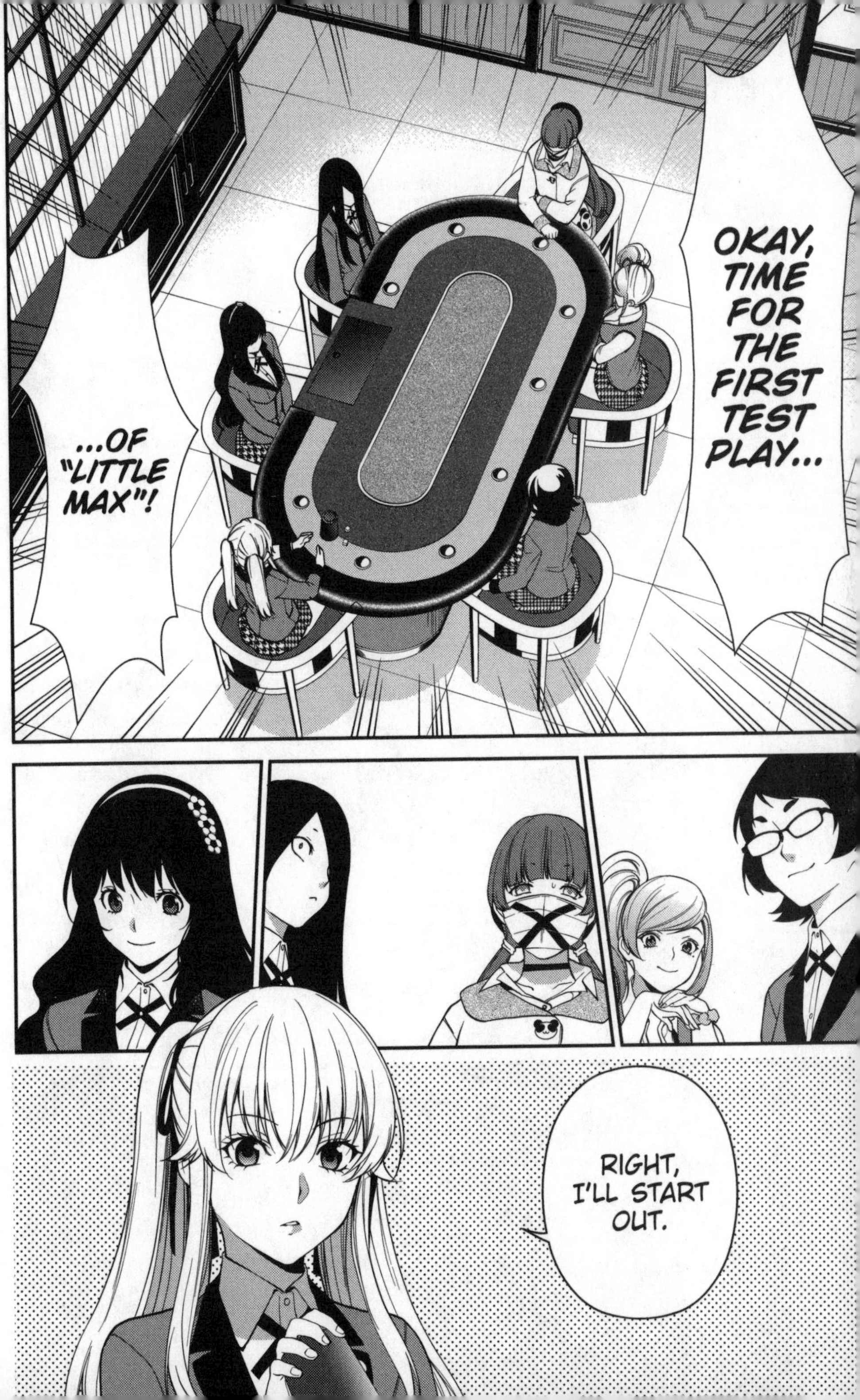
OKAY, TIME FOR THE FIRST TEST PLAY...
...OF "LITTLE MAX"!
RIGHT, I'LL START OUT.

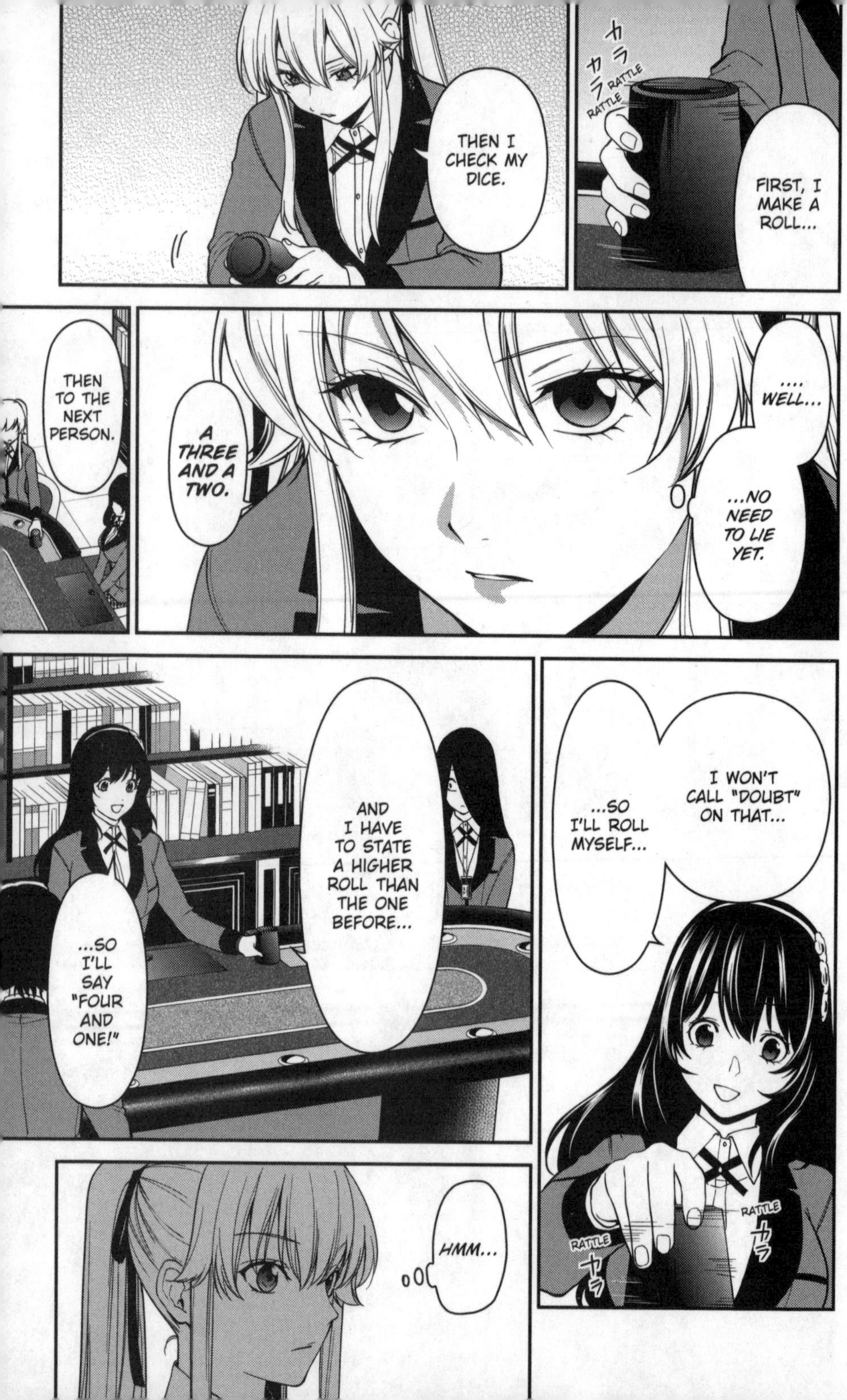
カラ
カラ
RATTLE
RATTLE
FIRST, I MAKE A ROLL...
THEN I CHECK MY DICE.
....WELL...
...NO NEED TO LIE YET.
A THREE AND A TWO.
THEN TO THE NEXT PERSON.
I WON'T CALL "DOUBT" ON THAT...
...SO I'LL ROLL MYSELF...
RATTLE
カラ
RATTLE
カラ
AND I HAVE TO STATE A HIGHER ROLL THAN THE ONE BEFORE...
...SO I'LL SAY "FOUR AND ONE!"
HMM...

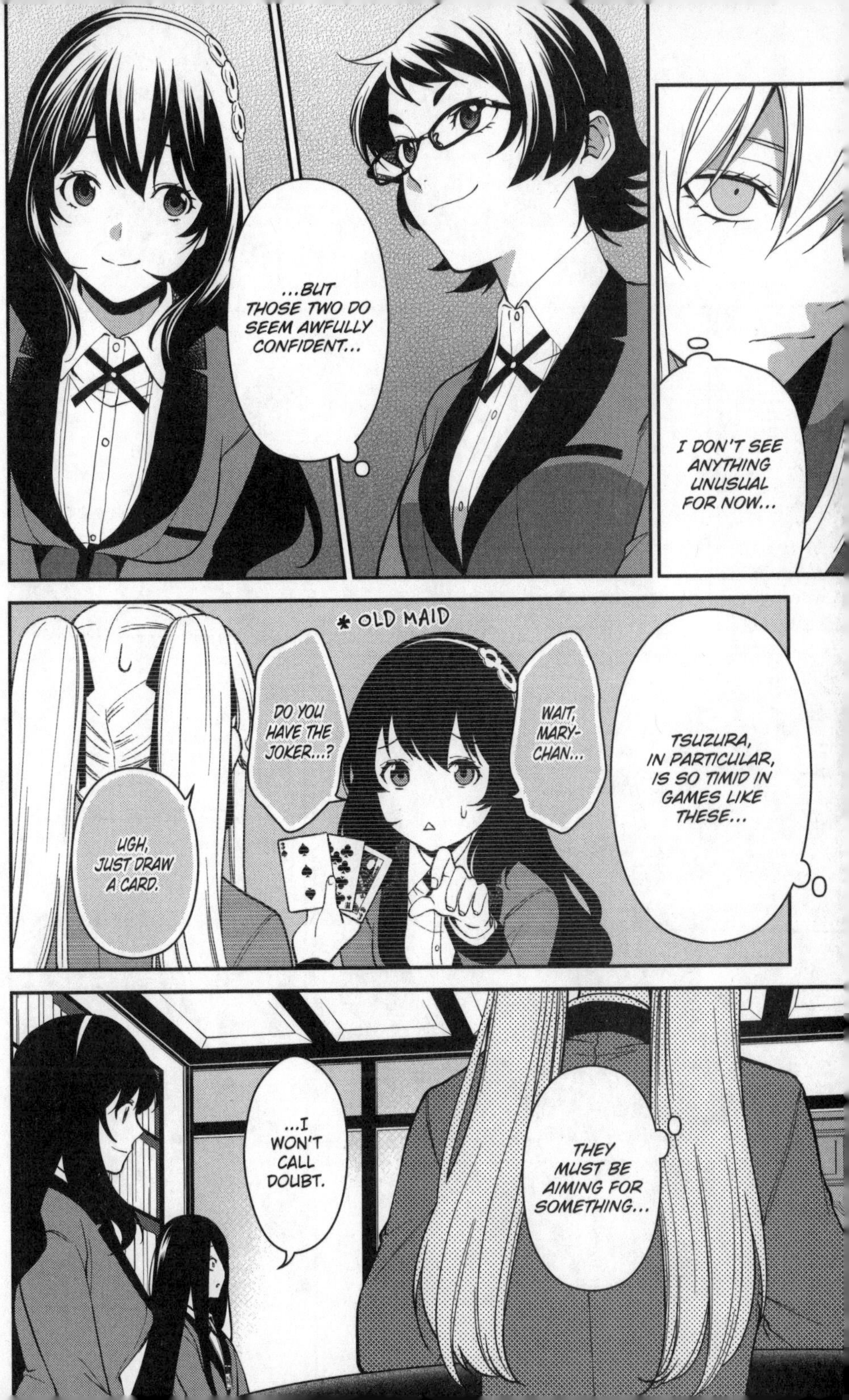
I DON'T SEE ANYTHING UNUSUAL FOR NOW...
...BUT THOSE TWO DO SEEM AWFULLY CONFIDENT...
TSUZURA, IN PARTICULAR, IS SO TIMID IN GAMES LIKE THESE...
WAIT, MARY-CHAN...
* OLD MAID
DO YOU HAVE THE JOKER...?
UGH, JUST DRAW A CARD.
THEY MUST BE AIMING FOR SOMETHING...
...I WON'T CALL DOUBT.

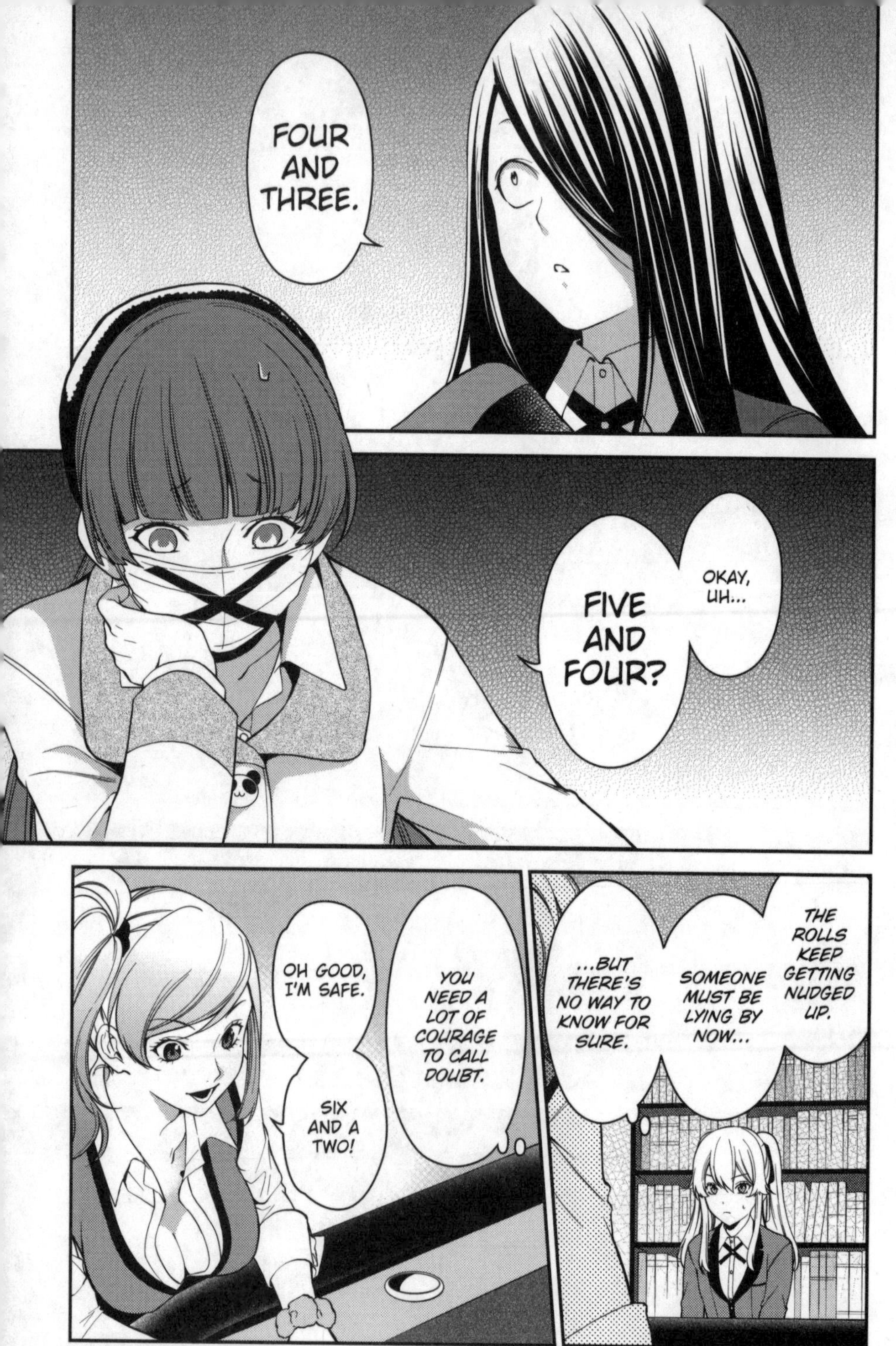
FOUR AND THREE.
OKAY, UH...
FIVE AND FOUR?
THE ROLLS KEEP GETTING NUDGED UP.
SOMEONE MUST BE LYING BY NOW...
...BUT THERE'S NO WAY TO KNOW FOR SURE.
YOU NEED A LOT OF COURAGE TO CALL DOUBT.
OH GOOD, I'M SAFE.
SIX AND A TWO!

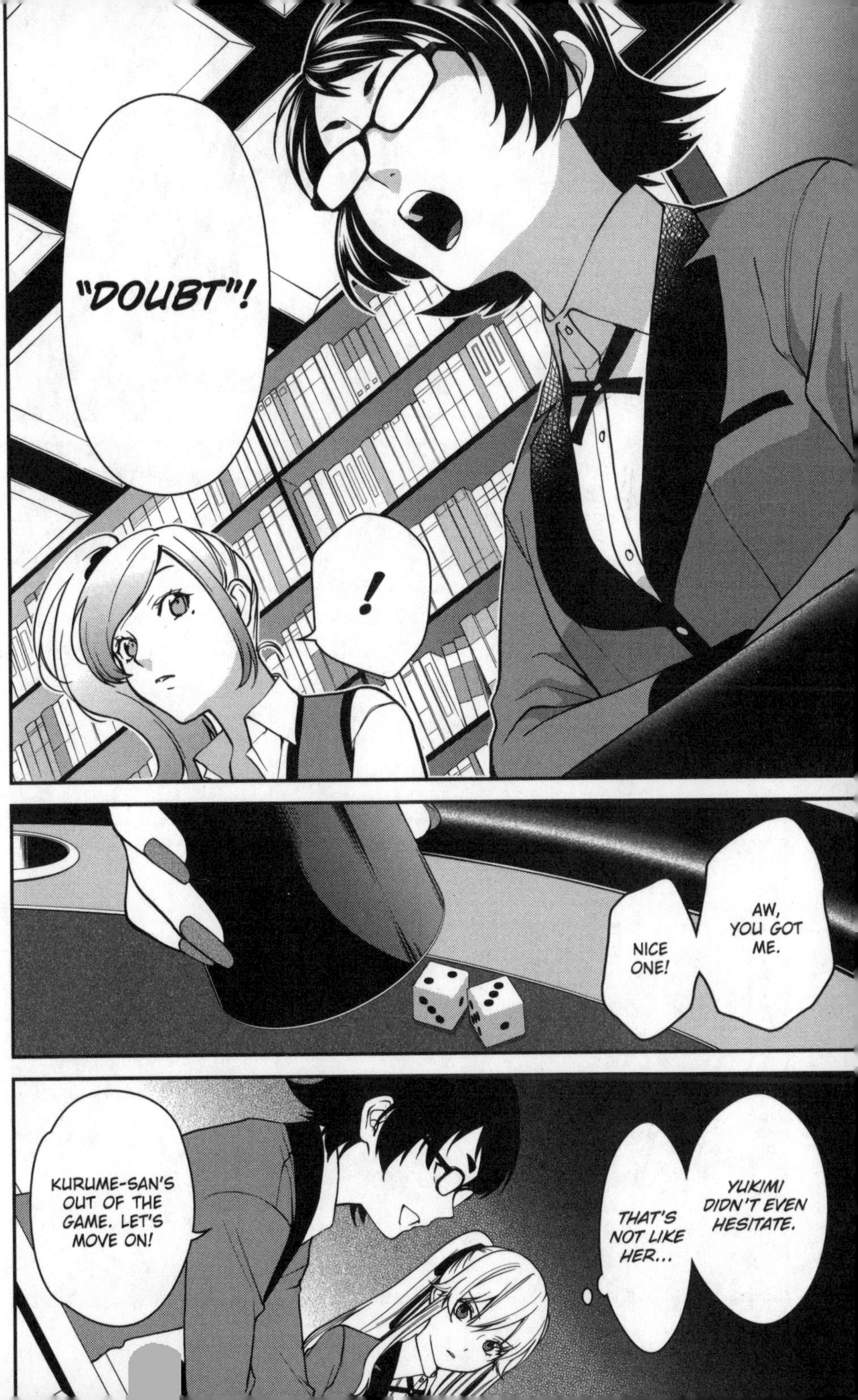
"DOUBT"!
!
AW, YOU GOT ME.
NICE ONE!
KURUME-SAN'S OUT OF THE GAME. LET'S MOVE ON!
YUKIMI DIDN'T EVEN HESITATE.
THAT'S NOT LIKE HER...

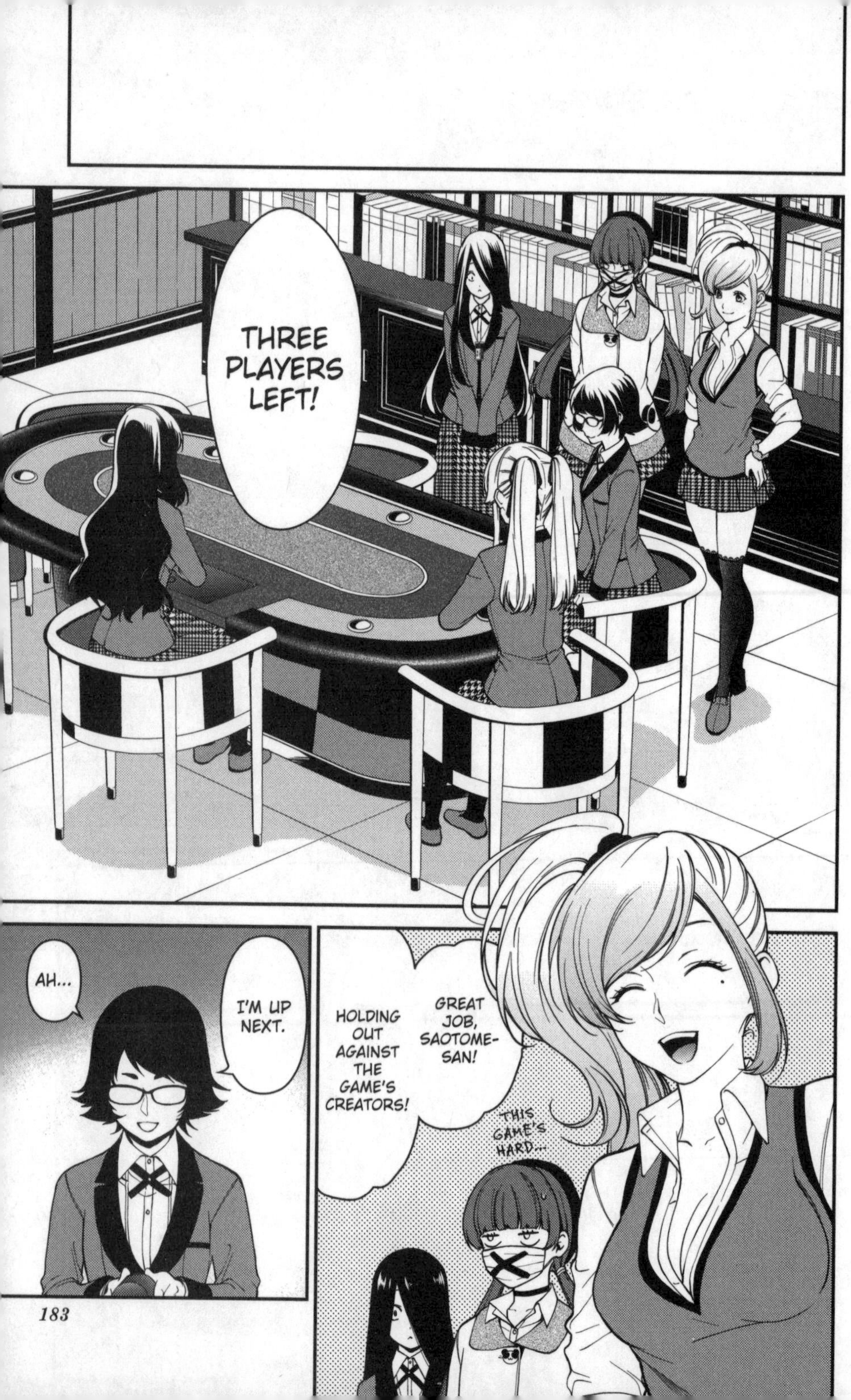
THREE PLAYERS LEFT!
GREAT JOB, SAOTOME-SAN!
HOLDING OUT AGAINST THE GAME'S CREATORS!
THIS GAME'S HARD...
AH...
I'M UP NEXT.

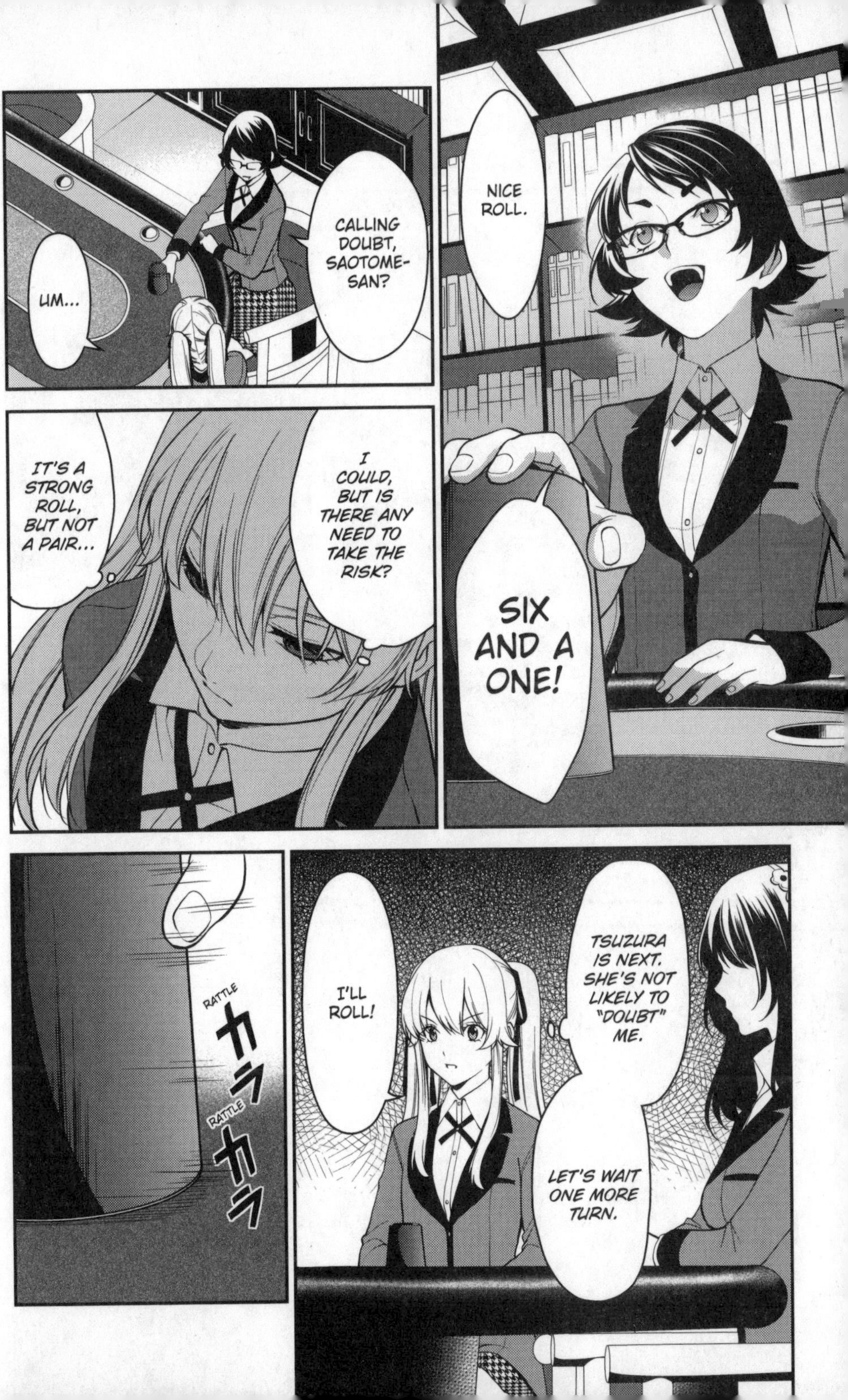
NICE ROLL.
SIX AND A ONE!
CALLING DOUBT, SAOTOME-SAN?
UM...
I COULD, BUT IS THERE ANY NEED TO TAKE THE RISK?
IT'S A STRONG ROLL, BUT NOT A PAIR...
TSUZURA IS NEXT. SHE'S NOT LIKELY TO "DOUBT" ME.
I'LL ROLL!
LET'S WAIT ONE MORE TURN.
RATTLE カラ
RATTLE カラ

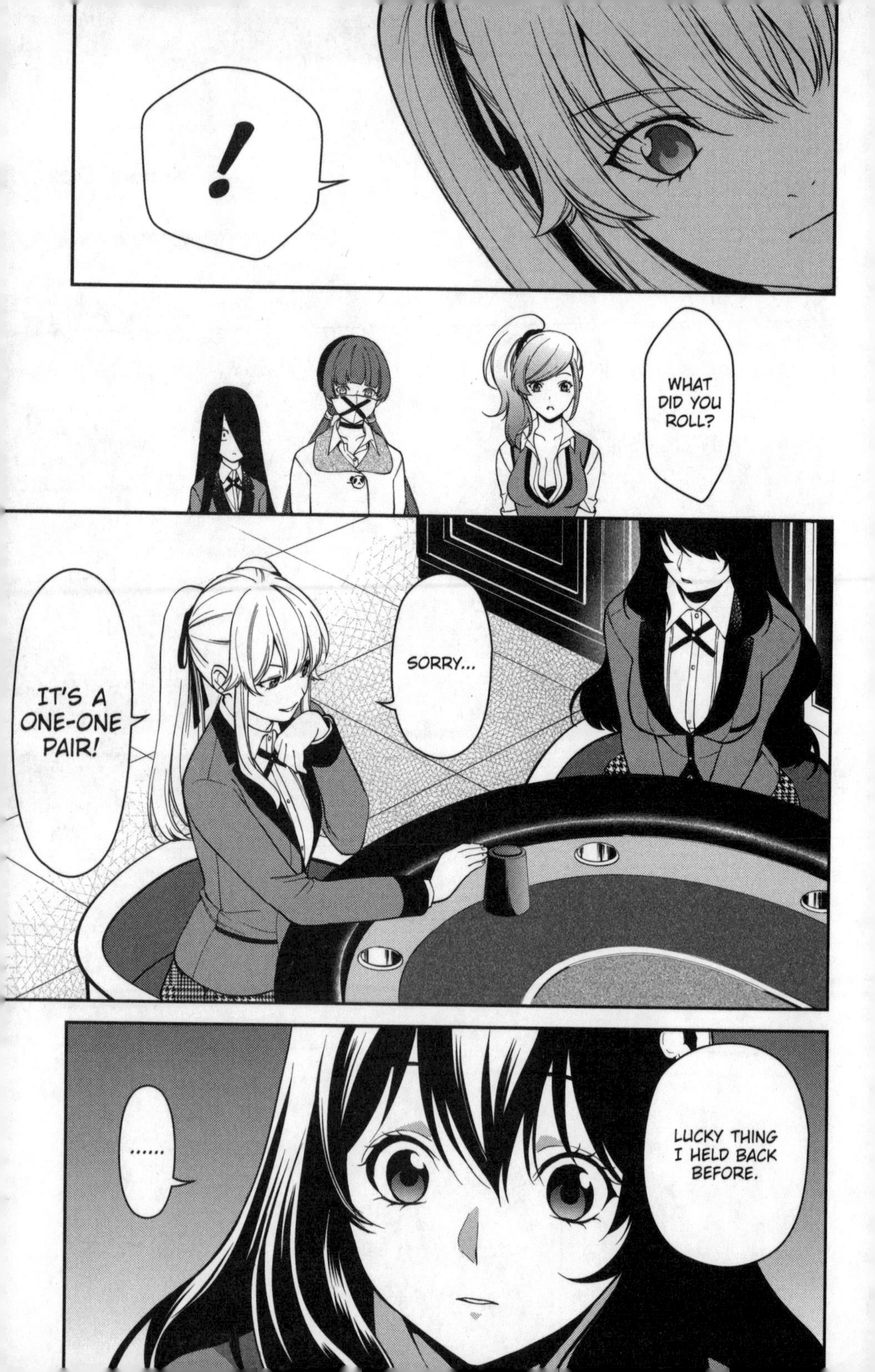
!
WHAT DID YOU ROLL?
SORRY...
IT'S A ONE-ONE PAIR!
LUCKY THING I HELD BACK BEFORE.
......

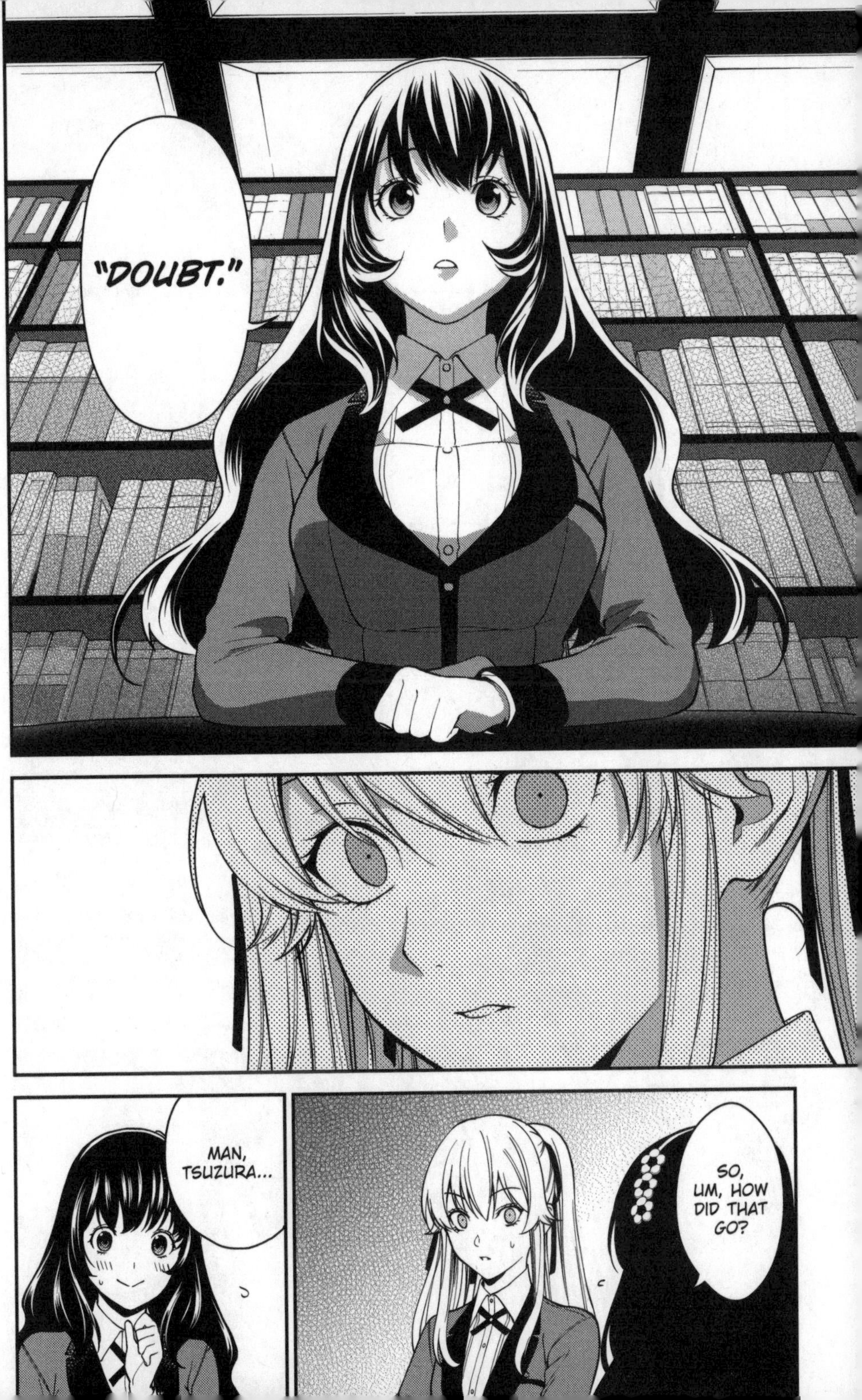
"DOUBT."
SO, UM, HOW DID THAT GO?
MAN, TSUZURA...

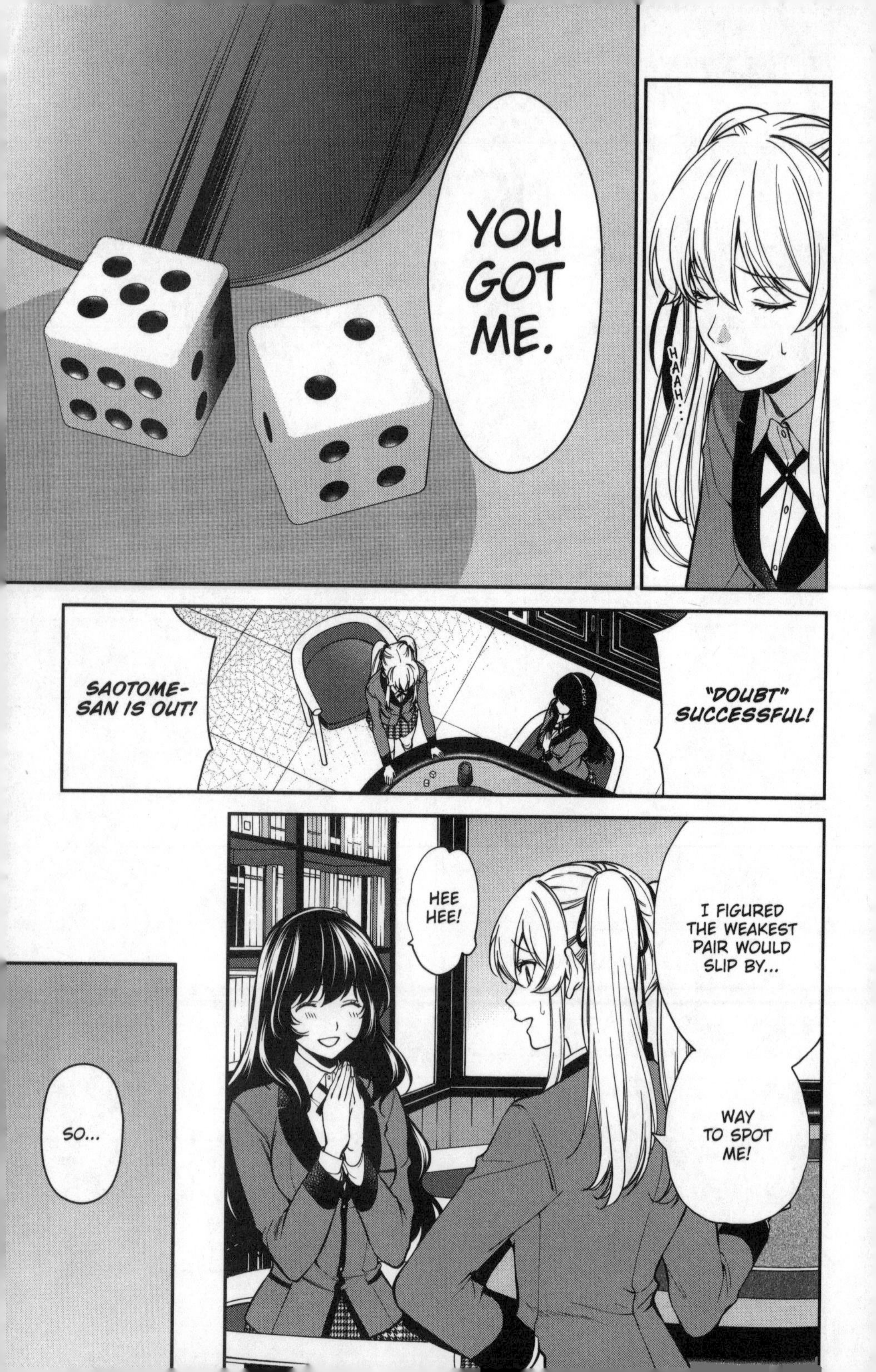
HAAH...
YOU GOT ME.
"DOUBT" SUCCESSFUL!
SAOTOME-SAN IS OUT!
I FIGURED THE WEAKEST PAIR WOULD SLIP BY...
WAY TO SPOT ME!
HEE HEE!
SO...

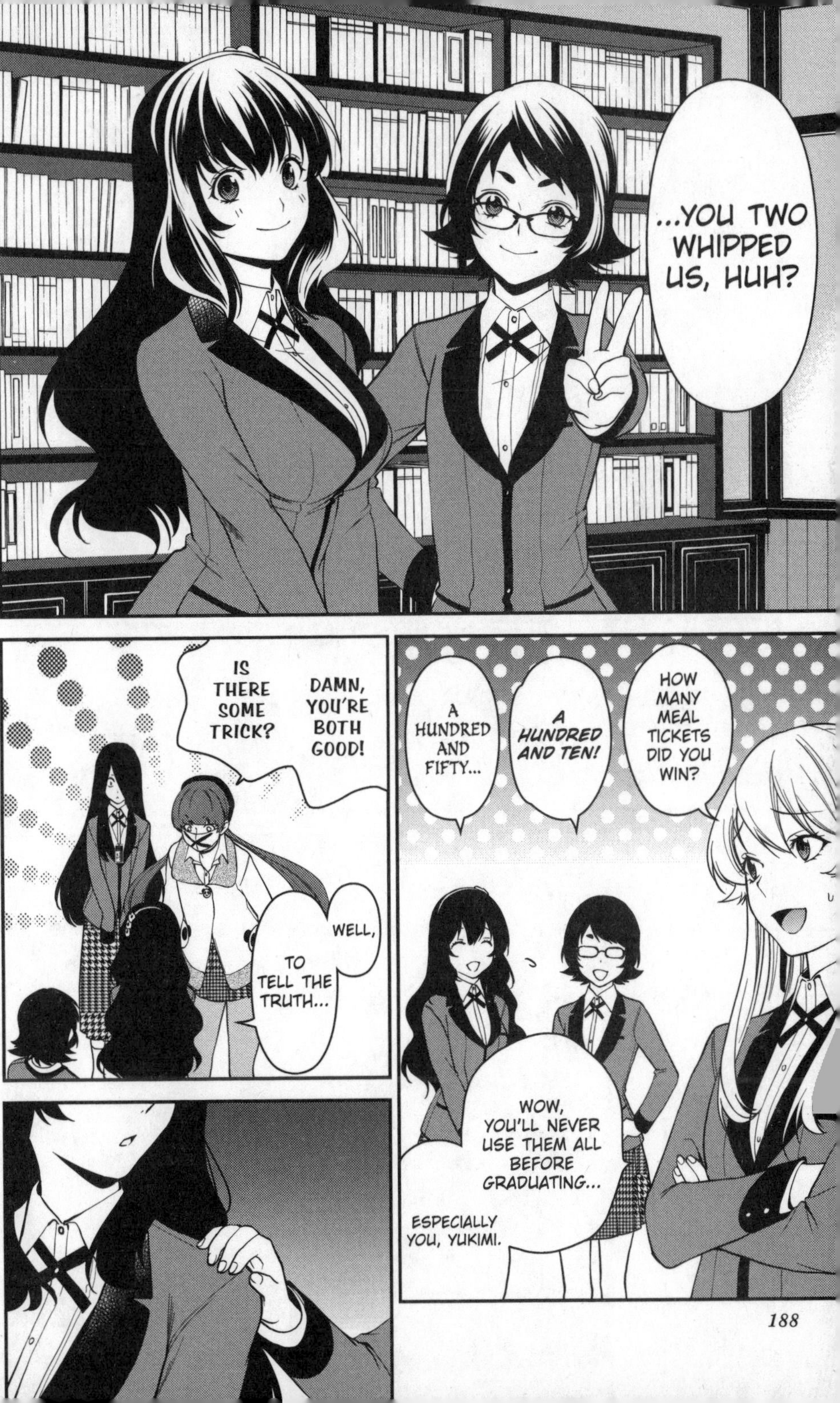

...YOU TWO WHIPPED US, HUH?
HOW MANY MEAL TICKETS DID YOU WIN?
A HUNDRED AND TEN!
A HUNDRED AND FIFTY...
WOW, YOU'LL NEVER USE THEM ALL BEFORE GRADUATING...
ESPECIALLY YOU, YUKIMI.
DAMN, YOU'RE BOTH GOOD!
IS THERE SOME TRICK?
WELL,
TO TELL THE TRUTH...

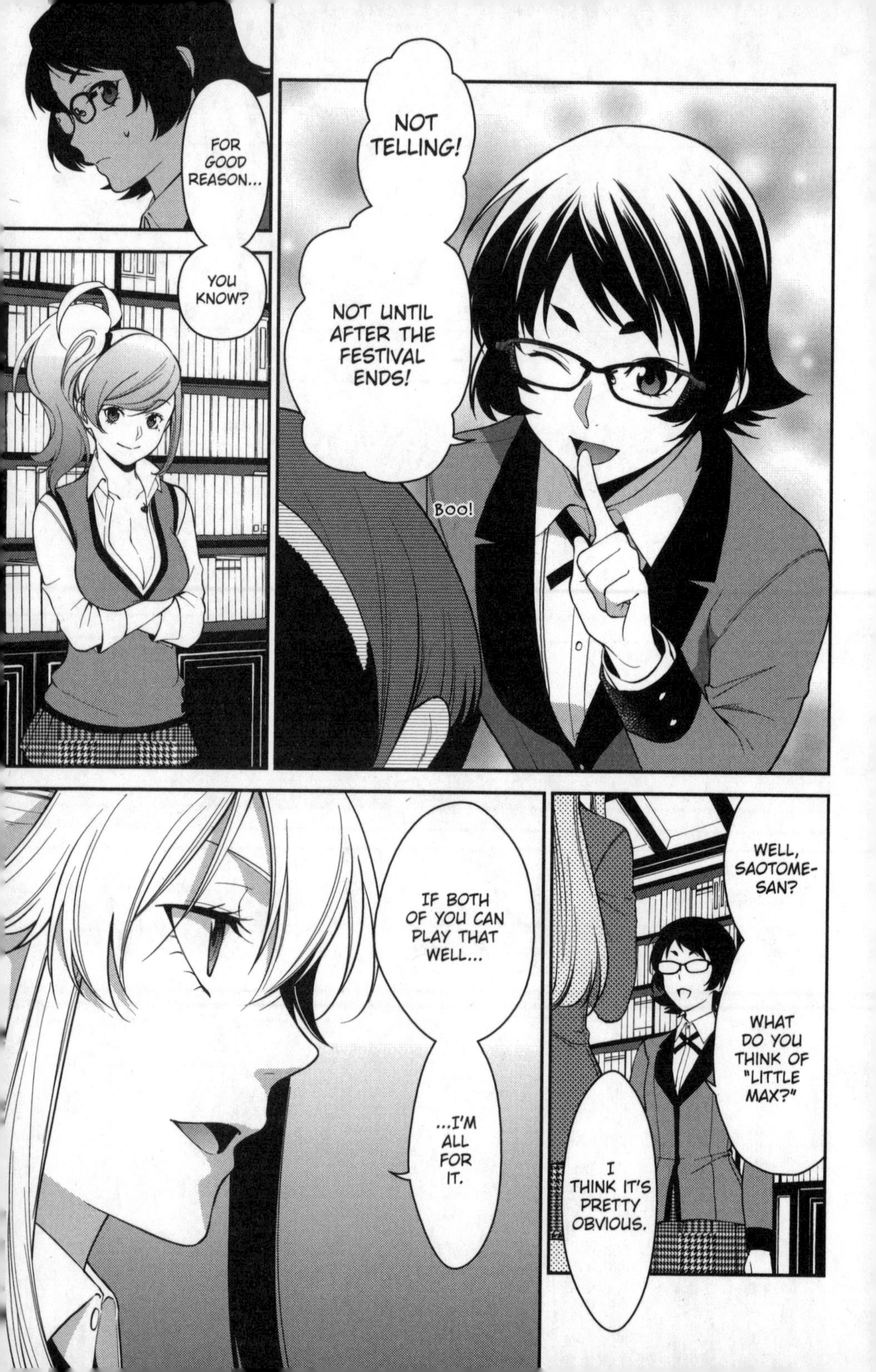
NOT TELLING!
NOT UNTIL AFTER THE FESTIVAL ENDS!
Boo!
FOR GOOD REASON...
YOU KNOW?
WELL, SAOTOME-SAN?
WHAT DO YOU THINK OF "LITTLE MAX?"
I THINK IT'S PRETTY OBVIOUS.
IF BOTH OF YOU CAN PLAY THAT WELL...
...I'M ALL FOR IT.

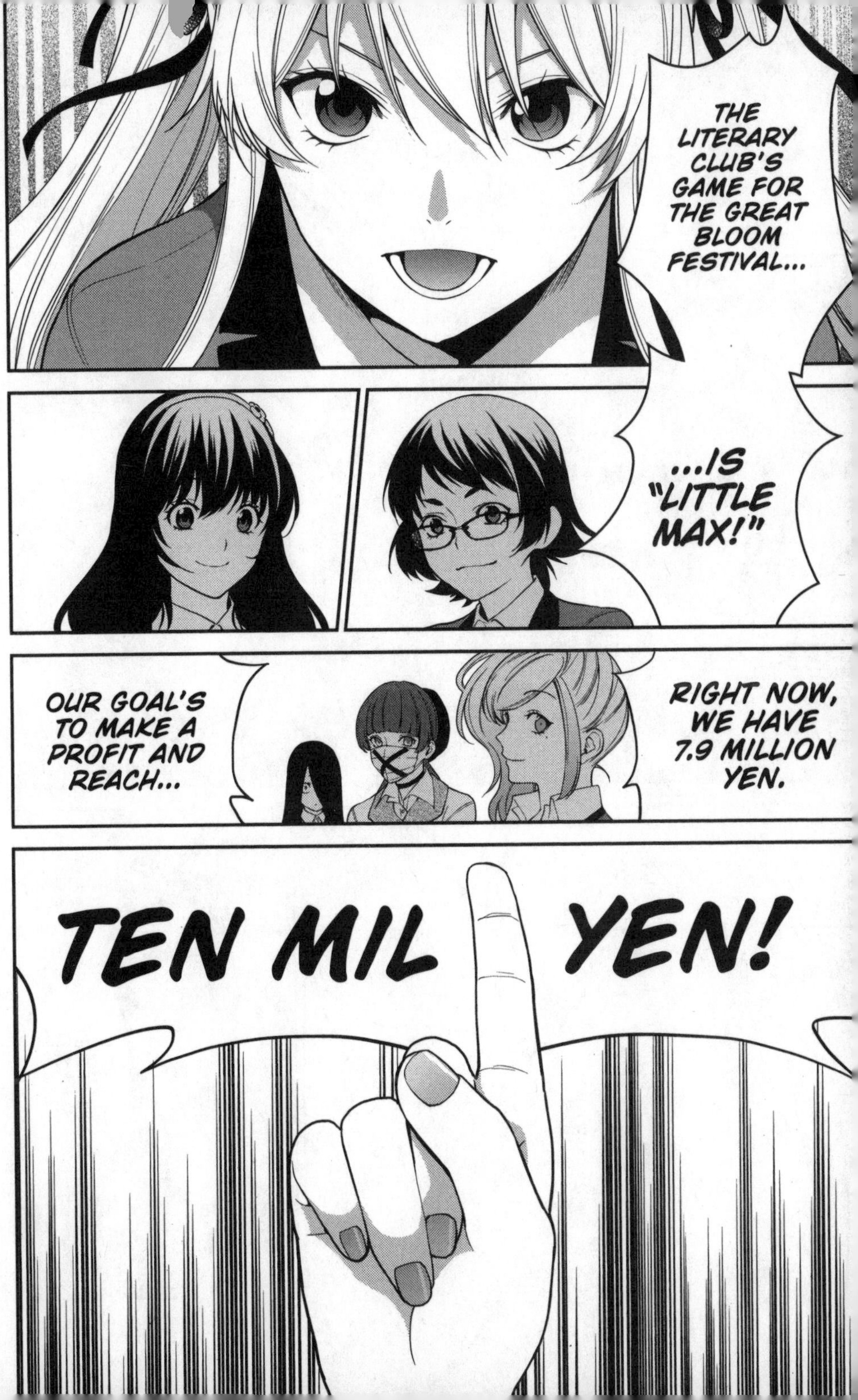
THE LITERARY CLUB'S GAME FOR THE GREAT BLOOM FESTIVAL...
...IS "LITTLE MAX!"
RIGHT NOW, WE HAVE 7.9 MILLION YEN.
OUR GOAL'S TO MAKE A PROFIT AND REACH...
TEN MIL YEN!

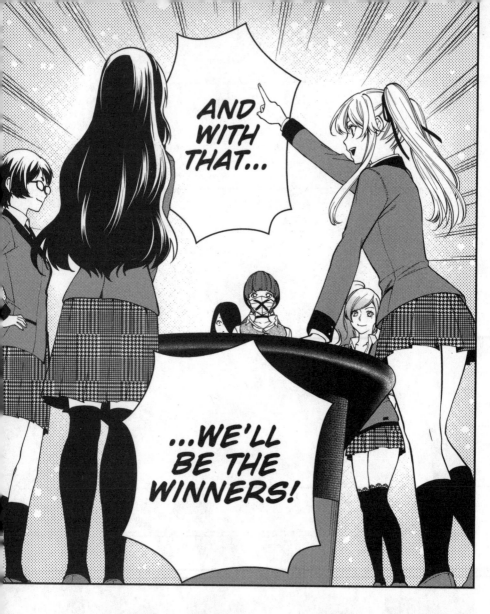

AND WITH THAT...

...WE'LL BE THE WINNERS!

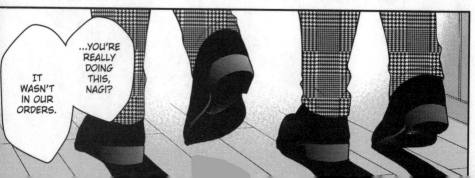

...YOU'RE REALLY DOING THIS, NAGI?

IT WASN'T IN OUR ORDERS.

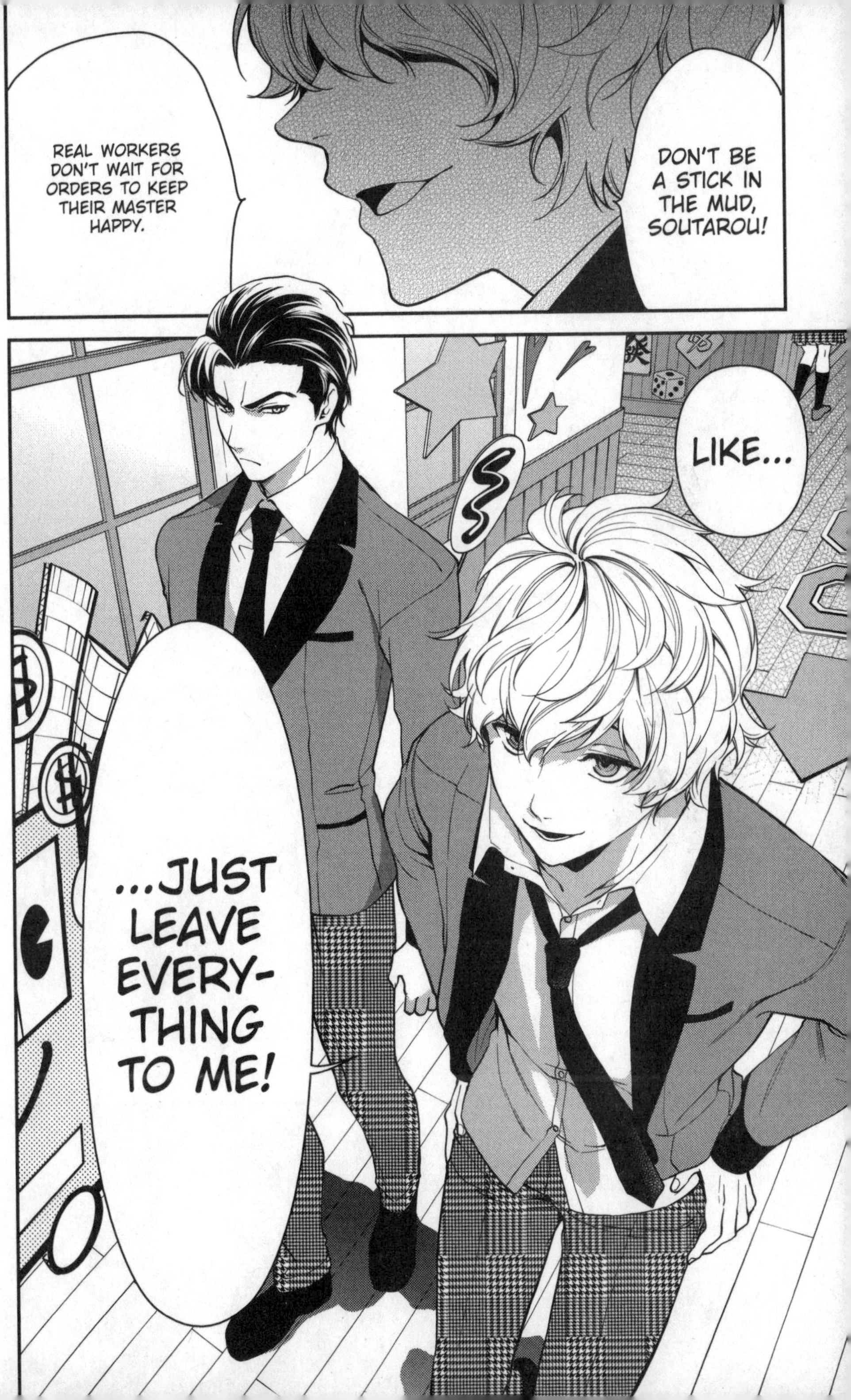
DON'T BE A STICK IN THE MUD, SOUTAROU!
REAL WORKERS DON'T WAIT FOR ORDERS TO KEEP THEIR MASTER HAPPY.
LIKE...
...JUST LEAVE EVERY-THING TO ME!

Kakegurui Twin

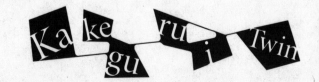

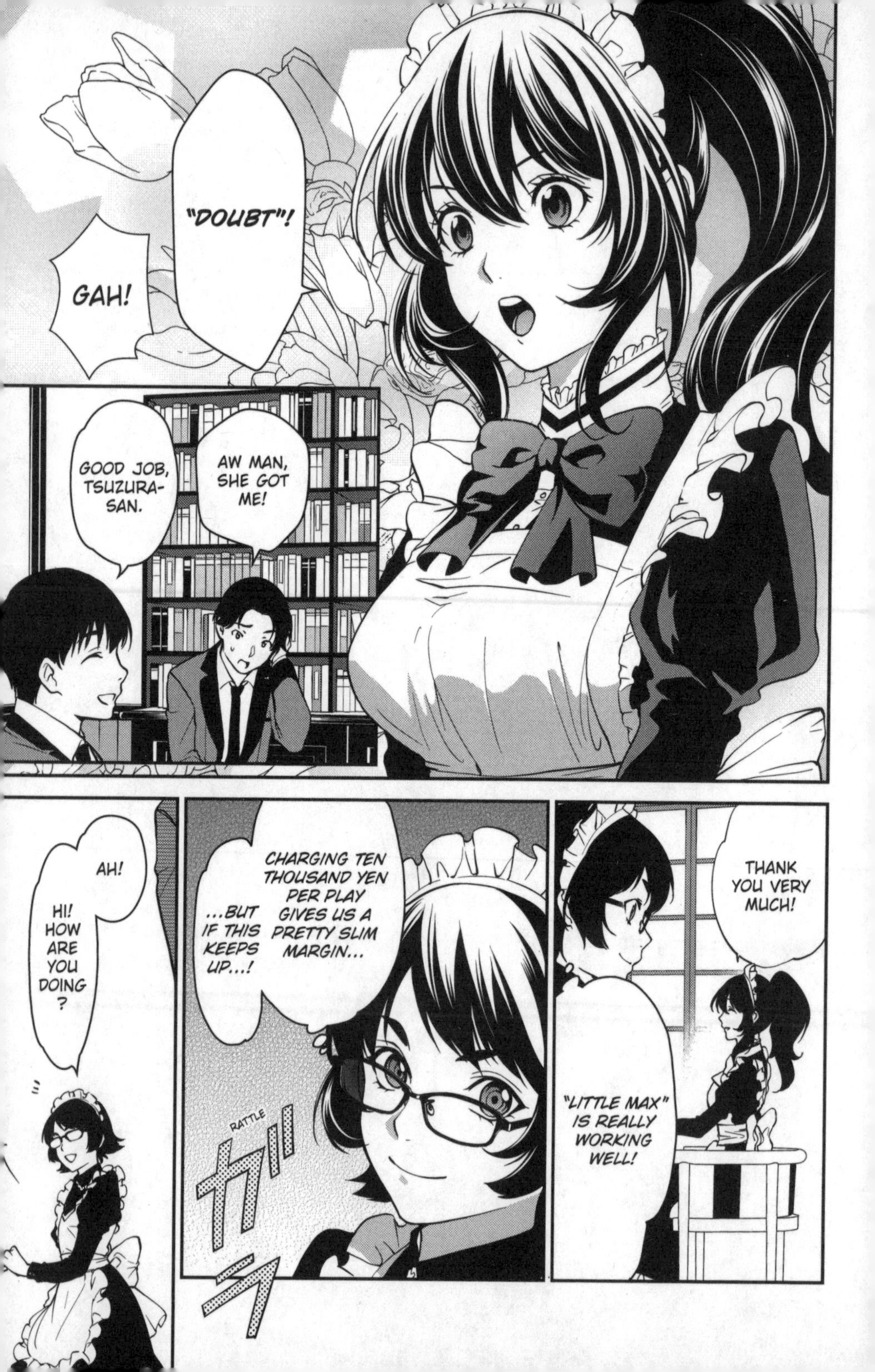
"DOUBT"!
GAH!
AW MAN, SHE GOT ME!
GOOD JOB, TSUZURA-SAN.
THANK YOU VERY MUCH!
"LITTLE MAX" IS REALLY WORKING WELL!
CHARGING TEN THOUSAND YEN PER PLAY GIVES US A PRETTY SLIM MARGIN...
...BUT IF THIS KEEPS UP...!
RATTLE
AH!
HI! HOW ARE YOU DOING?

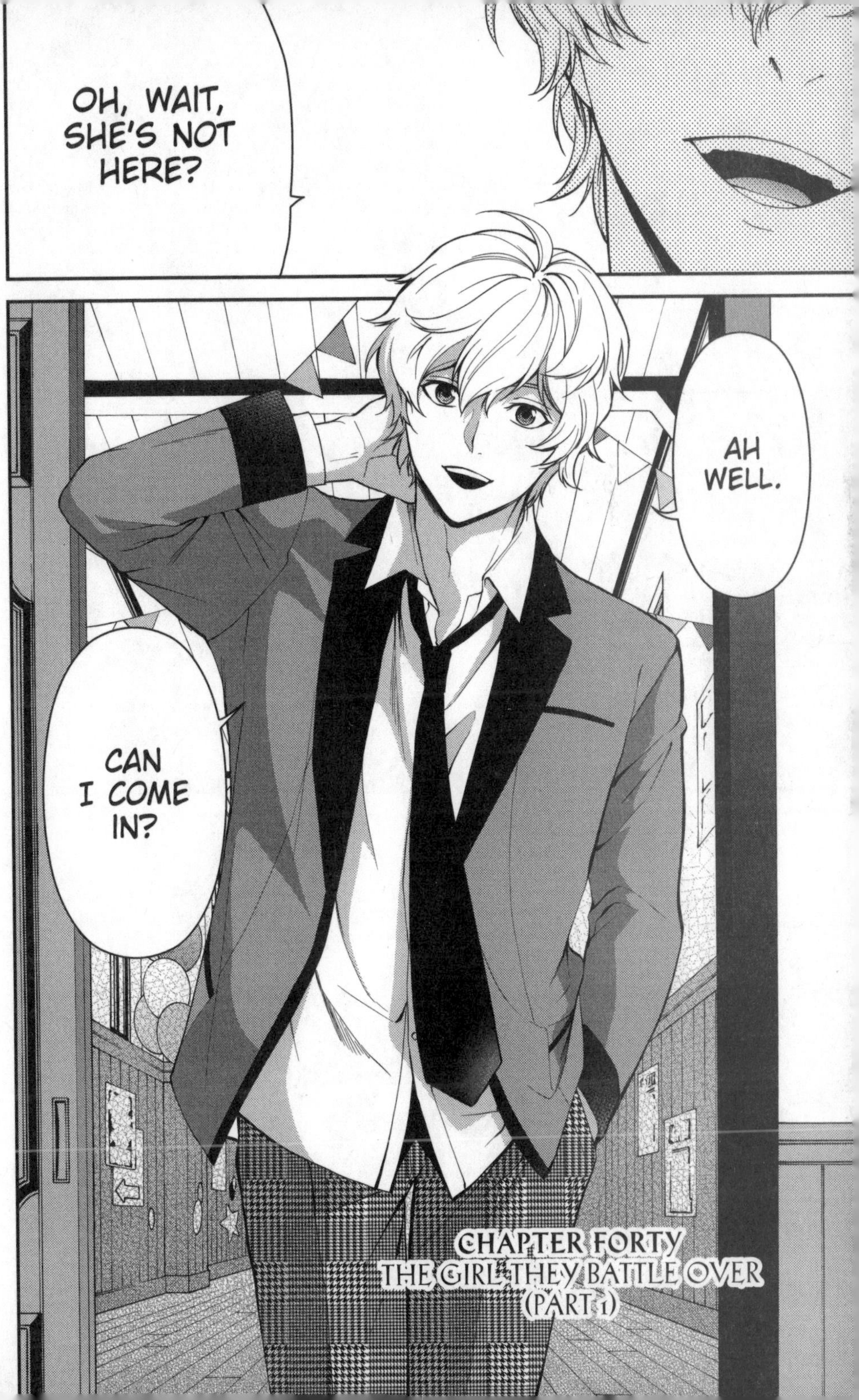
OH, WAIT, SHE'S NOT HERE?
AH WELL.
CAN I COME IN?
CHAPTER FORTY
THE GIRL THEY BATTLE OVER
(PART 1)

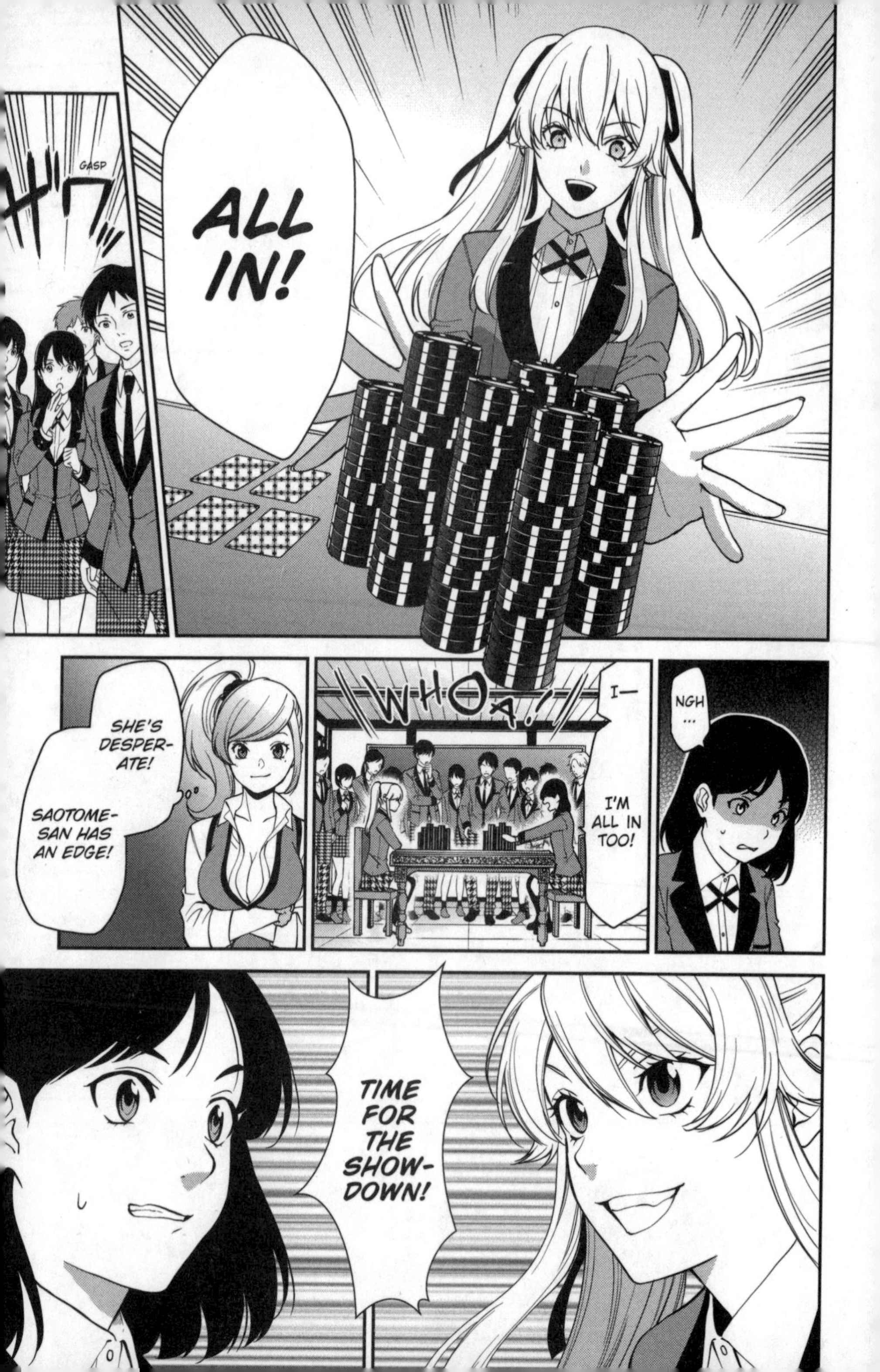
ALL IN!
GASP
NGH ...
WHOA!!
I—
I'M ALL IN TOO!
SHE'S DESPERATE!
SAOTOME-SAN HAS AN EDGE!
TIME FOR THE SHOWDOWN!

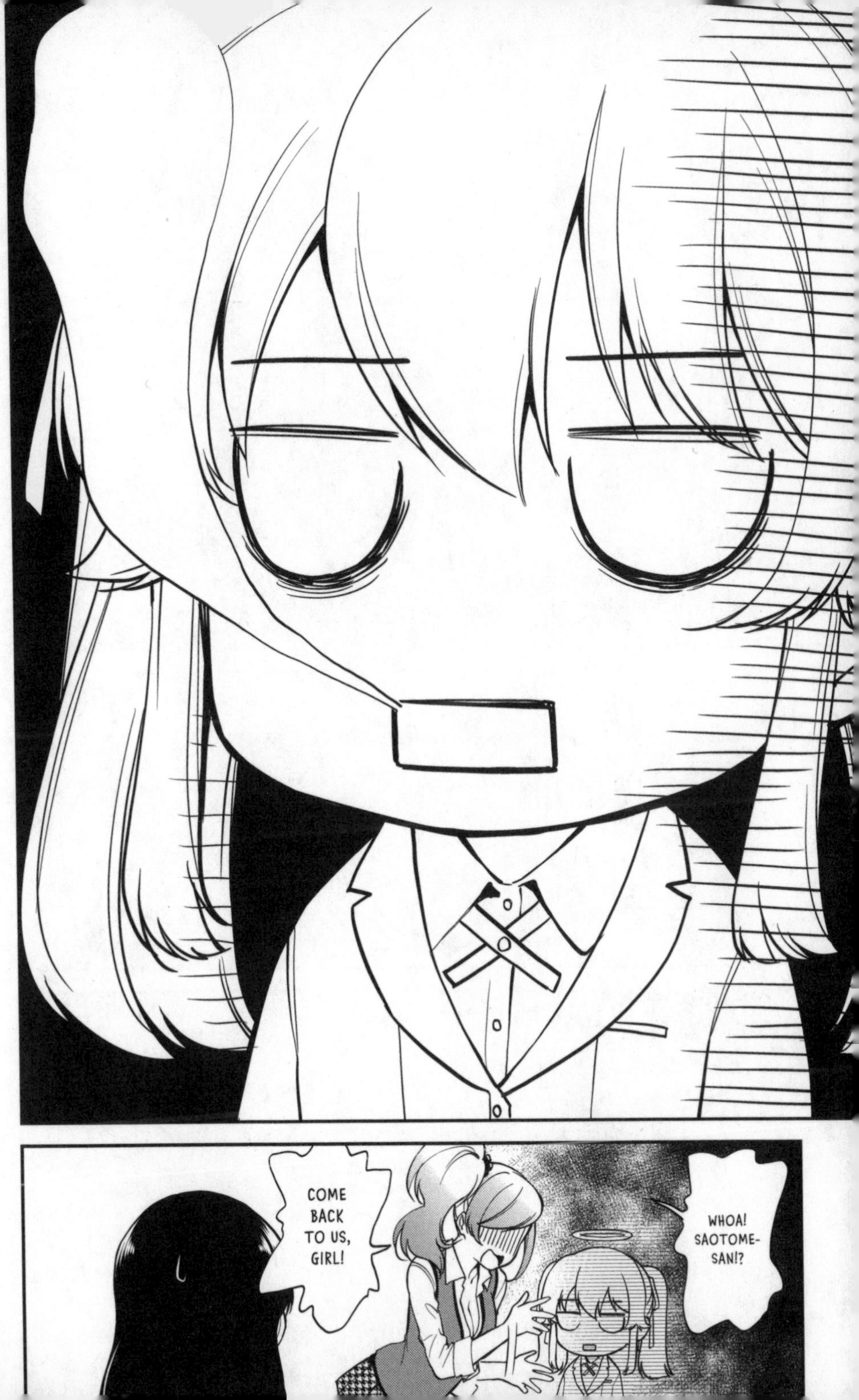
WHOA! SAOTOME-SAN!?
COME BACK TO US, GIRL!

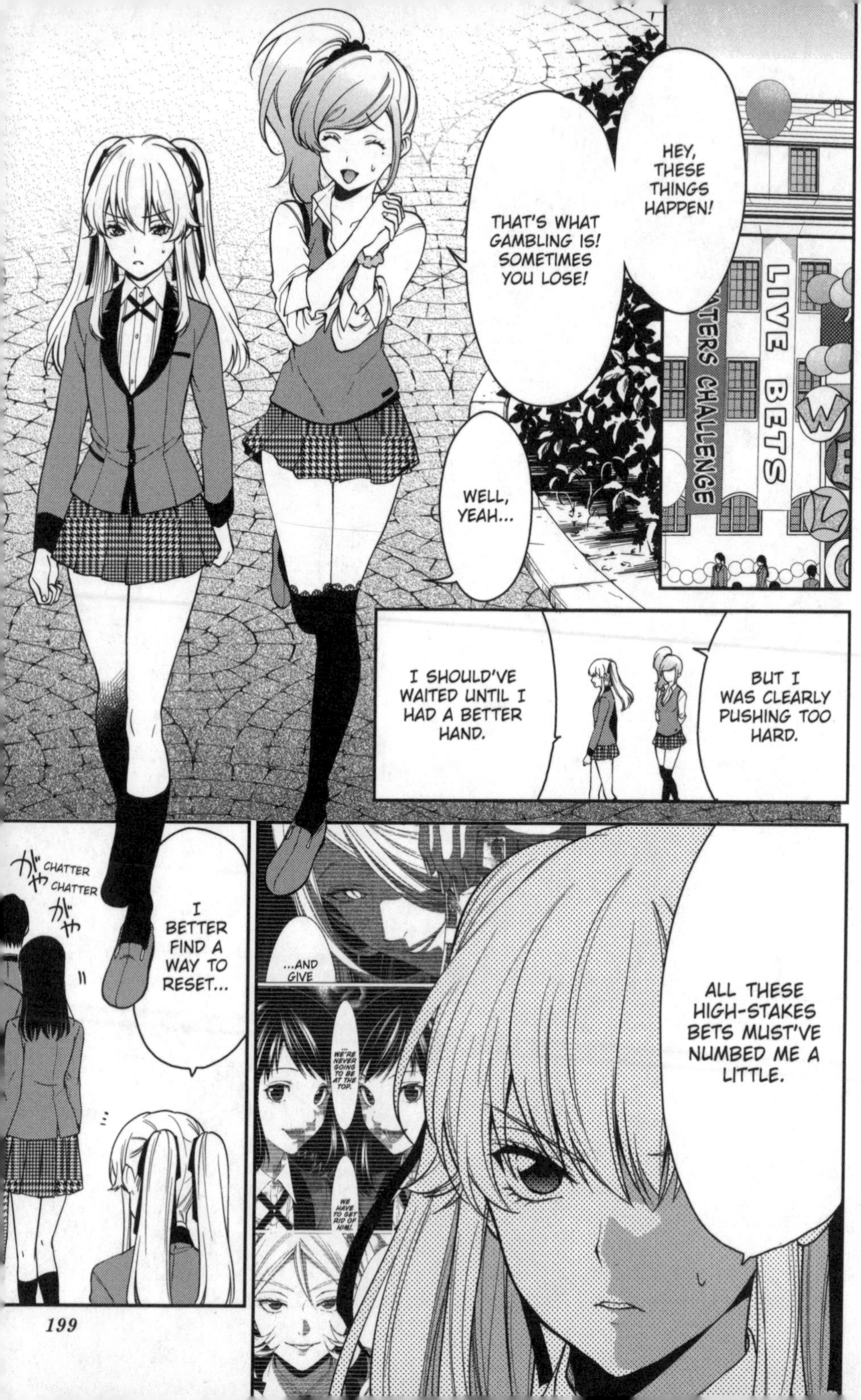
LIVE BETS
HEY, THESE THINGS HAPPEN!
THAT'S WHAT GAMBLING IS! SOMETIMES YOU LOSE!
WELL, YEAH...
BUT I WAS CLEARLY PUSHING TOO HARD.
I SHOULD'VE WAITED UNTIL I HAD A BETTER HAND.
ALL THESE HIGH-STAKES BETS MUST'VE NUMBED ME A LITTLE.
...AND GIVE
...WE'RE NEVER GOING TO BE AT THE TOP.
WE HAVE TO GET RID OF HIM!
がや CHATTER
がや CHATTER
I BETTER FIND A WAY TO RESET...

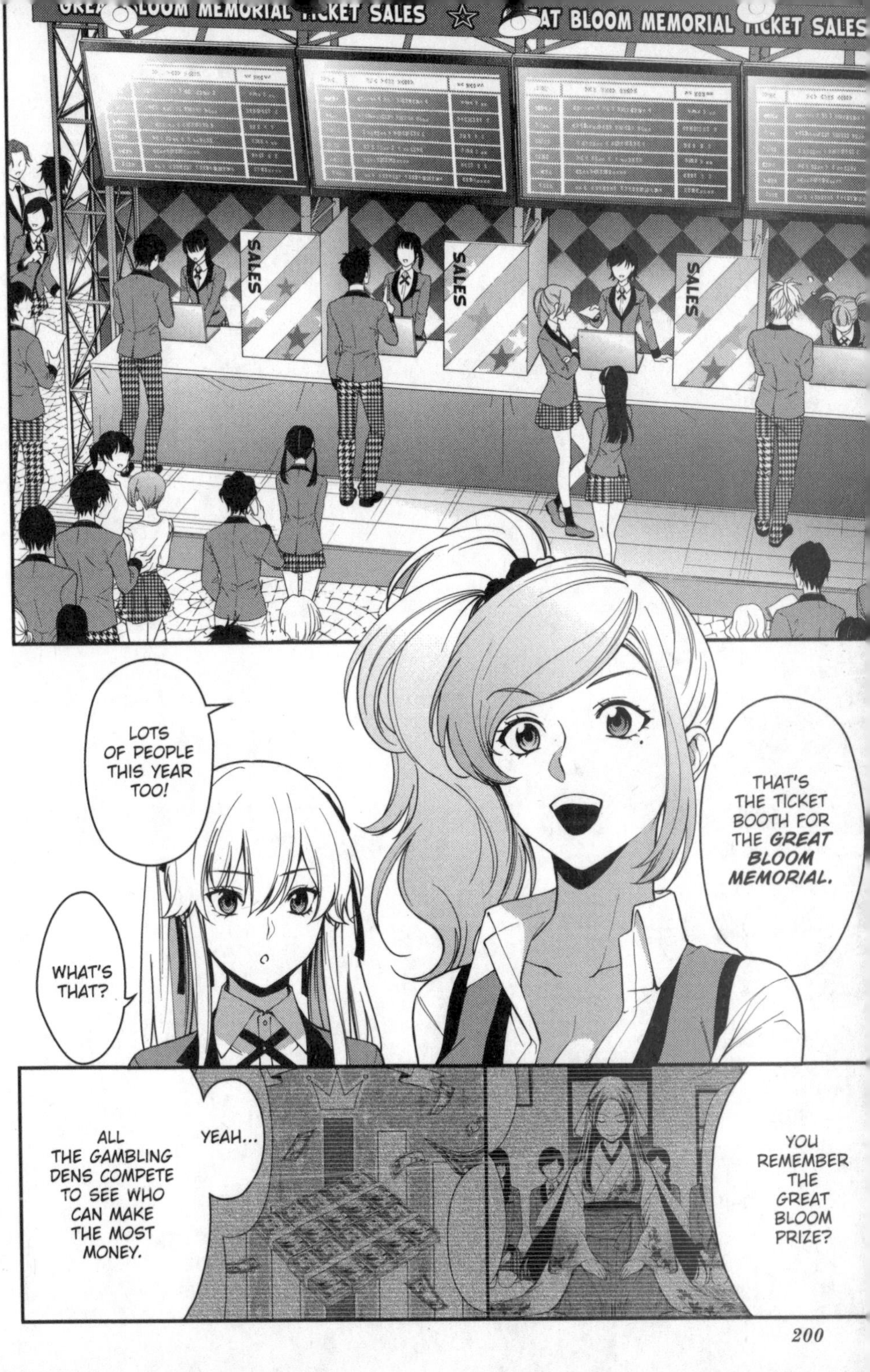
SALES
SALES
SALES
THAT'S THE TICKET BOOTH FOR THE ***GREAT BLOOM MEMORIAL.***
LOTS OF PEOPLE THIS YEAR TOO!
WHAT'S THAT?
YOU REMEMBER THE GREAT BLOOM PRIZE?
YEAH...
ALL THE GAMBLING DENS COMPETE TO SEE WHO CAN MAKE THE MOST MONEY.

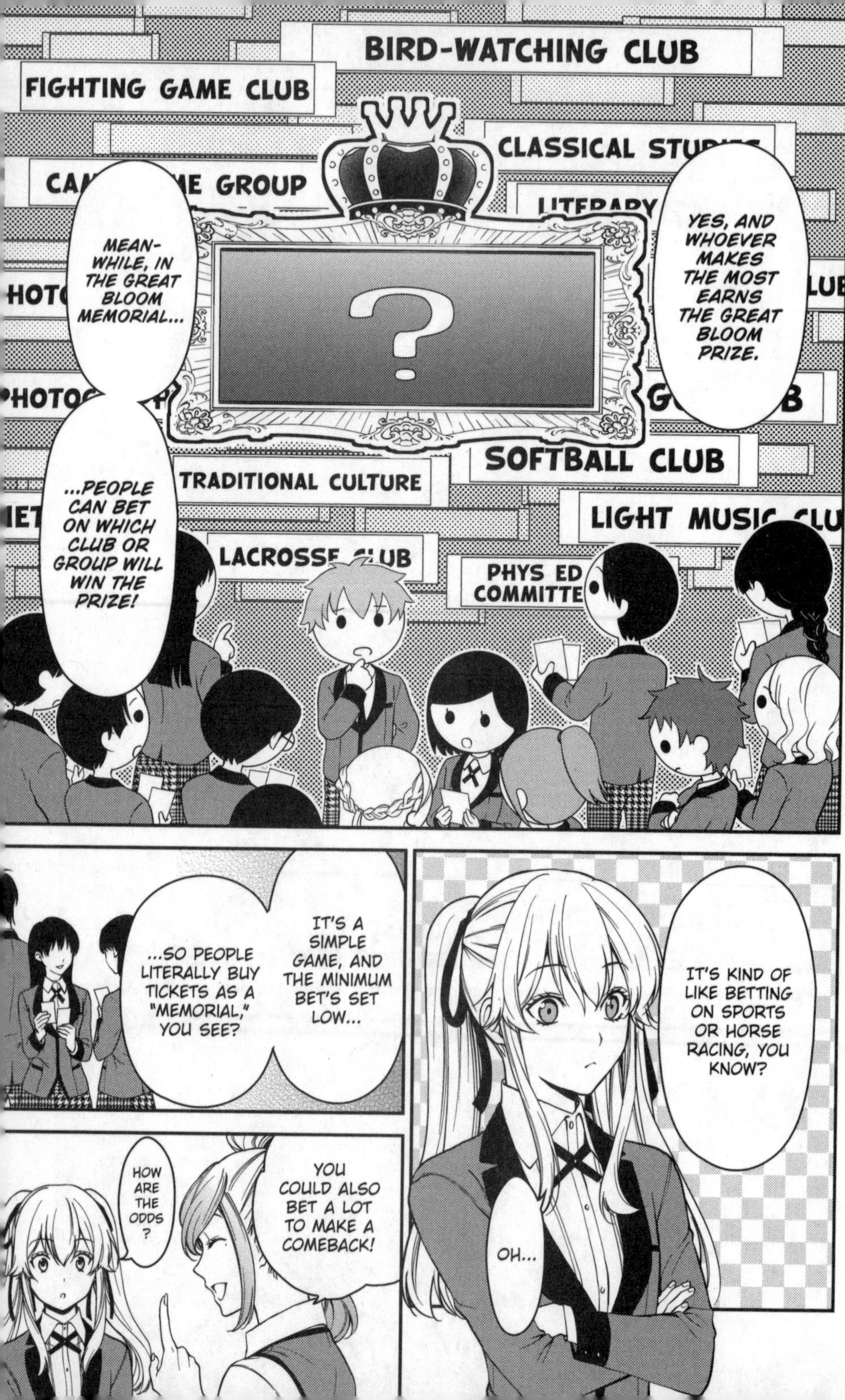
BIRD-WATCHING CLUB
FIGHTING GAME CLUB
CLASSICAL STU
ME GROUP
SOFTBALL CLUB
TRADITIONAL CULTURE
LIGHT MUSIC
LACROSSE
PHYS ED COMMITTE
?
YES, AND WHOEVER MAKES THE MOST EARNS THE GREAT BLOOM PRIZE.
MEAN-WHILE, IN THE GREAT BLOOM MEMORIAL...
...PEOPLE CAN BET ON WHICH CLUB OR GROUP WILL WIN THE PRIZE!
IT'S KIND OF LIKE BETTING ON SPORTS OR HORSE RACING, YOU KNOW?
OH...
IT'S A SIMPLE GAME, AND THE MINIMUM BET'S SET LOW...
...SO PEOPLE LITERALLY BUY TICKETS AS A "MEMORIAL," YOU SEE?
YOU COULD ALSO BET A LOT TO MAKE A COMEBACK!
HOW ARE THE ODDS?

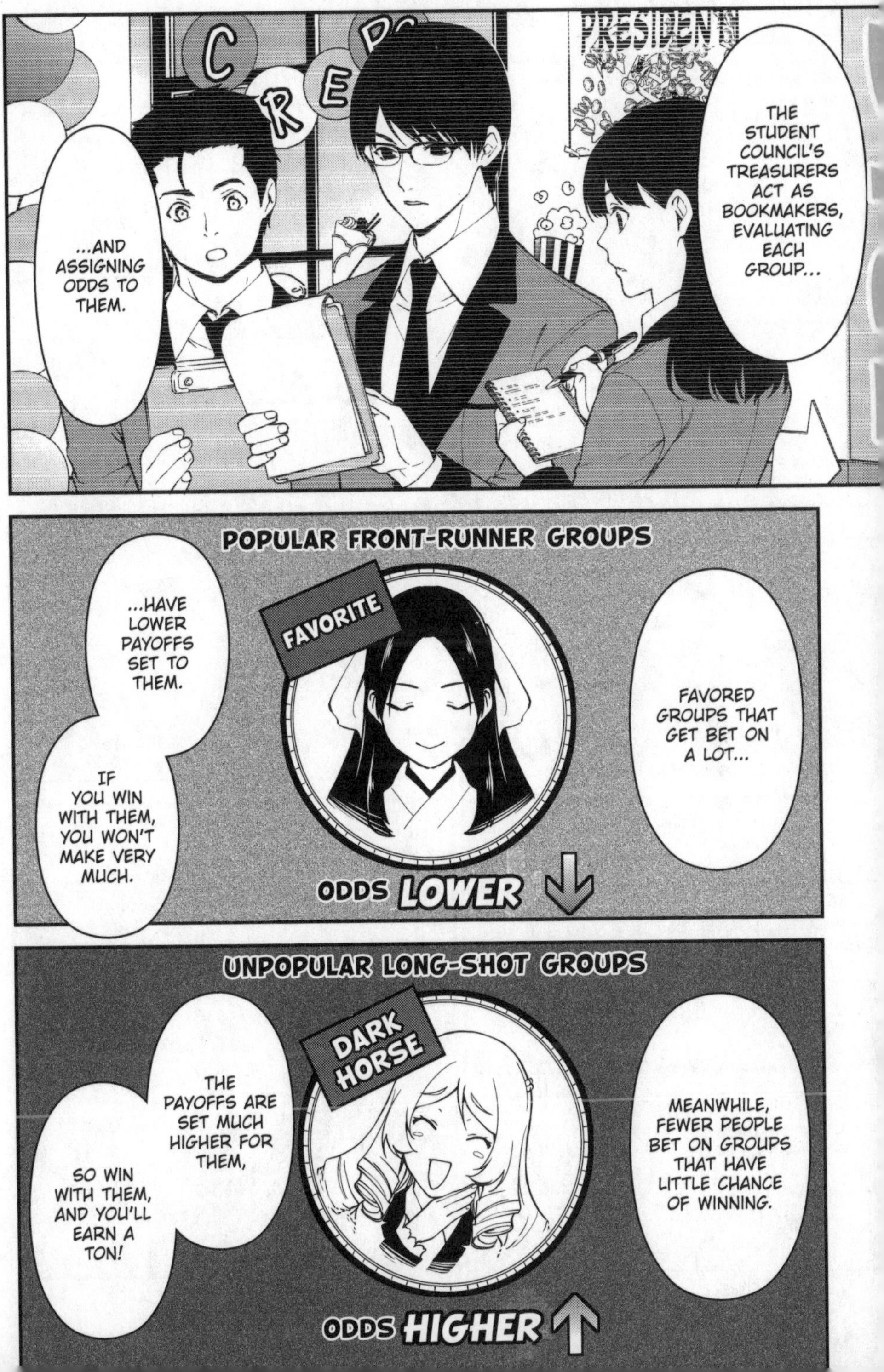
THE STUDENT COUNCIL'S TREASURERS ACT AS BOOKMAKERS, EVALUATING EACH GROUP...
...AND ASSIGNING ODDS TO THEM.
POPULAR FRONT-RUNNER GROUPS
FAVORED GROUPS THAT GET BET ON A LOT...
FAVORITE
...HAVE LOWER PAYOFFS SET TO THEM.
IF YOU WIN WITH THEM, YOU WON'T MAKE VERY MUCH.
ODDS LOWER
UNPOPULAR LONG-SHOT GROUPS
MEANWHILE, FEWER PEOPLE BET ON GROUPS THAT HAVE LITTLE CHANCE OF WINNING.
DARK HORSE
THE PAYOFFS ARE SET MUCH HIGHER FOR THEM,
SO WIN WITH THEM, AND YOU'LL EARN A TON!
ODDS HIGHER

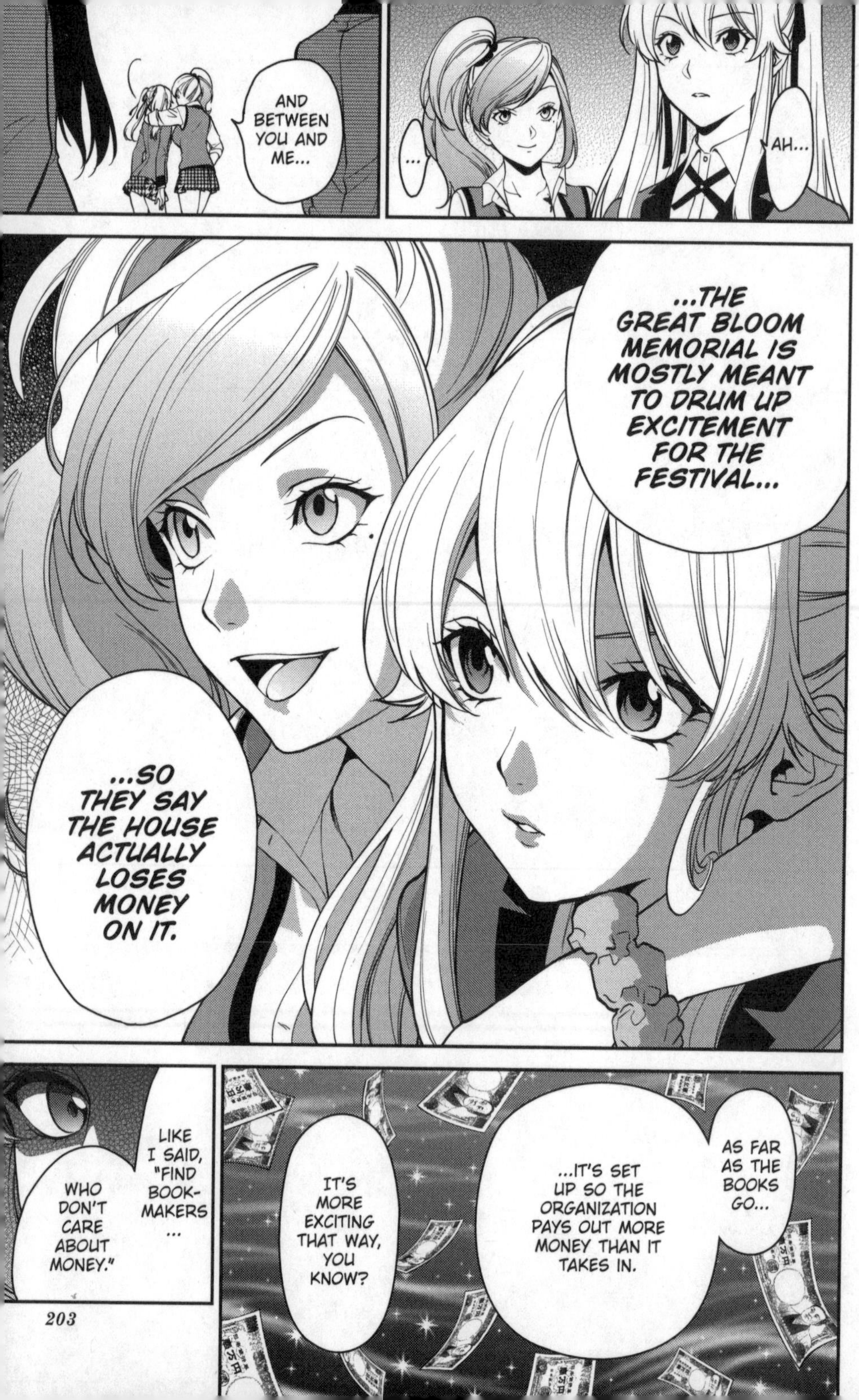
AH...
...
AND BETWEEN YOU AND ME...
...THE GREAT BLOOM MEMORIAL IS MOSTLY MEANT TO DRUM UP EXCITEMENT FOR THE FESTIVAL...
...SO THEY SAY THE HOUSE ACTUALLY LOSES MONEY ON IT.
AS FAR AS THE BOOKS GO...
...IT'S SET UP SO THE ORGANIZATION PAYS OUT MORE MONEY THAN IT TAKES IN.
IT'S MORE EXCITING THAT WAY, YOU KNOW?
LIKE I SAID, "FIND BOOK-MAKERS...
WHO DON'T CARE ABOUT MONEY."

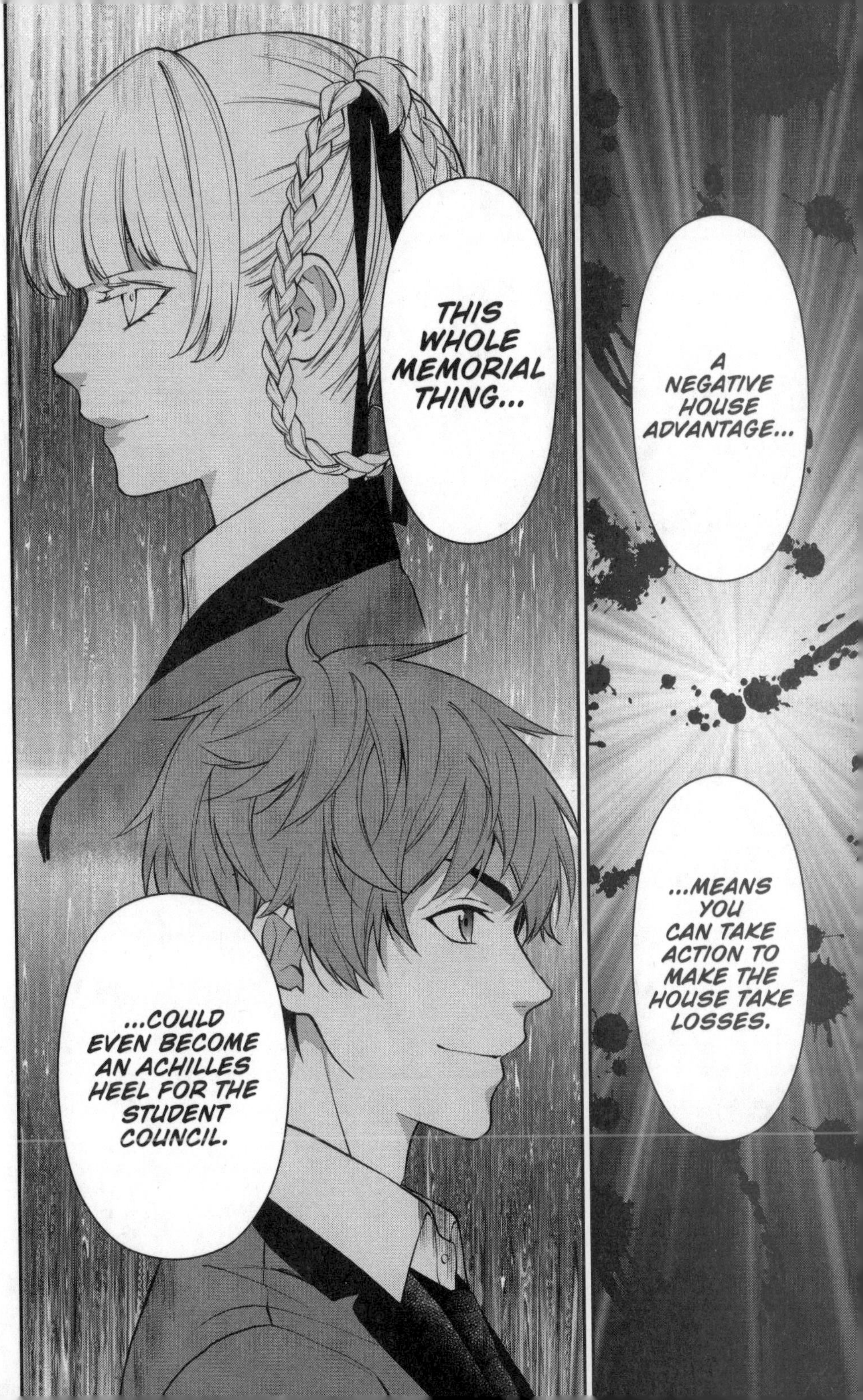
A NEGATIVE HOUSE ADVANTAGE...
...MEANS YOU CAN TAKE ACTION TO MAKE THE HOUSE TAKE LOSSES.
THIS WHOLE MEMORIAL THING...
...COULD EVEN BECOME AN ACHILLES HEEL FOR THE STUDENT COUNCIL.

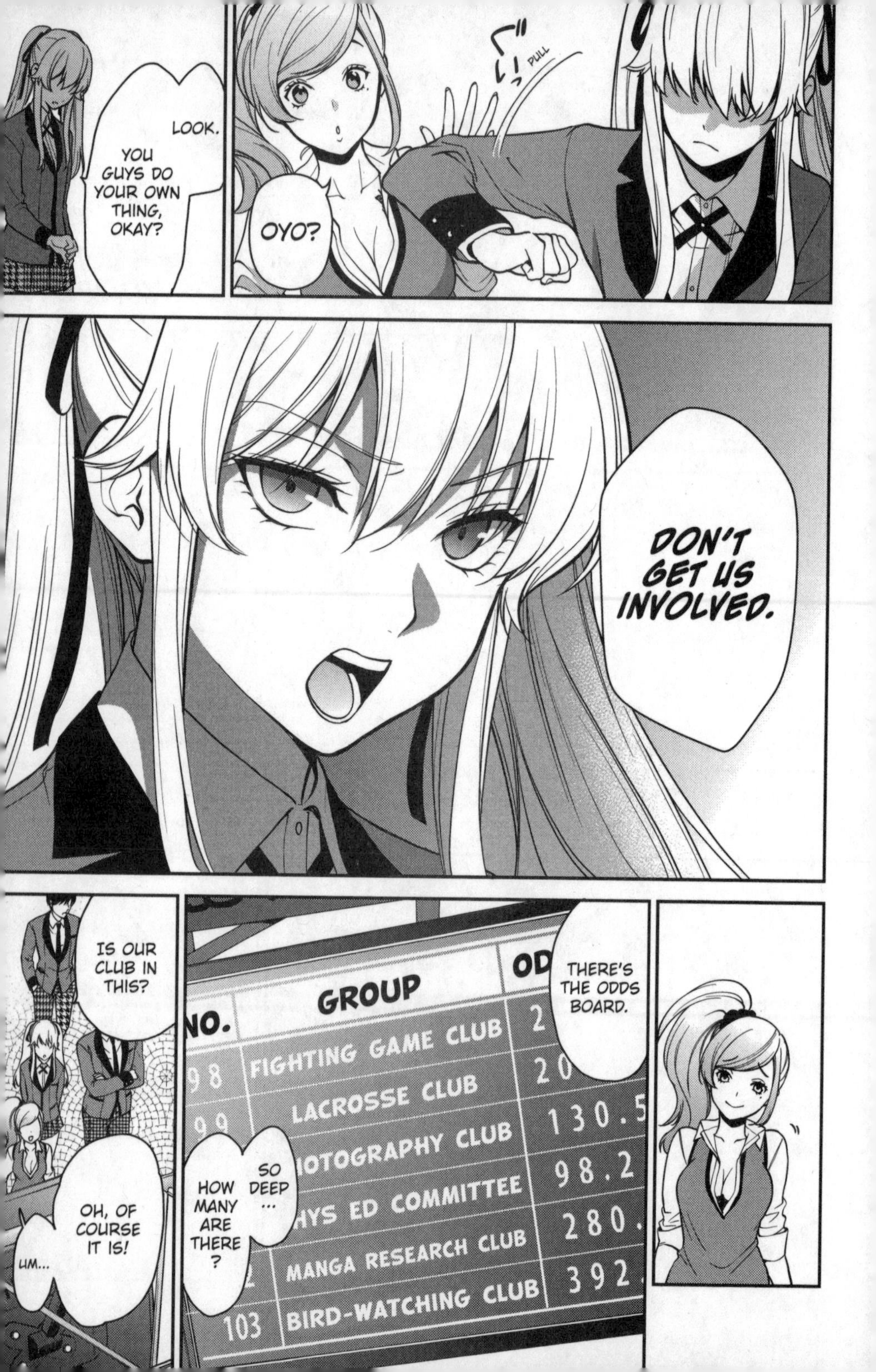
PULL
OYO?
LOOK.
YOU GUYS DO YOUR OWN THING, OKAY?
DON'T GET US INVOLVED.
THERE'S THE ODDS BOARD.
NO.
GROUP
OD
FIGHTING GAME CLUB
LACROSSE CLUB
130.5
HOTOGRAPHY CLUB
98.2
HYS ED COMMITTEE
280.
MANGA RESEARCH CLUB
392.
103
BIRD-WATCHING CLUB
SO DEEP...
HOW MANY ARE THERE?
IS OUR CLUB IN THIS?
OH, OF COURSE IT IS!
UM...

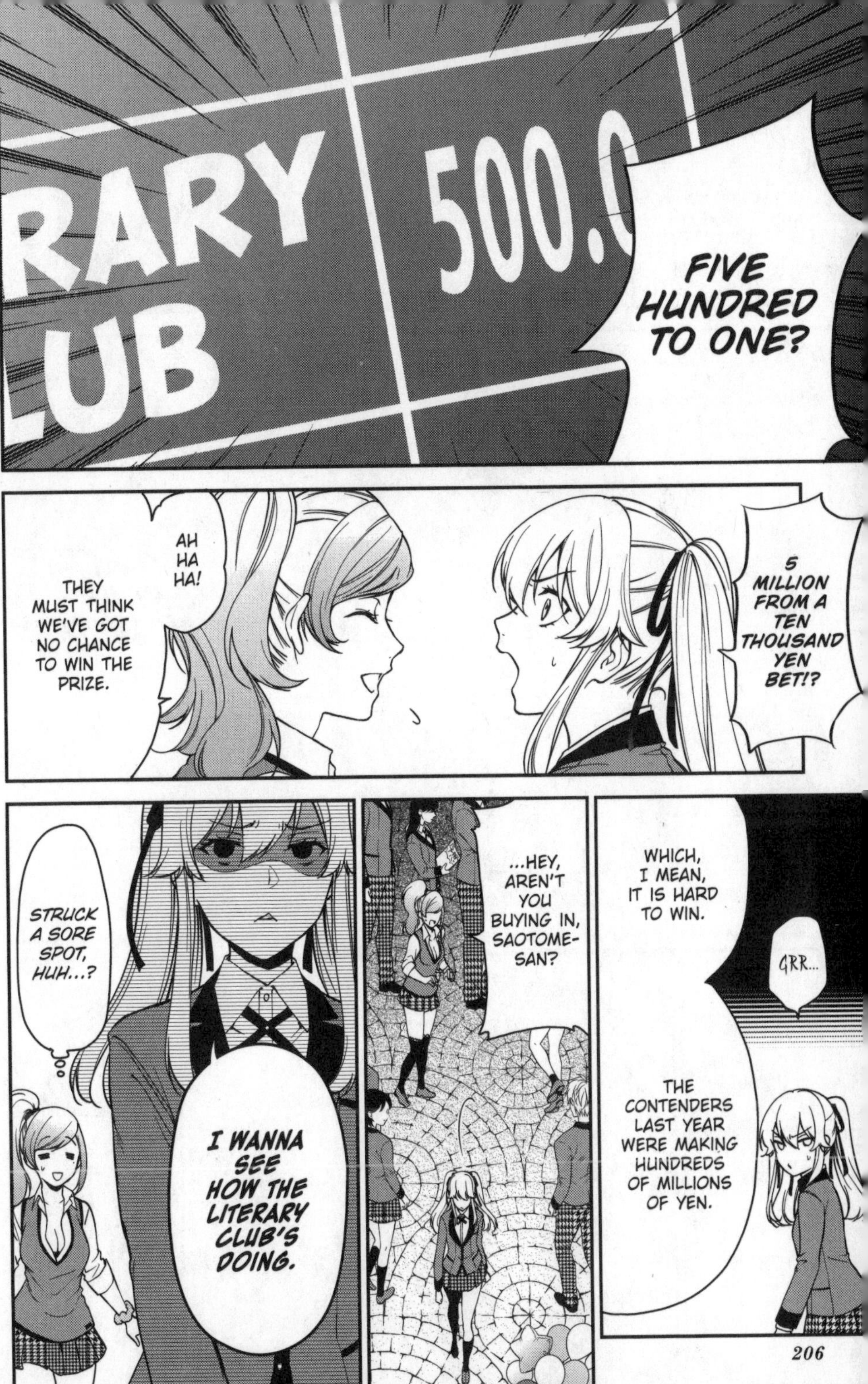
RARY
LUB
500.0
FIVE HUNDRED TO ONE?
5 MILLION FROM A TEN THOUSAND YEN BET!?
AH HA HA!
THEY MUST THINK WE'VE GOT NO CHANCE TO WIN THE PRIZE.
WHICH, I MEAN, IT IS HARD TO WIN.
GRR...
THE CONTENDERS LAST YEAR WERE MAKING HUNDREDS OF MILLIONS OF YEN.
...HEY, AREN'T YOU BUYING IN, SAOTOME-SAN?
STRUCK A SORE SPOT, HUH...?
I WANNA SEE HOW THE LITERARY CLUB'S DOING.

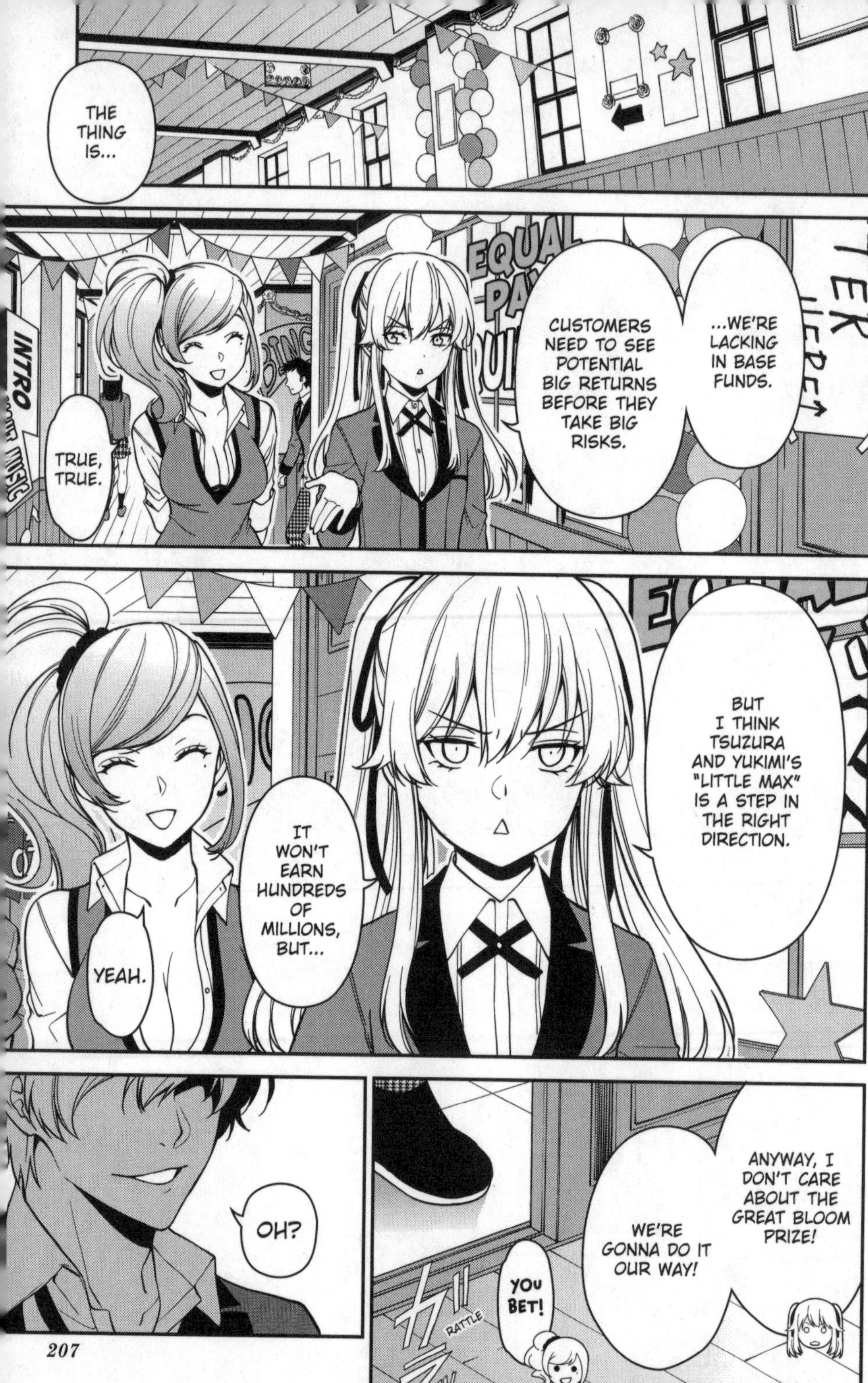
THE THING IS...
...WE'RE LACKING IN BASE FUNDS.
CUSTOMERS NEED TO SEE POTENTIAL BIG RETURNS BEFORE THEY TAKE BIG RISKS.
TRUE, TRUE.
BUT I THINK TSUZURA AND YUKIMI'S "LITTLE MAX" IS A STEP IN THE RIGHT DIRECTION.
IT WON'T EARN HUNDREDS OF MILLIONS, BUT...
YEAH.
ANYWAY, I DON'T CARE ABOUT THE GREAT BLOOM PRIZE!
WE'RE GONNA DO IT OUR WAY!
YOU BET!
RATTLE
OH?

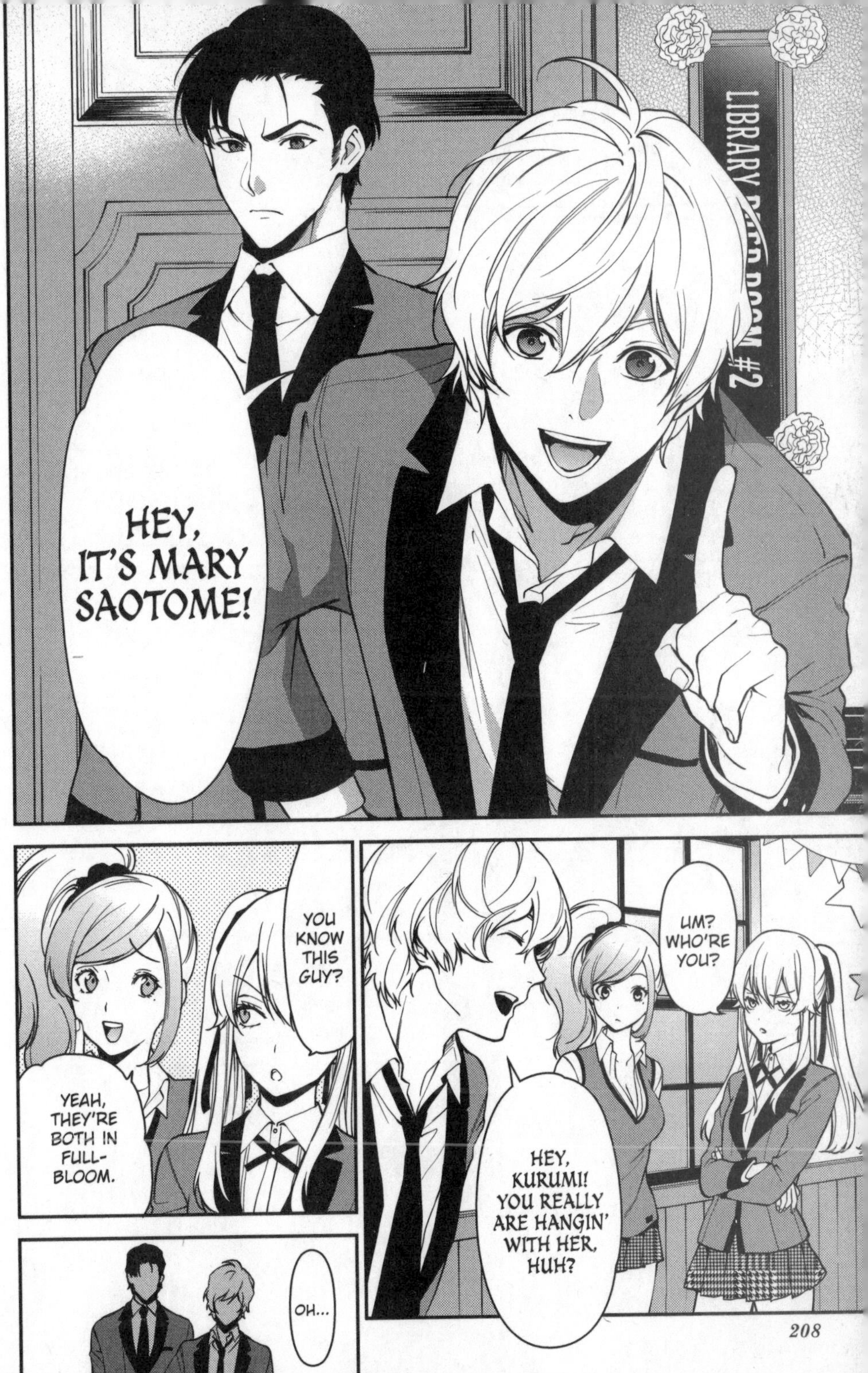

LIBRARY
HEY, IT'S MARY SAOTOME!
UM? WHO'RE YOU?
HEY, KURUMI! YOU REALLY ARE HANGIN' WITH HER, HUH?
YOU KNOW THIS GUY?
YEAH, THEY'RE BOTH IN FULL-BLOOM.
OH...

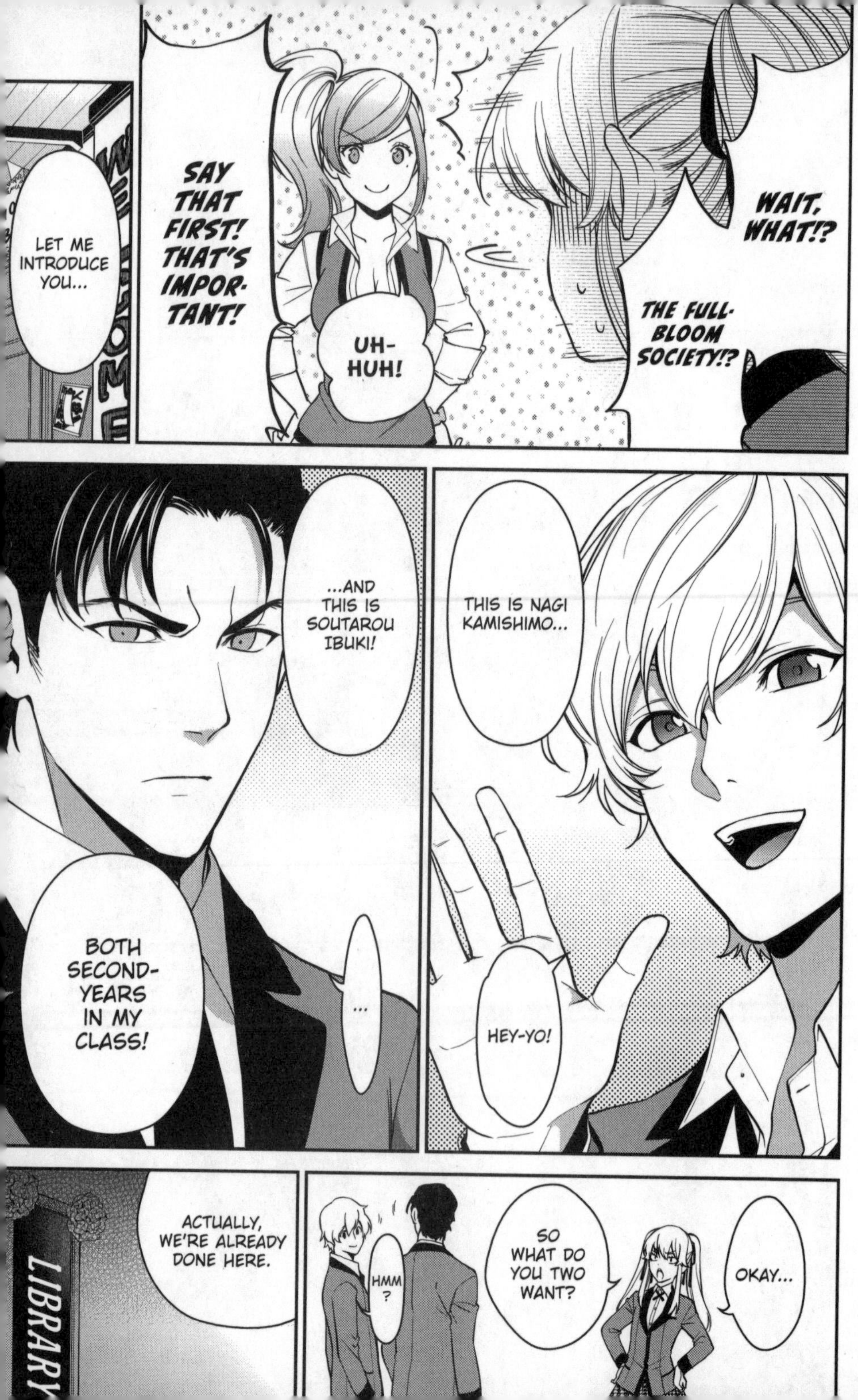
WAIT, WHAT!?
THE FULL-BLOOM SOCIETY!?
SAY THAT FIRST! THAT'S IMPORTANT!
UH-HUH!
LET ME INTRODUCE YOU...
THIS IS NAGI KAMISHIMO...
HEY-YO!
...AND THIS IS SOUTAROU IBUKI!
BOTH SECOND-YEARS IN MY CLASS!
...
OKAY...
SO WHAT DO YOU TWO WANT?
HMM?
ACTUALLY, WE'RE ALREADY DONE HERE.
LIBRARY

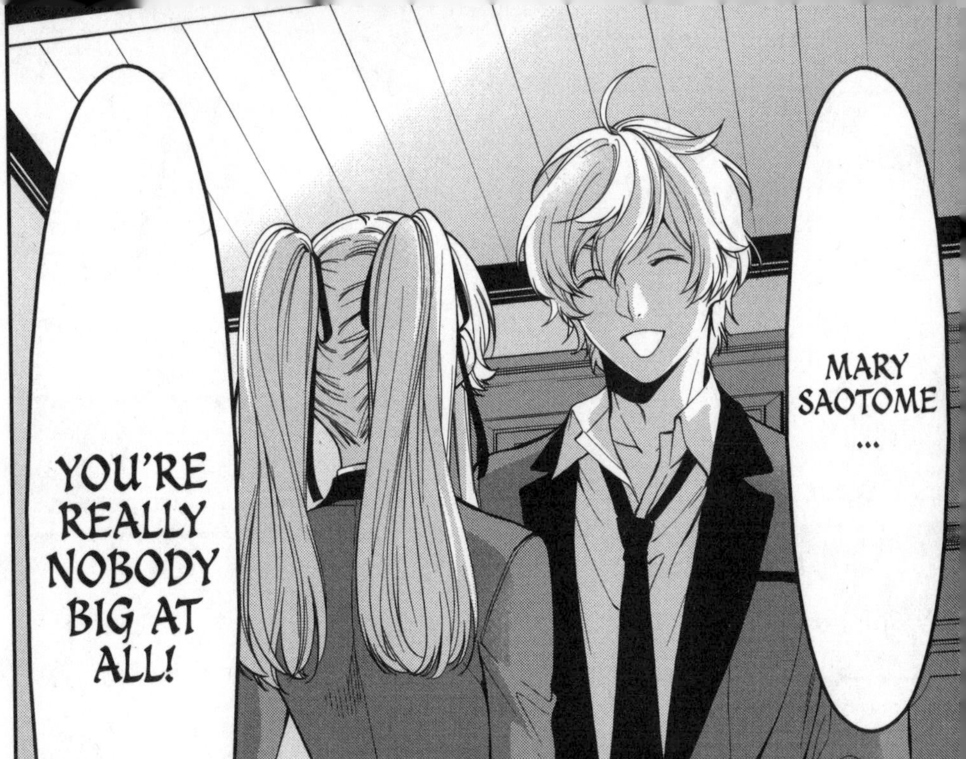
MARY SAOTOME ...
YOU'RE REALLY NOBODY BIG AT ALL!

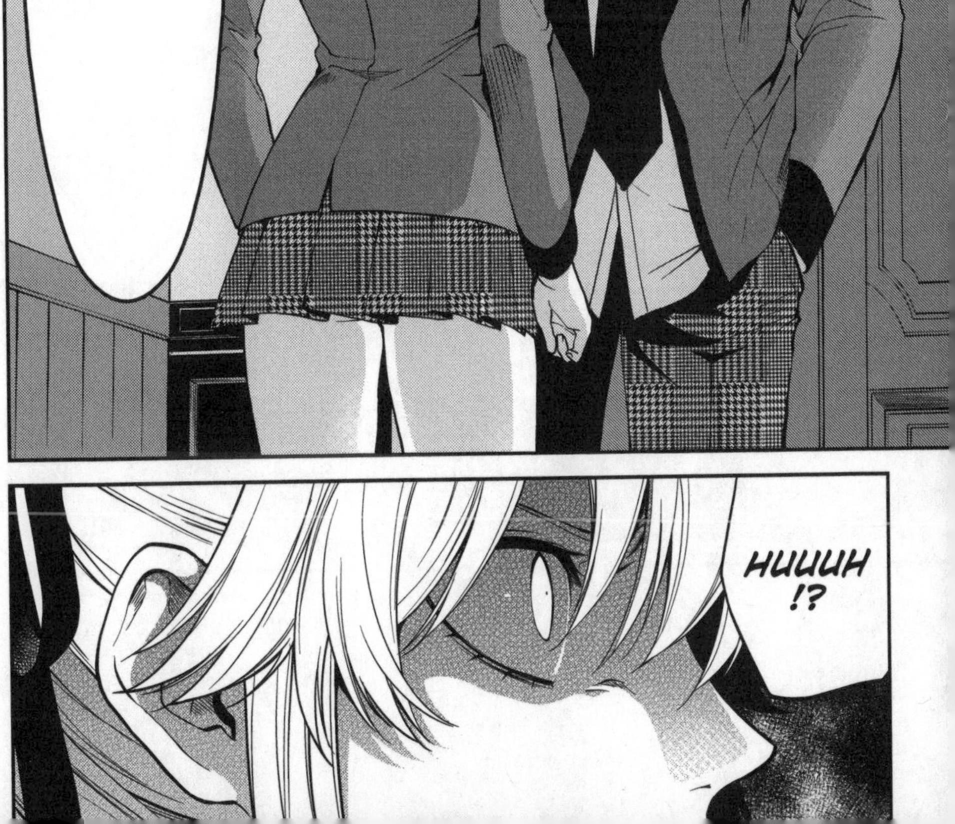
HUUUH !?

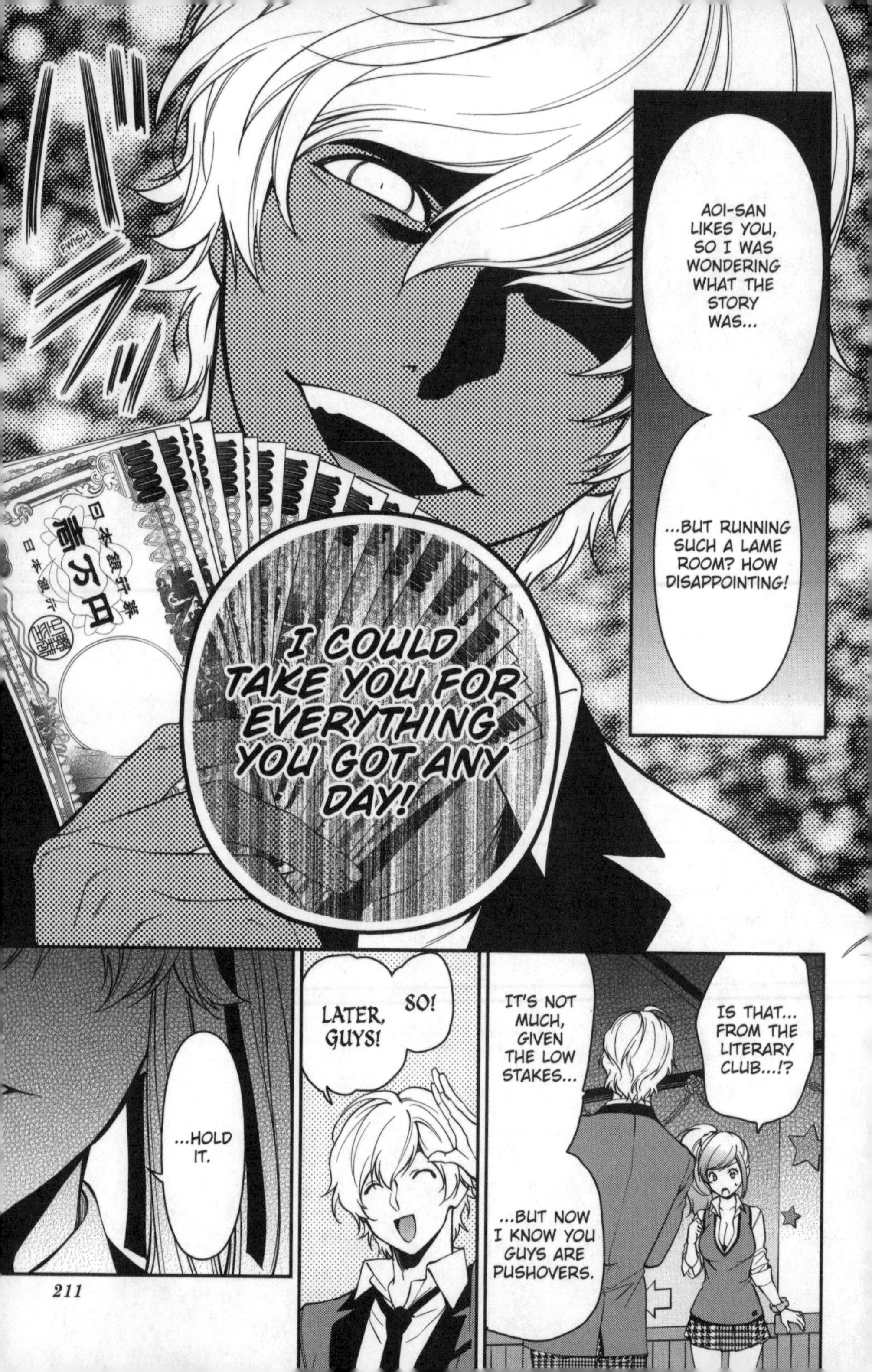
FWISH
AOI-SAN LIKES YOU, SO I WAS WONDERING WHAT THE STORY WAS...
...BUT RUNNING SUCH A LAME ROOM? HOW DISAPPOINTING!
I COULD TAKE YOU FOR EVERYTHING YOU GOT ANY DAY!
IS THAT... FROM THE LITERARY CLUB...!?
IT'S NOT MUCH, GIVEN THE LOW STAKES...
...BUT NOW I KNOW YOU GUYS ARE PUSHOVERS.
SO!
LATER, GUYS!
...HOLD IT.

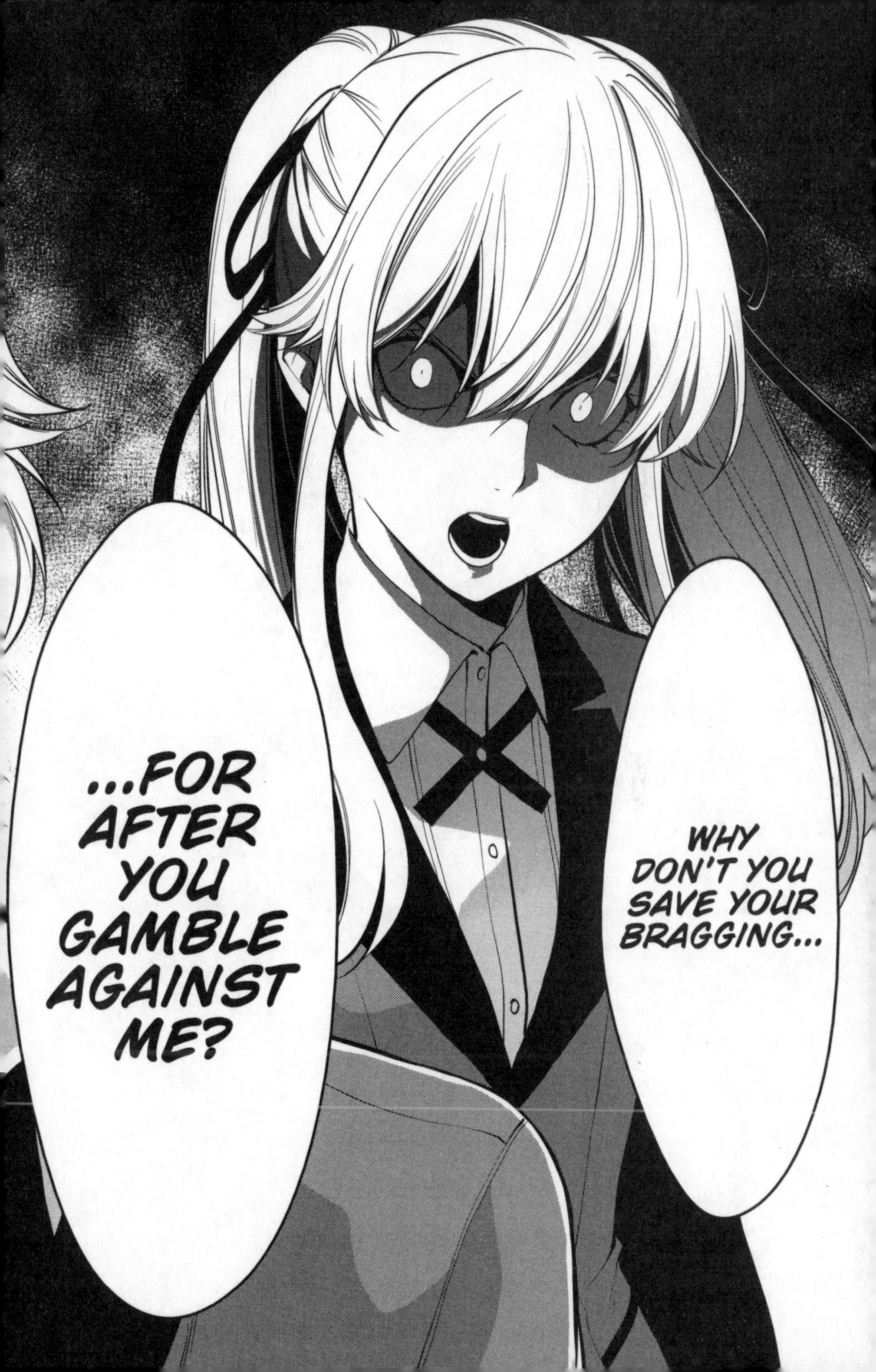
WHY DON'T YOU SAVE YOUR BRAGGING...
...FOR AFTER YOU GAMBLE AGAINST ME?

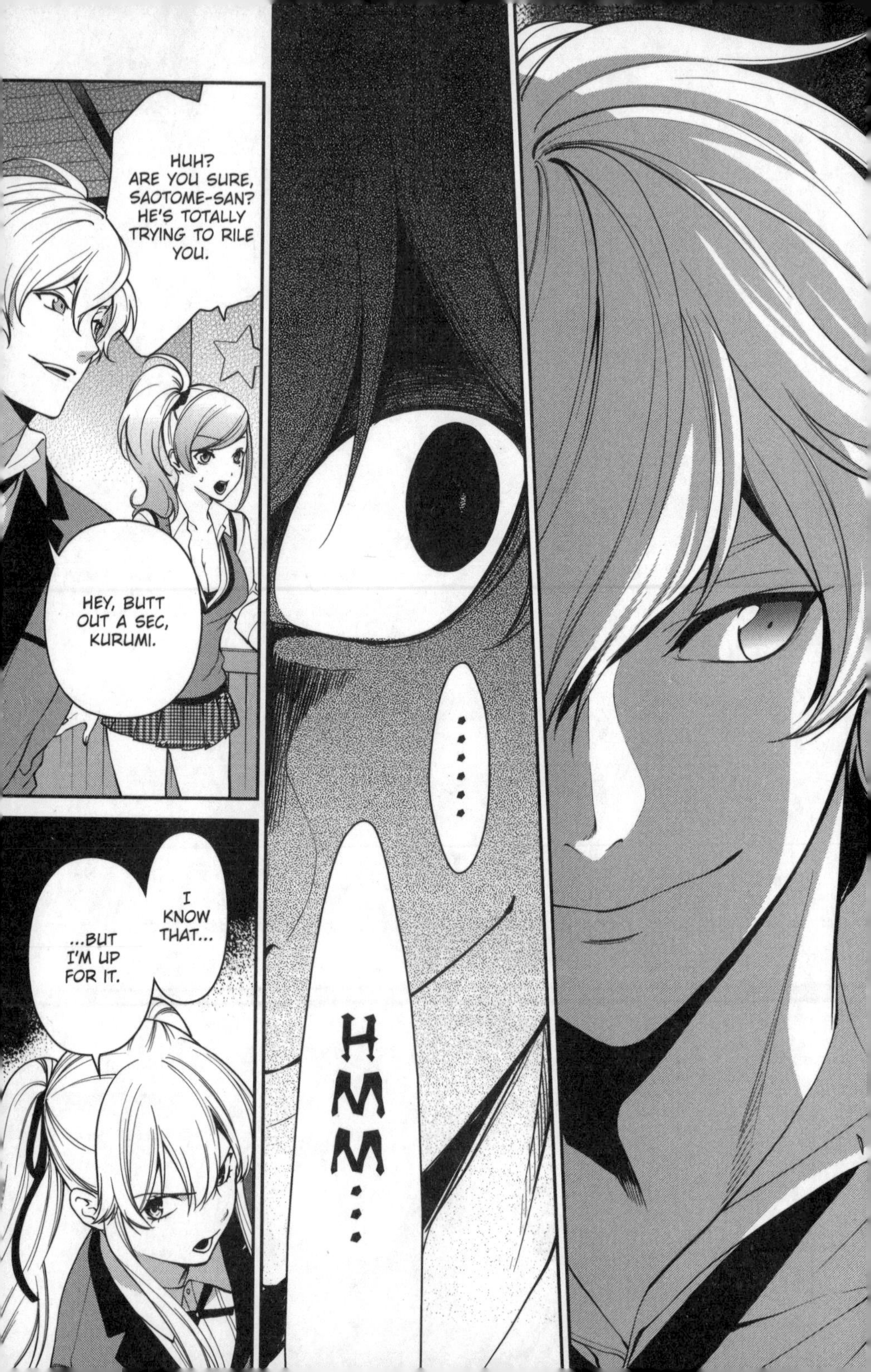
......
HMM...
HUH? ARE YOU SURE, SAOTOME-SAN? HE'S TOTALLY TRYING TO RILE YOU.
HEY, BUTT OUT A SEC, KURUMI.
I KNOW THAT...
...BUT I'M UP FOR IT.

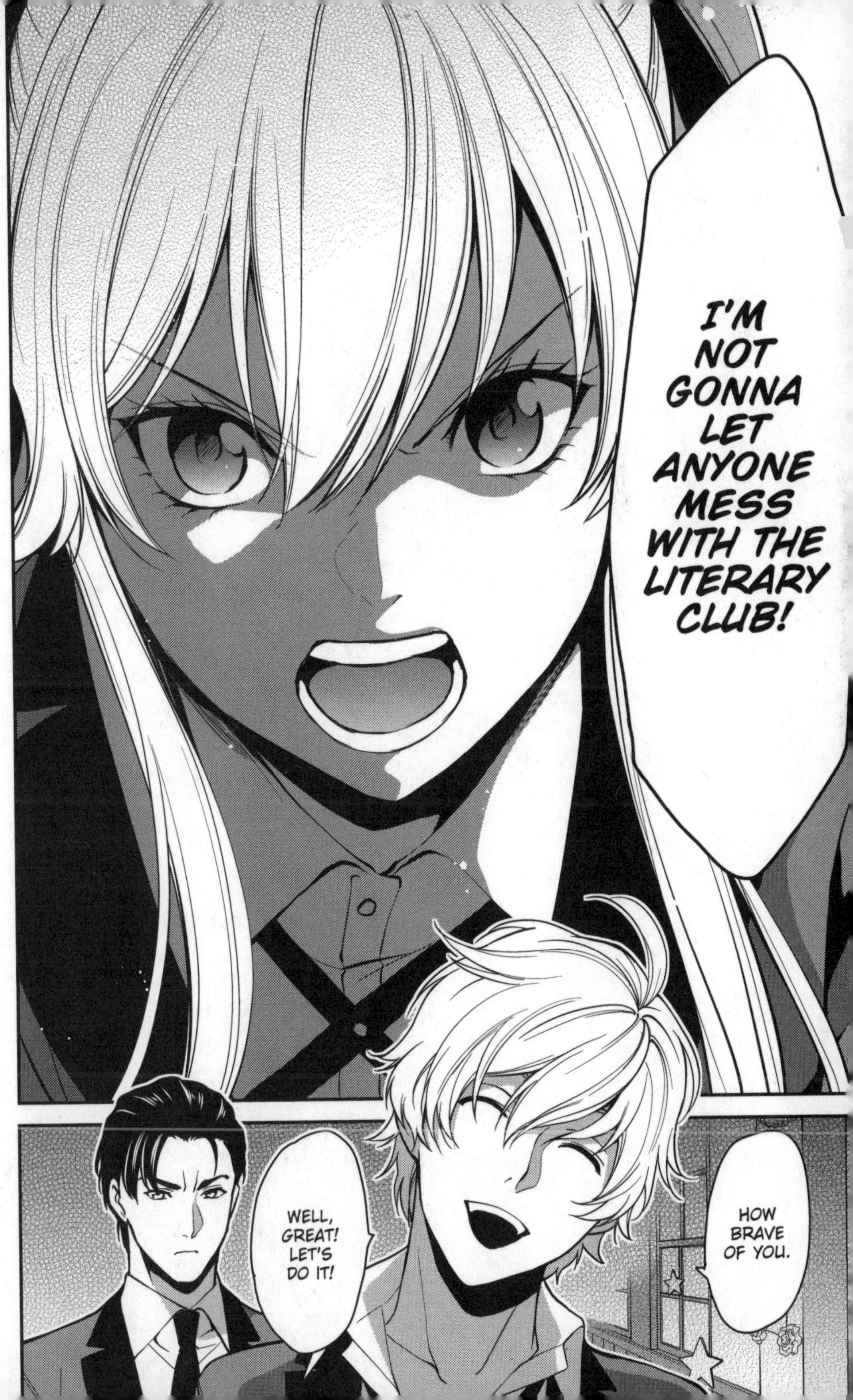
I'M NOT GONNA LET ANYONE MESS WITH THE LITERARY CLUB!
HOW BRAVE OF YOU.
WELL, GREAT! LET'S DO IT!

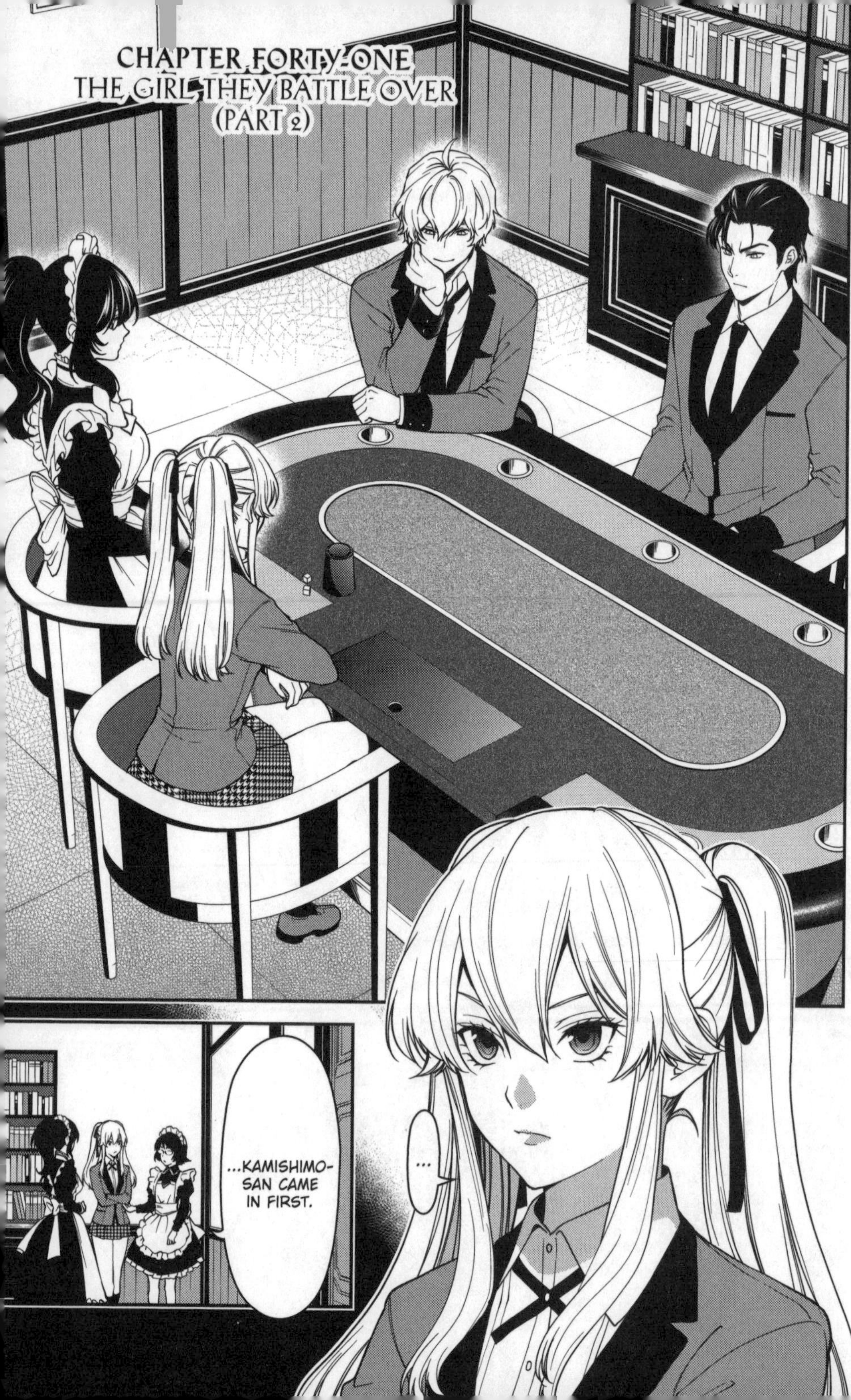
CHAPTER FORTY-ONE
THE GIRL THEY BATTLE OVER
(PART 2)
...
...KAMISHIMO-SAN CAME IN FIRST.

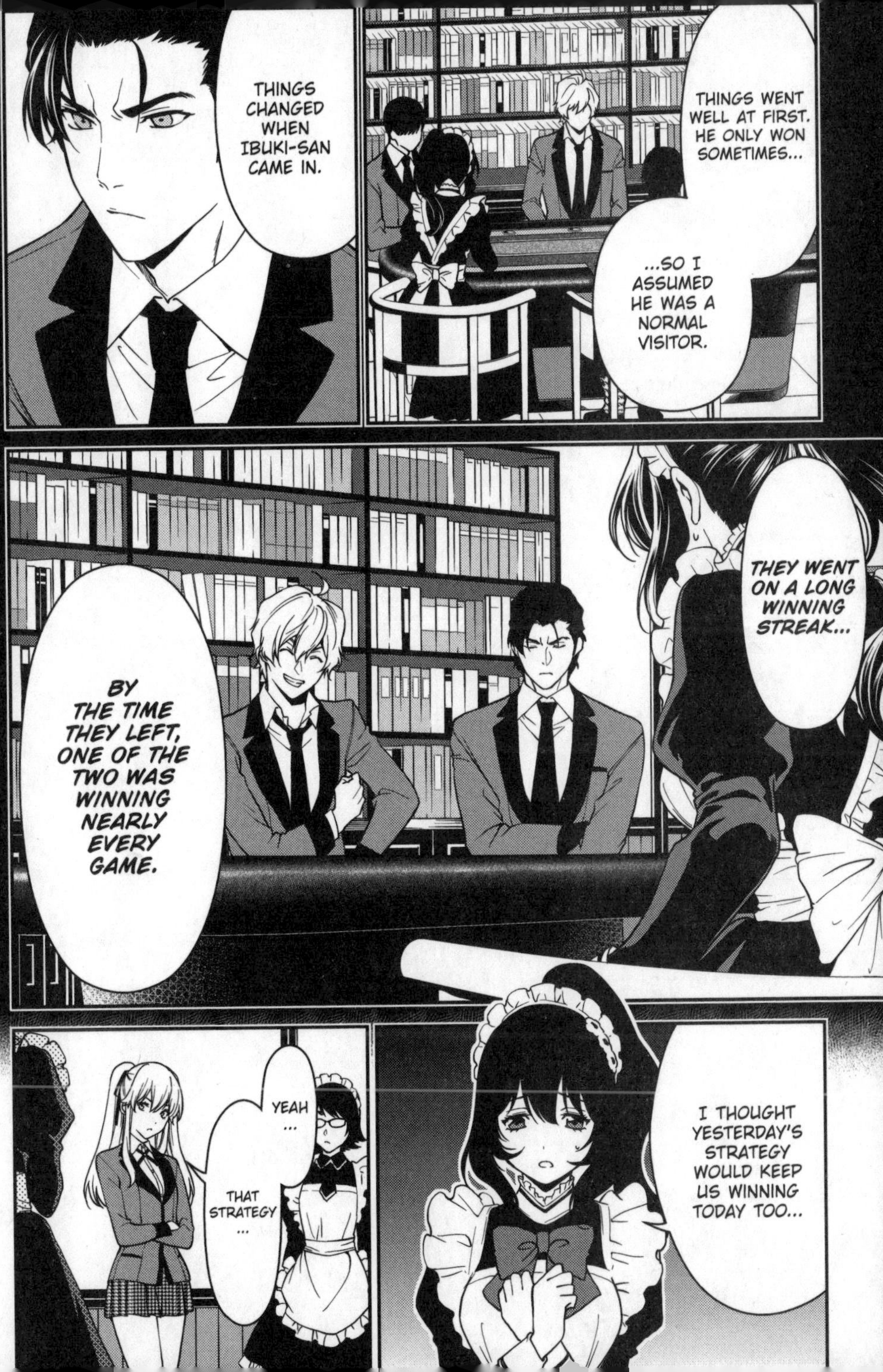
THINGS WENT WELL AT FIRST. HE ONLY WON SOMETIMES...
...SO I ASSUMED HE WAS A NORMAL VISITOR.
THINGS CHANGED WHEN IBUKI-SAN CAME IN.
THEY WENT ON A LONG WINNING STREAK...
BY THE TIME THEY LEFT, ONE OF THE TWO WAS WINNING NEARLY EVERY GAME.
I THOUGHT YESTERDAY'S STRATEGY WOULD KEEP US WINNING TODAY TOO...
YEAH...
THAT STRATEGY...

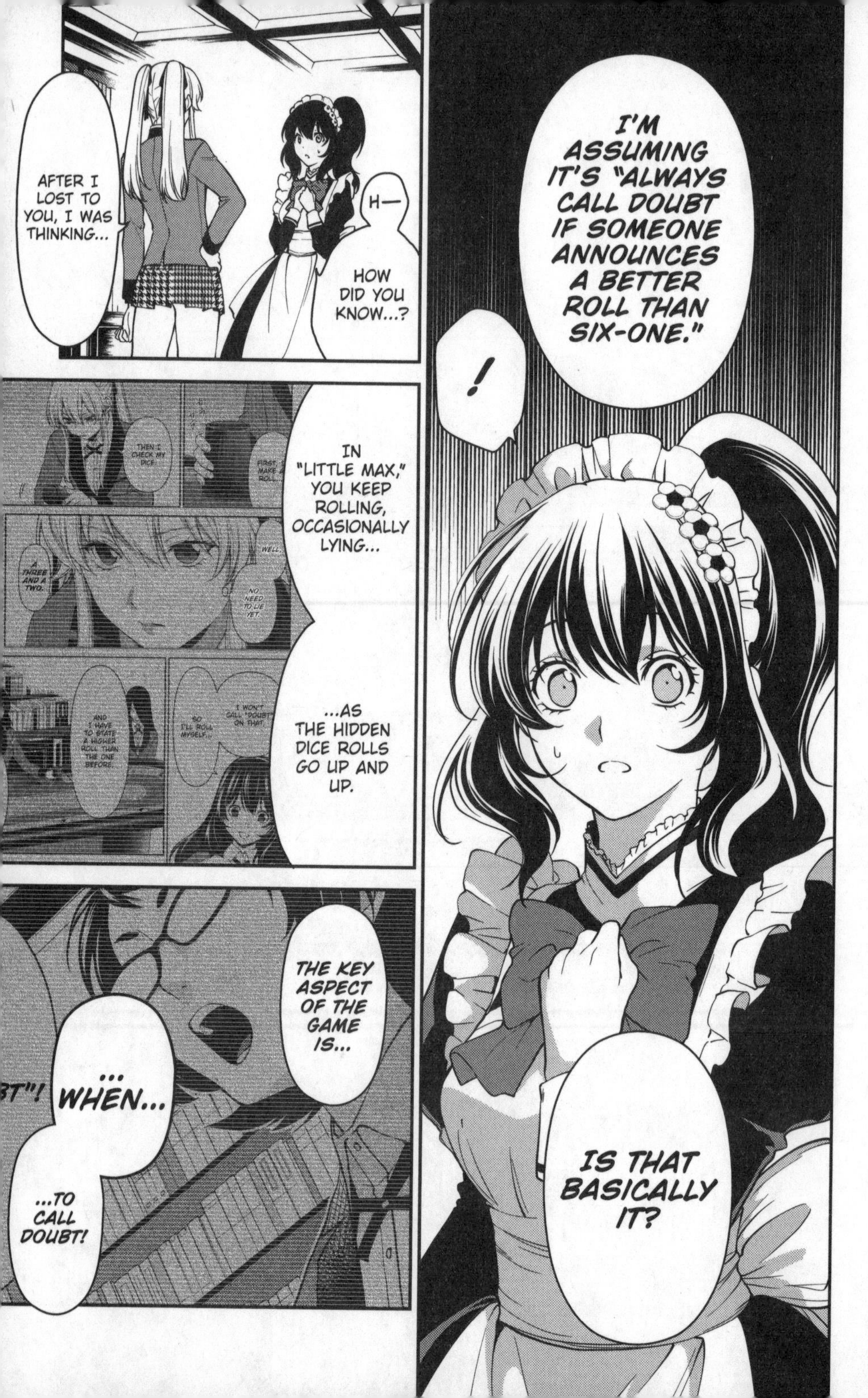
I'M ASSUMING IT'S "ALWAYS CALL DOUBT IF SOMEONE ANNOUNCES A BETTER ROLL THAN SIX-ONE."
!
IS THAT BASICALLY IT?
H—
HOW DID YOU KNOW...?
AFTER I LOST TO YOU, I WAS THINKING...
IN "LITTLE MAX," YOU KEEP ROLLING, OCCASIONALLY LYING...
FIRST, MAKE A ROLL...
THEN I CHECK MY DICE.
WELL,
NO NEED TO LIE YET.
A THREE AND A TWO.
I WON'T CALL "DOUBT" ON THAT.
SO I'LL ROLL MYSELF...
AND I HAVE TO STATE A HIGHER ROLL THAN THE ONE BEFORE.
...AS THE HIDDEN DICE ROLLS GO UP AND UP.
THE KEY ASPECT OF THE GAME IS...
... WHEN...
...TO CALL DOUBT!
BT"!

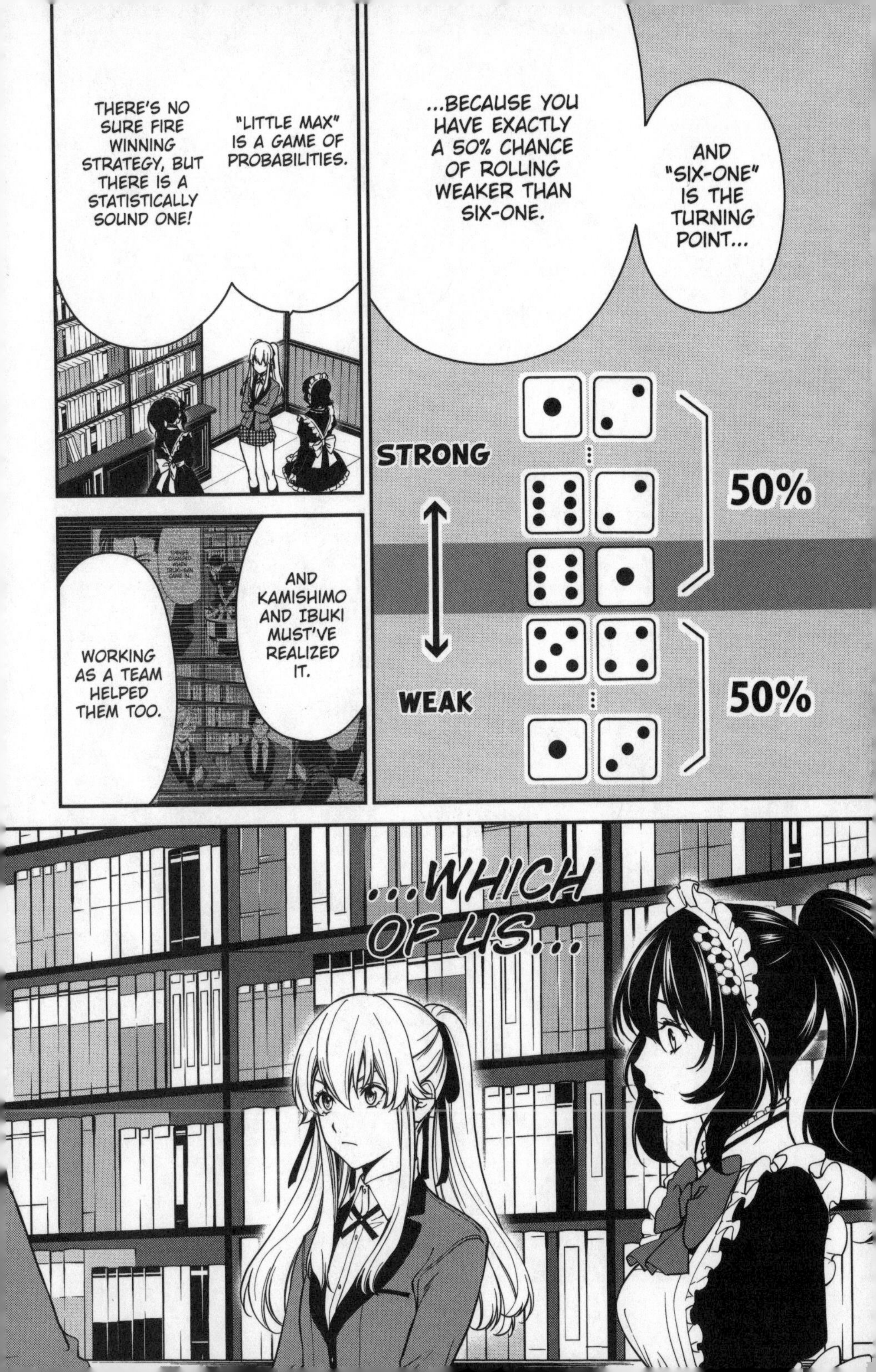
AND "SIX-ONE" IS THE TURNING POINT...
...BECAUSE YOU HAVE EXACTLY A 50% CHANCE OF ROLLING WEAKER THAN SIX-ONE.
STRONG
WEAK
50%
50%
"LITTLE MAX" IS A GAME OF PROBABILITIES.
THERE'S NO SURE FIRE WINNING STRATEGY, BUT THERE IS A STATISTICALLY SOUND ONE!
THINGS CHANGED WHEN IBUKI-SAN CAME IN.
AND KAMISHIMO AND IBUKI MUST'VE REALIZED IT.
WORKING AS A TEAM HELPED THEM TOO.
...WHICH OF US...

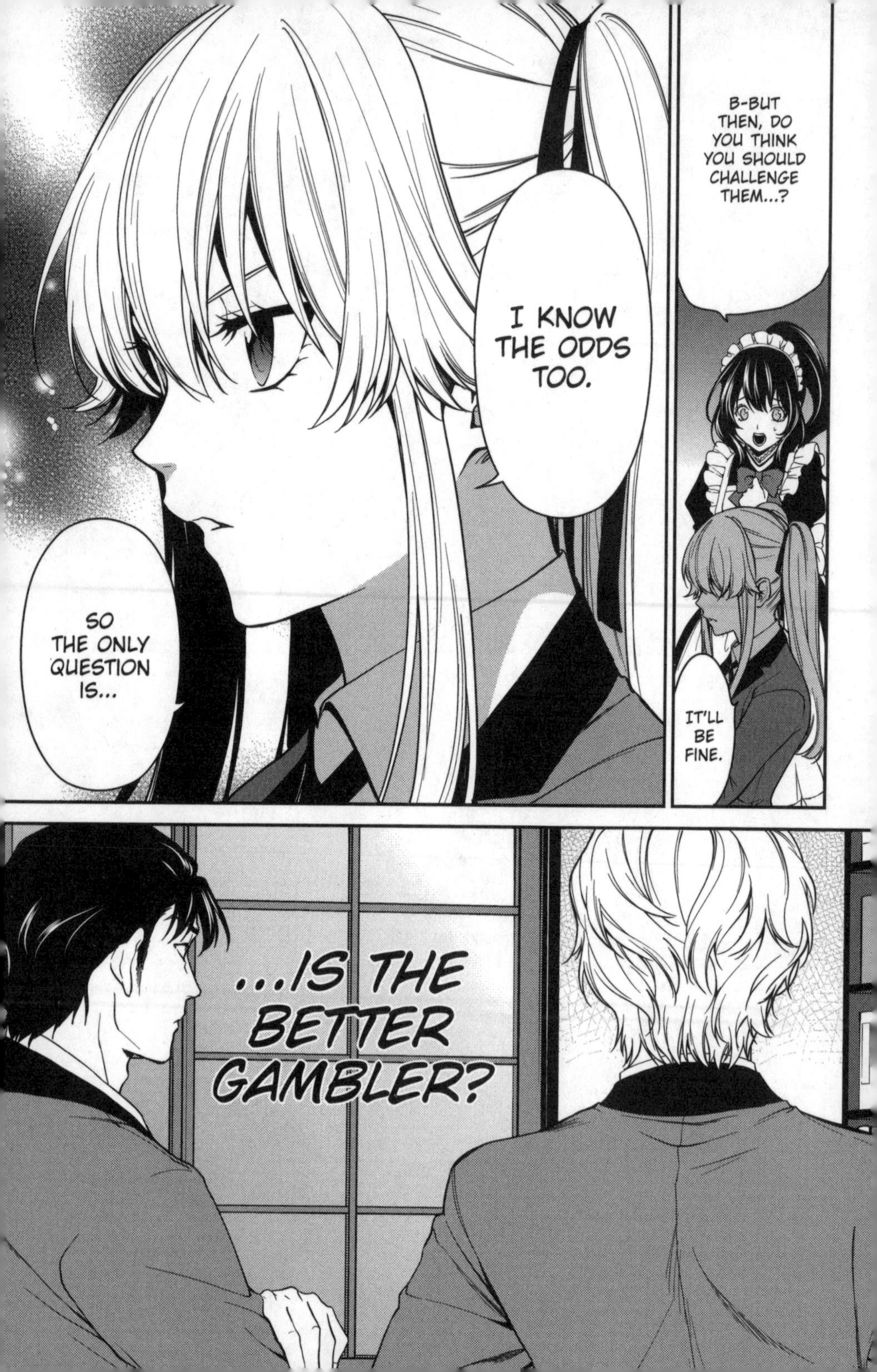
B-BUT THEN, DO YOU THINK YOU SHOULD CHALLENGE THEM...?
IT'LL BE FINE.
I KNOW THE ODDS TOO.
SO THE ONLY QUESTION IS...
...IS THE BETTER GAMBLER?

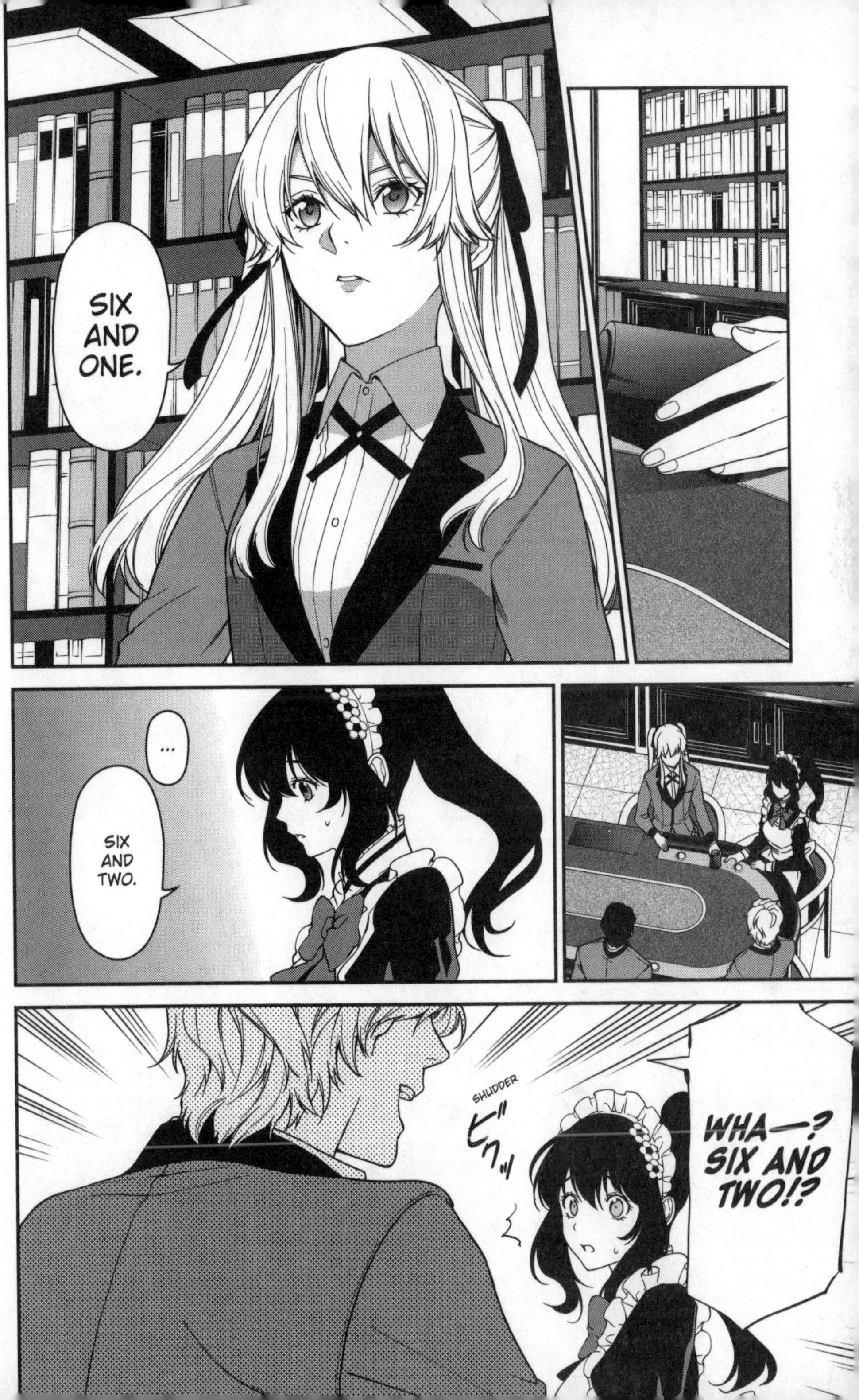
SIX AND ONE.
...
SIX AND TWO.
SHUDDER
WHA—? SIX AND TWO!?

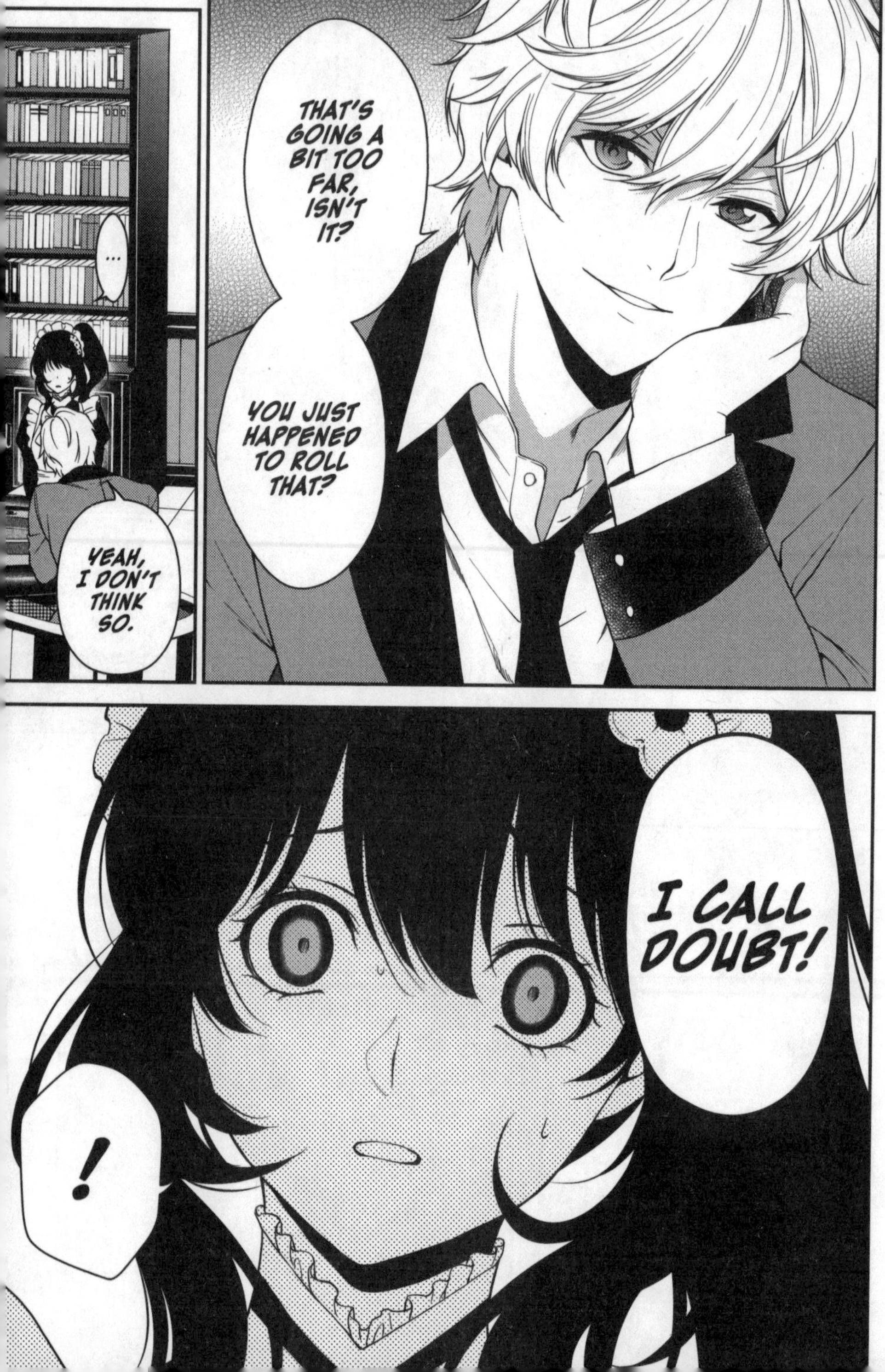
THAT'S GOING A BIT TOO FAR, ISN'T IT?
YOU JUST HAPPENED TO ROLL THAT?
...
YEAH, I DON'T THINK SO.
I CALL DOUBT!
!

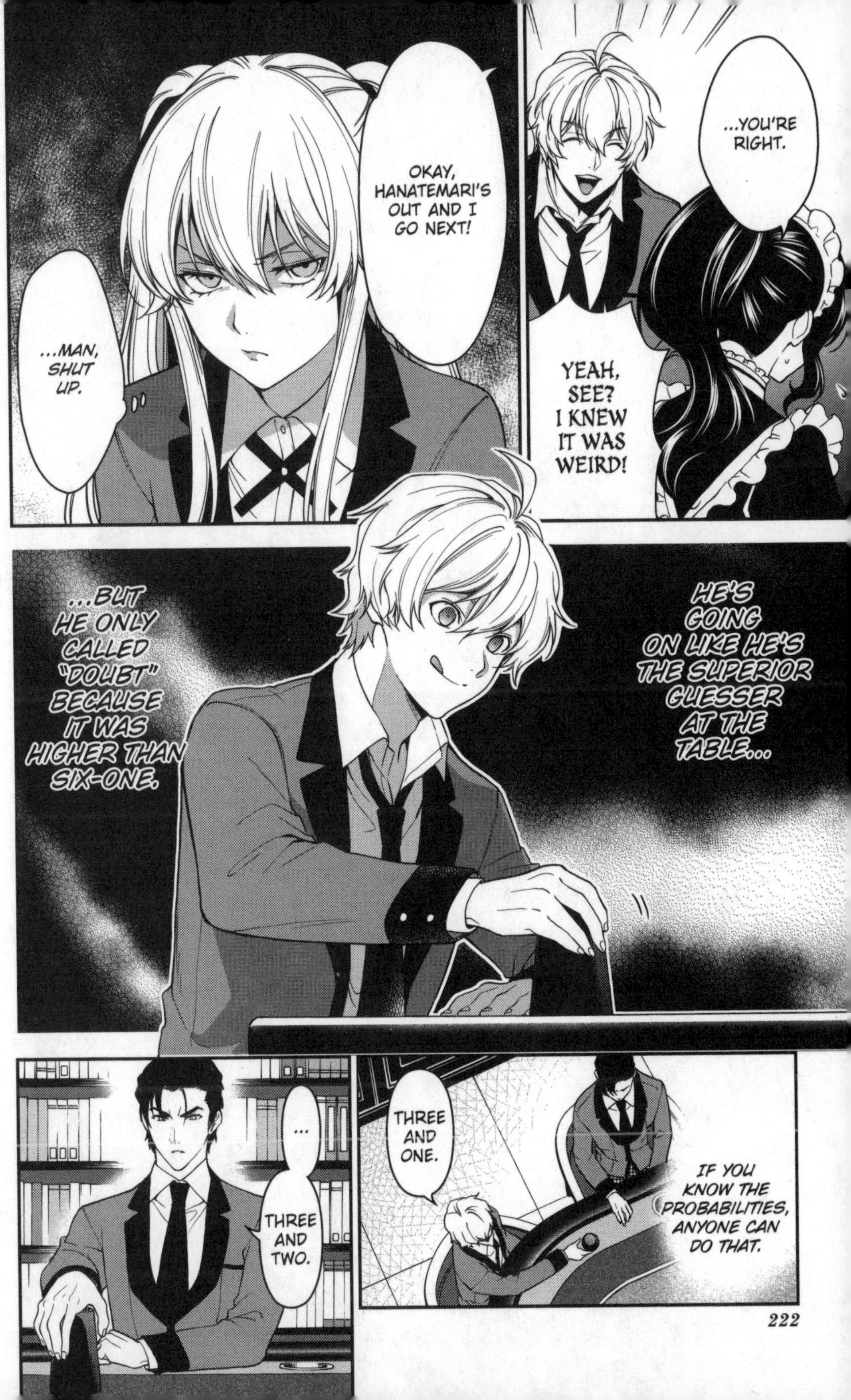
...YOU'RE RIGHT.
YEAH, SEE? I KNEW IT WAS WEIRD!
OKAY, HANATEMARI'S OUT AND I GO NEXT!
...MAN, SHUT UP.
HE'S GOING ON LIKE HE'S THE SUPERIOR GUESSER AT THE TABLE...
...BUT HE ONLY CALLED "DOUBT" BECAUSE IT WAS HIGHER THAN SIX-ONE.
THREE AND ONE.
IF YOU KNOW THE PROBABILITIES, ANYONE CAN DO THAT.
...
THREE AND TWO.

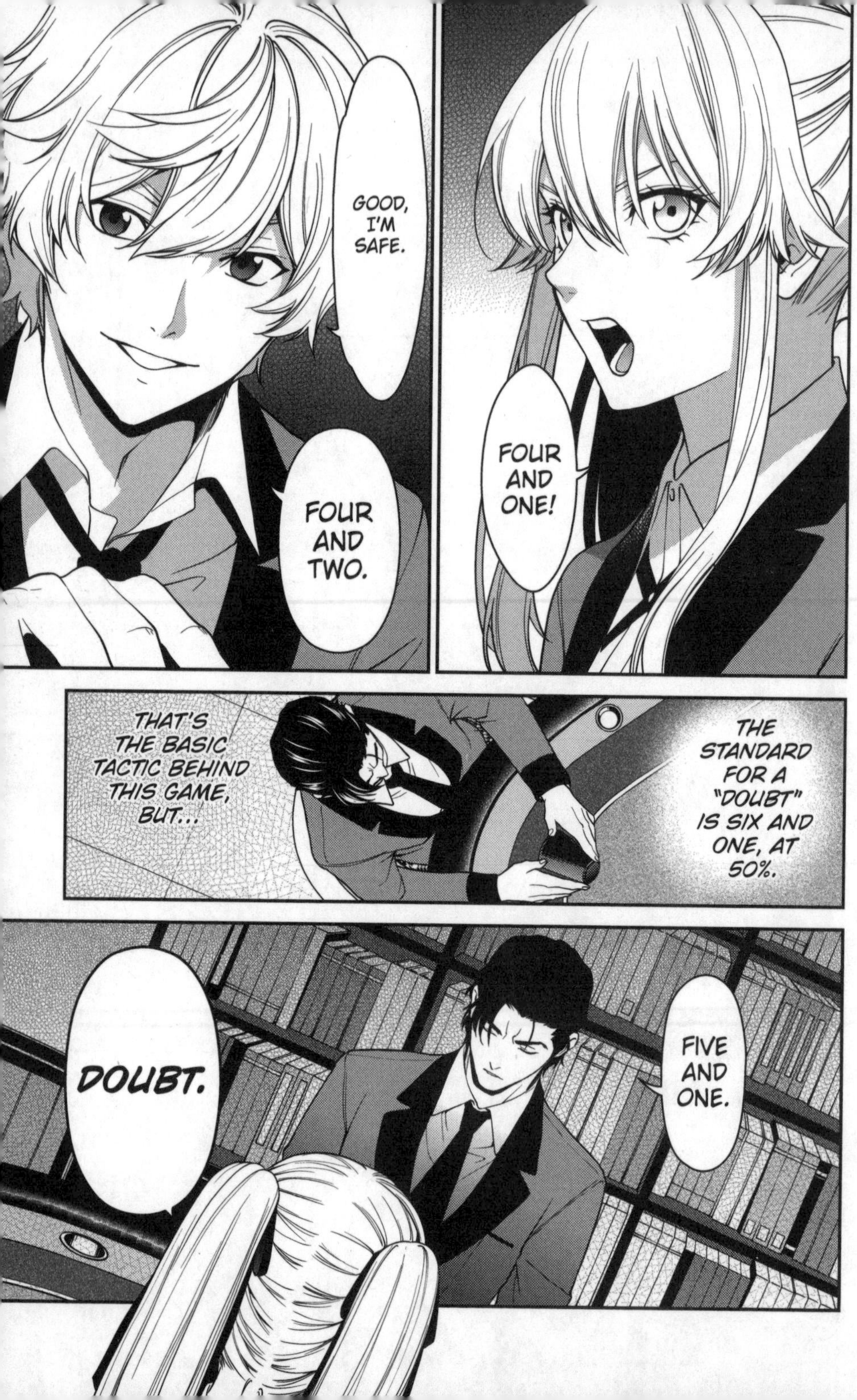
FOUR AND ONE!
GOOD, I'M SAFE.
FOUR AND TWO.
THE STANDARD FOR A "DOUBT" IS SIX AND ONE, AT 50%.
THAT'S THE BASIC TACTIC BEHIND THIS GAME, BUT...
FIVE AND ONE.
DOUBT.

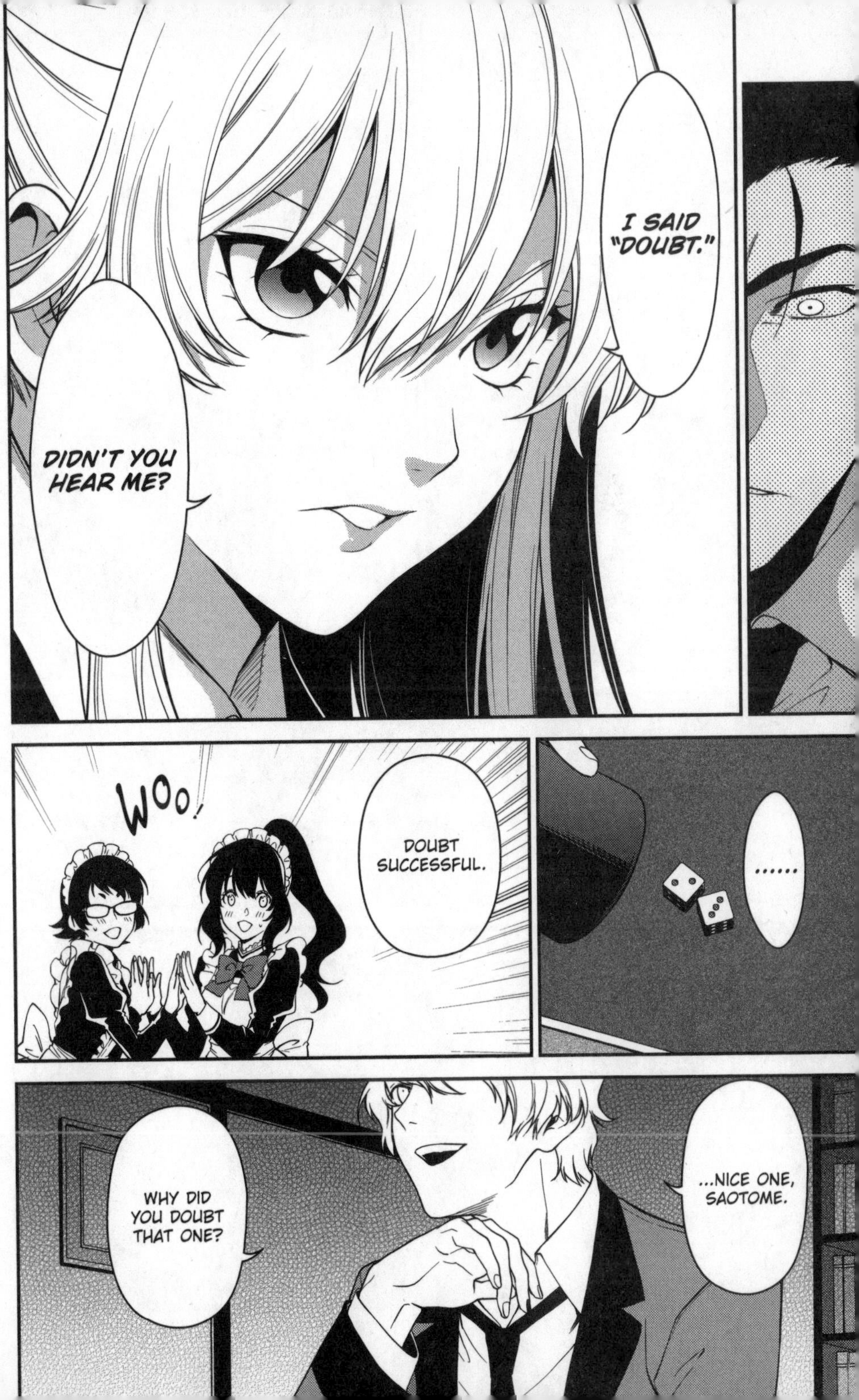
I SAID "DOUBT."
DIDN'T YOU HEAR ME?
......
DOUBT SUCCESSFUL.
WOO!
...NICE ONE, SAOTOME.
WHY DID YOU DOUBT THAT ONE?

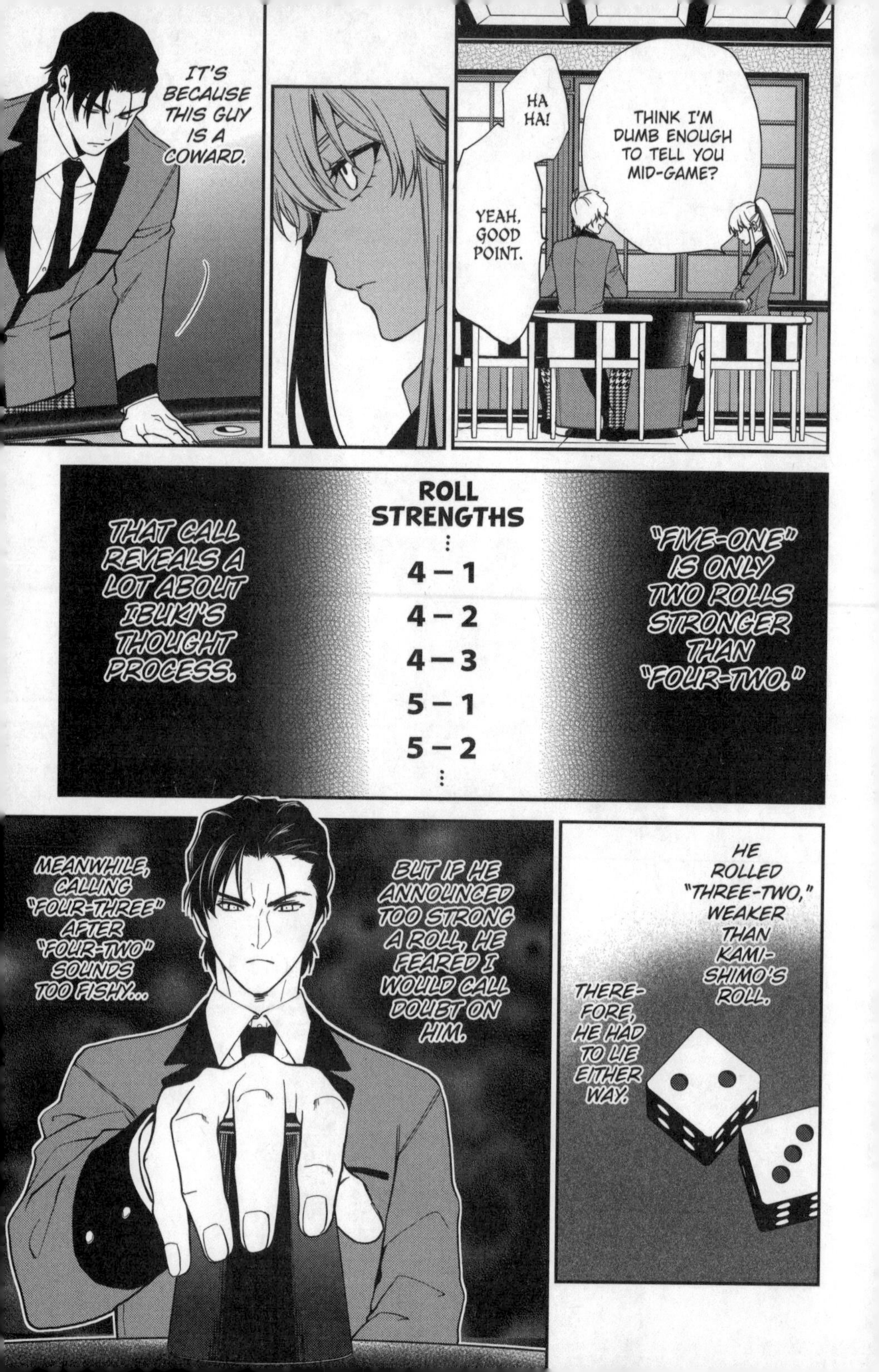

THINK I'M DUMB ENOUGH TO TELL YOU MID-GAME?
HA HA!
YEAH, GOOD POINT.
IT'S BECAUSE THIS GUY IS A COWARD.
"FIVE-ONE" IS ONLY TWO ROLLS STRONGER THAN "FOUR-TWO."
ROLL STRENGTHS
⋮
4—1
4—2
4—3
5—1
5—2
⋮
THAT CALL REVEALS A LOT ABOUT IBUKI'S THOUGHT PROCESS.
HE ROLLED "THREE-TWO," WEAKER THAN KAMI-SHIMO'S ROLL.
THERE-FORE, HE HAD TO LIE EITHER WAY.
MEANWHILE, CALLING "FOUR-THREE" AFTER "FOUR-TWO" SOUNDS TOO FISHY...
BUT IF HE ANNOUNCED TOO STRONG A ROLL, HE FEARED I WOULD CALL DOUBT ON HIM.

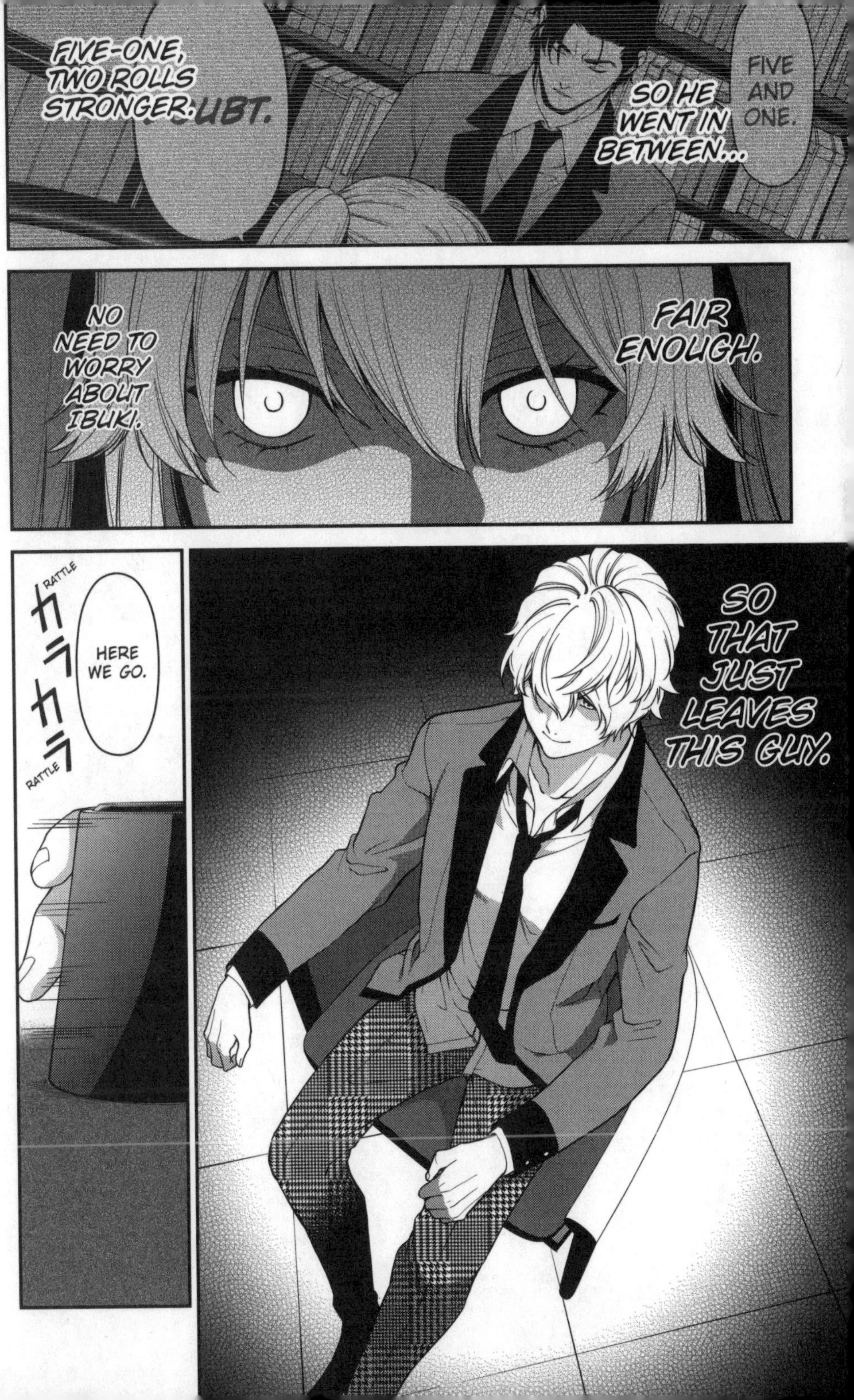
FIVE AND ONE.
SO HE WENT IN BETWEEN...
FIVE-ONE, TWO ROLLS STRONGER.
FAIR ENOUGH.
NO NEED TO WORRY ABOUT IBUKI.
SO THAT JUST LEAVES THIS GUY.
HERE WE GO.
カラカラ
RATTLE RATTLE

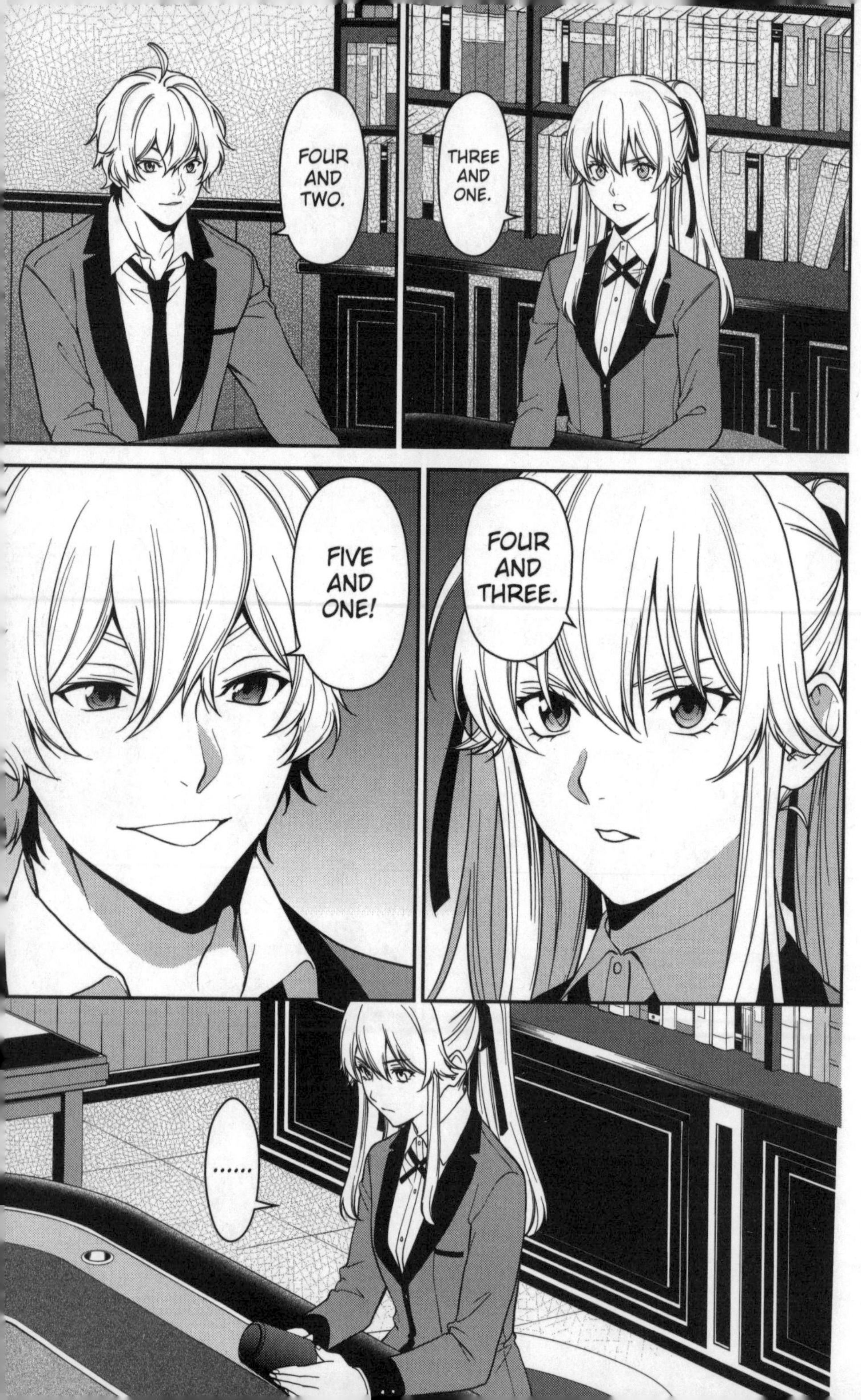
THREE AND ONE.
FOUR AND TWO.
FOUR AND THREE.
FIVE AND ONE!
......

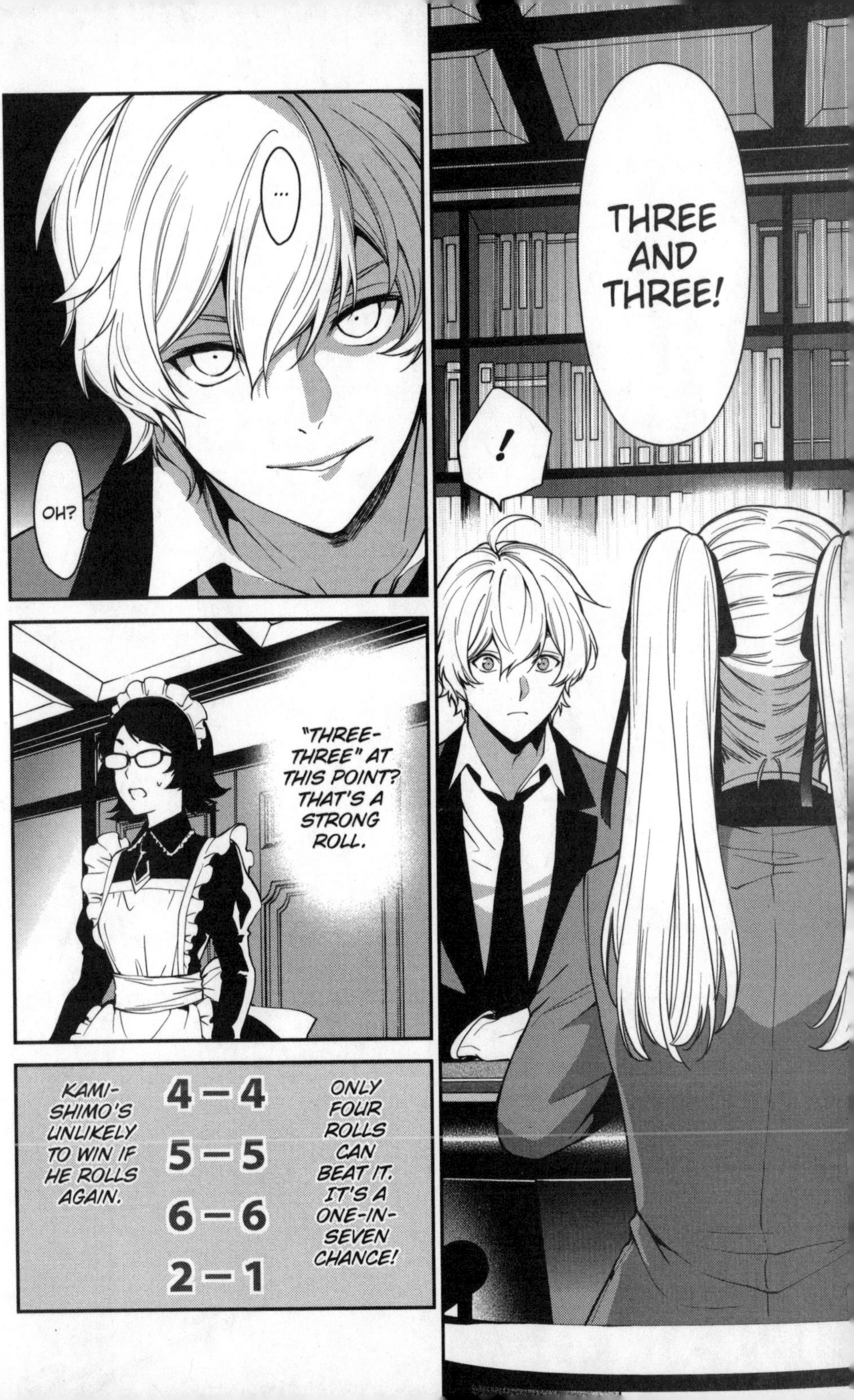
THREE AND THREE!
!
...
OH?
"THREE-THREE" AT THIS POINT? THAT'S A STRONG ROLL.
ONLY FOUR ROLLS CAN BEAT IT. IT'S A ONE-IN-SEVEN CHANCE!
4 – 4
5 – 5
6 – 6
2 – 1
KAMI-SHIMO'S UNLIKELY TO WIN IF HE ROLLS AGAIN.

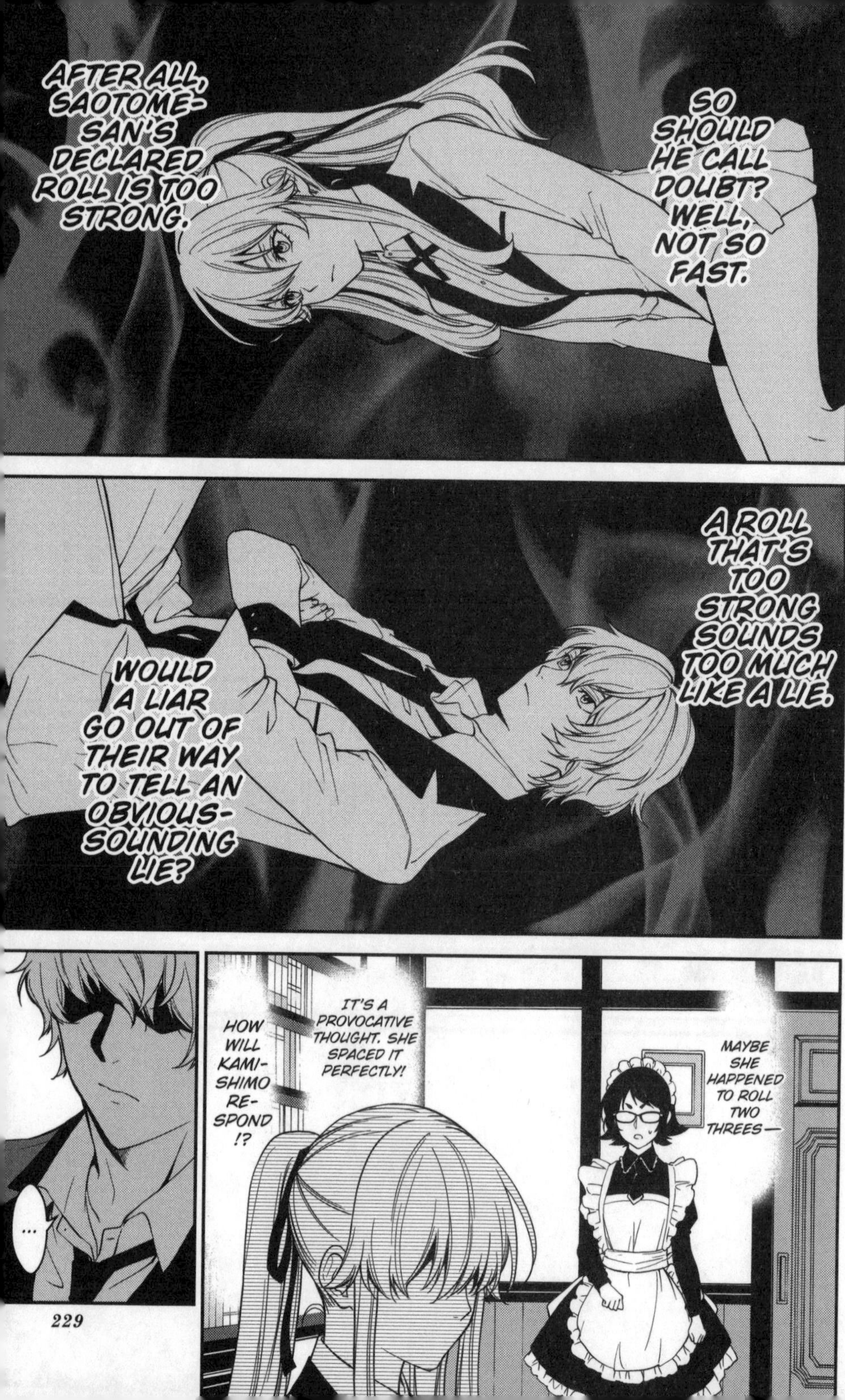
SO SHOULD HE CALL DOUBT? WELL, NOT SO FAST.
AFTER ALL, SAOTOME-SAN'S DECLARED ROLL IS TOO STRONG.
A ROLL THAT'S TOO STRONG SOUNDS TOO MUCH LIKE A LIE.
WOULD A LIAR GO OUT OF THEIR WAY TO TELL AN OBVIOUS-SOUNDING LIE?
MAYBE SHE HAPPENED TO ROLL TWO THREES—
IT'S A PROVOCATIVE THOUGHT. SHE SPACED IT PERFECTLY!
HOW WILL KAMI-SHIMO RE-SPOND!?
...

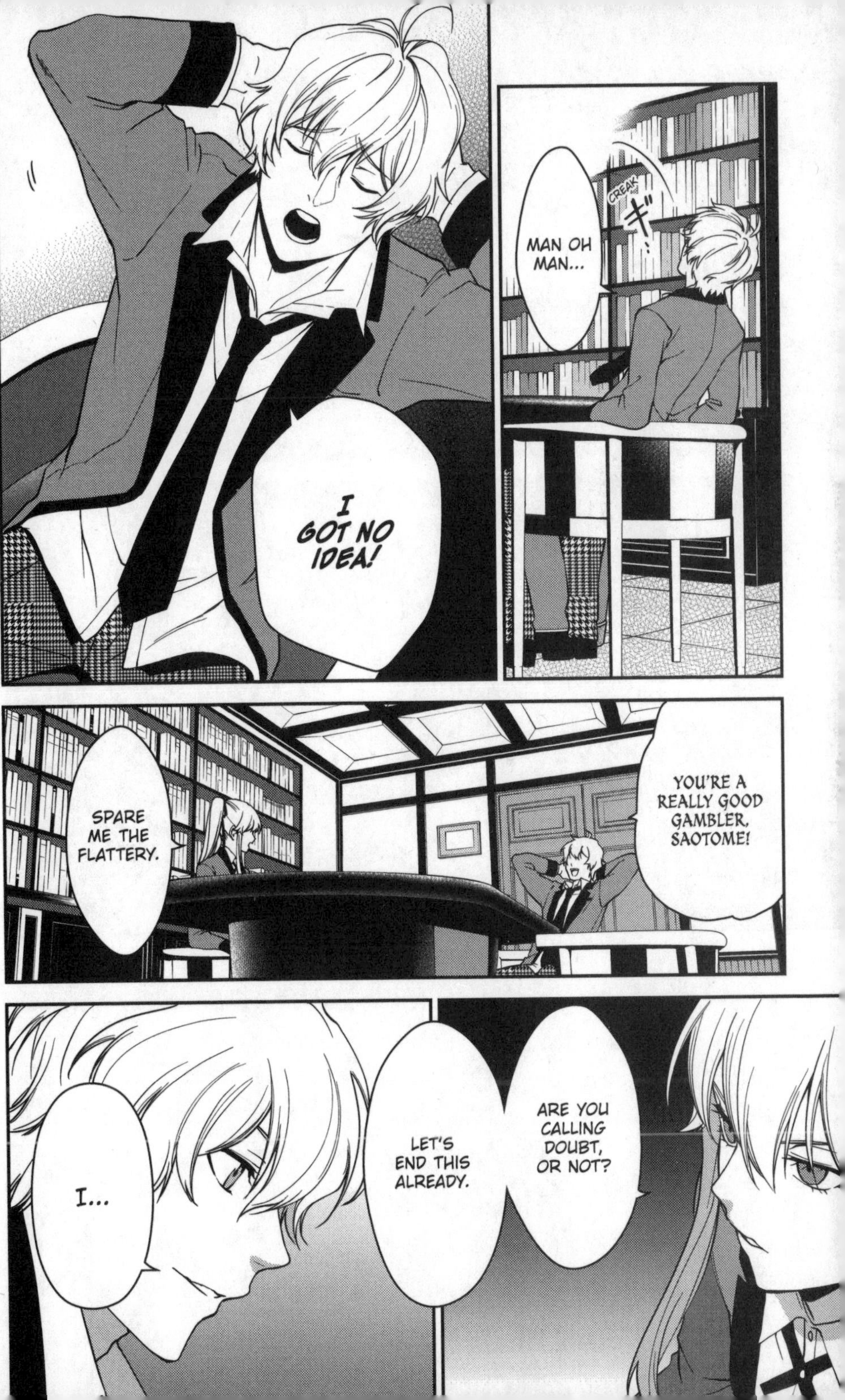
MAN OH MAN...
CREAK
ギ
I GOT NO IDEA!
YOU'RE A REALLY GOOD GAMBLER, SAOTOME!
SPARE ME THE FLATTERY.
ARE YOU CALLING DOUBT, OR NOT?
LET'S END THIS ALREADY.
I...

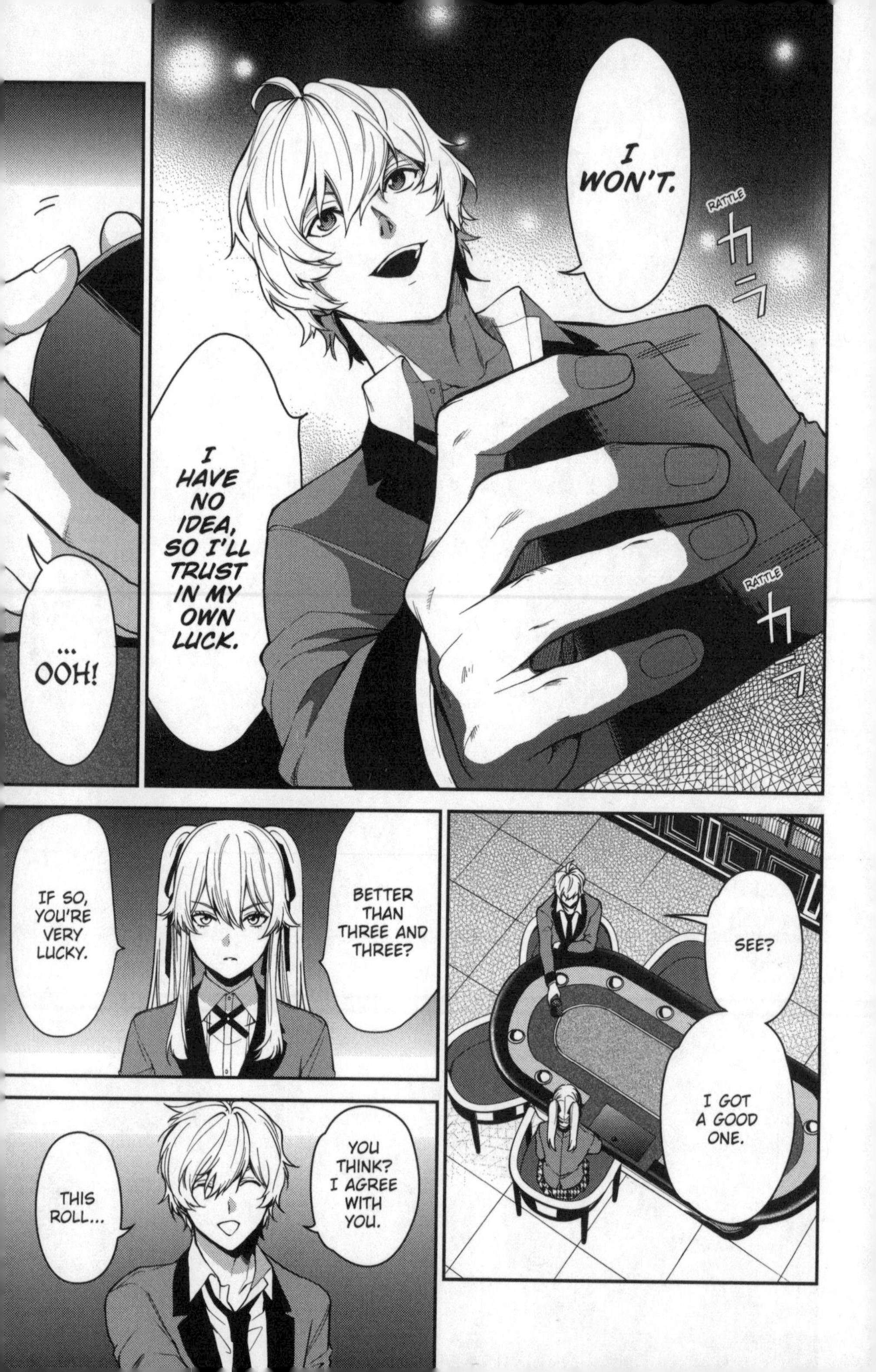
I WON'T.
RATTLE
カラ
I HAVE NO IDEA, SO I'LL TRUST IN MY OWN LUCK.
RATTLE
カラ
... OOH!
SEE?
I GOT A GOOD ONE.
BETTER THAN THREE AND THREE?
IF SO, YOU'RE VERY LUCKY.
YOU THINK? I AGREE WITH YOU.
THIS ROLL...

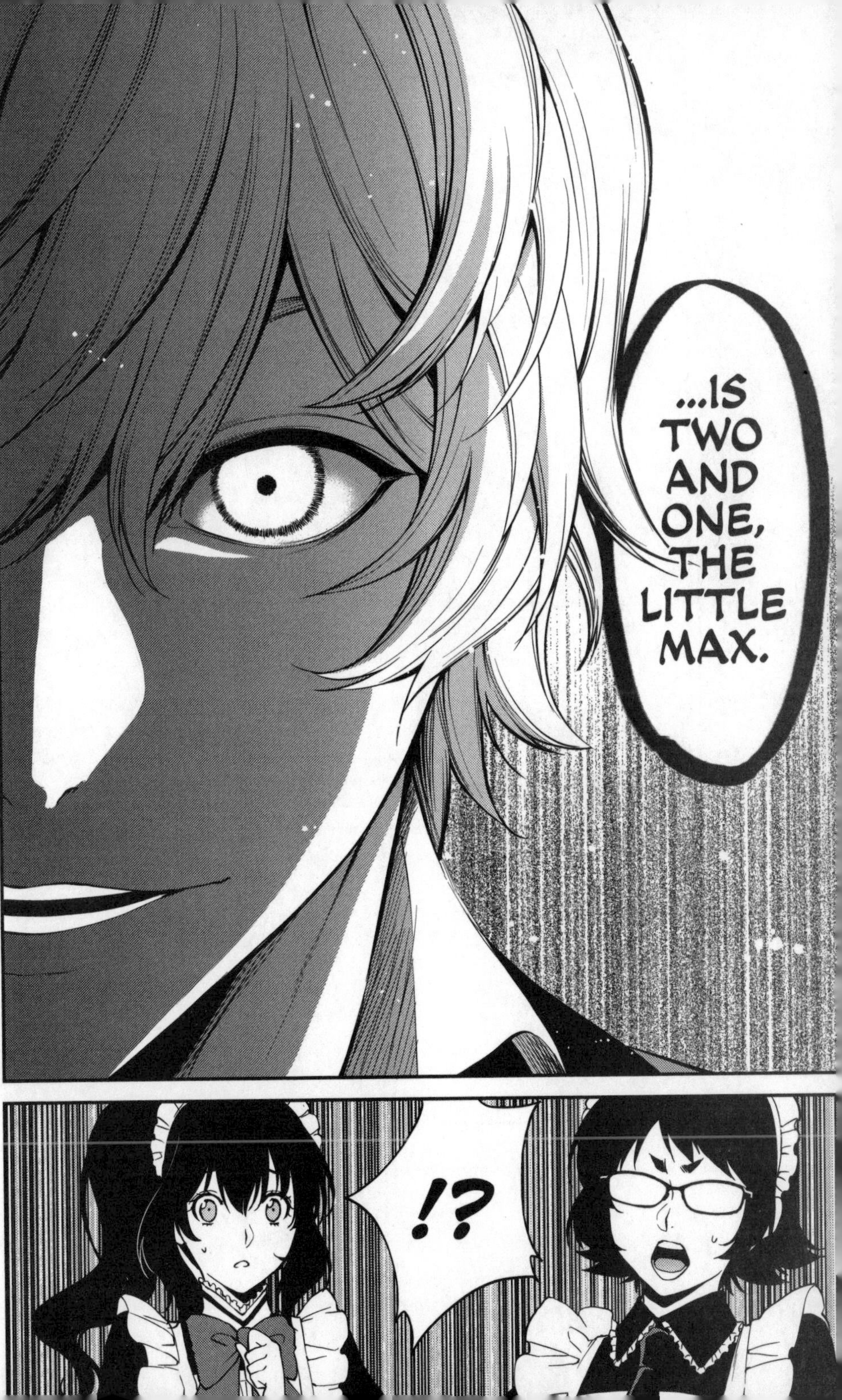
...IS TWO AND ONE, THE LITTLE MAX.
!?

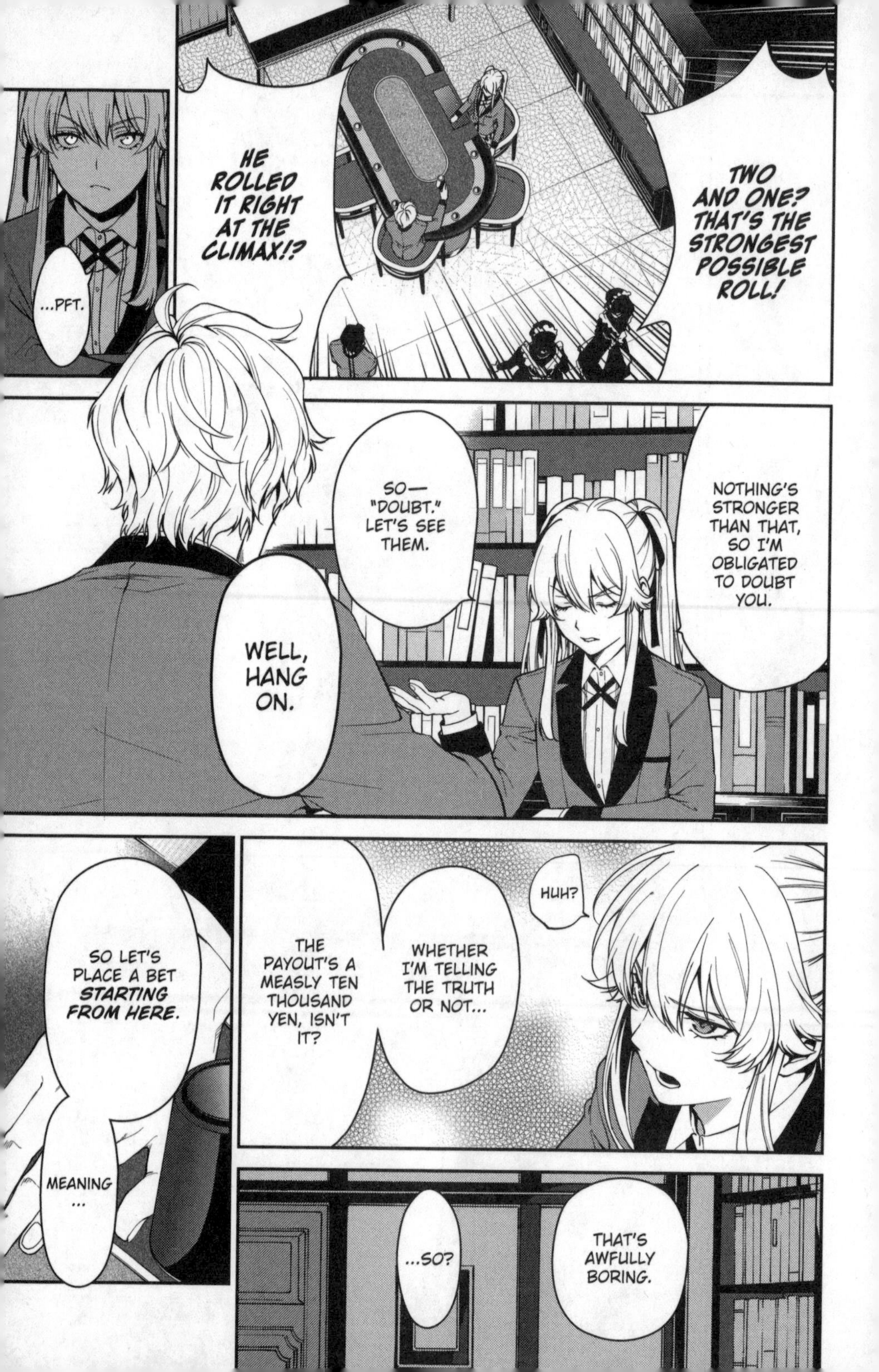
TWO AND ONE? THAT'S THE STRONGEST POSSIBLE ROLL!
HE ROLLED IT RIGHT AT THE CLIMAX!?
...PFT.
NOTHING'S STRONGER THAN THAT, SO I'M OBLIGATED TO DOUBT YOU.
SO— "DOUBT." LET'S SEE THEM.
WELL, HANG ON.
HUH?
WHETHER I'M TELLING THE TRUTH OR NOT...
THE PAYOUT'S A MEASLY TEN THOUSAND YEN, ISN'T IT?
THAT'S AWFULLY BORING.
...SO?
SO LET'S PLACE A BET STARTING FROM HERE.
MEANING...

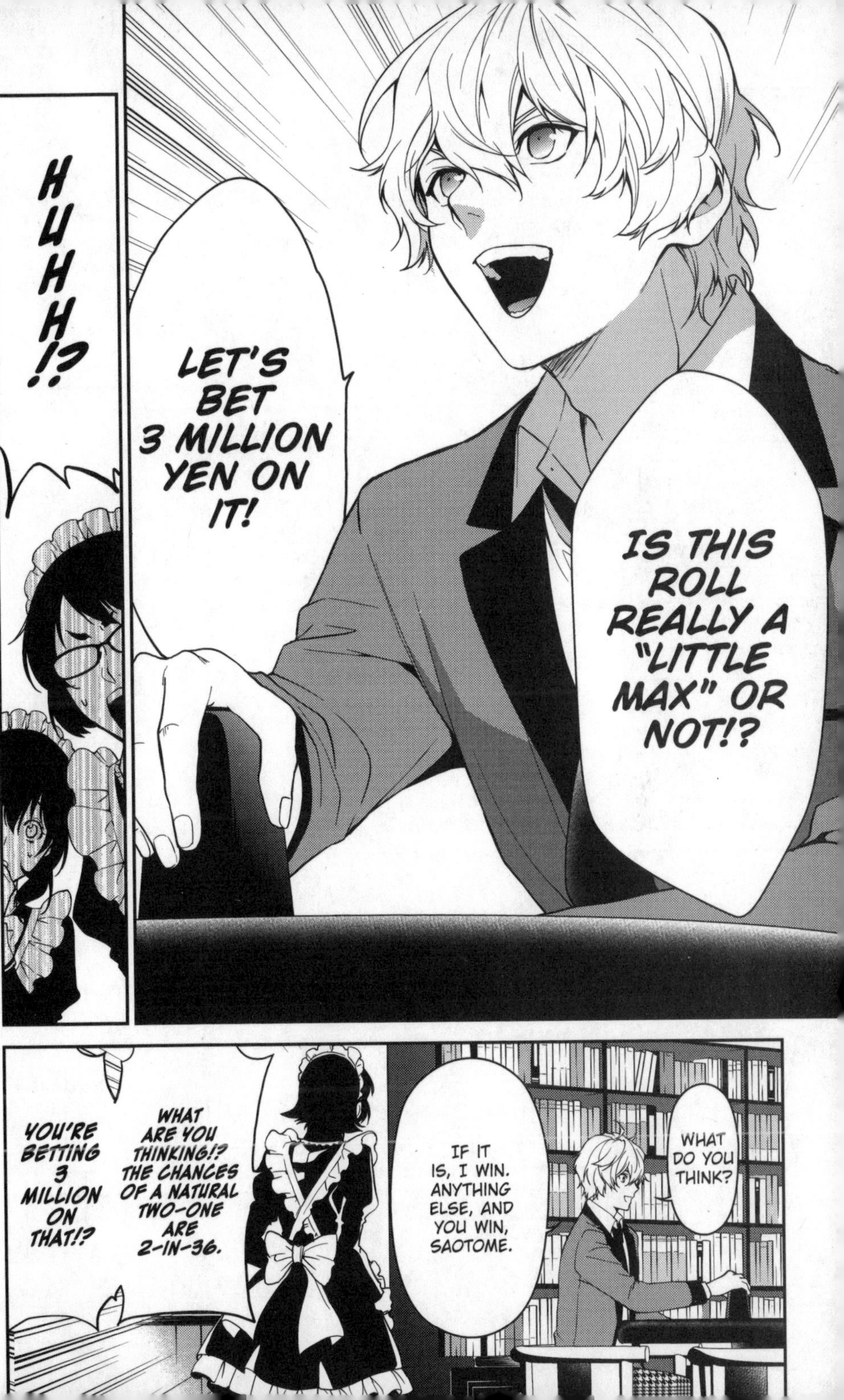
IS THIS ROLL REALLY A "LITTLE MAX" OR NOT!?
LET'S BET 3 MILLION YEN ON IT!
HUHHH!?
WHAT DO YOU THINK?
IF IT IS, I WIN. ANYTHING ELSE, AND YOU WIN, SAOTOME.
WHAT ARE YOU THINKING!? THE CHANCES OF A NATURAL TWO-ONE ARE 2-IN-36.
YOU'RE BETTING 3 MILLION ON THAT!?

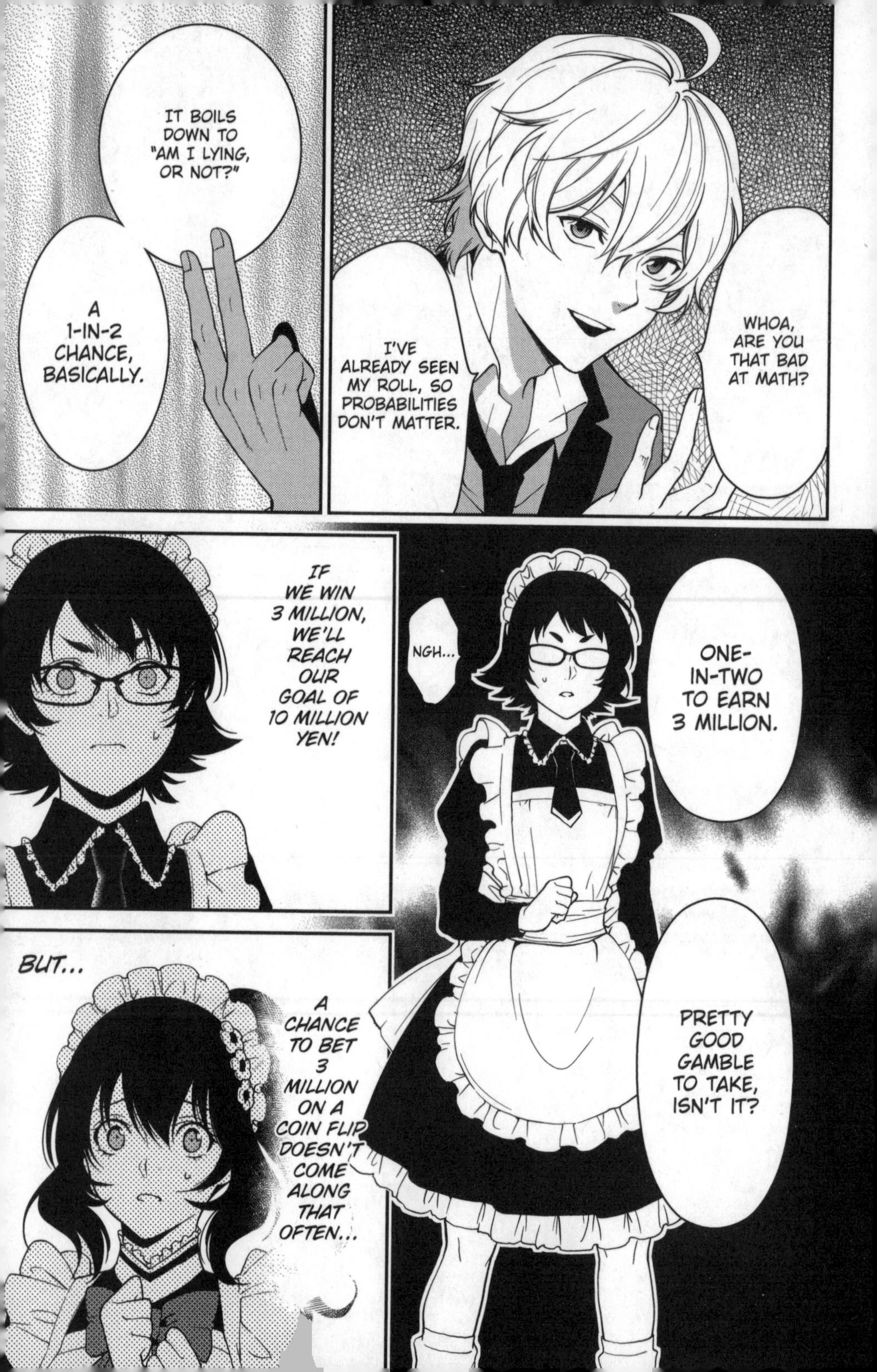
WHOA, ARE YOU THAT BAD AT MATH?
I'VE ALREADY SEEN MY ROLL, SO PROBABILITIES DON'T MATTER.
IT BOILS DOWN TO "AM I LYING, OR NOT?"
A 1-IN-2 CHANCE, BASICALLY.
ONE-IN-TWO TO EARN 3 MILLION.
NGH...
PRETTY GOOD GAMBLE TO TAKE, ISN'T IT?
IF WE WIN 3 MILLION, WE'LL REACH OUR GOAL OF 10 MILLION YEN!
BUT...
A CHANCE TO BET 3 MILLION ON A COIN FLIP DOESN'T COME ALONG THAT OFTEN...

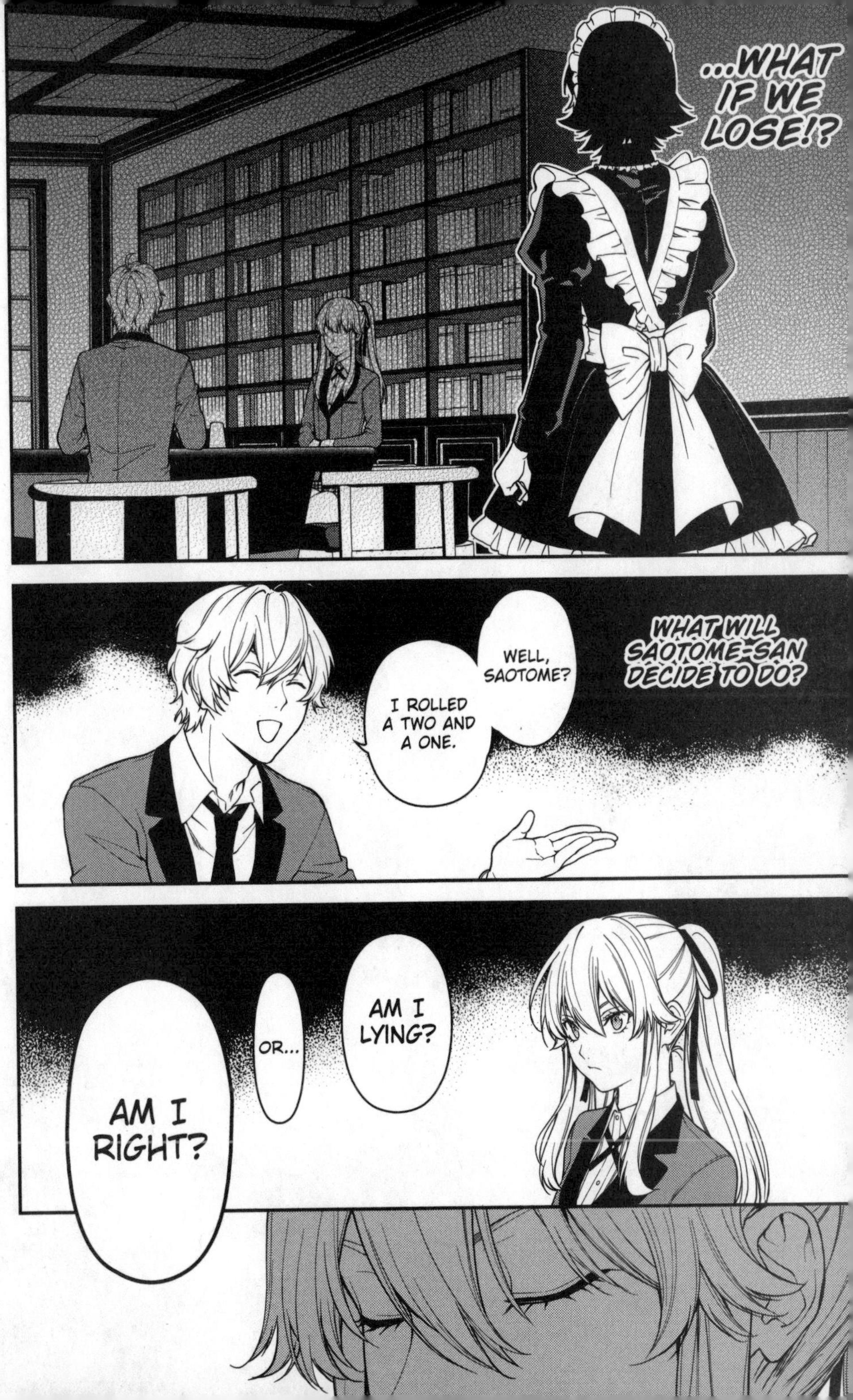
...WHAT IF WE LOSE!?
WHAT WILL SAOTOME-SAN DECIDE TO DO?
WELL, SAOTOME?
I ROLLED A TWO AND A ONE.
AM I LYING?
OR...
AM I RIGHT?

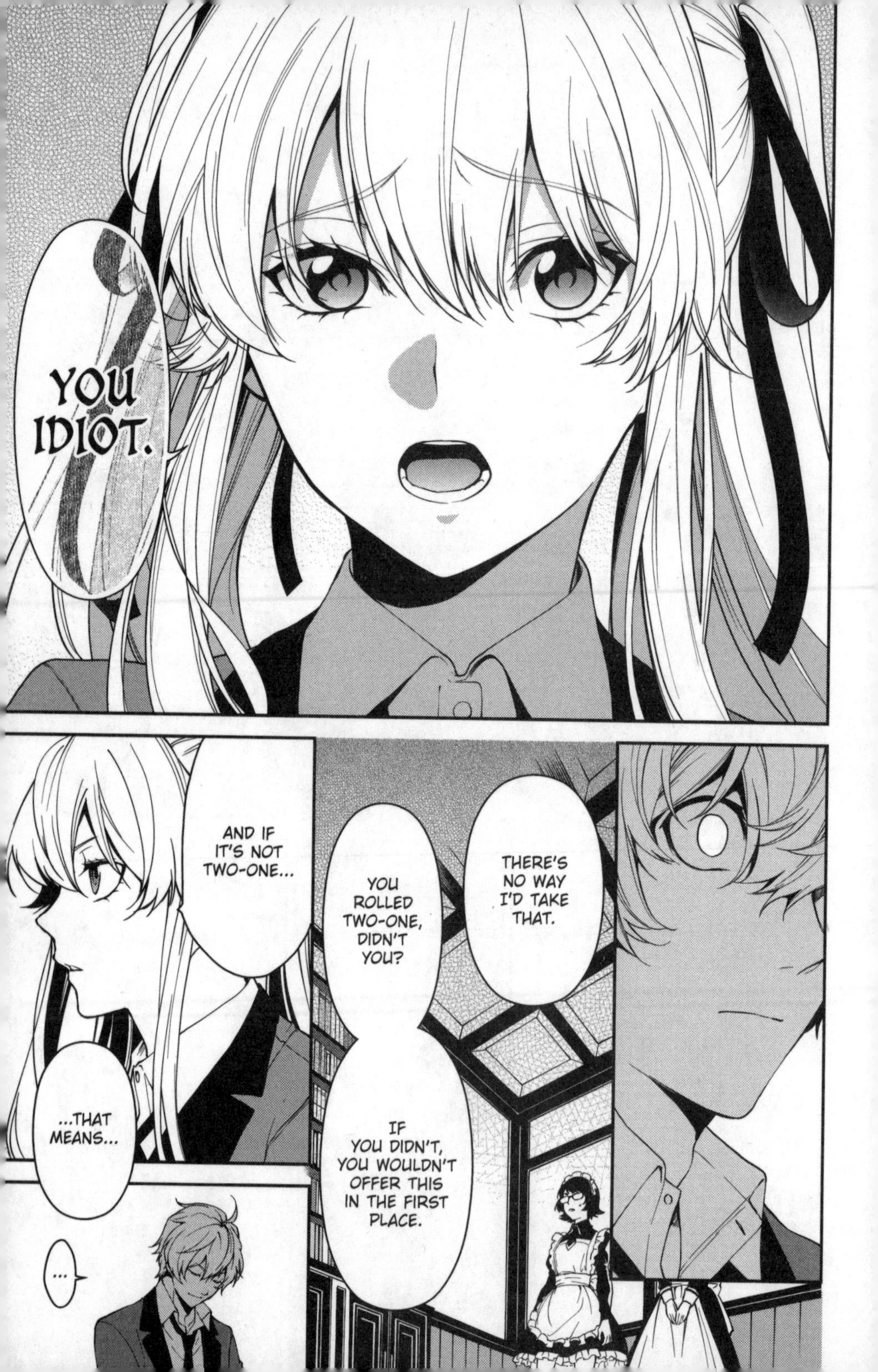
YOU IDIOT.
THERE'S NO WAY I'D TAKE THAT.
YOU ROLLED TWO-ONE, DIDN'T YOU?
IF YOU DIDN'T, YOU WOULDN'T OFFER THIS IN THE FIRST PLACE.
AND IF IT'S NOT TWO-ONE...
...THAT MEANS...
...

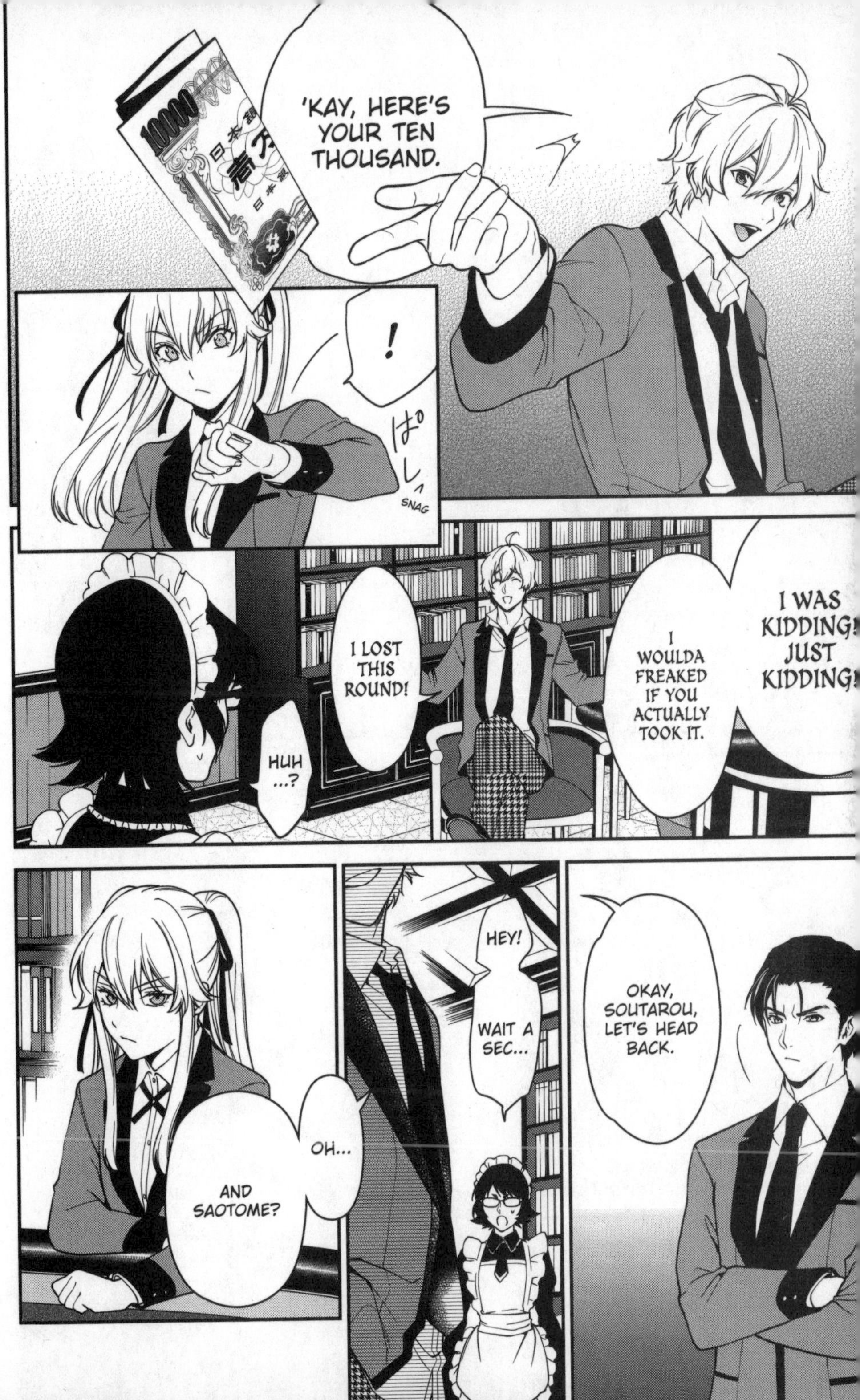
'KAY, HERE'S YOUR TEN THOUSAND.
!
ぱしっ
SNAG
I WAS KIDDING! JUST KIDDING!
I WOULDA FREAKED IF YOU ACTUALLY TOOK IT.
I LOST THIS ROUND!
HUH ...?
OKAY, SOUTAROU, LET'S HEAD BACK.
HEY!
WAIT A SEC...
OH...
AND SAOTOME?

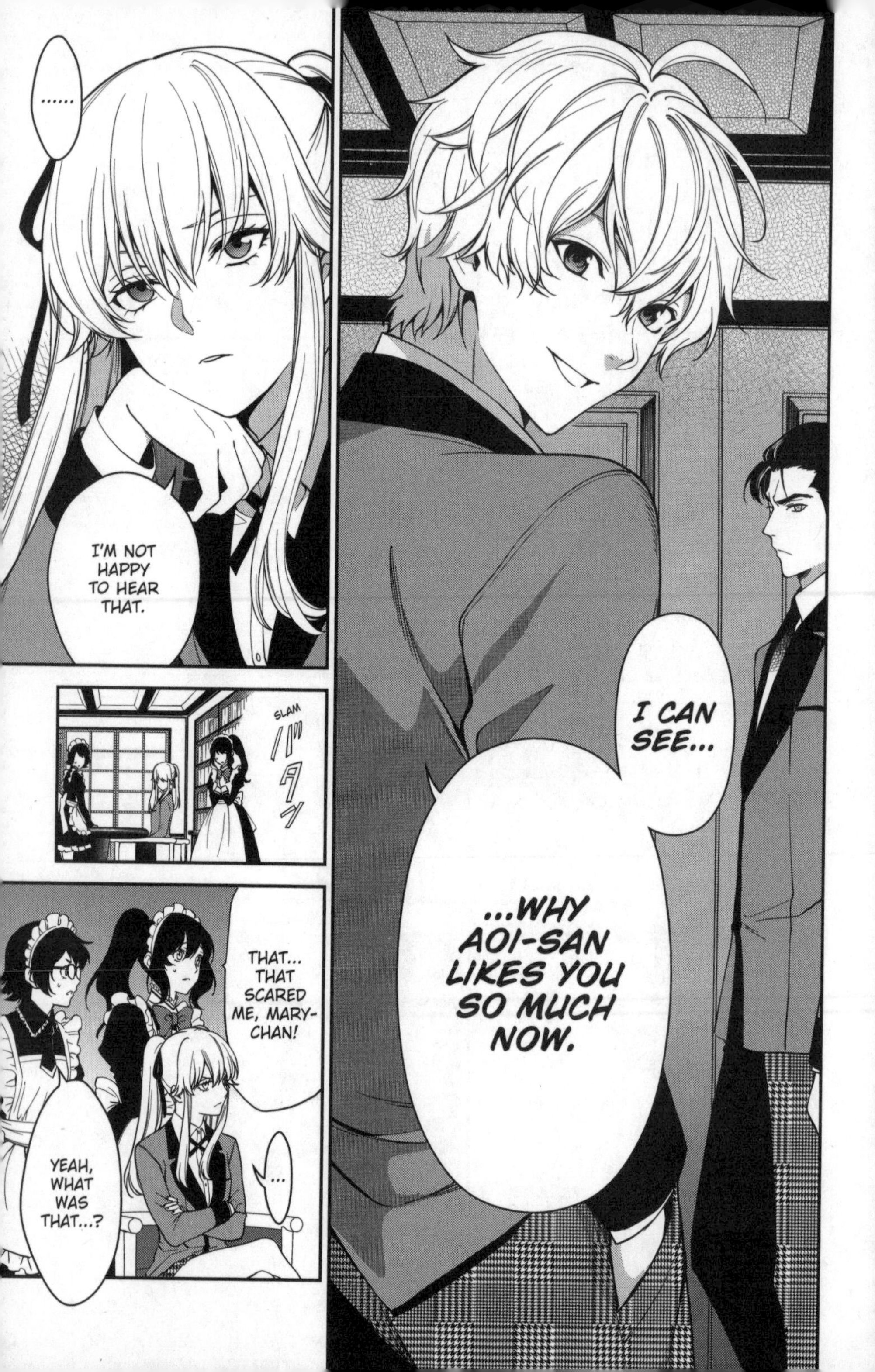
I CAN SEE...
...WHY AOI-SAN LIKES YOU SO MUCH NOW.
......
I'M NOT HAPPY TO HEAR THAT.
SLAM
THAT... THAT SCARED ME, MARY-CHAN!
...
YEAH, WHAT WAS THAT...?

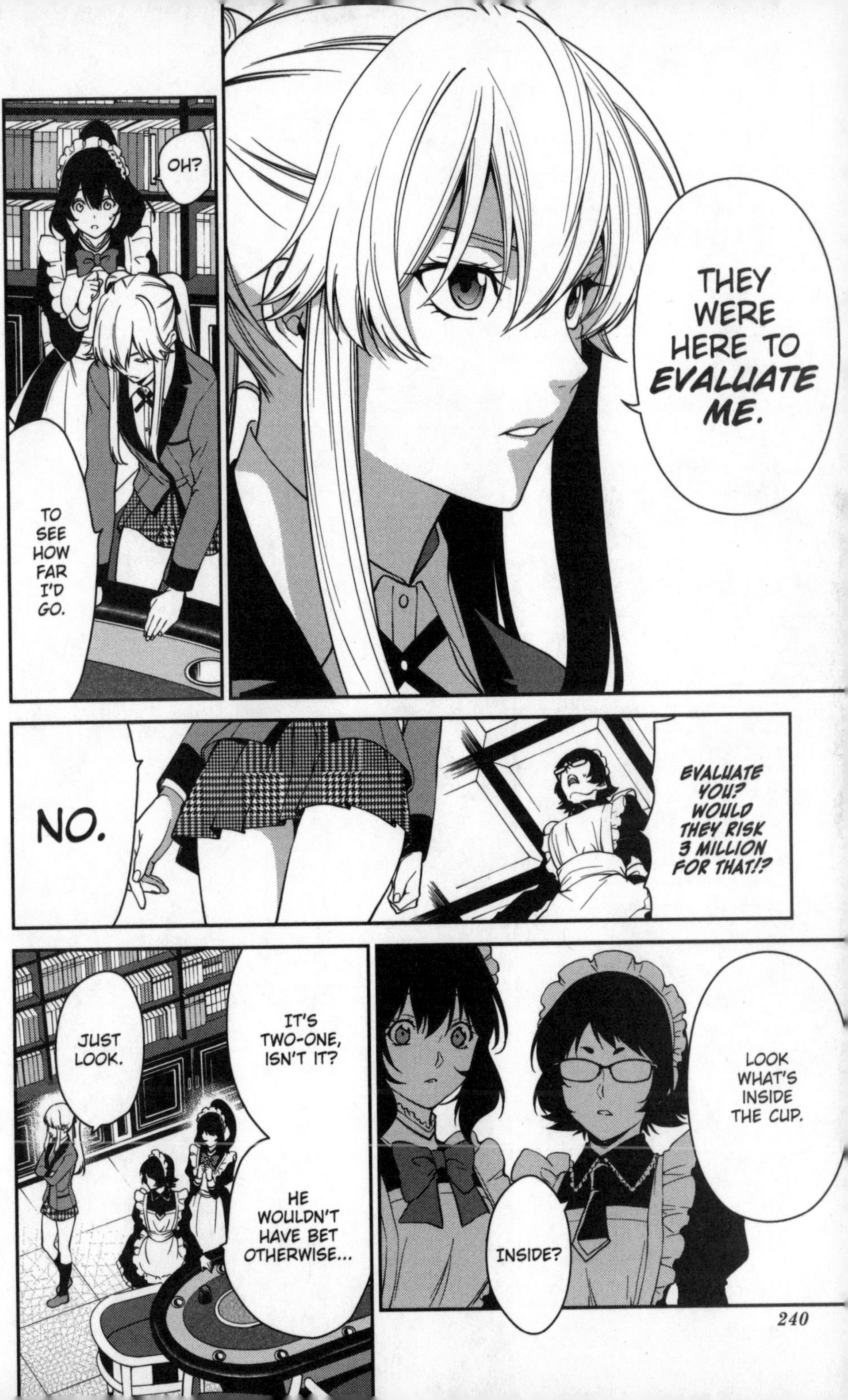
THEY WERE HERE TO EVALUATE ME.
OH?
TO SEE HOW FAR I'D GO.
EVALUATE YOU? WOULD THEY RISK 3 MILLION FOR THAT!?
NO.
LOOK WHAT'S INSIDE THE CUP.
INSIDE?
IT'S TWO-ONE, ISN'T IT?
HE WOULDN'T HAVE BET OTHERWISE...
JUST LOOK.

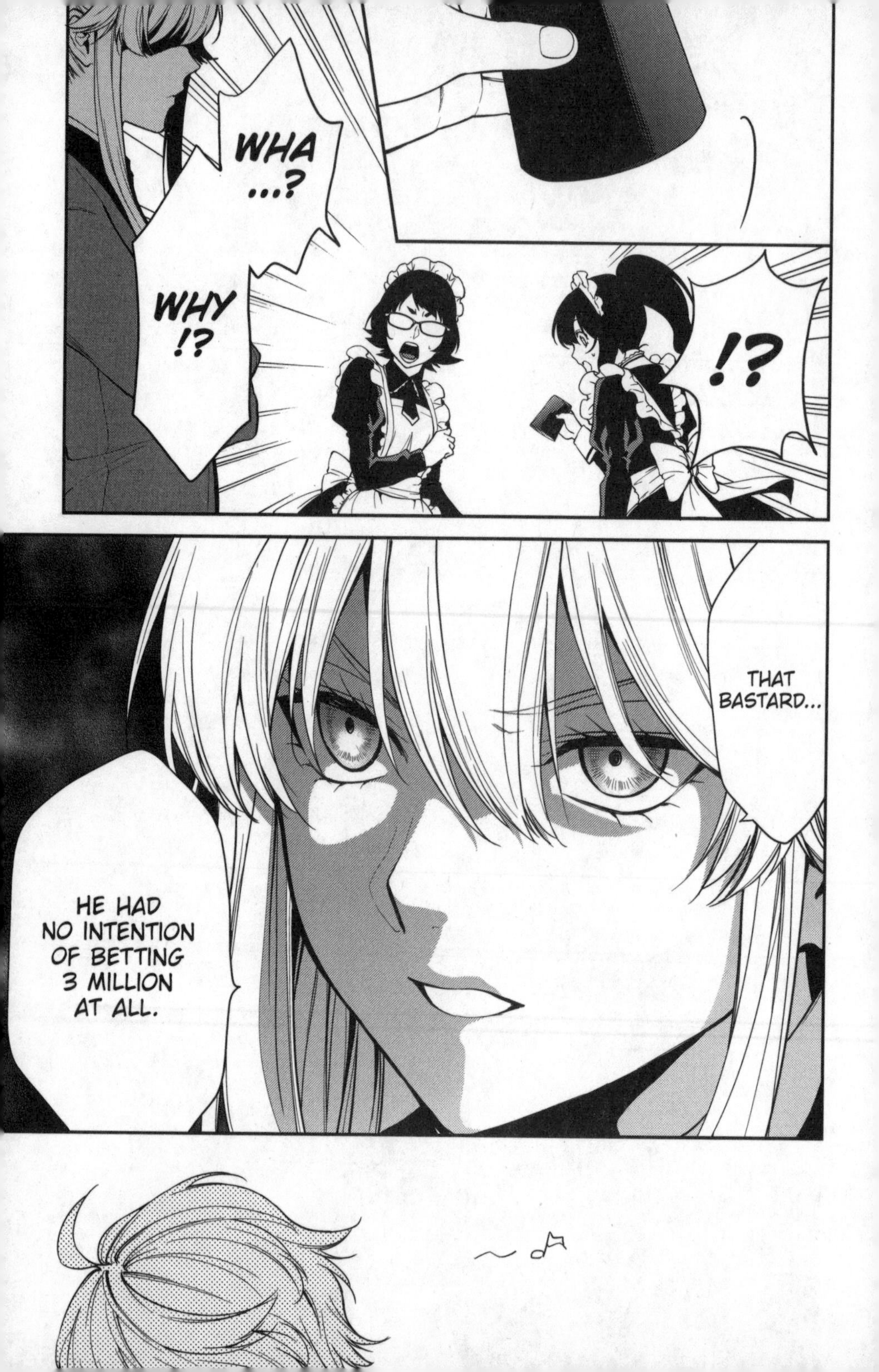
!?
WHA ...?
WHY !?
THAT BASTARD...
HE HAD NO INTENTION OF BETTING 3 MILLION AT ALL.
~

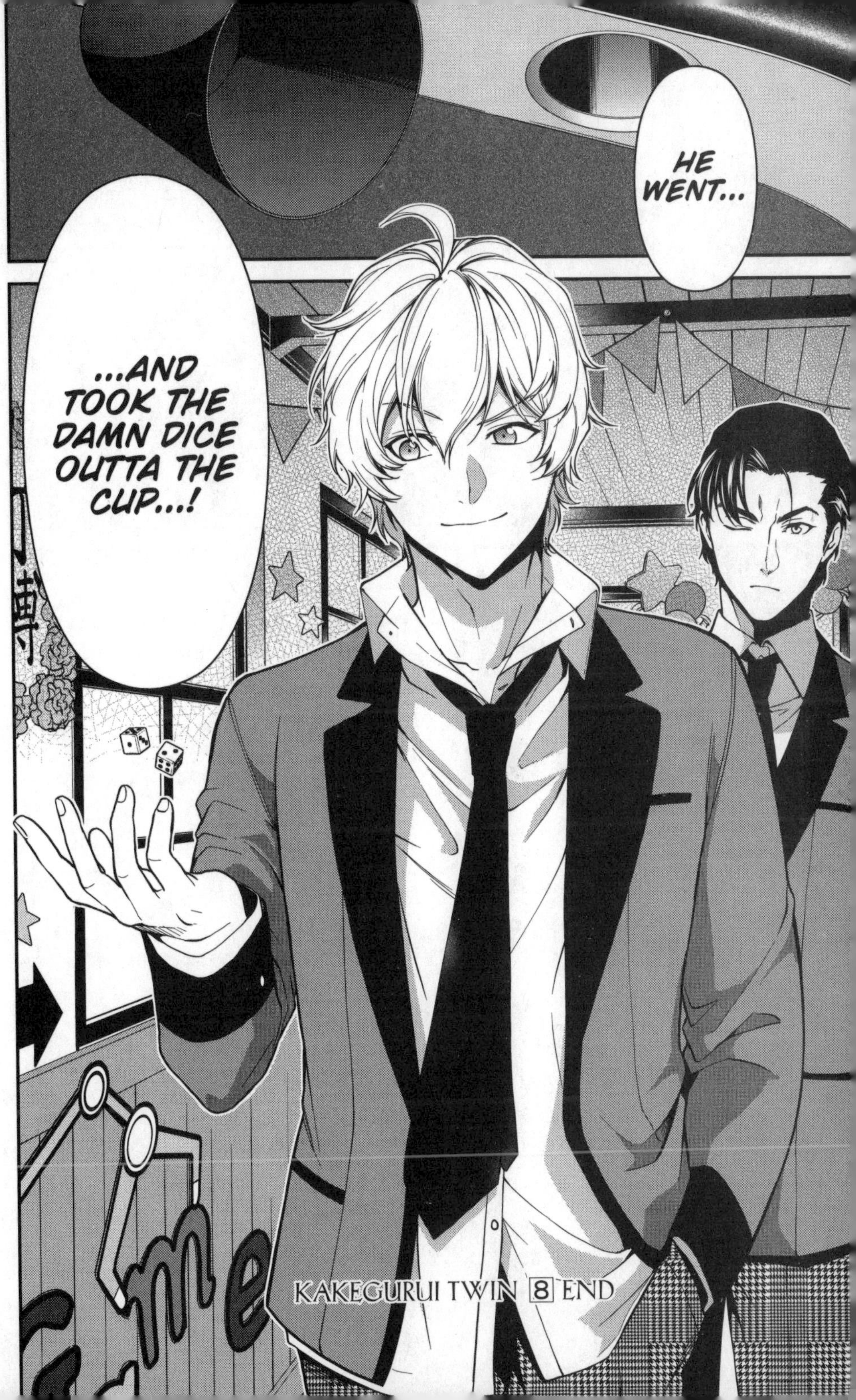
HE WENT...
...AND TOOK THE DAMN DICE OUTTA THE CUP...!
KAKEGURUI TWIN 8 END

# NADESHIKO RURICHOU MASTER CHEATER

TIME FOR SOME END-OF-THE-VOLUME BONUS COMICS!

* This has no relation to the actual story.

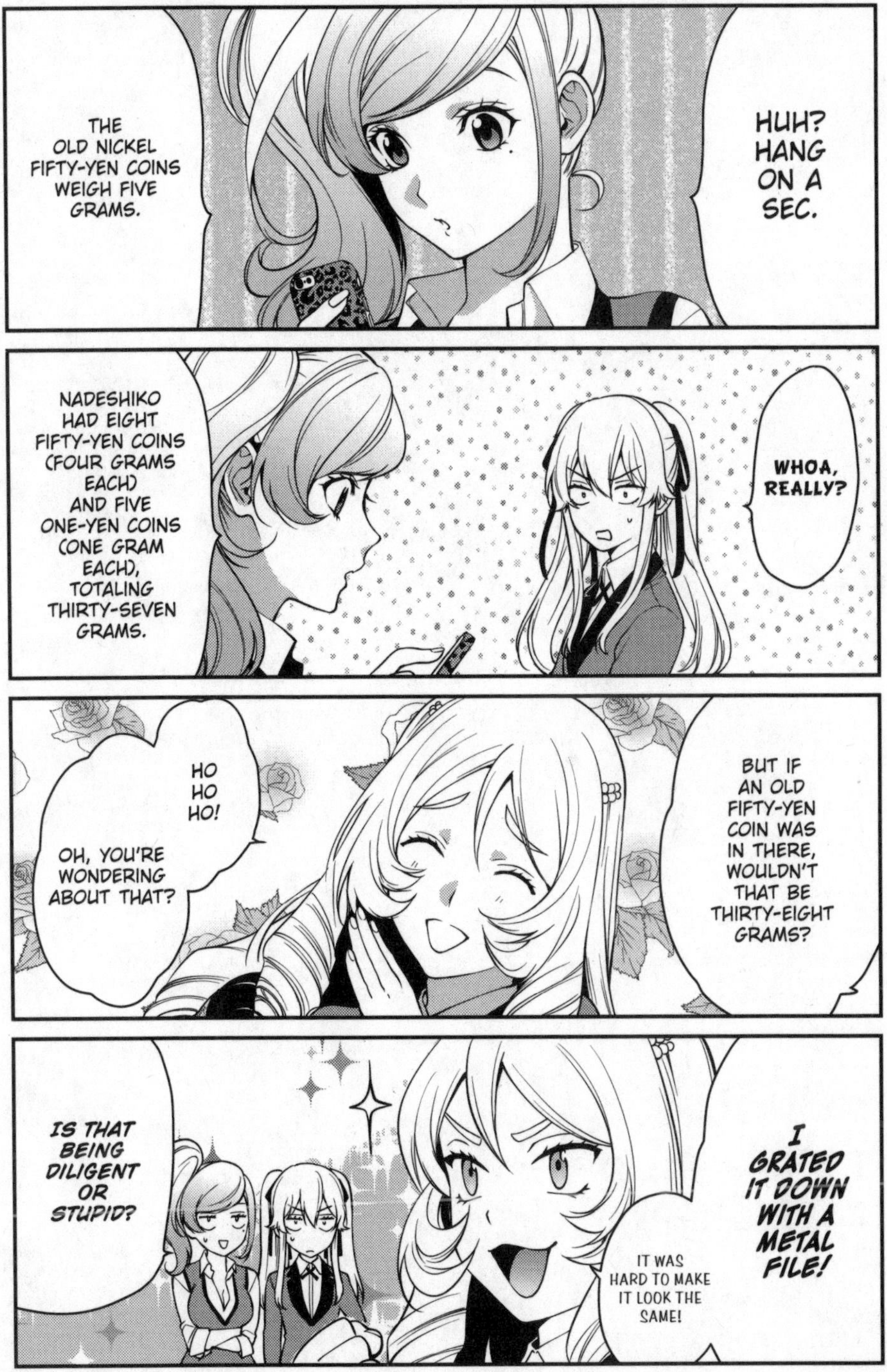
HUH? HANG ON A SEC.
THE OLD NICKEL FIFTY-YEN COINS WEIGH FIVE GRAMS.
WHOA, REALLY?
NADESHIKO HAD EIGHT FIFTY-YEN COINS (FOUR GRAMS EACH) AND FIVE ONE-YEN COINS (ONE GRAM EACH), TOTALING THIRTY-SEVEN GRAMS.
BUT IF AN OLD FIFTY-YEN COIN WAS IN THERE, WOULDN'T THAT BE THIRTY-EIGHT GRAMS?
HO HO HO!
OH, YOU'RE WONDERING ABOUT THAT?
I GRATED IT DOWN WITH A METAL FILE!
IT WAS HARD TO MAKE IT LOOK THE SAME!
IS THAT BEING DILIGENT OR STUPID?

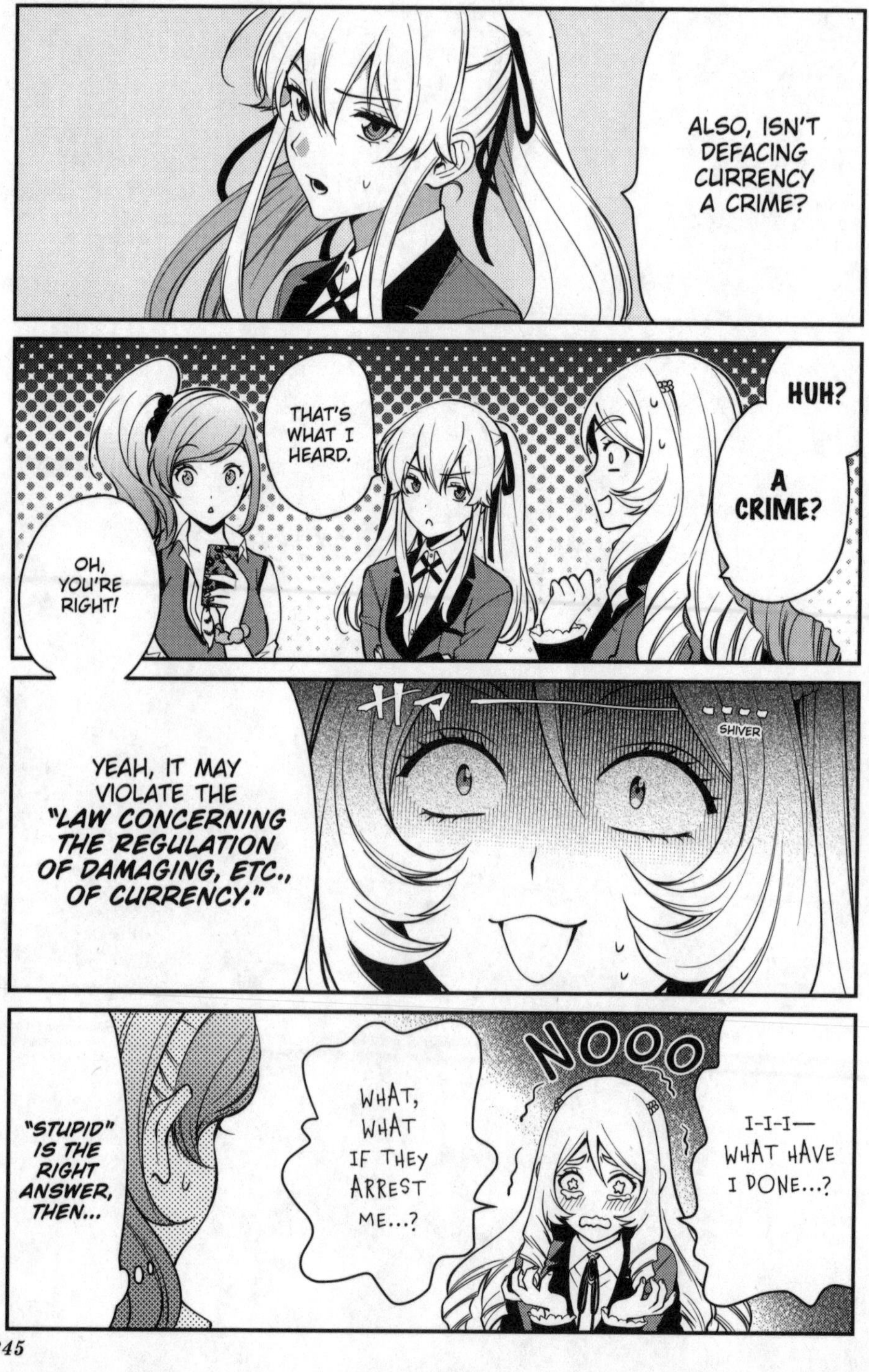
ALSO, ISN'T DEFACING CURRENCY A CRIME?
HUH?
A CRIME?
THAT'S WHAT I HEARD.
OH, YOU'RE RIGHT!
SHIVER
YEAH, IT MAY VIOLATE THE "LAW CONCERNING THE REGULATION OF DAMAGING, ETC., OF CURRENCY."
NOOO
I-I-I— WHAT HAVE I DONE...?
WHAT, WHAT IF THEY ARREST ME...?
"STUPID" IS THE RIGHT ANSWER, THEN...

# GAMBLING, THAT IS MY RAISON D'ÊTRE.

In this game, mastering the concepts of "sound" and "weight" is the key to victory. Turn that around, and if you aren't well-versed in both, it's likely impossible to seize the advantage. Under normal circumstances, the game would be more about reading your opponent than anything.

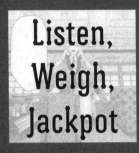

Listen, Weigh, Jackpot

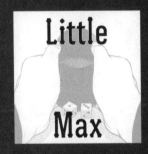

Little Max

Tsuzura and Yukimi came up with this game. It is, in a way, the kind of game they'd come up with—it takes a fair amount of time to play, you have a firm advantage if you know the probabilities, and it doesn't pay out much, making for a gamble you can enjoy without things getting too heated. If you actually play it, you'll find yourself swinging between joy and pain as the dice rolls gleefully ignore the odds, which is pretty fun.

Thank you for picking up Volume 8 of *Kakegurui Twin*.

Nadeshiko Rurichou appears! I love these spoiled little rich girl characters who go off on long stories about themselves and end them with "Ohhhh ho ho ho!" I love them even more if they're not the sharpest tool in the shed. If they are drawn pretty too, then it's perfect. Thus, bringing out a character I love as much as Nadeshiko makes me really happy. Here's hoping you'll enjoy her in action as well.

Now for some thanks. Thanks to Saiki-sensei and his assistants, who not only produce beautiful art but also regularly give me vital advice on story content. Thanks to our editors, Sasaki-sama and Yumoto-sama, for letting me do whatever I want. And, of course, thanks to our readers. It's thanks to all of you that we're able to keep going. Please continue to support us.

The Great Bloom Festival is nearing its climax. Will Hyakkaou Academy's school festival end without a hitch, or are there heavy seas on the horizon? I hope you'll want to see for yourselves.

See all of you in Volume 9.

Homura Kawamoto

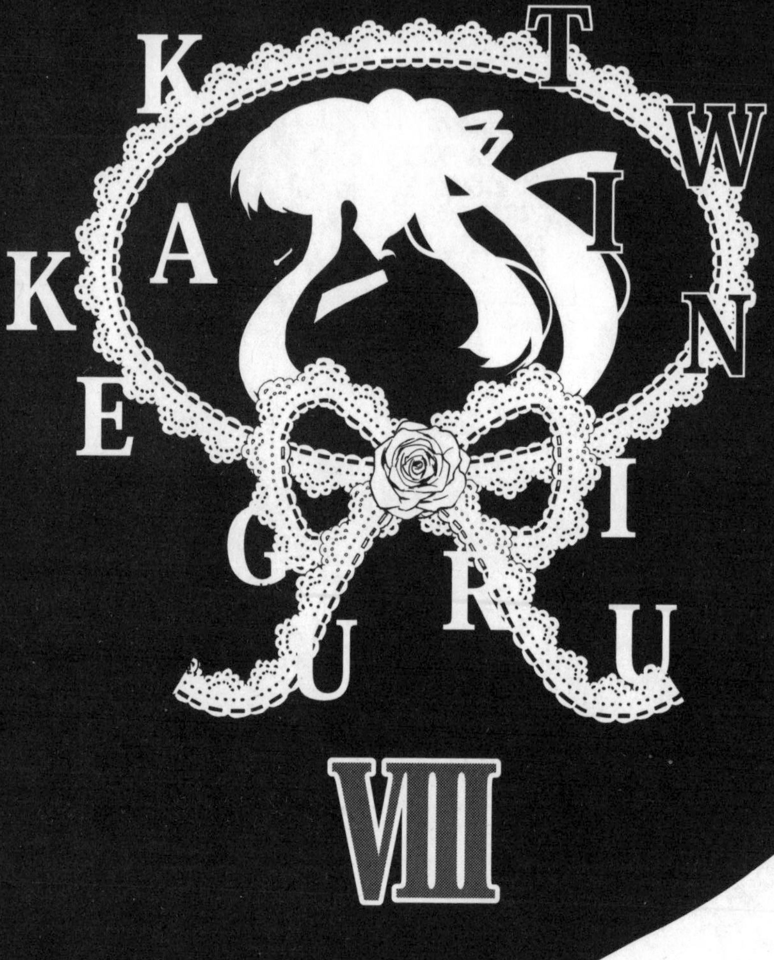
KAKEGURUI TWIN
VIII

◆ Special Thanks ◆

My editors
Kawamoto-sama

Ken'ichi Sato-sama
Kozue Tachikawa-sama

It's Volume 8!

Nadeshiko-chan is here, a cutie you can't help but love as she get carried away. Her original character design was meant to be more dignified, but she's done a 180 from that—and personally, I love the slightly sillier version you see here far more. We've got more male characters now too, adding even more to the excitement! I can't wait to see how all this develops!

Kei Saiki

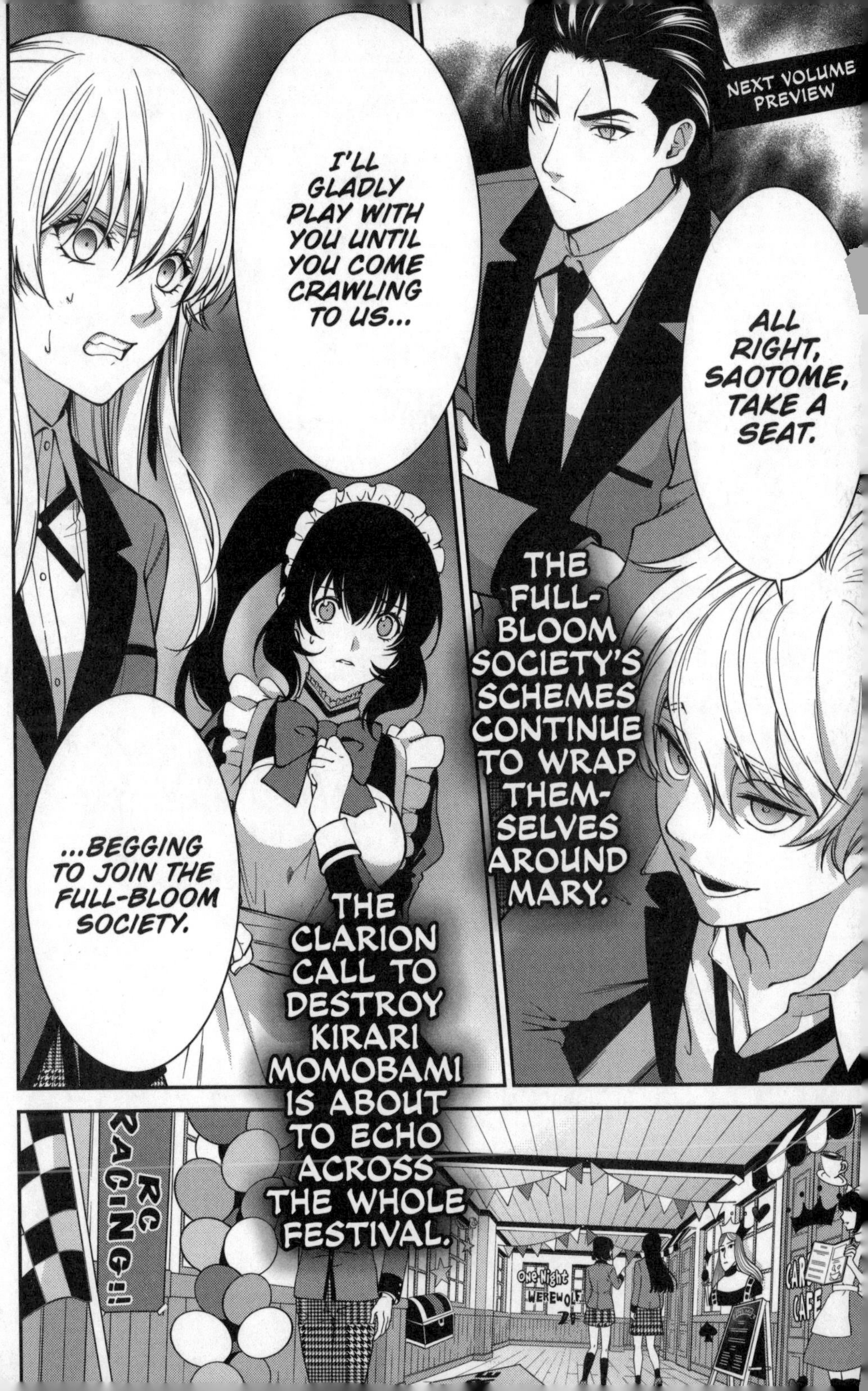
NEXT VOLUME PREVIEW
ALL RIGHT, SAOTOME, TAKE A SEAT.
I'LL GLADLY PLAY WITH YOU UNTIL YOU COME CRAWLING TO US...
...BEGGING TO JOIN THE FULL-BLOOM SOCIETY.
THE FULL-BLOOM SOCIETY'S SCHEMES CONTINUE TO WRAP THEMSELVES AROUND MARY.
THE CLARION CALL TO DESTROY KIRARI MOMOBAMI IS ABOUT TO ECHO ACROSS THE WHOLE FESTIVAL.
One Night WEREWOLF
RC RACING!!

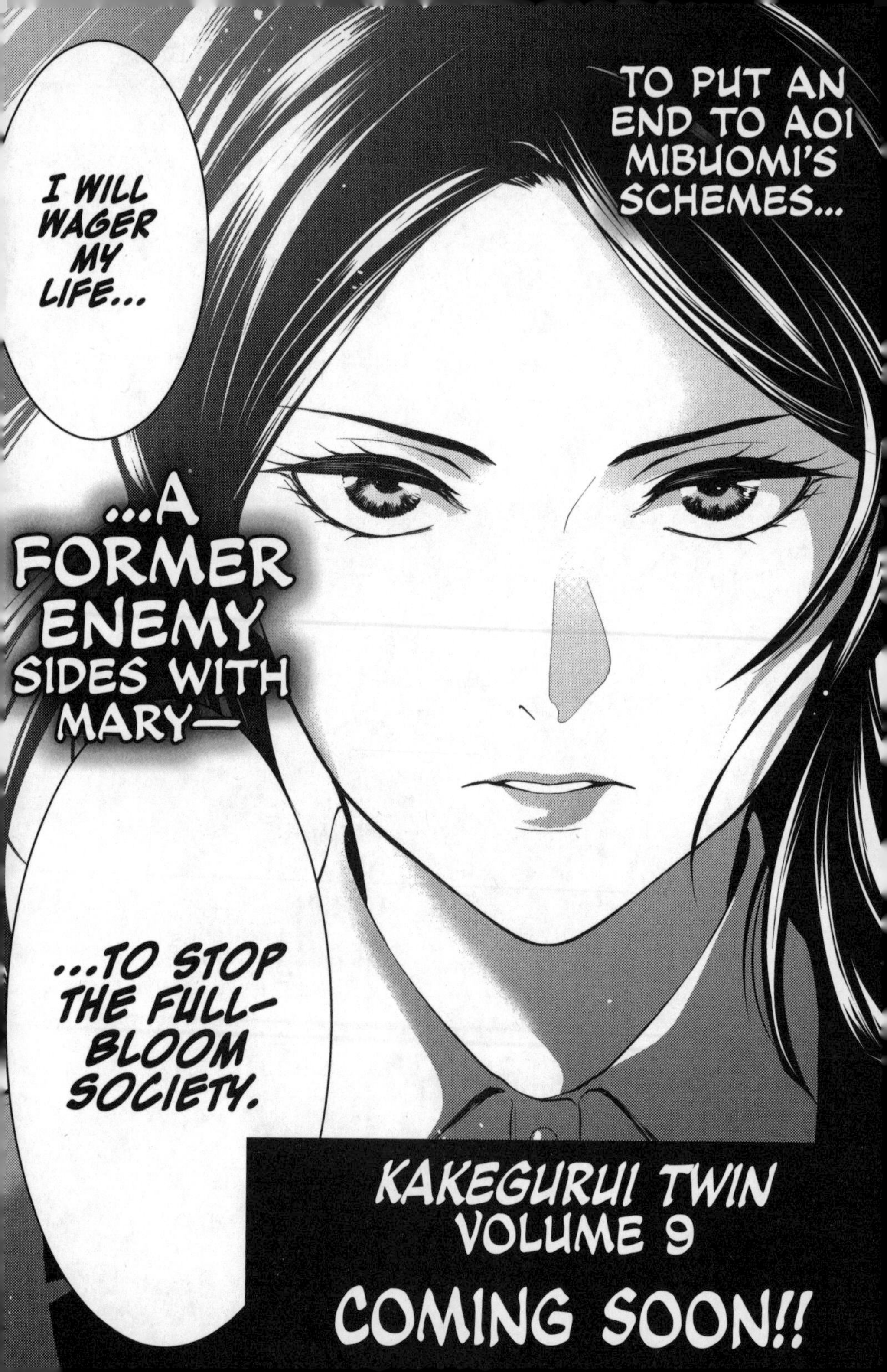
TO PUT AN END TO AOI MIBUOMI'S SCHEMES...
I WILL WAGER MY LIFE...
...A FORMER ENEMY SIDES WITH MARY—
...TO STOP THE FULL-BLOOM SOCIETY.
KAKEGURUI TWIN VOLUME 9
COMING SOON!!

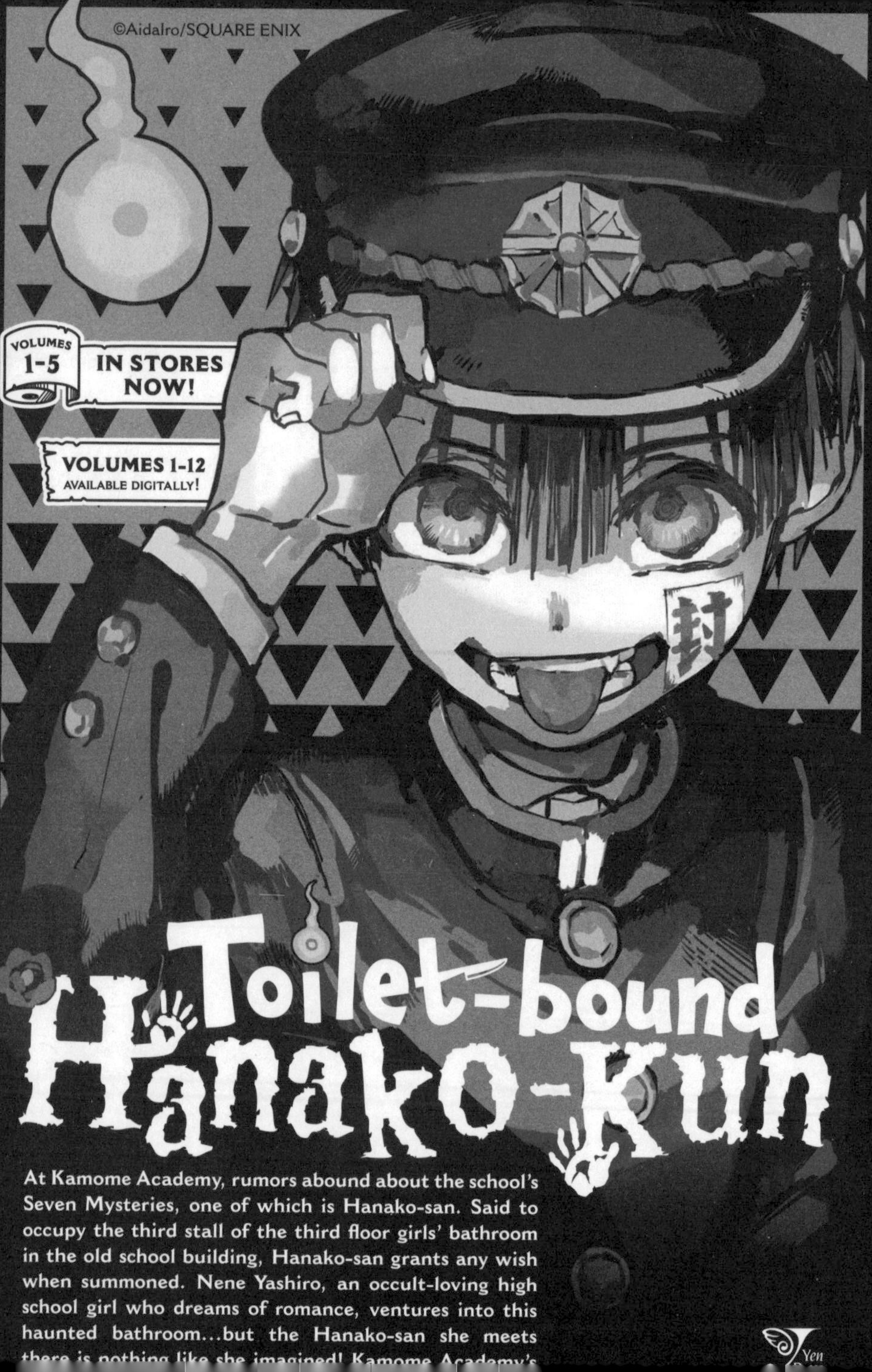

©AidaIro/SQUARE ENIX
VOLUMES 1-5
IN STORES NOW!
VOLUMES 1-12
AVAILABLE DIGITALLY!
封
Toilet-bound
Hanako-Kun
At Kamome Academy, rumors abound about the school's Seven Mysteries, one of which is Hanako-san. Said to occupy the third stall of the third floor girls' bathroom in the old school building, Hanako-san grants any wish when summoned. Nene Yashiro, an occult-loving high school girl who dreams of romance, ventures into this haunted bathroom...but the Hanako-san she meets there is nothing like she imagined! Kamome Academy's

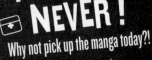
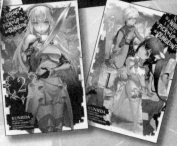
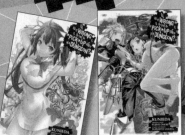
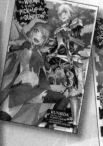
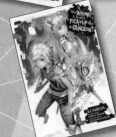
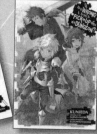

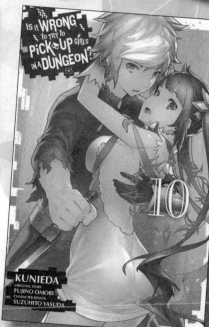

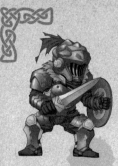

# HE DOES NOT LET ANYONE ROLL THE DICE.

A young Priestess joins her first adventuring party, but blind to the dangers, they almost immediately find themselves in trouble. It's Goblin Slayer who comes to their rescue—a man who has dedicated his life to the extermination of all goblins by any means necessary. A dangerous, dirty, and thankless job, but he does it better than anyone. And when rumors of his feats begin to circulate, there's no telling who might come calling next...

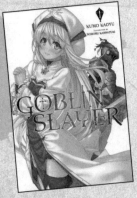

Light Novel
V. 1-10
Available
Now!

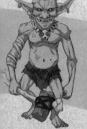

Check out the simul-pub manga chapters every month!

Yen Press  YEN ON
www.yenpress.com

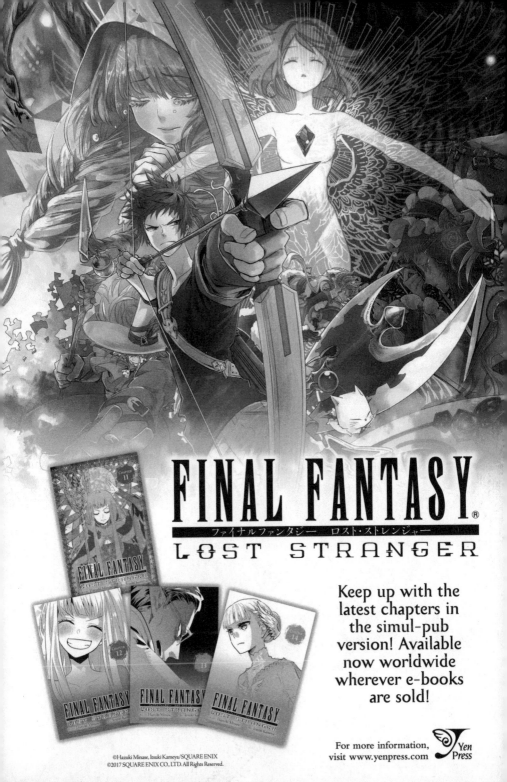

# FINAL FANTASY
ファイナルファンタジー　ロスト・ストレンジャー
## LOST STRANGER

Keep up with the latest chapters in the simul-pub version! Available now worldwide wherever e-books are sold!

For more information, visit www.yenpress.com

Yen Press

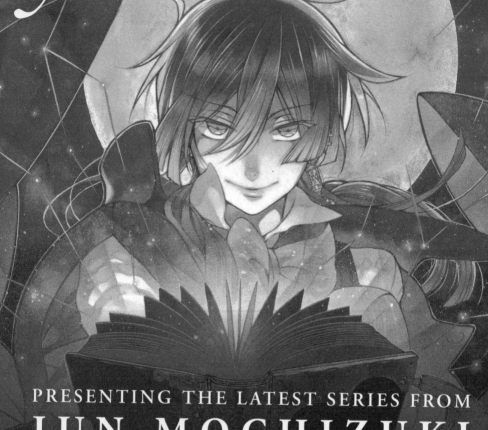
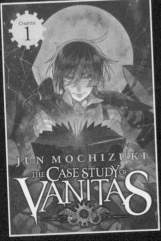

The Phantomhive family has a butler who's almost too good to be true...

...or maybe he's just too good to be human.

# Black Butler

YANA TOBOSO

**VOLUMES 1-29 IN STORES NOW!**

Karino Takatsu, creator of
**SERVANT × SERVICE**, presents:

# My Monster Girl's Too Cool For You

### Burning adoration melts her heart...literally!

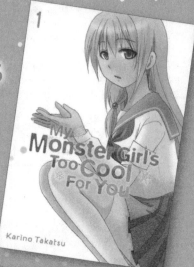

In a world where *youkai* and
humans attend school together,
a boy named Atsushi Fukuzumi
falls for snow *youkai* Muku Shiroishi. Fukuzumi's passionate feelings
melt Muku's heart...and the rest of her?! The first volume of an
interspecies romantic comedy you're sure to fall head over heels for
is now available!!

YenPress.com

### Read new installments of this series every month at the same time as Japan!

CHAPTERS AVAILABLE NOW AT E-TAILERS EVERYWHERE!

© Karino Takatsu/SQUARE ENIX CO., LTD.

STORY: **Homura Kawamoto**     ART: **Kei Saiki**

Translation: Kevin Gifford     Lettering: Anthony Quintessenza

KAKEGURUI TWIN Vol. 8 ©2019 Homura Kawamoto, Kei Saiki/ SQUARE ENIX CO., LTD.
First published in Japan in 2019 by SQUARE ENIX CO., LTD. English translation rights arranged with SQUARE ENIX CO., LTD. and Yen Press, LLC through Tuttle-Mori Agency, Inc.

English translation ©2020 by SQUARE ENIX CO., LTD.

Yen Press
150 West 30th Street, 19th Floor
New York, NY 10001

Visit us at yenpress.com
facebook.com/yenpress
twitter.com/yenpress
yenpress.tumblr.com
instagram.com/yenpress

First Yen Press Edition: November 20

Yen Press is an imprint of Yen Press
The Yen Press name and logo are trademarks of Yen Press

The publisher is not responsible for websites (or their con
that are not owned by the publis

Library of Congress Control Number: 2018961911

ISBNs: 978-1-9753-1386-9 (paperback)
978-1-9753-1385-2 (ebook)

10 9 8 7 6 5 4 3 2 1

WOR

Printed in the United States of America